THE ASSOCIATED PRESS
STYLEBOOK

56TH EDITION

2022–2024

Edited by
Paula Froke
Anna Jo Bratton
Andale Gross
Jeff McMillan
Pia Sarkar
Jerry Schwartz
Raghuram Vadarevu

apstylebook.com

BASIC BOOKS

New York

Basic Books
Hachette Book Group
1290 Avenue of the Americas, New York, NY 10104
www.basicbooks.com

Printed in the United States of America

First Edition: The Associated Press, August 1977
Fifty-Sixth Edition: July 2022

Published by Basic Books, an imprint of Perseus Books, LLC, a subsidiary of Hachette Book Group, Inc. The Basic Books name and logo is a trademark of the Hachette Book Group.

The Hachette Speakers Bureau provides a wide range of authors for speaking events. To find out more, go to www.hachettespeakersbureau.com or call (866) 376-6591.

The publisher is not responsible for websites (or their content) that are not owned by the publisher.

Design and content management by Stylebooks.com
Product management by Colleen Newvine

Library of Congress Control Number: 2022936222

ISBNs: 9781541601659 (trade paperback)

LSC-C

Printing 1, 2022

In memory

of

RACHEL ZOLL

A woman of valor whose devotion to the AP's religion beat over nearly two decades was boundless, whose contributions to the Stylebook were indispensable and whose heart was beyond measure.

Contents

Foreword

In 1953, The Associated Press introduced the first edition of the AP Stylebook. At 60 pages, it focused on matters of capitalization, punctuation, grammar and spelling. The audience was reporters and editors with the AP, a not-for-profit newsgathering cooperative whose journalists today cover news around the globe in words and compelling visuals.

Today's Stylebook, at 10 times the size, serves not only journalists but also communicators in a wide variety of fields and publications.

We still outline basic rules or guidance on grammar, punctuation, word usage and journalistic style, and strive to reflect changes in common usage.

But we have evolved to also offer guidelines on a number of significant topics of our times. Among them: race, gender, climate change, addiction, immigration, disabilities, sexual misconduct and more. We have added chapters on religion, health and science, polls and surveys, data journalism, digital security for journalists, and inclusive storytelling.

While we remain committed to our classic, practical, spiral-bound edition — now published every other year — AP Stylebook Online has become the primary way professional writers and editors access this definitive resource. With the shift to a digital environment, our online format allows AP Stylebook to remain a fundamental and easily accessible guide. It is constantly updated to reflect changes to news writing in real time.

A team of top AP editors meets throughout the year to make updates and improvements, many of which appear immediately in Stylebook Online. Contributions come from the AP staff, AP's member news organizations and subscribers, journalism teachers and students, specialists in a host of fields, and everyday readers. Indeed, some of the changes that are talked about most have come at the suggestion of @APStylebook's Twitter followers.

We are honored to help writers and editors in all fields in their commitment to clear and accurate writing, even in these times of profound and frequent change.

DAISY VEERASINGHAM
President and CEO
The Associated Press

What's new

This edition of the AP Stylebook features a new chapter on **inclusive storytelling**, emphasizing that such efforts are essential to accuracy and fairness and giving guidance on how to achieve those goals. We note that inclusive storytelling seeks to truly represent all people around the globe, giving voice and visibility to those who have been missing or misrepresented in traditional narratives of both history and daily journalism.

Among the chapter's focuses: recognizing and overcoming unconscious biases; being sensitive about specific words and phrases; reaching beyond your usual sources and story ideas; including the necessary context and background; avoiding tokenism; and making content accessible.

Other highlights:

Behind the Stylebook scenes: who we are, how we do it, why we do it. Also, an expanded list of **contributors** both inside and outside the AP, and an expanded **bibliography** with more online resources and other stylebooks.

Pronouns: As much as possible, AP now uses **they/them/their** as a way of accurately describing and representing a person who uses those pronouns for themself. This is an expansion on our more limited 2017 guidance.

Disabilities: Additions and revisions to updates made on AP Stylebook Online in 2021; the feedback we requested on those changes helped shape this version. Revisions include: **If individual or group preferences can't be determined, use a mix of identity-first language and person-first language.** As always, we recommend referring to a person's disability only when relevant to the story; being specific about what the disability is; and asking a person's preference about language. In addition to overview guidance, **we added or revised 35 disabilities-related entries** throughout the book.

Those revised entries include guidance that the **uppercase Deaf** is acceptable, if used by a person or group, in descriptions such as *the cultural Deaf community, Deaf education, Deaf culture,* etc. We use lowercase **deaf** for the audiological condition and for people with that condition.

Immigration, migration: Greatly expanded and revised, including discussion of language such as *crisis* and guidance to avoid imagery conjuring war or natural disaster such as *onslaught, tidal wave, flood, inundation, invasion, army, march, sneak* and *stealth.* Explanation of the terms **migrant** vs. **immigrant.** A detailed rundown on agencies dealing with immigration and migration. Also, 20 new or revised individual entries, including **refugees, asylum-seekers,** "**catch and release,**" **explusions, deportations, pushbacks, birthright citizenship, sanctuaries,** "**Dreamers**" and more.

Race-related coverage: Revised guidance to not use **Black(s)** or **white(s)** as either a singular or plural noun; previously we had said the plural use was acceptable in limited uses. New entries on **critical race theory** and **historically Black colleges and universities,** and new guidance on **Arab Americans.** The **Native Americans, American Indians** section now notes that the term **Natives** is acceptable on second reference, and adds entries including **Indian Country** and **tribal affiliation.** It changes the preferred spelling to **tipi,** rather than teepee.

And it advises: Do not use the word **squaw** in any sense, including quotes, to refer to individual Native Americans. The word is acceptable if necessary as a first reference to a place name, but limit its use.

The print book also adds **race-related coverage** updates made in Stylebook Online after the 55th Edition was published. Those include capitalizing **Black**; discussion of the terms **systemic/structural/institutional racism**; and a number of **Asian American**-related terms. See below for more.

Gender, sex and sexual orientation: A renamed umbrella entry, including more than 25 new or revised entries. They include **transgender, nonbinary, gender identity, sexual identity, gender expression, gender-fluid, gender-fluidity, genderqueer, gender dysphoria**. We now use **LGBTQ** instead of **LGBT**. The **deadnaming** entry says: Deadname a person very rarely and only if required to understand the news, or if requested by the person.

Female, woman: Revised guidance noting that some people object to the use of **female** as a descriptor for women because it can be seen as emphasizing biology and reproductive capacity over gender identity. It can also sometimes carry misogynistic tones that may vary in severity by race, class and other factors.

Religion chapter: Thoroughly updated and expanded, with 30 new entries including **African Methodist Episcopal Church; Sikhi, Sikhism; humanism, humanist; "nones."**

We now say that **Roman Catholic**, which refers to the Latin branch of Catholicism, is not the appropriate first reference when referring to the pope, the Vatican or the universal church. **Catholic Church** should be used instead, since it encompasses believers belonging to the Latin (Roman) and Eastern churches. Given the majority of Catholics belong to the Latin (Roman) rite, it is acceptable to use **Roman Catholic Church** on first reference if the context is clearly referring to the Latin rite. For example: *the Roman Catholic Archdiocese of Indianapolis.*

Social media and web-based reporting chapter: New chapter name, with updates throughout, such as how to guard against the misinformation that can easily be mistaken for fact on online platforms. Includes some detail that previously was in the **internet** entry.

Polls and surveys chapter: Adds more detail on **survey weighting** and **exit polling**, and makes other updates and edits throughout.

Coronavirus: Updates in that entry, along with separate entries including **anti-vaxxer** (don't use the term); **antiviral, antivirus; epidemic, pandemic, endemic; superspreader; vaccine, vaccination**. Many other terms are in the Coronavirus Topical Guide on Stylebook Online.

Cryptocurrency, blockchain, bitcoin, NFT, Web3: Renamed entry combines formerly separate entries, adds **NFT** and **Web3** and updates throughout. We now use lowercase **bitcoin** on all references.

Terrorism: New guidance saying to describe specific actions that are being perpetrated, and attribute the use of the word **terrorism** or **terrorist** to authorities or others except when talking about significant historical events widely acknowledged as terrorist actions.

Marijuana, cannabis: Renamed entry now says those terms can be used interchangeably. We also update to say don't use inaccurate terms like *synthetic marijuana* and we give guidance on alternative phrasing. Other updates throughout.

Japanese internment, incarceration: New entry notes that while **internment** has been applied historically to all these detainments, the broad use of the term is inaccurate. Instead: the **incarceration** of Japanese Americans and Japanese nationals.

Military terms: New entry cautions not to use the terms **military training** or **decorated** broadly. Be specific about the person's military roles or awards. Don't use the term **soldiers** broadly to describe members of the U.S. armed forces; it applies only to members of the Army. Use **former Marine** rather than **ex-Marine** for a Marine who has been honorably discharged.

Also:

Advice to limit use of **community** in reference to groups of people, because it implies homogeneity. An entry covering **electric, hybrid and plug-in hybrid vehicles**. An updated entry noting that **spongy moth** is the new term for **gypsy moth** and advising not to use **gypsy** in any sense. Guidance that the terms **pregnant people** or **people seeking abortions** should be confined to stories that specifically address the experiences of people who do not identify as women.

A new entry saying to avoid the terms **child-free** and **childless**. We say the terms **supervised injection sites, safe injection sites** and **overdose prevention centers** are acceptable.

We have removed most individual listings for companies, airlines and railroads. They remain available on Stylebook Online. We also removed individual listings for a number of cities; that guidance is included in the **datelines** entry. The **Broadcast chapter** is now online only (the **Food** and **Fashion** chapters were moved to online previously). Most words previously listed only for spelling have been removed from the print book.

2021 updates made on AP Stylebook Online and now in the print book:

A change in style to **antisemitism, antisemitic**.

In the **race-related coverage** entry, new entries in addition to those noted above: **Indigenous; brown; people of color; BIPOC; slaves, enslaved people; Black Lives Matter; Juneteenth**.

Additions to the overview of **race-related coverage: Be aware that some words and phrases that seem innocuous to one group can carry negative connotations, even be seen as slurs, to another. And: Do not write in a way that assumes *white* is the default.**

Guidance on the terms **riot, unrest, protest, demonstration, uprising, revolt; looting, looters; officer-involved, police-involved; defund**.

Revised guidance that although **temperatures** get higher or lower, phrasing such as **warmer temperatures** or **cold temperatures** is also acceptable.

A new **Uyghur** entry. A change in style to **TSA PreCheck**. Revised guidance that **injuries** may be suffered, sustained or received. Guidance to avoid the vague medical jargon **trauma** in many cases.

Contributors

Shelley Acoca
Ben Adlin
Ankur Ahluwalia
Nadia Ahmed
Frank Bajak
Amanda Barrett
Brian Barrett
Thalia Beaty
Sarah Blazucki
Seth Borenstein
Renata Brito
Rook Campbell
Alicia Chang
Stacy Christiansen
Tara Schupner Congdon
Alex Connor
David Crary
John Daniszewski
Jin Ding
Dan Fagin
Jon Fahey
Mariam Fam
Carole Feldman
Hannah Fingerhut
Felicia Fonseca
Bryan Gallion
Kathy Gannon
Kristin Gilger
Mary Gladstone
Sarah Glover
Deepti Hajela
David Hamilton
Alina Hartounian
Erika Check Hayden
Julie Hochgesang
Anick Jesdanun
Carla Johnson
James Jordan
Zeina Karam
Jamey Keaten

Ashraf Khalil
Tom Krisher
Ryan Kryska
Larry Lage
James LaPorta
Travis Loller
Karen Mahabir
Holly Meyer
Rebecca Miller
William Millios
Aaron Morrison
Geoff Mulvihill
Justin Myers
Stephanie Nano
Noreen Nasir
Lauran Neergaard
Ron Nixon
Ivan Oransky
Barbara Ortutay
Richard Ostling
Jon Poet
Bryan Pollard
Jenn Pollitt
Karl Ritter
Howard A. Rosenblum
Bobby Ross Jr.
David Scott
Amy Silverman
Peter Smith
Elliot Spagat
Mike Stobbe
Emily Swanson
Maia Szalavitz
Lindsey Tanner
Troy Thibodeaux
Tai Tomasi
Doris Truong
Marlon A. Walker
Nicole Winfield
Rachel Zoll

For a partial list of print and online resources used by the Stylebook team, including some other style guides, see the Bibliography.

Stylebook: how we do it

"The English language is fluid and changes incessantly. What last year may have been very formal, next year may be loosely informal. Word combinations, slogans and phrases are being added and becoming part of the language. ...

"Because of the constantly changing usage, no compilation can be called permanent. Nor can any one volume be infallible or contain all the wisdom and information of the ages."

That's what AP editors observed in introducing the first version of the AP Stylebook in 1953.

We say the same today.

Or, as a modern-day Stylebook subscriber put it: In a lot of ways, the Stylebook is a history book of sorts, a real-time reflection on the times in which we live.

Through all the changes in the world through the years, our work remains deeply rooted in respect for language and commitment to the goals of AP journalism in general: to be accurate, clear, fair and concise.

We're a combination of prescriptivist (rules rules rules) and descriptivist — capturing and conveying how the language is used, and adding some guidance around that.

There's not always a definitive right or wrong. Some of our guidance offers key points to consider in choosing language, and notes that there can be a lot of gray areas. Often, writers and editors may need to make judgment calls based on in-depth discussion and consideration.

Since AP style is grounded in guiding AP journalists, our approach considers a very broad audience, from all sorts of backgrounds, in cities large and small around the globe. We aim to make our guidance easy to apply for those outside the AP as well. But organizations, writers and editors who aren't with the AP can modify as needed for their own audiences.

The core Stylebook team consists of a lead editor plus several other editors from a variety of backgrounds. At this writing, we are: lead editor Paula Froke, also a manager on AP's Nerve Center; Anna Jo Bratton, U.S. enterprise editor; Andale Gross, leader of AP's Race & Ethnicity team; Jeff McMillan, an editor on AP's East Desk; Pia Sarkar, a news editor in AP's Business News Department; Jerry Schwartz, AP's editor at large and veteran of 44 years with the company; and Raghuram Vadarevu, news editor for digital storytelling on the Global Enterprise team.

Standards editor John Daniszewski weighs in on many issues. AP's senior news leaders make the final call on the biggest or most sensitive guidance.

We consult regularly with AP reporters and editors who are experts in the fields they cover. We do a great deal of research. We confer with people and organizations outside the AP. Often our AP specialists write the first drafts of our guidance — whether it's a single entry or an entire chapter — and work with us to revise and refine.

We get ideas for additions or changes from all over. Many come from those of us on the team, based on what we see and read in the world around us. Others on the AP staff regularly make suggestions.

We get many ideas from our Twitter and Facebook followers. Questions to

Stylebook Online's Ask the Editor feature and a separate suggestions link often point to a need for a new entry, or changes to existing entries. Organizations and regular readers email with ideas.

From all of that, we assess what we believe would be of the greatest broad interest or importance or usefulness.

For much of the year, the core Stylebook team meets once or twice a week by Zoom to discuss ideas for guidance, or drafts of new guidance, or proposals to change or delete existing guidance. Between the meetings, we review drafts in a shared document and do more research with experts inside and outside the AP.

Our discussions consider many points, including the need to be inclusive and respectful in our storytelling. We monitor the evolution of language and society, while avoiding calls for us to jump on every possible change that comes our way.

We carefully consider the perspectives offered in comments made directly to us and in commentary and factual stories from a diversity of sources.

We also consider our very wide variety of users — far beyond our original scope of straight-news journalists — and their even broader variety of readers.

We discuss at length every proposal, including those that appear to be fairly straightforward. Often those discussions extend for days, weeks, months or more. We revise, revise again, revise some more, discuss some more, and revise and revise again.

Once we make our updates public, we pay close attention to the feedback. Nothing, of course, is universally applauded. The reaction — both positive and negative — can be intense. Generally, the comments are points that we've already considered and discussed. At times, though, we will get feedback that causes us to revise again — even after all the thinking and talking we've already done.

"The end result of extensive exploration and consultation in this work necessarily represents many compromises between conflicting points of view," the editors noted in 1953.

We say that today as well.

Paula Froke
AP Stylebook editor

Key to Stylebook entries

This updated and revised version of The Associated Press Stylebook has been organized like a dictionary. Need the acronym for a government agency? Look under the agency's name. Should you capitalize a word? Check the word itself or the **capitalization** entry. What's the format for baseball boxes? See **baseball**.

Following is a key to the entries:

Entry words, in alphabetical order, are in **boldface**. They represent the accepted word forms unless otherwise indicated.

airport Capitalize as part of a proper name: *LaGuardia Airport, O'Hare International Airport.*

The first name of an individual and the word *international* may be deleted from a formal airport name while the remainder is capitalized: *John F. Kennedy International Airport, Kennedy International Airport* or *Kennedy Airport.* Use whichever is appropriate in the context.

Text explains usage.

Do not make up names, however. There is no *Boston Airport*, for example. The *Boston airport* (lowercase *airport*) would be acceptable if for some reason the proper name, *Logan International Airport*, were not used.

Examples of correct and incorrect usage are in italics. AP doesn't use italics in news stories.

airstrike

Many entries simply give the correct spelling, hyphenation and/or capitalization.

air traffic controller No hyphen.

airways The system of routes that the federal government has established for airplane traffic.

See the **airline, airlines** entry for its use in carriers' names.

Related topics are in **boldface**.

aka Abbreviation for *also known as.*

Other abbreviations used in the Stylebook:
n.: noun   **adj.:** adjective
v.: verb   **adv.:** adverb

a

a- The rules of **prefixes** apply, but in general, no hyphen. Some examples: *achromatic atonal*

AAA Formerly the American Automobile Association.

Headquarters is in Heathrow, Florida.

a, an Use the article *a* before consonant sounds: *a historic event, a one-year term* (sounds as if it begins with a *w*), *a united stand* (sounds like *you*).

Use the article *an* before vowel sounds: *an energy crisis, an honorable man* (the *h* is silent), *an homage* (the *h* is silent), *an NBA record* (sounds like it begins with the letter *e*), *an 1890s celebration.*

AARP Use only the initials for the organization formerly known as the American Association of Retired Persons.

abaya Robe-like outer garment worn by Muslim women.

abbreviations and acronyms A few universally recognized abbreviations are required in some circumstances. Some others are acceptable, depending on the context. But in general, avoid alphabet soup. Do not use abbreviations or acronyms that the reader would not quickly recognize.

Abbreviations and most acronyms should be avoided in headlines.

Guidance on how to use a particular abbreviation or acronym is provided in entries alphabetized according to the sequence of letters in the word or phrase.

An *acronym* is a word formed from the first letter or letters of a series of words: *laser (light amplification by stimulated emission of radiation)*. An *abbreviation* is not an *acronym*.

Some general principles:

BEFORE A NAME: Abbreviate titles when used before a full name: *Dr., Gov., Lt. Gov., Mr., Mrs., Rep., the Rev., Sen.* and certain military designations listed in the **military titles** entry.

For guidelines on how to use titles, see **courtesy titles; legislative titles; military titles; religious titles**; and the entries for the most commonly used titles.

AFTER A NAME: Abbreviate *junior* or *senior* after an individual's name. Abbreviate *company, corporation, incorporated* and *limited* when used after the name of a corporate entity. See entries under these words and **company names**.

In some cases, an academic degree may be abbreviated after an individual's name. See **academic degrees**.

WITH DATES OR NUMERALS: Use the abbreviations *A.D., B.C., a.m., p.m., No.,* and abbreviate certain months (Jan., Feb., Aug., Sept., Oct., Nov., Dec.) when used with the day of the month.

Right: *In 450 B.C.; at 9:30 a.m.; in room No. 6; on Sept. 16.*

Wrong: *Early this a.m. he asked*

a

for the No. of your room. The abbreviations are correct only with figures.

Right: *Early this morning he asked for the number of your room.*

See **months** and individual entries for these other terms:

IN NUMBERED ADDRESSES: Abbreviate *avenue, boulevard* and *street* in numbered addresses: *He lives on Pennsylvania Avenue. He lives at 1600 Pennsylvania Ave.*

See **addresses**.

STATES: The names of certain states and the *United States* are abbreviated with periods in some circumstances.

See **state names; datelines;** and individual entries.

AVOID AWKWARD CONSTRUCTIONS: Do not follow an organization's full name with an abbreviation or acronym in parentheses or set off by dashes. If an abbreviation or acronym would not be clear on second reference without this arrangement, do not use it.

Names not commonly before the public should not be reduced to acronyms solely to save a few words.

SPECIAL CASES: Many abbreviations are desirable in tabulations and certain types of technical writing. See individual entries.

CAPS, PERIODS: Use capital letters and periods according to the listings in this book. For words not in this book, use the first-listed abbreviation in Webster's New World College Dictionary. Generally, omit periods in acronyms unless the result would spell an unrelated word. But use periods in most two-letter abbreviations: *U.S., U.N., U.K., B.A., B.C.* (*AP*, a trademark, is an exception. Also, no periods in *GI, ID* and *EU,* among others.) In headlines, do not use periods in abbreviations,

unless required for clarity.

Use all caps, but no periods, in longer abbreviations when the individual letters are pronounced: *ABC, CIA, FBI.*

Use only an initial cap and then lowercase for abbreviations and acronyms of more than five letters, unless listed otherwise in this Stylebook or Webster's New World College Dictionary.

ABCs

able-bodied Use care in deciding whether to use this term for people who don't have disabilities. If necessary to make a distinction, the terms *nondisabled* or *people without disabilities* may be preferable. See **disabilities**.

ableism Discrimination or prejudice against people with disabilities; the belief that abilities of people who aren't disabled are superior. A concept similar to *racism, sexism* and *ageism* in that it includes stereotypes, generalizations, and demeaning views and language. It is a form of discrimination or prejudice against disabled people. See **disabilities**.

ABM, ABMs Acceptable in all references for *anti-ballistic missile(s),* but the term should be defined in the story. (The hyphen is an exception to Webster's New World College Dictionary.)

Avoid the redundant phrase *ABM missiles.*

abortion Use the modifiers *anti-abortion* or *abortion-rights;* don't use *pro-life, pro-choice* or *pro-abortion* unless they are in quotes or proper names. Avoid *abortionist,* which connotes a person who performs clandestine abortions.

Abu Sayyaf Muslim separatist group based in the southern islands of the Philippines. The name is Arabic for *father of the bearer of the sword.*

academic degrees If mention of degrees is necessary to establish someone's credentials, the preferred form is to avoid an abbreviation and use instead a phrase such as: *Fatima Kader, who has a doctorate in psychology.*

Use an apostrophe in *bachelor's degree, a master's*, etc., but there is no possessive in *Bachelor of Arts* or *Master of Science.*

Also: an *associate degree* (no possessive).

Use such abbreviations as *B.A., M.A., LL.D.* and *Ph.D.* only when the need to identify many individuals by degree on first reference would make the preferred form cumbersome. Use these abbreviations only after a full name — never after just a last name.

When used after a name, an academic abbreviation is set off by commas: *John Snow, Ph.D., spoke.*

Do not precede a name with a courtesy title for an academic degree and follow it with the abbreviation for the degree in the same reference.

See **doctor; Master of Arts, Master of Science, Master of Business Administration**.

academic departments Use lowercase except for words that are proper nouns or adjectives: *the department of history, the history department, the department of English, the English department,* or when *department* is part of the official and formal name: *University of Connecticut Department of Economics.*

academic titles Capitalize and spell out formal titles such as *chancellor, chair*, etc., when they precede a name. Lowercase elsewhere.

Lowercase modifiers such as *department* in *department Chair Jerome Wiesner.*

See **doctor** and **titles**.

Academy Awards Presented annually by the Academy of Motion Picture Arts and Sciences. Also known as the *Oscars.* (Both *Academy Awards* and *Oscars* are trademarks.)

Lowercase *the academy* and *the awards* whenever they stand alone.

accent marks Use accent marks or other diacritical marks with names of people who request them or are widely known to use them, or if quoting directly in a language that uses them: *An officer spotted him and asked a question: "Cómo estás?" How are you?* Otherwise, do not use these marks in English-language stories. Note: Many AP customers' computer systems ingest via the ANPA standard and will not receive diacritical marks published by the AP.

accept, except *Accept* means *to receive. Except* means *to exclude.*

accident, crash Generally acceptable for automobile and other collisions and wrecks. However, when negligence is claimed or proven, avoid *accident*, which can be read by some as a term exonerating the person responsible. In such cases, use *crash, collision* or other terms.

accommodate

accounts payable Current liabilities or debts of a business which must be

a

paid within one year.

accounts receivable Amounts due to a company for merchandise or services sold on credit. These are short-term assets.

accused, alleged, suspected A person is *accused of*, not *with*, a crime.

To avoid any suggestion that an individual is being judged before a trial, do not use a phrase such as *accused slayer John Jones* or *the accused slayer; alleged killer Ralph Hornsby* or *the alleged killer; suspected shooter Carmine Jablonski* or *the suspected shooter.* Instead: *John Jones, accused of the slaying* or *Ralph Hornsby, charged with killing the man.*

Also see separate **allege** and **suspect** entries. For guidance on related terms, see **arrest** and **indict**.

Ace A trademark for a brand of elastic bandage. *Elastic bandage* is preferred in all references.

Achilles tendon No apostrophe for the tendon connecting the back of the heel to the calf muscles. But it's *Achilles' heel*, with an apostrophe, for a vulnerable spot.

acknowledgment

acre Equal to 43,560 square feet or 4,840 square yards. The metric equivalent is 0.4 (two-fifths) of a hectare or 4,047 square meters.

One square mile is 640 acres.

See **wildfires** and **hectare**.

ACT Use only the initials in referring to the previously designated *American College Testing.*

act, amendment, bill, law, measure, ordinance, resolution, rule, statute The word *act* is sometimes included in a formal name for pending or implemented legislation. Capitalize when part of the name: *the Taft-Hartley Act.*

An *amendment* is a change or proposed change to a bill or law. Amendments are usually *passed* or *enacted.*

A *bill* is a draft proposal presented to a lawmaking body, such as a legislature, that requires debate, voting and final approval before it can become a *law.* Bills usually *pass* or *fail*, or are *approved* or *signed.* Do not capitalize when part of references to specific legislation: *the Kennedy bill.* Use conditional language for bills throughout the legislative process: *The bill would prohibit such activity; the bill seeks to legalize the drug.*

A *law* is a bill that has been approved by a lawmaking body, usually at the state or federal level, and that sometimes requires the signature of an executive such as a governor or president. Laws are usually *enacted* and don't necessarily *take effect* at the time they are enacted.

An *ordinance* is the municipal equivalent of a *law.* Ordinances are *enacted.* Before they become *ordinances*, they should usually be called *proposals* or *proposed ordinances.* Though terminology varies from place to place, it's usually best to avoid referring to such proposals as *bills*, to avoid confusion with higher levels of government.

A *resolution* is a sentiment or recommendation of a lawmaking body, often described as *binding* or *nonbinding* depending on whether it has the force of law. Resolutions are *adopted* or *fail*.

A *rule* is an authoritative regulation that can be *enacted*, *created* or *ordered* at various levels of government.

A *statute* is a written and enacted *law* or *ordinance*.

Any of the above terms can also be described generically as *measures*, provided no confusion would result.

acting Always lowercase, but capitalize any formal title that may follow before a name: *acting Mayor Peter Barry*.

See **titles**.

act numbers Use Arabic figures and capitalize *act*: *Act 1; Act 2, Scene 2*. But: *the first act, the second act*. See **numerals**.

A.D. Acceptable in all references for *anno Domini*: in the year of the Lord.

Because the full phrase would read *in the year of the Lord 96*, the abbreviation *A.D.* goes before the figure for the year: *A.D. 96*.

Do not write: *The fourth century A.D. The fourth century* is sufficient. If A.D. is not specified with a year, the year is presumed to be A.D.

See **B.C.**

addiction Addiction is a treatable disease that affects a person's brain and behavior. Drug and alcohol use can cause changes in the brain that lead to compulsive use, despite damage incurred to a person's health and relationships. Genetics, mental illness and other factors make certain people susceptible to addiction.

Addiction is the preferred term. The term *substance use disorder* is preferred by some health professionals and is acceptable in some uses, such as in quotations or scientific contexts. *Alcoholism* is acceptable for addiction to alcohol.

Avoid words like *abuse* or *problem* in favor of the word *use* with an appropriate modifier such as *risky, unhealthy, excessive* or *heavy. Misuse* is also acceptable. Don't assume all people who engage in risky use of drugs or alcohol have an addiction.

Avoid *alcoholic, addict, user* and *abuser* unless individuals prefer those terms for themselves or if they occur in quotations or names of organizations, such as Alcoholics Anonymous. Avoid derogatory terminology such as *junkie, drunk* or *crackhead* unless in quotations. Many researchers and organizations, including the Office of National Drug Control Policy and the International Society of Addiction Journal Editors, agree that stigmatizing or punitive-sounding language can be inaccurate by emphasizing the person, not the disease; can be a barrier to seeking treatment; and can prejudice even doctors. Instead, choose phrasing like *he was addicted, people with heroin addiction* or *he used drugs*.

Examples: *Keene had trouble keeping his job because of alcoholism*, not *Keene had trouble keeping his job because he was an alcoholic. Yang joined other people with heroin addictions at the conference*, not *Yang joined other heroin addicts at the conference*.

Avoid describing *sobriety* as *clean* unless in quotations, since it implies a previous state of dirtiness instead of disease.

Not all compulsive behaviors, including shopping, eating and sex, are considered addictions. Gambling is the only one classified as an addiction in the American

Psychiatric Association's diagnostic manual. The World Health Organization says excessive video gaming can be an addiction.

Do not use the terms *addiction* and *dependence* interchangeably. *Addiction* usually refers to a disease or disorder; *dependence* may not involve one, such as some babies born to mothers who use drugs or cancer patients who take prescribed painkillers.

The term *misuse* can be helpful in cases of legally prescribed medications, such as if a person with a painkiller prescription purposely takes too many to get high, or excessively uses medical marijuana. Such actions do not necessarily entail an addiction but can progress into one.

See **alcoholic**; **diseases**; **drugs**; **mental illness**; **naloxone**; **opiate, opioid**; and the **Health and Science chapter**.

addresses Use the abbreviations *Ave.*, *Blvd.* and *St.* only with a numbered address: *1600 Pennsylvania Ave.* Spell them out and capitalize when part of a formal street name without a number: *Pennsylvania Avenue*. Lowercase and spell out when used alone or with more than one street name: *Massachusetts and Pennsylvania avenues*.

All similar words (*alley*, *drive*, *road*, *terrace*, etc.) always are spelled out. Capitalize them when part of a formal name without a number; lowercase when used alone or with two or more names.

Always use figures for an address number: *9 Morningside Circle*.

Spell out and capitalize *First* through *Ninth* when used as street names; use figures for *10th* and above: *7 Fifth Ave.*, *100 21st St.*

Abbreviate compass points used to indicate directional ends of a street or quadrants of a city in a numbered address: *222 E. 42nd St.*, *562 W. 43rd St.*, *600 K St. NW.* Do not abbreviate if the number is omitted: *East 42nd Street, West 43rd Street, K Street Northwest.* No periods in quadrant abbreviations — NW, SE — unless customary locally.

See **highway designations**.

Use periods in the abbreviation *P.O.* for *P.O. Box* numbers.

See **numerals**.

adjustable-rate mortgage A mortgage that has a fixed interest rate for a short period of time and then resets, usually yearly, over the life of the loan, based on an index tied to changes in market interest rates. *ARM* should be used only in direct quotes.

ad-lib

administration Lowercase: *the administration, the president's administration, the governor's administration, the Biden administration.*

See **government, junta, regime, administration** for distinctions that apply in using these terms.

administrative law judge This is the federal title for the position formerly known as *hearing examiner*. Capitalize it when used as a formal title before a name.

To avoid the long title, seek a construction that sets the title off by commas: *The administrative law judge, John Williams, disagreed.*

administrator Never abbreviate. Capitalize when used as a formal title before a name.

See **titles**.

admissible

admit, admitted These words may in some contexts give the erroneous connotation of wrongdoing.

People who say they are recovering from alcoholism, for example, are not *admitting* it. *Said* is usually sufficient.

ad nauseam

adoption The adoptive status of children or their parents should be mentioned only when its relevance is made clear in the story. If relevant, use the term *biological* or *birth parents/mother/father*. Do not use *real* or *first parents/mother/father*. Write that a *child is placed for adoption*, rather than *given up for adoption*, unless people use the latter or other terms for their own situation: *She describes herself as given up for adoption.*

Adrenalin A trademark for the synthetic or chemically extracted forms of epinephrine, a substance produced by the adrenal glands.

The nonproprietary terms are *epinephrine hydrochloride* or *adrenaline*.

adult A person who has reached 18. See **privacy**.

Advanced Placement courses and exams College-level high school courses and exams offered in high school. *AP classes* and *AP exams* are acceptable on second reference.

adverse, averse *Adverse* means *unfavorable*: *He predicted adverse weather.*

Averse means *reluctant, opposed*: *She is averse to change.*

adviser Not *advisor*.

affect, effect *Affect*, as a verb, means *to influence*: *The game will affect the standings.*

Affect, as a noun, is best avoided. It occasionally is used in psychology to describe an emotion, but there is no need for it in everyday language.

Effect, as a verb, means *to cause*: *He will effect many changes in the company.*

Effect, as a noun, means *result*: *The effect was overwhelming. He miscalculated the effect of his actions. It was a law of little effect.*

Affordable Care Act Shorthand for the formal title of the health care overhaul that former President Barack Obama signed into law in 2010. The term is acceptable on first reference, but explain later in the story: *former President Barack Obama's health care law*. On second reference, *ACA* or *"Obamacare"* (the latter in quote marks) are acceptable. Its full name is Patient Protection and Affordable Care Act.

Afghan The term for the people and culture of Afghanistan. *Afghani* is the *Afghan* unit of currency.

AFL-CIO Acceptable in all references for the *American Federation of Labor and Congress of Industrial Organizations*. Headquarters is in Washington.

African Union The African Union, established in 2002 to succeed the Organization of African Unity, has the following 55 members:
Algeria, Angola, Benin,

a

Botswana, Burkina Faso, Burundi, Cameroon, Cape Verde, Central African Republic, Chad, Comoros, Congo, Djibouti, Egypt, Equatorial Guinea, Eritrea, Eswatini (formerly Swaziland), Ethiopia, Gabon, Gambia, Ghana, Guinea-Bissau, Guinea, Ivory Coast, Kenya, Lesotho, Liberia, Libya, Madagascar, Malawi, Mali, Mauritania, Mauritius, Morocco, Mozambique, Namibia, Niger, Nigeria, Republic of Congo, Rwanda, Sao Tome and Principe, Senegal, Seychelles, Sierra Leone, Somalia, South Africa, South Sudan, Sudan, Tanzania, Togo, Tunisia, Uganda, Western Sahara, Zambia, Zimbabwe. There are two Congos: *the Republic of Congo* and *the Democratic Republic of Congo*. The latter is *the Congo* in AP style.

after- No hyphen after this prefix when it is used to form a noun:
> *aftereffect   afterthought*

Follow *after* with a hyphen when it is used to form compound modifiers:
> *after-dinner drink*
> *after-theater snack*

afterward Not *afterwards*.

agent Lowercase unless it is a formal title used before a name.

In the FBI, the formal title is *special agent*. In most cases, make it *agent William Smith* or *FBI agent William Smith*.

See **titles**.

ages Use when deemed relevant to the situation. If someone is quoted as saying, "I'm too old to get another job," the age is relevant. Generally, use ages for profiles, obituaries, significant career milestones and achievements unusual for the age. Use ages for people commenting or providing information only if their age is relevant to their comments (e.g., a teenager's comment on video games aimed at that age group). Appropriate background, such as a *parent of two young children* or a *World War II veteran*, may suffice instead of the actual age.

Always use figures. *The girl is 15 years old; the law is 8 years old; the 101-year-old house.* When the context does not require *years* or *years old*, the figure is presumed to be *years*.

Use hyphens for ages expressed as adjectives before a noun or as substitutes for a noun.

Examples: *A 5-year-old boy*, but *the boy is 5 years old. The boy, 7, has a sister, 10. The woman, 26, has a daughter 2 months old. The race is for 3-year-olds. The woman is in her 30s* (no apostrophe).

See also **boy, girl**; **infant**; **youth**; **older adult(s), older person/people** and **numerals**.

See **comma** in punctuation guidelines.

agnostic, atheist An *agnostic* believes it is impossible to know whether any deities exist. An *atheist* believes that no deities exist.

aid, aide *Aid* is assistance.

An *aide* is a person who serves as an assistant.

AIDS Acceptable in all references for *acquired immune deficiency syndrome*, sometimes called *acquired immunodeficiency syndrome*.

AIDS is a disease that weakens the immune system, gradually destroying the body's ability to fight infections and certain cancers. It is caused by *human immunodeficiency virus*, or *HIV*. (*HIV virus* is redundant.)

HIV is spread most often through sexual contact; shared or contaminated needles or syringes; infected blood or blood products; and from infected women to their babies at birth or through breastfeeding.

Use the *HIV/AIDS* construction with care. People can be infected with the virus and not have *AIDS*; they do not have *AIDS* until they develop serious symptoms. Many remain infected but apparently healthy for years.

See **cocktail**.

air bag Two words.

air base Two words. Follow the practice of the U.S. Air Force, which uses *air force base* as part of the proper name for its bases in the United States and *air base* for its installations abroad. Some bases have become joint bases with other services.

On second reference: *the Air Force base, the air base,* or *the base.*

Do not abbreviate, even in datelines:

LACKLAND AIR FORCE BASE, Texas (AP) —

JOINT BASE ANDREWS, Md. (AP) —

air-condition, air-conditioned (v. and adj.) The nouns are: *air conditioner, air conditioning.*

aircraft names Use a hyphen when changing from letters to figures; no hyphen when adding a letter after figures.

Some examples of aircraft: *B-1, C-5A, FH-227, F-15 Eagle, F-16 Falcon, MiG-29, Tu-154, Il-96, Boeing 737-800, 747, 747B. Airbus A380, A380F* (no hyphen) is an exception.

This hyphenation principle is the one used most frequently by manufacturers and users. Apply it in all cases for consistency. For other elements of a name, use the form adopted by the manufacturer or user. If in doubt, consult IHS Jane's All the World's Aircraft.

NO QUOTES: Do not use quotation marks for aircraft with names: *Air Force One, the Spirit of St. Louis.*

AVOID PROMOTIONAL NAMES: *Boeing 787,* not *Dreamliner.*

PLURALS: *747s.* But: *747B's.* (As noted in plurals, the apostrophe is used in forming the plural of a single letter.)

SEQUENCE: Use Arabic figures to establish the sequence of aircraft, spacecraft and missiles: *Apollo 10.* Do not use hyphens.

See **numerals**.

aircraft terms Use *engine,* not *motor,* for the units that propel aircraft: a *twin-engine* plane (not *twin engined*).

Use *jet plane* or *jetliner* to describe only those aircraft driven solely by jet engines. Use *turboprop* to describe an aircraft on which the jet engine is geared to a propeller. Turboprops sometimes are called *propjets.*

See **engine, motor**.

aired, broadcast, televised *Televised* is the preferred term for shows and other programs shown on television. *Broadcast* and *aired* are acceptable for over-the-air channels.

airfare

air force Capitalize when referring to U.S. forces: *the U.S. Air Force, the Air Force, Air Force regulations.* Do not use the abbreviation *USAF.*

Use lowercase for the forces of

a

other nations: *the Israeli air force*.

This approach has been adopted for consistency, because many foreign nations do not use *air force* as the proper name.

See **military academies** and **military titles**.

Air Force One The Air Force applies this name to any of its aircraft the president of the United States may be using.

In ordinary usage, however, *Air Force One* is the name of the Air Force plane normally reserved for the president's use.

airline, airlines Capitalize *airlines*, *air lines* and *airways* when used as part of a proper airline name.

Companies that use *Airlines* in the title include Alaska, American, Hawaiian, Japan, Southwest and United.

Companies that use *Airways* include British, JetBlue and Qantas.

Delta uses *Air Lines*.

Companies that use none of these include Aer Lingus, Aeromexico, Air Canada, Air France, Air India, Emirates and Iberia.

On second reference, use just the proper name (*Delta*), an abbreviation if applicable, or *the airline*. Acceptable abbreviations are *ANA* for *All Nippon Airways*, *BA* for *British Airways* and *JAL* for *Japan Airlines*. Use *airlines* when referring to more than one line.

Do not use *air line*, *air lines* or *airways* in generic references to an airline.

Air National Guard

airport Capitalize as part of a proper name: *LaGuardia Airport*, *O'Hare International Airport*.

The first name of an individual and the word *international* may be deleted from a formal airport name while the remainder is capitalized: *John F. Kennedy International Airport*, *Kennedy International Airport*, or *Kennedy Airport*. Use whichever is appropriate in the context.

Do not make up names, however. There is no *Boston Airport*, for example. The *Boston airport* (lowercase *airport*) would be acceptable if for some reason the proper name, *Logan International Airport*, were not used.

airsoft gun A gun that commonly shoots plastic spheres, typically propelled by compressed air or springs. *Pellet gun* is acceptable on first reference.

airstrike

air traffic controller No hyphen.

aka Abbreviation for *also known as*.

Al-Aqsa Mosque See entry in the **Religion** chapter.

alarms Avoid referring to a fire in terms of the number of "alarms," which may mean little to a distant reader. Depending on the city or town, a two-alarm fire could involve widely varying numbers of firefighters. Instead, specify the number of firefighters or quantity of equipment.

Alaska Standard Time The time zone used in all of Alaska, except the western Aleutian Islands and St. Lawrence Island, which are on *Hawaii-Aleutian Standard Time*.

There is also an *Alaska Daylight Time*.

See **time zones**.

Alberta A province of western Canada. Do not abbreviate.
See **datelines**.

albinism (n.), **albino** (adj.) Albinism is a genetic condition that reduces the amount of melanin pigment in the skin, hair and/or eyes. People with albinism have vision problems that are not correctable with eyeglasses; the degree of vision loss varies. Describe a person as *having albinism* only if relevant to the story, and if a medical diagnosis has been made or the person uses the term. If relatives or others use the term, ask how they know, then consider carefully whether to include the information. Avoid referring to *people with albinism* as *albinos* or *an albino*, unless the person or group prefers that term. The adjective *albino* is acceptable for animals or plants with the condition. See **disabilities**.

alcoholic As an adjective, use it to describe beverages. For people, generally say *people* or *person with alcoholism*, or *person recovering from alcoholism*. Avoid *an alcoholic* unless individuals prefer that term for themselves or if they occur in quotations or names of organizations, such as Alcoholics Anonymous. Avoid describing people as *drunks*, though the word can be used as an adjective to describe someone who is temporarily intoxicated by alcohol. See **addiction**.

Alcoholics Anonymous *AA* is acceptable on second reference.

Alexa Name of Amazon's *voice assistant*. Do not refer to Alexa with feminine pronouns. Runs on devices such as Amazon's *Echo* smart speakers.

A-list

all- Use a hyphen:
all-around (*not all-round*)   *all-out*
all-clear   *all-star*
See **all right** and the **all time, all-time** entries.

Allah The Arabic word for God. The word *God* should be used, unless the Arabic name is used in a quote written or spoken in English.

Allahu akbar The Arabic phrase for *God is great.*

allege The word must be used with great care.
Some guidelines:
— Avoid any suggestion that the writer is making an allegation.
— Specify the source of an allegation. In a criminal case, it should be an arrest record, an indictment or the statement of a public official connected with the case.
— Use *alleged bribe* or similar phrase when necessary to make it clear that an unproved action is not being treated as fact. Be sure that the source of the charge is specified elsewhere in the story.
— Avoid, where possible, *alleged victim*. It is too easily construed as skepticism of a victim's account.
— Avoid redundant uses of *alleged*. It is proper to say: *The district attorney alleged that she took a bribe.* Or: *The district attorney accused her of taking a bribe.* But not: *The district attorney accused her of allegedly taking a bribe.*

a

— Do not use *alleged* to describe an event that is known to have occurred, when the dispute is over who participated in it. Do not say: *He attended the alleged meeting* when what you mean is: *He allegedly attended the meeting.*

— Do not use *alleged* as a routine qualifier. Instead, use a word such as *apparent, ostensible* or *reputed.* For guidelines on related words, see **accused, alleged, suspected; arrest;** and **indict.**

Allegheny Mountains Or simply: *the Alleghenies.*

alley Do not abbreviate. See **addresses.**

allies, allied Capitalize *allies* or *allied* only when referring to the combination of the United States and its Allies during World War I or World War II: *The Allies defeated Germany. He was in the Allied invasion of France.*

all right Never *alright.* Hyphenate only if used colloquially as a compound modifier: *He is an all-right guy.*

all-terrain vehicle *ATV* is acceptable on second reference.

all time, all-time An *all-time high*, but *the greatest runner of all time.* Avoid the redundant phrase *all-time record.*

allude, refer To *allude* to something is to speak of it without specifically mentioning it. To *refer* is to mention it directly.

allusion, illusion *Allusion* means *an indirect reference*: *The allusion was to his opponent's war record.* *Illusion* means *an unreal or false*

impression: *The scenic director created the illusion of choppy seas.*

al-Qaida Muslim militant group founded by Osama bin Laden that carried out the attacks in the United States on Sept. 11, 2001. Bin Laden was killed by U.S. forces in Pakistan in May 2011. Al-Qaida's current leader is Ayman al-Zawahri.

Affiliated groups include:
al-Qaida in the Arabian Peninsula, operating in Yemen and Saudi Arabia.

Nusra Front, operating in Syria.

al-Qaida in the Islamic Maghreb, operating in the Sahel region, a region along the Sahara Desert stretching across North Africa.

Khorasan group, an al-Qaida cell that the United States says operated in Syria to plot attacks on the U.S.

Al-Quds The Arabic name for Jerusalem; it means *the holy.*

al-Shabab The preferred spelling for the Somali militant group.

altar, alter An *altar* is a tablelike platform used in a religious service. *To alter* is to change.

"alt-right" A political grouping or tendency mixing racism, white nationalism, antisemitism and populism; a name currently embraced by some white supremacists and white nationalists to refer to themselves and their ideology, which emphasizes preserving and protecting the white race in the United States.

Avoid using the term generically and without definition, because it is not well known globally and the term may exist primarily as a public relations device to make its supporters' actual beliefs less clear and more acceptable to a broader audience. In AP stories discussing what the movement says about itself, the term *"alt-right"* (quotation marks, hyphen and lowercase) may be used in quotes or modified as in the *self-described "alt-right"* or *so-called alt-right*.

Depending on the specifics of the situation, such beliefs might be termed *racist, white supremacist* or *neo-Nazi*; be sure to describe the specifics. Whenever *"alt-right"* is used in a story, include a definition: *an offshoot of conservatism mixing racism, white nationalism, antisemitism and populism*, or, more simply, *a white nationalist movement*.

When writing on extreme groups, be precise and provide evidence to support the characterization. Report their actions, associations, history and positions to reveal their actual beliefs and philosophy, as well as how others see them.

Some related definitions:

racism The broad term for asserting racial or ethnic discrimination or superiority based solely on race, ethnic or religious origins; it can be by any group against any other group.

white nationalism A subset of racist beliefs that calls for a separate territory and/or enhanced legal rights and protections for white people. Critics accuse white nationalists of being white supremacists in disguise.

white separatism A term sometimes used as a synonym for *white nationalism* but differs in that it advocates a form of segregation in which races would live apart but in the same general geographic area.

white supremacy The racist belief that whites are superior to justify political, economic and social suppression of nonwhite people and other minority groups.

neo-Nazism Combines racist and white supremacist beliefs with admiration for an authoritarian, totalitarian style of government such as the German Third Reich to enforce its beliefs.

antifa Shorthand for *anti-fascists*, an umbrella description for the far-left-leaning militant groups that resist neo-Nazis and white supremacists at demonstrations and other events. Until the term becomes better known, include a definition in close proximity to first use of the word.

"alt-left" A term that some use to describe far-left factions. See "alt-right" for usage guidelines.

See **race-related coverage**.

Alzheimer's disease A progressive, irreversible neurological disorder and the most common form of dementia. Most victims are older than 65, but Alzheimer's can strike at earlier ages.

Symptoms may include memory loss, issues with judgment, disorientation, personality change, difficulty in learning and loss of language skills. Alzheimer's disease is defined by specific changes in the brain that occur before symptoms appear. Current drugs only ease symptoms and don't reverse the course of the disease.

The terms *younger-onset* or *early-onset Alzheimer's disease* applies to people diagnosed before age 65.

Do not use the terms *senile* or *demented*.

See **disabilities; dementia**.

ambassador Capitalize as a formal title before a name.

a See **titles**.

Amber Alert A procedure for rapidly publicizing the disappearance of a child.

America, American, Americans Can be used to refer to the *United States* and *U.S. citizens* if that meaning is clear in the context. Use the modifier *U.S.* in referring to the federal government and its officials in the United States.

American Bar Association *ABA* is acceptable on second reference. Headquarters is in Chicago.

American Civil Liberties Union *ACLU* is acceptable on second reference.
Headquarters is in New York.

American depositary receipt A negotiable certificate representing a foreign company's equity or debt. *ADR* is acceptable on second reference.

American depositary share A security issued by a foreign company representing an ownership interest in that company. It can represent a fixed number of securities on deposit, or a fraction of them. *ADS* is acceptable on second reference.

American Federation of Government Employees Use this full name on first reference to prevent confusion with other unions that represent government workers. *AFGE* is acceptable on second reference.
Headquarters is in Washington.

American Federation of Labor and Congress of Industrial Organizations *AFL-CIO* is acceptable in all references.
Headquarters is in Washington.

American Federation of State, County and Municipal Employees *AFSCME* is acceptable on second reference.
Headquarters is in Washington.

American Federation of Teachers *AFT* is acceptable on second reference.
Headquarters is in Washington.

American Hospital Association *AHA* is acceptable on second reference. Headquarters is in Chicago.

Americanisms Words and phrases that have become part of the English language as spoken in the United States are listed with a star in Webster's New World College Dictionary.
Most Americanisms are acceptable in news stories, but let the context be the guide.

American Legion Capitalize also *the Legion* in second reference. Members are *Legionnaires*, just as members of the Lions Club are *Lions*.
Legion and *Legionnaires* are capitalized because they are not being used in their common noun sense. A *legion* (lowercase) is a large group of soldiers or, by derivation, a large number of items: *His friends are legion*. A *legionnaire* (lowercase) is a member of such a legion.
See **fraternal organizations and service clubs**.

American Medical Association *AMA* is acceptable on second reference. Headquarters is in Chicago.

American Petroleum Institute *API* is acceptable on second reference. Headquarters is in Washington.

American Postal Workers Union This union represents clerks and similar employees who work inside post offices.

Use the full name on first reference to prevent confusion with the National Association of Letter Carriers. The shortened form *Postal Workers union* is acceptable on second reference.

Headquarters is in Washington.

American Sign Language A complete language consisting of manual signs and gestures, facial expressions, and body positions used by many deaf and hard-of-hearing people in the United States, Canada and a number of other countries. It does not parallel English grammatical structure. *ASL* is acceptable on second reference.

Some minority linguistic signing communities within the United States and some parts of Canada use either dialects of ASL or what are considered to be separate languages. Examples include *Black American Sign Language* and *North American Indian Sign Language*.

Other countries or regions may have their own sign languages, such as *British Sign Language* and *French Sign Language*.

When quoting someone who signs, explain on first reference: *The city's economic forecast is promising, Cauley said through a sign language interpreter*. On later references, simply *said* is sufficient.

See **deaf, Deaf, hard of hearing**; **disabilities**.

American Society of Composers,

Authors and Publishers *ASCAP* is acceptable on second reference. Headquarters is in New York.

Americans with Disabilities Act A 1990 U.S. law that prohibits discrimination on the basis of disability. *ADA* is acceptable on second reference. The law defines a disability as a physical or mental impairment that substantially limits one or more major life activities. It does not specifically name all disabilities that are covered. See **disabilities**.

AmeriCorps

amid Not *amidst*.

amok Not *amuck*.

among, between The maxim that *between* introduces two items and *among* introduces more than two covers most questions about how to use these words: *The choice is between fish and tofu. The funds were divided among Ford, Carter and McCarthy*.

However, *between* is the correct word when expressing the relationships of three or more items considered one pair at a time: *The games between the Yankees, Phillies and Mets have been rollicking ones*.

As with all prepositions, any pronouns that follow these words must be in the objective case: *among us, between him and her, between you and me*.

amount, number Use *amount* for things that cannot be counted individually: *the amount of milk in the refrigerator, the amount of courage it takes to climb Mount Everest*. For things that can be counted individually, use *number*: *The number*

a

of soldiers in an army, the number of books in a library. Similarly, use *less* for things that can't be counted — *less paper, less paint* — and *fewer* for things that can: *fewer days, fewer votes.* However, some expressions are exceptions: *Write the jingle in 25 words or less.*

ampersand (&) Use the ampersand when it is part of a company's formal name or composition title: *House & Garden, Procter & Gamble, Wheeling & Lake Erie Railway.*

The ampersand should not otherwise be used in place of *and,* except for some accepted abbreviations: *B&B, R&B.*

a.m., p.m. Lowercase, with periods. Avoid the redundant *10 a.m. this morning.*

Amtrak This acronym, drawn from the words *American travel by track,* may be used in all references to the *National Railroad Passenger Corp.* Do not use *AMTRAK.* Headquarters is in Washington.

AMVETS Acceptable in all references for *American Veterans,* the organization formerly known as *American Veterans of World War II, Korea, and Vietnam.*

Headquarters is in Washington.

Android The world's largest operating system for phones, tablets and other devices. Owned by Google. Google gives away the system for free; the company has drawn criticism for the way it previously bundled its own services with the operating system. Many device manufacturers use Google's app store and other Google apps on Android devices, giving Google more users — and data on those users.

Anglo- Always capitalized. No hyphen when the word that follows is in lowercase:

> *Anglomania   Anglophobe*
> *Anglophile*

Use a hyphen when the word that follows is capitalized:

> *Anglo-American   Anglo-Indian*
> *Anglo-Catholic   Anglo-Saxon*

animals Do not apply a personal pronoun to an animal unless its sex has been established or the animal has a name: *The dog was scared; it barked. Rover was scared; he barked. The cat, which was scared, ran to its basket. Susie the cat, who was scared, ran to her basket. The bull tosses his horns.*

Capitalize the name of a specific animal, and use Roman numerals to show sequence: *Bowser, Whirlaway II.*

For breed names, follow the spelling and capitalization in Webster's New World College Dictionary. For breeds not listed in the dictionary, capitalize words derived from proper nouns; use lowercase elsewhere: *basset hound, Boston terrier.*

In stories about animal attacks, especially by dogs, avoid stereotyping particular breeds. The breed should be included in such stories but does not necessarily need to be especially prominent unless newsworthy in itself.

animal welfare activist Use instead of *animal rights activist.*

anniversary Avoid terms such as *six-month anniversary* (or other time spans less than a year).

annual Avoid the term *first annual*.

annual meeting Lowercase in all uses.

anonymous sources Whenever possible, we pursue information on the record. When a source insists on background or off-the-record ground rules, we must adhere to a strict set of guidelines.

Under AP's rules, material from anonymous sources may be used only if:

— The material is information and not opinion or speculation, and is vital to the news report.
— The information is not available except under the conditions of anonymity imposed by the source.
— The source is reliable, and in a position to have accurate information.

Reporters who intend to use material from anonymous sources must get approval from their news managers.

Explain in the story why the source requested anonymity. And, when it's relevant, describe the source's motive for disclosing the information.

The story also must provide attribution that establishes the source's credibility; simply quoting *a source* is not allowed. Be as descriptive as possible about the source of information. If space is limited, use *source* as a last resort. *Official* or a similar word will often suffice, including in headlines. See **source**.

Examples:

Speaking on customary condition of anonymity in line with government rules, the official said the two sides were engaged "in very fierce" battles near the border crossing, and that one woman was wounded by a stray bullet.

Incorrect: Granting anonymity *"on customary condition ... in line with government rules"* is insufficient. Readers need a plausible explanation of such a condition, and why we're accepting it. For instance, *"The rules of the official's job did not allow him to be quoted by name."*

A security official, who requested anonymity because of the sensitivity of the case, said the suspect was monitoring and recording the movements of tourists before his arrest in July.

Incorrect: First, we grant anonymity only to those who insist on it, not those who *request* it. Second, granting anonymity because of the *sensitivity of the case* is insufficient explanation. Did the official insist on anonymity because he was not allowed to speak with reporters? Because he was not authorized to release information in advance of a public announcement of details of the case?

Speaking privately, a senior Foreign Ministry official said any further increase in tension could strengthen "warlike" sentiment on both sides and make a resolution of the problem even more difficult.

Incorrect: *Speaking privately* isn't the same thing as insisting on anonymity, so we cannot use the *privately* explanation. Moreover, the official is speculating on something that might happen. We grant anonymity for factual information, not speculation or opinion.

Sometimes a government or corporation intentionally leaks information, but insists we publish it attributed to an anonymous official. If we cannot convince the government or company to go on the

a

record, it's best to use a formulation that implies that the release of the information was official, even though anonymous. For instance: ... *according to the official, who insisted on anonymity because he was not allowed to use his own name in releasing the findings*.

For additional guidance, see **Statement of News Values**.

another *Another* is not a synonym for *additional*; it refers to an element that somehow duplicates a previously stated quantity.

Right: *Ten people took the test; another 10 refused.*

Wrong: *Ten people took the test; another 20 refused.*

Right: *Ten people took the test; 20 others refused.*

Antarctic, Antarctica, Antarctic Ocean

ante- The rules in **prefixes** apply, but in general, no hyphen. Some examples:

antebellum   antedate

anthems See **composition titles**. Lowercase the term *national anthem*.

anti- Hyphenate all except the following words, which have specific meanings of their own:

antibiotic	*antiperspirant*
antibody	*antiphon*
anticlimax	*antiphony*
anticoagulant	*antipollution*
antidepressant	*antipsychotic*
antidote	*antisemitic*
antifreeze	*antisemitism*
antigen	*antiseptic*
antihistamine	*antiserum*
antiknock	*antispyware*
antimatter	*antithesis*
antimicrobial	*antitoxin*
antimony	*antitrust*
antioxidant	*antitussive*
*antiparticle**	*antiviral*
antipasto	*antivirus*

*And similar terms in physics such as *antiproton*.

This approach has been adopted in the interests of readability and easily remembered consistency.

It's *anti-lock* in Webster's New World College Dictionary. But note these Stylebook exceptions to Webster's spellings:

anti-abortion anti-social
anti-aircraft   anti-war
anti-labor

See **Antichrist, anti-Christ** in **Religion** chapter.

anticipate, expect *Anticipate* means to expect and prepare for something; *expect* does not include the notion of preparation:

They expect a record crowd. They have anticipated it by adding more seats to the auditorium.

antisemitism (n.), **antisemitic** (adj.) Prejudice or discrimination against Jews. A 2021 change from previous style (*anti-Semitism* and *anti-Semitic*).

The term was coined in the 19th century by the German writer Wilhelm Marr, who opposed efforts to extend the full rights of German citizenship to Jews. He asserted that Jews were Semites — descended from the Semitic peoples of the Middle East and thus racially different from (and threatening to) Germany's Aryans. This racist pseudoscience was applied only to Jews, not Arabs.

The previous style was based on common usage. In recent years, that style has come under criticism from those who say it could give credence to the idea that Jews are a separate race. In response, a growing number of Jewish organizations and others have settled on the style *antisemitism*.

Avoid using the term *antisemite* for an individual other than in a direct quotation. Instead, be specific in describing the person's words or actions.

antitrust Any law or policy designed to encourage competition by curtailing monopolistic power and unfair business practices.

antiviral (n., adj.), **antivirus** (adj.) No hyphen in either term, an exception based on common usage to the general guidance to hyphenate *anti-* terms unless they have specific meanings of their own. Use *antiviral* in medical references: *an antiviral drug, antivirals to fight COVID-19.* Use *antivirus* in general references: *antivirus measures, antivirus controls.*

anti-vaxxer Do not use this term for someone who opposes or is hesitant about vaccinations. If necessary in a direct quotation, explain it.

anybody, any body, anyone, any one One word for an indefinite reference: *Anyone can do that.*

Two words when the emphasis is on singling out one element of a group: *Any one of them may speak up.*

AOL An online services provider owned by Verizon Communications Inc. Do not use its former name, America Online.

AP Acceptable on second reference for *The Associated Press.*

Either *AP* or *the AP* (no capital on *the*) may be used.

See **Associated Press**.

API Abbreviation for *application programming interface*, which is software code that allows one website, app or program to interact with another. Limit use of the term outside of technical references. *API* is acceptable on second reference.

apostrophe (') See entry in the **Punctuation** chapter.

app Short for *application* and acceptable on first reference. Typically used to refer to computer programs that run on phones, tablets and PCs, or as part of a larger online service — for instance, Facebook apps.

See **app, platform, service, site**.

Appalachia In the broadest sense, the word applies to the entire region along the Appalachian Mountains, which extend from Maine into northern Alabama.

In a sense that often suggests economic depression and poverty, the reference is to sections of eastern Tennessee, eastern Kentucky, southeastern Ohio and the western portion of West Virginia.

The Appalachian Regional Commission, established by federal law in 1965, has a mandate to foster development in 397 counties in 13 states — all of West Virginia and parts of Alabama, Georgia, Kentucky, Maryland, Mississippi, New York, North Carolina, Ohio, Pennsylvania, South Carolina, Tennessee and Virginia.

When the word *Appalachia* is used, specify the extent of the area in question.

Appalachian Mountains Or simply: *the Appalachians.*

a

20

a

apples Most varieties are capitalized, including *Cortland, Golden Delicious, Granny Smith, Honeycrisp* and *McIntosh*.

app, platform, service, site
Though these terms are often used interchangeably, they have different meanings:

An *app*, short for *application*, is software written for a mobile device or personal computer, typically for a specific task such as making an airline reservation or watching Netflix.

A *site*, short for *website*, is an online destination typically accessed via web browsers.

A *service* is a function that runs on the *app* or at the *site*. Just as lightbulbs tap electricity to work, *apps* and *sites* tap *services* to work.

A *platform* is a computing system composed of hardware, software, or both, on which *apps* and *services* can run, including those from third parties. The term is typically reserved for larger systems, such as the Facebook social network, Xbox video games and the Windows operating system for personal computers. Apps written for one platform would typically need to be adapted to work on another.

Some can be all four. For example, Facebook is a *site*, at Facebook.com, that accesses the Facebook *service*. Facebook's *service* can also be reached through a phone or tablet *app* called Facebook. And Facebook is a *platform* that lets third-party *apps* and *services* tap its tools.

app stores Lowercase references to *app stores* or a given company's *app store* are acceptable in most references. *The game is now available in both the Apple and Google app stores.*

The Justice Department is investigating whether policies of the Apple app store potentially violate antitrust law. If the formal name of a company's app store is required, it's *Apple App Store* and *Google Play Store*. Microsoft's is simply *Microsoft Store*, and Amazon's is *Amazon Appstore*.

April Fools' Day

Arab Spring Wave of pro-democratic protests, revolutions and civil wars that have swept some Arab nations since 2011.

Arabic names In general, use an English spelling that approximates the way a name sounds in Arabic.

If an individual has a preferred spelling in English, use that. If usage has established a particular spelling, use that.

Problems in transliteration of Arabic names often are traceable to pronunciations that vary from region to region. The *g*, for example, is pronounced like the *g* of *go* mainly in Egypt, and the *j* of *joy* in the rest of the Arab world. Thus it is *Gamal* in Egypt and *Jamal* in nations on the peninsula. Follow local practice in deciding which letter to use.

Arabs commonly are known by two names (*Hassan Nasrallah*), or by three (*Mohammed Mahdi Akef*). Follow the individual's preference on first reference. On second reference, use only the final name in the sequence.

The articles *al-* or *el-* may be used or dropped depending on the person's preference or established usage. (*Ayman al-Zawahri, al-Zawahri,* or *Moammar Gadhafi, Gadhafi*). The article *al-* or *el-* should not be capitalized.

The Arabic word for son (*ibn* or

bin) is sometimes part of a name. On second reference, it is often dropped, using only the final name. In cases of personal preference or common usage, it should be retained. (*Osama bin Laden, bin Laden; Abdul-Aziz bin Baz, bin Baz*).

The word *abu* or *abou*, meaning *father of*, occasionally is used as a last name (*Abdel-Halim Abou Ghazala*). Capitalize and repeat it on second reference: *Abou Ghazala*.

The word *abdul*, meaning "servant of (God)," generally does not stand alone as a name, except sometimes in South Asia and Afghanistan. It is used in combination with a second name (an Arabic word for an attribute of God). This combination should be hyphenated, unless the individual prefers otherwise, and capitalized (*Adil Abdul-Mahdi, Abdul-Mahdi*). In Egypt and some other countries, *Abdul* is often written *Abdel*, reflecting local pronunciation.

For royalty, the titles *king, emir, sheikh* and *imam* are used, but *prince* usually replaces *emir*. Some Arabs are known only by the title and a given name on first reference (*King Abdullah*). Others are known by a complete name (*Sheikh Mohammed bin Rashid Al Maktoum*). Follow the common usage on first reference. On second reference, drop the title and use only the first name (*Abdullah, Mohammed*). The full names of many Gulf royals include the word *Al*, which in their case should be capitalized without a hyphen since it means *family of*.

The *al* should be capitalized in front of most Muslim and Arab institutions, universities, newspapers and major mosques, as in *Al-Azhar*, the university in Cairo; *Al-Aqsa*, the Jerusalem mosque, the newspaper *Al-Ahram* and the satellite television news network *Al-Jazeera*.

Arabic numerals The numerical figures 0, 1, 2, 3, 4, 5, 6, 7, 8, 9.

In general, use Arabic forms unless denoting the sequence of wars or establishing a personal sequence for people or animals. See **Roman numerals**.

Separate entries list more details and examples. For a full list, see **numerals**.

arbitrage Buying currencies, commercial bills or securities in one market and selling them at the same time in another to make a profit on the price discrepancy.

arbitrate, mediate Both terms are used in reports about labor negotiations, but they should not be interchanged.

One who *arbitrates* hears evidence from all people concerned, then hands down a decision.

One who *mediates* listens to arguments of both parties and tries by the exercise of reason or persuasion to bring them to an agreement.

arch- No hyphen after this prefix unless it precedes a capitalized word:
archbishop   *arch-Republican*
archenemy   *archrival*

archaeology

arctic Lowercase for adjective meaning *frigid*; capitalize for region around the North Pole. **Arctic Circle, arctic fox, Arctic Ocean**

Argentine The preferred term for the people and culture of Argentina.

army Capitalize when referring to

U.S. forces: *the U.S. Army, the Army, Army regulations.* Do not use the abbreviation *USA.*

Use lowercase for the forces of other nations: *the French army.*

This approach has been adopted for consistency, because many foreign nations do not use *army* as the proper name.

See **military academies** and **military titles**.

arrest To avoid any suggestion that someone is being judged before a trial, do not use a phrase such as *arrested for killing.* Instead, use *arrested on a charge of killing.* If a charge hasn't been filed, *arrested on suspicion of,* or a similar phrase, should be used.

For guidelines on related words, see **accused; allege; indict; sue.**

artificial intelligence A computer system that emulates aspects of human cognition. Such systems are not sentient, but can accomplish human-level tasks such as visual perception, understanding and using speech, and learning — though only to a limited extent in many cases. *AI* is acceptable in headlines and on second reference in text. See **machine learning.**

artworks Lowercase *impressionism, modernism* and other art styles and movements unless used in formal titles of shows or exhibits with quotation marks. Exception: *Bauhaus* is capitalized as the name of a school. *Gothic, Renaissance* and other historical periods are capitalized for art and architecture from those ages. Titles of paintings are enclosed in quotes: *"Mona Lisa."* Sculptures are capitalized without quotes: *The Thinker, Michelangelo's Pieta.*

See **composition titles.**

Asian Used to describe people from Asia. Avoid using *Asian* as shorthand for *Asian American* when possible. See **race-related coverage.**

assassin, killer, murderer An *assassin* is one who kills a politically important or prominent person.

A *killer* is anyone who kills with a motive of any kind.

A *murderer* is one who is convicted of murder in a court of law.

Preferred use: *Joe Smith was convicted of second-degree murder.*

See **execute, execution** and the **homicide, murder, manslaughter** entry.

assassination Use the term only if it involves the murder of a politically important or prominent individual by surprise attack.

assassination, date of A prominent person is shot one day and dies the next. Which day was he assassinated? The day he was attacked.

assault, battery *Assault* almost always implies physical contact and sudden, intense violence.

Legally, however, *assault* means simply to threaten violence, as in pointing a pistol at an individual without firing it. *Assault and battery* is the legal term when the victim was touched by the assaulter or something the assaulter put in motion.

assembly Capitalize when part of the proper name for the lower house of a legislature: *the California Assembly.* Retain capitalization if the state name is dropped but the reference is specific:

SACRAMENTO, Calif. (AP) — The state Assembly ...

If a legislature is known as a general assembly: *the Missouri General Assembly, the General Assembly, the assembly. Legislature* also may be used as the proper name, however. See **legislature**.

Lowercase all plural uses: *the California and New York assemblies.*

assets Everything a company or an individual owns or is owed.

Assets may be broken down as:

Current assets: cash, investments, money due to a corporation, unused raw materials and inventories of finished but unsold products.

Fixed assets: buildings, machinery and land.

Intangible assets: patents and goodwill.

See **goodwill**.

asset-backed security A financial security backed by loans, leases, credit-card debt, royalties, a company's accounts receivables, etc. *ABS* should not be used in copy.

asset, fixed Plant, land, equipment, long-term investments that cannot be readily liquefied without disturbing the operation of the business.

assistant Do not abbreviate. Capitalize only when part of a formal title before a name: *Assistant Secretary of State Richard Boucher.* Whenever practical, however, an appositional construction should be used: *Richard Boucher, assistant secretary of state.*

See **titles**.

associate Never abbreviate. Apply the same capitalization norms listed under **assistant**.

Associated Press, The The newsgathering cooperative dating from 1846.

Use *The Associated Press* on first reference (the capitalized article is part of the formal name).

On second reference, *AP* or *the AP* (no capital on *the*) may be used.

Headquarters is in New York.

See **AP**.

Association Do not abbreviate. Capitalize as part of a proper name: *American Medical Association.*

assure, ensure, insure Use *assure* to mean *to make sure or give confidence*: *She assured us the statement was accurate.*

Use *ensure* to mean *guarantee*: *Steps were taken to ensure accuracy.*

Use *insure* for references to insurance: *The policy insures his life.*

asterisk Do not use the symbol. It rarely translates and in many cases cannot be seen by AP computers or received by newspaper or other computers.

asymptomatic Avoid this medical jargon; use *no symptoms, without symptoms* or the like.

athlete's foot

Atlantic Ocean

Atlantic Standard Time, Atlantic Daylight Time Used in the Maritime Provinces of Canada and in Puerto Rico.

See **time zones**.

at large Usually two words for an individual representing more than

a

a single district: *council member at large*.

But it is *ambassador-at-large* for an ambassador assigned to no particular country.

ATM Acceptable in all references for *automated teller machine*.

Do not use the redundant *ATM machine*.

attache It is not a formal title. Always lowercase.

attention-deficit/hyperactivity disorder One of the most common developmental disorders in children; often lasts into adulthood. People with *ADHD* may be overly active or may have trouble paying attention or controlling impulsive behavior. *ADHD* is acceptable on first reference, but spell out shortly thereafter. Describe a person as *having ADHD* only if relevant to the story, and if a medical diagnosis has been made or the person uses the term. If relatives or others use the term, ask how they know, then consider carefully whether to include the information. Generally, when relevant, say a person *has ADHD* rather than *is ADHD*, unless the person prefers the latter. Do not use the outdated terms *attention-deficit disorder* or *ADD*. See **disabilities**; **neurodiversity, neurodivergent, neurodiverse, neurotypical**.

attorney general, attorneys general Never abbreviate. Capitalize only when used as a title before a name: *Attorney General William Barr*.

See **titles**.

attorney, lawyer In common usage the words are interchangeable.

Technically, however, an *attorney* is someone (usually, but not necessarily, a lawyer) empowered to act for another. Such an individual occasionally is called an *attorney in fact*.

A *lawyer* is a person admitted to practice in a court system. Such an individual occasionally is called an *attorney at law*.

Do not abbreviate. Do not capitalize unless it is an officeholder's title: *defense attorney Perry Mason, attorney Perry Mason, District Attorney Hamilton Burger*.

Power of attorney is a written statement legally authorizing a person to act for another.

See **lawyer**.

attribution AP news reports must attribute facts not gathered or confirmed on our own, whether the pickup is from a newspaper, website, broadcaster or blog, U.S. or international, AP member or subscriber. AP reports must also credit other organizations when they break a story and AP matches or further develops it. News from a government, agency, organization, company or other recognized group may be attributed to that entity on first reference in the story: *the White House announced*. In a follow-up attribution, specify whether the information came from a spokesman or other named official or in a news release.

"Auld Lang Syne" Sung to greet the New Year, poem by Robert Burns set to Scottish music.

autism spectrum disorder, autism Umbrella terms for a broad range of developmental disorders that can involve widely varying degrees of intellectual, language and social difficulties, and repetitive behaviors. Describe a person as *autistic* only if relevant to the story, and if a medical diagnosis has been made or the person uses the term. If relatives or others use the term, ask how they know, then consider carefully whether to include the information.

Many autistic people strongly prefer identity-first language: *She is autistic; he is an autistic student.* Some prefer person-first language: *She has autism; people with autism.* Try to determine the preference.

When a preference isn't known, and in describing groups of autistic people, use identity-first language.

Do not use the term *an autistic* or *autistics* as a noun unless someone describes themself that way. Do not use *ASD.* Do not describe someone as being *on the spectrum.*

Asperger's syndrome, previously classified separately, is one form of autism. Do not refer to Asperger's syndrome unless an individual or family member uses the term. If used by others, explain that it is a form of *autism* and follow guidelines above.

See **disabilities**; **high functioning, low functioning**; **neurodiversity, neurodivergent, neurodiverse, neurotypical**.

author A noun. Do not use it as a verb.

autonomous vehicles Describes vehicles that can drive for all or part of a trip on public roads without the need for a human to monitor the road and surroundings. Also can be called *self-driving.* The term *driverless* should not be used unless there is no human backup driver.

As of early 2022 there were no *autonomous vehicles* for sale to the public in the U.S. Some autonomous vehicles are in use by ride-hailing and goods-delivery services.

If a human is expected to supervise or take action, the vehicle is not autonomous. In cases where a company is testing what it considers to be an autonomous vehicle on public roads with a human driver supervising, these should be called *autonomous test vehicles.* Some vehicles have *driver-assist systems* that can perform tasks such as changing lanes, driving at low speeds, or keeping a safe distance from vehicles ahead of them, but they still need human supervision. These should be referred to as *partially automated.*

Avoid the term *semi-autonomous* because it implies that these systems can drive themselves. As of early 2022, human drivers must be ready to intervene at any time.

Nearly all automakers now sell their own version of partially automated driving systems. Some of the best known are Tesla's *Autopilot*, General Motors' *Super Cruise* and Nissan's *ProPilot Assist. Autopilot, ProPilot Assist* and other trade names should be capitalized; the generic use of *autopilot* is lowercase.

Auto Train Rail service that carries passengers and their cars. Owned and operated by Amtrak.

autoworker, autoworkers One word when used generically.

But *United Auto Workers* when referring to the union.

avatar An image or other digital representation for a user in an online service or video game.

avenue Abbreviate only with a

a

numbered address. See **addresses**.

average, mean, median, norm
Average refers to the result obtained by dividing a sum by the number of quantities added together: *The average of 7, 9, 17 is 33 divided by 3, or 11.*

Mean, in its sense used in arithmetic and statistics, is an *average* and is determined by adding the series of numbers and dividing the sum by the number of cases: *The mean temperature of five days with temperatures of 67, 62, 68, 69, 64 is 66.*

Median is the middle number of points in a series arranged in order of size: *The median grade in the group of 50, 55, 85, 88, 92 is 85. The average is 74.*

Norm implies a standard of average performance for a given group: *The child was below the norm for his age in reading comprehension.*

average of The phrase takes a plural verb in a construction such as: *An average of 100 new jobs are created daily.*

awards and decorations Capitalize them: *Bronze Star*, *Medal of Honor*, etc.

See **Nobel Prize, Nobel Prizes** and **Pulitzer Prizes**.

awhile (adv.) **a while** *He plans to stay awhile* (adv.). *He plans to stay for a while* (n.).

AWOL Acceptable in all references for *absent without leave*.

ax Not *axe*.
The verb forms: *ax, axed, axing.*

Axis The alliance of Germany, Italy and Japan during World War II.

Aymara An ethnic group around Lake Titicaca, in Bolivia and Peru, or the language of these people.

b

baby boom, baby boomer See **generations**.

baby bump The rounded abdominal area of a pregnant woman. Avoid using.

babysit, babysitting, babysat, babysitter

baccalaureate

Bachelor of Arts, Bachelor of Science A *bachelor's degree* or *bachelor's* is acceptable in any reference.

See **academic degrees** for guidelines on when the abbreviations *B.A.* or *B.S.* are acceptable.

backfire In wildfires, this term is for a fire set along the inner edge of a fire line to consume the fuel in the fire's path or change its direction.

backstage Part of the stage or theater behind the proscenium, particularly the wings and dressing rooms. Also can refer to the press area where award winners meet with the news media.

backward Not backwards.

bad, badly *Bad* should not be used as an adverb. It does not lose its status as an adjective, however, in a sentence such as *I feel bad*. Such a statement is the idiomatic equivalent of *I am in bad health*. An alternative, *I feel badly*, could be interpreted as meaning that your sense of touch was bad.

See **good, well**.

Bahamas In datelines, give the name of the city or town followed by *Bahamas*:
NASSAU, Bahamas (AP) —
In stories, use *Bahamas, the Bahamas or the Bahama Islands* as the construction of a sentence dictates.

Identify a specific island in the text if relevant.

bail *Bail* is money or property that will be forfeited to the court if an accused individual fails to appear for trial. It may be posted as follows:
— The accused may deposit with the court the full amount or its equivalent in collateral such as a deed to property.
— A friend or relative may make such a deposit with the court.
— The accused may pay a professional bail bondsman a percentage of the total figure. The bondsman, in turn, guarantees the court that it will receive from him the full amount in the event the individual fails to appear for trial.

It is correct in all cases to say that an accused *posted bail* or *posted a bail bond* (the money held by the court is a form of bond). When a distinction is desired, say that the individual *posted his own bail*, that *bail was posted by a friend or relative*, or that *bail was obtained through a bondsman*.

baker's dozen 13, not 12.

b

balance of payments, balance of trade The *balance of payments* is the difference between the amount of money that leaves a nation and the amount that enters it during a period of time.

The *balance of payments* is determined by computing the amount of money a nation and its citizens send abroad for all purposes — including goods and services purchased, travel, loans, foreign aid, etc. — and subtracting from it the amount that foreign nations send into the nation for similar purposes.

The *balance of trade* is the difference between the monetary value of the goods a nation imports and the goods it exports.

An example illustrating the difference between the two:

The United States and its citizens might send $10 billion abroad — $5 billion for goods, $3 billion for loans and foreign aid, $1 billion for services and $1 billion for tourism and other purposes.

Other nations might send $9 billion into the United States — $6 billion for U.S. goods, $2 billion for services and $1 billion for tourism and other purposes.

The United States would have a *balance-of-payments* deficit of $1 billion but a *balance-of-trade* surplus of $1 billion.

balance sheet A listing of assets, liabilities and net worth showing the financial position of a company at the specific time. A bank balance sheet is generally referred to as a statement of condition.

ballclub, ballpark, ballplayer, ballroom

balloon mortgage A mortgage whose amortization schedule will not extinguish the debt by the end of the mortgage term, leaving a large payment (called balloon payment) of the remaining principal balance to be paid at that time.

baloney Foolish or exaggerated talk.
The sausage or luncheon meat is *bologna*.

Band-Aid A trademark for a type of adhesive bandage.

bankruptcy Federal courts have exclusive jurisdiction over bankruptcy cases and each of the 94 federal judicial districts handles bankruptcy matters. The primary purposes of the federal bankruptcy laws are to give honest debtors a fresh start in life by relieving them of most debts, and to repay creditors in an orderly manner to the extent debtors have property available for payment. Bankruptcies can be voluntary or involuntary.

Chapter 7 of the Bankruptcy Code is available to both individual and business debtors. Its purpose is to achieve a fair distribution to creditors of the debtor's available non-exempt property. It provides a fresh financial start for individuals, although not all debt is wiped away; debts for certain taxes, fraudulently incurred credit card debt, family support obligations — including child support and alimony — and most student loans must still be repaid. The bankruptcy law that took effect in October 2005 limits Chapter 7 as an option for many Americans: Those deemed by a "means test" to have at least $100 a month left over after paying certain debts and expenses must file a five-year repayment plan under the more restrictive Chapter 13 instead.

When a company files for Chapter 7, it usually leads to liquidation. But a company in Chapter 7 proceedings can continue to operate under the direction of a court trustee until the matter is settled, and if it can settle with creditors in the interim, it may not have to be liquidated.

Chapter 11 of the Bankruptcy Code is available for both business and consumer debtors. Its purpose is to rehabilitate a business as a going concern or reorganize an individual's finances through a court-approved reorganization plan. When referring to such a filing, say the company is seeking Chapter 11 protection. This action frees a company from the threat of creditors' lawsuits while it reorganizes its finances. The debtor's reorganization plan must be accepted by a majority of its creditors. Unless the court rules otherwise, the debtor remains in control of the business and its assets.

Chapter 12 of the Bankruptcy Code is designed to give special debt relief to a family farmer with regular income from farming.

Chapter 13 of the Bankruptcy Code is likely to be required for an increasing percentage of individuals seeking to wipe the slate clean. Those deemed by a "means test" to have at least $100 a month left over after paying certain debts and expenses will have to file a five-year repayment plan under Chapter 13 allowing unsecured creditors to recover part or all of what they are owed.

Chapter 15 was added to the Bankruptcy Code in 2005 and covers U.S. filings that are secondary to bankruptcy cases filed overseas. Courts can authorize trustees to act in a foreign country on behalf of a bankruptcy estate in a Chapter 15 proceeding. It represents the U.S. adoption of a model law on cross-border bankruptcy developed by the United Nations.

barbiturate

barrel A standard barrel in U.S. measure contains 31.5 gallons.

A standard barrel in British and Canadian measure contains 36 imperial gallons.

In international dealings with crude oil, a standard barrel contains 42 U.S. gallons or 35 imperial gallons.

See the **oil** entry online to compute the volume and weight of petroleum products.

barrel, barreled, barreling

BASE jumping Acceptable on first reference for the extreme sport, but explain later in the story. *BASE* is an acronym for *building, antenna, span* (such as a bridge) and *earth* (such as a cliff).

basis point One one-hundredth of 1 percentage point. Changes in interest rates are measured in basis points. If the Federal Reserve's target rate was 2% and it was cut by 50 basis points, the new rate would be 1.5%.

battalion Capitalize when used with a figure to form a name: *the 3rd Battalion, the 10th Battalion.*

battlefield Also: *battlefront, battleground, battleship.* But *battle station.*

battleground states States where candidates from both major political parties have a reasonable chance

b

for victory in a statewide race or presidential vote.

bay Capitalize as an integral part of a proper name: *Hudson Bay, San Francisco Bay*.

Capitalize also *San Francisco Bay Area* or *the Bay Area* as the popular name for the nine-county region that has San Francisco as its focal point.

B.C. Acceptable in all references to a calendar year in the period *before Christ*.

Because the full phrase would be *in the year 43 before Christ*, the abbreviation B.C. is placed after the figure for the year: *43 B.C.*

See **A.D.**

bear market A period of generally declining stock prices over a prolonged period, generally defined as a 20% or larger decline in broad stock indexes such as the S&P 500.

bearer bond A bond for which the owner's name is not registered on the books of the issuing company. Interest and principal is thus payable to the bondholder.

bearer stock Stock certificates that are not registered in any name. They are negotiable without endorsement and transferable by delivery.

because, since Use *because* to denote a specific cause-effect relationship: *He went because he was told.*

Since is acceptable in a causal sense when the first event in a sequence led logically to the second but was not its direct cause: *They went to the game, since they had been given the tickets.*

bed-and-breakfast *B&B* is acceptable

on second reference.

bellwether

benefit, benefited, benefiting

Ben-Gurion International Airport Located at Lod, Israel, about 10 miles southeast of Tel Aviv.

See **airport**.

Berlin Wall

beside, besides *Beside* means at the side of.

Besides means in addition to.

bestseller, bestselling No hyphen.

betting odds Use figures and a hyphen: *The odds were 5-4, he won despite 3-2 odds against him.* See **numerals**.

bettor A person who bets.

bi- The rules in **prefixes** apply, but in general, no hyphen. Some examples:
bifocal   bimonthly
bilateral   bipartisan
bilingual

biannual, biennial *Biannual* means *twice a year* and is a synonym for the word *semiannual*.

Biennial means *every two years*.

Bible See entry in the **Religion** chapter.

big brother One's older brother is a *big brother*. *Big Brother* (capitalized) means under the watchful eye of big government, from George Orwell's "1984."

Capitalize also in reference to members of Big Brothers Big Sisters of America Inc. The organization has headquarters in Philadelphia.

Big Tech A colloquial reference, similar to *Big Tobacco* or *Big Pharma*, for the technology companies that dominated global commerce throughout the 2010s. Generally this includes *Google, Apple, Microsoft, Meta* (formerly *Facebook*) and *Amazon*, although it should not be understood to specifically exclude other large U.S. tech companies.

The term is most appropriate in the context of legal, regulatory or market issues, particularly in the U.S. and Europe. Avoid if the deliberate ambiguity of the term risks confusion, particularly where Chinese technology giants are concerned.

Avoid related jargony terms often used by investors. Prior to Meta's rebranding, these terms included *FAANG* (Facebook, Apple, Amazon, Netflix, Google), *GAFAM* (Google, Apple, Facebook, Amazon, Microsoft) and *GAFA* (Google, Apple, Facebook, Amazon). No new consensus had formed as of early 2022.

billion A thousand million.
For forms, see **millions, billions, trillions**.

Bill of Rights The first 10 amendments to the Constitution. See **Constitution**.

bimonthly Means *every other month*. *Semimonthly* means *twice a month*.

bin Laden, Osama Use *bin Laden* on all second and later references except at the start of a sentence. It is the family preference for the last name, which is an exception to the general rule on Arabic names. He founded al-Qaida and was killed by U.S. forces in Pakistan in May 2011.

bioterrorism

bipolar disorder A mental illness that causes dramatic shifts in mood, energy, activity levels and concentration levels. These range from periods of extremely elated, irritable or energized behavior (known as manic episodes) to very sad, indifferent or hopeless periods (known as depressive episodes).

Describe a person as *having bipolar disorder* only if relevant to the story, and if a medical diagnosis has been made or the person uses the term. If relatives or others use the term, ask how they know, then consider carefully whether to include the information.

Do not use the terms *manic-depressive illness* or *manic depression*.
See **disabilities; depression; mental illness**.

bird flu Preferred term for *avian influenza*, viruses that mostly infect poultry and other birds. Several types are known to infect humans and the deadliest form so far appears to be H5N1. Other strains that have infected people include H7N9, H9N2 and H6N1. The viruses mainly infect people who have direct contact with sick birds but human-to-human transmission occasionally occurs.

birthday Capitalize as part of the name for a holiday: *Washington's Birthday*. Lowercase in other uses.

birth defect Acceptable in broad references such as *lessening the chances of birth defects* or *about 1 in 33 babies in the U.S. has a birth defect*. Do not use the term when referring to a specific person or to a group of people with a specific condition. Instead, be specific about the

b

condition and use only if relevant to the story. Some prefer the term *congenital disorder*. See **disabilities**.

bit Acceptable in all references as an abbreviation for *binary digit*, the digital 1 and 0 that represent data in modern computers.

bitcoin See **cryptocurrency, blockchain, bitcoin, NFT, Web3**.

biweekly Means *every other week*. *Semiweekly* means *twice a week*.

bizarre Unusual. A fair is a *bazaar*.

blackout, brownout A *blackout* is a total power failure over a large area or the concealing of lights that might be visible to enemy raiders.

The term *rolling blackout* is used by electric companies to describe a situation in which electric power to some sections temporarily is cut off on a rotating basis to assure that voltage will meet minimum standards in other sections.

A *brownout* is a small, temporary voltage reduction, usually from 2% to 8%, implemented to conserve electric power.

blind, limited vision, low vision/ partially sighted *Blind* describes a person with complete loss of sight. In addition, many people with some vision identify as *blind* because they feel an affinity with the blind community and are proud of their identities. *Blind*, along with terms such as *a person/people with low vision, person/people with limited vision, person/people with vision loss, partially sighted person/people* are acceptable if an individual or group uses them for themself. Try to determine a preference.

In referring to groups when a preference can't be determined: *blind or partially sighted people, or people with blindness or low vision*.

When possible, ask if a person or group uses identity-first language (*blind students*) or person-first language (*students who are blind*). If a preference can't be determined, aim to use a mix of those approaches.

It may not be relevant or necessary to specify the amount of vision a person has.

In order to be *legally blind*, a person must have a visual acuity of 20/200.

See **disabilities**.

bloc, block A *bloc* is a coalition of people, groups or nations with the same purpose or goal.

Block has more than a dozen definitions, but a political alliance is not one of them.

blockchain See **cryptocurrency, blockchain, bitcoin, NFT, Web3**.

blood alcohol content The concentration of alcohol in blood. It is usually measured as weight per volume. For example, 0.02% means 0.02 grams of alcohol per deciliter of an individual's blood. *The jury found he was driving with a blood alcohol level above the state's 0.08% limit.*

bloodbath One word, an exception to Webster's New World College Dictionary.

BLT Acceptable on first reference for a *bacon, lettuce and tomato sandwich*.

blue chip stock Stock in a company known for its long-established record of making money and paying dividends.

Bluetooth A standard for short-range wireless transmissions, commonly used to establish connections between such devices as smartphones, headsets, car audio systems and smartwatches.

Blu-ray Disc A successor to the DVD, *Blu-ray Disc* is a standard used to deliver high-definition video and other digital content.

board Capitalize only when an integral part of a proper name. See **capitalization**.

board of directors, board of trustees Always lowercase. See **organizations and institutions**.

boats, ships A *boat* is a watercraft of any size but generally is used to indicate a small craft. A *ship* is a large, seagoing vessel.

The word *boat* is used, however, in some words that apply to large craft: *ferryboat, PT boat.*

Use *it*, not the pronoun *she*, in references to boats and ships.

Use Arabic or Roman numerals in the names of boats and ships: *the Queen Elizabeth 2* or *QE2; Titan I, Titan II.*

The reference for military ships is IHS Jane's Fighting Ships; for nonmilitary ships, IHS Fairplay Register of Ships.

See **numerals**.

body camera Preferred for cameras mounted on clothing, generally of law enforcers. When the condensed version appears in headlines or in quotes, it is *bodycam*, one word.

body mass index A measurement calculated from weight and height. *BMI* is acceptable on second reference. To calculate: multiply weight in pounds by 703, divide by height in inches, divide again by height in inches.

Boko Haram Muslim militant group in northeast Nigeria.

bond ratings Standard & Poor's, Moody's Investors Service and Fitch Ratings sell information — mainly to institutional investors — about what they view as the relative risk of various issues of debt. They also charge companies, municipalities and even foreign governments that wish to sell debt and have it rated. The ratings are a fundamental way for investors to form an opinion on whether they are likely to be repaid, and then decide whether the interest rate is high enough to compensate for the risk that they may get back none or only a portion of their investment (in the case of a bankruptcy or some other adverse event). The ratings also effectively set benchmarks for how much interest companies will have to pay to sell bonds, commercial paper, preferred stock and for bank loans they obtain. The higher the grade, the lower the interest rate a borrower must pay.

Standard & Poor's bond ratings, for example, include 10 categories that are referred to as investment-grade, from AAA to BBB-, given to borrowers with the strongest ability to repay. Another six categories, from BB+ to CCC-, are assigned to more speculative securities that are commonly referred to as *junk* or *high-yield debt*. The lowest category, D, is for securities that are in payment default.

A reduction in the rating of a company's debt to non-investment-grade can force some mutual funds and pension funds to sell those bonds because they are prohibited from holding junk debt.

book value The difference between a company's assets and liabilities.

The *book value per share* of common stock is the *book value* divided by the number of common shares outstanding.

Bosnia-Herzegovina The country has been divided into a Bosnian Serb republic and a Muslim-Croat federation since 1995. Both have wide autonomy but share a common presidency, parliament and government. In datelines: *SARAJEVO, Bosnia-Herzegovina.* The people are *Bosnians.*

Bosniak, Bosniaks Use this term, rather than *Bosnian Muslims,* for the ethnic group in Bosnia-Herzegovina that is mainly Muslim but also includes atheists and people of other religions. *Bosniaks* are one of the three main ethnicities living in the Balkan state; the others are *Bosnian Serbs* and *Bosnian Croats.* Explain in the story that *Bosniaks* are primarily Muslims. The phrase a *Bosniak* is acceptable for one person. Use *Bosnian* for terms that can be linked to all ethnic groups in Bosnia. For example: *Bosnian language, Bosnian borders, Bosnian war, Bosnian national team, three-member Bosnian presidency,* etc. Use the full terms *Bosnian Serbs* and *Bosnian Croats* in BOSNIA-HERZEGOVINA-datelined stories to differentiate from those living in Serbia and Croatia.

Bosporus, the Not the Bosporus Strait.

boulevard Abbreviated only with a numbered address: *43 Park Blvd.* See **addresses**.

Boxing Day Post-Christmas holiday Dec. 26 in British Commonwealth countries. Term came from practice of giving gift boxes to employees and others.

box office (n.) **box-office** (adj.)

boy, girl Generally acceptable to describe males or females younger than 18. While it is always inaccurate to call people under 18 *men* or *women* and people 18 and older *boys* or *girls,* be aware of nuances and unintentional implications. Referring to Black males of any age and in any context as *boys,* for instance, can be perceived as demeaning and call to mind historical language used by some to address Black men. Be specific about ages if possible, or refer to *Black youths, child, teen* or similar. See **race-related coverage** and **gender, sex and sexual orientation**.

boycott, embargo A *boycott* is an organized refusal to buy a particular product or service, or to deal with a particular merchant or group of merchants.

An *embargo* is a legal restriction against trade. It usually prohibits goods from entering or leaving a country. The plural is *embargoes.*

Boy Scouts The full name of the national organization is *Boy Scouts of America.* Headquarters is in Irving, Texas.

See **Girl Scouts**.

brackets See the entry in **Punctuation** chapter.

brain-dead (adj.) **brain death** Complete absence of brain function based on a series of tests. Used as a legal definition of death. In the U.S., most organ transplants are done after the donor has been declared brain-dead. See **clinically dead, clinical death**.

brain injury, traumatic brain injury, brain damage, brain-damaged *Traumatic brain injury* usually results from a violent blow or jolt. Do not use *TBI* other than in direct quotations, and explain the acronym. Other brain injuries occur as a result of illnesses such as cancer, stroke and infection. Brain injuries vary in severity and duration. Describe a person as *having brain damage* or *having a traumatic brain injury* only if relevant to the story, and if a medical diagnosis has been made or the person uses the term. If relatives or others use the term, ask how they know, then consider carefully whether to include the information.

Do not say a person *is brain-damaged*. Instead, *has brain damage* or *has a brain injury*. See **disabilities**.

brand names When they are used, capitalize them.

Brand names normally should be used only if they are essential to a story.

Sometimes, however, the use of a brand name may not be essential but is acceptable because it lends an air of reality to a story: *He fished a Camel from his shirt pocket* may be preferable to the less specific *cigarette*.

When a company sponsors a sports or other event identified only by the company's name, use the name on first reference: Example: *Buick Open*.

However, when an event is clearly identifiable without the company's name, drop the name on first reference and include the sponsor name elsewhere in the story or at the bottom as an Editor's Note. Example: *FedEx Orange Bowl* would be identified in the story only as *Orange Bowl*.

Also use a separate paragraph to provide the name of a sponsor when the brand name is not part of the formal title.

See **trademark** entry.

Braunschweig The spelling of the German city. Not *Brunswick*.

break-in (n. and adj.) **break in** (v.)

breakup (n. and adj.) **break up** (v.)

breastfeed, breastfeeding, breastfed

Breathalyzer Trademarked name for a device to test blood alcohol level.

Brexit Shorthand for *"British exit"* — the United Kingdom's Jan. 31, 2020, departure from the European Union following a June 23, 2016, referendum. No quotation marks. Explain what it means when you use it. Britain's formal exit was followed by an 11-month transition period; as of Jan. 1, 2021, the U.K. left the EU's economic structures and a new Trade and Cooperation Agreement took effect, covering areas including economic relations and security.

bride, bridegroom, bridesmaid *Bride* is appropriate in wedding stories, but use *wife* or *spouse* in other circumstances.

Britain Acceptable in all references for *Great Britain*, which consists of England, Scotland and Wales.

See **United Kingdom**.

British, Briton(s) The people of Great

b

Britain: the English, the Scottish, the Welsh. *Brits* is slang.

British Broadcasting Corp. *BBC* is acceptable in all references.

British Columbia The Canadian province bounded on the west by the Pacific Ocean. Do not abbreviate. See **datelines**.

British thermal unit The amount of heat required to increase the temperature of a pound of water 1 degree Fahrenheit. *Btu* (the same for singular and plural) is acceptable on second reference.

British Virgin Islands Use with a community name in datelines on stories from these islands. Do not abbreviate.
Specify an individual island in the text if relevant. See **datelines**.

broadcast The past tense also is *broadcast*, not *broadcasted*.

Brothers Generally abbreviate as *Bros.* in formal company names: *Warner Bros.*, but follow the spelling preferred by the company.
For possessives: *Warner Bros.' profits*.

Btu The same in singular and plural. See **British thermal unit**.

Bubble Wrap A registered trademark. Unless the trademark name is important to the story, use *cushioning* or *packaging material*.

Budapest The capital of Hungary. In datelines, follow it with *Hungary*.

bug, tap A concealed listening device designed to pick up sounds in a room, an automobile, or such is a *bug*.
A *tap* is a device attached to a telephone circuit to pick up conversations on the line.

building Never abbreviate. Capitalize the proper names of buildings, including the word *building* if it is an integral part of the proper name: *the Empire State Building*.

buildup (n. and adj.) **build up** (v.)

bull's-eye

bullion Unminted precious metals of standards suitable for coining.

bull market A period of generally rising stock prices over a prolonged period, generally defined as a 20% or larger increase in broad stock indexes such as the S&P 500.

bureau Capitalize when part of the formal name for an organization or agency: *the Bureau of Labor Statistics*.
Lowercase when used alone or to designate a corporate subdivision: *the Washington bureau of The Associated Press*.

Bureau of Alcohol, Tobacco, Firearms and Explosives *ATF* is acceptable in subsequent references to this agency of the Department of Justice. (Note the *Explosives* part of the name.)

burglary, larceny, robbery, theft Legal definitions of *burglary* vary, but in general a *burglary* involves entering a building (not necessarily by breaking in) and remaining unlawfully with the intention of committing a crime.
Larceny is the legal term for the wrongful taking of property. Its

nonlegal equivalents are *stealing* or *theft*.

Robbery in the legal sense involves the use of violence or threat in committing larceny. In a wider sense it means *to plunder* or *rifle*, and may thus be used even if a person was not present: *His house was robbed while he was away.*

Theft describes a larceny that did not involve threat, violence or plundering.

USAGE NOTE: You *rob* a person, bank, house, etc., but you *steal* the money or the jewels.

burqa The all-covering dress worn by some Muslim women. See also other garments such as **niqab**; **hijab**; **chador**.

bus, buses Transportation vehicles. The verb forms: *bus, bused, busing.*

In a restaurant, to clear dishes from a table: *The busboy buses tables.* See **buss, busses.**

bushel A unit of dry measure equal to 4 pecks or 32 dry quarts. The metric equivalent is approximately 35.2 liters.

See **liter.**

buss, busses Kisses. The verb forms: *buss, bussed, bussing.*

See **bus, buses.**

by- The rules in **prefixes** apply, but in general, no hyphen. Some examples:

byline	*byproduct*
bypass	*bystreet*

By-election is an exception. See the next entry.

by-election A special election held between regularly scheduled elections. The term most often is associated with special elections to the British House of Commons.

bylines Our standard byline consists of *By*, followed by the name, in the byline field, and *Associated Press* as the bytitle. The bytitle can also be a special designation, like *AP Sports Writer*.

Use a byline only if the reporter was in the datelined community to gather the information reported.

Nicknames should not be used unless they specifically are requested by the writer.

In the case of a double byline, at least one of the bylined reporters must have reported in the datelined community. If the other reported from elsewhere, note that location in a tag line at the bottom of the story: *Smith reported from Washington.*

For materials or columns contributed by people like politicians or celebrities — cases in which we want to stress that the writer is not working for AP — use the bytitle *For The Associated Press.*

byte A unit of data storage frequently used to refer to the memory or storage capacity of phones, PCs and other digital gadgets. A byte is equal to 8 *bits*.

Larger storage values are typically measured in megabytes, terabytes and petabytes. In common usage, a kilobyte is 1,000 bytes, a megabyte is 1 million bytes; a terabyte is 1,000 gigabytes or 1 trillion bytes; and a petabyte is 1,000 terabytes, or 1 quadrillion bytes.

In uncommon instances, these terms may refer to binary storage values in which a kilobyte, for instance, is 1,024 bytes. Such usage is generally restricted to highly technical subjects.

Abbreviate *KB* for *kilobyte*, *MB* for *megabyte*, *GB* for *gigabyte*, *TB* for *terabyte* and *PB* for *petabyte* on

b

second and subsequent references: *a 300GB hard drive*.

b

C

cabinet Capitalize references to a specific body of advisers heading executive departments for a president, king, governor, etc.: *The president-elect said he has not made his Cabinet selections.*

See **department** for a listing of all the U.S. Cabinet departments.

caliber The form: *.38-caliber pistol.* See **weapons**.

campaign manager Do not treat as a formal title. Always lowercase. See **titles**.

Canada Montreal, Quebec City and Toronto stand alone in datelines. For all other datelines, use the city name and the name of the province or territory spelled out.

The 10 provinces of Canada are Alberta, British Columbia, Manitoba, New Brunswick, Newfoundland and Labrador (but usually known as just Newfoundland), Nova Scotia, Ontario, Prince Edward Island, Quebec and Saskatchewan.

The three territories are the Yukon, the Northwest Territories, and Nunavut (created April 1, 1999).

The provinces have substantial autonomy from the federal government.

The territories are administered by the federal government, although residents of the territories do elect their own legislators and representatives to Parliament. See **datelines**.

Canada goose

canal Capitalize as an integral part of a proper name: *the Suez Canal.*

Canal Zone Do not abbreviate. No longer used except when referring to the Panama Canal area during the time it was controlled by the United States, exclusively or jointly with Panama, 1904-1999.

cancel, canceled, canceling, cancellation

cannon, canon A *cannon* is a weapon; plural is *cannons*. See **weapons**.

A *canon* is a law or rule, particularly of a church, or a musical composition.

Canuck This reference to a Canadian is sometimes considered derogatory. It should be avoided except when in quoted matter or in terms used in Canada, such as references to the hockey team, the *Vancouver Canucks.*

canvas, canvass Canvas is heavy cloth.

Canvass is a noun and a verb denoting a survey.

cape Capitalize as part of a proper name: *Cape Cod, Cape Hatteras.* Lowercase when standing alone.

Although local practice may call for capitalizing *the Cape* when the rest of the name is clearly understood, always use the full name on first reference.

Cape Canaveral, Florida Formerly Cape Kennedy. See **John F. Kennedy**

Space Center.

capital The city where a seat of government is located. Do not capitalize.

When used in a financial sense, *capital* describes money, equipment or property used in a business by a person or corporation.

See **Capitol**.

capital gain, capital loss The difference between what a *capital* asset cost and the price it brought when sold.

capitalization In general, avoid unnecessary capitals. Use a capital letter only if you can justify it by one of the principles listed here.

Many words and phrases, including special cases, are listed separately in this book. Entries that are capitalized without further comment should be capitalized in all uses.

If there is no relevant listing in this book for a particular word or phrase, consult Webster's New World College Dictionary. Use lowercase if the dictionary lists it as an acceptable form for the sense in which the word is being used.

As used in this book, *capitalize* means to use uppercase for the first letter of a word. If additional capital letters are needed, they are called for by an example or a phrase such as *use all caps*.

Some basic principles:

PROPER NOUNS: Capitalize nouns that constitute the unique identification for a specific person, place, or thing: *John, Fatima, Mexico, Boston, England*.

Some words, such as the examples just given, are always proper nouns. Some common nouns receive proper noun status when they are used as the name of a particular entity: *General Electric, Gulf Oil*.

PROPER NAMES: Capitalize common nouns such as *party, river, street* and *west* when they are an integral part of the full name for a person, place or thing: *Democratic Party, Mississippi River, Fleet Street, West Virginia*.

Lowercase these common nouns when they stand alone in subsequent references: *the party, the river, the street*.

Lowercase the common noun elements of names in plural uses: *the Democratic and Republican parties, Main and State streets, lakes Erie and Ontario*. Exception: plurals of formal titles with full names are capitalized: *Presidents Jimmy Carter and Gerald R. Ford*.

Among entries that provide additional guidelines are:

animals	holidays and holy
brand names	days
building	legislature
committee	months
Congress	monuments
datelines	nicknames
days of the week	organizations and
directions and	institutions
regions	planets
food	plants
geographic names	police department
governmental	religious
bodies	references
heavenly bodies	seasons
historical periods	trademarks
and events	unions

POPULAR NAMES: Some places and events lack officially designated proper names but have popular names that are the effective equivalent: *the Combat Zone* (a section of downtown Boston), *the Main Line* (a group of Philadelphia suburbs), *the South Side* (of Chicago), *the Badlands* (of South Dakota), *the Street* (the financial community in the Wall Street area of New York).

The principle applies also to shortened versions of the proper names of one-of-a-kind events: *the Series* (for the World Series), *the Derby* (for the Kentucky Derby). This practice should not, however, be interpreted as a license to ignore the general practice of lowercasing the common noun elements of a name when they stand alone.

FAMILY NAMES: Capitalize words denoting family relationships when they substitute for a person's name: *I wrote Mom a letter. I wrote my father a letter.*

INFORMAL NAMES: Capitalize words such as *professor, doctor, coach,* etc., when they substitute for a person's name: *What's the diagnosis, Doctor? Put me in, Coach! She asked her doctor for a diagnosis.*

DERIVATIVES: Capitalize words that are derived from a proper noun and still depend on it for their meaning: *American, Christian, Christianity, English, French, Marxism, Shakespearean.*

Lowercase words that are derived from a proper noun but no longer depend on it for their meaning: *french fries, herculean, malapropism, pasteurize, quixotic, venetian blind.*

SENTENCES: Capitalize the first word in a statement that stands as a sentence. See **sentences** and **parentheses**.

In poetry, capital letters are used for the first words of some phrases that would not be capitalized in prose. See **poetry**.

COMPOSITIONS: Capitalize the principal words in the names of books, movies, plays, poems, operas, songs, radio and television programs, works of art, etc. See **composition titles**, **magazine names** and **newspaper names**.

TITLES: Capitalize formal titles when used immediately before a name. Lowercase formal titles when used alone or in constructions that set them off from a name by commas.

Use lowercase at all times for terms that are job descriptions rather than formal titles.

See **academic titles**, **legislative titles**, **military titles**, **nobility**, **religious titles** and **titles**.

ABBREVIATIONS: Capital letters apply in some cases. See **abbreviations and acronyms**.

Capitol Capitalize *U.S. Capitol* and *the Capitol* when referring to the building in Washington: *The meeting was held on Capitol Hill in the west wing of the Capitol.*

Follow the same practice when referring to state capitols: *The Virginia Capitol is in Richmond. Thomas Jefferson designed the Capitol of Virginia.*

See **capital**.

captain See **military titles** for military and police usage.

Lowercase and spell out in such uses as *team captain Carl Yastrzemski.*

carat, caret, karat The weight of precious stones, especially diamonds, is expressed in *carats*. A carat is equal to 200 milligrams or about 3 grains.

A *caret* is a writer's and a proofreader's mark.

The proportion of pure gold used with an alloy is expressed in *karats*.

cardholder, credit card holder

caregiver, caretaker A *caregiver* is a person who takes care of someone requiring close attention, such as a person with serious illnesses or age-related concerns. Generally use that term, rather than *caretaker*, in situations involving people receiving care. The term *caretaker* generally refers to a person who takes care of something, such as a house, when the owner isn't present, or to a person or entity carrying out duties temporarily (*a caretaker government*). See **diseases**; **disabilities**; **mental illness**; **older adult(s), older person/ people**.

Caribbean See **Western Hemisphere**.

Carioca A term applied to the people and culture of the city of Rio de Janeiro. The term for the state of the same name is *Fluminense*.

Carnival Capitalize when referring specifically to the revelry in many Roman Catholic countries preceding Lent. Otherwise, a *carnival* is lowercase. See **Mardi Gras**.

cash or collect on delivery The abbreviation *c.o.d.* is preferred in all references. This is an exception to Webster's New World College Dictionary.

caster, castor *Caster* is a roller. *Castor* is the spelling for the oil and the bean from which it is derived.

casualties Avoid using the word, which is vague and can refer to either injuries or deaths. Instead, be specific about what is meant. If authorities use the term, press for specifics. If specifics aren't available, say so: *Officer Riya Kumar said the crash resulted in casualties, but she said she did not know whether those were injuries or deaths.*

Caterpillar A trademark for a brand of crawler tractor. The formal name of the company is *Caterpillar Inc.* Headquarters is in Peoria, Illinois.

Use lowercase for the wormlike larva of various insects.

Catholic, Catholicism Use *Catholic Church*, *Catholic* or *Catholicism* in the first references to those who believe that the pope, as bishop of Rome, has the ultimate authority in administering an earthly organization founded by Jesus Christ.

Given the majority of Catholics belong to the Latin (Roman) rite, it is acceptable to use *Roman Catholic Church* on first reference if the context is clearly referring to the Latin rite. For example: *the Roman Catholic Archdiocese of Indianapolis.* However, when referring to the pope, the Vatican or the universal church, *Catholic Church* should be used since it encompasses believers belonging to the Latin and Eastern churches that are in communion with Rome. Similarly, the U.S. Conference of Catholic Bishops includes bishops from Eastern churches as well as Roman Catholic bishops.

Lowercase *catholic* where used in its generic sense of general or universal, meanings derived from a similar word in Greek.

See **Roman Catholic Church** and the **Religion** chapter.

Caucasus Mountains

cease-fire, cease-fires (n. and adj.) The verb form is *cease fire*.

cellphone

Celsius Use this term rather than *centigrade* for the temperature scale that is part of the metric system.

The Celsius scale is named for Anders Celsius, a Swedish astronomer who designed it. In it, zero represents the freezing point of water, and 100 degrees is the boiling point at sea level.

When giving a Celsius temperature, use these forms: *40 degrees Celsius* or *40 C* (note the space and no period after the capital *C*) if degrees and Celsius are clear from the context.

See **Fahrenheit** and **metric system**.

cement *Cement* is the powder mixed with water and sand or gravel to make *concrete*. The proper term is *concrete* (not *cement*) *pavement, blocks, driveways,* etc.

censer, censor, censure A *censer* is a container in which incense is burned.

To *censor* is to prohibit or restrict the use of something.

To *censure* is to condemn.

census Capitalize only in specific references to the *U.S. Census Bureau.* Lowercase in other uses: *The census data was released Tuesday.*

Centers for Disease Control and Prevention Located in Atlanta, the Centers for Disease Control and Prevention is part of the U.S. Department of Health and Human Services. On first reference, use *Centers for Disease Control and Prevention.* Precede with *national, federal* or *U.S.* if needed for clarity. Takes a singular verb. On second reference, *the CDC* is acceptable.

centi- A prefix denoting one-hundredth of a unit. Move a decimal point two places to the left in converting to the basic unit: *155.6 centimeters equals 1.556 meters.*

centimeter One-hundredth of a meter. There are 10 millimeters in a centimeter.

See **meter**; **metric system**; and **inch**.

Central Asia The region includes Kyrgyzstan, Kazakhstan, Turkmenistan, Tajikistan and Uzbekistan.

central bank A bank having responsibility for controlling a country's monetary policy.

Central Intelligence Agency *CIA* is acceptable in all references.

The formal title for the individual who heads the agency is *director of central intelligence.* On first reference: *Director Gina Haspel of the CIA* or *CIA Director Gina Haspel.*

cents Spell out the word *cents* and lowercase, using numerals for amounts less than a dollar: *5 cents, 12 cents.* Use the $ sign and decimal system for larger amounts: *$1.01, $2.50.* See **numerals**.

century Lowercase (unless part of a proper name). Spell out numbers under 10: *the first century, the 21st century.*

CEO, CFO, COO Leading executives of a company.

CEO is acceptable in all references for *chief executive officer,* who typically has the primary decision-making authority. This role is separate from *chief financial officer*

C

C

and *chief operating officer*, but an individual may hold more than one of these positions at a time.

Use *chief financial officer* on first reference and *CFO* thereafter. Typically handles major financial responsibilities, such as record-keeping and financial planning.

Use *chief operating officer* on first reference and *COO* thereafter. Often responsible for a company's day-to-day operations.

Spell out other *C-level* or *C-suite* positions, such as *chief administrative officer*, *chief information officer* or *chief risk officer*.

CES Annual technology show held in early January in Las Vegas. Do not call it by its former name, *Consumer Electronics Show*.

cesarean section *C-section* is acceptable on second reference.

chador A cloak worn by some Muslim women, mainly in Iran, which covers the hair, neck and shoulders but not the face. See also other garments such as **burqa; hijab; niqab**.

chair, chairperson, chairman, chairwoman In general, use terms such as *chair* or *chairperson*, *councilperson* unless the *-man* or *-woman* terms are specified by an organization.

Capitalize as a formal title before a name: *company Chair Henry Khan*, *committee Chairwoman Margaret Chase Smith*.

Do not capitalize as a casual, temporary position: *chair Dara Jackson*.

Chair is acceptable as a verb: *She chaired the meeting; he chairs the committee.*

See **titles; gender-neutral language**.

Champagne A sparkling wine from the Champagne region of France. If made elsewhere, call it *sparkling wine*.

chancellor The translation to English for the first minister in the governments of Germany and Austria. Capitalize when used before a name.

See **premier, prime minister** and **titles**.

chapters Capitalize *chapter* when used with a numeral in reference to a section of a book or legal code. Always use Arabic figures: *Chapter 1, Chapter 20*.

Lowercase when standing alone. See **numerals**.

character, reputation *Character* refers to moral qualities.

Reputation refers to the way a person is regarded by others.

charge-off A loan that no longer is expected to be repaid and is written off as a bad debt. Two words, no hyphen, as a verb.

Charleston, Charlestown, Charles Town *Charleston* is the name of the capital of West Virginia and a port city in South Carolina.

Charlestown is a section of Boston. *Charles Town* is the name of a small city in West Virginia.

checkup (n.) **check up** (v.)

Chemical Mace A trademark, usually shortened to *Mace*, for a brand of tear gas that is packaged in an aerosol canister and temporarily stuns its victims.

Chevy Not *Chevie* or *Chevvy*. This

nickname for the *Chevrolet* should be used only in automobile features or in quoted matter.

Chicago Board of Trade Commodity trading market where contracts are traded for Treasury bonds, corn, soybeans, wheat, gold, silver, etc. Owned by CME Group Inc. See **CME Group Inc.**

Chicago Board Options Exchange Originally set up by the Chicago Board of Trade, the CBOE is the world's largest options exchange. Not part of CME Group Inc., parent company of the Chicago Board of Trade.

chickenpox

chief Capitalize as a formal title before a name: *She spoke to police Chief Michael Codd. He spoke to Chief Michael Codd of the New York police.*

Lowercase when it is not a formal title: *union chief Walter Reuther.*

See **titles**.

chief justice Capitalize only as a formal title before a name: *Chief Justice John Roberts.* The officeholder is the chief justice of the United States, not of the Supreme Court. See **judge**.

child care Two words, no hyphen, in all cases.

child-free, childless Avoid these terms other than in direct quotes essential to the story. They may be viewed as loaded or demeaning. If you must mention a newsmaker's parental status and if it is relevant, use a neutral description such as *has no children.*

chile, chiles Any of a variety of spicy peppers or the sauces or gravies derived from them. The meat- and/or bean-based dish is *chili.*

China When used alone, it refers to the nation that includes the mainland, Hong Kong and Macao. Use China in mainland datelines; Hong Kong and Macao stand alone in datelines.

Use *People's Republic of China, Communist China* and *mainland China* only in direct quotations or when needed to distinguish the mainland and its government from Taiwan. Use *Red China* only in direct quotes.

For datelines on stories from the island of Taiwan, use the name of a community and *Taiwan.* In the body of a story, use *Taiwan* for references to the government based on the island. Use the formal name of the government, the *Republic of China,* when required for legal precision. See **"One China" policy**.

Chinese names A variety of systems are used for spelling Chinese names. For personal and place names from China, use the official Chinese spelling system known as *Pinyin: Senior leader Deng Xiaoping, Beijing,* or *Zhejiang province.*

In personal names, Chinese generally place surnames first and then given names, *Deng Xiaoping.* Second reference should be the family name, *Deng* in this case.

Some Chinese have Westernized their names, putting their given names or the initials for them first or sometimes using both an English name and a Chinese name: *P.Y. Chen, Jack Wang, Frank Hsieh Chang-ting.* In general, follow an individual's preferred spelling.

Normally Chinese women do not

take their husbands' surnames.

The Pinyin spelling system eliminates the hyphen or apostrophe previously used in many given names. Use the new spelling for *Mao Zedong* and *Zhou Enlai*, but keep the traditional American spelling for such historical figures as *Sun Yat-sen* and *Chiang Kai-shek*.

If the new Pinyin spelling of a proper noun is so radically different from the traditional American spelling that a reader might be confused, provide the Pinyin spelling followed by the traditional spelling in parentheses. For example, the city of *Fuzhou (Foochow)*. Or use a descriptive sentence: *Fuzhou, long known in the West as Foochow, is the capital of Fujian province, on China's eastern coast.*

Use the traditional American spellings for these place names: *China, Inner Mongolia, Shanghai, Tibet.*

Follow local spellings in stories dealing with Hong Kong and Taiwan.

Capitalize the animal names for years in the Chinese lunar calendar: *Year of the Sheep, Year of the Dog.*

chip In electronics, a sliver of semiconducting material (usually but not always silicon) on which an integrated circuit is fabricated. Chips perform a variety of functions, including processing information (microprocessors) and storing information (memory chips). *Semiconductor* is an acceptable substitute, although not recommended for first references except in technical publications.

chipmaker (n.) **chipmaking** (adj.)

Christmas, Christmas Day Dec. 25. The federal legal holiday is observed on Friday if Dec. 25 falls on a Saturday, on Monday if it falls on a Sunday.

Never abbreviate *Christmas* to *Xmas* or any other form.

Christmastime One word.

Christmas tree Lowercase *tree* and other seasonal terms with *Christmas*: *card, wreath, carol,* etc. Exception: *National Christmas Tree.*

Chromebook Laptop made by Google and other manufacturers. It ships with many Google services and is designed primarily to run software in the cloud, with little actually running or stored on the laptop. Operating system is called *Chrome OS.*

chronic traumatic encephalopathy A degenerative brain disease that researchers have linked to concussions or repeated blows to the head. It is most closely associated with football but also has been diagnosed in some athletes from other contact sports and military combat veterans. It can be identified only posthumously through an examination of the brain. *CTE* is acceptable on second reference, and in headlines if essential. See **disabilities; brain injury, traumatic brain injury, brain damage, brain-damaged**.

church Capitalize as part of the formal name of a building, a congregation or a denomination; lowercase in other uses: *St. Mary's Church, the Roman Catholic Church, the Catholic and Episcopal churches, a Roman Catholic church, a church.*

Lowercase in phrases where the church is used in an institutional sense: *She believes in the separation of* church and state. *The pope says climate change is a crucial issue for the church.*

See **religious titles** and the entry for the denomination in question in the **Religion** chapter.

Church of Jesus Christ of Latter-day Saints, The

Note the capitalization and punctuation of *Latter-day*. The church in 2018 began moving away from the widely recognized terms *Mormon church* and *LDS church*, and now prefers that its full name be used and that members be referred to as *Latter-day Saints*.

Use the full name of the church on first references, with *the church*, *church members*, *members of the faith* preferred on second and later reference. When necessary for space or clarity or in quotations or proper names, *Mormon*, *Mormons* and *Latter-day Saints* are acceptable.

The term *Mormon* is based on the church's sacred Book of Mormon and remains in common use by members of the faith. When using the church's full name, include a short explanation such as, *the church, widely known as the Mormon church* ...

For more detail, see **Church of Jesus Christ of Latter-day Saints, The** in the **Religion** chapter.

cities and towns

See **datelines** for guidelines on when they should be followed by a state or a country name.

Capitalize official names, including separate political entities such as *East St. Louis, Illinois*, or *West Palm Beach, Florida*.

The preferred form for the section of a city is lowercase: *the west end, northern Los Angeles*. But capitalize widely recognized names for the sections of a city: *South Side* (Chicago), *Lower East Side* (New York).

See **city**.

citizen, resident, subject, national, native, Native

A *citizen* is a person who has acquired the full civil rights of a nation either by birth or by naturalization. Cities and states in the United States do not confer citizenship. To avoid confusion, use *resident*, not *citizen*, in referring to inhabitants of states and cities.

Citizen is also acceptable for those in the United Kingdom, or other monarchies where the term *subject* is often used.

National is applied to a person residing away from the nation of which he or she is a citizen, or to a person under the protection of a specified nation.

The term *native* (lowercase) denotes that a person was born in a given location: *a Seattle native.*

The terms *Native* and *Natives* are acceptable on second reference for *Native Americans*. Also acceptable as an adjective — *Native music, Native art* — but if the story is not generally about *Native Americans*, use *Native American music, Native American art*, etc.

In Alaska, the Indigenous groups are collectively known as *Alaska Natives*.

city

Capitalize *city* if part of a proper name, an integral part of an official name, or a regularly used nickname: *Kansas City, New York City, Windy City, City of Light, Fun City.*

Lowercase elsewhere: *a Texas city*; *the city government*; *the city Board of Education*; and all *city of* phrases: *the city of Boston.*

Capitalize when part of a formal title before a name: *City Manager*

C

48

Francis McGrath. Lowercase when not part of the formal title: *city Health Commissioner Frank Smith.*

See **city council** and **governmental bodies**.

city council Capitalize when part of a proper name: *the Boston City Council.*

Retain capitalization if the reference is to a specific council but the context does not require the city name:

BOSTON (AP) — *The City Council* ...

Lowercase in other uses: *the council, the Boston and New York city councils, a city council.*

Use the proper name if the body is not known as a city council: *the Miami City Commission, the City Commission, the commission; the Louisville Board of Aldermen, the Board of Aldermen, the board.*

Use *city council* in a generic sense for plural references: *the Boston, Louisville and Miami city councils.*

city hall Capitalize with the name of a city, or without the name of a city if the reference is specific: *Boston City Hall, City Hall.*

Lowercase plural uses: *the Boston and New York city halls.*

Lowercase generic uses, including: *You can't fight city hall.*

citywide

civil cases, criminal cases A *civil case* is one in which an individual, business or agency of government seeks damages or relief from another individual, business or agency of government. Civil actions generally involve a charge that a contract has been breached or that someone has been wronged or injured.

A *criminal case* is one that the state

or the federal government brings against an individual charged with committing a crime.

claim This verb implies doubt, and its use in stories — *Smith claimed* — can imply the reporter does not believe something. Generally, *said* is a better term. *Claim* is most appropriate when an assertion is open to question and the story presents an alternative point of view: *Pro-government forces claimed they seized the town, but rebels denied it.*

cliches, jargon It is tempting to advise writers to avoid cliches like the plague; they are the bane of our existence. Right there, you can see why they are so difficult to shun: Cliches are the junk food of the literary pantry, much loved by lazy writers. But platitudes and shopworn phrases serve as signals to the reader to move along, there's nothing to see here.

Don't push readers away, or lull them to sleep. Engage them with original, specific phrasing.

Jargon presents other issues. It has its place in specialized worlds whose inhabitants use jargon-speak as shortcuts (and sometimes, as code words for those in the know, or as tools to disguise, euphemize or editorialize). To a doctor, "symptomatology" is a patient's set of symptoms; to a businessperson, "due diligence" is putting the necessary effort into research before making a decision; to a military officer, "collateral damage" is the accidental killing of innocent people. To the rest of us, these words may be befuddling.

William Strunk Jr. and E.B. White put it simply in "The Elements of Style": "Be clear." Jargon is the opposite of clarity. Don't just repeat the words. Translate them, and push for the true meaning when necessary.

climate change The terms *global warming* and *climate change* are often used interchangeably. But *climate change* is the more accurate scientific term to describe the various effects of increasing levels of greenhouse gases on the world because it includes extreme weather; storms; and changes in rainfall patterns, ocean acidification and sea level. *Global warming,* the increase of average temperature around the world, is one aspect of climate change.

The terms *climate crisis* and *climate emergency* are used by some scientists, policymakers and others, and are acceptable.

Avoid attributing single occurrences to *climate change* unless scientists have established a connection. At the same time, stories about individual events should make it clear that they occur in a larger context. *Scientists say without extensive study they cannot directly link a single weather event to climate change, but climate change is responsible for more intense and more frequent extreme events such as storms, droughts, floods and wildfires.*

According to the vast majority of peer-reviewed studies, science organizations and climate scientists: The world is warming, mainly due to rising levels of carbon dioxide and other greenhouse gases in the atmosphere. By far, most of the increase in temperature is the result of human activity. That includes the burning of coal, oil and natural gas; deforestation; and raising livestock.

Identify the source for specific climate change data, and for any detailed predictions of how climate change will affect Earth.

Avoid false balance — giving a platform to unqualified claims or sources in the guise of balancing a story by including all views. For example, coverage of a study describing effects of climate change need not seek "other side" comment that humans have no influence on the climate.

The *Paris Agreement* of 2015 set two goals to limit global warming to 2 degrees Celsius (3.6 degrees Fahrenheit) and if possible to limit it to no more than 1.5 degrees Celsius (2.7 degrees Fahrenheit) compared to pre-industrial temperatures. The world has already warmed about 1.1 degrees Celsius (2 degrees Fahrenheit). Countries and scientists have recently emphasized the more stringent goal, which many scientists say the world is unlikely to achieve.

Do not use terms like *climate change deniers, climate change skeptics* or *climate change doubters.* Be specific about an individual or group of people's beliefs. For instance: *people who do not agree with mainstream science that says the climate is changing.* Or *people who do not believe that human activity is responsible for the bulk of climate change.* Or *people who disagree with the severity of climate change projected by scientists.*

See the **Health and Science chapter** and **weather terms**.

clinically dead, clinical death Avoid these terms and seek explanation if used by a medical professional. There is no standard definition, though generally means the heart and breathing have stopped. It's possible in some cases to resuscitate a person, such as a victim of sudden cardiac arrest. See **brain-dead, brain death**.

Clinton, Hillary Rodham She prefers to use her full name, *Hillary Rodham Clinton*. On second reference: *Clinton*.

closely held corporation A corporation in which stock shares and voting control are concentrated in the hands of a small number of investors, but for which some shares are available and traded on the market.

cloture Not *closure*, for the parliamentary procedure for closing debate.

Whenever practical, use a phrase such as closing debate or ending debate instead of the technical term.

cloud computing The use of remote servers to store data and provide related computing services to large numbers of users. *Cloud* and *the cloud* are acceptable references. Consumer cloud services include social media, streaming video and *Google Drive* and Apple's *iCloud*. There are similar services for business, government and, increasingly, military use.

CME Group Inc. Parent of the Chicago Board of Trade, the Chicago Mercantile Exchange, the New York Mercantile Exchange and COMEX, which operates the CME Globex electronic trading platform and live trading floors in Chicago and New York. Headquarters is in Chicago.

co- Retain the hyphen when forming nouns, adjectives and verbs that indicate occupation or status:

co-author	*co-defendant*
co-chair	*co-host*
co-owner	*co-signer*
co-partner	*co-sponsor*
co-pilot	*co-star*
co-respondent (in a divorce suit)	*co-worker*

(Several are exceptions to Webster's New World College Dictionary in the interests of consistency.)

As part of a formal title before a name: *co-President Alexa Manola, co-Executive Director Alfredo Hudson*. But *Smith Electric Co-Op* if that is the formal name.

Use no hyphen in other combinations:

coeducation	*cooperative*
coequal	*coordinate*
coexist	*coordination*
coexistence	*copay*
cooperate	

Cooperate, coordinate and related words are exceptions to the rule that a hyphen is used if a prefix ends in a vowel and the word that follows begins with the same vowel.

coast Lowercase when referring to the physical shoreline: *Atlantic coast, Pacific coast, east coast*.

Capitalize when referring to regions of the United States lying along such shorelines: *the Atlantic Coast states, a Gulf Coast city, the West Coast, the East Coast*.

Do not capitalize when referring to smaller regions: *the Virginia coast*.

Capitalize *the Coast* when standing alone only if the reference is to the West Coast.

Coast Guard Capitalize when referring to this branch of the U.S. armed forces, a part of the Department of Homeland Security: the *U.S. Coast Guard, the Coast Guard, Coast Guard policy*. Do not use the abbreviation *USCG*, except in quotes.

Use lowercase for similar forces of other nations.

This approach has been adopted for consistency, because many foreign nations do not use *coast guard* as the proper name.

See **military academies**.

Coast Guardsman Capitalize as a proper noun when referring to an individual in a U.S. Coast Guard unit: *He is a Coast Guardsman.*

Lowercase *guardsman* when it stands alone.

See **military titles**.

cocktail Do not use *cocktail* in reference to a mixture of drugs. Instead: *drug combination* or simply *drugs* or *medications*: *HIV drugs.*

c.o.d. Preferred in all references for *cash on delivery* or *collect on delivery*. This is an exception to Webster's New World College Dictionary.

Cold War Capitalize when referring specifically to the post-World War II rivalry between the United States and the former Soviet Union. Use only in the historic sense.

collateral Stock or other property that a borrower is obliged to turn over to a lender if unable to repay a loan.

See **loan terminology**.

collateralized debt obligations
Debt, including bonds or mortgages, that is pooled, sliced up and resold to investors.

collectibles

collective nouns Nouns that denote a unit take singular verbs and pronouns: *class, committee, crowd, family, group, herd, jury, orchestra, team.*

Some usage examples: *The committee is meeting to set its agenda. The jury reached its verdict. A herd of cattle was sold.*

Team names and musical group names that are plural take plural verbs. *The Yankees are in first place. The Jonas Brothers are popular.*

Team or group names with no plural forms also take plural verbs: *The Miami Heat are battling for third place.* Other examples: *Orlando Magic, Oklahoma City Thunder, Utah Jazz, Alabama Crimson Tide.*

Most singular names take singular verbs, including places and university names in sports: *Coldplay is on tour. Boston is favored in the playoffs. Stanford is in the NCAA Tournament.*

Some proper names that are plural in form take a singular verb: *Brooks Brothers is holding a sale.*

PLURAL IN FORM: Some words that are plural in form become collective nouns and take singular verbs when the group or quantity is regarded as a unit.

Right: *A thousand bushels is a good yield.* (A unit.)

Right: *A thousand bushels were created.* (Individual items.)

collectors' item

college Capitalize when part of a proper name: *Dartmouth College.*

See **organizations and institutions**.

College Board Not-for-profit organization that administers the SAT and Advanced Placement, or AP, exams, which assess college-level high school courses.

colloquialisms The word describes the informal use of a language. It is not local or regional in nature, as dialect is.

Webster's New World College Dictionary identifies many words as colloquial with the label *Informal*.

Many colloquial words and phrases characteristic of informal writing and conversation are acceptable in some contexts but out of place in others.

Other colloquial words normally should be avoided because they are pejorative.

See **dialect**.

colon See entry in the **Punctuation** chapter.

colonial Capitalize *Colonial* as a proper adjective in all references to the *Colonies*. (See the next entry.)

colonies Capitalize only for the British dependencies that declared their independence in 1776, now known as the United States.

Columbus Day A federal legal holiday, first proclaimed on Oct. 12, 1892, to mark the 400th anniversary of Christopher Columbus' sighting of what came to be known as the Americas. Oct. 12 is still celebrated in Italy, Spain and some Latin American countries; in the United States, the holiday is now observed on the second Monday of October. Some U.S. localities have renamed the holiday *Indigenous Peoples Day*, recognizing that the lands "discovered" by Columbus were already inhabited and that Columbus dealt brutally with those populations. In 2021, President Joe Biden issued the first-ever presidential proclamation of Indigenous Peoples Day, observed along with Columbus Day. See **Indigenous Peoples Day**.

coma A state of unconsciousness in which the eyes are closed and the patient can't be aroused as if simply asleep. There is no sign of a sleep-wake cycle, or of any awareness of self or environment. The patient cannot communicate or hear, and shows no emotion. Any movement is purely reflex. This is the first stage after a severe brain injury; the patient may recover partially or completely, die, or progress to a vegetative or minimally conscious state.

See **minimally conscious state** and **vegetative state**.

combat, combated, combating

combustible

comma See entry in the **Punctuation** chapter.

commander in chief Capitalize only if used as a formal title before a name.

See **titles**.

commercial paper Short-term loans, issued primarily by corporations, to finance their daily needs, such as making payroll. Historically, a lower cost alternative to bank loans.

commissioner Do not abbreviate. Capitalize when used as a formal title.

See **titles**.

commitment

committee Do not abbreviate. Capitalize when part of a formal name: *the House Appropriations Committee.*

Do not capitalize committee in shortened versions of long committee names: *The Senate Banking, Housing and Urban Affairs Committee,* for example, became *the Senate banking committee.*

See **subcommittee.**

commodities futures contract A contract to purchase or sell a specific amount of a given commodity at a specified future date.

commodity The products of mining or agriculture before they have undergone extensive processing.

Common Core educational standards First adopted by most states beginning in 2010, a uniform set of learning standards that established benchmarks for reading and math skills across grade levels from kindergarten through high school. The standards are intended to ensure college readiness. They were developed by the National Governors Association and Council of Chief State School Officers, not the federal government. Standards do not determine curriculum; those decisions are made by local school boards and educators.

common stock, preferred stock An ownership interest in a corporation.

If other classes of stock are outstanding, the holders of common stock are the last to receive dividends and the last to receive payments if a corporation is dissolved. The company may raise or lower common stock dividends as its earnings rise or fall.

When preferred stock is outstanding and company earnings are sufficient, a fixed dividend is paid. If a company is liquidated, holders of preferred stock receive payments up to a set amount before any money is distributed to holders of common stock.

Commonwealth of Independent States Founded Dec. 8, 1991, the organization is made up of 11 of the former republics of the USSR, or Soviet Union. Russia is the largest and richest. Three other former republics — Latvia, Lithuania and Estonia — became independent nations earlier in 1991. (The Soviet Union was formally dissolved in December 1991. Its last leader, Mikhail Gorbachev, resigned on Dec. 25, 1991.)

The republics (with adjective form in parentheses):

Armenia (Armenian); Azerbaijan (Azerbaijani); Belarus (Belarusian); Kazakhstan (Kazakh); Kyrgyzstan (Kyrgyz); Moldova (Moldovan); Russia (Russian); Tajikistan (Tajik); Turkmenistan (Turkmen); Ukraine (no *the*) (Ukrainian); Uzbekistan (Uzbek). Georgia (Georgian) quit the CIS in 2009.

DATELINES: *MOSCOW* stands alone. Follow all other datelines with the name of the state. *ALMATY, Kazakhstan.*

Commonwealth, the Formerly the British Commonwealth. The members of this free association of sovereign states recognize the British sovereign as head of the Commonwealth. Some also recognize the sovereign as head of their state; others do not.

The members are: Antigua and Barbuda, Australia, Bahamas, Bangladesh, Barbados, Belize, Botswana, Brunei, Cameroon,

53

Canada, Cyprus, Dominica, Fiji, Gambia, Ghana, Grenada, Guyana, India, Jamaica, Kenya, Kiribati, Lesotho, Malawi, Malaysia, Maldives, Malta, Mauritius, Mozambique, Namibia, Nauru, New Zealand, Nigeria, Pakistan, Papua New Guinea, Rwanda, St. Kitts and Nevis, St. Lucia, St. Vincent and the Grenadines, Samoa, Seychelles, Sierra Leone, Singapore, Solomon Islands, South Africa, Sri Lanka, Swaziland, Tanzania, Tonga, Trinidad and Tobago, Tuvalu, Uganda, United Kingdom, Vanuatu and Zambia.

Communications Workers of America *CWA* is acceptable on second reference.

Headquarters is in Washington.

community Limit use of this term in reference to groups of people. It implies homogeneity and the idea that all members of a particular "community" think and act alike. This is similar to the concept of avoiding any type of generalization or stereotype.

commutation A legal term for a change of sentence or punishment to one that is less severe.

See **pardon, parole, probations**.

compact disc *CD* is acceptable in all references.

company, companies Use *Co.* or *Cos.* when a business uses either word at the end of its proper name: *Ford Motor Co., United Tandem Bicycle Cos.*

If *company* or *companies* appear alone in second reference, spell the word out.

The forms for possessives: *Ford Motor Co.'s profits, United Tandem Bicycle Cos.' profits.*

company (military) Capitalize only when part of a name: *Company B.* Do not abbreviate.

company names For a company's formal name, consult the New York Stock Exchange, Nasdaq or filings with the Securities and Exchange Commission.

Do not use a comma before *Inc.* or *Ltd.*, even if it is included in the formal name.

You must include the full company name in the body of any story in which the subject matter could affect a company's business, although not necessarily on first reference when the informal name can be used. For example, *Costco* is acceptable for *Costco Wholesale Corp.* on first reference as long as the full name appears elsewhere in the story. This ensures the story will be among the search results on major websites.

Include the corporate name, for example, in a story on an earnings report, or in a story on a plane crash that could affect the airline's stock price. However, the corporate name might be irrelevant in a story about a political candidate's appearance at a local retail store.

If "The" is part of the formal company name it should be included. For example: *The Walt Disney Co.*

Generally, follow the spelling preferred by the company, but capitalize the first letter of company names in all uses: e.g., *Adidas, Lululemon.* Exceptions include company names such as *eBay,* which have a capital letter elsewhere in the name. However, company names should always be capitalized at the beginning of a sentence. For corporate news, AP may use the legal name from the Securities and Exchange Commission filing rather than a company's preference.

Do not use all-capital-letter names unless the letters are individually pronounced: *BMW*. Others should be uppercase and lowercase. *Ikea*, not *IKEA*; *USA Today*, not *USA TODAY*.

The + symbol is acceptable when it is pronounced as part of a company, brand or event name: *Disney+, Apple TV+, ESPN+, CompTia Network+*. Do not use in slugs of AP stories.

Use an ampersand only if it is part of the company's formal name, but not otherwise in place of *and*. Do not use in slugs of AP stories.

Do not use other symbols such as exclamation points or asterisks that form contrived spellings that might distract or confuse a reader. Use *Yahoo*, not *Yahoo!*; *Toys R Us*, not *Toys "R" Us*; *E-Trade*, not *E*Trade*.

Use *the* lowercase unless it is part of the company's formal name.

Notes on some individual companies:

FedEx No space.

Johnson & Johnson *J&J* is acceptable on second reference.

Procter & Gamble Co. *P&G* is acceptable on second reference.

IBM Acceptable in all references for *International Business Machines Corp.*

MGM Acceptable in all references for *Metro-Goldwyn-Mayer Inc.*

3M Trademark and name of the company formerly known as *Minnesota Mining & Manufacturing.*

UPS Acceptable in all references for *United Parcel Service Inc.*

Volkswagen of America Inc. The U.S. subsidiary of the German company *Volkswagen AG. Volkswagen* is acceptable for either on second

reference as long as the specific company is clear in the context.

Walmart Inc. It changed its legal name from Wal-Mart Stores Inc. in 2018.

compared to, compared with

Use *compared to* when the intent is to assert, without the need for elaboration, that two or more items are similar: *She compared her work for women's rights to Susan B. Anthony's campaign for women's suffrage.*

Use *compared with* when juxtaposing two or more items to illustrate similarities and/or differences: *His time was 2:11:10, compared with 2:14 for his closest competitor.*

compatible

complacent, complaisant

Complacent means *self-satisfied*. Complaisant means *eager to please*.

complement, compliment

Complement is a noun and a verb denoting completeness or the process of supplementing something: *The ship has a complement of 200 sailors and 20 officers. The tie complements his suit.*

Compliment is a noun or a verb that denotes praise or the expression of courtesy: *The captain complimented the sailors. She was flattered by the compliments on her project.*

complementary, complimentary

The husband and wife have complementary careers.

They received complimentary tickets to the show.

compose, comprise, constitute

Compose means *to create or put together*. It commonly is used in both the active and passive voices: *She composed a song. The United States is composed of 50 states. The zoo is composed of many animals.*

Comprise means *to contain, to include all* or *embrace*. It is best used only in the active voice, followed by a direct object: *The United States comprises 50 states. The jury comprises five men and seven women. The zoo comprises many animals.*

Constitute, in the sense of *form or make up*, may be the best word if neither *compose* nor *comprise* seems to fit: *Fifty states constitute the United States. Five men and seven women constitute the jury. A collection of animals can constitute a zoo.*

Use *include* when what follows is only part of the total: *The price includes breakfast. The zoo includes lions and tigers.*

composition titles Apply these guidelines to the titles of books, movies, plays, poems, albums, songs, operas, radio and television programs, lectures, speeches, and works of art:

— Capitalize all words in a title except articles (*a, an, the*); prepositions of three or fewer letters (*for, of, on, up*, etc.); and conjunctions of three or fewer letters (*and, but, for, nor, or, so, yet*, etc.) unless any of those start or end the title.

  More detail:

— Capitalize prepositions of four or more letters (*above, after, down, inside, over, with*, etc.) and conjunctions of four or more letters (*because, while, since, though*, etc.)

— Capitalize both parts of a phrasal verb: "What to Look For in a Mate"; "Turn Off the Lights in Silence." But: "A Life of

Eating Chocolate for Stamina"; "Living With Both Feet off the Ground." (Note the different uses of *for* and *off*, and thus the different capitalization, in those examples.)

— Capitalize *to* in infinitives: "What I Want To Be When I Grow Up." Also:

— Put quotation marks around the names of all such works except the Bible, the Quran and other holy books, and books that are primarily catalogs of reference material. In addition to catalogs, this category includes almanacs, directories, dictionaries, encyclopedias, gazetteers, handbooks and similar publications.

— Do not use quotation marks around such software titles as WordPerfect or Windows; apps; or around names of video, online or analog versions of games: FarmVille, Pokemon Go, The Legend of Zelda, Monopoly.

— Do not use quotation marks for sculptures: The Thinker, Michelangelo's Pieta.

— Translate a foreign title into English unless a work is generally known by its foreign name. An exception to this is reviews of musical performances. In those instances, generally refer to the work in the language it was sung in, so as to differentiate for the reader. However, musical compositions in Slavic languages are always referred to in their English translations.

  EXAMPLES: "The Star-Spangled Banner," "The Rise and Fall of the Third Reich," "Gone With the Wind," "Of Mice and Men," "For Whom the Bell Tolls," "Time After Time," the "Today" show, the "CBS

Evening News," "This Is Us," "A Star Is Born," "Star Wars," "Game of Thrones." See **television program titles** for further guidelines and examples.

REFERENCE WORKS: IHS Jane's All the World's Aircraft; Encyclopaedia Britannica; Webster's New World College Dictionary, Fifth Edition.

FOREIGN WORKS: Rousseau's "War," not Rousseau's "La Guerre." But: Leonardo da Vinci's "Mona Lisa." Mozart's "The Marriage of Figaro" if sung in English but "Le Nozze di Figaro" if sung in Italian. Mozart's "The Magic Flute" if sung in English but "Die Zauberfloete" if sung in German. "Die Walkuere" and "Goetterdaemmerung" from Wagner's "Der Ring des Nibelungen" if sung in German but "The Valkyrie" and "The Twilight of the Gods" from "The Ring of the Nibelung" if sung in English. Janacek's "From the House of the Dead," not Janacek's "Z Mrtveho Domu."

— For other classical music titles, use quotation marks around the composition's nicknames but not compositions identified by its sequence.

EXAMPLES: Dvorak's "New World Symphony." Dvorak's Symphony No. 9.

compound adjectives See the **hyphen** entry in the **Punctuation** chapter.

comptroller, controller *Comptroller* generally is the accurate word for government financial officers.

The U.S. comptroller of the currency is an appointed official in the Treasury Department who is responsible for the chartering, supervising and liquidation of banks organized under the federal government's National Bank Act.

Controller generally is the proper word for financial officers of businesses and for other positions such as *air traffic controller.*

Capitalize *comptroller* and *controller* when used as the formal titles for financial officers. Use lowercase for *air traffic controller* and similar occupational applications of the word.

See **titles**.

concentration camps For World War II camps in countries occupied by Nazi Germany, do not use phrases like *Polish death camps* or *death camps in Poland* that confuse the location and the perpetrators. Use instead, for example, *death camps in Nazi Germany-occupied Poland.*

Confederate States of America The formal name of the states that seceded during the Civil War. The shortened form *the Confederacy* is acceptable in all references.

Conference Board, The The capitalized article is part of the formal name of the business organization.

confess, confessed In some contexts the words may be erroneous.
See **admit, admitted**.

conglomerate A corporation that has diversified its operations, usually by acquiring enterprises in widely varied industries.

Congo Note the two countries in Africa: the Democratic Republic of Congo, whose capital is Kinshasa, and the Republic of Congo, whose capital is Brazzaville.

In datelines:

KINSHASA, Congo (AP) —
BRAZZAVILLE, Republic of Congo
(AP) —
Use *Congo* when referring to the
Democratic Republic of Congo.
If referring to the country whose
capital is Brazzaville, the full name
— *Republic of Congo* — should be
used.

Congress Capitalize *U.S. Congress*
and *Congress* when referring to
the U.S. Senate and House of
Representatives. Although *Congress*
sometimes is used as a substitute for
the House, it properly is reserved
for reference to both the Senate and
House.
Capitalize *Congress* also if
referring to a foreign body that
uses the term, or its equivalent in
a foreign language, as part of its
formal name: *the Argentine Congress,
the Congress.*
Lowercase when used as a
synonym for *convention* or in second
reference to an organization that
uses the word as part of its formal
name: *the Congress of Racial Equality,
the congress.*

congressional Lowercase unless
part of a proper name: *congressional
salaries, the Congressional Quarterly,
the Congressional Record.*

Congressional Directory Use this as
the reference source for questions
about the federal government that
are not covered by this stylebook.

congressional districts Use figures
and capitalize district when joined
with a figure: *the 1st Congressional
District, the 1st District.*
Lowercase *district* whenever it
stands alone.
See **numerals**.

Congressional Record A daily
publication of the proceedings of
Congress including a complete
stenographic report of all remarks
and debates.

congressman, congresswoman Use
only in reference to members of the
U.S. House of Representatives.
The terms *U.S. representative,
representative, member of Congress*
are preferred. *Congressman* and
congresswoman are acceptable
because of their common use. Do
not use *congressperson.*
Rep. and *U.S. Rep.* are the
preferred first-reference forms
when a formal title is used before
the name of a U.S. House member.
Congressman and *congresswoman*
should appear as capitalized formal
titles before a name only in direct
quotation.
See **legislative titles; gender-
neutral language**.

connote, denote *Connote* means *to
suggest or imply something beyond the
explicit meaning*: *To some people, the
word "marriage" connotes too much
restriction.*
Denote means *to be explicit about
the meaning*: *The word "demolish"
denotes destruction.*

constable Capitalize when used as a
formal title before a name.
See **titles**.

Constitution The U.S. Constitution
is made up of the original preamble
that begins "We the people" and
seven articles that took effect in
1789, and 27 amendments added
between 1791 and 1992. The first 10
of those amendments are known as
the *Bill of Rights.*
The articles establish the system

of government; the Bill of Rights mainly lays out rights guaranteed to the people. The rest of the amendments expand on the original document (prohibiting slavery, expanding the right to vote, limiting a president's terms, for example). Some reflect society's changing values, such as Prohibition and its repeal.

The articles and many amendments are divided into sections, but the most important elements of articles and amendments often are identified as *clauses*. Clauses get their names from key words or phrases, like the commerce clause in Article 1, Section 8, the free speech clause in the First Amendment or the equal protection clause in Section 1 of the 14th Amendment.

Capitalize references to the U.S. Constitution, with or without the *U.S.* modifier: *The president said he supports the Constitution.*

When referring to constitutions of other nations or of states, capitalize only with the name of a nation or a state: *the French Constitution, the Massachusetts Constitution, the nation's constitution, the state constitution, the constitution.*

Lowercase in other uses: *the organization's constitution.*

Lowercase *constitutional* in all uses. See **constitutional amendments, clauses**.

constitutional amendments, clauses Use this style of uppercase and lowercase for amendments to the U.S. Constitution: *the First Amendment guarantee of free speech, the Eighth Amendment prohibition on cruel and unusual punishment.*

Shorthand such as *the First Amendment* or *the Eighth Amendment*

may be used on first reference, but explain later in the text. Colloquial references to the Fifth Amendment's protection against self-incrimination are best avoided, but where appropriate: *He took the Fifth seven times.*

Lowercase clauses in the Constitution: *the due process clause, the commerce clause, the equal protection clause.* Limit use of the term *clause*. It is better to explain a clause's meaning. For example, instead of: *The court said the law is unconstitutional under the First Amendment's free speech clause,* say: *The court said the law violates the First Amendment's guarantee of free speech,* or *The court said the law violates the First Amendment right to speak free of government interference.*

Some of the more frequently cited constitutional clauses and what they mean:

THE COMMERCE CLAUSE: From Article 1, Section 8, giving Congress broad authority to regulate business among the states.

THE SUPREMACY CLAUSE: From Article 6, the Constitution and federal law take precedence over state laws.

THE FREE SPEECH CLAUSE: From the First Amendment, guaranteeing the right to speak, free of interference by the government.

THE FREE EXERCISE CLAUSE: From the First Amendment, guaranteeing the right to practice religion, free of interference by the government.

THE ESTABLISHMENT CLAUSE: From the First Amendment, prohibiting government from favoring one religion over others.

THE DUE PROCESS CLAUSE: From the Fifth and 14th amendments, safeguarding life, liberty and property from arbitrary actions

C

by the government. The Fifth Amendment applies to the federal government and the 14th, to the states. All people, not just citizens, are afforded due process.

THE EQUAL PROTECTION CLAUSE: From the 14th Amendment, requiring that people (not just citizens) in similar circumstances be treated the same under the law. The Supreme Court has invoked equal protection under the law to strike down official discrimination.

See **constitution**.

consulate A *consulate* is the residence of a consul in a foreign city. It handles the commercial affairs and personal needs of citizens of the appointing country.

Capitalize with the name of a nation; lowercase without it: *the French Consulate, the U.S. Consulate, the consulate.*

See **embassy** for the distinction between a consulate and an embassy.

consul, consul general, consuls general Capitalize when used as a formal title before a noun.

See **titles**.

consumer credit Loans extended to individuals or small businesses usually on an unsecured basis, and providing for monthly repayment. Also referred to as installment credit or personal loans.

Consumer Financial Protection Bureau Created by Congress under the 2010 financial overhaul to oversee mortgages, payday loans and other consumer borrowing. It aimed to close regulatory gaps exposed by the 2008 financial crisis. *CFPB* is acceptable on second reference.

consumer price index A measurement of changes in the retail prices of a constant marketbasket of goods and services. It is computed by comparing the cost of the marketbasket at a fixed time with its cost at subsequent or prior intervals.

It is issued monthly by the Bureau of Labor Statistics, an agency of the Labor Department. It should not be referred to as a *cost-of-living index*, because it does not include the impact of income taxes and Social Security taxes on the cost of living, nor does it reflect changes in buying patterns that result from inflation. It is, however, the basis for computing cost-of-living raises in many union contracts.

The preferred form for second reference is *the index*. Confine *CPI* to quoted material.

The *chained consumer price index* is a version of the CPI used by the government to account for substitutions consumers typically make in their purchases when prices of certain goods change. Some consider it a more accurate gauge of consumer prices than the conventional CPI. Avoid using the term *chained CPI* in stories.

Consumer Product Safety Commission *CPSC* is acceptable on second reference. Headquarters is in Bethesda, Maryland.

contemptible

content All forms of digital media, whether text, music, podcasts, images, video, games, augmented reality, virtual reality or others. Use this jargony term with caution; be specific about the format(s) involved if possible.

continent The seven continents, in order of their land size: Asia, Africa, North America, South America, Europe, Antarctica and Australia.

Capitalize *the Continent* and *Continental* only when used as synonyms for Europe or European. Lowercase in other uses such as: *the continent of Europe, the European continent, the African and Asian continents.*

Continental Divide The ridge along the Rocky Mountains that separates rivers flowing east from those that flow west.

continental shelf, continental slope Lowercase. The *shelf* is the part of a continent that is submerged in relatively shallow sea at gradually increasing depths, generally up to about 600 feet below sea level.

The *continental slope* begins at the point where the descent to the ocean bottom becomes very steep.

continual, continuous *Continual* means *a steady repetition, over and over again*: *The merger has been the source of continual litigation.*

Continuous means *uninterrupted, steady, unbroken*: *All she saw ahead of her was a continuous stretch of desert.*

Contra, Contras Uppercase when used to describe former Nicaraguan rebel groups.

contractions Contractions reflect informal speech and writing. Webster's New World College Dictionary includes many entries for contractions: *aren't* for *are not*, for example.

Avoid excessive use of contractions. Contractions listed in the dictionary are acceptable,

however, in informal contexts where they reflect the way a phrase commonly appears in speech or writing.

See **colloquialisms** and **quotations in the news**.

contrasted to, contrasted with Use *contrasted to* when the intent is to assert, without the need for elaboration, that two items have opposite characteristics: *He contrasted the appearance of the house today to its ramshackle look last year.*

Use *contrasted with* when juxtaposing two or more items to illustrate similarities and/or differences: *He contrasted the Republican platform with the Democratic platform.*

control, controlled, controlling

controversial An overused word. Most issues that are described as controversial are obviously so, and the word is not necessary.

convention Capitalize as part of the name for a specific national or state political convention: *the Democratic National Convention, the Republican State Convention.*

Lowercase in other uses: *the national convention, the state convention, the convention, the annual convention of the American Medical Association.*

convict (v.) Follow with preposition *of*, not *for*: *He was convicted of murder.*

cooperate, cooperative But *co-op* as a short term of *cooperative*, to distinguish it from *coop*, a cage for animals.

cop Be careful in the use of this

colloquial term for *police officer*. It may be used in lighter stories and in casual, informal descriptions, but often is a derogatory term out of place in serious police stories.

Copenhagen The city in Denmark carries the country name in datelines.

copter Acceptable shortening of *helicopter*. But use it only as a noun or adjective. It is not a verb.

copyright (n., v. and adj.) *A copyright story.*

Use *copyrighted* only as the past tense of the verb: *He copyrighted the article.*

See **Copyright Infringement** in **Briefing on Media Law** section.

cord cutting, cord-cutters A general term for canceling cable- or satellite-television service in favor of internet *streaming*. Does not require a definition on first reference unless the context is unclear. The term has generally evolved to include those who have never subscribed to cable or satellite, rather than just those who dropped service. This group is also known as *cord-nevers*, though that term should not be used without explanation.

co-respondent In a divorce suit.

Corn Belt The region in the north-central Midwest where much corn and corn-fed livestock are raised. It extends from western Ohio to eastern Nebraska and northeastern Kansas.

coronaviruses A family of viruses, some of which cause disease in people and animals, named for the crownlike spikes on their surfaces.

Coronaviruses can cause the common cold or more severe diseases such as *SARS* (severe acute respiratory syndrome) and *MERS* (Middle East respiratory syndrome). A new coronavirus emerged in cases first reported in late 2019 in Wuhan, China. It causes a respiratory illness now called *COVID-19*, which stands for *coronavirus disease 2019*.

The virus itself is named *SARS-CoV-2* but avoid using that name.

Referring to simply *the coronavirus* is acceptable on first reference in stories about the pandemic that began in 2019. While the phrasing incorrectly implies there is only one coronavirus, the meaning is clear in this context.

The term *coronavirus* is generally acceptable in references to the pandemic: *coronavirus cases, coronavirus tests, coronavirus variants*. Use the term *COVID-19* when referring specifically to the disease: *COVID-19 treatments, COVID-19 patients, COVID-19 deaths, recovering from COVID-19*.

Passages and stories focusing on the science of the disease require sharper distinctions.

When referring specifically to the virus, *the COVID-19 virus* and *the virus that causes COVID-19* are acceptable, as is simply *the coronavirus*.

But, because *COVID-19* is the name of the disease, not the virus, it is not accurate to write *a virus called COVID-19*.

Lowercase names of variants: the *omicron variant*, or simply *omicron* on later references.

The shortened form *COVID* is acceptable if necessary for space in headlines, and in direct quotations and proper names.

Omitting *the* is acceptable in headlines and in uses such as: *He said coronavirus concerns are increasing.*

corporation An entity that is treated as a person in the eyes of the law. It is able to own property, incur debts, sue and be sued.

Abbreviate *corporation* as *Corp.* when a company or government agency uses the word at the end of its name: *the Federal Deposit Insurance Corp.*

Spell out *corporation* when it occurs elsewhere in a name: *the Corporation for Public Broadcasting.*

Spell out and lowercase *corporation* whenever it stands alone.

The form for possessives: *Chevron Corp.'s profits.*

corps Capitalize when used with a word or a figure to form a proper name: *the Marine Corps, the Signal Corps, the 9th Corps, the Army Corps of Engineers.*

Capitalize when standing alone only if it is a shortened reference to *U.S. Marine Corps* or *Army Corps of Engineers.*

The possessive form is *corps'* for both singular and plural: *one corps' location, two corps' assignments.*

Corsica Use instead of *France* in datelines on stories from communities on this island.

Cortes The Spanish parliament. See **legislative bodies**.

cosmonaut A Russian or Soviet astronaut.

cost of living The amount of money needed to pay taxes and to buy the goods and services deemed necessary to make up a given standard of living, taking into account changes that may occur in tastes and buying patterns.

The term often is treated incorrectly as a synonym for the *U.S. Consumer Price Index,* which does not take taxes into account and measures only price changes, keeping the quantities constant over time.

Hyphenate when used as a compound modifier: *The cost of living went up, but he did not receive a cost-of-living raise.*

See **consumer price index** and **inflation**.

cost-plus

Cotton Belt The region in the South and Southwestern sections of the United States where much cotton is grown.

council, counsel A *council* is a body of people or organizations, often appointed or elected. Capitalize councilor, councilman and councilwoman when used as a formal title before a name; otherwise, lowercase.

Counsel (n. or v.) refers to guidance, sometimes legal in nature and given by a lawyer, or a person or people who provide such guidance. *He sought counsel from former bosses as he considered the job offer. Her counsel advised her not to answer questions. The attorney counseled her client.*

Counselor is often synonymous with *lawyer,* shortened from *counselor at law. The lawyer greeted his fellow counselors before the trial began.* It also is a person who gives advice, such as a school guidance counselor or an investment counselor.

A *special counsel* is an official, often

appointed, who fulfills a temporary legal duty. *The Justice Department appointed a special counsel to lead the federal investigation.*

Lowercase counsel and special counsel whether before or after a name.

See **lawyer**.

Council of Economic Advisers

A group of advisers who help the U.S. president prepare his annual economic report to Congress and recommend economic measures to him throughout the year.

counter- The rules in **prefixes** apply, but in general, no hyphen. Some examples:

counteract	*counterproposal*
countercharge	*counterspy*
counterfoil	

country music The music genre is *country*. Lowercase *western* if the full but antiquated term is needed, as in a quote: *country-western*; *country and western*. See **West, Western, west, western**.

county Capitalize when an integral part of a proper name: *Dade County, Nassau County, Suffolk County*.

Capitalize the full names of county governmental units: *the Dade County Commission, the Orange County Department of Social Services, the Suffolk County Legislature*.

Retain capitalization for the name of a county body if the proper noun is not needed in the context; lowercase the word *county* if it is used to distinguish an agency from state or federal counterparts: *the Board of Supervisors, the county Board of Supervisors; the Department of Social Services, the county Department of Social Services*. Lowercase *the*

board, the department, etc. whenever they stand alone.

Capitalize *county* if it is an integral part of a specific body's name even without the proper noun: *the County Commission, the County Legislature*. Lowercase *the commission, the legislature*, etc. when not preceded by the word *county*.

Capitalize as part of a formal title before a name: *County Manager John Smith*. Lowercase when it is not part of the formal title: *county Health Commissioner Frank Jones*.

Avoid *county of* phrases where possible, but when necessary, always lowercase: *the county of Westchester*.

Lowercase plural combinations: *Westchester and Rockland counties*.

Apply the same rules to similar terms such as *parish*.

See **governmental bodies**.

county court In some states, it is not a court but the administrative body of a county. In most cases, the *court* is presided over by a *county judge*, who is not a judge in the traditional sense but the chief administrative officer of the county.

The terms should be explained if they are not clear in the context.

Capitalize all references to a specific *county court*, and capitalize *county judge* when used as a formal title before a name. Do not use *judge* alone before a name except in direct quotations.

EXAMPLES:

SEVIERVILLE, Tenn. (AP) — A reluctant County Court approved a school budget today that calls for a 10% tax increase for property owners.

The county had been given an ultimatum by the state: Approve the budget or shut down the schools.

The chief administrative officer, County Judge Ray Reagan, said ...

coup d'etat The word *coup* usually is sufficient.

couple When used in the sense of two people, the word takes plural verbs and pronouns: *The couple were married Saturday and left Sunday on their honeymoon. They will return in two weeks.*

In the sense of a single unit, use a singular verb: *Each couple was asked to give $10.*

couple of The *of* is necessary. Never use *a couple tomatoes* or a similar phrase.

The phrase takes a plural verb in constructions such as: *A couple of tomatoes were stolen.*

coupon See **loan terminology** for its meaning in a financial sense.

course numbers Use Arabic numerals and capitalize the subject when used with a numeral: *History 6, Philosophy 209.* Otherwise, lowercase: *calculus, world history.*

court decisions Use figures and a hyphen: *The Supreme Court ruled 5-4, a 5-4 decision.* The word *to* is not needed, but use hyphens if it appears in quoted matter: *The court ruled 5-to-4, the 5-to-4 decision.*

courtesy titles In general, do not use courtesy titles except in direct quotations. When it is necessary to distinguish between two people who use the same last name, as in married couples or brothers and sisters, use the first and last name.

courthouse Capitalize with the name of a jurisdiction: *the Cook County Courthouse, the U.S. Courthouse.* Lowercase in other uses: *the county courthouse, the courthouse, the federal courthouse.*

Court House (two words) is used in the proper names of some communities: *Appomattox Court House, Virginia.*

court-martial, court-martialed, courts-martial

court names Capitalize the full proper names of courts at all levels.

Retain capitalization if *U.S.* or a state name is dropped: *the U.S. Supreme Court, the Supreme Court, the state Superior Court, the Superior Court, Superior Court.*

For courts identified by a numeral: *2nd District Court, 8th U.S. Circuit Court of Appeals.*

For additional details on federal courts, see **judicial branch** and separate listings under **U.S.** and the court name.

See **judge** for guidelines on titles before the names of judges.

Court of St. James's Note the *'s.* The formal name for the royal court of the British sovereign. Derived from St. James's Palace, the former scene of royal receptions.

courtroom

coworking (n., adj.) Sharing workspace and amenities, such as Wi-Fi, a printer, fax machine and the like, when people don't actually work for the same company but instead are self-employed or remote workers. No hyphen for this use. But: *co-worker* for a colleague within the same company.

CPR Acceptable in all references for *cardiopulmonary resuscitation.*

crawfish Not *crayfish*. An exception to Webster's New World College Dictionary based on the dominant spelling in Louisiana, where it is a popular delicacy.

credit default swaps A form of insurance that promises payment to investors in mortgage securities and other bonds if borrowers default.

Creutzfeldt-Jakob disease A rare degenerative brain disorder. The most common type has no known risk factors. In some cases, the disease can be hereditary or related to a gene mutation. A rare type, called *variant Creutzfeldt-Jakob disease*, can be acquired from eating meat from cattle affected by mad cow disease. The word *variant* is needed. Do not use *CJD* or *vCJD*.
See **dementia; mad cow disease**.

Crimea A Black Sea peninsula seized from Ukraine by Russia and annexed in March 2014. The international community has refused to recognize the Russian annexation, while tacitly acknowledging that Ukraine has lost control over Crimea for the foreseeable future. The capital is Simferopol. In stories, the dateline should be Crimea, without reference to Ukraine or Russia: *SIMFEROPOL, Crimea.*

criminal cases See **civil cases, criminal cases** and **privacy**.

crisis, crises

CRISPR A gene-editing technique. Stands for *clustered regularly interspaced short palindromic repeats*. A widely used version is called CRISPR-Cas9 to indicate a specific enzyme used in the process. *CRISPR* is acceptable in all uses, but provide a brief definition: *the gene-editing tool CRISPR.*

criterion, criteria

cross-examination (n.) **cross-examine** (v.)

crossfire

cross rate The rate of exchange between two currencies calculated by referring to the rates between each and a third currency.

crowdfunding A financing method in which money is raised through soliciting relatively small individual contributions from a large number of people, often via a website.

crowdsourcing The practice of asking people online to help gather information, produce ideas or conduct other tasks.

cryptocurrency, blockchain, bitcoin, NFT, Web3
    cryptocurrency A type of digital money secured via encryption technology in an unalterable — at least for now — and publicly viewable way. *Cryptocurrency* is not the same as *virtual currency*, which is used in online games and other virtual worlds.
    The shorthand *crypto* is acceptable in headlines and direct quotations, but should be avoided in story text to avoid confusion with *cryptography*.
    As of early 2022, *bitcoin* was the most popular cryptocurrency system. Others include *ethereum, litecoin, dogecoin* and a large number of rivals, some created for specific purposes. Lowercase all references to *bitcoin* and other cryptocurrencies,

consistent with the style for conventional currency.

References to individual cryptocurrencies should use the singular form — *bitcoin, ethereum, litecoin*. Example: *Thieves reportedly stole litecoin worth $15 million.* Use plural forms for specific quantities of cryptocurrency — *six bitcoins, 58.7 ethers* — analogous to style for traditional currency. Acronyms for particular cryptocurrencies — for instance, *USDC* for *U.S. digital coin* — should still be fully capitalized.

Unlike dollars, euros and other traditional currencies, cryptocurrencies are not backed by governments, central banks or, for the most part, physical assets. As a result, their value is often determined largely via supply and demand, which can cause wild swings in their value. The exception is a class of cryptocurrencies known as *stablecoins* whose values are pegged, often to traditional currencies like the U.S. dollar or commodities like gold.

Individual units of cryptocurrency, called *tokens*, can be traded for other tokens or for traditional currencies via online *exchanges*. Many investors trade these tokens much like they'd trade stocks.

Cryptocurrency owners typically store their tokens in virtual wallets offered by a variety of vendors, including some online services that resemble bank accounts. Tokens can be used to pay for goods and services at participating merchants, although as of early 2022 few vendors accepted cryptocurrency.

In technical terms, tokens exist as chunks of data that are digitally signed each time they travel from one owner to the next. These transactions are stored in data blocks; when the transactions are verified, those blocks are chained to previous blocks, forming a digital ledger called a *blockchain*. Copies of each blockchain are stored in multiple locations, making them extremely difficult to tamper with.

Blockchains are constructed by people known as *miners* who lend their computing power to verify cryptocurrency transactions so that no one can spend the same token twice. Miners receive new cryptocurrency tokens — bitcoins or ethers (the ethereum token), for instance — as rewards. The mining process consumes a great deal of electricity, much of it carbon-based as of early 2022.

Although it's possible to trace bitcoins and some other cryptocurrencies as they are spent, owners of the accounts behind those transactions aren't always easily identifiable. Criminals favor cryptocurrency for that reason and employ various methods to launder it. It is the currency of *ransomware* attacks, in which malicious software locks a computer and its data until the target pays a ransom.

Investigators, however, are increasingly able to link cryptocurrency transactions to real people, especially when the cryptocurrency is converted to a traditional currency.

The world of cryptocurrency and blockchain continues to evolve rapidly. The Associated Press will update style for these subjects on a regular basis.

bitcoin The first *cryptocurrency* to attain significant popularity. It was designed by an unknown person or group using the pseudonym Satoshi Nakamoto and launched in 2009. As of early 2022, *bitcoin* was the most popular cryptocurrency system available. Lowercase all references to *bitcoin* and other cryptocurrencies, consistent with the style for conventional currency.

As with other cryptocurrencies, bitcoins do not exist as physical bills or coins. Rather, they exist as blocks of data that are digitally signed each time they travel from one owner to the next. The value of bitcoin has risen considerably over the past several years, although it continues to experience wild price swings.

blockchain A distributed digital ledger of cryptocurrency transactions that is maintained across a worldwide network. In general, different cryptocurrencies use different blockchains, although some new cryptocurrencies have been established on existing blockchains.

Some blockchains can store other kinds of data, such as hyperlinks and files. *Smart contracts*, for instance, exist as software code stored on a blockchain that can self-execute once the contract terms have been met.

Blockchain records are stored in a "peer-to-peer" network that updates continually so that copies of these records are stored across computers around the world.

Blockchain records are secured through *cryptography*. Participants have their own private keys that act as personal digital signatures for accessing their funds. Cryptocurrency transactions are digitally signed each time cryptocurrency changes hands.

Web3 A catchall term for the prospect of a new stage of the internet driven by the *cryptocurrency*-related technology *blockchain*.

Although blockchain is best known as a mechanism that makes *bitcoin* and other cryptocurrencies possible, it can also store data and even software code that can self-execute under certain conditions.

Some see this latter feature as the key to building a new, distributed internet based on blockchain technology, one that's effectively owned by no one, answerable to no authority and "owned" in a sense by the holders of cryptocurrencies. Many proponents consider Web3 the natural successor to both the early World Wide Web (Web 1.0) and the current internet of interactive websites and services, sometimes called Web 2.0.

As of early 2022, Web3 remained a distant vision. Critics argue that it has yet to generate any widely useful applications and decry the fact that any systems built on blockchain will be "financialized" and thus likely to be warped by speculators trading the cryptocurrency *tokens* associated with the blockchain.

Do not use the term *Web3* without explanation. For instance: *Many proponents believe that a new version of the internet based on blockchain, known by some as Web3, will be key to undermining the power of giant tech companies such as Google and Meta, the company formerly known as Facebook.*

non-fungible token, NFT Artificially scarce digital objects created by using *blockchain* technology to mint "unique" versions of digital artwork, sports memorabilia, famous photographs and anything else that can be digitized. *NFT* is acceptable on first reference, but use the full term high in the story and explain what it means.

Digital objects such as these can typically be copied or altered without limit. Turning them into

NFTs involves placing a declaration of ownership on a blockchain, typically the *ethereum* blockchain. That creates a permanent record of "ownership." It's possible to create a series of NFTs for a single digital object, each uniquely numbered, theoretically increasing the value of the lowest numbers.

In March 2021 the artist Beeple sold an NFT of one of his pieces for almost $70 million, kicking off an NFT boom.

Critics point out that NFTs don't actually involve putting digital artworks directly on the blockchain; most are far too large for that. Instead, the data placed on the blockchain typically includes a series number and a simple hyperlink pointing to a non-unique version of the art.

The Associated Press has conducted some trial sales of NFTs made from its archival photographs.

CT scan *Computerized tomography*, a method of making a series of X-ray images of the body or parts of the body and using those images to construct cross-sectional views. (Formerly known as *CAT scan*.)

cup Equal to 8 fluid ounces. The approximate metric equivalents are 240 milliliters or 0.24 of a liter. See **liter**.

cupful, cupfuls

currency conversions Currency conversions are necessary in stories that use foreign currency to make clear for readers how a number translates into dollars. But conversions should be used sparingly and preferably not in the lead unless it's a significant part of a story.

A conversion is generally needed only the first time a currency is mentioned. The reader can make the necessary conversions after that.

Do not convert amounts that are not current because exchange rates change over time.

If necessary for clarity in the story, specify that the conversion is at current exchange rates.

EXAMPLES:

AMSTERDAM (AP) — Anheuser-Busch InBev, the world's largest brewer, says its third-quarter profits rose as the takeover of new brands and higher selling prices offset the impact of lower sales volumes.

The company, based in Leuven, Belgium, said Thursday that net profit was up 31% to $2.37 billion (1.73 billion euros), from $1.81 billion in the same period a year earlier.

The gain largely reflects the company's $20 billion purchase in June of the 50% of Mexico's Grupo Modelo it didn't already own.

PARIS (AP) — French cosmetics giant L'Oreal says sales of its Maybelline makeup, Garnier shampoo and other beauty aids helped lift earnings to a new record in 2013.

The company behind Lancome cosmetics and the Body Shop retail chain reported net profit of 2.96 billion euros ($4 billion) last year, up 3.2% from 2.87 billion in 2012.

For all other currencies, following the amount, spell out the name of the currency followed in parentheses by the equivalent in U.S. dollars. *Japan approved a 1.8 trillion yen ($18 billion) extra budget to partially finance an economic stimulus package.*

When dealing with a dollar currency of a country other than the United States, use the following abbreviations before the amount on second and subsequent references:

C

AU$ Australian dollars
CA$ Canadian dollars
SG$ Singapore dollars
NZ$ New Zealand dollars
HK$ Hong Kong dollars
NT$ New Taiwan dollars
ZW$ Zimbabwe dollars
*Treasurer Wayne Swan approved
a 16 billion Australian dollar ($10.74
billion) deal. Swan said AU$8
billion would be reserved for capital
expenditure.*

currency depreciation, currency devaluation A nation's money *depreciates* when its value falls in relation to the currency of other nations or in relation to its own prior value.

A nation's money is *devalued* when its value is reduced in relation to the currency of other nations, either deliberately by the government or through market forces.

When a nation devalues its currency, the goods it imports tend to become more expensive. Its exports tend to become less expensive in other nations and thus more competitive.

See **devaluations**.

cyberattack A computer operation carried out over a device or network that causes physical damage or significant and wide-ranging disruption.

The term is routinely overused.

A computer intrusion that causes damage — i.e., to machinery at a steel mill — or injury or death is unquestionably a *cyberattack*.

Low-tech trickery aimed at robbing people of their passwords by using spam emails or social engineering is not a *cyberattack*. Avoid using the terms *cyberattack* or *attack* in cases where data has

merely been stolen or leaked unless the consequences are catastrophic. Also avoid using where the damage is limited (as in the case when a single device is affected); virtual (as in the case when only data is destroyed); or short-term (as in the case when a network is temporarily rendered inoperable through denial of service.)

If authorities or others term something a *cyberattack*, push for details and be specific in describing what happened or what is alleged. If it doesn't rise to the level of a cyberattack, avoid using the term, even in direct quotations, unless the quote is essential. Avoid putting a number to cyberattacks unless someone can explain in detail how such a figure was derived. Cyberattacks can be counted in so many different ways that figures are only rarely meaningful.

For help in determining whether to call something a *cyberattack*, consider an action's equivalent in the physical world.

— Defacing of a company's website: The physical world equivalent would be someone spraying graffiti or leaving a taunting message on the headquarters building. Typical language would be *vandalize* or *deface*, not *attack*.
— Electronic theft of government data or an official's email: The physical equivalent might be someone stealing sensitive records from filing cabinets. Typical language would be *theft* or *break-in*, but not *attack*.
— A factory's controls are remotely compromised and rogue commands cause an explosion: The physical equivalent here might involve placing a bomb somewhere. Whether electronic

or physical, such acts could properly be termed an *attack*.

— A huge amount of data is stolen — data of such sensitivity that its theft or release causes panic or dramatic financial losses. This might happen for example with the sudden publication of millions of medical records or credit card numbers: Imagine simultaneous break-ins at scores of hospitals or repeated bank robberies across the country. At a catastrophic scale, thefts or leaks can be described as *cyberattacks*.

Other examples of wording:

A *denial of service* can range in severity from a nuisance to a major attack. If disruption is minimal, use wording such as *the website was hit by a denial of service* and explain what that means. It's akin to having many people call the same phone number at once so that legitimate callers would get busy signals. However, a *denial of service* that blocks millions of customers and businesses from making payments or receiving money for an extended length of time might be described as a cyberattack.

Someone who breaks into a network and copies data is *breaching a network*, *committing cyberespionage* or *engaged in electronic theft*.

Someone who remotely wipes a smartphone or trashes a company's webpage is an *online vandal* or *a cybercriminal*. But someone who wipes thousands of computers at critical infrastructure provider could be described as a *cyberattacker* given the severity of the potential damage.

cyber- Use sparingly. In general, *internet*, *digital* or a similar term is preferred, as in *internet shopping* or *online security*. When necessary to use, follow the general rule for prefixes, which calls for no hyphen in most cases. For example: *cyberattack, cyberbullying, cybercafe, cybersecurity, cyberspace*. But *Cyber Monday, cyber shopping, cyber liability insurance*. Our decisions on when to use one word or two words is case by case, based largely on prevailing usage if the term isn't in Webster's New World College Dictionary.

Cyclone A trademark for a brand of chain-link fence.

cynic, skeptic A *skeptic* is a doubter. A *cynic* is a disbeliever.

czar Not *tsar*. It was a formal title only for the ruler of Russia and some other Slavic nations.

Lowercase in all other uses.

Czech Republic, the Use the official country name in all instances. Also: *Czech* as an adjective, and *Czechs* for the people. The government has said that *Czechia* can be used in English-language communications, and registered it at the United Nations, but as of early 2022 that name had yet to catch on in common usage.

d

dam Capitalize when part of a proper name: *Hoover Dam*.

damage, damages *Damage* is destruction or loss: *Authorities said the storm caused more than $1 billion in damage.*

Damages are awarded by a court as compensation for injury, loss, etc.: *The woman received $25,000 in damages.*

damn it Use instead of *dammit*, but like other profanity it should be avoided unless there is a compelling reason.

See **obscenities, profanities, vulgarities**.

dangling modifiers Avoid modifiers that do not refer clearly and logically to some word in the sentence.

Dangling: *Taking our seats, the game started.* (*Taking* does not refer to the subject, *game*, nor to any other word in the sentence.)

Correct: *Taking our seats, we watched the opening of the game.* (*Taking* refers to *we*, the subject of the sentence.)

Dardanelles, the Not *the Dardanelles Strait*.

dark horse

darknet A part of the internet hosted within an encrypted network and accessible only through specialized anonymity-providing tools, most notably the Tor Browser. Examples of *darknets* include the *Tor network*, *I2P* and *Freenet*. Do not confuse with *deep web*.

dash See entry in the **Punctuation** chapter.

dashcam

data The word typically takes singular verbs and pronouns when writing for general audiences and in data journalism contexts: *The data is sound.* In scientific and academic writing, plural verbs and pronouns are preferred.

Use *databank* and *database*, but *data processing* (n. and adj.) and *data center*.

date line Two words for the imaginary line that separates one day from another.

See the **international date line** entry.

datelines Datelines on stories should contain a place name, entirely in capital letters, followed in most cases by the name of the state, country or territory where the city is located.

DOMESTIC DATELINES: A list of domestic cities that stand alone in datelines:

ATLANTA	MILWAUKEE
BALTIMORE	MINNEAPOLIS
BOSTON	NEW ORLEANS
CHICAGO	NEW YORK
CINCINNATI	OKLAHOMA CITY
CLEVELAND	PHILADELPHIA
DALLAS	PHOENIX
DENVER	PITTSBURGH

DETROIT	ST. LOUIS	BEIRUT	MOSCOW
HONOLULU	SALT LAKE CITY	BERLIN	MUNICH
HOUSTON	SAN ANTONIO	BRUSSELS	NEW DELHI
INDIANAPOLIS	SAN DIEGO	CAIRO	PANAMA CITY
LAS VEGAS	SAN FRANCISCO	DJIBOUTI	PARIS
LOS ANGELES	SEATTLE	DUBLIN	PRAGUE
MIAMI	WASHINGTON	GENEVA	QUEBEC CITY
		GIBRALTAR	RIO DE JANEIRO
		GUATEMALA CITY	ROME
		HAVANA	SAN MARINO
		HELSINKI	SAO PAULO
		HONG KONG	SHANGHAI
		ISLAMABAD	SINGAPORE
		ISTANBUL	STOCKHOLM
		JERUSALEM	SYDNEY
		JOHANNESBURG	TOKYO
		KUWAIT CITY	TORONTO
		LONDON	VATICAN CITY
		LUXEMBOURG	VIENNA
		MACAO	ZURICH
		MADRID	

Stories from all other U.S. cities should have both the city and state name in the dateline, including *KANSAS CITY, Mo.*, and *KANSAS CITY, Kan.*

Spell out *Alaska*, *Hawaii*, *Idaho*, *Iowa*, *Maine*, *Ohio*, *Texas* and *Utah*. Abbreviate others as listed in this book under the full name of each state.

Use *Hawaii* on all cities outside Honolulu. Specify the island in the text if needed.

Follow the same practice for communities on islands within the boundaries of other states: *EDGARTOWN, Mass.*, for example, not *EDGARTOWN, Martha's Vineyard*.

Use *BEVERLY HILLS, Calif.* It's an incorporated city and the dateline for the Golden Globes movie awards, sponsored by the Hollywood Foreign Press Association and held at the Beverly Hilton Hotel.

STATE SERVICES: Additional cities in a state or region may stand alone.

U.S. POSSESSIONS: Apply the guidelines listed below in the ISLAND NATIONS AND TERRITORIES section and the OVERSEAS TERRITORIES section.

INTERNATIONAL DATELINES: These international locations stand alone in datelines:

AMSTERDAM	MEXICO CITY
BAGHDAD	MILAN
BANGKOK	MONACO
BEIJING	MONTREAL

In addition, use *UNITED NATIONS* alone, without an *N.Y.* designation, in stories from *U.N.* headquarters.

BALKANS: With the independence of Montenegro from Serbia-Montenegro formalized in 2006, use a Montenegro-only dateline, such as *PODGORICA, Montenegro*. Stories originating in Serbia carry a Serbia-only dateline: *BELGRADE, Serbia*. With the independence of Kosovo in 2008, use Kosovo in the dateline, such as *PRISTINA, Kosovo*.

CANADIAN DATELINES: Datelines on stories from Canadian cities other than Montreal, Quebec City and Toronto should contain the name of the city in capital letters followed by the name of the province. Do not abbreviate any province or territory name.

COMMONWEALTH OF INDEPENDENT STATES: For cities in the former Soviet Union, datelines include city and republic name: *ALMATY,*

d

Kazakhstan.

OTHER NATIONS: Stories from other international cities that do not stand alone in datelines should contain the name of the country or territory (see the next section) spelled out.

SPELLING AND CHOICE OF NAMES: In most cases, the name of the nation in a dateline is the conventionally accepted short form of its official name: *Argentina*, for example, rather than *Republic of Argentina*. (If in doubt, look for an entry in this book. If none is found, follow Webster's New World College Dictionary.)

Note these special cases:
— Instead of *United Kingdom*, use *England, Northern Ireland, Scotland* or *Wales*.
— For divided nations, use the commonly accepted names based on geographic distinctions: *North Korea, South Korea*.
— Use an article only with *El Salvador*. For all others, use just a country name — *Gambia, Netherlands, Philippines*, etc.

See **geographic names** for guidelines on spelling the names of international cities and nations not listed here or in separate entries.

ISLAND NATIONS AND TERRITORIES: When reporting from nations and territories that are made up primarily of islands but commonly are linked under one name, use the city name and the general name in the dateline. Identify an individual island, if needed, in the text:

Examples:
British Virgin Islands
Netherlands Antilles
Indonesia   Philippines

OVERSEAS TERRITORIES: Some overseas territories, colonies and other areas that are not independent nations commonly have accepted separate identities based on their geographic character or special status under treaties. In these cases, use the commonly accepted territory name after a city name in a dateline.

Examples:
Bermuda   Martinique
Corsica   Puerto Rico
Crimea   Sardinia
Faeroe Islands   Sicily
Greenland   Sikkim
Guadeloupe   Tibet
Guam

WITHIN STORIES: In citing other cities within the body of a story:
— No further information is necessary if a city is in the same state as the datelined city. Make an exception only if confusion would result.
— Follow the city name with further identification in most cases where it is not in the same state or nation as the dateline city. The additional identification may be omitted, however, if no confusion would result. For example, *Boston* stands alone without Massachusetts in a story datelined *NEW YORK*.
— Provide a state or nation identification for the city if the story has no dateline. However, cities that stand alone in datelines may be used alone in those stories if no confusion would result.

dateline selection A dateline should tell the reader that the AP obtained the basic information for the story in the datelined place.

Do not, for example, use a Washington dateline on a story written primarily from information that a newspaper reported under a Washington dateline. Use the home city of the newspaper instead.

This rule does not preclude

the use of a story with a dateline different from the home city of a newspaper if it is from the general area served by the newspaper.

Use an international dateline only if the basic information in a story was obtained by a full- or part-time correspondent physically present in the datelined community.

If a radio broadcast monitored in another city was the source of information, use the dateline of the city where the monitoring took place and mention the fact in the story.

When a story has been assembled from sources in widely separated areas, or when a reporter gathered the material remotely, it is acceptable to use no dateline.

Datelines should convey the spirit of the reporting; they are not restricted to cities and towns. Census-designated places, townships, parks, counties, or datelines such as ABOARD AIR FORCE ONE or ON THE MISSISSIPPI RIVER may be used if appropriate. But do not designate neighborhoods or other places within a better-known jurisdiction as the dateline. For instance, NEW YORK should be the dateline, not BROOKLYN or CENTRAL PARK.

For bylined stories, a reporter must be reporting from the dateline on the story. When there are multiple bylines, at least one reporter must have been at the scene, and a note at the end of the story should explain the locations of all bylined reporters. If the story has no dateline, no note is needed at the end of the story explaining the reporters' locations.

The dateline for video or audio must be the location where the events depicted actually occurred. For voice work, the dateline must be the location from which the reporter is speaking; if that is not possible, the reporter should not use a dateline. If a reporter covers a story in one location but does a live report from a filing point in another location, the dateline is the filing point.

dates Always use Arabic figures, without *st*, *nd*, *rd* or *th*. See **years** and **months**.

daughter-in-law, daughters-in-law

Daughters of the American Revolution *DAR* is acceptable on second reference.

Headquarters is in Washington.

day care Two words, no hyphen, in all uses.

daylight saving time Not *savings*. No hyphen.

When linking the term with the name of a time zone, use only the word *daylight*: *Eastern Daylight Time*, *Pacific Daylight Time*, etc.

Lowercase *daylight saving time* in all uses and *daylight time* whenever it stands alone.

A federal law specifies that daylight time applies from 2 a.m. on the second Sunday of March until 2 a.m. on the first Sunday of November in areas that do not specifically exempt themselves.

See **time zones**.

daylong, dayslong

Day One Capitalize and spell out as a chronological device for summarizing multiday events such as Day One, Day Two. Lowercase in casual or conversational references.

days of the week Capitalize them. Do not abbreviate, except when needed in a tabular format: *Sun, Mon, Tue, Wed, Thu, Fri, Sat* (three letters, without periods, to facilitate tabular composition).

See **time element** and **today, tonight**.

daytime

D-Day June 6, 1944, the day the Allies invaded Western Europe in World War II.

DDT Preferred in all references for the insecticide *dichlorodiphenyltrichloroethane.*

Dead Sea Scrolls

deaf, Deaf, hard of hearing Use the lowercase form *deaf* for the audiological condition of total or major hearing loss and for people with total or major hearing loss, when relevant to the story. *Hard of hearing* can be used to describe people with a lesser degree of hearing loss. The phrase *deaf and hard of hearing* encompasses both groups. Do not use *hearing-impaired, hearing impairment* or *partially deaf* unless a person uses those terms for themself.

Many deaf people who use sign language have a deeply ingrained sense of culture and community built around the experience of deafness and sign language, and use the uppercase form *Deaf* to signify that culture. The uppercase is acceptable, if used by the person or group, in descriptions such as *the cultural Deaf community, Deaf education, Deaf culture*, etc.

Do not use the uppercase form for a person; use lowercase *deaf,* the standard style for medical conditions: *Lagier, who is deaf, said the Deaf community is a powerful force in his life.*

Not all people with hearing loss use sign language or identify with the Deaf culture and community; such identification can be a deeply personal choice.

When possible, ask if a person or group uses identity-first language (*deaf students*) or person-first language (*students who are deaf*). In the United States, the National Association of the Deaf recommends identity-first language unless an individual or a group uses person-first language.

The adjective *deaf-blind* or *deafblind* is acceptable to describe a person who uses either for themself. Try to determine which term the person uses. Also acceptable: *deaf-blindness* or *deafblindness.*

Do not use the terms *deaf-mute* or *deaf and dumb.*

Hyphenate *hard-of-hearing* as a modifier: *hard-of-hearing students.* But: *They are hard of hearing.* Do not use *deaf-mute* or *deaf and dumb.*

See **American Sign Language; disabilities**.

dean Capitalize when used as a formal title before a name: *Dean John Jones, Deans John Jones and Susan Smith.*

Lowercase in other uses: *John Jones, dean of the college; the dean.*

dean's list Lowercase in all uses: *He is on the dean's list. She is a dean's list student.*

deathbed (n. and adj.)

death, die Don't use euphemisms like *passed on* or *passed away* except in a direct quote.

death row

debt The money a company or individual owes a creditor.

debt service The outlay necessary to meet all interest and principal payments during a given period.

decades Use Arabic figures to indicate decades of history. Use an apostrophe to indicate numerals that are left out; show plural by adding the letter *s*: *the 1890s, the '90s, the Gay '90s, the 1920s, the mid-1930s*.
See **historical periods and events**.

deci- A prefix denoting one-tenth of a unit. Move the decimal point one place to the left in converting to the basic unit: 15.5 decigrams = 1.55 grams.

decimal units Use a period and numerals to indicate decimal amounts. Decimalization should not exceed two places in textual material unless there are special circumstances.
For amounts less than 1, use the numeral zero before the decimal point: 0.03.
See **fractions** and **numerals**.

Declaration of Independence Lowercase *the declaration* whenever it stands alone.

deepfake (n., adj.) A manipulated video or other digital representation produced by sophisticated machine-learning techniques that yield seemingly realistic, but fabricated, images and sounds. Deepfake video can, for instance, make it appear that people said or did something that they did not. *Deepfake* or *deepfake video* is acceptable, but it must be explained on first reference. See **misinformation, fact checks, fake news**.

deep-sea (adj.)

Deep South Capitalize both words when referring to the region that consists of Alabama, Georgia, Louisiana, Mississippi and South Carolina.

deep water (n.) **deep-water** (adj.)

default The failure to meet a financial obligation, the failure to make payment either of principal or interest when due or a breach or nonperformance of the terms of a note or mortgage.

defendant

defense Do not use it as a verb.

defense attorney Always lowercase, never abbreviate.
See **attorney, lawyer** and **titles**.

defense spending *Military spending* usually is the more precise term.

definitely Overused as a vague intensifier. Avoid it.

deflation A decrease in the general price level, which results from a decrease in total spending relative to the supply of available goods on the market. Deflation's immediate effect is to increase purchasing power.

defund To stop providing or to reduce funds, especially government funds, for a program, group, etc. The term *defund the police* often refers to taking funds from police departments to spend on other priorities such as employment programs, mental health services and social services to increase public safety. The term is sometimes misrepresented as abolishing police. Avoid using the term other than in a direct quotation; if used in a quotation, explain and provide detail about what is being sought.

dek- (before a vowel), **deka-** (before a consonant) A prefix denoting 10 units of a measure.

delegate The formal title for members of the lower houses of legislatures in states including Delaware, Maryland, Virginia and West Virginia. Capitalize only before their names. Abbreviate as a formal title before names, as local usage allows.

Always lowercase in other uses: *convention delegate Richard Henry Lee.*

demagogue, demagoguery

dementia A general term for the impaired ability to remember, think or make decisions that interferes with doing everyday activities. It is not a disease itself. *Alzheimer's disease* is the most common cause of dementia. Other causes include *Huntington's disease, Parkinson's disease, Creutzfeldt-Jakob disease* and *traumatic brain injury.* Though dementia mostly affects older adults, it is not a part of normal aging. Describe a person as *having dementia* only if relevant to the story, and if a medical diagnosis has been made or the person uses the term. If relatives or others use the term, ask how they know, then consider carefully whether to include the information.

The terms *younger-onset* or *early-onset Alzheimer's disease* applies to people diagnosed before age 65.

Do not use the terms *senile* or *demented.* See **Alzheimer's disease**; **disabilities.**

democrat, Democrat, democratic, Democratic, Democratic Party For the U.S. political party, capitalize *Democrat* and *Democratic* in references to the *Democratic Party* or its members. Lowercase in generic uses: *He champions the values of a democratic society.* Use *Democratic*, not *Democrat*, in usages such as *the Democratic-controlled Legislature* and *the Democratic senator* (except in direct quotations that use *Democrat*). See the **political parties and philosophies** entry.

Democratic Governors Association No apostrophe.

Democratic National Committee On the second reference: *the national committee, the committee* or *the DNC.*

Similarly: *Democratic State Committee, Democratic County Committee, Democratic City Committee, the state committee, the city committee, the committee.*

demolish, destroy Both mean *to do away with something completely.* Something cannot be partially *demolished* or *destroyed.* It is redundant to say *totally demolished* or *totally destroyed.*

Denali Tallest peak in North America at 20,310 feet. Located in Alaska. Formerly *Mount McKinley.*

depart Follow it with a preposition: *He will depart from LaGuardia. She will depart at 11:30 a.m.*

department The following are the U.S. Cabinet departments:

Department of Agriculture (*USDA* acceptable on second reference); *Department of Commerce*; *Department of Defense* (*DOD* or *Pentagon* acceptable on second reference); *Department of Education*; *Department of Energy* (*DOE* acceptable on second reference); *Department of Health and Human Services* (*HHS* acceptable on second reference); *Department of Homeland Security* (*DHS* acceptable on second reference); *Department of Housing and Urban Development* (*HUD* acceptable on second reference); *Department of the Interior*; *Department of Justice* (*DOJ* acceptable on second reference); *Department of Labor*; *Department of State*; *Department of Transportation* (*DOT* acceptable on second reference); *Department of the Treasury*, and *Department of Veterans Affairs* (*VA* acceptable on second reference).

It is preferable to list the subject first in stories, such as the *Agriculture Department* and *Commerce Department*. Exceptions are *Department of Health and Human Services*, *Department of Homeland Security*, *Department of Housing and Urban Development* and *Department of Veterans Affairs*.

Avoid acronyms when possible. A phrase such as *the department* is preferable on second reference because it is more readable and avoids alphabet soup.

Lowercase *department* in plural uses, but capitalize the proper name element: *the departments of Labor and Justice*.

A shorthand reference to the proper name element also is capitalized: *Kissinger said, "State and Justice must resolve their differences."* But: *Henry Kissinger, the secretary of state*.

Lowercase *the department*

whenever it stands alone.

Do not abbreviate *department* in any usage.

TITLES: In stories with U.S. datelines, do not include U.S. before the titles of Secretary of State or other government officials, except where necessary for clarity. Examples: *Secretary of State John Kerry, Attorney General Eric Holder*.

In stories with international datelines, include U.S. before the titles: *U.S. Secretary of State John Kerry, U.S. Attorney General Eric Holder*. Exceptions: *President Joe Biden, Vice President Kamala Harris*.

See **academic departments**.

dependent (n. and adj.)

depreciation The reduction in the value of capital goods due to wear and tear or obsolescence.

Estimated depreciation may be deducted from income each year as one of the costs of doing business.

depression (mental health) A serious mood disorder characterized by a range of symptoms. Those include a persistent sad, anxious or "empty" mood; feelings of hopelessness, worthlessness, guilt, pessimism; loss of interest in activities; difficulty concentrating and making decisions.

Describe a person as *having depression* only if relevant to the story, and if a medical diagnosis has been made or the person uses the term. If relatives or others use the term, ask how they know, then consider carefully whether to include the information. Be clear on the type of depression if relevant, such as *He was diagnosed with bipolar disorder* or *She has postpartum depression or she is being treated for depression*.

Medically diagnosed *depression* is called *clinical depression* or *major depressive disorder*.

The terms *depressing* or *depressed* are acceptable in general uses if not intended as a slur, though alternatives are often better: *She found the results disheartening, discouraging, disturbing*, etc.

See **disabilities; bipolar disorder; postpartum depression; seasonal affective disorder; mental illness**.

depression (financial) Capitalize *Depression* and *the Great Depression* when referring to the worldwide economic hard times generally regarded as having begun with the stock market collapse of Oct. 28-29, 1929.

Lowercase in other uses: *the depression of the 1970s*.

deputy Capitalize as a formal title before a name. See **titles**.

derivative A contract whose value depends on the financial performance of its underlying assets, such as mortgages, stock or traded commodities. Credit default swaps are one form of derivative.

derogatory terms Do not use a derogatory term except in extremely rare circumstances — when it is crucial to the story or the understanding of a news event. Flag the contents in an editor's note.

See **obscenities, profanities, vulgarities**.

-designate Do not capitalize *designate* if used as part of a formal title before a name: *Attorney General-designate Whitney Smith*.

See **titles**.

detective Do not abbreviate. Capitalize before a name only if it is a formal rank: *police Detective Frank Serpico, private detective Richard Diamond*.

See **titles**.

detente

devaluations Occur when a country's government pushes down the value of its currency in relation to another currency. (When market forces, not the government, push a currency down, it is known as depreciation.)

Suppose China devalues its currency, the yuan, against the U.S. dollar. To calculate the devaluation, you'd look at the value of 1 yuan to the U.S. dollar before the devaluation and the value afterward and calculate the percentage difference.

Example: On Day One, 1 yuan is worth 16.1 cents (or $0.161). The next day, the Chinese government devalues the currency and 1 yuan is equal to 15.8 cents ($0.158). That is a 1.9% devaluation — the yuan has dropped 1.9% against the U.S. dollar.

Currencies are often reported the other way, showing how much $1 is worth in another currency. In the example above, $1 went from being worth 6.21 yuan to being worth 6.32 yuan. To find out what 1 yuan is worth — so you can show the yuan dropping, not the dollar rising — divide 1 by 6.21 and 6.32 respectively.

device memory, device storage The *memory* of a computer, phone or other digital device holds data needed for current operations; it is typically wiped clean when the device shuts down.

Device *storage*, by contrast, holds data for the long term.

Memory and *storage* are both measured in bytes. *Device memory* is sometimes referred to as *RAM,* an older acronym for *random access memory. Storage* can be in the form of a traditional, magnetic hard drive or a solid-state drive, which keeps data on semiconductor chips and is widely used on smartphones and other portable electronics.

devil But capitalize *Satan.*

diabetes A disease in which the body doesn't make enough or properly use insulin, a hormone that turns food into energy. There are two main forms: *Type 1 diabetes,* formerly called juvenile diabetes, and *Type 2 diabetes,* the most common kind, formerly called adult-onset diabetes. Include the type when relevant or necessary, for example, when discussing specific treatments.

dialect The form of language peculiar to a region or a group, usually in matters of pronunciation or syntax. Dialect should be avoided, even in quoted matter, unless it is clearly pertinent to a story.

There are some words and phrases in everyone's vocabulary that are typical of a particular region or group. Quoting dialect, unless used carefully, implies substandard or illiterate usage.

When there is a compelling reason to use dialect, words or phrases are spelled phonetically, and apostrophes show missing letters and sounds: *"Din't ya yoosta live at Toidy-Toid Street and Sekun' Amya? Across from da moom pitchers?"*

See **colloquialisms** and **quotes in the news**.

dialogue (n.)

dictionaries For spelling, style and usage questions not covered in this stylebook, consult Webster's New World College Dictionary, Fifth Edition, Houghton Mifflin Harcourt, Boston and New York, 2016.

Use the first spelling listed in Webster's New World College Dictionary unless a specific exception is listed in this book.

If Webster's New World College Dictionary provides different spellings in separate entries (*tee shirt* and *T-shirt,* for example), use the spelling that is followed by a full definition (*T-shirt*).

If Webster's New World College Dictionary provides definitions under two spellings for the same sense of a word, either use is acceptable.

Webster's New World College Dictionary is also the first reference for geographic names not covered in this stylebook. See **geographic names**.

Diet The Japanese parliament. See **legislative bodies**.

dietitian

different Takes the preposition *from,* not *than.*

differ from, differ with To *differ from* means *to be unlike.*

To *differ with* means *to disagree.*

digital advertising, internet advertising, online advertising Advertising delivered digitally, such as on a website or an app, often targeted to a person's location, interests and other preferences. Ad revenue finances many free tech services, such as Facebook and Google, but it has also drawn

d

scrutiny over data collection and privacy. See **internet privacy**.

Types of digital advertising include:

search advertising: Ads, usually text ads, that appear alongside search results, targeted to the specific keywords typed by the user. They can also appear on third-party websites, such as news sites, based on keywords in an article.

display advertising: An ad in the form of graphic or video displayed on a website or app. It can be targeted based on keywords in an article or the specific user's personal profile.

video advertising: Can include traditional television commercials shown over the internet. It can appear before or during breaks in streaming video, or appear embedded or as a pop-up window when visiting a website.

affiliate advertising: An advertising model in which a company pays a third party for bringing traffic or leads to its service or products. For example, if a third-party website posts a link to Amazon, it could receive commissions for products bought through that link.

With most types of digital advertising, an advertiser can specify the intended audience based on location, demographics, hobbies, interests and other factors.

With some services, including Google and Facebook, a business can share a list of its existing customers, based on unique identifiers such as email address, and have the service find other customers with similar demographics, behavior and other attributes. Facebook calls this *lookalike audience*. Google calls it *similar audience*.

Other types of targeting include:

retargeting: A method of targeting an audience based on previous behavior. For example, if someone clicks on an ad or visits a shopping site but does not buy, an ad for that same product could appear later when visiting another website or app.

microtargeting: The practice of targeting ads to even smaller groups of people, sometimes even individuals, by increasing the attributes that must match. For example, advertisers can seek users who live in specific ZIP codes, have kids, like football, watch "Saturday Night Live" and went to a specific school. The more specific the requirements, the narrower the audience.

Additional advertising terms:

pay per click: A form of paid advertising in which an advertiser pays the service for every click made by visitors. Hyphenate as a modifier: *pay-per-click advertising*.

pay per impression: A form of paid advertising in which an advertiser pays the service every time the ad is shown, regardless of whether the user clicks on the ad. Hyphenate as a modifer: *pay-per-impression advertising*.

click-through rate: The number of clicks based on a set number of impressions.

Many services now let advertisers specify how much they are willing to pay per impression or click. The service would then display the highest bidder for a particular set of keywords or other targeting attributes. This approach is often referred to as an auction, or *real-time bidding*.

digital assistant, virtual assistant, voice assistant Artificial intelligence software that responds to spoken questions or commands. Some systems allow questions or commands to be typed. Major *voice assistants* include *Alexa* from Amazon, *Siri* from Apple, *Google Assistant* from Google, *Bixby* from Samsung and *Cortana* from Microsoft. Although many of these assistants have female names, do not use female pronouns.

Devices that come with voice assistants often go by different names, such as Amazon's *Echo* and Google's *Nest Hub*. Such devices come with microphones that continually listen for command words, such as "Hey, Siri" or "OK, Google." After hearing such word, the device sends the subsequent command to the company's voice assistant servers for processing and response.

However, there have been cases of a device mishearing the word and sending background conversations online anyway. Some devices have a mute button that turns off the mic entirely, even for the command word.

Audio recordings of voice commands are typically kept online and can be sought in investigations and lawsuits. Major companies offer users a chance to review and delete recordings. Some tech companies allow their employees or contractors to review voice interaction for quality control. Following revelation of leaked conversations and a backlash over the review practice, some companies have made it clearer and easier for consumers to opt out of this review.

digital wallet, mobile wallet A phone app used to store credit cards, gift cards, loyalty cards, tickets and other transactional items. Such a *wallet* can include cards used for *mobile payments* and other digital items such as vaccination records.

The terms *digital wallets* or *mobile wallets* are acceptable, but depending on the audience, the *wallet* terminology may require explanation on first use. Avoid *e-wallet*. See **mobile payment**.

digitize, digitalize *Digitize* generally has a more narrow meaning, reflecting a conversion of something to digital form: *to digitize a document*. *Digitalize* can be broader, referring to a transformation by embracing digital technologies: *to digitalize an industry*.

dilemma It means more than *a problem*. It implies a choice between two unattractive alternatives.

dimensions Use figures and spell out *inches, feet, yards*, etc., to indicate depth, height, length and width. Hyphenate adjectival forms before nouns.

EXAMPLES: *He is 5 feet, 6 inches tall, the 5-foot-6-inch man, the 5-foot man, the basketball team signed a 7-footer.*

The car is 17 feet long, 6 feet wide and 5 feet high. The rug is 9 feet by 12 feet, the 9-by-12 rug.

The storm left 5 inches of snow.

The building has 6,000 square feet of floor space.

Use an apostrophe to indicate feet and quote marks to indicate inches (5'6") only in very technical contexts.

Diners Club No apostrophe, in keeping with the practice the company has adopted for its public identity.

directions and regions In general, lowercase *north, south, northeast, northern,* etc., when they indicate compass direction; capitalize these words when they designate regions. Some examples:

COMPASS DIRECTIONS: *He drove west. The cold front is moving east.*

REGIONS: *A storm system that developed in the Midwest is spreading eastward. It will bring showers to the East Coast by morning and to the entire Northeast by late in the day. Showers and thunderstorms were forecast in the Texas Panhandle. High temperatures will prevail throughout the Western states.*

Settlers from the East went to the West in search of new lives. The customs of the East are different from those of the West. The Northeast depends on the Midwest for its food supply.

She has a Southern accent. He is a Northerner. Asian nations are opening doors to Western businessmen. The candidate developed a Southern strategy.

The storm developed in the South Pacific. European leaders met to talk about supplies of oil from Southeast Asia. She studied Eastern civilizations. He was a student of Western philosophy.

WITH NAMES OF NATIONS: Lowercase unless they are part of a proper name or are used to designate a politically divided nation: *northern France, eastern Canada, the western United States.*

But: *Northern Ireland, South Korea.*

WITH STATES AND CITIES: The preferred form is to lowercase directional or area descriptions when referring to a section of a state or city: *western Montana, southern Atlanta.*

But capitalize compass points:

— When part of a proper name: *North Dakota, West Virginia.*
— When used in denoting widely known sections: *Southern California, West Texas, the South Side of Chicago, the Lower East Side of New York.* If in doubt, use lowercase.

IN FORMING PROPER NAMES: When combining with another common noun to form the name for a region or location: *the North Woods, the South Pole, the Far East, the Middle East, the West Coast* (the entire region, not the coastline itself — see **coast**), *the Eastern Shore* (see separate entry), *the Western Hemisphere.*

See **Midwest region; Northeast region; South; West, Western, west, western.**

direct message A private message sent via an online service such as Twitter or Slack. *DM* is acceptable on second reference. Can also be used as a verb: *to direct-message* or *DM* someone.

dis- The rules in **prefixes** apply, but in general, no hyphen. Some examples:

dismember   disservice
dissemble   dissuade

dis, dissing, dissed

disabilities The terms *disabilities* and *disabled* include a broad range of physical, psychological, developmental and intellectual conditions both visible and invisible.

Perceptions of disabilities vary widely. Language about disabilities is both wide-ranging and evolving. Disabled people are not monolithic. They use diverse terms to describe themselves. Many, for example, use the term *people with disabilities.* Both *people with disabilities* and *disabled people* are acceptable terms, but try to determine the preference of a person or group.

Use care and precision, considering the impact of specific words and the terms used by the people you are writing about.

When possible, ask people how they want to be described. Be mindful that the question of *identity-first* vs. *person-first language* is vital for many.

The terms *disabilities* and *disabled* are generally embraced by disabled people and are acceptable when relevant. Do not use euphemisms such as *handi-capable, differently abled* or *physically challenged*, other than in direct quotations or in explaining how an individual describes themself. Do not use *handicap* for a disability or *handicapped* for a person.

Limit use of the term *disorder* other than in the names of specific conditions, as well as words such as *impairment, abnormality* and *special.*

In general, refer to a disability only if relevant to the story, and if a medical diagnosis has been made or the person uses the term. If relatives or others use the term, ask how they know, then consider carefully whether to include the information.

Avoid writing that implies *ableism*: the belief that abilities of people who aren't disabled are superior. *Ableism* is a concept similar to *racism, sexism* and *ageism* in that it includes stereotypes, generalizations, and demeaning views and language. It is a form of discrimination or prejudice against people with disabilities.

Don't limit coverage of disabled people to coverage of disabilities. People with disabilities are experts in as many fields as nondisabled people are. Include their voices and their images in your regular coverage of any topic.

Avoid "inspiration porn" — stories or photos meaning to portray something positive or uplifting, with the unintended implication that a disability is negative and that disabled people are objects of pity or wonder.

If a disability is pertinent to the story, provide brief details explaining that relevance. For example: *Merritt, who is blind and walks with the help of a guide dog, said she is pleased with the city's walkway improvements. Feldman said the airline kicked her family off a plane after her 3-year-old refused to wear a mask. She said the mask refusal relates to her son's autism.* But not: *Zhang, who has paraplegia, is a fan of the Philadelphia Phillies.*

Some people use *person-first language* in describing themselves: *a man with Down syndrome* or *a woman with schizophrenia.*

Others view their disability as central to their identity and use *identity-first language,* such as *an autistic woman* or *deaf students.* Autistic people and deaf people often — but not always — use *identity-first language.*

When preferences of an individual or group can't be determined, try to use a mix of *person-first* and *identity-first language.*

Avoid using disability-related words lightly or in unrelated situations, and avoid direct quotations using such wording unless essential to the story. Some examples: calling a person or an idea *demented, psychotic, lame, blind, catatonic, moronic, retarded, on the spectrum,* etc.; saying *the warning falls on deaf ears* or *he turned a blind eye* or *the awards show is schizophrenic.*

d

As in all writing, consider word choice carefully. Words that seem innocuous to some people can have specific and deeply personal or offensive meanings to others. Alternative phrasing is almost always possible.

Do not write in a way that implies a person's condition or disability is related to a crime or other wrongdoing unless that link has been firmly established by experts in the specific case and is explained in the story.

Other language or constructions not to use:

— Words that suggest pity, such as *afflicted with, battling* or *suffers from* any disability or illness, or that a person *overcame her disability*. Instead: *has cancer, being treated for ADHD*. Bear in mind that disabilities can be a combination of both challenges and assets. Generally avoid *living with* constructions unless a person uses that for themselves.
— Cliches such as *inspiring* and *brave*.
— Dehumanizing mass terms such as *the disabled, the blind, the mentally ill*, etc. As with all writing, avoid broad generalizations, labels and stereotypes.
— Terms such as *normal* or *typical* for someone who does not have a disability. Instead: *People without a disability, nondisabled*. Use care in deciding whether to use the term *able-bodied*, although the term has specific meaning in contexts such as some government reports and is appropriate in such references.
— Negative or condescending language such as *wheelchair-bound* or *Alzheimer's victim*. Instead use accurate, neutral language such as *uses a wheelchair* or a *person with Alzheimer's disease*.

For a partial list of print and online resources used by the Stylebook team, see the **Bibliography**.

See the **Inclusive Storytelling** chapter; and individual entries including:

able-bodied
ableism
albinism, albino
Alzheimer's disease
American Sign Language
Americans with Disabilities Act
attention-deficit/ hyperactivity disorder
autism spectrum disorder, autism
bipolar disorder
birth defect
blind, limited vision, low vision/partially sighted/visually impaired
brain injury, traumatic brain injury, brain damage, brain-damaged
caregiver, caretaker
chronic traumatic encephalopathy
deaf, Deaf, hard of hearing
dementia
depression
Down syndrome
dwarf, dwarfism, little people
dyslexia, dyslexic
handicap, handicapped
high functioning, low functioning
Individuals with Disabilities Education Act
mental illness
neurodiversity, neurodivergent, neurodiverse, neurotypical
obsessive-compulsive disorder
Paralympics
paraplegia/ paraplegic, quadriplegia/ quadriplegic
postpartum depression
post-traumatic stress disorder
seasonal affective disorder
service animal, assistance animal, guide dog
special needs, special education
Special Olympics
stutter
wheelchair user

disc jockey *DJ* is acceptable in all references.

discount Interest withheld when a note, draft or bill is purchased.

discount rate The rate of interest charged by the Federal Reserve on loans it makes to member banks. This rate has an influence on the rates banks then charge their customers.

discreet, discrete *Discreet* means *prudent, circumspect*: "I'm afraid I was not very discreet," she wrote.
   Discrete means *detached, separate*: There are four discrete sounds from a quadraphonic system.

diseases Do not capitalize diseases such as *cancer, emphysema, leukemia, hepatitis*, etc.
   When a disease is known by the name of a person or geographical area identified with it, capitalize only the proper noun element: *Alzheimer's disease, Parkinson's disease, Ebola virus disease*, etc.
   Other than in direct quotations, avoid such expressions as: *He is battling cancer. She is a stroke victim.* Use neutral, precise descriptions: *He has stomach cancer. She had a stroke. They are being treated for malaria.*
   See **disabilities; addiction; mental illness**; and the **Health and Science chapter**.

disinterested, uninterested
Disinterested means *impartial*, which is usually the better word to convey the thought.
   Uninterested means that someone lacks interest.

disk, disc Use *disk* for computer-related references (*diskette*) and medical references, such as a *slipped disk*. Use the *disc* spelling for optical and laser-based devices (a *Blu-ray Disc, CD, DVD*) and for *disc brake*.

dispel, dispelled, dispelling

disposable personal income The income that a person retains after deductions for income taxes, Social Security taxes, property taxes and for other payments such as fines and penalties to various levels of government.

Disposall A trademark for a type of mechanical garbage disposer.

dissociate Not *disassociate*.

distance learning (n., adj.) *Schools are turning to distance learning. He is taking a distance learning class.*

distances Always use figures: *He walked 4 miles.* See **numerals**.

district Always spell it out. Use a figure and capitalize *district* when forming a proper name: *the 2nd District.*

district attorney Capitalize when used as a formal title before a name: *District Attorney Hamilton Burger.*
   DA acceptable on second reference.
   See **titles**.

district court See **court names** and **U.S. District Court**.

District of Columbia In datelines Washington doesn't take *D.C.* Generally use *District of Columbia* within a story only for official designations, such as local government names, or to avoid

d

confusion with other localities of that name. *Washington* should be used in most story references to the U.S. capital because of the name recognition globally. Use *Washington, D.C.*, with the added abbreviation only if the city might be confused with the state. Do not use *D.C.* standing alone other than in quotations. On second reference, *the district* is acceptable. Postal code: *DC*. See **state names**.

dive, dived or **dove, diving**

dividend In a financial sense, the word describes the payment per share that a corporation distributes to its stockholders as their return on the money they have invested in its stock.
See **profit terminology**.

division See **organizations and institutions**; **military units**; and **political divisions**.

divorce Use the same standards for men and women in deciding whether to mention marital status in a story. Avoid describing a woman as a *divorcee*, or a man as a *divorce*, unless used in an essential quote. When the news isn't about a marital breakup, but marital status is relevant, say in the body of the story that the woman or man is divorced.

Dixie cup A trademark for a paper drinking cup.

DNA Acceptable for all reference to deoxyribonucleic acid, which carries genetic information in the cell.

DNS Abbreviation for the *domain name system*, an international network of directories that keep track of internet names and addresses. Spell out on first reference. See **domain name**.

doctor Use *Dr.* in first reference as a formal title before the name of an individual who holds a doctor of dental surgery, doctor of medicine, doctor of optometry, doctor of osteopathic medicine, doctor of podiatric medicine, or doctor of veterinary medicine: *Dr. Jonas Salk*.

The form *Dr.*, or *Drs.* in a plural construction, applies to all first-reference uses before a name, including direct quotations. Do not continue the use of *Dr.* in subsequent references.

Do not use *Dr.* before the names of individuals who hold other types of doctoral degrees. Instead, when necessary or appropriate: *Cassandra Karoub, who has a doctorate in mathematics, was lead researcher. U.S. first lady Jill Biden, who has a doctorate in education, plans to continue teaching. U.S. second gentleman Doug Emhoff, a lawyer, is joining the faculty of Georgetown Law.* In a list: *Stephanie Sanchez, Ph.D.*
See **academic degrees**; **shorthand descriptions**.

Doctors Without Borders Use the full English name on first reference. *MSF* is acceptable in quotations and second references, noting that it is the abbreviation for the French name of the group, *Medecins Sans Frontieres*. Do not use *MSF* in headlines.

dollars Always lowercase. Use figures and the *$* sign in all except casual references or amounts without a figure: *The book cost $4. Dad, please* *give me a dollar. Dollars are flowing overseas.*

For specified amounts, the word takes a singular verb: *He said $500,000 is what they want.*

For amounts of more than $1 million, use up to two decimal places. Do not link the numerals and the word by a hyphen: *He is worth $4.35 million. He proposed a $300 billion budget.*

The form for amounts less than $1 million: *$4, $25, $500, $1,000, $650,000.*

See **cents**.

domain name The address used to locate a particular website or reach an email system. In email addresses, it is the portion to the right of the @ sign. It includes a suffix that often defines the type of entity, such as *.com* (for commerce), *.gov* (for U.S. government), *.fr* (for France) and *.bank* (for financial institutions). There are also domains that use non-Latin characters such as Arabic and Japanese.

Some domain suffixes are restricted to specific types of institutions, such as banks, but institutions aren't required to use any particular suffix. Though domain names are less prominent these days as more people reach websites using search engines and apps, they are still important for email addresses, billboards and other nondigital advertising.

When writing about the suffix, use *.com, .org*, etc. Reserve *dot-com* for references to companies that do business mainly on the internet. See **DNS**; **dot-com**.

domino, dominoes

do's and don'ts

dot-com An older and informal description of companies that do business mainly on the internet. Usually reserved for companies that thrived in the years 1995-2001, a period often known as the *dot-com era*. When referring to the domain name itself, use *.com, .org*, etc.

d

Dow Jones Industrial Average
The market indicator comprises 30 leading U.S. stocks. The average is calculated and published by S&P Dow Jones Indices LLC, which is jointly owned by S&P Global Inc. and CME Group Inc. The average is maintained by S&P Dow Jones Indices' averages committee, comprising representatives of S&P Dow Jones Indices and The Wall Street Journal. Always use the full name on first reference in stories. On subsequent references, use *the Dow*.

-down Follow Webster's New World College Dictionary. Some examples, all nouns and/or adjectives:

   breakdown   *pat-down*
   countdown   *sit-down*

All are two words when used as verbs.

down- The rules in **prefixes** apply, but in general, no hyphen. Some examples:

   downgrade   *downtown*

Down East Use only in reference to Maine.

down payment

downside risk The probability that the price of an investment will fall.

downstage

downstate Lowercase unless part of a proper name: *downstate Illinois*. But: *the Downstate Medical Center*.

Down syndrome A condition in which a person is born with an extra chromosome, causing mild to moderate cognitive disability, developmental delays and physical challenges. Do not use the term *mentally retarded*. Describe a person as *having Down syndrome* only if relevant to the story, and if a medical diagnosis has been made or the person uses the term. If relatives or others use the term, ask how they know, then consider carefully whether to include the information. The condition is named for Dr. J. Langdon Down, who first reported it in 1866. Not *Down's syndrome*. See **disabilities**.

Down Under Australia, New Zealand and environs.

Dramamine A trademark for a brand of motion sickness remedy.

dreidel Toy spinning top used in games played during Hanukkah.

dressing room

dressing, stuffing *Dressing* is cooked outside of the bird; *stuffing* is cooked inside. Use of the terms also varies regionally in the U.S., with one preferred over the other in some places regardless of how it's prepared.

drive-by (adj.) A *drive-by shooting*.

driver's license(s)

drive-thru (n. and adj.)

drop-down (adj.)

dropout (n.) **drop out** (v.)

drowned, was drowned If a person suffocates in water or other fluid, the proper statement is that the individual *drowned*. To say that someone *was drowned* implies that another person caused the death by holding the victim's head under the water.

Drug Enforcement Administration *DEA* on second reference.

drugmaker

drugs Acceptable as a term for both prescribed products and illicit substances. Avoid *narcotic* or *narcotics* in general references since narcotics can be prescribed or illegal. Capitalize brand names; lowercase generics.

The names used for some street drugs can often be misleading, so ensure they are described correctly. Details on some drugs:

bath salts Any of a number of drugs that contain synthetic chemicals related to the natural stimulant cathinone and sometimes marketed as *bath salts*. Ensure that stories explain they are unrelated to actual bathing products.

cannabis See **marijuana, medical marijuana** below.

cocaine The slang term *coke* should appear only in quotations. *Crack* is a refined cocaine in crystalline rock form; mention it separately from *cocaine* only if pertinent.

ecstasy, molly, MDMA All acceptable shorthand for *methylenedioxymethamphetamine*, commonly used as a party drug, though *molly* refers to a purer form. Lowercase (other than *MDMA*) unless it's a brand name. Use *MDMA* in medical contexts.

fake pot See **synthetic cannabinoids** below.

fentanyl An opioid painkiller many times more powerful than heroin, and typically prescribed to treat severe pain. Now frequently appears as an illegal street drug mixed with other substances, such as *heroin*, *metonitazene* or *para-fluorofentanyl*, the latter of which is sometimes known as *China white*. Experts say the growing prevalence of fentanyl in the illicit drug supply is a top driver of the increasing number of overdose deaths in the U.S.

heroin An opioid related to morphine, but more potent and addictive.

LSD Acceptable on first reference for the hallucinogenic drug *lysergic acid diethylamide*. Also known as *acid*.

marijuana, medical marijuana *Marijuana* may be used interchangeably with *cannabis* and, in colloquial references, *pot*. *Cannabis* is the usual term outside North America. Slang terms such as *weed*, *reefer*, *ganja* or *420* are acceptable in limited, colloquial cases or in quotations. In the United States, many states have legalized *medical marijuana* for a variety of ailments and conditions; others have legalized the drug for recreational use. Possession and distribution of marijuana remain federal offenses. See separate full entry **marijuana, cannabis** for more detail.

meth Usually acceptable on first reference for *methamphetamine* unless it could be confused with

other drugs, such as *methcathinone* or *methadone*.

mushrooms When referring to the fungi that are commonly used as a recreational drug, call them *psychedelic mushrooms* in the first reference and *mushrooms* in subsequent references. *Magic mushrooms* is acceptable in quotations.

PCP Acceptable on first reference for the hallucinogenic drug *phencyclidine*. Also known as *angel dust*.

synthetic cannabinoids Drugs made of synthetic cannabis compounds that are added to plant material and sold for recreational use in products such as Spice and K2, often described as dangerous. Use the full term only if necessary. Do not refer to it by the inaccurate terms *fake pot* or *synthetic marijuana*. See separate full entry **marijuana, cannabis** for more detail. Also see **naloxone**; **opiate, opioid**.

drugstore

drunk, drunken, drunkenness

Drunk is the spelling of the adjective used after a form of the verb *to be*: *He was drunk*.

Drunken is the spelling of the adjective used before nouns: *a drunken driver, drunken driving*.

DUI, *driving under the influence*; *DWI*, *driving while intoxicated*; follow official state usage. See **addiction**.

dual-class stocks
Some companies sell different classes of stock to boost the voting power of their founders, family members and others. For example, the regular class may come with one vote per share, while the special class gets 10 votes per share. Or the regular class

may get no voting rights, while the special class gets one. Those with the special class can control a company without having majority ownership. Alphabet has three classes: one with regular voting power, one with more and one with none at all.

The New York Times Co., Meta Platforms Inc. and Ford Motor Co. are among the companies with dual-class stocks, but only one is traded.

When multiple classes are traded, each has its own stock symbol. When citing stock prices, use the class that's more common, which is usually the one with regular or zero voting power. See the longer **dual-class stocks** entry in Stylebook Online for the stock symbols to use for some of the companies with dual-class stocks.

duel A contest between two people. Three people cannot duel.

duffel

DUI, DWI Abbreviations for *driving under the influence* or *driving while intoxicated*. Acceptable in all references. See **drunk, drunken, drunkeness**.

dumping The selling of a product in a foreign market at a price lower than the domestic price. It is usually done by a monopoly when it has such a large output that selling entirely in the domestic market would substantially reduce the price.

durable goods Long-lasting goods such as appliances that are bought by consumers.

Dutch auction A bidding process where the price is lowered until the lowest price at which all securities

will sell becomes the set price. Used on Treasury auctions and in risk arbitrage.

DVD Abbreviation for *digital video disc* (or *digital versatile disc*), similar to CD-ROMs, but able to hold more music, video or data.

The abbreviation is acceptable in all references.

DVR Acceptable on second reference for *digital video recorder*. *TiVo* is the trademark for one type of DVR. Do not use *TiVo* to describe the generic DVRs offered by many cable systems. Although standalone DVRs are becoming less prevalent in the age of streaming video, some services now offer internet-based DVRs as part of television subscription services, including cable-like packages of channels delivered over the internet.

dwarf, dwarfism, little people *Dwarfism* is a genetic condition resulting in an adult height below 4'10." Refer to the condition only if relevant to the story. Some people prefer the term *dwarf* to describe themselves. Others prefer *person with dwarfism* or *little person*, both of which are used by the Little People of America organization. Try to determine an individual's preference, and briefly explain the condition. Use *person with dwarfism* if the preference isn't known. Do not use *midget*. See **disabilities**.

dyeing, dying *Dyeing* refers to changing colors.
Dying refers to death.

dyslexia, dyslexic *Dyslexia* is a learning disability characterized by problems identifying speech sounds and learning how to connect them to letters and words. Describe a person as *dyslexic* or *having dyslexia* only if relevant to the story, and if a medical diagnosis has been made or the person uses the term. If relatives or others use the term, ask how they know, then consider carefully whether to include the information. Don't use *a dyslexic* as a noun unless someone describes themself that way. See **disabilities**.

d

e

each Takes a singular verb.

each other, one another Two people look at *each other*.

More than two look at *one another*.

Either phrase may be used when the number is indefinite: *We help each other. We help one another.*

earbuds, earphones, headphones, headsets

Earth Capitalize when used as the proper name of the planet, lowercase for other uses. *The astronauts returned to Earth. He hopes to move heaven and earth. She is down-to-earth. The moon, Earth and sun lined up to create the only total lunar eclipse this year.*

See **planets**.

earthquakes The best source for information on major earthquakes is the National Earthquake Information Center, operated by the U.S. Geological Survey, in Golden, Colorado.

Earthquake magnitudes are measures of earthquake size calculated from ground motion recorded by seismometers. The Richter scale, named for Charles F. Richter, is no longer widely used.

Magnitudes are usually reported simply as *magnitude 6.7* (or *6.7 magnitude*), for example. Do not use hyphens when the magnitude is used as a modifier: *a magnitude 6.7 quake, a 6.7 magnitude quake.*

In the first hours after a quake, earthquake size should be reported as a *preliminary magnitude* at a *preliminary depth*.

The most commonly used measure is the *moment magnitude*, related to the area of the fault on which an earthquake occurs and the amount the ground slips.

The magnitude scale used should be specified only when necessary. An example would be when two centers are reporting different magnitudes because they are using different scales. The various scales usually differ only slightly.

When comparing quakes, every increase of one number means that the quake is 10 times bigger and releases 32 times more energy. For example, a magnitude 7 quake shakes 10 times as hard and is 32 times stronger than a magnitude 6 quake. To determine the difference in size and strength, use the U.S. Geological Survey's calculator: https://earthquake.usgs.gov/learn/topics/calculator.php.

Some indications of earthquake size:

Magnitude 2.5 to 3: The smallest generally felt by people.

Magnitude 4: Can cause moderate damage.

Magnitude 5: Can cause considerable damage.

Magnitude 6: Can cause severe damage.

Magnitude 7: A major earthquake, capable of widespread, heavy damage.

Magnitude 8: An earthquake capable of tremendous damage.

Depth is a key factor in

determining how damaging an earthquake will be. The closer to the surface an earthquake starts, the more ground shaking and potential damage it will cause, particularly in places without strict building codes. Two different earthquakes of the same magnitude can result in vastly different damage and deaths depending on the depth.

Quakes are divided into three categories: shallow, intermediate and deep. Shallow quakes are at depths of less than 70 km (43 miles) and are the ones that have broader damage. Intermediate quakes are between 70 km and 300 km in depth (43 miles to 186 miles). Deep quakes are deeper than 300 km (186 miles).

The deadliest quake on record occurred in Shaanxi province of China on Jan. 23, 1556. It killed 830,000 people.

Initial earthquake reports from seismic monitoring networks are usually generated automatically and should be confirmed if the reporter did not feel the tremor. Some reports result from system errors and will be deleted after review by a seismologist. A very large earthquake anywhere in the world may cause a seismic network to produce erroneous reports of one or more quakes in its monitoring area.

The USGS' "Did You Feel It" webpages collect unvetted reports from the public. These may be useful in characterizing how widely a quake was felt but singular reports from distant locations should be confirmed.

OTHER TERMS: The word *temblor* (not tremblor) is a synonym for *earthquake*.

The word *epicenter* refers to the point on Earth's surface above the underground center, or focus, of an earthquake.

Earthquake early warning systems do not predict earthquakes. When an earthquake begins they provide warning to distant locations where the shaking has not yet begun.

Easter Christian holy day commemorating the resurrection of Jesus Christ. Christians believe Jesus was raised from the dead three days after his crucifixion.

Western Christian churches and most Orthodox Christian churches follow different calendars and observe Easter on different dates.

Eastern Europe No longer a separate political unit, but can be used in specific references to the region. Use only in historic sense. (Also *Western Europe*.)

Eastern Hemisphere The half of the Earth made up primarily of Africa, Asia, Australia and Europe.

Eastern Seaboard Synonym for *East Coast*.

Eastern Shore A region on the east side of Chesapeake Bay, including parts of Maryland and Virginia.

Eastern Shore is not a synonym for *East Coast*.

eBay Inc. The online auctioneer is based in San Jose, California. Lowercase *e* unless it's the start of a sentence.

Ebola A virus that causes a severe and often fatal illness. It is named for a river in the Democratic Republic of Congo, where one of the first outbreaks of the disease occurred in 1976. An outbreak in West Africa that began in 2014 killed more than

e

11,000 people.

Ebola virus comes from wild animals and then spreads person to person through direct contact with an infected person or contaminated materials. Symptoms can include sudden fever, muscle pain, headache, sore throat, vomiting, diarrhea, rash, kidney or liver problems and bleeding. People are not infectious until they develop symptoms, and the incubation period is two to 21 days.

e-book A book or publication in electronic form, often sold digitally and commonly read on a hand-held device called an *e-reader* or on an *e-reader app* on a smartphone, tablet or PC.

E. coli Acceptable in all references for the bacteria called *Escherichia coli O157:H7 bacteria*. Infections can be caused by contaminated food or water.

ecology The study of the relationship between organisms and their surroundings. It is not synonymous with *environment*.

Right: *The laboratory is studying the ecology of man and the desert.*

Wrong: *Even so simple an undertaking as maintaining a lawn affects ecology.* (Use *environment* instead.)

ecosystem

ecotourism

Ecuadorian The term for the people and culture of Ecuador.

editor Capitalize *editor* before a name only when it is an official corporate or organizational title. Do not capitalize as a job description.

See **titles**.

editor-in-chief Use hyphens and capitalize when used as a formal title before a name: *Editor-in-Chief Horace Greeley*. The hyphens, reflecting industry usage, are an exception to Webster's New World College Dictionary.

See **titles**.

eerie

e.g. Meaning *for example*, it is always followed by a comma.

Eglin Air Force Base, Florida

Eid al-Adha Meaning "Feast of Sacrifice," this most important Islamic holiday marks the willingness of the Prophet Ibrahim (Abraham to Christians and Jews) to sacrifice his son. During the holiday, which in most places lasts four days, Muslims slaughter sheep or cattle, distribute part of the meat to poor people and eat the rest. The holiday begins on the 10th day of the Islamic lunar month of Dhul-Hijja, during the annual hajj pilgrimage to Mecca.

Eid al-Fitr A three-day holiday marking the end of Ramadan, Islam's holy month of fasting.

either Use it to mean *one or the other*, not *both*.

Right: *She said to use either door.*

Wrong: *There were lions on either side of the door.*

Right: *There were lions on each side of the door. There were lions on both sides of the door.*

either ... or, neither ... nor The nouns that follow these words do not constitute a compound subject; they are alternate subjects and require a verb that agrees with the nearer subject:

Neither they nor he is going. Neither he nor they are going.

-elect Always hyphenate and lowercase: *President-elect Joe Biden.* For a newly elected candidate, the term can be used as soon as the race is called. After a name or standing alone: *the president-elect* or *Biden, the president-elect.* Also: *Vice President-elect Kamala Harris, Gov.-elect Sue Ahmad, Sen.-elect D'Shawn Washington, Attorney General-elect Melissa Rubin,* etc.

Election Day, election night The first Tuesday after the first Monday in November.

election returns Use figures, with commas every three digits starting at the right and counting left. Use the word *to* (not a hyphen) in separating different totals listed together: *Jimmy Carter outpolled Gerald Ford 40,827,292 to 39,146,157 in 1976.*

Use the word *votes* if there is any possibility that the figures could be confused with a ratio: *Nixon outpolled McGovern 16 votes to 3 votes in Dixville Notch.*

Do not attempt to create adjectival forms such as *the 40,827,292-39,146,157 vote.*
See **vote tabulations**.

Electoral College But *electoral vote(s).* The process by which the United States selects its president. The "college" consists of 538 electors from the states. Each state gets as many electoral votes as it has members of Congress, and the District of Columbia gets three. To be elected president, the winner must get at least half the total plus one — or 270 electoral votes. Most states give all their electoral votes to whichever candidate wins that state's popular vote. The electoral system has delivered a split verdict five times, most recently in 2016, with one candidate winning the popular vote and another the presidency.

electrocardiogram A test measuring the heart's electrical activity. *EKG* is acceptable on second reference.

electronic cigarette A battery-operated device that typically heats a flavored nicotine solution into a vapor, which is inhaled. The term *e-cigarette* is acceptable on second reference. Do not use *e-cig.* See **vape, vaping.**

electric, hybrid, plug-in hybrid vehicles The term *electric vehicles* describes vehicles that are powered by a battery linked to an electric motor. Sometimes these are called *battery-electric vehicles.*

Other vehicles can run on electricity but also have internal combustion engines. Those are *hybrid vehicles,* which use both an electric motor and a gasoline engine and can shift back and forth for efficiency; and *plug-in hybrid vehicles,* which can run on battery power alone before reverting to hybrid operation. Do not call these *electric vehicles.*

EV is acceptable on second reference when referring to vehicles that run only on electricity and have no internal combustion engine. Do not use *HEV* on second reference for hybrids or *PHEV* for plug-in hybrids.

eleventh Spell out only in the phrase *the eleventh hour*, meaning at the last moment; otherwise use the numeral.

ellipsis See entry in the **Punctuation** chapter.

El Salvador The use of the article in the name of the nation helps to distinguish it from its capital, *San Salvador*.

Use *Salvadoran(s)* in references to citizens of the nation.

email Acceptable in all references for *electronic mail*. Also: *esports*. Use a hyphen with other *e-* terms: *e-book, e-reader, e-commerce*.

embargo times Embargoed copy contains *HFR* (Hold for Release) in the keyword.

embarrass, embarrassing, embarrassed, embarrassment

embassy An *embassy* is the official office of an ambassador in a foreign country and the office that handles the political relations of one nation with another.

A *consulate*, the office of a consul in a foreign city, handles the commercial affairs and personal needs of citizens of the appointing country.

Capitalize with the name of a nation; lowercase without it: *the French Embassy, the U.S. Embassy, the embassy*.

embryo, fetus, unborn baby, unborn child While the terms are essentially interchangeable in many common uses, each has become politicized by the abortion debate even in uses not involving abortion. Anti-abortion advocates say *fetus* devalues a human life; abortion-rights supporters argue *unborn child* or *baby* equate termination of a pregnancy with murder by emphasizing the fetus's humanity.

Write clearly and sensitively, using any of the terms when appropriate:

Fetus, which refers to the stage in human development from the eighth week of pregnancy to birth, is preferred in many cases, including almost all scientific and medical uses: *The virus can be disastrous to a fetus. The lawsuit alleges harm to a fetus that prosecutors claim was viable. The research was conducted on fetal tissue.*

In scientific uses referring to the first seven weeks of human development after conception, use *embryo*.

The context or tone of a story can allow for *unborn baby* or *child* in cases where *fetus* could seem clinical or cold: *Weiss said her love for her unborn baby was the strongest feeling she had ever felt. The expectant mother lost her baby in the seventh month of pregnancy.*

See **abortion**.

emcee, emceed, emceeing A phrase such as: *He was the master of ceremonies* is preferred.

emergency room *ER* is acceptable on second reference.

emeritus This word often is added to formal titles to denote that individuals who have retired retain their rank or title.

When used, place *emeritus* after the formal title, in keeping with the general practice of academic institutions: *Professor Emeritus Samuel Eliot Morison, Dean Emeritus Ashanti Washington.* Or: *Samuel Eliot*

Morison, *professor emeritus of history*; *Ashanti Washington, dean emeritus.* See **gender-neutral language**; **professor**.

Emmy, Emmys The annual awards by the Academy of Television Arts & Sciences (for prime-time programming; based in Los Angeles) and the National Academy of Television Arts and Sciences (for daytime, news and sports; based in New York).

emoji (s. and pl.) A symbol, such as a cartoon face, hand gesture, animal or other object, that might be used instead of a word or as an illustration in text messages or on social media. For guidance on quoting social media posts with emoji, see **quotations in the news**.

emoticon A typographical cartoon or symbol generally used to indicate mood or appearance, as :-) and sometimes looked at sideways. Also known as *smileys.* See **emoji**.

end user (n.) **end-user** (adj.) A phrase used by technology developers when imagining the audience for software or hardware. *End-user experience.*

enforce But *reinforce.*

engine, motor An *engine* develops its own power, usually through internal combustion or the pressure of air, steam or water passing over vanes attached to a wheel: *an airplane engine, an automobile engine, a jet engine, a missile engine, a steam engine, a turbine engine.*

A *motor* receives power from an outside source: *an electric motor, a hydraulic motor.*

England Part of *Great Britain*, which also includes *Scotland* and *Wales. Great Britain* and *Northern Ireland* are part of the *United Kingdom.* Do not refer to *England* as the *United Kingdom*, and vice versa. *LONDON* stands alone in datelines. Use *England* after the names of other English communities in datelines. See **datelines** and **United Kingdom**.

enroll, enrolled, enrolling

en route Always two words.

entitled Use it to mean *a right to do or have something.* Do not use it to mean *titled.*
Right: *She was entitled to the promotion.*
Right: *The book was titled "Gone With the Wind."*

envelop (v.) Other verb forms: *enveloping, enveloped.* But: *envelope* (n.)

Environmental Protection Agency *EPA* is acceptable on second reference.

envoy Not a formal title. Lowercase. See **titles**.

epicenter The point on the Earth's surface above the underground center, or focus, of an earthquake. See **earthquakes**.

epidemic (n., adj.), **pandemic** (n., adj.), **endemic** (adj.) An *epidemic* is the rapid spreading of disease in a certain population or region; a *pandemic* is an epidemic that has spread wider, usually to multiple countries or continents, affecting a large number of people. Follow declarations of public health officials in terminology. On March 11, 2020, the World Health Organization declared the COVID-19 outbreak a *pandemic*. Do not write *global pandemic* for the COVID-19 pandemic; the adjective is unnecessary as this pandemic is widely known to be global.

Endemic as an adjective refers to the constant presence of a disease. For example, malaria is *endemic* in some tropical regions. Health experts say the coronavirus that causes COVID-19 is unlikely to go away, and as of early 2022 they expected it to eventually become *endemic*. Do not use the noun phrase *an endemic*.

equal An adjective without comparative forms.

When people speak of a *more equal* distribution of wealth, what is meant is *more equitable*.

Equal Employment Opportunity Commission *EEOC* is acceptable on second reference.

equal, equaled, equaling

equally as Do not use the words together; one is sufficient.

Omit the *equally* shown here in parentheses: *She was (equally) as wise as Marilyn.*

Omit the *as* shown here in parentheses: *She and Marilyn were equally (as) wise.*

equal time *Equal time* applies to the U.S. law that requires a radio or television station to offer a candidate for political office airtime equal to any time that an opponent receives beyond news coverage.

equator Always lowercase.

equity When used in a financial sense, *equity* means the value of property beyond the amount that is owed on it.

A *stockholder's equity* in a corporation is the value of the shares he holds.

A *homeowner's equity* is the difference between the value of the house and the amount of the unpaid mortgage.

ERA Acceptable in all references to baseball's *earned run average*.

e-reader Or *e-book reader*. A device used to display electronic books and other digital publications. Other devices such as phones can use e-reader software that performs similar functions.

escalator clause A clause in a contract providing for increases or decreases in wages, prices, etc., based on fluctuations in the cost of living, production, expenses, etc.

Eskimo In general, avoid the term *Eskimo* for the native peoples of northern North America except when paired with a group's ethnic name in Alaska: *Inupiat Eskimos*, a *Yup'ik Eskimo community*, a *Cu'pik Eskimo*, etc. Follow the preference of those involved in the story, such as identifying someone simply as *Yup'ik*. The term *Eskimo* was assigned by non-native people and in some cultures, has since taken on offensive connotations. The term *Inuit* is used in Canada and Greenland and by some groups in northern Alaska.

ESOP Acronym for *employee stock ownership plan*. Spell out on first reference.

essential clauses, nonessential clauses

These terms are used in this book instead of *restrictive clause* and *nonrestrictive clause* to convey the distinction between the two in a more easily remembered manner.

Both types of clauses provide additional information about a word or phrase in the sentence.

The difference between them is that the *essential clause* cannot be eliminated without changing the meaning of the sentence — it so *restricts* the meaning of the word or phrase that its absence would lead to a substantially different interpretation of what the author meant.

The *nonessential clause*, however, can be eliminated without altering the basic meaning of the sentence — it does not *restrict* the meaning so significantly that its absence would radically alter the author's thought.

PUNCTUATION: An essential clause must not be set off from the rest of a sentence by commas. A nonessential clause must be set off by commas.

The presence or absence of commas provides the reader with critical information about the writer's intended meaning. Note the following examples:

— *Reporters who do not read the Stylebook should not criticize their editors.* (The writer is saying that only one class of reporters, those who do not read the Stylebook, should not criticize their editors. If the *who ... Stylebook* phrase were deleted, the meaning of the sentence would be changed substantially.)

— *Reporters, who do not read the Stylebook, should not criticize their editors.* (The writer is saying that all reporters should not criticize their editors. If the *who*

... Stylebook phrase were deleted, this meaning would not be changed.)

USE OF WHO, WHOM, THAT, WHICH. See separate entries on **that (conjunction); that, which (pronouns); who, whom.**

That is the preferred pronoun to introduce essential clauses that refer to an inanimate object or an animal without a name. *Which* is the only acceptable pronoun to introduce a nonessential clause that refers to an inanimate object or an animal without a name.

The pronoun *which* occasionally may be substituted for *that* in the introduction of an essential clause that refers to an inanimate object or an animal without a name. In general, this use of *which* should appear only when *that* is used as a conjunction to introduce another clause in the same sentence: *He said Monday that the part of the army which suffered severe casualties needs reinforcement.*

See **that (conjunction)** for guidelines on the use of *that* as a conjunction.

essential phrases, nonessential phrases

These terms are used in this book instead of *restrictive phrase* and *nonrestrictive phrase* to convey the distinction between the two in a more easily remembered manner.

The underlying concept is the one that also applies to clauses:

An *essential phrase* is a word or group of words critical to the reader's understanding of what the author had in mind.

A *nonessential phrase* provides more information about something. Although the information may be helpful to the reader's comprehension, the reader would not be misled if the information were not there.

PUNCTUATION: Do not set an essential phrase off from the rest of a sentence by commas:

We saw the award-winning movie "Green Book." (No comma, because many movies have won awards, and without the name of the movie the reader would not know which movie was meant.)

They ate dinner with their daughter Julie. (Because they have more than one daughter, the inclusion of Julie's name is critical if the reader is to know which daughter is meant.)

Set off nonessential phrases by commas:

We saw the 2019 winner of the Academy Award competition for best picture, "Green Book." (Only one movie won the award. The name is informative, but even without the name no other movie could be meant.)

They ate dinner with their daughter Julie and her husband, Jesse. (Julie has only one husband. If the phrase read *and her husband Jesse*, it would suggest that she had more than one husband.)

The company chair, Camie Garcia, spoke. (In the context, only one person could be meant.)

Indian corn, or maize, was harvested. (*Maize* provides the reader with the name of the corn, but its absence would not change the meaning of the sentence.)

DESCRIPTIVE WORDS: Do not confuse punctuation rules for nonessential clauses with the correct punctuation when a nonessential word is used as a descriptive adjective. The distinguishing clue often is the lack of an article or pronoun:

Right: *Julie and husband Jesse went shopping. Julie and her husband, Jesse, went shopping.*

Right: *Company Chair Camie Garcia made the announcement. The company chair, Camie Garcia, made the announcement.*

Eswatini A country in southern Africa that changed its name from Swaziland in 2018. In stories, note that the country was formerly known as Swaziland.

ETF Abbreviation for *exchange-traded fund*. A security that tracks a benchmark much as a mutual fund does, but trades throughout market days like a stock on the exchange. Spell out on first reference.

ethanol Fuel additive distilled from mashed and fermented grain. Gasoline blends are written as a percentage of *ethanol*, e.g., *E85* for 85% ethanol and 15% gasoline.

ethnic cleansing Euphemism for a campaign to force a population from a region by expulsions and other violence often including killings and rapes. The term came to prominence in former Yugoslavia during the 1990s to whitewash atrocities of warring ethnic groups, then usage spread to other conflicts. AP does not use the term *ethnic cleansing* on its own. It must be enclosed in quotes, attributed and explained. Don't use the term as a keyword or in headlines.

euro The common currency of 19 members of the European Union, known as the *eurozone*: Austria, Belgium, Cyprus, Estonia, Finland, France, Germany, Greece, Ireland, Italy, Latvia, Lithuania, Luxembourg, Malta, Netherlands, Portugal,

Slovakia, Slovenia and Spain. Some smaller countries and territories also use the euro, either through agreement with the EU or as a de facto currency.

Plural is *euros*. Write euro amounts in the form *100 euros*. Do not use the "€" sign. See **currency conversions**.

eurodollar A U.S. dollar on deposit in a European bank, including foreign branches of U.S. banks.

European Union *EU* (no periods). The multination European Union, based in Brussels, Belgium, was created by the Treaty on European Union, which took effect Nov. 1, 1993. Its executive body is the European Commission, which runs the EU's day-to-day affairs, drafts European laws and, after their adoption by governments, ensures their enforcement across the bloc. It also represents the EU in international trade negotiations and conducts antitrust investigations. The six founding members are: France, Germany, Italy, Netherlands, Belgium and Luxembourg. Other members are: Austria, Bulgaria, Croatia, Cyprus, Czech Republic, Denmark, Estonia, Finland, Greece, Hungary, Ireland, Latvia, Lithuania, Malta, Poland, Portugal, Romania, Slovakia, Slovenia, Spain and Sweden. Britain's 2016 Brexit vote resulted in its exit from the EU on Jan. 31, 2020, though an 11-month transition period followed. As of Jan. 1, 2021, the U.K. left the EU's economic structures and a new Trade and Cooperation Agreement took effect, covering areas including economic relations and security. See **Brexit**.

Eve Capitalize when used with *New Year's Eve*, *Christmas Eve*.

events Titles of special events, such as art exhibits and touring displays, are enclosed in quotes with primary words capitalized: *"Mummies: New Secrets From the Tombs"* at Chicago's Field Museum. Names of annually recurring events are capitalized without quotes: *North American International Auto Show in Detroit*; *Calgary Stampede*. For athletic events, refer to **sports sponsorship** in the Sports section.

every day (adv.) **everyday** (adj.)

every one, everyone Two words when it means *each individual item*: *Every one of the clues was worthless.*

One word when used as a pronoun meaning *all people*: *Everyone wants their life to be happy.* (Don't use *his* with everyone; it presumes maleness. *They/them/their* may be used as singular in such constructions if essential, but rewriting is preferred: *All people want their lives to be happy.*) See **pronouns**.

Every Student Succeeds Act The federal education law signed by President Barack Obama in 2015. The previous version of the law, the No Child Left Behind Act, was enacted in 2002. Use *ESSA* and *NCLB* only in direct quotations.

ex- Use no hyphen for words that use *ex-* in the sense of *out of*:
    excommunicate   *expropriate*

Hyphenate when using *ex-* in the sense of *former*:
    ex-convict   *ex-president*
Do not capitalize *ex-* when attached to a formal title before a name: *ex-President Richard Nixon*.

e

The prefix modifies the entire term: *ex-New York Gov. Mario Cuomo*; not *New York ex-Gov.*

Usually *former* is better.

exclamation point See entry in the **Punctuation** chapter.

execute, execution To *execute* a person is to kill that person in compliance with a military order or judicial decision.

See **assassin, killer, murderer** and **homicide, murder, manslaughter**.

execution-style Avoid use of this term to describe how people are killed, since it means different things to different people. Be specific as to how the person was killed, if that information is necessary.

executive branch Always lowercase.

executive director Capitalize before a name only if it is a formal corporate or organizational title.

See **titles**.

Executive Mansion Capitalize only in references to the White House.

expel, expelled, expelling

exponential growth Used when something has grown by increasing amounts. For instance, a population might increase by 5% from 1980 to 1990, 10% from 1990 to 2000 and 15% from 2000 to 2010. Not simply a synonym for a large increase.

Export-Import Bank of the United States *Export-Import Bank* is acceptable in all references; *Ex-Im Bank* is acceptable on second reference.

Headquarters is in Washington.

extol, extolled, extolling

extra- Do not use a hyphen when *extra* means *outside of* unless the prefix is followed by a word beginning with *a* or a capitalized word:

extralegal　　　*extraterrestrial*
extramarital　　*extraterritorial*

Follow *extra-* with a hyphen when it is part of a compound modifier describing a condition beyond the usual size, extent or degree:

extra-base hit　　*extra-large book*
extra-dry drink　*extra-mild taste*

extrasensory perception *ESP* is acceptable on second reference.

f

Facebook (company) Former name of the company *Meta Platforms Inc.*, which owns the world's most popular social network — also called Facebook. The company adopted the name *Meta Platforms Inc.* in October 2021 to signal its intention of building the *metaverse*, a proposed immersive digital environment that could supplant the internet.

See **Meta Platforms Inc.**; **Facebook (social platform)**; **Family of Apps**; **metaverse**.

Facebook (social platform) The world's most popular social network, with about 2.9 billion monthly active users as of December 2021. It is owned by *Meta Platforms Inc.*, the company formerly known as Facebook.

Facebook connects billions of users and tracks their activity closely, allowing it to build individual profiles it can use for selling *targeted advertising*. That business has been hugely profitable for the social network, but has also drawn significant criticism for fomenting hate speech, genocide and extremism, invading the privacy of users and promoting dangerous misinformation.

Facebook is also under scrutiny for alleged anticompetitive practices, and has been sued by the Federal Trade Commission and several states on those grounds.

During the 2020 U.S. presidential election, Facebook took small and grudging steps to curb misinformation and violent rhetoric

from then-President Donald Trump, largely by attaching labels to Trump posts with links to accurate information or rebuttals. Following the Jan. 6 insurrection, Facebook banned Trump from its service indefinitely. After a nonbinding ruling by the company's oversight board held that indefinite bans were inconsistent with Facebook rules, the company instead banned Trump for two years, after which it will review his case.

See **Meta Platforms Inc.**; **Facebook (company)**.

face recognition A technology for automatically detecting human faces in an image and identifying individual people. It is a form of biometric technology that relies on comparing selected aspects of a face against a database of images to find a match. Techniques for comparing facial features to recognize individual faces have existed since the 1960s, but the technology has improved through advancements in computer vision, machine learning and data processing.

Face recognition raises privacy concerns because governments and others can scan images from video cameras or the internet and track individual people without their knowledge. Some lawmakers have sought to curtail the technology as it becomes more widely used by law enforcement, businesses and consumers.

Similar technologies include *gait recognition*, for detecting people in video images based on their body shape and how they move; and *object recognition*, for detecting objects in an image, such as a traffic cone in the path of a self-driving car.

Face recognition technology is sometimes called *face scanning*. Apple's version of face recognition on iPhones and other devices is known as *Face ID*.

See **machine learning; artificial intelligence**.

fact-finding (adj.)

factor A financial organization whose primary business is purchasing the accounts receivable of other firms, at a discount, and taking the risk and responsibilities of making collection.

Faeroe Islands Use in datelines after a community name in stories from this group of Danish islands in the northern Atlantic Ocean between Iceland and the Shetland Islands.

Fahrenheit The temperature scale commonly used in the United States.

The scale is named for Gabriel Daniel Fahrenheit, a German physicist who designed it. In it, the freezing point of water is 32 degrees and the boiling point is 212 degrees.

To convert to Celsius, subtract 32 from Fahrenheit figure, multiply by 5 and divide by 9 (77 - 32 = 45, times 5 = 225, divided by 9 = 25 degrees Celsius.)

To convert a temperature difference from Fahrenheit to Celsius, multiply by 5 and divide by 9. A difference of 18 degrees F is a 10-degree C difference.

In cases that require mention of the scale, use these forms: *86 degrees Fahrenheit* or *86 F* (note the space and no period after the *F*) if degrees and Fahrenheit are clear from the context.

See **Celsius** and **Kelvin scale**.

For guidelines on when Celsius temperatures should be used, see **metric system** entry.

fallout (n.)

family names Capitalize words denoting family relationships only when they substitute for a person's name: *I wrote Mom a letter. I wrote my father a letter.*

Family of Apps *Meta Platforms Inc.'s* name for its social apps and services. It includes the *Facebook* social network, *Messenger*, *Instagram* and *WhatsApp*.

See **Meta Platforms Inc.; Facebook (social platform)**.

Fannie Mae A government-controlled company that helps provide money for the U.S. housing market by buying residential mortgages and packaging pools of those loans for sale to investors. The company, whose name is short for *Federal National Mortgage Association*, was seized by the government in September 2008 and is overseen by the Federal Housing Finance Agency.

FAQ Acceptable in all uses for *frequently asked questions*.

farmers market No apostrophe.

farmworker

far-ranging (adj.)

farsighted When used in a medical sense, it means that a person can see objects at a distance but has difficulty seeing materials at close range.

farther, further Farther refers to physical distance: *He walked farther into the woods.*
Further refers to an extension of time or degree: *She will look further into the mystery.*

Far West For the U.S. region, generally west of the Rocky Mountains.

FASB Abbreviation for *Financial Accounting Standards Board*. Spell out on first reference.

fashion week Capitalize in an official name, such as *New York Fashion Week* or *London Fashion Week*.

fast fashion (n.), **fast-fashion** (adj.) An approach to the design, creation and marketing of clothing fashions that emphasizes making fashion trends quickly and cheaply available to consumers.

Fatah A secular Palestinian party and former guerrilla movement founded by Yasser Arafat. Do not use with the prefix *al-*.

father Use *the Rev.* in first reference before the names of Episcopal, Orthodox and Catholic priests. Use *Father* before a name only in direct quotations. Capitalize *Father* in *God the Father* and similar phrases.
See **religious titles** in the **Religion** chapter.

Father's Day The third Sunday in June.

father-in-law, fathers-in-law

Father Time

faze, phase *Faze* means *to embarrass or disturb*: *The snub did not faze her.*
Phase denotes *an aspect or stage*: *They will phase in a new system.*

FBI Acceptable in all references for *Federal Bureau of Investigation*.

featherbedding The practice of requiring an employer to hire more workers than needed to handle a job.

federal Use a capital letter for the architectural style and for corporate or governmental bodies that use the word as part of their formal names: *the Federal Trade Commission.* (See separate entries for governmental agencies.)
Lowercase when used as an adjective to distinguish something from state, county, city, town or private entities: *federal assistance, federal court, the federal government, a federal judge.*
Also: *federal court* (but *U.S. District Court* is preferred) and *federal Judge Ann Aldrich* (but *U.S. District Judge Ann Aldrich* is preferred).

Federal Aviation Administration *FAA* is acceptable on second reference.

Federal Bureau of Investigation *FBI* is acceptable in all references. To avoid alphabet soup, however, use *the bureau* in some references.

Federal Communications Commission *FCC* is acceptable on second reference.

federal court Always lowercase. The preferred form for first reference is to use the proper name of the court. See entries under **U.S.** and the court name.

Do not create nonexistent entities such as *Manhattan Federal Court*. Instead, use *a federal court in Manhattan*.

See **judicial branch**.

Federal Deposit Insurance Corp.
The government agency that insures deposits in banks and thrifts. *FDIC* is acceptable on second reference.

Federal Emergency Management Agency *FEMA* is acceptable on second reference.

Federal Energy Regulatory Commission The government agency that regulates interstate natural gas and electricity transactions.

FERC is acceptable on second reference, but *the agency* or *the commission* is preferred.

Federal Farm Credit System The
federally chartered cooperative banking system that provides most of the nation's agricultural loans. The system is cooperatively owned by its farm borrowers and is made up of the regional banks that issue operating and mortgage loans through local land bank associations and production credit associations.

federal funds, federal funds rate
Money in excess of what the Federal Reserve says a bank must have on hand to back up deposits. The excess can be lent overnight to banks that need more cash on hand to meet their reserve requirements. The interest rate of these loans is the *federal funds rate*. Its target rate is set by the Federal Reserve's policymaking panel, the Federal Open Market Committee. See **Federal Reserve**.

Federal Highway Administration
Reserve the *FHA* abbreviation for the *Federal Housing Administration*.

Federal Housing Administration
FHA is acceptable on second reference.

Federal Mediation and Conciliation Service Do not abbreviate. Use *the mediation service* on second reference.

Federal Register This publication, issued every workday, is the legal medium for recording and communicating the rules and regulations established by the executive branch of the federal government.

Individuals or corporations cannot be held legally responsible for compliance with a regulation unless it has been published in the Register.

In addition, executive agencies are required to publish in advance some types of proposed regulations.

Federal Reserve The central bank of the United States. It comprises the Federal Open Market Committee, which sets interest rates; the Federal Reserve Board, the regulatory body made up of Fed governors in Washington; and the Federal Reserve System, which includes the Fed in Washington and 12 regional Fed banks. Use *Federal Reserve* on first reference, *the Fed* on second reference.

Federal Trade Commission *FTC* is acceptable on second reference.

felony, misdemeanor A *felony* is a serious crime. A *misdemeanor* is a minor offense against the law.

A fuller definition of what constitutes a felony or misdemeanor depends on the governmental jurisdiction involved.

At the federal level, a *misdemeanor* is a crime that carries a potential penalty of no more than a year in jail. A *felony* is a crime that carries a potential penalty of more than a year in prison. Often, however, a statute gives a judge options such as imposing a fine or probation in addition to or instead of a jail or prison sentence.

A *felon* is a person who has been convicted of a *felony*, regardless of whether the individual actually spends time in confinement or is given probation or a fine instead.

Convicted felon is redundant. See **prison, jail**.

female, male In general, *female* and *male* are adjectives that can describe people of any age and are used only rarely as nouns, such as for a range of ages or an unknown age. *The study included males ages 10-21. She is the first female governor of North Carolina.*

Woman, women, man and *men* are usually reserved for use as a noun to describe adults, while *girl, girls, boy* and *boys* are typically used as a noun for people under age 18.

Be aware of nuances and pitfalls in the use of *female* and *woman/women*.

Since *female* primarily describes sex, not gender, some people object to its use as a descriptor for women because it can be seen as emphasizing biology and reproductive capacity over *gender identity*. It can also sometimes carry misogynistic tones that may vary in severity by race, class and other factors.

For this reason, *woman* or *women* is increasingly common an adjective.

But its use as such can often be awkward, especially if the words *man* or *men* would not be used adjectivally in a parallel sense.

For instance: *He is the only man construction worker on the otherwise all-woman crew* is awkward, and *He is the only male construction worker on the all otherwise all-woman crew* is not parallel. Options for being both sensitive and eloquent include *He is the only man on the otherwise all-woman construction crew.* See **boy, girl; gender, sex and sexual orientation; gender-neutral language**.

Ferris wheel

ferryboat

fertility rate As calculated by the federal government, it is the number of live births per 1,000 females age 15 through 44 years.

fewer, less In general, use *fewer* for individual items, *less* for bulk or quantity.

Wrong: *The trend is toward more machines and less people.* (People in this sense refers to individuals.)

Wrong: *She was fewer than 60 years old.* (Years in this sense refers to a period of time, not individual years.)

Right: *Fewer than 10 applicants called.* (Individuals.)

Right: *I had less than $50 in my pocket.* (An amount.) But: *I had fewer than 50 $1 bills in my pocket.* (Individual items.)

Fez The preferred spelling for the city in Morocco.

fiance (man) **fiancee** (woman) Generally acceptable to describe anyone who is engaged to be married, regardless of sexual orientation. If a couple requests not to use those terms or if a gender-neutral option is needed, describe couples as *engaged* or *planning to marry* or use similar phrasing.

Fiberglas Note the single *s*. A trademark for fiberglass or glass fiber.

field house

figuratively, literally *Figuratively* means *in an analogous sense, but not in the exact sense. He bled them white.*

   Literally means *in an exact sense*; do not use it figuratively.

   Wrong: *He literally bled them white.* (Unless the blood was drained from their bodies.)

figure The symbol for a number: *the figure 5.*

   See **numerals**.

filibuster To *filibuster* is to make long speeches to obstruct the passage of legislation.

   A legislator who used such methods also is a *filibuster*, not a *filibusterer*.

Filipinos The people of the Philippines. *Filipina* is acceptable as the feminine form.

film, movie The terms *film* and *movie* often are interchangeable. *Movie* is more often used to refer to mass-market motion pictures. *Film* remains an acceptable term for a *movie*, even though many movies these days use digital recording rather than film. Likewise, old-school terms such as *filmed* and *taped* are acceptable, even without the use of film and videotapes. However, use *recorded* when possible.

film noir

filmgoer

filmmaker

Finland A Nordic state, not part of Scandinavia.

fintech Short for *financial technology*, *fintech* loosely refers to products and services designed to let consumers and businesses conduct banking and other financial services digitally. It can include the technology behind mobile and online banking, money transfers among friends and tools for finding cheaper loans. *Fintech* can involve both consumer-facing products and back-end services and can come from both startups and established financial institutions. *Fintech* can be used on first reference but should be defined in the story if it isn't clear from context.

   Use lowercase except at the start of sentences or in the formal name of a company.

Fire Name of Amazon tablets. Do not use the term *Kindle Fire* to describe recent models. Amazon also makes video streaming devices called *Fire TV*.

fire department See the **governmental bodies** entry for the basic rules on capitalization.

   See **titles** and **military titles** for guidelines on titles.

firefight

firefighter The preferred term to describe a person who fights fire.

fire names Use descriptors to identify a fire. For example: *the deadly fire* *burning near San Diego.* While local media may choose to use the names of fires given by local agencies, the AP generally does not use those names because they are not widely known to a global audience. On some occasions, when a fire is particularly significant, the AP may use the name of the fire lower in the story. See **storm names** in the **weather terms** entry.

firewall A device or software designed to stop malicious or unauthorized internet traffic from reaching a computer or local data network. Many firewalls also inspect outgoing traffic.

firm A business partnership is correctly referred to as a *firm*: *He joined a law firm.*

Do not use *firm* in references to an incorporated business entity. Use *the company* or *the corporation* instead.

first aid (n.) **first-aid** (adj.)

first class, first-class Hyphenate as a modifier before a noun. *The restaurant was first class. It was a first-class restaurant.*

first degree, first-degree Hyphenate when used as a compound modifier: *It was murder in the first degree. He was convicted of first-degree murder.*

first family Always lowercase.

firsthand (adj. and adv.)

first lady , first gentleman An informal reference for the spouse of the president; not an official title. Always lowercase. Also: *second lady* or *second gentleman* for the spouse of the vice president. Usually reserved

for families of heads of state, but acceptable at lower levels such as governor or mayor if that is the local custom. Should the individual hold or have held an official title of high office, that title takes precedence: *Former Secretary of State Hillary Rodham Clinton ran for president,* not *former first lady Hillary Rodham Clinton ran for president.*

first responder(s) Acceptable in general references to police, fire, medical, hazmat or other professionals who respond to emergencies.

Each class of responders may prefer more specific job descriptions that can be difficult to verify in breaking news situations or be irrelevant. Writers and editors must decide how much detail is required and assess how realistic it is to verify.

For instance, first medical responders are often called *emergency medical services* and may include *emergency medical technicians, paramedics, firefighters* and *police officers.* If necessary, *EMT* may be used in all references and *EMS* may be used in second and subsequent references. *Paramedics* undergo advanced training and may be *EMTs,* but not all *EMTs* are *paramedics.* Some firefighters are *paramedics* called *firefighter medics.*

If it is difficult or unnecessary to describe a first medical responder's specific title, *medic* is acceptable shorthand.

Examples: *Medics treated the burn victims at the fire scene and took them away in ambulances. First responders said as many as 20 people were injured. Firefighters extinguished the blaze while medics treated the injured.*

Avoid *ambulance driver* unless

necessary to distinguish who was driving; drivers are generally also medical workers.

Hazmat worker or *hazmat team* is acceptable in all references for hazardous-material responders.

fiscal, monetary *Fiscal* applies to budgetary matters.

Monetary applies to money supply.

fiscal year The 12-month period that a corporation or governmental body uses for bookkeeping purposes.

The federal government's fiscal year starts three months ahead of the calendar year — fiscal 2007, for example, ran from Oct. 1, 2006, to Sept. 30, 2007.

fitful It means restless, not a condition of being fit.

flack, flak *Flack* is slang for *press agent*. Avoid using in copy.

Flak is a type of anti-aircraft fire, hence figuratively a barrage of criticism.

flagpole, flagship

flail, flay To *flail* is to swing the arms widely.

To *flay* is, literally, to strip off the skin by whipping. Figuratively, *to flay* means to tongue-lash a person.

flair, flare *Flair* is conspicuous talent or style.

Flare is a verb meaning to blaze with sudden, bright light, to burst out in anger, or to curve or spread outward. It is also a noun meaning a flame.

flare-up (n.) **flare up** (v.) See **flair, flare**.

flash mob A gathering of people performing an action in a public place designated by a text message, email, social media post or other notification.

flaunt, flout To *flaunt* is to make an ostentatious or defiant display: *She flaunted her intelligence.*

To *flout* is to show contempt for: *He flouts the law.*

fleet Use figures and capitalize *fleet* when forming a proper name: *the 6th Fleet.*

Lowercase *fleet* whenever it stands alone.

flip-flop (n. and v.)

float Money that has been committed but not yet credited to an account, like a check that has been written but has not yet cleared.

flood plain

floodwaters

floor leader Treat it as a job description, lowercased, rather than a formal title: *Republican floor leader Mariana Morales.*

Do not use when a formal title such as *majority leader, minority leader* or *whip* would be the accurate description.

See **legislative titles** and **titles**.

Florida Keys A chain of small islands extending southwest from the southern tip of mainland Florida.

Cities, or the islands themselves, are followed by *Fla.* in datelines: *KEY WEST, Fla. (AP)* —

flounder, founder A *flounder* is a fish; to *flounder* is to move clumsily or jerkily, to flop about: *The fish floundered on land.*

To founder is to bog down, become disabled or sink: *The ship floundered in the heavy seas for hours, then foundered.*

fluid ounce Equal to 1.8 cubic inches, 2 tablespoons or 6 teaspoons. The metric equivalent is approximately 30 milliliters. See **liter**.

flu-like

flyer, flier *Flyer* is the preferred term for a person flying in an aircraft, and for handbills: *He used his frequent flyer miles; they put up flyers announcing the show.* Use *flier* in the phrase *take a flier*, meaning *to take a big risk.*

f.o.b. Acceptable on first reference for *free on board*, meaning a seller agrees to put a commodity on a truck, ship, etc., at no charge, but transportation costs must be paid by the buyer.

-fold No hyphen: *twofold, fourfold* and *hundredfold.*

food Most food names are lowercase: *apples, cheese, peanut butter.*

Capitalize brand names and trademarks: *Roquefort cheese, Tabasco sauce.*

Most proper nouns or adjectives are capitalized when they occur in a food name: *Boston brown bread, Russian dressing, Swiss cheese, Waldorf salad.*

Lowercase is used, however, when the food does not depend on the proper noun or adjective for its meaning: *french fries.*

If a question arises, check the separate section on **Food Guidelines** on Stylebook Online. If there is

no entry, follow Webster's New World College Dictionary. Use lowercase if the dictionary lists it as an acceptable form for the sense in which the word is used.

The same principles apply to foreign names for foods: *mousse de saumon* (salmon mousse), *pomme de terre* (literally, "apple of the earth" — for potato), *salade Russe* (Russian salad).

Food and Agriculture Organization Not *Agricultural.* FAO is acceptable on second reference to this U.N. agency.

Food and Drug Administration *FDA* is acceptable on second reference.

foot The basic unit of length in the measuring system used in the United States. Its origin was a calculation that this was the length of the average human foot.

The metric equivalent is exactly 30.48 centimeters, which may be rounded to 30 centimeters for most comparisons.

For most conversions to centimeters, it is adequate to multiply 30 (5 feet x 30 equals 150 centimeters). For more exact figures, multiply by 30.48 (5 feet x 30.48 equals 152.4 centimeters).

To convert to meters, multiply by 0.3 (5 feet x 0.3 equals 1.5 meters).

See **centimeter; meter;** and **dimensions**.

forbear, forebear *To forbear* is to avoid or shun.

A forebear is an ancestor.

forbid, forbade, forbidding

force majeure A condition permitting a company to depart from the strict terms of a contract because of an event or effect that can't be reasonably controlled.

forcible rape A redundancy that usually should be avoided. It may be used, however, in stories dealing with both rape and statutory rape, which does not necessarily involve the use of force. See **sexual abuse, sexual assault, sexual harassment, sexual misconduct**.

fore- The rules in **prefixes** apply, but in general, no hyphen. Some examples:

forebrain	foregoing
forefather	foretooth

There are three nautical exceptions, based on long-standing practice:

fore-topgallant	fore-topsail
fore-topmast	

forecast Use *forecast* also for the past tense, not *forecasted*.

See **weather terms**.

foreclosure The process by which a lender seizes property from a mortgage holder who has failed to make payments and is in default.

forego, forgo To *forego* means to go before, as in *foregone conclusion*.

To *forgo* means to abstain from, as in: *He decided to forgo his senior year of eligibility*.

foreign names For foreign place names, use the primary spelling in Webster's New World College Dictionary. If it has no entry, follow the National Geographic Atlas of the World.

For personal names, follow the individual's preference for an English spelling if it can be determined. Otherwise:

— Use the nearest phonetic equivalent in English if one exists: *Alexander Solzhenitsyn*, for example, rather than *Aleksandr*, the spelling that would result from a transliteration of the Russian letters into the English alphabet.

If a name has no close phonetic equivalent in English, express it with an English spelling that approximates the sound in the original language: *Anwar Sadat*.

In general, lowercase particles such as *de, der, la, le*, and *van, von* when part of a given name: *Charles de Gaulle, Baron Manfred von Richthofen*. But follow individual preferences, as in *bin Laden*, or Dutch names such as *Van Gogh* or *Van der Graaf*. Capitalize the particles when the last names start a sentence: *De Gaulle spoke to von Richthofen*.

For additional guidelines, see **Arabic names; Chinese names; Portuguese names; Russian names; Spanish names**.

foreign words Some foreign words and abbreviations have been accepted universally into the English language: *bon voyage*; *versus, vs.*; *et cetera, etc.*

Many foreign words and their abbreviations are not understood universally, although they may be used in special applications such as medical or legal terminology. If such a word or phrase is needed in a story, place it in quotation marks and provide an explanation: *"ad astra per aspera," a Latin phrase meaning "to the stars through difficulty."*

former Always lowercase. But retain capitalization for a formal title used immediately before a name: *former President Bill Clinton*. Do not use *former* for job titles or descriptions that are bestowed in perpetuity, such as *bishop*, unless those designations have been officially revoked. Instead use language like *retired bishop* to indicate that people are no longer actively serving.

formula, formulas Use figures in writing formulas. See **metric system**.

fort Do not abbreviate for cities or for military installations.

In datelines for cities:

FORT LAUDERDALE, Fla. (AP) —

In datelines for military installations:

FORT BRAGG, N.C. (AP) —

forward Not *forwards*.

foul, fowl *Foul* means offensive, out of line.

A *fowl* is a bird, especially the larger domestic birds used as food: chickens, ducks, turkeys.

Founding Fathers Capitalize when referring to the creators of the U.S. Constitution.

4G, 5G, LTE Types of cellular technology.

5G, which stands for *fifth generation*, refers to a more robust system that in early 2022 was still starting to offer service. Besides faster speeds, the network promises reduced signal lag, improving performance for some services. 5G will require new phones capable of tapping the new network. The dominant system as of early 2022 was *4G*.

3G refers to *4G's* predecessor and was still in use in some pockets around the world as of early 2022.

LTE, which stands for *Long Term Evolution*, is often used interchangeably with *4G*, although early versions of *LTE* didn't meet all of the technical requirements of *4G*. *LTE* refers to one of the ways a phone company can deliver *4G* technology. The other, *WiMax*, is rarely used.

3G, 4G, 5G and *LTE* are acceptable on first reference, but should be explained in stories as *cellular networks*. *5G* should be described as *faster, emerging* or *next-generation network*, rather than *fifth generation*.

No certification is required for a phone company to use any of these terms in marketing materials, and some companies have used the *5G* label for services that aren't technically *5G*.

Do not confuse these with *Wi-Fi*, which is a separate wireless technology from cellular and has its own nomenclature.

4K The term typically refers to video with 2,160 lines of vertical resolution, producing sharper images than high-definition video. The name comes from a version that offers 4,096 lines of horizontal resolution, though the term now usually refers to a version with just 3,840 horizontal lines, also known as *ultra-high definition*, or *UHD*. Many TVs now come with 4K capabilities, even though not all movies and shows are available in 4K. 4K is considered a successor to *high-definition video*.

Fourth of July, July Fourth Also *Independence Day*. The federal legal holiday is observed on Friday if July 4 falls on a Saturday, on Monday if it falls on a Sunday.

4x4 *Four-wheel drive* is preferred,

unless *4x4* is part of the car model's proper name.

401(k) (no space)

fracking Acceptable with brief explanation. The energy industry uses the technique to extract oil and gas from rock by injecting high-pressure mixtures of water, sand or gravel and chemicals. See **hydraulic fracturing**.

fractions Generally spell out amounts less than 1 in stories, using hyphens between the words: *two-thirds, four-fifths, seven-sixteenths*, etc.

Use figures for precise amounts larger than 1, converting to decimals whenever practical.

When using fractional characters, use a forward-slash mark (/): 1/8, 1/4, 5/16, 9/10, etc. For mixed numbers, use 1 1/2, 2 5/8, etc. with a full space between the whole number and the fraction. AP systems may automatically replace some fractions with single-character versions: 1/2 may be replaced by ½. These can be left in the form the system changes them to. (You may also choose to set the options on your system so that these replacements are not made.)

See **numerals** and **percent, percentage, percentage points**.

fragment, fragmentary *Fragment* describes a piece or pieces broken from the whole: *She sang a fragment of the song.*

Fragmentary describes disconnected and incomplete parts: *Early returns were fragmentary.*

fraternal organizations and service clubs Capitalize the proper names: *American Legion, Lions Club, Independent Order of Odd Fellows,* *Rotary Club.*

Capitalize also words describing membership: *He is a Legionnaire, a Lion, an Odd Fellow, an Optimist and a Rotarian.* See **American Legion** for the rationale on *Legionnaire.*

Capitalize the formal titles of officeholders when used before a name.

See **titles**.

Freddie Mac A government-controlled company that helps provide money for the U.S. housing market by buying residential mortgages and packaging pools of those loans for sale to investors. The company, whose name is short for *Federal Home Loan Mortgage Corp.,* was seized by the government in September 2008 and is overseen by the Federal Housing Finance Agency.

freelancer (n.) **freelance** (v. and adj.)

freely floating Describes an exchange rate that is allowed to fluctuate in response to supply and demand in the foreign markets.

French Canadian A Canadian whose native language, though not necessarily family origin, is French. In Quebec, the term refers to shared French culture and language among diverse citizens rather than strictly dual heritage. No hyphen.

French Foreign Legion Retain capitalization if shortened to the Foreign Legion.

Lowercase *the legion* and *legionnaires.* Unlike the situation with the American Legion, the French Foreign Legion is a group of active soldiers.

french fries Lowercase *french* because

it refers to the style of cut, not the nation.

frequent flyer

friend, follow, like Acceptable in a social media context as both nouns and verbs. Actions by which users connect to other users on social networks and engage with their content.

Frisbee A trademark for a plastic disc thrown as a toy. Use *Frisbee disc* for the trademarked version and *flying disc* for other generic versions.

front line (n.) front-line (adj.)

front-runner

frosting, icing Either term can be used to describe a topping of sugar, butter and other ingredients applied to cookies, cakes and other pastries. Use of the terms varies regionally in the U.S. Both cookies and cakes can be *glazed* (drizzled with a thin sugar mixture).

fulfill, fulfilled, fulfilling

full- Hyphenate when used to form compound modifiers:

full-dress	*full-page*
full-fledged	*full-scale*
full-length	

See the listings that follow and Webster's New World College Dictionary for the spelling of other combinations.

full-body scanner

full time, full-time Hyphenate when used as a compound modifier: *He works full time. She has a full-time job.*

fulsome It means disgustingly excessive. Do not use it to mean lavish or profuse.

fundraising, fundraiser One word in all cases.

fusillade

futures *Futures* contracts are agreements to deliver a quantity of goods, generally commodities, at a specified price at a certain time in the future. *Options*, which also are widely traded on the nation's commodities exchanges, give buyers the right but not the obligation to buy or sell something at a certain price within a specified period.

The purpose of the futures exchanges is to transfer the risk of price fluctuations from people who don't want the risk, such as farmers or metals processors, to speculators who are willing to take a gamble on making big profits.

Major U.S. commodities markets are the Chicago Board Options Exchange, Chicago Board of Trade, Chicago Mercantile Exchange, New York Mercantile Exchange, the New York Cotton Exchange, and the Coffee, Sugar and Cocoa Exchange.

f

g

GAAP The acronym stands for *generally accepted accounting principles*. Spell out on first reference.

gage, gauge A *gage* is a security or a pledge.

A *gauge* is a measuring device.

Gauge is also a term used to designate the size of shotguns. See **weapons**.

gallon Equal to 128 fluid ounces. The metric equivalent is approximately 3.8 liters. See **imperial gallon**; **liter**; and **metric system**.

gambling Preferred term instead of *gaming* for risking money or some other stake on the outcome of an event: *gambling on blackjack at a casino; gambling on a chess match, gambling on football. Betting* and *wagering* are also acceptable: *betting on a horse race; the friends wagered on a footrace; a betting pool for the NCAA Tournament.* Avoid using the term *gaming* except in direct quotations, in proper names or when referring to video games, as it is often used as a euphemism to downplay gambling.

The terms *sports gambling* and *sports betting* are essentially interchangeable.

gambling revenue Do not confuse gambling revenue with *handle*. Revenue is the money kept by casinos after paying out winners on their wagers. *Handle*, also sometimes known as *drop*, is casino jargon for the amount of money wagered. The difference between revenue and handle in legislative contexts is important because the numbers are vastly different with implications for taxes, fees and other elements of proposed laws.

game plan

gamut, gantlet, gauntlet A *gamut* is a scale of notes or any complete range or extent.

A *gantlet* is a flogging ordeal, literally or figuratively.

A *gauntlet* is a glove. *To throw down the gauntlet* means to issue a challenge. To *take up the gauntlet* means to accept a challenge.

garnish (v. and n.) **garnishee** (n.) *Garnish* means to adorn or decorate. The noun *garnish* is a decoration or ornament. In a legal context, *garnish* means to attach property or wages as a result of a legal action. A *garnishee* is an individual whose property was attached, or garnished.

Gazprom Russia's state-controlled gas monopoly. Corporate name is *OAO Gazprom*. Headquarters is in Moscow.

GED A trademark abbreviation for *General Educational Development* tests, a battery of five exams designed by the American Council on Education to measure high school equivalency. *GED* should be used as an adjective, not as a noun. Those passing the tests earn a *GED diploma* or *certificate*, not a *GED*.

gender, sex and sexual orientation

Gender refers to internal and social identity and often corresponds with but is not synonymous with *sex*. Experts say *gender* is a spectrum, not a *binary* structure consisting of only males and females, that can vary by society and change over time.

Sex refers to biological characteristics, such as chromosomes, hormones and reproductive anatomy, which can also vary or change in understanding over time, or be medically and legally altered.

Since not all people fall under one of two categories for *sex* or *gender* — as in the cases of *nonbinary* and *intersex* people — avoid references to *both*, *either* or *opposite sexes* or *genders*.

Relatedly, not all people use gendered pronouns such as *his* or *hers*. Such pronouns are often an example of *gender expression*, but they do not always align with typical or stereotypical expectations of gender and are not certain indicators of someone's *gender identity*.

Language around gender is ever-evolving. Newsrooms and organizations outside the AP may need to make decisions, based on timing, necessity and audience, on terms that differ from or are not covered by the AP's specific recommendations.

More details and key terms:

gender A social construct encompassing a person's behaviors, intrinsic identity and appearance. Gender often corresponds with but is not synonymous with *sex*. A person's sex and gender are usually assigned at birth by parents or attendants and can turn out to be inaccurate. Experts say gender is a spectrum, not a binary structure consisting of only men and women, that can vary among societies and can change over time. See **gender expression; gender identity; sex; transgender**.

gender identity A person's sense of feeling male, female, neither or some combination of both. Often just *gender* will suffice: *She spent a lot of time explaining her gender* may work just as well as *She spent a lot of time explaining her gender identity*. Examples of gender identities include *man* or *boy*; *woman* or *girl*; *nonbinary*; *bigender*; *agender*; *gender-fluid*; *genderqueer*; and combinations of identities, such as *nonbinary woman*. See **gender; gender expression; LGBTQ; nonbinary; pronouns; transgender**.

gender expression How people outwardly convey their gender, intentionally or not, such as through fashion choices, mannerisms or pronouns. Gender stereotypes can lead others to incorrectly perceive someone's *gender* or *sexual orientation*. See **gender identity; gender-nonconforming; pronouns**.

gender-fluid, gender-fluidity Refers to a gender identity or expression that changes over time. Include the hyphen.

gender-nonconforming (adj.) Acceptable in broad references to describe people whose identities or expressions do not follow gender norms. May include but is not synonymous with *transgender*. Avoid dated terminology such as *gender-bending* or *tomboy*.

genderqueer (adj.) An identity describing people whose gender expression does not follow norms; use only if the person or group identifies as such. Not synonymous with *nonbinary*.

nonbinary (adj.) Describes people

g

g

who don't identify as strictly *male* or *female*; can include *agender* (having no gender), *gender-fluid* (an identity that fluctuates) or a combination of male and female. Not synonymous with *transgender*, though some *nonbinary* people are also *transgender*. See **gender expression**; **gender identity**; **pronouns**.

pronouns See the separate **pronouns** entry.

transgender (adj.) Describes people whose gender does not match the one usually associated with the sex they were assigned at birth. Identify people as *transgender* only when relevant, and use the name by which they live publicly. Unless it is central to the story, avoid mention of a person's *gender transition* or *gender-confirmation surgery* in news coverage, which can be intrusive and insensitive.

Avoid references to a transgender person being born a boy or girl, or phrasing like *birth gender*. *Sex* (or *gender*) *assigned at birth* is the accurate terminology. The shorthand *trans* is acceptable on second reference and in headlines.

Do not use as a noun, such as referring to someone as *a transgender*, or use the term *transgendered*.

Not synonymous with terms like *cross-dresser* or *drag queen*. Do not use the outdated term *transsexual* unless a source specifically asks to be identified as such.

Avoid derogatory terms such as *tranny*. Follow guidelines for **obscenities, profanities, vulgarities** as appropriate.

Refer to a transgender person's previous name, also called a *deadname*, only in the rare instance it is relevant to the story. See **biological**; **deadnaming**; **gender confirmation**; **transition, gender transition**.

cisgender Describes people whose *gender identity* matches the sex they were assigned at birth; that is, not *transgender*. Explain if necessary. Do not use terms like *normal* to describe people who are not *transgender*. Not synonymous with *heterosexual*, which refers to *sexual orientation*. See **transgender**.

deadnaming The practice, widely considered insensitive, offensive or damaging, of referring to transgender people who have changed their name by the name they used before their transition. Use a person's previous name very rarely and only if required to understand the news, or if requested by the person.

The issue of *deadnaming* often arises when public figures announce a gender transition. In such cases, generally use the *deadname* only once and not in the opening paragraph, with future coverage using only the new name.

When naming suspects or victims in stories about crimes or accidents, be cognizant that authorities or family members may be ignorant of or be disregarding the person's wishes; when possible, take into account information given by the person or by current friends or others who may have better information about how the person lived and identified. See **transgender**.

transition (n., v.), **gender transition** The legal, medical or social processes some transgender or nonbinary people undergo to match their *gender identity*. Examples can include a formal or informal change to names or pronouns, makeup and hairstyles, hormone therapy, or gender-confirmation surgery.

Mention or describe it only when relevant. See **gender confirmation**; **transgender**.

gender dysphoria Use this term, not *gender identity disorder*, for the distress felt when someone's *gender expression* does not match their *gender identity*. It is also a medical diagnosis often required for people to undergo *gender confirmation* procedures.

gender confirmation The medical treatments that *transgender* and *nonbinary* people sometimes use to transition, or alter their sexual characteristics. Can include surgery and/or hormone therapy. Sometimes rendered *gender-confirming* as an adjective. Alternatives such as *gender affirmation* and *sex reassignment* are acceptable in quotes and in proper names. If surgery is involved, *gender-confirmation surgery*. Do not use abbreviations such as *GCS* or *SRS* unless in quotes, and introduce the full term before the quote. Do not use the outdated term *sex change*, and avoid describing someone as *pre-op* or *post-op*.

Refer to a person's *gender-confirmation surgery* only when relevant. Surgery is not necessary for people to transition.

transsexual Some people who have undergone *gender-confirmation* procedures refer to themselves as *transsexual*; use the term only if a person requests it. See **gender confirmation**.

biological A word often best confined to medical or scientific contexts, especially in stories or passages about gender. While sex is a biological feature, terms like *biological male, man, female* or *woman* are sometimes used by opponents of transgender rights to portray sex as more simplistic than

scientists assert, and to downplay the significance of *gender* and how it differs from *sex*.

hormones Avoid references to *male* or *female hormones*. All humans have varying levels of sex hormones, including testosterone and estrogen. Hormone replacement therapy may be an element of a person's *gender transition*. See **transition, gender transition**.

cross-dresser Use this term instead of the outdated *transvestite* for someone who wears clothing associated with a different gender, and only when the subject identifies as such. Not synonymous with *drag performer* or *transgender*.

drag performer, drag queen, drag king Entertainers who dress and act as a different gender. *Drag queens* act as women; *drag kings* act as men. *Male impersonator* and *female impersonator* are also acceptable. Not synonymous with *cross-dresser* or *transgender*.

sex Refers to biological and physiological characteristics, including but not limited to chromosomes, hormones and reproductive organs. A person's *sex* is usually assigned at birth by parents or attendants, sometimes inaccurately. *Sex* often corresponds with but is not synonymous with *gender*, which is a social construct. See **gender**; **hormones**; **biological**.

female, male In general, *female* and *male* are adjectives that can describe people of any age and are used only rarely as nouns, such as for a range of ages or an unknown age. *The study included males ages 10-21. She is the first female governor of North Carolina.*

Woman, women, man and *men* are usually reserved for use as a noun to describe adults, while *girl, girls, boy* and *boys* are typically used as a noun

g

for people under age 18.

Be aware of nuances and pitfalls in the use of *female* and *woman/women*.

Since *female* primarily describes sex, not gender, some people object to its use as a descriptor for women because it can be seen as emphasizing biology and reproductive capacity over *gender identity*. It can also sometimes carry misogynistic tones that may vary in severity by race, class and other factors.

For this reason, *woman* or *women* is increasingly common as an adjective. But its use as such can often be awkward, especially if the words *man* or *men* would not be used adjectivally in a parallel sense.

For instance: *He is the only man construction worker on the otherwise all-woman crew* is awkward, and *He is the only male construction worker on the all otherwise all-woman crew* is not parallel. Options for being both sensitive and eloquent include *He is the only man on the otherwise all-woman construction crew*. See **boy, girl**; **gender-neutral language**.

intersex Describes people born with genitalia, chromosomes or reproductive organs that don't fit typical definitions for males or females. Do not use the outdated term *hermaphrodite*. Not synonymous with *nonbinary*.

sexual orientation Not *sexual preference*. Examples include *lesbian* (women attracted to women), *gay* (men attracted to men), *bisexual* (attraction to men and women), *pansexual* (attraction regardless of gender), *asexual* (people who don't experience sexual attraction), and *straight* or *heterosexual* (women attracted to men, and vice versa). Mention a person's *sexual orientation* only when relevant to the subject matter, and do so only if the information is verified.

Avoid references to a *gay* or *alternative lifestyle*. Avoid *homosexual* to describe people, though *homosexuality* is acceptable as a noun for the concept of same-sex attraction. *Gays* is acceptable as a plural noun when necessary, but use the singular *gay* only as an adjective, not as a noun. *Lesbian* is acceptable as an adjective or as a noun in singular or plural form.

Avoid salacious terminology and unnecessary modifiers in phrasing like *gay lovers* or *lesbian kiss*; instead use neutral terms like *couple* or *kiss*.

Transgender is not a sexual orientation. Like anyone, transgender people can have any sexual orientation. See **asexual**; **bisexual**; **LGBTQ**.

LGBTQ (adj.) Acceptable in all references for *lesbian, gay, bisexual, transgender and queer and/or questioning*. In quotations and the formal names of organizations and events, other variations such as *LGBTQIA* are also acceptable with the other letters explained. *I* generally stands for *intersex*, and *A* can stand for *asexual* (a person who doesn't experience sexual attraction), *ally* (some activists decry this use of the abbreviation for a person who is not LGBTQ but who actively supports LGBTQ communities) or both. Use of *LGBTQ* is best as an adjective and an umbrella term: *Walters joined the LGBTQ business association*. Avoid it to describe individuals or, for instance, if the group you're referring to is limited to bisexuals. *Queer* is often used as an umbrella term covering people who are not *heterosexual* or *cisgender* and is acceptable for people and organizations that use the term to identify themselves. Do not use it when intended as a slur. Follow guidelines for **obscenities, profanities, vulgarities** as appropriate. See **sexual orientation; gender identity**.

asexual Describes people who don't experience sexual attraction, though they may feel other types of attraction, such as romantic or aesthetic. Not synonymous with and does not assume celibacy. A person's asexuality can be constant or change over time. See **sexual orientation**.

bisexual (n. and adj.) Describes people attracted to men and women. The shortened form *bi* is acceptable in quotations. See **sexual orientation**.

conversion therapy The scientifically discredited practice of using therapy to "convert" LGBTQ people to heterosexuality or traditional gender expectations. Either refer to it as *so-called conversion therapy* or put quotation marks around it. Do not do both. *Gay conversion therapy* should take no hyphen. Always include the disclaimer that it is discredited. See **so called, so-called**.

homophobia, homophobic Acceptable in broad references or in quotations to the concept of fear or hatred of gays, lesbians and bisexuals. *The governor denounced homophobia.* In individual cases, be specific about observable actions; avoid descriptions or language that assume motives. *The leaflets contained an anti-gay slur. The voters opposed same-sex marriage.* Related terms include *biphobia* (fear or hatred of bisexuals) and *transphobia* (fear or hatred of transgender people).

openly, out The terms *out* and *openly* can imply that to identify as *LGBTQ* is inherently shameful, so use them only when relevant: *Xiong is the group's first openly gay president* (which would allow for the possibility that previous presidents were gay but not *out*) or *Xiong, who came out at age 29, wishes he had done so sooner.*

Do not use terms like *avowed* or *admitted*.

Don't assume that because news figures address their *sexual orientation* or *gender transition* publicly, it qualifies as *coming out*; public figures may consider themselves *out* even if they haven't previously addressed their identity or orientation publicly.

Outing or *outed* is usually used when someone's identity or orientation is revealed against their knowledge or will.

same-sex marriage The preferred term over *gay marriage*, because it is more inclusive and because the laws generally don't address sexual orientation. Where legal, *same-sex marriages* do not differ from other marriages, so the term should be used only when relevant and needed to distinguish from marriages of other couples.

sexual identity People's awareness of themselves in a sexual sense. It incorporates a person's *sex, gender identity, gender expression* and *sexual orientation*. See **SOGI**.

SOGI Increasingly popular shorthand for the concept of *sexual orientation and gender identity*. Avoid using the acronym unless necessary, as in a quote or name of an organization, and explain the term if used. See **sexual identity**.

For a partial list of print and online resources used by the Stylebook team, see the **Bibliography**.

gender-neutral language In general, use terms for jobs and roles that can apply to any gender. Such language aims to treat people equally and is inclusive of people whose gender identity is not strictly male or female.

Balance these aims with common sense, respect for the language, and an understanding that gender-neutral or gender-inclusive language is evolving and in some cases is challenging to achieve.

Consider any word or term that has the effect of emphasizing one gender over another. Is there another word that could be substituted? For example: *search* instead of *manhunt. Police officer* instead of *policeman. Door attendant* instead of *doorman.*

A true gender-neutral noun often presents itself easily: *chair* or *chairperson, firefighter, workforce.* In other cases, a noun may technically not be gender-neutral but instead be a masculine noun that assumes the generic case under English language convention: *actor, host.*

In general, use terms such as *chair* or *chairperson, councilperson* or *council member,* and *spokesperson* unless the *-man* or *-woman* terms are specified by an organization. *Councilmember* is acceptable in jurisdictions that have adopted the one-word version.

Mother/father, son/daughter, sister/ brother, husband/wife, girlfriend/ boyfriend and other relationship terms are generally acceptable. But *parent, child, sibling, spouse* are acceptable if preferred by an individual. Also: *fiance/fiancee* and *divorce/divorcee* are acceptable if relevant.

While some *-person* constructions, such as *chairperson* and *spokesperson,* are commonly used, avoid tortured or unfamiliar constructions such as *snowperson, baseperson* or *freshperson.* Similarly, don't use *siblinghood* in place of *brotherhood* or *sisterhood.*

The terms *U.S. representative, representative, member of Congress* are preferred. *Congressman* and *congresswoman* are acceptable because of their common use. Do not use *congressperson.*

Sports terms such as *man-to-man defense* and *third baseman* are acceptable for both men's and women's events, though often rephrasing is better: *She plays third base.* Royal titles such as *princess, duchess* and *lady* are standard. Also acceptable: *goddess* in religious or mythology references.

Unless *city leaders* (not *city fathers*) decide otherwise, Philadelphia remains the *City of Brotherly Love.* History recognizes the seven *Founding Fathers* of the United States. *Frosty the Snowman* is the character's name, though *Frosty* can work as shorthand.

Here are some other examples of preferred usage. Some are new to the Stylebook. Others are changes from past style. This list is not all-inclusive; it can serve as a framework by which to consider other words. Multiple terms are not necessarily interchangeable. Choose what is appropriate and accurate in the context.

actor In general, use this term for any gender. Use *actress* for a woman only in stories about the Oscars, Emmys or Tonys, all of which use the word *actress* in their awards.

alumnus, alumni, alumna, alumnae, alum The terms *alumnus* (s.) and *alumni* (pl.) for men, and *alumna* (s.) and *alumnae* (pl.) for women, are acceptable. If a gender-neutral term is desired, *alum* or *alums* is acceptable.

blond Use *blond* as an adjective in all applications when relevant: *She has blond hair.* Avoid using either *blond* or *blonde* as a noun: *He has blond hair*, not *he is a blond.* If necessary to use as a noun in a direct quote, use *blond* for any gender.

brown (hair) Use *brown* as an adjective in all applications when relevant: *She has brown hair.* Avoid using *brunette* as a noun unless in a direct quote. *She has brown hair*, not *she is a brunette.*

business owner, businessperson Not *businessman/businesswoman.*

busser Not *busboy* or *busgirl.*

city leaders Not *city fathers.*

confidant Not *confidante.*

crew, staff, workforce, workers Not *manpower.*

dancer, ballet dancer But *ballerina* is acceptable because of broad use by dancers.

firefighter Not *fireman.*

first-year student *Freshman* is acceptable. Do not use *freshperson* or *freshwoman. First-term lawmakers* is preferred over *freshman lawmakers.*

hero Not *heroine.*

host Not *hostess.*

humanity, humankind, humans, human beings, people Not *mankind.*

human-made, human-caused, artificial, synthetic Not *man-made.*

maintenance hole Not *manhole.*

mail carrier or **letter carrier** Not *mailman.*

police officer Not *policeman/policewoman* or *patrolman.*

salesperson, sales associate, sales clerk, sales executive Not *salesman/saleswoman.*

search Not *manhunt.*

server Not *waiter/waitress.*

singer, songwriter, singer/songwriter Not *songstress.*

gender-nonconforming (adj.) See **gender and sexuality**.

general assembly See **legislature** for its treatment as the name of a state's legislative body.

Capitalize when it is the formal name for the ruling or consultative body of an organization: *the General Assembly of the World Council of Churches.*

General Assembly (U.N.) *General Assembly* may be used on the first reference in a story under a United Nations dateline.

Use *U.N. General Assembly* in other first references, *the General Assembly* or *the assembly* in subsequent references.

general court Part of the official proper name for the legislatures in Massachusetts and New Hampshire. Capitalize specific references with or without the state name: *the Massachusetts General Court, the General Court.*

In keeping with the accepted practice, however, *Legislature* may be used instead and treated as a proper name. See **legislature**.

Lowercase *legislature* in a generic use such as: *The General Court is the legislature in Massachusetts.*

general manager Capitalize only as a formal title before a name: corporate *General Manager Jim Smith.* Lowercase as a job description for sports teams: *Giants general manager Jerry Reese.*

See **titles**.

General Services Administration *GSA* is acceptable on second reference.

g

generations First there was the *Silent Generation*, the children of the Great Depression. Then, more than 16 million Americans fought in World War II, and their pent-up desire to start families at war's end unleashed the *baby boom* — more than 78 million births between the years 1946 and 1964, as defined by the U.S. Census Bureau.

The *baby boomers* begat *Generation X*, which begat *millennials*, also known as *Generation Y*, which begat *Generation Z* (*Gen X, Gen Y* and *Gen Z* are acceptable on second reference, and their members are called *Gen Xers, Gen Yers* and *Gen Zers*). The next generation, the first born wholly in the 21st century, has been called *Generation Alpha*.

The generations that preceded and followed the baby boom have no officially designated beginnings or endings. The Pew Research Center defines the *Silent Generation* as those born between 1928 and 1945, *Generation X* as 1965 to 1980, *millennials* as 1981 to 1996, and *Generation Z* as 1997 to 2012. But it also cautions that those eras are inexact. The time period should be specified when possible.

While each of these generations shares common experiences — many baby boomers recall the day President John F. Kennedy was assassinated, and Sept. 11, 2001, is a millennial milestone — they are too often stereotyped as sharing common characteristics. Avoid pronouncements that any generation is materialistic or apathetic or altruistic.

Geneva Conventions Note the final *s*.

gentile Generally, any person not Jewish; often, specifically a Christian.

gentleman Do not use as a synonym for *man*. See **lady**.

genus, species In scientific or biological names, capitalize the first, or generic, Latin name for the class of plant or animal and lowercase the species that follows: *Homo sapiens, Tyrannosaurus rex.*

In second references, use the abbreviated form: *P. borealis, T. rex.*

geographic names The basic guidelines:

DOMESTIC: Do not use the postal abbreviations for state names. For acceptable abbreviations, see entries in this book under each state's name. See **state names** for rules on when the abbreviations may be used.

Abbreviate *Saint* as *St.* (But abbreviate *Sault Sainte Marie* as *Sault Ste. Marie.*)

FOREIGN: The first source for the spelling of all foreign place names is Webster's New World College Dictionary as follows:

— Use the first-listed spelling if an entry gives more than one.
— If the dictionary provides different spellings in separate entries, use the spelling that is followed by a full description of the location.

If the dictionary does not have an entry, use the first-listed spelling in the National Geographic Atlas of the World.

Online: http://maps.nationalgeographic.com/maps

NEW NAMES: Follow the styles adopted by the United Nations and the U.S. Board on Geographic Names for new cities, new independent nations and nations that change their names.

DATELINES: See the **datelines** entry.

CAPITALIZATION: Capitalize common nouns when they form an integral part of a proper name, but lowercase them when they stand alone: *Pennsylvania Avenue, the avenue; the Philippine Islands, the islands; the Mississippi River, the river.*

Lowercase common nouns that are not a part of a specific name: *the Pacific islands, the Swiss mountains, Zhejiang province.*

For additional guidelines, see **addresses; capitalization; directions and regions;** and **island.**

geolocation, geotagging The act of adding geographical metadata to pieces of media, social media updates or other digital content. Also, the use of a user's physical location to determine access to certain information. The metadata itself is an item's *geolocation* or *geotag.* A *geotagged* tweet, post, photo or video would contain information about the latitude and longitude of the location where the photo was taken, or possibly the name of the city and/or country, or of a landmark or establishment where the user has chosen to check in.

German measles Also known as *rubella.*

ghetto, ghettos Do not use indiscriminately as a synonym for the sections of cities inhabited by minorities or poor people. *Ghetto* has a connotation that government decree has forced people to live in a certain area.

In most cases, *section, district, slum area* or *quarter* is the more accurate word. See **race-related coverage.**

gibe, jibe To *gibe* means *to taunt or sneer*: *They gibed him about his mistakes.*

Jibe means *to shift direction* or, colloquially, *to agree*: *They jibed their ship across the wind. Their stories didn't jibe.*

Gibraltar, Strait of Not *Straits.* The entrance to the Mediterranean from the Atlantic Ocean. The British colony on the peninsula that juts into the strait stands alone in datelines as *GIBRALTAR.*

GIF Acronym for *Graphics Interchange Format,* a compression format for images. *GIF* is acceptable in copy but should be explained in the story. Use lowercase in a file name. For guidance on quoting social media posts with *GIFs,* see **quotations in the news.**

giga- A prefix denoting 1 billion units of a measure.

gig economy Job-to-job employment with little security and few employment rights. Include a brief explanation in the text if used.

GI, GIs Believed to have originated as an abbreviation for *government issue* supplies, it describes military personnel in general, but normally is used for the Army. (No periods is an exception to the general rule for two-letter abbreviations.)

Soldier is preferred unless the story contains the term in quoted matter or involves a subject such as the *GI Bill of Rights.*

Ginnie Mae Commonly used for *Government National Mortgage Association.*

Girl Scouts The full name of the national organization is *Girl Scouts of the United States of America.* Headquarters is in New York. Note that *Girl Scout Cookies* is a trademark name.
See **Boy Scouts**.

glamour One of the few *our* endings still used in American writing. But the adjective is *glamorous.*

globe-trotter, globe-trotting But the proper name of the basketball team is the *Harlem Globetrotters.*

GMT For *Greenwich Mean Time.* Also referred to as *Coordinated Universal Time* or *UTC.* See **time zones** and **meridians.**

godchild, goddaughter Also: *godfather, godliness, godmother, godsend* and *godson.* Always lowercase.

gods and goddesses Capitalize *God* in references to the deity of all monotheistic religions. Capitalize all noun references to the deity: *God the Father, Holy Ghost, Holy Spirit, Allah,* etc. Lowercase personal pronouns.
Lowercase *gods* and *goddesses* in references to the deities of polytheistic religions.
Lowercase *god, gods* and *goddesses* in references to false gods: *He made money his god.*
See **religious references** section of the **Religion** chapter.

Godspeed

-goer One word. Examples: *concertgoer, moviegoer, partygoer, theatergoer.*

Good Friday The Friday before Easter.

good Samaritan But uppercase when used in a title: *Good Samaritan Hospital.*

good, well *Good* is an adjective that means something is as it should be or is better than average.
When used as an adjective, *well* means suitable, proper, healthy. When used as an adverb, *well* means in a satisfactory manner or skillfully.
Good should not be used as an adverb. It does not lose its status as an adjective in a sentence such as *I feel good.* Such a statement is the idiomatic equivalent of *I am in good health.* An alternative, *I feel well,* could be interpreted as meaning that your sense of touch is good.
See **bad, badly.**

goodwill One word in all uses.

Google Cloud, Google Docs, Google Drive, Google Sheets But *Google's cloud services.*

GOP Grand Old Party. *GOP* is acceptable on second reference for *Republican Party.*

Gospel(s), gospel Capitalize when referring to any or all of the first four books of the New Testament: *the Gospel of St. John, the Gospels.*
Lowercase in other references: *She is a famous gospel singer.*

gourmand, gourmet A *gourmand* is a person who likes good food and tends to eat to excess; a *glutton.* A *gourmet* is a person who likes fine food and is an excellent judge of food and drink.

government Always lowercase, never abbreviate: *the federal government, the state government, the U.S. government.*

Government Accountability Office

A nonpartisan congressional agency that audits federal programs. *GAO* is acceptable on second reference.

governmental bodies Follow these guidelines:

FULL NAME: Capitalize the full proper names of governmental agencies, departments and offices: *The U.S. Department of State, the Georgia Department of Human Resources, the Boston City Council, the Chicago Fire Department.*

WITHOUT JURISDICTION: Retain capitalization in referring to a specific body if the dateline or context makes the name of the nation, state, county, city, etc. unnecessary: *The Department of State* (in a story from Washington), *the Department of Human Resources* or *the state Department of Human Resources* (in a story from Georgia), *the City Council* (in a story from Boston), *the Fire Department* or *the city Fire Department* (in a story from Chicago).

Lowercase further condensations of the name: *the department, the council*, etc.

For additional guidance see **assembly**; **city council**; **committee**; **Congress**; **legislature**; **House of Representatives**; **Senate**; **Supreme Court of the United States**; and **supreme courts of the states**.

FLIP-FLOPPED NAMES: Retain capital names for the name of a governmental body if its formal name is flopped to delete the word *of*: *the State Department, the Human Resources Department.*

GENERIC EQUIVALENTS: If a generic term has become the equivalent of a proper name in popular use, treat it as a proper name: *Walpole State Prison*, for example, even though the proper name is the *Massachusetts Correctional Institute-Walpole.*

For additional examples, see **legislature**; **police department**; and **prison, jail**.

PLURALS, NONSPECIFIC REFERENCES: All words that are capitalized when part of a proper name should be lowercased when they are used in the plural or do not refer to a specific, existing body. Some examples:

All states except Nebraska have a state senate. The town does not have a fire department. The bill requires city councils to provide matching funds. The president will address the lower houses of the New York and New Jersey legislatures.

NON-U.S. BODIES: The same principles apply.

Capitalize the names of the specific governmental agencies and departments, either with the name of the nation or without it if clear in the context: *French Foreign Ministry, the Foreign Ministry.*

Lowercase *the ministry* or a similar term when standing alone.

government, junta, regime, administration A *government* is

an established system of political administration: *the U.S. government.*

A *junta* is a group or council that often rules after a coup: *A military junta controls the nation.* A *junta* becomes a government after it establishes a system of political administration.

A *regime* is a form of political system, generally an oppressive or undemocratic one: *an authoritarian regime, a communist regime.* The word regime should be used only in general terms. Do not use in references to a specific country or leader: *the North Korean regime,*

Assad's regime.

An *administration* consists of officials who make up the executive branch of a government: *the Reagan administration.*

governor Capitalize and abbreviate as *Gov.* or *Govs.* when used as a formal title before one or more names.

See the next entry and **titles**.

governor general, governors general The formal title for the British sovereign's representatives in Canada and some other countries of the Commonwealth.

Do not abbreviate in any use.

GPA Acceptable in all references for *grade-point average.*

GPS Acceptable in all references to *Global Positioning System*. If a descriptive word is used following, use it in lowercase: *the GPS satellite.*

grade, grader No hyphen in most cases: *a fourth grade student, first grader, she is in the fifth grade.* (A change in 2019.) Do hyphenate if needed to avoid confusion, such when combined with another ordinal number: *He was the sixth fourth-grade student to win the prize; she is the 10th third-grader to join.*

graduate (v.) *Graduate* is correctly used in the active voice: *She graduated from the university.*

It is correct, but unnecessary, to use the passive voice: *He was graduated from the university.*

Do not, however, drop *from*: *John Adams graduated from Harvard.* Not: *John Adams graduated Harvard.*

grain The smallest unit in the system of weights that has been used in the United States. It originally was defined as the weight of 1 grain of wheat.

It takes 437.5 grains to make an ounce. There are 7,000 grains to a pound.

See **ounce (weight)** and **pound**.

gram The basic unit of mass in the metric system. It is equal to approximately one-twenty-eighth of an ounce. See **metric system**.

Grammy Awards Presented annually by the Recording Academy. Also known as *the Grammys*. The Latin Grammys celebrate the best in Latin music from across the globe.

granddad, granddaughter Also: *grandfather, grandmother, grandson, grandma*, etc. See **family names**.

grand jury Always lowercase: *a Los Angeles County grand jury, the grand jury.*

This style has been adopted because, unlike the case with city council and similar governmental units, a jurisdiction frequently has more than one grand jury session.

grant-in-aid, grants-in-aid

grassroots (n., adj.) One word for uses such as: *The candidate launched a grassroots campaign; she hopes to appeal to the grassroots.*

gray Not *grey*. But: *greyhound*.

great- Hyphenate *great-grandfather, great-great-grandmother*, etc.

Use *great grandfather* only if the intended meaning is that the grandfather was a great man.

Great Britain It consists of England,

Scotland and Wales, but not Northern Ireland.

Britain is acceptable in all references.

See **United Kingdom**.

greater Capitalize when used to define a community and its surrounding region: *Greater Boston*.

Great Plains Capitalize *Great Plains* or *the Plains* when referring to the U.S. prairie lands that extend from North Dakota to Texas and from the Rocky Mountains east to the Mississippi River valley. Use *northern Plains, southwestern Plains*, etc., when referring to a portion of the region.

Great Recession The recession that began in December 2007 and became the longest and deepest since the Great Depression of the 1930s. It occurred after losses on subprime mortgages battered the U.S. housing market. The National Bureau of Economic Research said it officially ended in June 2009, having lasted 18 months.

gringo A derogatory term for a foreigner, especially an American, in parts of Latin America. Use only in direct quotes when essential to the story.

grisly, grizzly *Grisly* is horrifying, repugnant.

Grizzly means grayish or is a short form for *grizzly bear*.

gross domestic product The sum of all goods and services produced within a nation's borders. In the U.S., it is calculated quarterly by the Commerce Department.

Lowercase in all uses, but *GDP* is acceptable in later references.

Groundhog Day Feb. 2.

groundswell

ground zero

group Takes singular verbs and pronouns: *The group is reviewing its position.*

G-7 Use a hyphen in the abbreviated form for the *Group of Seven*, made up of representatives of the major industrial nations, Britain, Canada, France, Germany, Italy, Japan and the United States. Russia was suspended from the Group of Eight in March 2014. A general description rather than the full name is preferred on first reference: *Leading industrial nations*. See **G-20**.

G-20 Use a hyphen in the abbreviated form for the *Group of 20*, made up of representatives of industrial and emerging-market nations. A general description rather than the full name is preferred on first reference: *Leading rich and developing nations*. Members are the European Union and the following 19 countries: Argentina, Australia, Brazil, Britain, Canada, China, France, Germany, India, Indonesia, Italy, Japan, Mexico, Russia, Saudi Arabia, South Africa, South Korea, Turkey and the United States.

Guadalupe (Mexico)

Guadeloupe (West Indies)

Guam Use in datelines after the name of a community. See **datelines**.

Guangzhou City in China formerly known as Canton.

guarantee Preferred to *guaranty*, except in proper names.

guardsman See **National Guard** and **Coast Guardsman**.

gubernatorial

guerrilla Unorthodox soldiers and their tactics.

guest Do not use as a verb except in quoted matter.

Guinness World Records The book is published by Guinness World Records Ltd.

Gulf Cooperation Council A regional bloc, based in Riyadh, Saudi Arabia, and representing Bahrain, Kuwait, Oman, Qatar, Saudi Arabia and the United Arab Emirates. Formed in 1981, the council makes economic policies across these Gulf nations and serves as a Sunni-led Arab counterweight to Shiite power Iran. *GCC* is acceptable on second reference.

Gulf, Gulf Coast Capitalize when referring to the region of the United States lying along the Gulf of Mexico. Also: *Mexico's Gulf Coast* or *Gulf Coast of Mexico*.
     See **coast**.

Gulf Stream But the racetrack is *Gulfstream Park*.

gunbattle, gunboat, gunfight, gunfire, gunpoint, gunpowder

h

habeas corpus A writ ordering a person in custody to be brought before a court. It places the burden of proof on those detaining the person to justify the detention.

When *habeas corpus* is used in a story, define it.

hacker The term is commonly used to describe someone who penetrates computer systems without authorization, although the term originally referred to anyone with expertise in programming and tinkering with technology to explore new uses.

Hades But lowercase *hell*.

Hague, The In datelines:
THE HAGUE, *Netherlands* (AP) —
In text: *The Hague.*

hajj The pilgrimage to Mecca required once in a lifetime of every Muslim who can afford it and is physically able to make it. Some Muslims make the journey more than once. The hajj occurs once a year during the Islamic lunar month of Dhul-Hijja, the 12th and final month of the Islamic calendar year. The person making the *hajj* is a *hajji* (male) or *hajjah* (female).

half It is not necessary to use the preposition *of*: *half the time* is correct, but *half of the time* is not wrong.

half- Follow Webster's New World College Dictionary. Hyphenate if not listed there.

Some frequently used words without a hyphen:
halfback	*halftone*
halfhearted	*halftrack*

Also: *halftime*, in keeping with widespread practice in sports copy.

Some frequently used combinations that are two words without a hyphen:
half brother	*half size*
half dollar	

Some frequently used combinations that include a hyphen:
half-baked	*half-life*
half-cocked	*half-mile*
half-dozen	*half-moon*
half-hour	*half-truth*

half-mast, half-staff On ships and at naval stations ashore, flags are flown at *half-mast*.

Elsewhere ashore, flags are flown at *half-staff*.

hallelujah Lowercase the biblical praise to God, but capitalize in composition titles: Handel's "Hallelujah" chorus.

Halley's comet After Edmund Halley, an English astronomer who predicted the comet's appearance once every 75 years. It was last seen in 1985-86.

Hamas A Palestinian Islamic political party, which has an armed wing of the same name. The word is an acronym for the Arabic words for *Islamic Resistance Movement.*

handicap, handicapped Do not use those terms for a disability or a person. Avoid uses such as *handicapped parking*; instead, *accessible parking*. Terms such as *golf handicap* or *handicapping a race* are acceptable. See **disabilities**.

handle A self-selected, public-facing username on a social network. May be used interchangeably with *username*.

hangar, hanger A *hangar* is a building. A *hanger* is used for clothes.

hang, hanged, hung One *hangs* a picture, a criminal or oneself.
For past tense or the passive, use *hanged* when referring to executions or suicides, *hung* for other actions.

Hannover The spelling of the German city.

Hanukkah The Jewish Festival of Lights, an eight-day commemoration of rededication of the Temple by the Maccabees after their victory over the Syrians.
Usually occurs in December but sometimes falls in late November.

happy holidays, merry Christmas, season's greetings, happy birthday, happy new year Lowercase except in exclamations (*Christmas* is always capitalized): *Have a happy new year, wishing you a merry Christmas, sending season's greetings your way.* In exclamations: *Happy holidays! Merry Christmas! Season's greetings! Happy New Year!* (*New Year* is up in this use for the Jan. 1 holiday.) *Happy birthday!* See **New Year's, New Year's Day, New Year's Eve, Happy New Year**.

Haqqani network Militant Islamic group based in Pakistan that seeks to establish Islamic law in Afghanistan.

harass, harassment

harelip Avoid. *Cleft lip* is preferred.

hard line (n.) **hard-liner** (n.) **hard-line** (adj.)

hashtag A term starting with a number or hash sign (#) in a social network post. It conveys the subject of the post so that it can be easily found by users interested in that subject. For example, the hashtag #UNGA is commonly used for the annual meeting of the U.N. General Assembly. A hashtag needs to be an uninterrupted string of characters, with no spaces.
The use of hashtags has evolved to also reflect a post's tone. For example, a user may add #sarcasm or #feelingstupid to help describe the nature of a post.
When tweeting or posting, take note that the use of a hashtag associated with a movement or cause could be interpreted as a sign of support. AP journalists should avoid this, unless the hashtag itself is the subject of the post. In stories, write the hashtag as it would appear on a social network: *The #Jan25 hashtag was credited with spreading support for the Egyptian uprising in its early days.*

Hawaii Standard Time The time zone used in Hawaii. There is no daylight saving time in Hawaii.

HDMI Acceptable on all references for *high-definition multimedia interface*, a system of cables and connectors used to transmit and receive high-definition video. Commonly used to connect DVD players, digital video recorders and other video devices to television sets.

HDR Abbreviation for high-dynamic range. *HDR* is acceptable on first reference, but should be explained in the story.
In video playback: A display feature that permits brighter whites and darker blacks. *HDR* can refer to television sets, tablets and other displays with the capability. Video adapted for *HDR* use such formats as *HDR10* and *Dolby Vision*. *HDR* displays and video also typically produce a wider range of colors, although that is technically not part of *HDR*.
In photography: A camera feature that automatically blends multiple shots of the same subject taken at different exposures in order to prevent bright areas from being too bright and dark areas from being too dark. Some smartphones now have the feature on by default, so the user doesn't need to activate it ahead of time.

headlines Headlines are key to any story. A vivid, accurate and fair headline can entice people to dig in for more. A bland, vague or otherwise faulty headline can push readers away. Often, a headline and photo are all that many readers see of a story. Their entire knowledge of the piece may be based on those elements.
Headlines must stand on their own in conveying the story fairly, and they must include key context. They should tempt readers to want to read more, without misleading or overpromising.
Other points:
— Match the headline's tone to the story's: Most serious, hard news stories demand serious headlines; lighter stories call for clever, witty and creative approaches. Sometimes a lighter headline can work on serious stories, but use judgment.
— Attribute carefully. Attribution is as important in headlines as in stories.
— Think carefully about keywords, search engine optimization and social media optimization. What terms are readers likely to be searching for, or what will be easily recognizable and compelling in a print headline? Include keywords that are central to the story's content, and consider what keywords relevant to the story are trending in search engines and social media.
— Update headlines intended for online use as often as needed to reflect the latest news.
— Capitalize only the first word and proper nouns in headlines that use AP style. Exception: The first word after a colon is always uppercase in headlines.
— Always capitalize the first letter of a headline, even if it starts with a proper name such as *iPhone* or *eBay*, though recasting may be the better choice.
— Avoid abbreviations and alphabet soup. Use only very universally recognized abbreviations. US, UK, UN and EU (no periods) are acceptable. Other acceptable shorthand includes *FBI, CIA, IRS, SEC.*
— Avoid abbreviating state names when possible in headlines on AP stories. If the shorter version is essential for space reasons, do not use periods in those abbreviated with two capital

h

letters: *NY, NJ, NH, NM, NC, SC, ND, SD* and *RI*. Also *DC*. Other state abbreviations retain periods: *Ga., Ky., Mont., Conn.,* etc. Do not use postal codes.

— Use numerals; do not spell out numbers except in casual uses or formal names: *hundreds* instead of *100s*; *Big Ten*; *one of the first*. Use numerals for ordinals: *2nd, 9th*, etc.

— Use single quote marks, never double quote marks.

— Label opinion or analysis pieces. AP headlines for news analyses must begin with *Analysis:* and reviews must begin with *Review:*

— Make every word and every character count. AP headlines are limited to 60 characters; use those characters wisely. Try to make each headline as close to the maximum length as possible.

— For AP audiences, write headlines with a global online audience in mind. Locators are not needed for every headline. But use locators when the place name is likely to increase the chances of someone wanting to read the story, likely to be searched for by readers online, or when needed to understand the story (i.e, to differentiate between a federal Supreme Court vs. state Supreme Court decision).

Other headline tips:

— Co. Try not to use this or *cos.* to abbreviate for company or companies.

— Federal Reserve. *Fed* is acceptable in headlines.

— Government. Do not abbreviate.

— Millions, billions. These figures can be abbreviated in headlines. For example, *$45 million* would be *$45M*, and *$5 billion* would be *$5B*.

— Periods: Avoid using them when abbreviations are necessary: *AP* (a trademark), *GI, ID, EU*, etc.

— Quarters. Use Q4, not 4Q.

head-on (adj. and adv.)

headquarters May take a singular or a plural verb.

headscarf, headscarves

health care

hearsay

heart attack, heart failure, cardiac arrest A *heart attack* (myocardial infarction) occurs when one or more arteries supplying blood to the heart become blocked. *Heart failure* is a chronic condition that occurs when a weakened heart can no longer effectively pump blood. *Cardiac arrest*, or *sudden cardiac arrest*, occurs when the heart suddenly stops beating. It can be due to a *heart attack*, a heart rhythm problem, or as a result of trauma.

heaven

heavenly bodies Capitalize the proper names of planets, stars, constellations, etc.: *Mars, Arcturus, the Big Dipper, Aries*. See **Earth**.

Lowercase *red planet* when referring to Mars.

For comets, capitalize only the proper noun element of the name: *Halley's comet*.

Lowercase *sun* and *moon*.

Capitalize nouns and adjectives derived from the proper names of planets: *Martian, Venusian*, but lowercase adjectives derived from other heavenly bodies: *solar, lunar*.

hect- (before a vowel), **hecto-** (before

a consonant) A prefix denoting 100 units of a measure.

hectare A unit of surface measure in the metric system equal to 100 acres or 10,000 square meters.
See **acre** and **metric system**.

hedge fund Unregulated funds that pool money from wealthy investors and trade in everything from commodities to real estate to complex derivative investments. The private investment funds use sophisticated techniques to try to achieve higher returns than the stock market.

hedging The act of protecting an investment (in a stock, commodity or other) from potential losses by simultaneously investing in another asset that tends to appreciate in value when the first investment falls. For example, to protect an investment in stocks, one could invest part of a portfolio in bonds, which tend to move in the opposite direction of stocks.

hell But capitalize *Hades*.

Hells Angels

hemisphere Capitalize *Northern Hemisphere*, *Western Hemisphere*, etc.
Lowercase *hemisphere* in other uses: *the Eastern and Western hemispheres, the hemisphere*.

hemorrhage The word *bleed* can be used instead in most cases.

her Do not use this pronoun in reference to nations, ships, storms or voice assistants except in direct quotes. Use *it* instead.

here The word is frequently redundant, particularly in the lead of a datelined story. Use only if there is some specific need to stress that the event being reported took place in the community.
If the location must be stressed in the body of the story, repeat the name of the datelined community, both for the reader's convenience and to avoid problems if the story is topped with a different dateline.

Her Majesty Capitalize when it appears in quotations or is appropriate before a name as the long form of a formal title.
For other purposes, use the woman's name or *the queen*.
See **nobility**.

heroes

hertz This term, the same in singular or plural, has been adopted as the international unit of frequency equal to one cycle per second.
In contexts where it would not be understood by most readers, it should be followed by a parenthetical explanation: *15,400 hertz (cycles per second)*.
Do not abbreviate.

Hezbollah The Lebanese Shiite Muslim political party, which has an armed wing of the same name. The word means *party of God* in Arabic.

high blood pressure Preferred term. Avoid using *hypertension*.

high definition (n.) **high-definition** (adj.) The term refers to video with at least 720 lines of vertical resolution. *HD* is acceptable on second reference. *HDTV* is acceptable on second reference for a

h

high-definition television set. A U.S. DVD or analog TV broadcast has 480 lines of vertical resolution — neither is HD. Many newer TVs have even sharper resolution, with 2,160 lines of vertical resolution, also known as *4K*, although not all movies and shows are available in *4K*.

high functioning, low functioning

Avoid these vague terms in reference to people with disabilities. Instead, be specific about the condition, and use descriptions of people's ability levels only when relevant to the story. See **disabilities**.

high tech (n.) high-tech (adj.)

highway designations

Use these forms, as appropriate in the context, for highways identified by number: *U.S. Highway 1, U.S. Route 1, U.S. 1, state Route 34, Route 34, Interstate Highway 495, Interstate 495*. On second reference only for *Interstate*: *I-495*.

When a letter is appended to a number, capitalize it but do not use a hyphen: *Route 1A*.

See **addresses** and **numerals**.

hijab

The headscarf worn by some Muslim women. The *h* is pronounced, so it takes the article *a*: *She wore a hijab*. See also other garments such as **niqab**; **burqa**; **chador**.

hike

Acceptable as a verb for increasing or raising prices sharply.

hillbilly

Usually a derogatory term for an Appalachian backwoods or mountain person. Avoid unless in direct quotes or special context.

HIPAA

Where possible avoid using the term, which is an acronym for the Health Insurance Portability and Accountability Act of 1996. Instead refer to *privacy laws* or *the federal law restricting release of medical information*. If *HIPAA* is used in a quote, explain it.

Hiroshima

On Aug. 6, 1945, this Japanese city and military base were the targets of the first atomic bomb dropped as a weapon. The explosion had the force of 15,000 tons (15 kilotons) of TNT. It destroyed more than 4 square miles and killed 140,000 people, according to an official count taken between August and December 1945. Hiroshima city officials say the toll may exceed 290,000 if including those who died after December 1945 of non-acute injuries or radiation.

Three days later, on Aug. 9, 1945, the U.S. dropped a second atomic bomb, on Nagasaki. The explosion, which had the force of 22,000 tons (22 kilotons) of TNT, destroyed one-third of the city and killed more than 70,000 people by December 1945, according to an official count.

his, her, he, she

Do not presume maleness in constructing a sentence. Do not use constructions such as *his/her, his or her, he or she*, etc.

As much as possible, AP uses *they/them/their* as a way of accurately describing and representing a person who uses those pronouns for themself. See the **pronouns** entry for more detail and guidance.

That entry also says:

When necessary, use *they* rather than *he/she* or *he or she* for an unspecified or unknown gender (*a person, the victim, the winner*) or indefinite pronoun (*anyone, everyone, someone*). But rewording to avoid a pronoun is preferable. For example: *The foundation gave grants to anyone who lost a job this year* (instead of *anyone who lost their job*).

A singular *they* may also be used when an anonymous source's gender must be shielded: *The person feared for their own safety and spoke on condition of anonymity.*

His Majesty Capitalize when it appears in quotations or is appropriate before a name as the long form of a formal title.

For other purposes, use the man's name or *king*.

See **nobility**.

Hispaniola The island shared by the Dominican Republic and Haiti.
See **Western Hemisphere**.

historical periods and events Capitalize the names of widely recognized epochs in anthropology, archaeology, geology and history: *the Bronze Age, the Dark Ages, the Middle Ages, the Pliocene Epoch.*

Capitalize also widely recognized popular names for the periods and events: *the Atomic Age, the Boston Tea Party, the Civil War, the Exodus* (of the Israelites from Egypt), *the Great Depression, Prohibition.*

Lowercase *century*: *the 18th century.*

Capitalize only the proper nouns or adjectives in general descriptions of a period: *ancient Greece, classical Rome, the Victorian era, the fall of Rome.*

For additional guidance, see separate entries in this book for other epochs, events and historical periods. If this book has no entry, follow the capitalization in Webster's New World College Dictionary, using lowercase if the dictionary lists it as

an acceptable form for the sense in which the word is used.

historic, historical A *historic* event is an important occurrence, one that stands out in history.

Any occurrence in the past is a *historical* event.

history Avoid the redundant *past history*.

hit-and-run (n. and adj.) **hit and run** (v.) *The coach told him to hit and run. He scored on a hit-and-run.*

Hitler, Adolf Not *Adolph.*

Hodgkin lymphoma After Dr. Thomas Hodgkin, the English physician who first described the disease of the lymph nodes. Formerly called *Hodgkin's disease.*

Non-Hodgkin lymphoma, spelled without a possessive, is the more common type and spreads rapidly, especially among older people and those with HIV infections.

holding company A company whose principal assets are the securities it owns in companies that actually provide goods or services.

The usual reason for forming a holding company is to enable one corporation and its directors to control several companies by holding a majority of their stock.

holidays and holy days Capitalize them: *New Year's Eve, New Year's Day, Groundhog Day, Easter, Hanukkah,* etc.

The federal legal holidays are New Year's, Martin Luther King Jr. Day, Washington's Birthday, Memorial Day, Juneteenth, Independence Day, Labor Day, Columbus Day, Veterans

Day, Thanksgiving and Christmas. See individual entries for the official dates and when they are observed if they fall on a weekend.

The designation of a day as a federal legal holiday means that federal employees receive the day off or are paid overtime if they must work. Other requirements that may apply to holidays generally are left to the states. Many follow the federal lead in designating a holiday, but they are not required to do so.

Hollywood District of the city of Los Angeles where the film industry used to be centered and where film studios and other production facilities, as well as landmark theaters, are still located. It is not a dateline and is most commonly used to describe Southern California's entertainment industry.

Holocaust Capitalize when referring to the mass murder of European Jews and other groups by the Nazi Germans before and during World War II. Lowercase in other references.

homebuilder

homebuyer, homeowner

home equity line of credit A line of credit secured by a home. Borrowers can draw on it for a fixed period set by the lender, usually five to 10 years. *HELOC* is acceptable on second reference.

homefront

homeless, homelessness *Homeless* is generally acceptable as an adjective to describe people without a fixed residence. Avoid the dehumanizing collective noun *the homeless*, instead using constructions like *homeless people, people without housing* or *people without homes*.

Mention that a person is homeless only when relevant. Do not stereotype *homeless people* as dirty, mentally ill, addicted to drugs or alcohol, reliant on charity, or criminals. Those conditions can often contribute to or be byproducts of *homelessness*, but many *homeless people* also hold jobs and are self-sufficient.

Homeless shelter is an acceptable term for a building that provides free or very inexpensive but temporary indoor refuge for people without homes, generally run by a government or charity. Do not use *flophouse*.

Government agencies do not always agree on what legally constitutes *homelessness*, but the term generally refers to people staying in shelters or on the street.

Avoid disparaging terminology such as *derelict, bum, beggar, tramp* and *hobo*. Terms like *couch surfing* (staying temporarily in various households) or *transient* (someone who moves from city to city but is not necessarily *homeless*) can be useful to describe specific situations. Avoid *vagrant*.

A *migrant* is someone who moves from place to place for temporary work or economic advantage and is usually not considered *homeless*.

Indigent describes someone who is very poor and is not synonymous with *homeless*.

homepage The "front" page of a website.

hometown Use a comma to set off an individual's hometown (both the city and, when needed, the state) when it is placed in apposition to a name, whether *of* is used or not: *Tim Johnson, of Sioux Falls, South Dakota, was arrested Thursday; Mary Richards, Minneapolis.* See **state names** and the **Within Stories** section of **datelines**.

homicide, murder, manslaughter

Homicide is a legal term for slaying or killing.

Murder is malicious, premeditated homicide. Some states define certain homicides as murder if the killing occurs in the course of armed robbery, rape, etc.

Generally speaking, *manslaughter* is homicide without malice or premeditation.

A *homicide* should not be described as murder unless a person has been convicted of that charge.

Do not say that a victim was *murdered* until someone has been convicted in court. Instead, say that a victim *was killed* or *slain*. Do not write that X was charged with *murdering* Y. Use the formal charge — *murder* — and, if not already in the story, specify the nature of the killing – shooting, stabbing, beating, poisoning, drowning, etc.: *Jones was charged with murder in the shooting of his girlfriend.*

Examples:

An officer pulled over 29-year-old John White, who was arrested and charged with murder, according to Andrew Johnson, the county sheriff's spokesman.

The 66-year-old amateur photographer has pleaded not guilty to four counts of first-degree murder in the slaying of four women.

The killings occurred between 1977 and 1979. Prosecutors say Adams raped, tortured and robbed some of them before killing them.

Cook County Sheriff James Jones says a shooting that left a man and a woman dead appears to be a murder-suicide.

See **execute** and **assassin, killer, murderer**.

homophobia, homophobic

Acceptable in broad references or in quotations to the concept of fear or hatred of gays, lesbians and bisexuals. *The governor denounced homophobia.* In individual cases, be specific about observable actions; avoid descriptions or language that assumes motives. *The leaflets contained an anti-gay slur. The voters opposed same-sex marriage.* Related terms include *biphobia* (fear or hatred specifically of bisexuals) and *transphobia* (fear or hatred of transgender people). See **phobia**; **gender, sex and sexual orientation**.

homosexual (adj.), homosexuality

(n.) See **gender, sex and sexual orientation**.

Honolulu
The city in Hawaii is on the island of Oahu.

honorary degrees
All references to honorary degrees should specify that the degree was honorary.

Do not use *Dr.* before the name of an individual whose only doctorate is honorary.

hooky

hopefully
The traditional meaning is *in a hopeful manner.* Also acceptable is the modern usage: *it's hoped, we hope.*

horsepower
A unit of power. It is not abbreviated. See **watt**.

hotel Capitalize as part of the proper name for a specific hotel: *the Waldorf-Astoria Hotel.*

Lowercase when standing alone or used in an indefinite reference to one hotel in a chain: *The city has a Sheraton hotel.*

hot spot Two words. Used to describe an area where computers can connect wirelessly, a troubled global locale, or an area of intense heat in general.

hourlong, hourslong

household, housing unit In the sense used by the Census Bureau, a *household* is made up of all occupants of a *housing unit*. A *household* may contain more than one family or may be used by one person.

A *housing unit*, as defined by the bureau, is a group of rooms or single room occupied by people who do not live and eat with any other person in the structure. It must have either direct access from the outside or through a common hall, or have a kitchen or cooking equipment for the exclusive use of the occupants.

House of Commons, House of Lords The two houses of the British Parliament.

On second reference: *Commons* or *the Commons, Lords* or *the Lords.*

House of Representatives Capitalize when referring to a specific governmental body: *the U.S. House of Representatives, the Massachusetts House of Representatives.*

Capitalize shortened references that delete the words *of Representatives*: *the U.S. House, the Massachusetts House.*

Retain capitalization if *U.S.* or the name of a state is dropped but the reference is to a specific body.

BOSTON (AP) — The House has adjourned for the year.

Lowercase plural uses: *the Massachusetts and Rhode Island houses.*

Apply the same principle to similar legislative bodies such as *the Virginia House of Delegates.*

See **organizations and institutions** for guidelines on how to handle the term when it is used by a nongovernmental body.

HPV Acceptable on first reference for *human papillomavirus*, which can cause cervical and other types of cancer. *HPV virus* is redundant. Short-term HPV infections are very common, especially in sexually active young people, and usually clear on their own. Infection must persist for several years to pose a cancer risk.

HTML For *hypertext markup language.* In stories, describe as *the web programming language known as HTML.*

HTTP Abbreviation for *hypertext transfer protocol.* It's traditionally used to signal the start of internet addresses, such as http://apnews. com, though modern browsers generally no longer display or require users to add that text. However, *http://* is still required in other cases, such as embedding links in web pages. A related term, *HTTPS*, stands for *hypertext transfer protocol secure*, which is used to create a link to websites that cannot be easily eavesdropped on. The language for coding web pages is known as *HTML*, for *hypertext markup language.* These abbreviations are acceptable on first reference with explanation.

human, human being *Human* is preferred, but either is acceptable.

Humane Society of the United States An animal protection agency headquartered in Washington. It operates 10 regional offices across the country, but has no formal affiliation with the many local organizations that use the name *Humane Society*.

human smuggling/people smuggling, human trafficking/people trafficking *Human smuggling* or *people smuggling* typically involves transporting people across an international border illegally, and with their consent, in exchange for a fee. *Human trafficking* or *people trafficking* involves the use of force or coercion, typically for labor or commercial sex. Make clear what type of trafficking is involved or alleged in a given situation. No hyphen in the modifiers: *a suspected people smuggling operation*; *a human trafficking gang*.

Humvee A trademark for a four-wheeled military vehicle, built by AM General and used by U.S. and allied forces. *Hummer* is the sport utility vehicle.

hurricane Capitalize *hurricane* when it is part of the name that weather forecasters assign to a storm: *Hurricane Harvey*.

But use *it* and *its* — not *she, her* or *hers* or *he, him* or *his* — in pronoun references.

Storms lose strength and are downgraded to tropical storm or tropical depression status after being widely known as hurricanes. Depending on the context, it may be more clear to use simply the storm's name on first reference: *Officials released more water Monday from Houston-area reservoirs overwhelmed by Harvey*. Give the storm's current status and history high in the story: *Harvey came ashore Friday night as a major hurricane and has been downgraded to a tropical storm*. Phrasing such as *storm Harvey* or *the remnants of Hurricane Harvey* is also acceptable on first reference, with background later. In broad references to a hurricane and its aftermath: *The damage and economic impact from Hurricane Harvey is substantial* or *the damage and economic impact from Harvey is substantial*. See **weather terms**.

husband, wife Regardless of sexual orientation, *husband* for a man or *wife* for a woman is acceptable in all references to individuals in any legally recognized marriage. *Spouse* or *partner* may be used if requested or as a gender-neutral option.

hydraulic fracturing A technique used by the energy industry to extract oil and gas from rock by injecting high-pressure mixtures of water, sand or gravel and chemicals. The short form is *fracking*. Although the industry considers the short form pejorative, AP accepts *fracking* with a brief definition. See **fracking**.

hydro- The rules in **prefixes** apply, but in general, no hyphen. Some examples:
hydroelectric   hydrophobia

hyper- The rules in **prefixes** apply, but in general, no hyphen. Some

examples:
hyperactive   hypercritical

hypertension Preferred term is *high blood pressure*.

hyphen See entry in the **Punctuation** chapter.

h

i

ICBM, ICBMs Abbreviation for *intercontinental ballistic missile(s)*. *ICBM* is acceptable on second reference. Avoid the redundant *ICBM missiles*.

ice age Lowercase, because it denotes not a single period but any of a series of cold periods marked by extensive glacial growth alternating with periods of relative warmth.

ICU Acceptable on second reference for an *intensive care unit*. If *ICU* is used on first reference, give the full term quickly thereafter.

ID Acceptable abbreviation for *identification*, including *ID card*. However, spell out verb forms such as *identified*. See **abbreviations and acronyms**.

i.e. Abbreviation for the Latin *id est* or *that is (to say)* and is always followed by a comma.

IED Abbreviation for *improvised explosive device*. *IED* is acceptable on second reference. *Roadside bomb* is preferable.

illegal Except in sports and game contexts, use *illegal* only to mean a violation of the law. Be especially careful in labor-management disputes, where one side often calls an action by the other side illegal. Usually it is a charge that a contract or rule, not a law, has been violated.

illegitimate Do not refer to the child of unmarried parents as *illegitimate*. If it is pertinent to the story at all, use an expression such as *whose parents were not married*.

IM Acceptable on second reference for *instant message*. Sometimes used as a verb: *IM'ing, IM'd*. An *instant message* is similar but not identical to a *direct message*; both offer person-to-person communication, but *instant messages* are usually associated with apps such as Apple's iMessage whose primary purpose is to connect individuals or small groups. *Direct messages* are generally associated with broader communication platforms such as Facebook or Twitter; there, they represent an alternative to public communications.

immigration, migration Political rhetoric and high passion are a large part of discussions and debate about migration and immigration worldwide. Language that is both neutral and accurate is essential in news coverage. At the same time, be aware that definitions or perceptions of some terms can vary around the world. Globally, for example, there is no uniform legal definition of the term *migrant*. Be as specific as possible in describing an event, and provide both specific detail and broader context.

Governments around the world limit access to border operations, making it harder to know the reality of what is going on. Describing current restrictions helps explain gaps in what we know and why.

Some guidance on language:

crisis Use caution and judgment in deciding whether to call a specific immigration or migration situation a *crisis*, a vague and subjective term.

If quoting others who use the word *crisis*, ask for specifics about what is meant. There could be a humanitarian crisis if the numbers grow so large that officials cannot house the migrants safely or in sanitary conditions. Migrants may face humanitarian crises in their home countries. In theory, there could be a security or a border crisis if officials lose control of the border, allowing people to enter unencumbered in large numbers. But, in general, avoid hyperbole in calling anything a *crisis* or an *emergency*.

other descriptions Avoid imagery conjuring war or natural disaster such as *onslaught, tidal wave, flood, inundation, invasion, army, march, sneak* and *stealth*.

Instead, use numbers and facts. For example: *Biden is contending with the largest number of migrant encounters at the border in 20 years. It is the largest number of unaccompanied children encountered at the border on record. Overcrowded detention facilities have sent U.S. authorities scrambling for space and prompted the administration to dispatch FEMA to the border.*

Using words like *rise, increase, upturn, uptick, spike, surge, fall, decrease* or *downturn* is legitimate to describe the change in numbers of people entering across the border as long as it is supported by facts. But try to be precise about what time period these terms refer to and, again, provide details and context.

Other terms

illegal immigration Entering or living in a country without authorization in violation of civil or criminal law. Except in direct quotes essential to the story, use *illegal* only to refer to an action, not a person: *illegal immigration*, but not *illegal immigrant*.

Acceptable variations include *living in* or *entering a country illegally* or *without legal permission*. For people: *immigrants lacking permanent legal status*. The European Union and some U.N. agencies use the term *irregular migration*; that term is acceptable in areas where it is commonly used. Do not use *irregular migrants*.

When space is a consideration, such as in a headline, simply *migrant(s)* or *immigrant(s)* is acceptable as long as the context is clear in the first few paragraphs of the story.

Do not use the terms *alien, unauthorized immigrant, irregular migrant, an illegal, illegals* or *undocumented* (except when quoting people or government documents that use these terms). Many immigrants have some sort of documents, but not the necessary ones.

In the U.S., the Biden administration has replaced the word *alien* in government documents with *noncitizen*. Limit use of the term, which can be misleading: *Noncitizen* makes no distinction between those who have legal status and those who don't. Many people are in the country with legal status, such as green-card holders, people on student visas, tourists and temporary workers. Do not use the term *alien*.

Do not describe without attribution people as violating immigration laws.

Specify wherever possible how someone entered the country illegally and from where. Crossed the border? Overstayed a visa? What nationality?

Consider carefully when deciding whether a person's immigration status is relevant to a story. Often such decisions should involve discussions with managers. Include immigration status only when it is relevant and that relevance is explicit in the story.

immigration, immigrant, migration, migrant

Immigrants generally are people who move to a different country with the intention of settling there. This term, rather than *migrants*, is most commonly used for people established in the U.S., which usually is their final destination. It also is used when another specific country is the final destination. For example: *British immigration statistics show how many people settled in the country last year*.

Migrants generally are people who are on the move, sometimes for economic reasons, either within one country or across borders. The term is generally preferred over *immigrant* in Europe, Africa, the Mideast and Asia, where a person's destination country may be undecided or in flux.

The term *migrant* also may be used for those whose reason for leaving their home country is not clear, or to cover people who may also be *refugees* or *asylum-seekers*.

But be specific whenever possible, or use other phrasing such as *people struggling to enter Europe, Cubans seeking new lives in the United States, families seeking to join relatives in the U.S.* If a given group of people is known to include both *migrants* and *refugees*, say so.

People moving within the 50 U.S. states, or from a U.S. territory to one of the 50 states, should not be referred to as immigrants, because they are moving within a single country.

Migrant children/child migrants may travel alone or with family members; make the distinction if possible. *Migrant children* traveling alone may also be described as *unaccompanied migrant children*. Use *migrant* in this context to reflect their status of moving from one place to another.

Refugees People compelled to leave their home or country to escape war, natural disaster, or persecution on the grounds of race, religion, nationality, political beliefs or some other grounds, which may include sexual orientation, gender identity, or gang or domestic violence.

Asylum-seekers People who have left their country of origin and have applied or intend to apply for asylum status. Asylum, under U.S. and international law, is permission granted to refugees to remain within the country to which they have fled. It is not intended for people leaving for economic reasons.

Use specific terms such as *political asylum* or *religious asylum* only when the person's reason for seeking asylum is known.

In the United States, people fleeing their home countries who do not qualify for asylum may be eligible for "withholding of removal" or the U.N. Convention Against Torture, which offer similar protections.

internally displaced person/people

Avoid this jargon. Refer simply to *people who are displaced* within their own countries or otherwise describe their situation. Limited use of the terms *displaced person* and *displaced people* is acceptable on later references. Do not call them *refugees* if they are within their own country.

"anchor babies" A pejorative term in the U.S. for children who are born to noncitizen parents wanting to take advantage of *birthright citizenship*. Avoid it unless part of an essential quote; enclose it in quote marks and explain it if used.

birthright citizenship A country's policy and practice of granting citizenship to anyone born within its borders. In the United States, the Constitution guarantees that any child born in and under jurisdiction of the United States is a U.S. citizen. The term is acceptable, but include an explanation.

"birth tourism" A term sometimes used for traveling to another country specifically to give birth in that country. Avoid it unless part of a quote; instead, describe the action. For example: *visiting the U.S. with intent to give birth to a U.S. citizen child.* Enclose the term in quote marks if used.

"catch and release" A term favored by advocates of immigration restriction for people who are taken into custody at the border for being in the United States illegally and released in the U.S., typically with notices to appear in immigration court. Do not use this misleading and dehumanizing term unless in direct quotations; enclose it in quote marks and explain the term when used.

"chain migration" A term applied by those who favor strict immigration limits to what the U.S. government calls *family-based immigration*, a long-standing program granting preference to people with close relatives who already have legal residency or U.S. citizenship. Avoid the term, which is vague and may imply unfettered immigration, which is not allowed under U.S. law. If needed in a direct quotation, enclose the term in quote marks and explain it.

deportation, expulsion The term *deportation* can be used generically for the forced removal of someone from a country for violating immigration laws or having been declared by authorities to have no legal right to remain. But be aware that the term may have specific legal meaning in some cases.

In the United States, *deportation* is synonymous with the legal term *removal* and is predicated on a formal order to leave the country, which carries legal consequences in terms of bans on legally returning to the country and exposure to criminal charges if arrested for returning illegally.

Expedited removal is a legal term by which a U.S. agency formally removes, or deports, someone without an appearance before an immigration judge. It also can be termed *fast-track deportation*. Either is acceptable, with an explanation.

Some people are offered *voluntary return* or *voluntary departure*, which carry lesser consequences in exchange for agreeing to leave the country voluntarily.

Avoid the term *self-deportation*, referring to people in a country illegally who leave without any pressure from authorities.

Since the onset of the coronavirus pandemic in March 2020, many immigrants to the U.S. have been *expelled* under authority of Title 42, a 1944 public health law that justifies immediate removal without an opportunity to seek asylum. *Expulsions* carry no legal consequences.

In the United States, the Border Patrol uses the term *turnback* to refer to someone who enters the country illegally, turns around and leaves, typically in anticipation of being arrested by authorities. If the term is used, explain it.

pushbacks Though there is no universally agreed-on definition, the term is used primarily in Europe to refer to the forcible return of migrants and refugees across an international border without an assessment of their rights to apply for asylum or other forms of protection. International law prohibits sending people back to a country where they risk being persecuted on certain grounds, including race, religion and political opinion. If the term is used, explain it.

green card (n.), green-card (adj.) Acceptable in all references for a U.S. card showing an immigrant has permanent legal status. It is a required step toward becoming a naturalized citizen. Hyphenate as a modifier: *green-card holder*.

sanctuaries, sanctuary jurisdictions Local and state governments that limit cooperation with federal immigration authorities. There are no firm criteria for what qualifies a jurisdiction as *sanctuary*. Some are self-described that way as a matter of pride, while those who favor immigration restrictions use the label as criticism. Provide details in each situation.

visas The general term often suffices for documents showing permission to visit, work or study in another country. If relevant, use the classification and/or a brief description. For example: *H-1B visas used for high-tech workers* or *visas used for high-tech workers*. More detail is here: https://travel.state.gov/content/travel/en/us-visas/visa-information-resources/all-visa-categories.html.

immigration detention centers, detention facilities, immigration jails, holding facilities Among the terms for places where people are held for reasons related to immigration status and are not free to leave. Conditions vary considerably, from modern prisons fully equipped with medical services to makeshift campsites. Choose the term that seems to best apply, be as descriptive as possible and name the managing agency.

In the United States, the Department of Health and Human Services manages what it calls *shelters* for unaccompanied migrant children. Avoid the term unless in direct quotations. Instead: *holding facilities*.

immigration raid Use the term *raid* only when there is a major show of force, such as a large number of officials with guns drawn or forced entry into a home or business with a judicial order. Avoid *sweep*, which may be interpreted to mean removal of something undesirable. *Operation* is an acceptable term but be specific as possible in describing what happened. For example: *The arrests were made outside homes and in traffic stops*.

human smuggling/people smuggling, human trafficking/people trafficking *Human smuggling* or *people smuggling* typically involves transporting people across an international border illegally, and with their consent, in exchange for a fee. *Human trafficking* or *people trafficking* involves the use of force or coercion, typically for labor or commercial sex. Make clear what type of trafficking is involved or alleged in a given situation. No hyphen in the modifiers: *a suspected people smuggling operation; a human trafficking gang.*

arrests, apprehensions, encounters In the United States, Customs and Border Protection has historically reported *apprehensions*, which is synonymous with *arrests*, as a primary barometer of illegal crossings. Either term is acceptable. Figures for arrests and apprehensions are not synonymous with the number of people arrested; some have more than one arrest during the specified time period.

Under authority derived from the coronavirus pandemic, CBP began using the term *encounters* to describe the number of times it stopped migrants because those expelled under those powers were not formally arrested. Limit use of the term; instead, *stops* or *stopped xx number of times.*

Deferred Action for Childhood Arrivals program A program introduced by then-President Barack Obama in 2012 that has allowed hundreds of thousands of people who were brought to the United States as children to temporarily remain in the country and obtain work permits. It does not confer legal status but provides protection from deportation. The program has survived legal challenges but faced an uncertain future as of July 2021, when a federal judge prohibited new enrollments but invited President Joe Biden's administration to make another attempt to pass legal muster. Use the acronym *DACA* sparingly and only on second reference.

"Dreamers" An often-used term for people who were brought to the United States illegally as children by family. The term is derived from never-passed legislation called the DREAM Act, short for Development, Relief and Education for Alien Minors. It would have allowed young immigrants in the United States illegally who were brought to the country as children to remain if they met certain criteria. Some also use the term "Dreamers" for those covered under the Obama-era Deferred Action for Childhood Arrivals act. That program, known as DACA, continues for those who have or had DACA status but was closed to new applicants in July 2021. The program does not convey legal status but conveys temporary protection from deportation and permission to legally work, similar to protections offered under DREAM Act proposals.

Use the term "Dreamers" sparingly and in quotation marks in all references. Define the term soon after use: *They are commonly referred to as "Dreamers," based on never-passed proposals in Congress called the DREAM Act.*

—

U.S. IMMIGRATION LAW ENFORCEMENT AND AGENCIES

The departments of **Homeland Security**, **Justice**, and **Health and Human Services** play key roles in immigration in the United States.

Many who come to the United States encounter any or all of these departments and perhaps multiple agencies within them. Strike a balance to sufficiently identify agencies without a jumble of names and abbreviations that may be difficult for readers to follow. When appropriate, use *U.S. authorities* or *U.S. immigration authorities* to avoid having to distinguish between departments and agencies.

Here is more detail, for use when needed:

The **Department of Health and Human Services**, through its *Office of Refugee Resettlement*, is responsible for taking custody of unaccompanied children within 72 hours and placing them with "sponsors" in the United States, most often parents or close relatives. *HHS* is acceptable on second reference if needed to avoid confusion with other departments in a story. Use *the department* if only one is mentioned.

The Department of Justice operates immigration courts through its *Executive Office for Immigration Review*. The office employs judges and operates courtrooms. It is an administrative office within the Justice Department, not part of the independent judiciary. Judges are under guidance of the attorney general and the immigration review office's *Board of Immigration Appeals*.

Generally use *immigration courts*. If appropriate, mention that immigration courts are an administrative agency within the Justice Department. Use *Executive Office for Immigration Review* if it is part of a person's job title. Do not use *EOIR*.

Immigrants are called *respondents* in immigration court. Avoid the jargon but do not use *defendant*. Instead: *immigrants, people seeking to remain in the U.S., asylum-seekers* (if applicable).

Homeland Security attorneys represent the government. Call them *government lawyers*, not *prosecutors*.

The Department of Homeland Security has three agencies dealing with immigration: *U.S. Immigration and Customs Enforcement, U.S. Customs and Border Protection*, and *U.S. Citizenship and Immigration Services*.

Generally use the relevant agency name on first reference, rather than the *Homeland Security Department*, since these agencies are commonly recognized by readers.

The abbreviations *ICE, CBP* and *USCIS* may be used in headlines and sparingly on second reference. For stories on the Homeland Security Department, *DHS* may be used in headlines, and on second reference if needed to avoid confusion with other departments in a story. Use *the department* if only one is mentioned.

For stories on *U.S. Immigration and Customs Enforcement, U.S. Customs and Border Protection*, and *U.S. Citizenship and Immigration Services*, generally avoid references to units within them on second reference if possible.

If it is necessary to refer to a specific unit, here are some details:

U.S. Immigration and Customs Enforcement has two main units: *Homeland Security Investigations* and *Enforcement and Removal Operations*:

— **Homeland Security Investigations** Investigates any criminal activity that crosses international lines, which includes trafficking of humans or goods; money laundering; and cybersecurity, intellectual property theft and trade fraud. *HSI* is acceptable on second reference if necessary. Do not call it *Homeland Security*. Explain in the story that it is a unit of *Immigration and Customs Enforcement*. It employs *agents*; do not call them *officers*.

— **Enforcement and Removal Operations** Arrests and detains people in the U.S. illegally and returns them to their homelands by chartered or commercial flights or through a land crossing with Mexico or Canada. The agency manages the world's largest immigration detention system. Its *fugitive operations* teams go into communities to arrest people, but it mostly relies on city, county and state law enforcement agencies to turn over people who are booked into jail and flagged in databases as wanted by immigration authorities. So-called *sanctuary jurisdictions* have varying degrees of limitations on the extent of cooperation with immigration authorities. *ERO* is acceptable on second reference if necessary. Explain in the story that it is a unit of *Immigration and Customs Enforcement*. It employs *officers*; do not call them *agents*.

ICE also has an **Office of Principal Legal Advisor** that, among other things, represents Homeland Security in immigration court.

U.S. Customs and Border Protection holds people for up to 72 hours in *jails* or *holding cells*. Do not call them *detention centers*, which implies they are designed for longer-term custody. *CBP* is acceptable on second reference when necessary to distinguish from other agencies. Do not use the stand-alone terms *Customs* or *customs* in reference to this agency.

CBP includes the *Border Patrol*, the *Office of Field Operations*, and the *Office of Air and Marine*.

The **Border Patrol** polices areas outside the more than 300 official land crossings, airports and sea landings. Its employees are *agents*; do not call them *officers*.

The **Office of Field Operations** polices all official ports of entry to the United States, including land crossings, airports and sea landings. Its employees are *officers*; do not call them *agents*. They may be referred to generically as *border inspectors* or *airport inspectors*.

U.S. Citizenship and Immigration Services grants citizenship, green cards, temporary work visas and other immigration benefits.

—

INTERNATIONAL AGENCIES
Frontex The European Union agency tasked with helping member states protect the EU's external borders. Based in Warsaw, Poland. Its formal name is the European Border and Coast Guard Agency, but it is widely known as Frontex, an acronym derived from its name in French. EU countries are responsible for protecting their own borders, but Frontex can assist countries facing intense migratory pressure with border guards, aircraft, boats, surveillance technology and other equipment. It can also assist EU member states with deportations.

International Organization for Migration An intergovernmental, U.N.-related organization based in Geneva, promoting international cooperation on migration, advising governments on migration issues and providing humanitarian assistance to migrants in need. *IOM* is acceptable on second reference.

UNHCR Acceptable in all references for the United Nations High Commissioner for Refugees, with a brief explanation that it is the U.N. refugee agency: *UNHCR, the U.N. refugee agency*. The agency, based in Geneva, protects and assists displaced people around the world. The abbreviation UNHCR now refers to the agency as a whole, rather than just the commissioner. The head of the agency is *the U.N. high*

commissioner for refugees; the term
U.N. refugee chief is also acceptable.

impassable, impassible, impassive

Impassable means that passage
is impossible: *The bridge was
impassable.*

Impassible and *impassive* describe
lack of sensitivity to pain or
suffering. Webster's New World
College Dictionary notes, however,
that *impassible* suggests an inability
to be affected, while *impassive*
implies only that no reaction
was noticeable: *She was impassive
throughout the ordeal.*

impeachment Impeachment by
the U.S. House is the first part of
a two-step process set out by the
Constitution for the removal of a
federal official, up to and including
the president. Though this is a
political process, not a legal process,
impeachment is the equivalent of an
indictment — a determination that
there is enough evidence to proceed
to a trial, which would be conducted
by the Senate.

The Constitution does not
describe the process in great detail.
Article 1, Section 2, says merely
that "The House of Representatives
shall ... have the sole Power of
Impeachment."

An official may be impeached
for "Treason, Bribery, or other high
Crimes and Misdemeanors." The
Constitution does not define "high
Crimes and Misdemeanors." But
there is general agreement that they
need not be criminal activities in a
legal sense, and that "high Crimes"
are abuses of power.

Do not use as a synonym for
conviction or *removal from office.*

impel, impelled, impelling

imperial gallon The standard British
gallon, equal to 277.42 cubic inches
or about 1.2 U.S. gallons.

The metric equivalent is
approximately 4.5 liters.
See **liter**.

imperial quart One-fourth of an
imperial gallon.

implausible

imply, infer Writers or speakers *imply*
in the words they use.

A listener or reader *infers*
something from the words.

impostor

improvised explosive device *IED*
is acceptable on second reference.
Roadside bomb is preferable.

-in Precede with a hyphen:

break-in	*walk-in*
cave-in	*write-in*

in- No hyphen when it means *not*:

inaccurate	*insufferable*

Other uses without a hyphen:

inbound	*infighting*
indoor	*inpatient (n., adj.)*
infield	

A few combinations take a
hyphen, however:

in-depth	*in-house*
in-group	*in-law*

Follow Webster's New World
College Dictionary when in doubt.

"in" When employed to indicate that
something is in vogue, use quotation
marks only if followed by a noun: *It
was the "in" thing to do. Raccoon coats
are in again.*

Inauguration Day Capitalize only
when referring to the total collection

of events that include inauguration of a U.S. president; lowercase in other uses: *Inauguration Day is Jan. 20. The inauguration day for the change has not been set.*

inbox

inch Equal to one-twelfth of a foot. The metric equivalent is exactly 2.54 centimeters.
See **centimeter**; **foot**; and **dimensions**.

incident A minor event. Anything that causes death, injury, notable damage and the like is not an incident.

include Use *include* to introduce a series when the items that follow are only part of the total: *The price includes breakfast. The zoo includes lions and tigers.*
Use *comprise* when the full list of individual elements is given: *The zoo comprises 100 types of animals, including lions and tigers.*
See **compose, comprise, constitute**.

incorporated Abbreviate and capitalize as *Inc.* when used as a part of a corporate name. Do not set off with commas: *Tyson Foods Inc. announced ...*
See **company names**.

incorporator Do not capitalize when used before a name.
See **titles**.

incredible, incredulous *Incredible* means unbelievable.
Incredulous means skeptical.

incur, incurred, incurring

Independence Day *July Fourth* or *Fourth of July* also are acceptable.

The federal legal holiday is observed on Friday if July 4 falls on a Saturday, on Monday if it falls on a Sunday.

index, indexes

Index of Leading Economic Indicators A composite of 10 economic measurements developed to help forecast shifts in the direction of the U.S. economy.
It is compiled by the Conference Board, a private business-sponsored research group, which took it over from the Commerce Department in 1995.

indict Use *indict* only in connection with the legal process of bringing charges against an individual or corporation.
To avoid any suggestion that someone is being judged before a trial, do not use phrases such as *indicted for killing* or *indicted for bribery*. Instead, use *indicted on a charge of killing or indicted on a bribery charge.*
For guidelines on related words, see **accused**; **allege**; and **arrest**.

indie Short for *independent film* or *recorded music*, meaning that it was originally made without the support of a major studio or company.

Indigenous Peoples Day A holiday celebrating the original inhabitants of North America, observed instead of *Columbus Day* in some U.S. localities. Usually held on the second Monday of October, coinciding with the federal Columbus Day holiday. See **Columbus Day**.

indiscreet, indiscrete *Indiscreet* means *lacking prudence*. Its noun form is *indiscretion*.

Indiscrete means *not separated into distinct parts*.

indiscriminate, indiscriminately

individual retirement account *IRA* is acceptable on second reference.

Individuals with Disabilities Education Act The federal law that guarantees a free appropriate public education to eligible children with disabilities. Use the acronym *IDEA* only in direct quotations. See **disabilities**.

indispensable

indo- Usually hyphenated and capitalized:

Indo-Aryan   Indo-Hittite
Indo-German Indo-Iranian
But: *Indochina*.

Indonesia Use after the name of a community in datelines on stories from this nation.

Specify an individual island, if needed, in the text.

indoor (adj.) **indoors** (adv.)

infant Applicable to children through 12 months old.

infantile paralysis The preferred term is *polio*.

inflation A sustained increase in prices. The result is a decrease in the purchasing power of money.

There are two basic types of inflation:

— *Cost-push inflation* occurs when increases in the price of specific items, such as oil or food, are big enough to drive up prices overall.

— *Demand-pull inflation* occurs when the amount of money available exceeds the amount of goods and services available for sale.

infra- The rules in **prefixes** apply, but in general, no hyphen. Some examples:

infrared   infrastructure

infrastructure An economy's capital in the form of roads, railways, water supplies, educational facilities, health services, etc., without which investment in factories can't be fully productive.

initial public offering *IPO* acceptable on second reference.

initials Use periods and no space when an individual uses initials instead of a first name: *H.L. Mencken*.

Do not give a name with a single initial (*J. Jones*) unless it is the individual's preference or a first name cannot be learned.

See **middle initials**.

injuries They may be suffered, sustained or received (a 2021 change). Often, simpler wording is possible: *She was injured in the crash*, rather than *she sustained injuries in the crash*.

innocent, not guilty In court cases, plea situations and trials, *not guilty* is preferable to *innocent*, because it is more precise legally. (However, special care must be taken to prevent omission of the word *not*.) When possible, say a defendant was *acquitted* of criminal charges.

innocuous

innuendo

inoculate

input Do not use as a verb in
describing the introduction of data
into a computer.

inquire, inquiry Not *enquire, enquiry.*

insignia Same form for singular and
plural.

Instagram Photo- and video-sharing
service owned by Meta Platforms
Inc.

Institute for Supply Management
Produces monthly reports on
manufacturing and service sectors.
ISM acceptable on second reference.

inter- The rules in **prefixes** apply,
but in general, no hyphen. Some
examples:

   inter-American   interstate
   interracial

Internal Revenue Service *IRS* is
acceptable in all references.
   Capitalize also *Internal Revenue
Service*, but lowercase *the revenue
service.*

**International Brotherhood
of Teamsters, Chauffeurs,
Warehousemen and Helpers
of America** *Teamsters* union is
acceptable in all references. See
Teamsters union.

International Court of Justice The
principal judicial organ of the United
Nations, established at The Hague
in 1945.
   The court is not open to
individuals. It has jurisdiction over
all matters specifically provided
for either in the U.N. charter or in
treaties and conventions in force.

It also has jurisdiction over cases
referred to it by U.N. members and
by nonmembers such as Switzerland
that subscribe to the court statute.
   The court serves as the successor
to the Permanent Court of
International Justice of the League
of Nations, which also was known as
the World Court.
   On second reference use
international court or *world court* in
lowercase. Do not abbreviate.

**International Criminal Police
Organization** *Interpol* is acceptable
in all references.
   Headquarters is in Lyon, France.

international date line The
imaginary line drawn north and
south through the Pacific Ocean,
largely along the 180th meridian.
   By international agreement, when
it is 12:01 a.m. Sunday just west of
the line, it is 12:01 a.m. Saturday just
east of it.
   See **time zones**.

International Energy Agency Paris-
based energy adviser for developed
nations. *IEA* acceptable on second
reference.

International Labor Organization
ILO is acceptable on second
reference.
   Headquarters is in Geneva.

International Monetary Fund *IMF*
is acceptable on second reference.
Headquarters is in Washington.
   A supply of money supported by
subscriptions of member nations,
for the purpose of stabilizing
international exchange and
promoting orderly and balanced
trade. Member nations may obtain
foreign currency needed, making

it possible to correct temporary maladjustments in their balance of payments without currency depreciation.

International Space Station Use *space station* on second reference. Don't use *ISS*.

internet A decentralized, worldwide network of computers and other devices that can communicate with one another.

The *web*, like *email*, is a subset of the internet. They are not synonymous and should not be used interchangeably in stories.

In stories, use the name of the website or service rather than the web address — so it's *Facebook*, not *Facebook.com*.

See the **Social Media and Web-Based Reporting** chapter; **misinformation, fact checks, fake news**.

Internet of Things General term used to describe devices, appliances, sensors and anything else with an internet connection, apart from traditional gadgets such as PCs and phones. Abbreviate as *IoT*. It's a technical term that should be avoided in stories for general readers. Instead, use *internet-connected* or *smart*, such as *internet-connected thermostat* or *smart light bulb*. See **smart devices**.

internet privacy Several leading tech companies have come under scrutiny in recent years over the way they collect data and build profiles on their users, primarily to target advertising to a user's interests, political views and other attributes. The issue gained prominence following the disclosure in March 2018 that a political consulting firm, Cambridge Analytica, had mined data on millions of Facebook users through a Facebook app that purported to be a psychological research tool.

Some of the information comes from data the user submits directly on a profile, but much of it comes from the use of technologies such as browser cookies and mobile device IDs to follow individual users as they visit websites and use apps. Data collected and used for ad targeting include location, hobbies, recreations, shopping habits, favorite sports teams and celebrities, vacation destinations, publications read and television shows watched. Companies can also infer race or political views based on the types of news outlets visited online.

Proponents of data collection and targeted advertising say the practice makes ads more relevant to users, as the alternative is to see an ad someone might not care about, rather than no ad at all. Proponents say advertisers save money overall by having to show the ad to fewer people to get the same result.

But critics say companies often don't tell users clearly what they are doing, even though companies say they have users' permission. See **opt in, opt out**.

Companies often say they don't sell data to third parties, though that still leaves open the possibility of sharing data for free. In addition, companies often do in-house targeting on behalf of customers, allowing them to make money off users' data without any need to sell data. See **digital advertising, internet advertising, online advertising**.

internet security As many aspects of

daily life and business have moved online, so have thieves, vandals and spies. Keeping organizations, individuals and their data protected online is an increasingly challenging task that has acquired a specialized vocabulary. Some terms:

encryption The mathematical scrambling of messages in order to shield them from unauthorized view or modification. Such *encrypted* messages can typically be read only by the sender and the intended recipient, although in the case of commercial messaging systems, the service provider can usually also decrypt and access messages and data such as files, photos or video.

end-to-end encryption A way of encrypting messages such that only the sender and recipient can read them. The messaging service does not have the ability to read or modify such messages. That also means it cannot respond to requests from law enforcement; in response, government agencies have been pushing services to create a backdoor just for them, though security experts warn that any backdoor for governments could also be exploited by criminals and other parties. Services that offer end-to-end encryption include *Signal*, Apple's *iMessage* and Meta's *WhatsApp* and *Messenger*.

No *encryption* method is foolproof, and advances in computing power and cryptographic methods can often unlock messages encrypted by older technologies. *Hackers* can also sometimes exploit undiscovered bugs in encryption software to illicitly read supposedly secure messages or files.

Attackers often break into seemingly secure systems by exploiting *vulnerabilities* — software or hardware flaws that can be used to bypass security protections. A *zero-day vulnerability* is such a flaw that has gone undetected by the system's creators and security reviews; explain this term when used in stories for general audiences.

malware A general term for software that takes harmful or surreptitious actions, usually to steal data or money, access secure systems, or disrupt organizations. Malware can spread via *phishing*, "poisoned" websites that resemble familiar destinations, apps, or by exploiting *vulnerabilities* in computer systems.

phishing Exploits the trust of users to attack computer systems or to commit fraud by stealing personal information such as credit card numbers, Social Security numbers, user IDs and passwords. The technique typically involves doctored emails often apparently sent by friends, family or co-workers that contain attachments or links to sites that infect a user's computer with malware.

spyware Designed to ransack personal information, track the online activity of individuals and sometimes to conduct surveillance via device microphones and cameras.

ransomware Essentially holds a target computer or computer system hostage by *encrypting* its files and demanding payment, often via bitcoin. Ransomware can target individuals, businesses and governments alike.

denial-of-service attack Entails targeting an internet site with enormous volumes of spurious data traffic. When successful, such attacks can knock a *site* or *service* offline until their operators find a way to divert the traffic elsewhere.

Sometimes abbreviated *DoS*, although this shorthand is best avoided. A *distributed denial-of-service attack*, sometimes abbreviated *DDoS*, employs a network of distributed computers to direct junk traffic at the target site.

botnet A collection of computers infected with malware that can be centrally controlled to conduct cyberattacks. Botnets have been used to carry out *denial-of-service* attacks, spread *malware*, send *spam* and steal data. Botnets can include a variety of devices, from desktop PCs to servers to household smart devices such as internet-connected video cameras.

See **cyberattack**; **Digital Security for Journalists**.

internet service provider *ISP* is acceptable on second reference.

Interpol Acceptable in all references for *International Criminal Police Organization*.

intifada An Arabic term for the Palestinian uprising against Israel.

intra- Within, inside. The rules in **prefixes** apply, but in general, no hyphen. Some examples:
intracity   *intraparty*

intranet A private network inside a company or organization, only for internal use.

in vitro fertilization Creating embryos by mixing eggs and sperm in a lab dish. Do not hyphenate; *IVF* acceptable on second reference. Use *test-tube babies* sparingly.

iOS The operating system used by Apple's *iPhone* and *iPod Touch*. The iPad's operating system is no longer *iOS* but goes by *iPadOS*. Use *IOS* when the word starts a sentence or headline.

IP address *Internet Protocol address*, a numeric address given to a computer connected to the internet. Most users type in domain names as stand-ins for *IP addresses*, and domain name servers help with the translation in the background. *IP addresses* can sometimes be used to identify the location of a computer, the company or organization it belongs to, and where it was registered. Avoid the term in most stories. If necessary, *IP address* is acceptable on first reference with explanation, such as: *Hackers targeted the site's IP address, a numeric designation that identifies its location on the internet*. See **domain name**.

iPad A touch-screen tablet sold by Apple Inc. that is much like an *iPhone* but with a larger screen. Use *IPad* when the word starts a sentence or headline. Do not use as a generic term for *tablet*.

iPhone Apple Inc.'s smartphone. Capitalize as *IPhone* when the word starts a sentence or headline. For clarity, capitalize individual letters that appear in iPhone model names: the *iPhone 7S*, not *iPhone 7s*.

iPod A digital media player sold by *Apple Inc.* Capitalize as *IPod* when the word starts a sentence or headline. For clarity, capitalize names of submodels such as the *iPod Touch* and *iPod Nano*. Apple no longer makes models other than the *iPod Touch*.

IQ Acceptable in all references for

intelligence quotient.

Iran A Middle East nation bordered by Afghanistan, Armenia, Azerbaijan, Iraq, Pakistan, Turkey and Turkmenistan. Home to over 80 million people. Iran lies along the northern edge of the Persian Gulf and the strategic Strait of Hormuz. It is known officially as the Islamic Republic of Iran.

Iran is predominantly Shiite nation with minority Christian, Jewish, Sunni and Zoroastrian populations. After its 1979 Islamic Revolution, Iran is governed by a Shiite theocracy with a supreme leader at its helm who has final say on all state matters. Iran holds elections for president and parliament, though candidates and proposed laws must be approved by a 12-member Guardian Council of clerics and jurists. Iran's official language is *Farsi*, also known as *Persian*. Its ethnic groups include Arab, Azeri, Baloch, Kurdish, Lur, Fars, Turkic and Turkmen people.

Iran's Revolutionary Guard A paramilitary organization formed in the wake of Iran's 1979 Islamic Revolution to defend its clerically overseen government. The force answers only to Iran's supreme leader, operates independently of the regular military and has vast economic interests across the country. Its branches include the expeditionary Quds — or Jerusalem — Force, the Basij volunteer militia and the country's ballistic missile force. *The Revolutionary Guard* is acceptable on first reference if the context makes Iran clear. *The Guard* is acceptable on second reference.

Iraq A Middle East nation bordered by Turkey, Iran, Kuwait, Saudi Arabia, Jordan and Syria home to nearly 40 million people. Iraq is home to diverse ethnic groups including Arabs, Kurds, Assyrians, Yazidis, Turkmen, Shabaks, Armenians and Circassians. It is a predominantly Muslim nation with minority Christian, Yazidi, Mandean and other religious communities.

It is a federal parliamentary republic consisting of 19 governorates and an autonomous Kurdish region in the northeast. Iraq's official languages are Arabic and Kurdish. The oil-rich country has been devastated by decades of conflict, including the eight-year Iraq-Iran war, the 2003 U.S.-led invasion that toppled dictator Saddam Hussein and ensuing sectarian strife, and a ruinous war against the Islamic State group.

Ireland Acceptable in most references to the independent nation known formally as the *Irish Republic*. Use *Irish Republic* when a distinction must be made between this nation and *Northern Ireland*, a part of the *United Kingdom*. See **datelines**, **United Kingdom** and **Northern Ireland**.

Irish Republican Army An outlawed paramilitary group committed to overthrowing Northern Ireland and its links with Britain. Its formal name is *Provisional IRA*. It was founded in 1969 with the aim of abolishing Northern Ireland as a predominantly British Protestant state. Its members claim direct lineage to the old IRA, which wrested the predominantly Catholic rest of Ireland from British control following a 1919-21 rebellion.

IRA is acceptable, but *Irish*

Republican Army should be spelled out somewhere in the story.

Sinn Fein (pronounced "shin fane") is a legal political party that is linked with the *IRA*, but not technically a wing of it.

irregardless A double negative. *Regardless* is correct.

IRS Acceptable in all references for *Internal Revenue Service*. Capitalize *Internal Revenue Service*, but lowercase *the revenue service*.

Islamic State group Islamic militant organization that broke with the al-Qaida network and took control of large parts of Iraq and Syria, where it declared a caliphate, a traditional form of Islamic rule, in 2014. It is largely made up of extremist Sunni militants from Iraq and Syria but has drawn jihadi fighters from across the Muslim world and Europe. The group lost its hold on territory in 2019 and its leader, Abu Bakr al-Baghdadi, died in a U.S. raid in Syria in October of the same year. The group is abbreviated as *IS* and is also known by its Arabic-language acronym, *Daesh*. To avoid giving the impression that it is a nation, do not refer to it as the *Islamic State*; it is the *Islamic State group*.

Islamist An advocate or supporter of a political movement that favors reordering government and society in accordance with laws prescribed by Islam. Do not use as a synonym for *Islamic fighters*, *militants*, *extremists* or *radicals*, who may or may not be Islamists. Where possible, be specific and use the name of militant affiliations: *al-Qaida-linked*, *Hezbollah*, *Taliban*, etc. Those who view the Quran as

a political model encompass a wide range of Muslims, from mainstream politicians to militants known as jihadis.

island Capitalize *island* or *islands* as part of a proper name: *Prince Edward Island, the Hawaiian Islands.*

Lowercase *island* and *islands* when they stand alone or when the reference is to the islands in a given area: *the Pacific islands.*

Lowercase all *island of* constructions: *the island of Nantucket.*

U.S. DATELINES: For communities on islands within the boundaries of the United States, use the community name and the state name:

EDGARTOWN, Mass. (AP) — *Honolulu* stands alone, however.

DATELINES ABROAD: If an island has an identity of its own (*Bermuda, Prince Edward Island, Puerto Rico, Sardinia, Taiwan,* etc.) use the community name and the island name:

HAMILTON, Bermuda (AP) — *Havana, Hong Kong, Macao* and *Singapore* stand alone, however.

If the island is part of a chain, use the community name and the name of the chain:

MANILA, Philippines (AP) — Identify the name of the island in the text if relevant: *Manila is on the island of Luzon.*

For additional guidelines, see **datelines**.

IT Abbreviation for *information technology*. For general audiences, use *IT* only on second reference. For more technically oriented audiences, *IT* is acceptable on all references.

italics AP does not italicize words in news stories. Italics are used in Stylebook entries to highlight examples of correct and incorrect usage.

it's, its *It's* is a contraction for *it is* or *it has*: *It's up to you. It's been a long time.*
Its is the possessive form of the neuter pronoun: *The company lost its assets.*

IUD Acceptable on first reference for *intrauterine device*. Explain on subsequent reference.

IV Acceptable in all references for *intravenous*.

i

j

jack-o'-lantern

Jacuzzi Trademark for a brand of whirlpool products. Generic terms are *whirlpool bath* or *whirlpool spa*.

jail Not interchangeable with *prison*. See **prison, jail**.

Japan Current A warm current flowing from the Philippine Sea east of Taiwan and northeast past Japan.

Japanese internment, incarceration During World War II, the United States — fearful that internal enemies would represent a fifth column in the battle against the Axis powers — set out to isolate people considered security risks. Under the rules of war, foreign nationals were taken into custody, or interned, at facilities operated by the Justice Department. But acting under Executive Order 9066, issued by President Franklin D. Roosevelt, authorities also detained an estimated 120,000 Japanese Americans and Japanese nationals, most of them living on the West Coast. They were placed in camps operated by the War Relocation Authority.

Though *internment* has been applied historically to all these detainments, the broad use of the term is inaccurate — about two-thirds of those who were relocated were U.S. citizens, and thus could not be considered interns — and many Japanese Americans find it objectionable.

It is better to say that they were *incarcerated* or *detained*, and to describe the larger event as the *incarceration* of Japanese Americans.

jargon The special vocabulary and idioms of a particular class or occupational group.

In general, avoid jargon. When it is appropriate in a special context, include an explanation of any words likely to be unfamiliar to most readers.

See **cliches, jargon** and **dialect**.

Jaws of Life Trademark name for the tool used to pry open parts of a vehicle to free those trapped inside.

Jaycees Members of the U.S. Junior Chamber of Commerce, affiliated with the worldwide body, Junior Chamber International.

See **fraternal organizations and service clubs** and **Junior Chamber of Commerce**.

jeep, Jeep Lowercase the military vehicle. Capitalize the civilian vehicle, a brand of Stellantis.

Jemaah Islamiyah Southeast Asian Islamic radical group. The words are Arabic for *Islamic congregation*, or *Islamic group*.

jerry-built To be made poorly, or of cheap materials: *flimsy houses were jerry-built on the hillside*. Sometimes confused with *jury-rig*, which means to be set up for temporary or emergency use: *a courtroom jury-*

rigged in a corner of the factory.

Jesus The central figure of Christianity, he also may be called *Jesus Christ* or *Christ.*

Personal pronouns referring to him are lowercase.

Jet Ski A registered trademark of Kawasaki for a type of personal watercraft.

jihad Arabic noun used to refer to the Islamic concept of the struggle to do good. In particular situations, that can include holy war, the meaning extremist Muslims commonly use. Use *jihadi* and *jihadis.* Do not use *jihadist.*

job descriptions Always lowercase. See **titles**.

John F. Kennedy Space Center
Located in Cape Canaveral, Florida, it is NASA's principal launch site for astronauts. *Kennedy Space Center* is acceptable in all references. Dateline: *CAPE CANAVERAL, Fla.*

See **Lyndon B. Johnson Space Center**.

Johns Hopkins University No apostrophes.

Joint Chiefs of Staff Also: *the Joint Chiefs.* But lowercase *the chiefs* or *the chiefs of staff.*

JPEG, JPG Acronyms for *Joint Photographic Experts Group*, a common image format used on the World Wide Web. Acronyms acceptable in all references.

judge Capitalize before a name when it is the formal title for an individual who presides in a court of law. Do

not continue to use the title in second reference.

Do not use *court* as part of the title unless confusion would result without it:

— No *court* in the title: *U.S. District Judge Jalen Garner, District Judge Jalen Garner, federal Judge Jalen Garner, Judge Jalen Garner, U.S. Circuit Judge Priscilla Owen, appellate Judge Priscilla Owen.*

— *Court* needed in the title: *Juvenile Court Judge Gabriela Cabrera, Criminal Court Judge John Jones, Superior Court Judge Robert Harrison, state Supreme Court Judge Keri Liu.*

When the formal title *chief judge* is relevant, put the court name after the judge's name: *Chief Judge Royce Lamberth of the U.S. District Court in Washington, D.C.; Chief Judge Karen Williams of the 4th U.S. Circuit Court of Appeals.*

Do not pile up long court names before the name of a judge. Make it *Judge John Smith of Allegheny County Common Pleas Court.* Not: *Allegheny County Common Pleas Court Judge John Smith.*

Lowercase *judge* as an occupational designation in phrases such as *contest judge Simon Cowell.*

See **administrative law judge; court names; judicial branch; justice;** and **magistrate**.

judge advocate The plural: *judge advocates.* Also: *judge advocate general, judge advocates general.*

Capitalize as a formal title before a name.

See **titles**.

judgment

judicial branch Always lowercase.
The federal court system that

exists today as the outgrowth of Article 3 of the Constitution is composed of the Supreme Court of the United States, the U.S. Court of Appeals, U.S. District Courts and the U.S. Customs Court. There are also four district judges for U.S. territories.

U.S. bankruptcy and magistrate judges are fixed-term judges serving in U.S. District Courts. Magistrate judges are generalist judges who preside in cases referred from U.S. district judges. Bankruptcy judges are specialized judges whose authority is restricted to bankruptcy issues.

The U.S. Tax Court and the U.S. Court of Military Appeals for the Armed Forces are not part of the judicial branch as such.

For more detail on all federal courts, see separate entries under the names listed here.

Judicial Conference of the United States This policymaking body for the courts of the judicial branch meets twice a year. Its 27 members are the chief justice of the United States, the chief judges of the 12 regional circuit courts of appeals, the chief judge of the Federal Circuit Court of Appeals, a district judge from each of the regional circuits, and the chief judge of the Court of International Trade.

Day-to-day functions are handled by the Administrative Office of U.S. Courts.

jumbo jet Any very large jet plane, including the Airbus A380 and Boeing 747.

Junior Chamber of Commerce A volunteer organization of young men and women involved in civic service and leadership training.

Members are called *Jaycees*.

U.S. headquarters is in Tulsa, Oklahoma; international headquarters in Coral Gables, Florida.

See **Jaycees**.

junior, senior Abbreviate as *Jr.* and *Sr.* and do not precede by a comma: *Martin Luther King Jr.*

The notation *II* or *2nd* may be used if it is the individual's preference. Note, however, that *II* and *2nd* are not necessarily the equivalent of *junior*; they often are used by a grandson or nephew.

Be clear in distinguishing between father and son on second reference if both names appear in a story. *The elder Smith* and *the younger Smith* is one option; *Smith Sr.* and *Smith Jr.* is also acceptable. The possessive form: *Smith Jr.'s career*.

See **names**.

junk bonds Also known as non-investment-grade bonds, these corporate debt securities provide high yields to investors to compensate for their higher-than-normal credit risk. They are typically issued by companies with a lot of debt to repay loans, fund takeovers or buy out stockholders.

jury The word takes singular verbs and pronouns: *The jury has been sequestered until it reaches a verdict*.

Include racial and gender breakdown only if relevant.

Do not capitalize: *a U.S. District Court jury, a federal jury, a Massachusetts Superior Court jury, a Los Angeles County grand jury*.

See **grand jury**.

jury-rig To set up something for

temporary or emergency use: *a courtroom jury-rigged in a corner of the factory*. Sometimes confused with *jerry-built*, which means to be made poorly, or of cheap materials: *flimsy houses were jerry-built on the hillside*.

justice Capitalize before a name when it is the formal title. It is the formal title for members of the U.S. Supreme Court and for jurists on some state courts. In such cases, do not use *judge* in first or subsequent references.

See **judge**; **Supreme Court of the United States**; and **titles**.

justice of the peace Capitalize as a formal title before a name. Do not abbreviate.

See **titles**.

justify *Smith justified his actions* means Smith demonstrated that his actions were right. If the actions are still controversial, say *Smith sought to justify his actions*.

juvenile delinquent Juveniles may be declared delinquents in many states for anti-social behavior or for breaking the law. In some states, laws prohibit publishing or broadcasting the names of juvenile delinquents.

Follow the local law unless there is a compelling reason to the contrary. Consult with regional editors if you believe such an exception is warranted.

See **privacy**.

juveniles See **names**; **privacy**.

k

K The *K* abbreviation is acceptable in headline and statistical references to kilometers, such as *a 10K race*; in baseball for strikeouts: *pitcher records 12 K's*; and monetary amounts in thousands: *employee earns $80K*.

kaffiyeh The men's headdress in Arab countries.

Kathmandu Preferred spelling for the capital of Nepal.

Kelvin scale A scale of temperature based on, but different from, the *Celsius scale*. It is used primarily in science to record very high and very low temperatures. The Kelvin scale starts at zero and indicates the total absence of heat (absolute zero).

Temperatures on the Kelvin scale are called *kelvins*, not *degrees*. The symbol, a capital K, stands alone with no degree symbol (*10 K*).

See **Celsius** and **Fahrenheit**.

keynote address Also: *keynote speech*.

keywords Terms used to define an online search.

KGB Acceptable on first reference, but the story should contain a phrase identifying it as the former Russian secret police and intelligence agency.

The initials stand for the Russian words meaning *Committee for State Security*.

kibbutz An Israeli collective settlement.

The plural is *kibbutzim*.

kidnap, kidnapped, kidnapping, kidnapper

kilo- A prefix denoting 1,000 units of a measure.

kilogram The metric term for 1,000 grams. A kilogram is equal to approximately 2.2 pounds or 35 ounces.

See **gram**; **metric system**; and **pound**.

kilohertz Equals 1,000 hertz (1,000 cycles per second). Spell out on first reference. Abbreviate *kHz*.

kilometer The metric term for 1,000 meters. Abbreviate *km*. A kilometer is equal to approximately 3,281 feet, or five-eighths (0.62) of a mile.

See **meter**; **metric system**; and **miles**.

kilometers per hour The abbreviation *kph* is acceptable in all references.

kiloton, kilotonnage A unit used to measure the power of nuclear explosions. One kiloton has the explosive force of 1,000 tons of TNT.

The atomic bomb dropped Aug. 6, 1945, on Hiroshima, Japan, in the first use of the bomb as a weapon had an explosive force of 20 kilotons.

A *megaton* has the force of a million tons of TNT. A *gigaton* has the force of a billion tons of TNT.

kilowatt-hour The amount of electrical energy consumed when

1,000 watts are used for one hour. The abbreviation *kWh* is acceptable on second reference. See **watt**.

king, queen Capitalize only when used before the name of royalty: *Queen Elizabeth II, King Felipe VI*. In subsequent references, use only the given name: *Elizabeth, Felipe*.

Lowercase *king* and *queen* when they stand alone: *The queen's birthday is Monday.* Capitalize in plural uses before names: *Kings George and Edward.* Lowercase in phrases such as *strikeout king Nolan Ryan*. See **nobility**.

kindergarten, kindergartners But pre-K, K-12.

Kindle Name of e-reader sold by Amazon. Older Amazon tablets were known as the *Kindle Fire*, although newer models are simply known as *Fire tablets*. *Kindle* is also the name of the proprietary e-book format for Kindle e-readers and the app for reading such books on phones and other devices.

Kitty Litter A brand of absorbent material used in cat litter boxes. Use a generic term such as *cat litter*.

Kleenex A trademark for a brand of facial tissue.

Knesset The Israeli parliament.

K-9

Kolkata Indian city formerly known as Calcutta.

Koran Use *Quran* in all references except when preferred by an organization or in a specific title or name. See **Quran**.

Korea The Korean Peninsula remains in a technical state of war, divided by the *Demilitarized Zone* into *North Korea*, officially the *Democratic People's Republic of Korea*, and *South Korea*, officially the *Republic of Korea*. On follow-ups, the *North* and the *South* are acceptable. The abbreviations *NKorea* and *SKorea* are used only in headlines. *DMZ* is acceptable on second reference.

Korean names The style and spelling of names in North Korea and South Korea follow each government's standard policy for transliterations unless the subject has a personal preference.

North Korean names are written as three separate words, each starting with a capital letter: *Kim Jong Un.* Use *Kim* on second reference.

South Korean names are written as two names, with the given name hyphenated and a lowercase letter after the hyphen: *Moon Jae-in.* Use *Moon* on second reference.

For South Korean place names, use the revised Romanized spellings introduced by the South Korean government in 2000: *Incheon* (formerly Inchon), *Busan* (formerly Pusan).

In both Koreas, the family name comes first.

Korean War But lowercase *Korean conflict*.

kosher Always lowercase.

K-pop Music performed by music stars and bands originating from South Korea. It's an amalgamation of pop, R&B and hip-hop sounds from the West but also blends cultural elements of the country. K-pop can be traced back to the early 1990s. The music groups were initially popular only in Asia, but K-pop has grown into a global phenomenon, particularly after the success of boy band BTS in late 2010s.

Kriss Kringle Not *Kris*. Derived from the German word *Christkindl*, or baby Jesus. See **Santa Claus, Santa**.

K2 World's second-tallest mountain. No hyphen. Part of the Karakoram range on the border of Pakistan, India and China. The Karakoram range is among a complex of ranges including the Himalayas.

kudos It means *credit or praise for an achievement*.
  The word is singular and takes singular verbs.

Ku Klux Klan A secretive society organized in the South after the Civil War to assert white supremacy, often using violence. The organization splintered, and not all successor groups use the full name. But each may be referred to as *the Ku Klux Klan. The klan* or *the KKK* may be used on second reference.

Kuomintang The Chinese Nationalist political party. Do not follow with the word *party*. *Tang* means party.

Kuril Islands Use in datelines after a community name in stories from these islands. Name an individual island, if needed, in the text.
  Explain in the text that a small portion of the archipelago is claimed by Japan but most are part of Russia.

Kyiv Capital of Ukraine. A 2019

change in style, in line with the Ukrainian government's preferred transliteration to English and increasing usage. Pronunciation: KEE'-yeev. The style for the food dish remains *chicken Kiev*.

k

L The name of the Chicago train system. Not *El*.

Labor Day The first Monday in September.

Labrador The mainland portion of the Canadian province of Newfoundland and Labrador.

Use *Newfoundland* in datelines after the name of a community. Specify in the text that it is in Labrador.

lady Do not use as a synonym for *woman*. *Lady* may be used when it is a title for members of the nobility.

See **nobility**.

lake Capitalize as part of a proper name: *Lake Erie, Canandaigua Lake, the Finger Lakes*.

Lowercase in plural uses: *lakes Erie and Ontario; Canandaigua and Seneca lakes*.

lame duck (n.) **lame-duck** (adj.)

laptop

last Avoid the use of *last* as a synonym for *latest* if it might imply finality. *The last time it rained, I forgot my umbrella*, is acceptable. But: *The last announcement was made at noon* may leave the reader wondering whether the announcement was the final announcement, or whether others are to follow.

The word *last* is not necessary to convey the notion of most recent when the name of a month or day is used:

Preferred: *It happened Wednesday. It happened in April*. Correct, but redundant: *It happened last Wednesday*.

But: *It happened last week. It happened last month*.

late Do not use it to describe someone's actions while alive.

Wrong: *Only the late senator opposed this bill*. (The senator was not dead at that time.)

Latin American A person who hails from or whose family background is in Mexico, Central America, parts of the West Indies or South America, where Spanish, Portuguese and French are the official languages derived from Latin.

latitude and longitude *Latitude*, the distance north or south of the equator, is designated by parallels. *Longitude*, the distance east or west of Greenwich, England, is designated by meridians.

Use these forms to express degrees of latitude and longitude: *New York City lies at 40 degrees 45 minutes north latitude and 74 degrees 0 minutes west longitude; New York City lies south of the 41st parallel north and along the 74th meridian west*.

lawsuit *Civil lawsuit* is redundant. See **sue**.

lawyer A generic term for all members of the bar.

An *attorney* is someone legally

appointed or empowered to act for another, usually, but not always, a lawyer. An *attorney at law* is a lawyer.

A *barrister* is an English lawyer who is specially trained and appears exclusively as a trial lawyer in higher courts. He is retained by a solicitor, not directly by the client. There is no equivalent term in the United States.

Counselor, when used in a legal sense, means a person who conducts a case in court, usually, but not always, a lawyer. A *counselor at law* is a lawyer. *Counsel* frequently is used collectively for a group of counselors.

A *solicitor* in England is a lawyer who performs legal services for the public. A solicitor appears in lower courts but does not have the right to appear in higher courts, which are reserved to barristers.

A *solicitor* in the United States is a lawyer employed by a governmental body. *Solicitor* is generally a job description, but in some agencies it is a formal title.

Solicitor general is the formal title for a chief law officer (where there is no attorney general) or for the chief assistant to the law officer (when there is an attorney general). Capitalize when used before a name.

Do not use *lawyer* as a formal title. See **attorney, lawyer** and **titles**.

lay, lie The action word is *lay*. It takes a direct object. *Laid* is the form for its past tense and its past participle. Its present participle is *laying*.

When *lie* means *to make an untrue statement*, the verb forms are *lie, lied, lying*.

Lie also has various other meanings, including *to recline, to be situated* or *to exist*. It does not take a direct object. Its past tense is *lay*. Its past participle is *lain*. Its present

participle is *lying*.

Some examples:

PRESENT OR FUTURE TENSES:

Right: *I will lay the book on the table. The prosecutor tried to lay the blame on him.*

Wrong: *He lays on the beach all day. I will lay down.*

Right: *He lies on the beach all day. I will lie down. The village lies beyond the hills. The answer lies in the stars.*

IN THE PAST TENSE:

Right: *I laid the book on the table. The prosecutor has laid the blame on him.*

Right: *He lay on the beach all day. He has lain on the beach all day. I lay down. I have lain down. The secret lay in the fermentation process.*

WITH THE PRESENT PARTICIPLE:

Right: *I am laying the book on the table. The prosecutor is laying the blame on him.*

Right: *He is lying on the beach. I am lying down.*

layoff (n.) **lay off** (v.)

Leaning Tower of Pisa

leatherneck Lowercase this nickname for a member of the U.S. Marine Corps. It is derived from the leather lining that was formerly part of the collar on the Marine uniform.

lectern, podium, pulpit, rostrum A speaker stands *behind a lectern, on a podium* or *rostrum*, or *in the pulpit*.

lectures Capitalize and use quotation marks for their formal titles, as described in **composition titles**.

LED Short for *light-emitting diodes*, LED is a form of lighting created when electrical currents run through semiconductor materials. Unlike traditional lightbulbs, LED produces light in one direction and is often more energy-efficient. *LED* is acceptable on first reference.

LEED Acronym for *Leadership in Energy and Environmental Design*, the rating system used by the U.S. Green Building Council to measure a building's sustainability and resource-efficiency. *LEED* is acceptable on first reference, but spell out and explain later in the story. Uppercase a LEED rating level: *LEED certified, LEED Gold certified.* Also: *LEED Silver, LEED Platinum,* the highest rating.

leftist, ultra-leftist In general, avoid these terms in favor of a more precise description of an individual's political philosophy.

Ultra-leftist suggests an individual who subscribes to a communist view or one holding that liberal or socialist change cannot come within the present form of government.

See **radical** and **rightist, ultra-rightist**.

left wing (n.) **left-winger** (n.) **left-wing** (adj.) Generally try to avoid in describing political leanings.

legion, legionnaire See **American Legion** and **French Foreign legion**.

Legionnaires' disease The respiratory disease takes its name from an outbreak at the Pennsylvania American Legion convention held at the Bellevue-Stratford Hotel in Philadelphia in July 1976. The bacterium believed to be responsible is found in soil and grows in water, such as air-conditioning ducts, storage tanks and rivers.

legislative bodies In general, capitalize the proper name of a specific legislative body abroad: *the Knesset, the Diet.*

The most frequent names in use are *Congress, National Assembly* and *Parliament.*

GENERIC USES: Lowercase *parliament* or a similar term only when used generically to describe a body for which the formal name is being given: *the Diet, Japan's parliament.*

PLURALS: Lowercase *parliament* and similar terms in plural constructions: *the parliaments of England and France, the English and French parliaments.*

INDIVIDUAL HOUSES: The principle applies also to individual houses of the nation's legislature, just as *Senate* and *House* are capitalized in the United States:

ROME (AP) — New leaders have taken control in the Chamber of Deputies.

Lowercase *assembly* when used as a shortened reference to *national assembly*.

In many countries, *national assembly* is the name of a unicameral legislative body. In some, such as France, it is the name for the lower house of a legislative body known by some other name such as *parliament*.

legislative titles FIRST-REFERENCE FORM: Use *Rep., Reps., Sen.* and *Sens.* as formal titles before one or more names. Spell out and lowercase *representative* and *senator* in other uses.

Spell out other legislative titles in all uses. Capitalize formal titles such as *chair, city councilor, delegate,* etc., when they are used before a name. Lowercase in other uses.

Add *U.S.* or *state* before a title

only if necessary to avoid confusion: *Former state Attorney General Dan Sullivan, a Republican, defeated U.S. Sen. Mark Begich, a Democrat from Alaska, during the 2014 general election.*

In stories with international datelines, include *U.S.* before legislative titles.

FIRST-REFERENCE PRACTICE: The use of a title such as *Rep.* or *Sen.* in first reference is normal in most stories. It is not mandatory, however, provided an individual's title is given later in the story.

Deletion of the title on first reference is frequently appropriate, for example, when an individual has become well known: *Barack Obama declared Americans were ready to "cast aside cynicism" as he looked for a convincing win in the Democratic contest. The Illinois senator was leading in the polls.*

SECOND REFERENCE: Do not use legislative titles before a name on second reference unless they are part of a direct quotation.

CONGRESSMAN, CONGRESSWOMAN: *Rep.* and *U.S. Rep.* are the preferred first-reference forms when a formal title is used before the name of a U.S. House member.

In stand-alone references, the terms *U.S. House representative, representative, member of Congress* are preferred. *Congressman* and *congresswoman* are acceptable. Do not use *congressperson. Congressman* and *congresswoman* should appear as capitalized formal titles before a name only in direct quotation.

ORGANIZATIONAL TITLES: Capitalize titles for formal, organizational offices within a legislative body when they are used before a name: *House Speaker Paul Ryan, Senate Majority Leader Mitch McConnell,* *House Minority Leader Nancy Pelosi, House Minority Whip Steny Hoyer, President Pro Tem Orrin Hatch, Senate Judiciary Committee Chairman Charles Grassley.*

See **party affiliation**; **titles**; **gender-neutral language**.

legislature Capitalize when preceded by the name of a state: *the Kansas Legislature.*

Retain capitalization when the state name is dropped but the reference is specifically to that state's legislature:

TOPEKA, Kan. (AP) — Both houses of the Legislature adjourned today.

Capitalize *legislature* in subsequent specific references and in such constructions as: *the 100th Legislature, the state Legislature.*

If a given context or local practice calls for the use of a formal name such as *Missouri General Assembly,* retain the capital letters if the name of the state can be dropped, but lowercase the word *assembly* if it stands alone. Lowercase *legislature* if a story uses it in a subsequent reference to a body identified as a general assembly.

Lowercase *legislature* when used generically: *No legislature has approved the amendment.*

Use *legislature* in lowercase for all plural references: *The Arkansas and Colorado legislatures are considering the amendment.*

In 49 states the separate bodies are a *senate* and a *house* or *assembly.* The *Nebraska Legislature* is a unicameral body. All members are *senators.*

See **assembly**; **general assembly**; **governmental bodies**; **House of Representatives**; and **Senate**.

-less No hyphen before this suffix:

tailless
weightless
waterless

leverage The use of debt to enhance returns. The expectation is that the cost of the debt will be lower than the earnings generated.

leveraged buyout A corporate acquisition in which the bulk of the purchase price is paid with borrowed money. The debt then is repaid with the acquired company's earnings, money raised by the sale of some of its assets or by the later sale of the entire company.

Levi's A trademark for a brand of jeans.

LGBTQ (adj.) See **gender, sex and sexual orientation**. Follow guidelines for **obscenities, profanities, vulgarities** as appropriate.

liabilities When used in a financial sense, the word means all the claims against a corporation.

They include accounts payable, wages and salaries due but not paid, dividends declared payable, taxes payable, and fixed or long-term obligations such as bonds, debentures and bank loans.

See **assets**.

liaison

lidar (n., adj.) Short for Light Detection and Ranging. A sensing method that sends pulses of laser light to determine the presence, shape and distance of objects, often in great detail. Lidar is on many autonomous vehicles and is used for a variety of uses related to the Earth and its surface. It can detect objects in darkness and at times in bad weather. The term is acceptable on first reference, but explain what it means. As an adjective: *lidar sensors* or *lidar lasers*.

lie in state Only people who are entitled to a state funeral may formally lie in state. In the United States, this occurs in the rotunda in the Capitol.

Those entitled to a state funeral are a president, a former president, a president-elect or any other person designated by the president.

Members of Congress may lie in state, and a number have done so. The decision is either house's to make, although the formal process normally begins with a request from the president.

Those entitled to an official funeral, but not to lie in state, are the vice president, the chief justice, Cabinet members and other government officials when designated by the president.

lieutenant governor Capitalize and abbreviate as *Lt. Gov.* or *Lt. Govs.* when used as a formal title before one or more names both inside and outside quotations. Lowercase and spell out in all other uses.

See **titles**.

life-size

life span

lifestyle

lifetime

light, lighted, lighting *Lit* is acceptable as the past tense form.

lightning The electrical discharge.

light-year The distance that light travels in one year at the rate of 186,282 miles per second. It works out to about 5.88 trillion miles (5,878,612,800,000 miles).

likable

-like Do not precede this suffix by a hyphen unless the letter l would be tripled or the main element is a proper noun:

> bill-like   Norwalk-like
> businesslike   shell-like
> An exception is flu-like.

like- Follow with a hyphen when used as a prefix meaning similar to:

> like-minded   like-natured
> No hyphen in words that have meanings of their own:
> likelihood   likewise
> likeness

like, as Use like as a preposition to compare nouns and pronouns. It requires an object: Jim blocks like a pro.

The conjunction as is the correct word to introduce clauses: Jim blocks the linebacker as he should.

linage, lineage Linage is the number of lines.

Lineage is ancestry or descent.

Lincoln's Birthday Capitalize birthday in references to the holiday.

Lincoln was born Feb. 12. His birthday is not a federal legal holiday.

Line Messaging service operated by Tokyo-based Line Corp., which is a subsidiary of South Korean tech company Naver Corp. It's primarily used for sharing text, photos and video and making calls with other individuals and small groups on the service, though it also has several non-messaging features including payments and games.

line numbers Use figures and lowercase the word line in naming individual lines of a text: line 1, line 9. But: the first line, the 10th line. See **numerals**.

LinkedIn A social media network owned by Microsoft Corp. that's used mainly for professional networking. Based in Mountain View, California.

link shortener A tool that allows users to shorten a URL to make it easier to share. Some link shorteners also allow users to track statistics related to clicks on those links, and they may allow "vanity" addresses that carry a brand's name.

liquefied natural gas Natural gas that has been cooled to minus 260 degrees Fahrenheit, making it liquid. The process reduces the volume of the gas, making it easier to transport. LNG is acceptable on second reference.

liquefy

liquidation When used in a financial sense, the word means the process of converting stock or other assets into cash.

When a company is liquidated, the cash obtained is first used to pay debts and obligations to holders of bonds and preferred stock. Whatever cash remains is distributed on a per-share basis to the holders of common stock.

liquidity The ease with which assets

can be converted to cash without loss in value. The faster it can be sold, the more liquid it is.

lists, bulleted lists AP uses dashes instead of bullets to introduce individual sections of a list; others may choose to use bullets. Put a space between the dash or bullet and the first word of each item in the list. Capitalize the first word following the dash or bullet. Use periods, not semicolons, at the end of each section, whether it is a full sentence or a phrase.

Use parallel construction for each item in a list:

— *Start with the same part of speech for each item (in this example, a verb).*

— *Use the same voice (active or passive) for each item.*

— *Use the same verb tense for each item.*

— *Use the same sentence type (statement, question, exclamation) for each item.*

— *Use just a phrase for each item, if desired.*

Introduce the list with a short phrase or sentence: *Our partners:* or *These are our partners:* or *Our partners are:*

Listserv A trademark for a software program for setting up and maintaining discussion groups through email. Do not use for generic list management software.

liter The basic unit of volume in the metric system. It is defined as the volume occupied by 1 kilogram of distilled water at 4 degrees Celsius. It works out to a total of 1,000 cubic centimeters (1 cubic decimeter).

It takes 1,000 milliliters to make a liter.

A liter is equal to approximately 34

fluid ounces or 1.06 liquid quarts. A liter equals 0.91 of a dry quart. The metric system makes no distinction between dry volume and liquid volume.

See **gallon**; **kilogram**; **metric system**; **quart (dry)**; and **quart (liquid)**.

literature See **composition titles**.

Little League, Little League Baseball The official name of the worldwide youth baseball and softball organization and its affiliated local leagues.

livable

livestream, livestreaming One word in all uses.

Lloyd's of London A self-regulating market of insurance. Founded in Britain in 1680, it relies on individual investors worldwide, known as Names, along with several hundred companies, to provide the money for underwriting insurance.

loan terminology Note the meanings of these terms in describing loans by governments and corporations:

bond A certificate issued by a corporation or government stating the amount of a loan, the interest to be paid, the time for repayment and the collateral pledged if payment cannot be made. Repayment generally is not due for a long period, usually seven years or more.

collateral Stock or other property that a borrower is obligated to turn over to a lender if unable to repay a loan.

convertible bond A bond carrying the stipulation that it may be exchanged for a specific amount of stock in the company that issued it.

coupon The interest rate stated on a bond and paid to a bondholder, usually semiannually.

debenture A certificate stating the amount of a loan, the interest to be paid and the time for repayment, but not providing collateral. It is backed only by the corporation's reputation and promise to pay.

default A person, corporation or government is in default if it fails to meet the terms for repayment.

full faith and credit bond An alternate term for general obligation bond, often used to contrast such a bond with a moral obligation bond.

general obligation bond A bond that has had the formal approval of either the voters or their legislature. The government's promise to repay the principal and pay the interest is constitutionally guaranteed on the strength of its ability to tax the population.

maturity The date on which a bond, debenture or note must be repaid.

moral obligation bond A government bond that has not had the formal approval of either the voters or their legislature. It is backed only by the government's "moral obligation" to repay the principal and interest on time.

municipal bond A general obligation bond issued by a state, county, city, town, village, possession or territory, or a bond issued by an agency or authority set up by one of these governmental units. In general, interest paid on municipal bonds is exempt from federal income taxes. It also usually is exempt from state and local taxes if held by someone living within the state of issue.

note A certificate issued by a corporation or government stating the amount of a loan, the interest to be paid and the collateral pledged in the event payment cannot be made. The date for repayment is generally more than a year after issue but not more than seven or eight years later. The shorter interval for repayment is the principal difference between a note and a bond.

revenue bond A bond backed only by the revenue of the airport, turnpike or other facility that was built with the money it raised.

Treasury borrowing A *Treasury bill* is a certificate representing a loan to the federal government that matures in three, six or 12 months. A *Treasury note* may mature in one to 10 years or more. A *Treasury bond* matures in more than 10 years. Because Treasurys carry the full backing of the government, they are viewed as the safest investment.

loan (n.) **lend** (v.) The preferred usage.

loath (adj.) **loathe** (v.) Note the difference. She is *loath* to leave. He *loathes* bureaucracy.

local Avoid the irrelevant use of the word.

Irrelevant: *The injured people were taken to a local hospital.*

Better: *The injured people were taken to a hospital.*

local of a union Always use a figure and capitalize *local* when giving the name of a union subdivision: *Local 123 of the United Auto Workers.*

Lowercase *local* standing alone in plural uses: *The local will vote Tuesday. He spoke to locals 2, 4 and 10.* See **union names**.

lodges See **fraternal organizations and**

service clubs.

login, logon, logoff (n.) But use as two words in verb form: *I log in to my computer.*

long shot Use two words for this term describing a big underdog.

long time, longtime *They have known each other a long time. They are longtime partners.*

long ton Also known as a *British ton.* Equal to 2,240 pounds. See **ton**.

looting, looters The taking or carrying off of plunder, or to burglarize or steal, during a riot, civil unrest or natural disaster. Apply the word *looters* carefully and specifically to those who engage in looting, do not overuse, and avoid the labeling and the stigmatizing of larger communities, groups or all protesters. The word *looters* applied to large groups has carried racial overtones in the past.

Whenever possible, explain circumstances. For example, *A group of people at the protest broke into the store and took whatever was on the shelves.* People engaged in looting may be petty criminals, individual community members or criminal gangs who have no relation to any nearby protests. In severe emergencies, such as hurricanes and floods that disrupt supplies, people sometimes steal to obtain water, food, medicine or essentials to survive. In all cases, it is important to explain the actions and the context in detail.

Los Angeles The city in California stands alone in datelines. *LA* is acceptable on second reference.

Hollywood is a district of the city of Los Angeles where the film industry used to be centered and where film studios and other production facilities, as well as landmark theaters, are still located. It is not a dateline and is most commonly used to describe Southern California's entertainment industry. *Beverly Hills* is an incorporated city and the dateline for the Golden Globes movie awards.

Lou Gehrig's disease Also called *amyotrophic lateral sclerosis*, or *ALS.* A progressive disease that attacks nerve cells that control muscles throughout the body. It became known as Lou Gehrig's disease after the star baseball player was diagnosed in 1939. Use *Lou Gehrig's disease* on first reference, but include the medical name later. *ALS* is acceptable in headlines and on second reference. Outside of the U.S., it is known as *motor neuron/ neurone disease.* See **disabilities**; **diseases**.

lowercase One word (n., v., adj.) when referring to the absence of capital letters. Originally from printers' practice.

Lucite A trademark for an acrylic plastic.

Lunar New Year The most important holiday in several East Asian countries, marking the start of the Chinese lunar calendar. The holiday starts anytime from mid-January to mid-February depending on the year. In China it is marked by a weeklong public holiday and mass travel by Chinese to their hometowns for family reunions. Also celebrated among Chinese communities overseas, especially in Southeast Asia. *Lunar New Year* is preferred over *Chinese New Year* or *Spring Festival*, the name it is known by in China. The holiday is also observed in South Korea, where it is known as *Seollal*, and Vietnam, where it is known as *Tet*.

-ly Do not use a hyphen between adverbs ending in -*ly* and adjectives they modify: *an easily remembered rule, a badly damaged island, a fully informed voter*.

See the compound modifiers section of the **hyphen** entry.

Lycra Unless referring to the trademark fiber or fabric, use a generic term such as *spandex* or *elastic* or *stretch fabric*.

Lyme disease An inflammatory disease caused by a tick bite.

Lyndon B. Johnson Space Center

Located in Houston, it is NASA's principal control and training center for astronauts. *Johnson Space Center* is acceptable in all references. Use HOUSTON dateline.

See **John F. Kennedy Space Center**.

m

Macao A spelling change (from Macau) in 2019, reflecting usage.

Mace A trademark, shortened from *Chemical Mace,* for a brand of tear gas that is packaged in an aerosol canister and temporarily stuns its victims.

machine gun (n.) **machine-gun** (v. and adj.) **machine-gunner, machine-gun fire**
    See **weapons**.

machine learning A form of *artificial intelligence* in which computers are "trained" to make humanlike decisions without being explicitly programmed for them. Examples of machine-learning applications include face recognition, language translation and self-driving cars. See **artificial intelligence; autonomous vehicles; face recognition**.

Mach number Named for Ernst Mach, an Austrian physicist, the figure represents the ratio of the speed of an object to the speed of sound in the surrounding medium, such as air, through which the object is moving.
    A rule of thumb for speed of sound is approximately 750 mph at sea level and approximately 660 mph at 30,000 feet above sea level.
    A body traveling at *Mach* 1 would be traveling at the speed of sound. *Mach 2* would equal twice the speed of sound.

mad cow disease Acceptable for bovine spongiform encephalopathy, a progressive neurological disease that afflicts cattle. The disorder caused in humans by eating meat from diseased cattle is called *variant Creutzfeldt-Jakob disease.* See **Creutzfeldt-Jakob disease**.

Mafia Secret criminal organization operating mainly in the U.S. and Italy and engaged in illegal activities such as gambling, drug-dealing and prostitution. Lowercase as a synonym for *organized crime.*

magazine names Capitalize the initial letters of the name but do not place it in quotes. Lowercase *magazine* unless it is part of the publication's formal title: Harper's Magazine, Newsweek magazine, Time magazine.
    Check the masthead if in doubt.

Magi Wise men who brought gifts to the infant Jesus at Epiphany, celebrated Jan. 6.

magistrate Capitalize when used as a formal title before a name. Use *magistrate judge* when referring to the fixed-term judge who presides in U.S. District Court and handles cases referred by U.S. district judges. See **titles**.

majority leader Capitalize when used as a formal title before a name: *Majority Leader Nancy Pelosi.* Lowercase elsewhere.
    See **legislative titles** and **titles**.

majority, plurality *Majority* means more than half of an amount.

Plurality means more than the next highest number.

COMPUTING MAJORITY: To describe how large a majority is, take the figure that is more than half and subtract everything else from it: If 100,000 votes were cast in an election and one candidate received 60,000 while opponents received 40,000, the winner would have a *majority* of 20,000 votes.

COMPUTING PLURALITY: To describe how large a plurality is, take the highest number and subtract from it the next highest number: If, in the election example above, the second-place finisher had 25,000 votes, the winner's *plurality* would be 35,000 votes.

Suppose, however, that no candidate in this example had a majority. If the first-place finisher had 40,000 votes and the second-place finisher had 30,000, for example, the leader's *plurality* would be 10,000 votes.

USAGE: When *majority* and *plurality* are used alone, they take singular verbs and pronouns: *The majority has made its decision.*

If a plural word follows an *of* construction, the decision on whether to use a singular or plural verb depends on the sense of the sentence: *A majority of two votes is not adequate to control the committee. The majority of the houses on the block were destroyed.*

-maker Follow Webster's New World College Dictionary. For words not in this book, if the word combination is not listed, use two words for the verb form and hyphenate any noun or adjective forms. Exceptions: *chipmaker, drugmaker, policymaker,* *coffee maker.*

makeup (n. and adj.) **make up** (v.)

Maldives Use this official name with a community name in a dateline: *MALE, Maldives.* Refer to the country in the body of the story as *the Maldives: The president won a referendum on the Maldives' future form of government.*

Mallorca Use instead of Spain in datelines on stories from communities on this island.

manageable

manager Capitalize when used as a formal title before a name: *City Manager Dick O'Connell.*

Do not capitalize in job descriptions, including sports teams: *Mets manager Terry Collins.*
See **titles**.

Manitoba A province of central Canada. Do not abbreviate.
See **datelines**.

mantel, mantle A *mantel* is a shelf. A *mantle* is a cloak.

Maoism (Maoist) The communist philosophy and policies of Mao Zedong. See **political parties and philosophies**.

Mardi Gras Literally *Fat Tuesday*, the term describes a day of merrymaking on the Tuesday before Ash Wednesday, the first day of Lent.

In New Orleans and many Roman Catholic countries, the Tuesday celebration is preceded by a week or more of parades and parties. See **Carnival**.

m

margin The practice of purchasing securities in part with borrowed money, using the purchased securities as collateral in anticipation of an advance in the market price. If the advance occurs, the purchaser may be able to repay the loan and make a profit. If the price declines, the stock may have to be sold to settle the loan. The margin is the difference between the amount of the loan and the value of the securities used as collateral.

marijuana, cannabis The terms *marijuana* and *cannabis* may be used interchangeably. The term *pot* is acceptable in headlines and generally in stories, though it may not be appropriate in some stories. *Cannabis* is the usual term outside North America. Some prefer *cannabis* because of arguments the term *marijuana* has anti-Mexican roots. Slang terms such as *weed, bud, reefer* or *ganja* are acceptable in limited, colloquial cases or in quotations.

Other cannabis-related terminology:

420 Slang for pot smoking, particularly at 4:20 p.m. or on April 20. Its origins are debated. No colon or slash is necessary unless referring specifically to the time or date.

budtender An employee who interacts with and sells products to customers at businesses that sell the drug. The term is acceptable in quotes and colloquial references; often terms like *employee, worker* or *staff member* will suffice.

cannabinoids Refers to the more than 100 chemical compounds found in the *cannabis* plant. The term is usually awkward in all but scientific contexts. Refer to them as *compounds, chemicals* or *derivatives* if needed. Spell out the name of all cannabinoids except *CBD* and *THC* on first reference. Use of other abbreviations, such as *CBGA* for *cannabigerolic acid*, is acceptable in subsequent references in limited use and only if necessary. See **synthetic cannabinoids** below.

CBD Acceptable in all references to *cannabidiol*. *CBD* does not cause a high and is often sold as a dietary supplement or included in creams and other personal care products. CBD products are legal, with some restrictions, in almost all states.

decriminalization A governmental policy of reducing or eliminating penalties for drug-related crimes, usually when dealing with small amounts for personal use. Not synonymous with legalization.

delta Lowercase the word *delta* and include a hyphen before the number when needed in references to specific *THC* compounds: *delta-8*. Uppercase *Delta-8*, though, in a brand name.

dispensary Acceptable term for establishments that provide marijuana for medical purposes. In states that have legalized the sale of recreational pot, words like *shop*, *store* or *retailer* suffice.

edibles Food into which marijuana has been incorporated. Acceptable in all references when the drug-related context is clear.

hashish A concentrated form of marijuana, sometimes colloquially shortened to *hash*. *Hashish oil* or *hash oil* is an extract that can be smoked, vaporized or infused into *edibles*.

hemp A plant in the *cannabis* family that is low in *THC*. Not synonymous with *cannabis* or *marijuana*. Its fibers are used in making rope, clothing, paper and other products.

medical marijuana, medical

cannabis Preferred term for the drug when prescribed by a doctor or otherwise used medicinally; *medicinal marijuana* is also acceptable. Do not use to refer to federally approved prescription drugs that contain cannabis compounds, such as Epidiolex. See **recreational marijuana**.

    recreational marijuana, recreational cannabis Acceptable term for the drug when taken for most nonmedical purposes; *casual* or *nonmedical use* are also acceptable. Other uses include *spiritual* and *therapeutic*. Be specific if needed. Avoid the euphemism *adult-use*.

    synthetic cannabinoids Drugs made of synthetic cannabis compounds that are added to plant material and sold for recreational use in products such as Spice and K2, often described as dangerous. Use the full term only if necessary; otherwise call them *synthetic cannabis compounds*. Do not refer to it by the inaccurate terms *fake pot* or *synthetic marijuana*.

    THC Acceptable in all references for *tetrahydrocannabinol*, the compound that gives pot its high. Include an explanation of the term in stories if unclear from the context. See **drugs**.

Marines Capitalize when referring to U.S. forces: *the U.S. Marines, the Marines, the Marine Corps, Marine regulations*. Do not use the abbreviation *USMC*.

    Capitalize *Marine* when referring to an individual in a Marine Corps unit: *He is a Marine.*

    Do not describe *Marines* as *soldiers*, which is generally associated with the Army. Use *troops* if a generic term is needed.

    Use the term *former Marine*, not *ex-Marine*, for those who have been honorably discharged.

Maritime Provinces The Canadian provinces of Nova Scotia, New Brunswick and Prince Edward Island.

marketbasket, marketplace

mark to market An accounting requirement that securities must be valued at their current price, rather than the purchase price or the price they might fetch later. Also called "fair value."

Marseille Preferred spelling for the French city.

Marshall Islands In datelines, give the name of a city and *Marshall Islands*. List the name of an individual island in the text.

marshal, marshaled, marshaling, Marshall *Marshal* is the spelling for both the verb and the noun: *Marilyn will marshal her forces. Erwin Rommel was a field marshal.*

    Marshall is used in proper names: *George C. Marshall, John Marshall, the Marshall Islands.*

Martin Luther King Jr. Day Federal holiday honoring the Rev. Martin Luther King Jr., who was born Jan. 15, 1929, is on the third Monday in January.

Marxism (Marxist) The system of thought developed by Karl Marx and Friedrich Engels. See **political parties and philosophies**.

Mason-Dixon Line The boundary line between Pennsylvania and Maryland, generally regarded as separating

m

the North from the South. (Named for 18th-century surveyors Charles Mason and Jeremiah Dixon, the line later was extended to West Virginia.)

Master of Arts, Master of Science, Master of Business Administration Abbreviated *M.A.*, *M.S.* but *MBA*. A *master's degree* or a *master's* is acceptable in any reference.

    See **academic degrees**.

matrimony See **sacraments** in Religion Guidelines.

maturity In a financial sense, the date on which a bond, debenture or note must be repaid. See **loan terminology**.

May Day, mayday *May Day* is May 1, often observed as a political or festive holiday.

    The compound *mayday* is the international distress signal, from the French *m'aider*, meaning "help me." It is lowercase in *mayday call* and capitalized as an exclamation: "*Mayday!*"

M.D. A word such as *physician* or *surgeon* is preferred. The periods in the abbreviation are an exception to Webster's New World College Dictionary.

    See **doctor** and **academic titles**.

mecca Lowercase in the metaphorical sense; capitalize the city in Saudi Arabia.

Medal of Honor The nation's highest military honor, awarded by Congress for risk of life in combat beyond the call of duty. Use *Medal of Honor recipient* or a synonym, but not *winner*.

There is no *Congressional Medal of Honor*.

medevac Acceptable abbreviation for *medical evacuation*, especially in referring to aircraft used to transport wounded military personnel. The verb form is *medevaced*. It's often better use the noun form: *He was taken from the crash site in a medevac helicopter.*

Medfly Mediterranean fruit fly. The capital *M* is an exception to Webster's New World College Dictionary.

media Generally takes a plural verb, especially when the reference is to individual outlets: *Media are lining up for and against the proposal.* The word is often preceded by "the." Sometimes used with a singular verb when referring to media as a monolithic group: *The media plays a major role in political campaigns.*

Medicaid The federal-state health care insurance program that helps pay for health care for low-income people of any age. Coverage varies by state; each state determines eligibility and the full scope of services covered. The federal government reimburses a percentage of the state's expenditures.

Medicare The federal health care insurance program for people who are age 65 or older or have certain severe disabilities or illnesses, regardless of income. Medicare helps pay charges for hospitalization, doctors' services, tests, prescription drugs, hospice and other care. Medicare does not pay for long-term care but covers limited nursing home stays when the patient needs medically skilled services, such as rehabilitation. In Canada, *Medicare* refers to the nation's national health insurance program.

"Medicare for All" The term means different things to different people but is generally thought of as a national program that would guarantee health insurance for every American. If applicable, explain how the subject of the story defines the term. Use quote marks on first reference. On later references: *Medicare for All*, no quote marks.

medieval

mega- A prefix denoting 1 million units of a measure.

megahertz A measure of radio frequency or the speed of a computer processor, equal to a million hertz, or cycles per second. Spell out on first reference. Abbreviate *MHz*.

melee

Memorial Day The federal legal holiday is the last Monday in May.

menswear Not *men's wear*.

mental illness The terms *mental illness* and *mentally ill* include a broad range of conditions. For guidance on specific conditions, see individual entries throughout the Stylebook.

Do not describe an individual as having a mental illness unless it is clearly pertinent to a story and the diagnosis is properly sourced.

When used, identify the source for the diagnosis. Seek firsthand knowledge derived from a medical examination; ask how the source knows. Don't rely on hearsay or speculate on a diagnosis. Avoid anonymous sources. On-the-record sources may be family members, mental health professionals, medical authorities, law enforcement officials or court records.

If someone says a person has a *history of mental illness*, seek details. If those details aren't immediately available, say so in the story and do additional reporting to follow up. Include those details in later stories. Specify the time frame for the diagnosis and ask about treatment. A person's condition can change over time, so a diagnosis of mental illness might not currently apply.

If used, comments about a *history of mental illness* must be attributed to law enforcement authorities, medical professionals, family members or others who have knowledge of the history and can authoritatively speak to its relevance. In the absence of definitive information, there should be a disclaimer that a link to a crime or other event had yet to be established.

Do not assume that mental illness is a factor in a violent crime, and avoid unsubstantiated statements by witnesses or first responders attributing violence to mental illness.

Studies have shown that the vast majority of people with mental illnesses are not violent, and experts say most people who are violent do not have mental illnesses.

Avoid interpreting behavior common to many people as symptoms of mental illness. Sadness, anger, exuberance and the occasional desire to be alone are normal emotions experienced by people who have mental illness as well as those who don't.

m

When practical, let people with mental illness talk about their own diagnoses.

Other points:

Be specific about the condition whenever possible and include sourcing: *The man accused in the killing was diagnosed with schizophrenia, according to court documents. She was diagnosed with anorexia, according to her parents. He said he was treated for depression.* Avoid wording such as *he is a schizophrenic* or *he is mentally ill* unless a person describes themself that way.

Avoid descriptions that connote pity, such as *afflicted with, suffers from, victim of, battling* and *demons.* Rather, *he has obsessive-compulsive disorder.*

Avoid dehumanizing "the" terms such as *the mentally ill.* Instead: *people with mental illnesses.*

Do not use derogatory terms, such as *insane, crazy/crazed, nuts* or *deranged,* unless they are part of a quotation that is essential to the story.

Avoid using mental illness-related words lightly or in unrelated situations. Some examples: calling a person or an idea *demented, psychotic, catatonic,* etc.; or saying an awards show was *schizophrenic.* Alternatives include: The idea is *deeply flawed* or *misguided*; the pressure is *intense*; the schedule is *demanding*; the strategy is *ineffective.*

See **disabilities; addiction; bipolar disorder; depression; diseases; obsessive-compulsive disorder; phobia; postpartum depression; post-traumatic stress disorder; seasonal affective disorder.** See the **Health and Science** chapter.

merchant marine Lowercase in referring to the ships of a nation used in commerce. Capitalize only in references to the organization the Merchant Marine or the U.S. Merchant Marine Academy. Members are *merchant mariners* or *merchant crewmen,* but not marines.

merger Few business combinations are truly a merger of equals, so be precise and sparing in the use of the word *merger.* It is not a synonym for acquisition or takeover, which should be the preferred descriptives in most stories. Use the following rules for deciding whether it's a merger or acquisition, and as a guide in concluding who is the acquirer and the company being taken over:

— Is one of the companies' stock being used as the currency? If the answer is yes, that's usually a good sign that company is the acquirer and it is not a merger.

— What is the message from the exchange ratio in stock transactions? Typically when shareholders of Company A are offered new shares in a combined company at a 1-for-1 ratio, and Company B shares are exchanged at something less or more (i.e., each Company B will be exchanged for 0.47% of a share of the new company), it's an indication that Company A's stock is being used as the basis for the transaction. But it also could be a sign that the companies' boards have agreed to a merger that uses a formula to compensate for the differing market value (total number of shares multiplied by the closing stock price the day before the announcement) of the two companies to come up with an exchange ratio for stock in the

new company.
— What is the message from the stock movements after the announcement? Shares of companies being acquired typically rise and shares of the acquirer often fall after the announcement. Not always, of course, but that's usually the case because most bidders pay a premium, or an above-market price, for the shares of the company being acquired, and investors often are worried about the amount of debt the acquirer is taking on to complete the transaction.
— Whose cash is being used to fund the cash portion of a transaction? If the announcement says Company A's cash will be used or that its existing lines of credit will be tapped to pay for Company B's shares, that's a strong indication that Company A is the acquirer.
— Which company's executives are filling most of the top management roles? The key distinction usually is who gets the CEO slot. But if one of the two CEOs is named to head the company for a limited period (say two years or less) before his fellow CEO takes over, that's a good sign of a political compromise to paper over the fact that the second CEO's company is going to be in charge long term.
— Which company will end up with the majority of the seats on the new board of directors? This is often a key tie breaker. When Company A and Company B insist it's a merger of equals and other checklist items are inconclusive, if one ends up with 60% of the board seats and the other gets 40%, that's a good indication of which is going to be in charge. Also, make sure you get not only the short-term makeup of the board of the combined company, but also whether there were any deals cut for some members to retire in short order.
— Where will the company be headquartered? Since CEOs typically do the negotiating and they typically aren't anxious to move, this can be an informative tell.

meridians Use numerals and lowercase to identify the imaginary locater lines that ring the globe from north to south through the poles. They are measured in units of 0 to 180 degrees east and west of the *prime meridian*, which runs through Greenwich, England.
Examples: *33rd meridian* (if location east or west of Greenwich is obvious), *1st meridian west, 100th meridian.*
See **latitude and longitude**.

Messenger Messaging service connected to the Facebook social platform, which is now owned by Meta Platforms Inc., formerly Facebook. *Messenger* is acceptable in all contexts; if necessary for clarity, use *Facebook's Messenger*.

messiah Capitalize in religious uses, such as references to the promised deliverer of the Jews or to Jesus in Christianity. Lowercase when referring to the liberator of a people or country.

metadata Behind-the-scenes data that provides important information about a piece of content. Examples include information about when or where information was created, by whom and in what format. If you refer to metadata in a story, explain what information is being revealed: *Investigators determined that Johnson wrote the document by analyzing its metadata, which indicated that it had been saved on his computer.*

Meta Platforms Inc. The company formerly known as Facebook, renamed in October 2021 to emphasize Mark Zuckerberg's new goal of building the *metaverse. Meta* is acceptable on first reference, but use the full name somewhere in the story. Describe it as *the parent company of Facebook* if the context isn't clear.

Based in Menlo Park, California, the company also owns *Instagram*, a photo and video-sharing service; the *WhatsApp* messaging service and Messenger. *Meta* calls this collection of businesses *Family of Apps*. Its other business segment, *Reality Labs*, includes virtual and augmented reality hardware and software such as the Oculus VR headset.

See **Facebook (social platform)**; **metaverse**.

metaverse A term minted by the science fiction writer Neal Stephenson in his 1992 novel *Snow Crash*, now used to describe a proposed immersive version of the internet accessed via virtual-reality headsets, augmented reality glasses, phone apps or other devices.

Think of the *metaverse* as the internet brought to life, or at least rendered in 3D. Mark Zuckerberg is now one of its biggest proponents; he even renamed *Facebook* the company to *Meta Platforms Inc.*, underscoring his determination to build a place where people can meet, work and play with others in virtual surroundings from any location in the world.

meter The basic unit of length in the metric system. It is equal to approximately 39.37 inches, which may be rounded off to 39.5 inches in most comparisons. It takes 100 centimeters to make a meter. It takes 1,000 meters to make a kilometer.

See **inch**; **metric system**; and **yard**.

#MeToo, #MeToo movement Aims to hold accountable those involved in sexual misconduct and those who cover it up.

metric system The Associated Press typically includes both metric and imperial figures in copy to serve customers throughout the world. Use the figure widely accepted in the location of the dateline, then the conversion in parentheses after the original figure. Round numbers up or down to avoid decimals unless a greater level of precision is important. For a story out of the U.S.: *He vowed to walk 62 miles (100 kilometers) in a week.* For a story out of France: *He vowed to walk 100 kilometers (62 miles) in a week.*

To avoid the need for long strings of figures, prefixes are added to the metric units to denote fractional elements or large multiples. The prefixes are: *pico-* (one-trillionth), *nano-* (one-billionth), *micro-* (one-millionth), *milli-* (one-thousandth), *centi-* (one-hundredth), *deci-* (one-tenth), *deka-* (10 units), *hecto-* (100 units), *kilo-* (1,000 units), *mega-* (1 million units), *giga-* (1 billion units), *tera-* (1 trillion units). Entries for each prefix show how to convert a unit preceded by the prefix to the basic unit.

m

In addition, separate entries for **gram**, **meter**, **liter**, **Celsius** and other frequently used metric units define them.

ABBREVIATIONS: The abbreviation mm for millimeter is acceptable in references to film widths (*8 mm film*) and weapons (*a 105 mm cannon*). (Note space between numeral and abbreviation.)

The principal abbreviations, for reference in the event they are used by a source, are: *g* (gram), *kg* (kilogram), *t* (metric ton), *m* (meter), *cm* (centimeter), *km* (kilometer), *mm* (millimeter), *L* (liter, capital L to avoid confusion with the figure 1) and *mL* (milliliter).

metric ton Equal to approximately 2,204.62 pounds. See **ton**.

Mexico There are 31 states and Mexico City, the capital and an independent federal district run by a city government. The states are Aguascalientes, Baja California, Baja California Sur, Campeche, Chiapas, Chihuahua, Coahuila, Colima, Durango, Guanajuato, Guerrero, Hidalgo, Jalisco, Mexico, Michoacan, Morelos, Nayarit, Nuevo Leon, Oaxaca, Puebla, Queretaro, Quintana Roo, San Luis Potosi, Sinaloa, Sonora, Tabasco, Tamaulipas, Tlaxcala, Veracruz, Yucatan and Zacatecas.

Mexican states elect their own governor and legislators. Congress is made up of two houses: the lower House of Deputies, with 500 members, and the Senate, with 128 members.

In datelines, use only the city and country.

mic (n.) Informal form of *microphone*.

micro- A prefix denoting one-millionth of a unit.

microtargeting The practice of targeting ads to small groups of people, sometimes even individuals, based on data collected by advertisers and internet companies like Meta and Google.

mid- No hyphen unless a capitalized word follows: *midair*, *mid-America*, *mid-Atlantic*, *midsemester* and *midterm*.

But use a hyphen when *mid-* precedes a figure: *mid-30s*.

Middle Ages A.D. 476 to approximately A.D. 1450.

Middle Atlantic States As defined by the U.S. Census Bureau, they are New Jersey, New York and Pennsylvania.

Less formal references often consider Delaware part of the group. See **Northeast**.

middle class (n.) **middle-class** (adj.)

Middle East The term generally applies to southwest Asia west of Pakistan and Afghanistan (Iran, Iraq, Israel, Kuwait, Jordan, Lebanon, Oman, Bahrain, Qatar, Saudi Arabia, Syria, the eastern part of Turkey known also as Asia Minor, United Arab Emirates and Yemen), and northeastern Africa (Egypt and Sudan).

Some consider Libya and other Arabic-speaking countries of the Maghreb to be part of the region.

Popular usage once distinguished between the *Near East* (the westerly nations in the listing) and the *Middle East* (the easterly nations), but the two terms now overlap, with current practice favoring *Middle East* for both areas.

Use *Middle East* unless *Near East* is used by a source in a story.

Mideast is also acceptable, but *Middle East* is preferred.

middle initials Include middle initials in stories where they help identify a specific individual. Examples include casualty lists and stories naming someone accused in a crime.

See **names**.

middle names Use them only with people who are publicly known that way (*James Earl Jones*), or to prevent confusion with people of the same name.

See **middle initials; names**.

midnight Avoid using the term if it would create ambiguity about what day something is taking place, since some users' understandings may vary. Instead: *11:59 p.m. Thursday* or *12:01 a.m. Friday*.

Midwest Use *Midwest*, not *Middle West*, for the 12-state region as defined by the U.S. Census Bureau (previously designated the North Central region) that is broken into two divisions. Capitalize *Midwestern* as an adjective describing the region.

The five *East North Central* states are Indiana, Illinois, Michigan, Ohio and Wisconsin.

The seven *West North Central* states are Iowa, Kansas, Minnesota, Missouri, Nebraska, North Dakota and South Dakota.

See **Northeast**, **South** and **West** for the bureau's other regional breakdowns.

See **directions and regions**.

MiG The *i* in this designation for a type of Russian fighter jet is lowercase because it is the Russian word for *and*. The initials are from the last names of the designers, Arten Mikoyan and Mikhail Gurevich.

The forms: *MiG-19*, *MiG-21s*.

See **aircraft names**.

mile Also called a statute mile, it equals 5,280 feet. The metric equivalent is approximately 1.6 kilometers.

See **foot**; **kilometer**; **nautical miles, knots**; **nautical mile** and **numerals**.

miles per gallon The abbreviation *mpg* is acceptable in all references when paired with a figure: *The car got 40 mpg.* But write out in general uses: *"My car gets a lot of miles per gallon,"* he said.

miles per hour The abbreviation *mph* is acceptable in all references. No hyphen when used with a figure: *60 mph*.

military academies Capitalize *U.S. Air Force Academy, U.S. Coast Guard Academy, U.S. Merchant Marine Academy, U.S. Military Academy, U.S. Naval Academy.* Retain capitalization if the *U.S.* is dropped: *the Air Force Academy*, etc.

Lowercase *academy* whenever it stands alone.

Cadet is the proper title on first reference for men and women enrolled at the Army, Air Force, Coast Guard and Merchant Marine academies. *Midshipman* is the proper title for men and women enrolled at the Naval Academy.

Use the appropriate title on first reference. On second reference, use only the last name.

military terms

military training Do not use the term *military training* broadly. Be specific as to what the person's job was or is. For example: *The candidate pointed to her six years as a Marine captain in Iraq*, not *the candidate pointed to her military training. Police said the suspect was a cook at Eglin Air Force Base* or *Police said the suspect was an Army sniper for five years*, not *police said the suspect had military training.*

decorated Do not use this term broadly in describing someone's military background unless it is merited by the nature of the award. Some awards, badges and ribbons are routine. For instance, all services award badges or ribbons for annual weapons qualification. A marksmanship badge or ribbon does not mean that a person is a sniper or an expert. Be specific.

soldiers Don't use this term to broadly describe members of the U.S armed forces. *Soldiers* are members of the Army. *Marines* are Marines. The Navy has *sailors*. Air Force personnel are *airmen*. Space Force members are *Guardians*. Members of the Coast Guard are *Coast Guardsmen*.

Stolen Valor Act A 2013 law making it unlawful to profit off fraudulent military service. People found simply wearing badges, rank or claiming service they did not earn are not subject to the law unless they profit in some way. The lowercase term *stolen valor* is sometimes used to describe a person's lies about military service. Avoid unless in a direct quotation.

military titles Capitalize a military rank when used as a formal title before an individual's name.

See the lists that follow to determine whether the title should be spelled out or abbreviated in regular text.

On first reference, use the appropriate title before the full name of a member of the military.

In subsequent references, do not continue using the title before a name. Use only the last name.

Spell out and lowercase a title when it is substituted for a name: *Gen. John Jones is the top U.S. commander in Afghanistan. The general endorsed the idea.*

In some cases, it may be necessary to explain the significance of a title: *Army Sgt. Maj. John Jones described the attack. Jones, who holds the Army's highest rank for enlistees, said it was unprovoked.*

In addition to the ranks listed on the next page, each service has ratings such as *machinist, radarman, torpedoman*, etc., that are job descriptions. Do not use any of these designations as a title on first reference. If one is used before a name in a subsequent reference, do not capitalize or abbreviate it.

Moreover, each service branch has its own systems of abbreviating officer and enlisted ranks — e.g., COL for colonel in the Army, CMDR for Navy commander — that vary widely from AP style. However, the Department of Defense uses AP's military titles in news releases because the abbreviations are easily understood.

ABBREVIATIONS: The abbreviations, with the highest ranks listed first:

m

MILITARY TITLES

Rank	Usage before a name

ARMY

Commissioned Officers

general	Gen.

lieutenant general	Lt. Gen.
major general	Maj. Gen.
brigadier general	Brig. Gen.
colonel	Col.
lieutenant colonel	Lt. Col.
major	Maj.
captain	Capt.
first lieutenant	1st Lt.
second lieutenant	2nd Lt.

Warrant Officers

chief warrant officer five (CW5)	Chief Warrant Officer 5
chief warrant officer four (CW4)	Chief Warrant Officer 4
chief warrant officer three (CW3)	Chief Warrant Officer 3
chief warrant officer two (CW2)	Chief Warrant Officer 2
warrant officer (WO1)	Warrant Officer

Enlisted Personnel

sergeant major of the Army	Sgt. Maj. of the Army
command sergeant major	Command Sgt. Maj.
sergeant major	Sgt. Maj.
first sergeant	1st Sgt.
master sergeant	Master Sgt.
sergeant first class	Sgt. 1st Class
staff sergeant	Staff Sgt.
sergeant	Sgt.
corporal	Cpl.
specialist	Spc.
private first class	Pfc.
private	Pvt.

NAVY, COAST GUARD

Commissioned Officers

admiral	Adm.
vice admiral	Vice Adm.
rear admiral upper half	Rear Adm.
rear admiral lower half	Rear Adm.
captain	Capt.
commander	Cmdr.
lieutenant commander	Lt. Cmdr.
lieutenant	Lt.
lieutenant junior grade	Lt. j.g.
ensign	Ensign

Warrant Officers

chief warrant officer	Chief Warrant Officer

Enlisted Personnel

master chief petty officer of the Navy	Master Chief Petty Officer of of the Navy
master chief petty officer	Master Chief Petty Officer
senior chief petty officer	Senior Chief Petty Officer
chief petty officer	Chief Petty Officer
petty officer first class	Petty Officer 1st Class
petty officer second class	Petty Officer 2nd Class
petty officer third class	Petty Officer 3rd Class
seaman	Seaman
seaman apprentice	Seaman Apprentice
seaman recruit	Seaman Recruit

MARINE CORPS

Ranks and abbreviations for commissioned officers are the same as those in the Army. Warrant officer ratings follow the same system used in the Navy. There are no specialist ratings.

Others

sergeant major of the Marine Corps	Sgt. Maj. of the Marine Corps
sergeant major	Sgt. Maj.
master gunnery sergeant	Master Gunnery Sgt.
first sergeant	1st Sgt.
master sergeant	Master Sgt.
gunnery sergeant	Gunnery Sgt.
staff sergeant	Staff Sgt.
sergeant	Sgt.
corporal	Cpl.
lance corporal	Lance Cpl.
private first class	Pfc.
private	Pvt.

AIR FORCE

Ranks and abbreviations for commissioned officers are the same as those in the Army.

Enlisted Designations

chief master sergeant of the Air Force	Chief Master Sgt. of the Air Force
chief master sergeant	Chief Master Sgt.

senior master sergeant	Senior Master Sgt.
master sergeant	Master Sgt.
technical sergeant	Tech. Sgt.
staff sergeant	Staff Sgt.
senior airman	Senior Airman
airman first class	Airman 1st Class
airman	Airman
airman basic	Airman

PLURALS: Add *s* to the principal element in the title: *Majs. John Jones and Robert Smith; Maj. Gens. John Jones and Robert Smith; Spcs. John Jones and Robert Smith.*

RETIRED OFFICERS: A military rank may be used in first reference before the name of an officer who has retired if it is relevant to a story. Do not, however, use the military abbreviation *Ret.*

Instead, use *retired* just as *former* would be used before the title of a civilian: *They invited retired Army Gen. John Smith.*

FIREFIGHTERS, POLICE OFFICERS: Use the abbreviations listed here when a military-style title is used before the name of a firefighter or police officer outside a direct quotation. Add *police* or *fire* before the title if needed for clarity: *police Sgt. William Smith, fire Capt. David Jones.*

Spell out titles such as *detective* that are not used in the armed forces.

military units Use Arabic figures and capitalize the key words when linked with the figures: *1st Infantry Division* (or *the 1st Division*), *5th Battalion, 395th Field Artillery, 7th Fleet.*

But: *the division, the battalion, the artillery, the fleet.*

See **numerals**.

milli- A prefix denoting one-thousandth of a unit.

milligram One-thousandth of a gram.

See **metric system**.

milliliter One-thousandth of a liter. See **liter** and **metric system**.

millimeter One-thousandth of a meter. It takes 10 millimeters to make a centimeter.

May be abbreviated as *mm* when used with a numeral in first or subsequent references to film or weapons: *35 mm film, 105 mm artillery piece.* (Note space after numeral.)

See **meter; metric system;** and **inch.**

millions, billions, trillions Use figures with *million, billion* or *trillion* in all except casual uses: *I'd like to make a billion dollars.* But: *The nation has 1 million citizens. I need $7 billion. The government ran a deficit of more than $1 trillion.*

Do not go beyond two decimal places. *7.51 million people, $256 billion, 7,542,500 people, $2,565,750,000.* Decimals are preferred where practical: *1.5 million.* Not: *1 1/2 million.*

Do not mix *millions* and *billions* in the same figure: *2.6 billion.* Not: *2 billion 600 million.*

Do not drop the word *million* or *billion* in the first figure of a range: *He is worth from $2 million to $4 million.* Not: *$2 to $4 million,* unless you really mean $2.

Note that a hyphen is not used to join the figures and the word *million* or *billion,* even in this type of phrase: *The president submitted a $300 billion budget.*

In headlines, abbreviate only *millions, billions: $5M lawsuit, $17.4B trade deficit*

See **numerals**.

mini- The rules in **prefixes** apply, but

in general, no hyphen.

minimally conscious state In this
condition, the eyes are open, but
the patient shows only minimal
or intermittent signs of awareness
of self and environment and often
responds only inconsistently when
asked to gesture, move or speak. At
times, the patient may be able to
reach for objects, indicate yes or no
and follow objects with the eyes, but
a given patient may not be able to do
all these things.

See **coma** and **vegetative state**.

minister It is not a formal title in
most religions, with exceptions such
as the Nation of Islam, and is not
capitalized. Where it is a formal title,
it should be capitalized before the
name: *Minister John Jones*.

See **religious titles** and the entry
for an individual's denomination in
the **Religion** chapter.

minority leader Treat the same as
majority leader. See that entry and
legislative titles.

minuscule

minus sign Use a hyphen, not a dash,
but use the word *minus* if there is
any danger of confusion.

Use a word, not a minus sign, to
indicate temperatures below zero:
minus 10 or *5 below zero*.

MIRV, MIRVs Acceptable on first
reference for *multiple independently
targetable reentry vehicle(s)*.

Explain in the text that a *MIRV* is
an intercontinental ballistic missile
with several warheads, each of which
can be directed to a different target.

mishap A minor misfortune. People
are not killed in *mishaps*.

**misinformation, fact checks, fake
news** The term *misinformation*
refers to false information shared
about a particular topic that could
be mistaken as truth. It can include
honest mistakes, exaggerations, and
misunderstandings of facts, as well
as *disinformation*, which refers to
misinformation created and spread
intentionally as a way to mislead or
confuse.

Misinformation can be transmitted
in any medium, including social
media, websites, printed materials
and broadcast. It includes
photography or video and audio
recordings that have been created,
manipulated or selectively edited.

The term typically excludes
opinions, as well as satire and
parody. It does include hoaxes,
propaganda and fabricated news
stories.

When used broadly, the term
misinformation is preferable to
the term *fake news*. The term *fake
news* may be used in quotes or as
shorthand for deliberate falsehoods
or fiction masked as news.

When using either term, be
specific in describing what is false
and back up that description with
facts. Avoid amplifying the false
claim.

Do not label as *fake news* specific
or individual news items that are
disputed. If *fake news* is used in
a quote, push for specifics about
what is meant. Alternative wording
includes *false reports, erroneous
reports, unverified reports, questionable
reports, disputed reports* or *false
reporting*, depending on the context.

Fact-checking is essential in
debunking fabricated stories or parts
of stories, or other misinformation.

This requires reporting or research to verify facts that affirm or disprove a statement, or that show a gray area.

The goal of fact-checking is to push back on falsehoods, exaggeration and political spin, and to hold politicians and public figures accountable for their words.

Basic fact-checking should always be part of the main story, including wording noting when an assertion differs with known facts. Often, however, additional reporting is required to explore disputed points or questions more fully. In those cases, a separate fact check piece should be done. Some points:

Present the assertion that's being checked, and quickly state what's wrong with it or what is correct. Use the exact quote or quotes that are being examined. Follow with the facts, backed by appropriate citations and attribution.

Stick to checking facts, rather than opinion. A person's personal tastes and preferences might lie outside the mainstream, but as opinions they are not a topic for a fact check.

Fact checks need not show statements to be clearly correct or clearly incorrect. Words can be true, false, exaggerated, a stretch, a selective use of data, partly or mostly true, etc. Use the most apt description that's supported by what the facts show.

If a statement can't be confirmed, or can't be immediately confirmed, say so. But describe the efforts made to confirm it.

Be skeptical of "first" and "only." It's often hard or impossible to verify that something is a first or an only. Or it may be a first for a certain facility or area yet has been done elsewhere. Or it may be a small step that's technically a first but of little importance overall.

Usage notes: *fact check* and *fact-checking* (n.), to *fact-check* (v.)

See **deepfake**.

missile names Use Arabic figures and capitalize the proper name but not the word *missile*: *Pershing 2 missile*.

See **ABM**; **ICBM**; **MIRV**; and **SAM**.

mistress Do not use this archaic and sexist term for a woman who is in a long-term sexual relationship with, and is financially supported by, a man who is married to someone else. Instead, use an alternative like *companion*, *friend* or *lover* on first reference and provide additional details later. *Smith, who is married to someone else, was accused of embezzling funds to support his lover*.

See **gender-neutral language**.

mobile payment Typically refers to a payment for goods or services made by tapping a phone or smartwatch near a card reader at a physical retail store or business. A form of payment previously provided to the service, usually a credit or debit card, gets charged. Not all card readers and businesses accept mobile payment, although the number is growing.

Apple Pay, *Google Pay* and *Samsung Pay* are among the major services. Although these services are typically for in-person payments, some also offer web and app payment options.

Such services often use a substitute card number on the phone or watch to increase security. While a customer's regular card account gets charged for transactions, hackers who steal the substitute number cannot use it without also having the device present to verify the transaction.

In a broader sense, mobile

m

payments can also refer to sending money to friends or family through an app using a payment service such as Venmo. In some developing countries, where credit cards and bank accounts aren't as widespread, mobile payments can refer to the use of text messaging and other means to transfer money or buy goods and services.

See **digital wallet, mobile wallet**.

model numbers See **serial numbers**.

Monaco After the Vatican, the world's smallest state.

The *Monaco* section stands alone in datelines. The other two sections, *La Condamine* and *Monte Carlo*, are followed by *Monaco*:

MONTE CARLO, Monaco (AP) —

monetary units See **cents**; **dollars**; and **pounds**.

moneymaker

Montessori method After Maria Montessori, a system of training young children. It emphasizes training of the senses and guidance to encourage self-education.

monthlong, monthslong One word as an adjective.

months Capitalize the names of months in all uses. When a month is used with a specific date, abbreviate only *Jan.*, *Feb.*, *Aug.*, *Sept.*, *Oct.*, *Nov.* and *Dec.* Spell out when using alone, or with a year alone.

When a phrase lists only a month and a year, do not separate the year with commas. When a phrase refers to a month, day and year, set off the year with commas.

EXAMPLES: *January 2016 was a cold month. Jan. 2 was the coldest day of the month. His birthday is May 8. Feb. 14, 2013, was the target date. She testified that it was Friday, Dec. 3, when the crash occurred.*

In tabular material, use these three-letter forms without a period: *Jan, Feb, Mar, Apr, May, Jun, Jul, Aug, Sep, Oct, Nov, Dec.*

See **dates** and **years**.

monuments Capitalize the popular names of monuments and similar public attractions: *Lincoln Memorial, Statue of Liberty, Washington Monument, Leaning Tower of Pisa*, etc.

moon Lowercase. See **heavenly bodies**.

more than, over Acceptable in all uses to indicate greater numerical value. *Salaries went up more than $20 a week. Salaries went up over $20 a week.* See **over**.

mortgage-backed security A bond backed by home or commercial mortgage payments. These provide income from payments of the underlying mortgages.

mosquito, mosquitoes

Mother's Day The second Sunday in May.

mother-in-law, mothers-in-law

Mother Nature

mount Spell out in all uses, including the names of communities and of mountains: *Mount Clemens, Michigan; Mount Everest.*

mountains Capitalize as part of a proper name: *Appalachian Mountains, Ozark Mountains, Rocky Mountains.*

Or simply: *the Appalachians, the Ozarks, the Rockies.*

Mountain States As defined by the U.S. Census Bureau, the eight are Arizona, Colorado, Idaho, Montana, Nevada, New Mexico, Utah and Wyoming.

moviegoer

movie ratings The ratings used by the Motion Picture Association are:
G — General audiences. All ages admitted.
PG — Parental guidance suggested. Some material may not be suitable for children.
PG-13 — Special *parental guidance* strongly suggested for children under 13. Some material may be inappropriate for young children.
R — Restricted. Under 17 requires accompanying parent or adult guardian.
NC-17 — No one 17 and under admitted.
When the ratings are used in news stories or reviews, use these forms as appropriate: *the movie has an R rating, an R-rated movie, the movie is R-rated.*

mpg Acceptable in all references for *miles per gallon* when paired with a figure: *The car got 40 mpg.* But write out in general uses: *"My car gets a lot of miles per gallon," he said.*

mph Acceptable in all references for *miles per hour* or *miles an hour.*

MRI Acceptable in all references for *magnetic resonance imaging,* a noninvasive diagnostic procedure used to render images of the inside of an object. It is primarily used in medical imaging to demonstrate pathological or other physiological alterations of living tissues.

MRSA Abbreviation for the bacteria called *methicillin-resistant Staphylococcus aureus. MRSA* is acceptable on all references.

Muhammad The chief prophet and central figure of the Islamic religion, *the Prophet Muhammad.* Use other spellings only if preferred by a specific person for his own name or in a title or the name of an organization.

mujahedeen Lowercase when using the Arabic for *holy warriors;* uppercase if it is part of the name of a group. The Iranian opposition group is *Mujahedeen-e-Khalq.* The singular for *holy warrior* is *mujahed.*

mullah An Islamic leader or teacher, often a general title of respect for a learned man.

multi- The rules in prefixes apply, but in general, no hyphen.

Mumbai India's largest city, formerly known as Bombay.

Murphy's law The law is: *If something can go wrong, it will.*

music Capitalize, but do not use quotation marks, on descriptive titles for orchestral works: Bach's Suite No. 1 for Orchestra; Beethoven's Serenade for Flute, Violin and Viola. If the instrumentation is not part of the title but is added for explanatory purposes, the names of the instruments are lowercased: Mozart's Sinfonia Concertante in E flat major (the common title) for violin and viola. If in

m

doubt, lowercase the names of the instruments.

Use quotation marks for nonmusical terms in a title: Beethoven's "Eroica" Symphony. If the work has a special full title, all of it is quoted: "Symphonie Fantastique," "Rhapsody in Blue."

In subsequent references, lowercase *symphony*, *concerto*, etc. See **composition titles**.

Muslim Brotherhood Pan-Arab Islamist political movement.

Muzak A trademark for a type of recorded background music.

Myanmar Use this name for the country (formerly *Burma*). Use *Myanmar's people* or *people of Myanmar* for the inhabitants. Use *Myanmar* for the country's dominant language.

myriad (adj.) Note word is not followed by *of*: *The myriad books in the library.*

m

n

NAACP Acceptable in all references for the *National Association for the Advancement of Colored People*. Define as the nation's oldest civil rights organization. Headquarters is in Baltimore.

naloxone Use the generic *naloxone* for the opioid-overdose antidote often carried by first responders and caretakers of people with heroin addiction, with explanation if necessary. Not synonymous with *Narcan*, which is a brand name for a device that delivers *naloxone*.

name changes In general, use the name by which a person currently lives or is widely known. Include a previous name or names only if relevant to story. See **names**; **pseudonyms, nicknames**; and the **deadnaming** section of **gender, sex and sexual orientation**.

names In general, use only last names on second reference. When it is necessary to distinguish between two people who use the same last name, generally use the first and last name on subsequent references. Generally use the name a person prefers: *Thomas* or *Tom*, depending on preference; Martine McCarthy Chang may prefer *McCarthy Chang* or *Chang* on second reference. If an individual requests it, a public name rather than a real name may be used for a political dissident, or a nom de guerre for a rebel leader, if the person's safety is an issue. In general, call children 15 or younger by their first name on second reference. Use the last name, however, if the seriousness of the story calls for it, as in a murder case, for example. For ages 16 and 17, use judgment, but generally go with the surname unless it's a light story. Use the surname for those 18 and older.

See **Arabic names**; **Chinese names**; **Korean names**; **Russian names**; **Spanish names**. Also: **anonymous sources**; **courtesy titles**; **middle initials**; **middle names**; **pseudonyms, nicknames**; **foreign names**; **name changes**.

nano- A prefix denoting one-billionth of a unit.

Nasdaq composite A major U.S. stock index, often referred to in conjunction with the Dow Jones Industrial Average and the S&P 500. The Nasdaq composite is an index of all the stocks listed on the Nasdaq Stock Market. On second reference: *the Nasdaq*.

Nasdaq Stock Market The world's first all-electronic stock market and a direct competitor to the New York Stock Exchange. Parent company is Nasdaq Inc.

National Aeronautics and Space Administration *NASA* is acceptable in all references.

national anthem Lowercase. But: "The Star-Spangled Banner."

National Education Association

NEA is acceptable on second reference.

Headquarters is in Washington.

National FFA Organization
Formerly the Future Farmers of America. *FFA* is acceptable on second reference.

Headquarters is in Alexandria, Virginia.

National Governors Association
Represents the governors of the 50 states and five territories.

Its office is in Washington.

National Guard Capitalize when referring to U.S. or state-level forces, or foreign forces when that is the formal name: *the National Guard, the Guard, the Iowa National Guard, Iowa's National Guard, National Guard troops, the Iraqi National Guard.* On second reference, *the guard.*

When referring to an individual in a National Guard unit, use *National Guard member* or *guard member.*

See **military titles**.

National Institutes of Health This agency within the Department of Health and Human Services is the principal biomedical research arm of the federal government. *NIH* is acceptable on second reference. There are 27 institutes or centers, including the National Cancer Institute, the National Institute on Drug Abuse and the National Institute of Mental Health.

nationalist Lowercase when referring to a partisan of a country. Capitalize only when referring to alignment with a political party for which this is the proper name.

See **political parties and philosophies**.

Nationalist China See **China**.

National Labor Relations Board
NLRB is acceptable on second reference.

National League of Cities Its members include the governments of about 2,000 U.S. cities and 48 state municipal leagues.

It is separate from the U.S. Conference of Mayors, whose membership is limited to mayors of cities with 30,000 or more residents. The office is in Washington.

National Organization for Women
Not *of. NOW* is acceptable on second reference.

Headquarters is in Washington.

National Park Service A bureau of the Interior Department, it manages the National Park System, which includes dozens of national parks as well as monuments, battlefields, historic sites and seashores, and the White House. The National Park Service also helps administer dozens of affiliated sites, the National Register of Historic Places, National Heritage Areas, National Wild and Scenic Rivers, National Historic Landmarks, and National Trails. On second reference, *park service.*

National Rifle Association *NRA* is acceptable on second reference.

Headquarters is in Fairfax, Virginia.

National Security Agency A U.S. intelligence agency that collects and analyzes signals from foreign and domestic sources for the purpose of intelligence and counterintelligence.

It also defends U.S. government signals and codes from intrusion. The NSA is based in Fort Meade, Maryland. *NSA* is acceptable on second reference.

National Weather Service Use *National Weather Service* on first reference and *weather service* on subsequent references.
See **weather terms**.

nationwide

Nativity scene Only the first word is capitalized.

NATO Acceptable in all references for the *North Atlantic Treaty Organization*.

Naugahyde A trademark for a brand of simulated leather.

nautical miles, knots *Nautical miles* are used in air and marine navigation. A *knot* is a unit of speed used in meteorology, and air and marine navigation.
One nautical mile is 6,080 feet, or a bit over 1.15 statute miles (1.85 km). One *knot* equals 1 *nautical mile* per hour.
These terms, based on measurement of the curvature of the Earth, assist pilots, captains and others in accurately tracking distances and speeds. But they are lost on a general readership; instead, use *miles* and *mph*. When nautical miles or knots appear in quotes, they should be converted immediately: *"We were traveling at 20 knots (23 mph) when we struck the reef,"* the *sailor said.* AP stories must follow the guidance for conversions in the **metric system** entry, as well.

naval, navel Use *naval* in copy pertaining to a navy.
A *navel* is a bellybutton.
A *navel orange* is a seedless orange, so named because it has a small depression, like a navel.

naval station Capitalize only as part of a proper name: *Naval Station Norfolk*.

navy Capitalize when referring to U.S. forces: *the U.S. Navy, the Navy, Navy policy*. Do not use the abbreviation *USN*.
Lowercase when referring to the naval forces of other nations: *the British navy*.
This approach has been adopted for consistency, because many foreign nations do not use *navy* as the proper name.
See **military academies** and **military titles**.

Nazi, Nazism Derived from the German for the National Socialist German Workers' Party, the fascist political party founded in 1919 and abolished in 1945. Under Adolf Hitler, it seized control of Germany in 1933.
See **political parties and philosophies**, **concentration camps** and **Holocaust**.

nearsighted When used in a medical sense, it means an individual can see well at close range but has difficulty seeing objects at a distance.

Nest Family of smart home devices owned by *Google*. Includes smart speakers, security cameras and thermostats designed for the home. Nest devices have the Google artificial intelligence system, *Assistant*, built in. Some of the devices used to be known as *Google Home*.

Netherlands In datelines, give the name of the community followed by *Netherlands*:

MAASTRICHT, *Netherlands* (AP) —
In stories: *the Netherlands* or *Netherlands* as the construction of a sentence dictates.

Netherlands Antilles In datelines, give the name of the community followed by *Netherlands Antilles*. Do not abbreviate.

Identify an individual island, if needed, in the text.

net neutrality The idea that internet service providers shouldn't favor or discriminate against some websites or services over others. U.S. internet service providers such as phone and cable companies typically oppose net neutrality regulations. During the Obama administration, the Federal Communications Commission barred ISPs from blocking or slowing access to internet sites or creating paid "fast lanes" for preferred services. The broadband industry lost a legal battle to stop those regulations, but the Trump-era FCC overturned them. An appeals court largely upheld the Trump administration's decision in October 2019.

neurodiversity, neurodivergent, neurodiverse, neurotypical
Neurodiversity is the concept that differences in brain functioning such as *autism*, *dyslexia* or *attention-deficit/hyperactivity disorder* are normal variations, with strengths and weaknesses. It is not a medical term. Individuals or groups that exhibit those variations are considered

neurodivergent or *neurodiverse*. The larger population is said to be *neurotypical*. While use of these terms has become more common, to many they remain unfamiliar; they should be used only in direct quotes. See **disabilities**.

New Brunswick One of the three Maritime Provinces of Canada. Do not abbreviate.
See **datelines**.

New England Connecticut, Maine, Massachusetts, New Hampshire, Rhode Island and Vermont. See **Northeast**.

Newfoundland This Canadian province, officially renamed Newfoundland and Labrador in 2001, comprises the island of Newfoundland and the mainland section of Labrador. Do not abbreviate.

In datelines, use Newfoundland after the names of all cities and towns. Specify in the text whether the community is on the island or in Labrador.
See **datelines**.

Newspaper Guild-Communications Workers of America, The
Formerly the American Newspaper Guild, it is a union for newspaper and news service employees, generally those in the news and business departments.

On second reference: *the Guild*. Headquarters is in Washington.

The News Media Guild, formerly the Wire Service Guild, is the local representing employees of The Associated Press.

newspaper names Capitalize *the* in a newspaper's name if that is the way

n

the publication prefers to be known. Do not place name in quotes.

Lowercase *the* before newspaper names if a story mentions several papers, some of which use *the* as part of the name and some of which do not.

It is unnecessary to provide state identification for a newspaper cited in the body of a story if the newspaper is in the same state as the dateline. For example, a story datelined Newport, R.I., would reference the Providence Journal, not the Providence (Rhode Island) Journal.

However, the state should be included and spelled out in the body of undated stories or stories datelined in other states.

Where location is needed but is not part of the official name, use parentheses: The Huntsville (Alabama) Times.

newsstand

New World The Western Hemisphere.

New Year's, New Year's Day, New Year's Eve, Happy New Year
Capitalize for the days of Dec. 31 and Jan. 1 and in exclamations. For resolutions made on or around Jan. 1, the phrase is *New Year's resolutions*. But lowercase general references to the coming year: *What will the new year bring?* The U.S. federal legal holiday is observed on Friday if Jan. 1 falls on a Saturday, on Monday if it falls on a Sunday. See **happy holidays, merry Christmas, season's greetings, happy birthday, happy new year**.

New York City Use *NEW YORK* in datelines, not the name of an individual community or borough such as *Flushing* or *Queens*.

Identify the borough in the body of the story if pertinent.

New York Stock Exchange *NYSE* is acceptable on second reference.

NGO *Nongovernmental organization.* Usually refers to a nonprofit, humanitarian organization. Use *NGO* sparingly and only on second reference.

9/11 For the Sept. 11, 2001, terrorist attacks, *9/11* is acceptable in all references. (Note comma to set off the year when the phrase refers to a month, date and year.)

911 Acceptable in all references for the U.S. emergency call number: *He called 911 to report a crash.* No hyphen in any use: *a 911 call; a 911 call problem.*

niqab The veil worn by the most conservative Muslim women, in which, at most, only the eyes show. See also other garments such as **hijab; burqa; chador**.

No. Use as the abbreviation for *number* in conjunction with a figure to indicate position or rank: *No. 1 man, No. 3 choice.*

Do not use in street addresses, with this exception: *No. 10 Downing St.*, the residence of Britain's prime minister.

Do not use in the names of schools: *Public School 19.*

See **numerals**.

Nobel Prize, Nobel Prizes The five established under terms of the will of Alfred Nobel are: Nobel Peace Prize, Nobel Prize in chemistry, Nobel Prize in literature, Nobel Prize

n

in physics, Nobel Prize in physiology or medicine. (Note the capitalization styles.)

The Nobel Memorial Prize in Economic Sciences (officially it is the cumbersome Bank of Sweden Prize in Economic Sciences in Memory of Alfred Nobel) is not a Nobel Prize in the same sense. The Central Bank of Sweden established it in 1968 as a memorial to Alfred Nobel. References to this prize should include the word *Memorial* to help make this distinction. Explain the status of the prize in the story when appropriate.

Nobel Prize award ceremonies are held on Dec. 10, the anniversary of Alfred Nobel's death in 1896. The award ceremony for peace is in Oslo and the other ceremonies are in Stockholm.

Capitalize *prize* in references that do not mention the category: *He is a Nobel Prize winner. She is a Nobel Prize-winning scientist.*

Lowercase *prize* when not linked with the word *Nobel*: *The peace prize was awarded Monday.*

nobility References to members of the nobility in nations that have a system of rank present special problems because nobles frequently are known by their titles rather than their given or family names. Their titles, in effect, become their names. Generally follow a person's preference, unless the person is widely known in another way.

The guidelines below relate to Britain's nobility. Adapt them as appropriate to members of nobility in other nations.

Orders of rank among British nobility begin with the royal family. The term *royalty* is reserved for the families of living and deceased sovereigns.

Next, in descending order, are dukes, marquesses or marquises, earls, viscounts and barons. There are also life peers who are appointed to the House of Lords and hold their titles only for their lifetimes. On first reference to a life peer, use the person's ordinary name, e.g., *Margaret Thatcher* or *Jeffrey Archer*. Elsewhere, if relevant, explain that the person has been appointed to the House of Lords.

Occasionally the sovereign raises an individual to the nobility and makes the title inheritable by the person's heirs, but the practice is rare. Sovereigns also confer honorary titles, which do not make an individual a member of the nobility. The principal designations are *baronet* and *knight*.

In general, the guidelines in **courtesy titles** and **titles** apply. However, honorary titles and titles of nobility are capitalized when they serve as an alternate name.

Some guidelines and examples:

ROYALTY: Capitalize *king, queen, prince* and *princess* when they are used directly before one or more names; lowercase when they stand alone:

Queen Elizabeth II. *The queen* or *Elizabeth* on second reference. Capitalize a longer form of the sovereign's title when its use is appropriate or in a quote: *Her Majesty Queen Elizabeth.*

Use *Prince* or *Princess* before the names of a sovereign's children: *Princess Anne, Prince Charles.*

In references to the queen's husband first reference should be *Prince Philip* (not *Duke of Edinburgh*, commonly used in Britain). He is *Philip* on second reference.

The male heir to the throne

normally is designated *Prince of Wales*, and the title becomes an alternate name. Capitalize when used: *The queen invested her eldest son as Prince of Wales. Prince Charles is now the Prince of Wales. The prince is married. His wife, Camilla, is called the Duchess of Cornwall* (Charles is also the *Duke of Cornwall*, among other titles).

Charles' older son is *Prince William*. He is also the *Duke of Cambridge*. Prince William's wife, the former Kate Middleton, is the *Duchess of Cambridge*. Their sons are *Prince George* and *Prince Louis* and their daughter is *Princess Charlotte*. A prince or princess is just *William, George* or *Harry* on second reference, as is a princess, whether she is *Charlotte, Beatrice* or *Eugenie*.

Charles' younger son is called *Prince Harry* on first reference, and then simply *Harry*. He is also the *Duke of Sussex*. His wife is called *Meghan, the Duchess of Sussex* on first reference and *Meghan* on second reference. She is not called *Meghan Markle*, though she can be referred to as *the former Meghan Markle*, and she is not *Princess Meghan* or *Duchess Meghan*. After leaving full-time royal duties in 2020, the couple do not use the titles *His Royal Highness* and *Her Royal Highness*.

DUKE: The full title — *Duke of York*, for example — is an alternate name, capitalized in all uses. Lowercase *duke* when it stands alone.

The wife of a duke is a *duchess*: *the Duchess of Kent, the duchess*, but never *Duchess Katherine* or *Lady Katherine*.

A duke normally also has a lesser title. It is commonly used for his eldest son if he has one. Use the courtesy titles *Lord* or *Lady* before the first names of a duke or earl's children. On second reference, the

children's given name would be used alone.

MARQUESS, MARQUIS, EARL, VISCOUNT, BARON: The full titles serve as alternate names and should be capitalized. In general, use the name the person goes by. Use *Lady* before the name of a woman married to a man who holds one of these titles, and use *Lady* before the first name of an earl's daughter — *Lady Diana Spencer*, for example. On second reference, *Lady Diana* or *Diana*.

Some examples:

Queen Elizabeth gave her sister's husband, Antony Armstrong-Jones, the title *Earl of Snowdon*. Their son, David, is the *Viscount Linley* — *Linley* on second reference. They also have a daughter, born Lady Sarah Armstrong-Jones. After her marriage she is now *Lady Sarah Chatto* — on second reference *Lady Sarah* or *Chatto*.

BARONET, KNIGHT: *Sir John Smith* on first reference and *Smith* on second. These are very common titles, and rarely are used in news copy. Do not use both an honorary title and a title of military rank or authority, such as prime minister, before a name.

Honorary titles for celebrities need not be used in every case. *Dame Maggie Smith* is correct, but *Maggie Smith* is preferred when writing about the actress. *Sir Paul McCartney* is correct, but *Paul McCartney* is preferred when writing about the former Beatle.

noisome, noisy *Noisome* means *offensive, noxious.*

Noisy means *clamorous.*

nolo contendere The literal meaning is, "I do not wish to contend." Terms such as *no contest* or *no-contest plea* are acceptable in all references.

When a defendant in a criminal case enters this plea, it means that he is not admitting guilt but is stating that he will offer no defense. The person is then subject to being judged guilty and punished as if he had pleaded guilty or had been convicted. The principal difference is that the defendant retains the option of denying the same charge in another legal proceeding.

non- The rules of **prefixes** apply, but in general no hyphen when forming a compound that does not have special meaning and can be understood if *not* is used before the base word. Use a hyphen, however, before proper nouns. Examples of compounds with special meaning include names with proper nouns: *Non-Aligned Movement, non-Euclidean geometry, non-Hodgkin lymphoma.*

nonaligned nations A political rather than economic or geographic term used primarily during the Cold War. Although nonaligned nations do not belong to Western or Eastern military alliances or blocs, they may take positions on international issues. Hyphenate in formal name *Non-Aligned Movement*, a political group representing more than 120 developing nations.

Do not confuse *nonaligned* with *developing nations*, which refers to the economic developing nations of Africa, Asia and Latin America. Avoid use of the term Third World.

noncombat, noncombatant

none It usually means *no single one*. When used in this sense, it always takes singular verbs and pronouns: *None of the seats was in its right place.* Mass nouns — things that can't be counted — also are singular: *None of the coffee was poured.*

Use a plural verb only if the sense is *no two* or *no amount of these things*: *None of the consultants agree on the same approach. None of the taxes have been paid.*

nonprofit

noon Do not put a 12 in front of it. See **midnight** and **times**.

North Atlantic Treaty Organization *NATO* is acceptable in all references.

Northeast Use *Northeast* for the nine-state region as defined by the U.S. Census Bureau that is broken into two divisions. Capitalize *Northeastern* as an adjective describing the region.

The six *New England* states are Connecticut, Maine, Massachusetts, New Hampshire, Rhode Island and Vermont.

The three *Middle Atlantic* states are New Jersey, New York and Pennsylvania. Also acceptable is mid-Atlantic.

See **Midwest**, **South** and **West** for the bureau's other regional breakdowns.

See **directions and regions**.

Northern Ireland Part of the *United Kingdom*, which also includes *Great Britain*. Use *Northern Ireland* after the names of all communities in datelines.

See **datelines**, **United Kingdom**, **Ireland** and **England**.

North Macedonia Name change effective in February 2019 for the country formerly known as Macedonia. North Macedonia's citizens are *Macedonians*.

north, northern, northeast, northwest See **directions and regions**.

North Slope The portion of Alaska north of Brooks Range, a string of mountains extending across the northern part of the state.

Northwest Territories A territorial section of Canada. Do not abbreviate. Use in datelines after the names of all cities and towns in the territory.
> See **Canada**.

note For use in a financial sense, see **loan terminology**.

notorious, notoriety Some understand these terms to refer simply to fame; others see them as negative terms, implying being well-known because of evil actions. Be sure the context for these words is clear, or use terms like *famous*, *prominent*, *infamous*, *disreputable*, etc.

Nova Scotia One of the three Maritime Provinces of Canada. Do not abbreviate.
> See **datelines**.

Novocain A trademark for a drug used as a local anesthetic.

Nuclear Non-Proliferation Treaty Global agreement intended to limit the spread of nuclear weapons. It provides civilian nuclear trade in exchange for a pledge from nations not to pursue nuclear weapons and for the United States and other nuclear weapons states to negotiate their nuclear disarmament.

Nuclear Regulatory Commission *NRC* is acceptable on second reference.

nuclear terminology In reporting on nuclear energy, include the definitions of appropriate terms, especially those related to radiation.

core The part of a nuclear reactor that contains its fissionable fuel. In a reactor core, atoms of fuel, such as uranium, are split. This releases energy in the form of heat which, in turn, is used to boil water for steam. The steam powers a turbine, and the turbine drives a generator to produce electricity.

fission The splitting of the nucleus of an atom, releasing energy.

gray (Gy) The standard measure of radiation a material has absorbed. It has largely replaced the *rad*. One gray equals 100 rads. This measure does not consider biological effect of the radiation.

meltdown The worst possible nuclear accident in which the reactor core overheats to such a degree that the fuel melts. If the fuel penetrates its protective housing, radioactive materials will be released into the environment.

rad See **gray**.

radiation Invisible particles or waves given off by radioactive material, such as uranium. Radiation can damage or kill body cells, resulting in latent cancers, genetic damage or death.

rem See **sievert**.

roentgen The standard measure of X-ray exposure.

sievert (Sv) The standard measure of radiation absorbed in living tissue, adjusted for different kinds of radiation so that a single sievert of any kind of radiation produces the same biological effect. The sievert has largely replaced the rem. One *Sv* equals 100 rem. A *millisievert* (mSv) is a thousandth of a sievert; a millirem is a thousandth of a rem. On average, a resident of United States receives about 3 mSv, or 300 mrem, every year from natural sources.

uranium A metallic, radioactive element used as fuel in nuclear reactors.

numerals In general, spell out one through nine: *The Yankees finished second. He had nine months to go.*

Use figures for 10 or above and whenever preceding a unit of measure or referring to ages of people, animals, events or things. Also in all tabular matter, and in statistical and sequential forms.

USE FIGURES FOR:

ACADEMIC COURSE NUMBERS: *History 6, Philosophy 209.*

ADDRESSES: *210 Main St.* Spell out numbered streets nine and under: *5 Sixth Ave.; 3012 50th St.; No. 10 Downing St.* Use the abbreviations *Ave., Blvd.* and *St.* only with a numbered address: *1600 Pennsylvania Ave.* Spell them out and capitalize without a number: *Pennsylvania Avenue.*

See **addresses**.

AGES: *a 6-year-old girl; an 8-year-old law; the 7-year-old house.* Use hyphens for ages expressed as adjectives before a noun or as substitutes for a noun. *A 5-year-old boy,* but *the boy is 5 years old. The boy, 5, has a sister, 10. The race is for 3-year-olds. The woman is in her 30s. 30-something,* but *Thirty-something* to start a sentence.

See **ages**.

PLANES, SHIPS AND SPACECRAFT DESIGNATIONS: *B-2 bomber, Queen Elizabeth 2, QE2, Apollo 9, Viking 2.* An exception: *Air Force One,* the president's plane. Use Roman numerals if they are part of the official designation: *Titan I, Titan II.*

See **aircraft names; boats, ships; spacecraft designations**.

CENTURIES: Use figures for numbers 10 or higher: *21st century.* Spell out for numbers nine and lower: *fifth century.* (Note lowercase.) For proper names, follow the organization's usage.

COURT DECISIONS: *The Supreme Court ruled 5-4, a 5-4 decision.* The word *to* is not needed, except in quotations: *"The court ruled 5 to 4."*

COURT DISTRICTS: *5th U.S. Circuit Court of Appeals.*

DATES, YEARS AND DECADES: *Feb. 8, 2007, Class of '66, the 1950s.* For the Sept. 11, 2001, terrorist attacks, *9/11* is acceptable in all references. (Note comma to set off the year when the phrase refers to a month, date and year.)

DECIMALS, PERCENTAGES AND FRACTIONS WITH NUMBERS LARGER THAN 1: *7.2 magnitude quake, 3 1/2 laps, 3.7% interest, 4 percentage points.* Decimalization should not exceed two places in most text material. Exceptions: blood alcohol content, expressed in three decimals: as in 0.056, and batting averages in baseball, as in .324. For amounts less than 1, precede the decimal with a zero: *The cost of living rose 0.03%.* Spell out fractions less than 1, using hyphens between the words: *two-thirds, four-fifths.* In quotations, use figures for fractions: *"He was 2 1/2 laps behind with four to go."*

See **decimal units; fractions; percent, percentage, percentage points**.

DIMENSIONS, TO INDICATE DEPTH, HEIGHT, LENGTH AND WIDTH: *He is 5 feet, 6 inches tall, the 5-foot-6 man* ("inch" is understood), *the 5-foot man, the basketball team signed a 7-footer. The* *car is 17 feet long, 6 feet wide and 5 feet high. The rug is 9 feet by 12 feet, the 9-by-12 rug. A 9-inch snowfall.* Exception: *two-by-four.* Spell out the noun, which refers to any length of untrimmed lumber approximately 2 inches thick by 4 inches wide.

See **dimensions**.

DISTANCES: *He walked 4 miles. He missed a 3-foot putt.*

GOLF CLUBS: *3-wood, 7-iron, 3-hybrid* (note hyphen).

HIGHWAY DESIGNATIONS: *Interstate 5, U.S. Highway 1, state Route 1A.* (Do not abbreviate *Route.* No hyphen between highway designation and number.)

See **highway designations**.

MATHEMATICAL USAGE: *Multiply by 4, divide by 6. He added 2 and 2 but got 5.*

MILITARY RANKS, USED AS TITLES WITH NAMES, MILITARY TERMS AND WEAPONS: *Petty Officer 2nd Class Alan Markow, Spc. Alice Moreno, 1st Sgt. David Triplett, M16 rifle, 9 mm* (note space) *pistol, 6th Fleet.* In military ranks, spell out the figure when it is used after the name or without a name: *Smith was a second lieutenant. The goal is to make first sergeant.*

See **military units**.

MILLIONS, BILLIONS, TRILLIONS: Use a figure-word combination. *1 million people; $2 billion,* NOT *one million/two billion.* (Also note no hyphen linking numerals and the word *million, billion* or *trillion.*)

See **millions, billions, trillions; dollars**.

MONETARY UNITS: *5 cents, $5 bill, 8 euros, 4 pounds.*

See **cents**.

ODDS, PROPORTIONS AND RATIOS: *9-1 long shot; 3 parts cement to 1 part water; a 1-4 chance; 1 chance in 3.*

See **betting odds; proportions; ratios**.

RANK: *He was my No. 1 choice.*

(Note abbreviation for "Number"). *Kentucky was ranked No. 3. The band had five Top 40 hits.*

SCHOOL GRADES: Use figures for grades 10 and above: *10th grade.* Spell out for first through ninth grades: *fourth grade, fifth grader.*

SEQUENTIAL DESIGNATIONS: *Page 1, Page 20A. They were out of sizes 4 and 5; magnitude 6 earthquake; Rooms 3 and 4; Chapter 2; line 1* but *first line; Act 3, Scene 4,* but *third act, fourth scene; Game 1,* but *best of seven.*

See **act numbers; chapters; earthquakes; line numbers; page numbers; scene numbers**.

POLITICAL DISTRICTS: *Ward 9, 9th Precinct, 3rd Congressional District.*

See **congressional districts; political divisions**.

RECIPES: *2 tablespoons of sugar to 1 cup of milk.*

See **recipes**.

SPEEDS: *7 mph, winds of 5 to 10 mph, winds of 7 to 9 knots.*

SPORTS SCORES, STANDINGS AND STANDARDS: *The Dodgers defeated the Phillies 10-3* (No comma between the team and the score); in golf, *3 up,* but *a 3-up lead; led 3-2; a 6-1-2 record* (six wins, one loss, two ties); *par 3; 5 handicap, 5-under-par 67* but *he was 5 under par* (or *5 under,* with "par" understood). In narrative, spell out nine and under except for yard lines in football and individual and team statistical performances: *The ball was on the 5-yard line. Seventh hole.* In basketball, *3-point play* and *3-point shot.* In statistical performances, hyphenate as a modifier: *He completed 8 of 12 passes. He made 5 of 6* (shots is understood). *He was 5-for-12 passing. He had a 3-for-5 day. He was 3-for-5. He went 3-for-5* (batting, shooting, etc., is understood).

TEMPERATURES: Use figures, except zero. *It was 8 degrees below zero* or

n

minus 8. *The temperature dropped from 38 to 8 in two hours.*

See **temperatures**.

TIMES: Use figures for time of day except for noon and midnight: *1 p.m.; 10:30 a.m.; 5 o'clock; 8 hours, 30 minutes, 20 seconds; a winning time of 2:17:3 (2 hours, 17 minutes, 3 seconds).* Spell out numbers less than 10 standing alone and in modifiers: *I'll be there in five minutes. He scored with two seconds left. An eight-hour day. The two-minute warning.*

See **times; time sequences**.

VOTES: *The bill was defeated by a vote of 6-4, but by a two-vote margin.*

SPELL OUT:

AT THE START OF A SENTENCE: In general, spell out numbers at the start of a sentence: *Forty years was a long time to wait. Fifteen to 20 cars were involved in the accident.* An exception is years: *1992 was a very good year.* Another exception: Numeral(s) and letter(s) combinations: *401(k) plans are offered. 4K TVs are flying off the shelves. 3D movies are drawing more fans.*

See **years**.

IN INDEFINITE AND CASUAL USES: *Thanks a million. He walked a quarter of a mile. One at a time; a thousand clowns; one day we will know; an eleventh-hour decision; dollar store; a hundred dollars.*

IN FANCIFUL USAGE OR PROPER NAMES: *Chicago Seven, Fab Four, Final Four, the Four Tops.*

IN FORMAL LANGUAGE, RHETORICAL QUOTATIONS AND FIGURES OF SPEECH: *"Fourscore and seven years ago ..." Twelve Apostles, Ten Commandments, high-five, Day One.*

IN FRACTIONS LESS THAN ONE THAT ARE NOT USED AS MODIFIERS: *reduced by one-third, he made three-fourths of his shots.*

ROMAN NUMERALS

They may be used for wars and to establish personal sequence for people and animals: *World War I, Native Dancer II, King George V.* Also for certain legislative acts (*Title IX*). Otherwise, use sparingly. Pro football Super Bowls should be identified by the year, rather than the Roman numerals: *1969 Super Bowl,* not *Super Bowl III.*

ORDINALS

Numbers used to indicate order (first, second, 10th, 25th, etc.) are called ordinal numbers. Spell out first through ninth: *fourth grade, first base, the First Amendment, he was first in line.* Use figures starting with 10th.

CARDINAL NUMBERS

Numbers used in counting or showing how many (2, 40, 627, etc.) are called cardinal numbers. The following separate entries provide additional guidance for cardinal numbers:

amendments to the Constitution
court names
decades
election returns
fleet
formula
latitude and longitude
mile
parallels
proportions
serial numbers
telephone numbers
weights

SOME OTHER PUNCTUATION AND USAGE EXAMPLES:
— *3 ounces*
— *4-foot-long*

— *4-foot fence*
— *"The president's speech lasted 28 1/2 minutes," she said.*
— *DC-10 but 747B*
— *the 1980s, the '80s*
— *the House voted 230-205* (fewer than 1,000 votes)
— *Jimmy Carter outpolled Gerald Ford 40,827,292 to 39,146,157* (more than 1,000 votes)
— *Carter outpolled Ford 10 votes to 2 votes in Little Junction* (to avoid confusion with ratio)
— *No. 3 choice,* but *Public School 3*
— *a pay increase of 12%-15%.* Or: *a pay increase of between 12% and 15%,* or *a pay increase of 12% to 15%*
But: *from $12 million to $14 million*
— *a ratio of 2-to-1, a 2-1 ratio*
— *1 in 4 voters*
— *seven houses 7 miles apart*
— *He walked 4 miles.*
— *minus 10, zero, 60 degrees* (spell out minus)

OTHER USES: For uses not covered by these listings, spell out whole numbers below 10, and use figures for 10 and above: *They had three sons and two daughters. They had a fleet of 10 station wagons and two buses.*

IN A SERIES: Apply the standard guidelines: *They had 10 dogs, six cats and 97 hamsters. They had four four-room houses, 10 three-room houses and 12 10-room houses.*

Nuremberg Use this spelling for the city in Germany, instead of *Nuernberg,* in keeping with widespread practice.

N-word Do not use this term or the racial slur it refers to, except in extremely rare circumstances — when it is crucial to the story or the understanding of a news event. Flag the contents in an editor's note. See **obscenities, profanities, vulgarities** and **race-related coverage**.

nylon Not a trademark.

n

O

oasis, oases

OB-GYN Acceptable in all references for *obstetrics and gynecology*, a medical specialty.

obscenities, profanities, vulgarities Do not use them in stories unless they are part of direct quotations and there is a compelling reason for them.

Try to find a way to give the reader a sense of what was said without using the specific word or phrase. For example, an *anti-gay* or *sexist slur*.

If a profanity, obscenity or vulgarity must be used, flag the story at the top for editors, being specific about what the issue is:

Eds: Note use of vulgarity "f---" [or "s---"] However, online readers receiving direct feeds of the stories will not see that warning, so consider whether the word in question truly needs to be in the story at all.

When possible, confine the offending language, in quotation marks, to a separate paragraph that can be deleted easily by editors.

In reporting profanity that normally would use the words *damn* or *god*, lowercase *god* and use the following forms: *damn, damn it, goddamn it.*

If the obscenity involved is particularly offensive but the story requires making clear what the word was, replace the letters of the offensive word with hyphens, using only an initial letter: *f---, s---.*

In some stories or scripts, it may be better to replace the offensive word with a generic descriptive in parentheses, e.g., *(vulgarity)* or *(obscenity).*

When the subject matter of a story may be considered offensive or disturbing, but the story does not contain quoted profanity, obscenities or vulgarities, flag the story at the top:

Eds: Graphic details of the killings could be offensive or disturbing to some readers.

For guidelines on racial or ethnic slurs, see **race-related coverage**.

obsessive-compulsive disorder An anxiety disorder characterized by uncontrollable, recurring thoughts and fears that lead to repetitive and often ritualized behaviors or compulsions. *OCD* is acceptable on second reference; avoid in headlines. Describe a person as *having OCD* only if relevant to the story, and if a medical diagnosis has been made or the person uses the term. If relatives or others use the term, ask how they know, then consider carefully whether to include the information. Say someone *has OCD* or *has obsessive-compulsive disorder*, not *is OCD* or *is obsessive-compulsive* unless the person prefers the latter. See **disabilities**.

Occupational Safety and Health Administration *OSHA* is acceptable on second reference.

occupational titles They are always lowercase. See **titles**.

occur, occurred, occurring Also: *occurrence*.

ocean The five, from the largest to the smallest: Pacific Ocean, Atlantic Ocean, Indian Ocean, Antarctic Ocean, Arctic Ocean.
Lowercase *ocean* standing alone or in plural uses: *the ocean, the Atlantic and Pacific oceans*.

oceangoing

odd- Follow with a hyphen:
odd-looking   odd-numbered
See **betting odds**.

oddsmaker

offering The issue or sale of a company stock or bond. A company usually will sell financial securities to the public to raise capital.

office Capitalize *office* when it is part of an agency's formal name: *Office of Management and Budget*.
Lowercase all other uses, including phrases such as: *the office of the attorney general, the U.S. attorney's office*.
See **Oval Office**.

Office Software package made by Microsoft Corp. The main components include *Word* for word processing, *Excel* for spreadsheets, *PowerPoint* for presentations, *Outlook* for email and *OneNote* for note-taking. Less-used programs include *Access* for database management and *Publisher* for desktop publishing.
The company has also extended Office to include such collaborative tools as *SharePoint* and *Teams* and the cloud-storage service *OneDrive*. Microsoft has historically sold Office as programs that get installed on individual PCs, but it now favors an online subscription called *Office 365*. Although it is typically lumped with other internet-based services, Office 365 offers versions of programs that can be downloaded and installed the traditional way.

officeholder

Office of Thrift Supervision U.S. Treasury Department bureau that regulates the nation's savings and loan industry. *OTS* is acceptable on second reference.

officer-involved, police-involved Avoid this vague jargon for shootings and other cases involving police. Be specific about what happened. If police use the term, ask for detail. How was the officer or officers involved? Who did the shooting? If the information is not available or not provided, spell that out.

offline No hyphen is an exception to Webster's New World College Dictionary.

off of The *of* is unnecessary: *He fell off the bed*. Not: *He fell off of the bed*.

off-, -off Follow Webster's New World College Dictionary. Hyphenate if not listed there.
Some commonly used combinations with a hyphen:
off-color   off-white
off-peak   send-off

Some combinations without a hyphen:
cutoff   offside
liftoff   offstage
offhand   playoff
offset   standoff
offshore   takeoff

O

off-site Hyphenated. Also: *on-site*.

oil field

OK, OK'd, OK'ing, OKs Do not use *okay*.

Old City of Jerusalem The walled part of the city.

older adult(s), older person/people
Preferred over *senior citizens, seniors* or *elderly* as a general term when appropriate and relevant.

It is best used in general phrases that do not refer to specific individuals: *concern for older people; a home for older adults.* Aim for specificity when possible: *new housing for people 65 and over; an exercise program for women over 70.*

Definitions and understandings vary about the age range denoted by the term *older adult*, as well as by the terms *senior citizen, senior* and *elderly*. When an official or organization uses one of these terms, ask for specifics.

Provide context and specifics to make the meaning clear. For example, a story might begin by referring to *cuts in programs for older adults*, but explain soon thereafter that *the programs are for people 62 and older.* Another example: *The researchers found that weekly exercise decreased the risk of diabetes among people in their 70s and 80s.*

The term *elderly* is acceptable in headlines when relevant and necessary because of space constraints. But aim for specificity when space allows: *Couple in their 90s die in Manhattan luxury high-rise blaze* rather than *Elderly couple die in Manhattan luxury high-rise blaze.*

Terms like *senior citizen* and *elderly* are acceptable in reference to an individual if that person prefers them.

Do not use *the elderly* in reference to a group.

Old South The South before the Civil War.

Old West The American West as it was being settled in the 19th century.

Old World The Eastern Hemisphere: Asia, Europe, Africa. The term also may be an allusion to European culture and customs.

on Do not use *on* before a date or day of the week when its absence would not lead to confusion, except at the beginning of a sentence: *The meeting will be held Monday. He will be inaugurated Jan. 20. On Sept. 3, the committee will meet to discuss the issue.*

Use *on* to avoid an awkward juxtaposition of a date and a proper name: *John met Mary on Monday. He told Biden on Thursday that the bill was doomed.*

onboard One word as a modifier: *There was onboard entertainment.* But: *he jumped on board the boat.*

one- Hyphenate when used in writing fractions:

one-half   one-third

Use phrases such as *a half* or *a third* if precision is not intended.
See **fractions**.

"One China" policy The U.S. policy under which the U.S. recognizes Beijing as representing China. The U.S. shifted diplomatic recognition to Beijing from Taipei in 1979. Under the policy, the U.S. acknowledges Beijing's view that it has sovereignty over Taiwan, but considers Taiwan's

O

status as unsettled. Taiwan split from the Chinese mainland in 1949 and is self-governing. The policy is distinct from the *"One China" principle*, which is China's view that it has sovereignty over the mainland, Hong Kong, Macao and Taiwan. See **China**; **Taiwan**.

one person, one vote The adjective form: *one-person, one-vote. He supports the principle of one person, one vote. The one-person, one-vote rule.*

Supreme Court rulings all use the phrase *one person, one vote*, not *one man, one vote*.

one-sided

onetime, one-time, one time *He is the onetime (former) heavyweight champion. She is the one-time (once) winner in 2003. He did it one time.*

One World Trade Center Skyscraper opened in 2014 on the site of the twin towers destroyed in the 9/11 attacks. Spell out *One* as used by the Port Authority of New York and New Jersey, which owns both the building and the 16-acre World Trade Center site. Other buildings in the complex are named with numerals 2, 3, etc., as designated by the company that leased them. See **World Trade Center**.

online One word in all cases for the computer connection term.

online petitions Be cautious about quoting the number of signers on such petitions. Some sites make it easy for the person creating the petition or others to run up the number of purported signers by clicking or returning to the page multiple times.

online trading Buying or selling financial securities and/or currencies through a brokerage's internet-based proprietary trading platforms.

onstage

Ontario This Canadian province is the nation's first in total population and second to Quebec in area. Do not abbreviate.

See **datelines**.

OPEC Acceptable in all references for the Organization of the Petroleum Exporting Countries.

Founded in 1960, OPEC has 13 members: Algeria, Angola, Republic of Congo, Equatorial Guinea, Gabon, Iran, Iraq, Kuwait, Libya, Nigeria, Saudi Arabia, United Arab Emirates, Venezuela.

Headquarters is in Vienna, Austria. See **OPEC+**.

OPEC+ A group of nations that allied with OPEC to cut production in order to boost oil prices beginning in 2016. While not formally members of the cartel, the countries have worked with OPEC on production quotas through the coronavirus pandemic. OPEC+, led by Russia, has included Azerbaijan, Bahrain, Brunei, Kazakhstan, Malaysia, Mexico, Oman, South Sudan and Sudan. See **OPEC**.

opiate, opioid *Opiate* refers to drugs derived directly from the poppy plant, such as morphine and codeine.

Opioids are synthetic or partially synthetic manufactured drugs that mimic the properties of opiates. Heroin can be made different ways but is generally considered an opioid, as are more common prescription painkillers such as

O

OxyContin and Vicodin.

When referring to just prescription medications, a general term like *powerful prescription painkillers* can be more accurate. But when referring to the overall class of drugs, *opioid* is the better choice.

The brand name or generic name of a drug can be acceptable, depending on the context and how any given drug is most commonly known. In some cases, it is useful to use both names. *Doctors were urged to limit prescriptions for hydrocodone, an ingredient in painkillers like Vicodin. He was prescribed Percocet after he complained that over-the-counter pain medications like ibuprofen were not working.* See **addiction**; **drugs**.

opt in, opt out (v.)**, opt-in, opt-out** (adj.) Terms used to describe how a service obtains permission for collecting and sharing data. The *opt-in* option requires explicit permission, while the *opt-out* approach typically assumes permission unless someone takes the step to withdraw consent.

When writing about *opt-in* permission, it's better to specify how permission is obtained. For instance, a company with an *opt-in* approach may count as approval the acceptance of a lengthy document that isn't prominent or easy to understand.

Also, be mindful that while a company may promise the ability to *opt out* of a practice, it requires the consumer knowing that it is happening and finding out how to do so. See **internet privacy**.

option In the financial world, it is a contract that gives an investor the right, but not the obligation, to buy (call) or sell (put) a security or other financial asset at an agreed-upon price (strike price) during a certain period of time or on a specific date (exercise date).

Organization of American States
OAS is acceptable on second reference. Headquarters is in Washington.

organizations and institutions
Capitalize the full names of organizations and institutions: *the American Medical Association; First Presbyterian Church; General Motors Corp.; Harvard University, Harvard University Medical School; the Procrastinators Club; the Society of Professional Journalists.*

Retain capitalization if *Co., Corp.* or a similar word is deleted from the full proper name: *General Motors.* **company, companies; corporation;** and **incorporated**.

SUBSIDIARIES: Capitalize the names of major subdivisions: *the Pontiac Motor Division of General Motors.*

INTERNAL ELEMENTS: Use lowercase for internal elements of an organization when they have names that are widely used generic terms: *the board of directors of General Motors, the board of trustees of Columbia University, the history department of Harvard University, the sports department of the Daily Citizen-Leader.*

Capitalize internal elements of an organization when they have names that are not widely used generic terms: *the General Assembly of the World Council of Churches, the House of Delegates of the American Medical Association, the House of Bishops and House of Deputies of the Episcopal Church.*

FLIP-FLOPPED NAMES: Retain capital letters when commonly accepted practice flops a name to delete the word of: *Harvard School of Dental Medicine, Harvard Dental School.*

Do not, however, flop formal names that are known to the public with the word of: *Massachusetts Institute of Technology,* for example, not *Massachusetts Technology Institute.*

ABBREVIATIONS AND ACRONYMS: Some organizations and institutions are widely recognized by their abbreviations: *GOP, NAACP, NATO.* For guidelines on when such abbreviations may be used, see the individual listings and the entries under **abbreviations and acronyms** and **second reference.**

original equipment manufacturer A company that builds components or systems that are used in production of another company's systems or products. *OEM* is acceptable on second reference.

Ottawa The capital of Canada carries Ontario, the province name, in datelines.

ounce (dry) Units of dry volume are not customarily carried to this level. See **pint (dry).**

ounce (weight) It is defined as 437.5 grains. The metric equivalent is approximately 28 grams.
See **grain** and **gram.**

-out Follow Webster's New World College Dictionary. Hyphenate nouns and adjectives not listed there.
Some frequently used words (all nouns):

cop-out	*hideout*
fade-out	*pullout*
fallout	*walkout*
flameout	*washout*

Two words for verbs:

fade out	*walk out*
hide out	*wash out*
pull out	

out- Follow Webster's New World College Dictionary. Hyphenate if not listed there.
Some frequently used words:

outargue	*outpost*
outbox	*output*
outdated	*outscore*
outfield	*outstrip*
outfox	*outtalk*
outpatient (n., adj.)	

outbreak For disease references, reserve for larger numbers of an illness, not a few cases.

Outer Banks The barrier islands along the North Carolina coast.

out of bounds But as a modifier: *out-of-bounds. The ball went out of bounds. He took an out-of-bounds pass.*

out of court, out-of-court *They settled out of court. He accepted an out-of-court settlement.*

outperform

outsourcing A business practice used by companies to reduce costs by transferring work previously performed in-house to outside suppliers.

outstanding shares Stock held by shareholders of a company.

Oval Office The White House office of the president.

-over Follow Webster's New World College Dictionary. Hyphenate if not listed there.

O

Some frequently used words (all are nouns, some also are used as adjectives):

carry-over *stopover*
holdover *walkover*
takeover

Use two words when any of these occurs as a verb.

See **suffixes**.

over Acceptable in all uses to indicate greater numerical value. *The crop was valued at over $5 billion.* See **more than, over**.

over- Follow Webster's New World College Dictionary. A hyphen seldom is used. Some frequently used words:

overbuy *overrate*
overexert *override*

See the **overall** entry.

overall A single word in adjectival and adverbial use: *Overall, the Democrats succeeded. Overall policy.*

The word for the garment is *overalls*.

over-the-counter stock A stock that isn't listed and traded on an organized exchange. OTC stocks are traditionally those of smaller companies that don't meet the listing requirements of the New York Stock Exchange or Nasdaq Stock Market. *OTC* is acceptable on second reference. See **Pink Sheets**.

owner Not a formal title. Always lowercase: *Dallas Cowboys owner Jerry Jones.*

Oyez Not *oyes*. The cry of court and public officials to command silence. *"Oyez! Oyez!"*

Ozark Mountains Or simply: *the Ozarks.*

O

p

PAC Acronym for *political action committee*. Raises money and makes contributions to campaigns of political candidates or parties. At the federal level, contribution amounts are limited by law and may not come from corporations or labor unions. Enforcement overseen by the Federal Election Commission. *PAC* acceptable on first reference; spell out in body of story. A *super PAC* is a political action committee that may raise and spend unlimited amounts of money, including from corporations and unions, to campaign independently for candidates for federal office. Its activities must be reported to the FEC, but are not otherwise regulated if not coordinated with the candidate or campaign.

pacemaker Formerly a trademark, now a generic term for a device that electronically helps a person's heart maintain a steady beat.

page numbers Use figures and capitalize *page* when used with a figure. When a letter is appended to the figure, capitalize it but do not use a hyphen: *Page 1, Page 10, Page 20A*. See **numerals**.

paintings See **composition titles**.

palate, palette, pallet *Palate* is the roof of the mouth.
　　A *palette* is an artist's paint board.
　　A *pallet* is a low platform. Also a small bed or pad filled with straw and used directly on the floor.

Palestine Use *Palestine* and *Palestinians* in the context of Palestine's activities in international bodies to which it has been admitted and the actions of the Palestinian Authority: *the Palestinian flag, Palestinian prime minister*. Do not use *Palestine* or *state of Palestine* in other situations, since it is not a fully independent, unified state. For territory, refer specifically to the *West Bank* or *Gaza*, or *the Palestinian territories* in reference to both.

Palestine Liberation Organization Not *Palestinian*. *PLO* is acceptable in all references.

pan- Prefix meaning "all" takes no hyphen when combined with a common noun:
　　panchromatic pantheism
　　Most combinations with *pan-* are proper nouns, however, and both *pan-* and the proper name it is combined with are capitalized:
　　Pan-African　Pan-Asiatic Pan-American

Pap test (or **smear**) A test for cervical cancer.

paparazzi (plural), **paparazzo** (singular) A photographer, often a freelancer, who takes candid shots, often in an intrusive manner, of celebrities.

parallel, paralleled, paralleling

parallels Use figures and lowercase to identify the imaginary locater lines that ring the globe from east to west. They are measured in units of 0 to 90 degrees north or south of the equator.

Examples: *4th parallel north*, *89th parallel south*, or, if location north or south of the equator is obvious: *19th parallel*.

See **latitude and longitude**.

Paralympics Multi-sport international competition for athletes with disabilities, held at the same sites as the Winter and Summer Olympics, usually two weeks after the end of the Olympic Games. Paralympic athletes have a wide range of disability categories, including intellectual, physical and visual. The athletes are *Paralympians*. See **disabilities**.

paraplegia/paraplegic, quadriplegia/quadriplegic
Paraplegia is the loss of movement in the lower extremities and torso. *Quadriplegia* is the paralysis of all four limbs as well as the torso. Both are typically caused by a spinal cord or brain injury. Refer to the condition only when relevant to the story. Do not use the term as a noun (*a quadriplegic*; *paraplegics*) unless someone describes themself that way. Do not use the shorthand *para* or *quad* unless someone uses those terms in direct quotes in reference to themself. See **disabilities**.

pardon, parole, probation The terms often are confused, but each has a specific meaning. Do not use them interchangeably.

A *pardon* forgives and releases a person from further punishment. It is granted by a chief of state or a governor. By itself, it does not expunge a record of conviction, if one exists, and it does not by itself restore civil rights.

A *general pardon*, usually for political offenses, is called *amnesty*.

Parole is the release of a prisoner before the sentence has expired, on condition of good behavior. It is granted by a parole board, part of the executive branch of government, and can be revoked only by the board.

Probation is the suspension of sentence for a person convicted, but not yet imprisoned, on condition of good behavior. It is imposed and revoked only by a judge.

parentheses See entry in the **Punctuation** chapter.

Parent Teacher Association *PTA* is acceptable in all references.

parish Capitalize as part of the formal name for a church congregation or a governmental jurisdiction: *St. John's Parish, Jefferson Parish*.

Lowercase standing alone or in plural combinations: *the parish, St. John's and St. Mary's parishes, Jefferson and Plaquemines parishes*.

See **county** for additional guidelines on governmental jurisdictions.

Parkinson's disease After James Parkinson, the English physician who described this degenerative disease of later life.

Parkinson's law After C. Northcote Parkinson, the British economist who came to the satirical conclusion that work expands to fill the time allotted to it.

parliament, Parliament Uppercase when referring to the legislative body in Great Britain or other countries.

parliamentary Lowercase unless part of a proper name.

partial quotes See **quotation marks** in the **Punctuation** chapter.

part time, part-time Hyphenate when used as a compound modifier: *She works part time. She has a part-time job.*

party affiliation A political figure's party affiliation is often relevant, but not always. Include party affiliation if a politician's actions could reasonably be seen as having an effect on policy or debate, or if readers need it for understanding. But reference to party affiliation is not necessary when a story has no link to politics. If in doubt, err on the side of including party affiliation.
— Party affiliation can be used on first reference when it is the most important element to connect with the subject: *Republican Sen. Tim Scott of South Carolina said …*
— On second reference to add context between the party affiliation and the rest of the story: *Rep. Frank Lucas of Oklahoma, the senior Republican on the House Agriculture Committee, said he supports the amendment.*
— Leave out when the story is clearly not political: *The governor attended the NCAA Tournament basketball game, having graduated from Villanova in 1995. The senator attended her daughter's high school graduation.*
— But use when a political connection exists: *The Democratic governor sat courtside next to the top donor to his campaign. The Republican senator spoke at her daughter's graduation two weeks after voting on the education bill.*
— In stories about party meetings, such as a report on the Republican National Convention, no specific reference to party affiliation is necessary unless an individual is not a member of the party in question.
   SHORT-FORM PUNCTUATION: Set short forms such as *R-S.C.* off from a name by commas: *Sen. Tim Scott, R-S.C., said …*
   Use the abbreviations listed in the entries for each state. (No abbreviations for *Alaska, Hawaii, Idaho, Iowa, Maine, Ohio, Texas* and *Utah.*)
   FORM FOR U.S. HOUSE MEMBERS: The normal practice for U.S. House members is to identify them by party and state. In contexts where state affiliation is clear and home city is relevant, such as a state election roundup, identify representatives by party and city: *U.S. Reps. Ander Crenshaw, R-Jacksonville, and Frederica Wilson, D-Miami.* If this option is used, be consistent throughout the story.
   FORM FOR STATE LEGISLATORS: Short-form listings showing party and home city are appropriate in state stories. For national stories, the normal practice is to say that the individual is a *Republican* or *Democrat.* Use a short-form listing only if the legislator's home city is relevant.
   See **legislative titles**.

passenger mile One passenger carried one mile, or its equivalent, such as two passengers carried one-half mile.

passerby, passersby

pasteurize

patrol, patrolled, patrolling

payload

PB&J Peanut butter and jelly sandwich.

PC Short for *personal computer*. Acceptable on first reference. The term typically refers to traditional desktop and laptop computers, though it sometimes includes tablets with detachable keyboards.

PDF Acceptable in all references for *Portable Document Format*. A file format that allows a document to be shared among several types of computers without losing its formatting.

peacekeeping

peacemaker, peacemaking

peace offering

peacetime

peasant Do not use the term, which is often derogatory, in referring to farm laborers (except in quotes or an organization name).

peck A unit of dry measure equal to 8 dry quarts or one-fourth of a bushel.
The metric equivalent is approximately 8.8 liters.
See **liter**.

pedal, peddle When riding a bicycle or similar vehicle, you *pedal* it.
When selling something, you may *peddle* it.

peddler

pedophilia Sexual desire felt by an adult for children. Do not use in a legal sense such as a *pedophilia conviction* or *convicted pedophile*. Instead, refer to the charges. For example, *convicted sexual offender; convicted of child sexual abuse; conviction on charges of sexually abusing children*.

peninsula Capitalize as part of a proper name: *the Florida Peninsula, the Upper Peninsula of Michigan, the Korean Peninsula, the Indochina Peninsula, the Crimean Peninsula*.

Pennsylvania Dutch The individuals are of German descent. The word *Dutch* is a corruption of *Deutsch*, the German word for "German."

people's Use this possessive form when the word occurs in the formal name of a nation: *the People's Republic of China*.
Use this form also in such phrases as *the people's desire for freedom*.

people, persons Use *person* when speaking of an individual: *One person waited for the bus.*
The word *people* is preferred to *persons* in all plural uses. For example: *Thousands of people attended the fair. What will people say? There were 17 people in the room.*
Persons should be used only when it is in a direct quote or part of a title as in *Bureau of Missing Persons*.
People also is a collective noun that takes a plural verb when used to refer to a single race or nation: *The people of the United States are not united.*
When relevant, use a more precise alternative to *people*. For example: *U.S. adults; likely voters in Ghana's presidential election; Chinese American*

college students.

Avoid general and often dehumanizing *"the"* labels such as *the poor, the homeless, the French, the disabled, the college-educated.*

percent, percentage, percentage points Use the % sign when paired with a number, with no space, in most cases (a change in 2019): *Average hourly pay rose 3.1% from a year ago; her mortgage rate is 4.75%; about 60% of Americans agreed; he won 56.2% of the vote.* Use figures: *1%, 4 percentage points.*

For amounts less than 1%, precede the decimal with a zero: *The cost of living rose 0.6%.*

In casual uses, use words rather than figures and numbers: *She said he has a zero percent chance of winning.*

At the start of a sentence: Try to avoid this construction. If it's necessary to start a sentence with a percentage, spell out both: *Eighty-nine percent of sentences don't have to begin with a number.*

Constructions with the % sign take a singular verb when standing alone or when a singular word follows an *of* construction: *The teacher said 60% was a failing grade. He said 50% of the membership was there.*

It takes a plural verb when a plural word follows an *of* construction: *He said 50% of the members were there.*

Use decimals, not fractions, in percentages: *Her mortgage rate is 4.5%.*

For a range, *12% to 15%, 12%-15%* and *between 12% and 15%* are all acceptable.

Use *percentage*, rather than *percent*, when not paired with a number: *The percentage of people agreeing is small.*

Be careful not to confuse *percent* with *percentage point*. A change from

10% to 13% is a rise of 3 percentage points. This is not equal to a 3% change; rather, it's a 30% increase.

Usage: *Republicans passed a 0.25 percentage point tax cut.* Not: *Republicans passed a 0.25 percentage points tax cut* or *Republicans passed a tax cut of 0.25 of a percentage point.*

periods See entry in the **Punctuation** chapter.

perk A shortened form of *perquisite* often used to describe fringe benefits.

permissible

per-share earnings Also: *earnings per share.*

Persian Gulf Use this long-established name for the body of water off the southern coast of Iran.

Some Arab nations call it the *Arabian Gulf.* Use *Arabian Gulf* only in direct quotations and explain in the text that the body of water is more commonly known as the *Persian Gulf.*

personifications Capitalize them: *Grim Reaper, Father Time, Mother Nature, Old Man Winter, Sol,* etc.

peshmerga A generic Kurdish term for a fighting group.

PFAS (n. and adj.; singular and plural) A group of synthetic, potentially harmful chemicals used in a wide variety of household products and industrial processes.

PFAS is acceptable on first reference as part of a phrase: *a group of chemicals known as PFAS.* Use the unabbreviated name on second reference or elsewhere in

p

the story: *PFAS is an abbreviation for perfluoroalkyl and polyfluoroalkyl substances.* The shorthand *per-* and *polyfluoroalkyl substances* is acceptable but not preferred.

PFAS were developed as coatings to protect consumer goods from stains, water and corrosion. Nonstick cookware, carpets, outdoor gear and food packaging are among items that contain the chemicals. They also are an ingredient in firefighting foams. PFAS are often described as *forever chemicals* because some don't degrade naturally and are believed capable of lingering indefinitely in the environment.

According to the U.S. Centers for Disease Control and Prevention, human health effects from exposure to low environmental levels of PFAS are uncertain. Studies of laboratory animals given large amounts of PFAS have found that some PFAS may affect growth and development, reproduction, thyroid function, the immune system, and the liver. PFAS have been found increasingly in ground and surface waters. The federal government does not regulate PFAS in drinking water, although some states are developing limits. They have been found in a variety of wildlife species, including fish, bald eagles and mink.

About 5,000 variations have been produced. The most common are known as PFOA (perfluorooctanoic acid) and PFOS (perfluorooctanesulfonic acid), which no longer are manufactured in the U.S. but remain widespread in soil and water. If needed to refer to them specifically, *PFOA* and *PFOS* are acceptable on all references in a story about PFAS.

Ph.D., Ph.D.s The preferred form is to say a person *holds a doctorate* and name the individual's area of specialty.

See **academic degrees** and **doctor**.

phenomenon, phenomena

Philippines In datelines, give the name of a city or town followed by *Philippines*:
    MANILA, Philippines (AP) —
    In stories: *the Philippines.*
    The people are *Filipinos. Filipina* is acceptable as the feminine form. The language is *Filipino*, an offshoot of Tagalog. *Philippine* is the adjective.

phishing A form of internet fraud that aims to steal personal information such as credit card numbers, Social Security numbers, user IDs and passwords.

phobia Irrational fear or hatred, sometimes a form of mental illness (*acrophobia, claustrophobia*) but also used more generally in political or social contexts: *homophobia, Islamophobia, xenophobia.* The latter terms are acceptable in broad references or quotations: *She said her prime goals are to fight xenophobia and racism.* In individual cases, be specific about observable actions; avoid descriptions or language that assumes motives.

Photoshop Trademark for a brand of photo-editing software. Use the generic form if the brand is uncertain, and don't use verbs like *photoshopped* except in direct quotations (in which case use lowercase).

physician assistant No possessive form in this medical profession title.

picket, pickets, picketed, picket line *Picket* is both the verb and the noun. Do not use *picketer*.

picnic, picnicked, picnicking, picnicker

pico- A prefix denoting one-trillionth of a unit.

pigeonhole (n. and v.)

Pikes Peak No apostrophe. After Zebulon Montgomery Pike, a U.S. general and explorer. The 14,115-foot peak is in the Rockies of central Colorado.

pileup (n. and adj.) **pile up** (v.)

pill Do not capitalize in references to oral contraceptives. Use *birth control pill* on first reference if necessary for clarity.

pingpong A synonym for *table tennis*. The trademark name is *Ping-Pong*.

Pink Sheets A daily publication compiled by the National Quotation Bureau with bid and ask prices of over-the-counter stocks. See **over-the-counter stock**.

pint (dry) Equal to 33.6 cubic inches, or one-half of a dry quart. The metric equivalent is approximately 0.55 of a liter.
See **liter** and **quart (dry)**.

pint (liquid) Equal to 16 fluid ounces, or two cups. The approximate metric equivalents are 470 milliliters or 0.47 of a liter.
See **liter**.

Pinterest A service in which users collect and share images in theme-based collections, also known as *pinboards* or simply *boards*. Images that are shared on Pinterest — or *pinned* — are sometimes referred to as *pins*. Headquarters is in San Francisco.

Pinyin The official Chinese spelling system.
See **Chinese names**.

planets Capitalize the proper names of planets. In order from the sun, they are *Mercury, Venus, Earth, Mars, Jupiter, Saturn, Uranus* and *Neptune*.
Capitalize *Earth* when used as the proper name of our planet: *The astronauts returned to Earth.*
Capitalize nouns and adjectives derived from the proper names of planets: *Martian, Venusian*. But lowercase adjectives derived from other heavenly bodies: *solar, lunar*.
See **Earth** and **heavenly bodies**.

planning Avoid the redundant *future planning*.

plants In general, lowercase the names of plants, but capitalize proper nouns or adjectives that occur in a name.
Some examples: *tree, fir, white fir, Douglas fir; Scotch pine; clover, white clover, white Dutch clover.*
If a botanical name is used, capitalize the first word; lowercase others: *pine tree (Pinus), red cedar (Juniperus virginiana), blue azalea (Callicarpa americana), Kentucky coffee tree (Gymnocladus dioica).*

plead, pleaded, pleading

Pledge of Allegiance

Plexiglas Note the single *s*. A trademark for plastic glass.

p

plurals Follow these guidelines in forming and using plural words:

MOST WORDS: Add *s*: *boys*, *girls*, *ships*, *villages*.

WORDS ENDING IN CH, S, SH, SS, X AND Z: Add *es*: *churches*, *lenses*, *parishes*, *glasses*, *boxes*, *buzzes*. (*Monarchs* is an exception.)

WORDS ENDING IN IS: Change *is* to *es*: *oases*, *parentheses*, *theses*.

WORDS ENDING IN Y: If *y* is preceded by a consonant or *qu*, change *y* to *i* and add *es*: *armies*, *cities*, *navies*, *soliloquies*. (See **PROPER NAMES** below for an exception.)

Otherwise add *s*: *donkeys*, *monkeys*.

WORDS ENDING IN O: If *o* is preceded by a consonant, most plurals require *es*: *buffaloes*, *dominoes*, *echoes*, *heroes*, *potatoes*. But there are exceptions: *pianos*. See individual entries in this book for many of these exceptions.

WORDS ENDINGS IN F: In general, change *f* to *v* and add *es*: *leaves*, *selves*. (*Roof*, *roofs* is an exception.)

LATIN ENDINGS: Latin-root words ending in *us* change *us* to *i*: *alumnus*, *alumni*. (Words that have taken on English endings by common usage are exceptions: *prospectuses*, *syllabuses*.)

Most ending in *a* change to *ae*: *alumna*, *alumnae* (*formula*, *formulas* is an exception).

Most ending in *um* add *s*: *memorandums*, *referendums*, *stadiums*. Among those that still use the Latin ending: *addenda*, *curricula*, *media*.

Use the plural that Webster's New World College Dictionary lists as most common for a particular sense of word.

FORM CHANGE: *man*, *men*; *child*, *children*; *foot*, *feet*; *mouse*, *mice*; etc.

Caution: When *s* is used with any of these words it indicates possession and must be preceded by an apostrophe: *men's*, *children's*, etc.

WORDS THE SAME IN SINGULAR AND PLURAL: *corps*, *chassis*, *deer*, *moose*, *sheep*, etc.

The sense in a particular sentence is conveyed by the use of a singular or plural verb.

WORDS PLURAL IN FORM, SINGULAR IN MEANING: Some take singular verbs: *measles*, *mumps*, *news*.

Others take plural verbs: *grits*, *scissors*.

COMPOUND WORDS: Those written solid add *s* at the end: *cupfuls*, *handfuls*, *tablespoonfuls*.

For those that involve separate words or words linked by a hyphen, make the most significant word plural:

— Significant word first: *adjutants general*, *aides-de-camp*, *attorneys general*, *courts-martial*, *daughters-in-law*, *passers-by*, *postmasters general*, *presidents-elect*, *secretaries-general*, *sergeants major*.
— Significant word in the middle: *assistant attorneys general*, *deputy chiefs of staff*.
— Significant word last: *assistant attorneys*, *assistant corporation counsels*, *deputy sheriffs*, *lieutenant colonels*, *major generals*.

WORDS AS WORDS: Do not use *'s*: *His speech had too many "ifs," "ands" and "buts."*

PROPER NAMES: Most ending in *es* or *s* or *z* add *es*: *Charleses*, *Joneses*, *Gonzalezes*.

Most ending in *y* add *s* even if preceded by a consonant: *the Duffys*, *the Kennedys*, *the two Kansas Citys*. Exceptions include *Alleghenies* and *Rockies*.

For others, add *s*: *the Carters*, *the McCoys*, *the Mondales*.

FIGURES: Add *s*: *The custom began in the 1920s. The airline has two 727s. Temperatures will be in the low 20s. There were five size 7s.*

(No apostrophes, an exception to Webster's New World College Dictionary guideline under "apostrophe.")

SINGLE LETTERS: Use *'s*: *Mind your p's and q's. He learned the three R's and brought home a report card with four A's and two B's. The Oakland A's won the pennant.*

MULTIPLE LETTERS: Add *s*: *She knows her ABCs. I gave him five IOUs. Four VIPs were there.*

PROBLEMS, DOUBTS: Separate entries in this book give plurals for troublesome words and guidance on whether certain words should be used with singular or plural verbs and pronouns. See also **collective nouns** and **possessives**.

For questions not covered by this book, use the plural that Webster's New World College Dictionary lists as most common for a particular sense of a word.

plus symbol (+) The symbol is acceptable when it is pronounced as part of a company, brand or event name: *Disney+, Apple TV+, ESPN+, CompTia Network+.* Do not use in slugs of AP stories; use *plus* in slugs. Use the word *plus* in other uses: *They expect 200-plus people. He is my plus-one. Flowers plus blue skies make for a nice day. She got a B-plus on the test.*

p.m., a.m. Lowercase, with periods. Avoid the redundant 10 *p.m. tonight.*

pocket veto Occurs only when Congress has adjourned. If Congress is in session, a bill that remains on the president's desk for 10 days becomes law without his signature. If Congress adjourns, however, a bill that fails to get his signature within 10 days is vetoed.

Many states have similar procedures, but the precise requirements vary.

podium See **lectern, podium, pulpit, rostrum**.

poetry See **composition titles** for guidelines on the names of poems.

Capitalize the first word in a line of poetry unless the author deliberately has used lowercase for a special effect. Do not, however, capitalize the first word on indented lines that must be created simply because the writer's line is too long for the available printing width. If quoting poetry within a single paragraph, use a slash with a space on each side: *Two roads diverged in a wood, and I — / I took the one less traveled by, / And that has made all the difference.*

poinsettia Note the *ia*.

point Do not abbreviate. Capitalize as part of a proper name: *Point Pleasant.*

poison pill In the financial world, any defensive measure to prevent the takeover of a corporation by making its acquisition prohibitively expensive for the party attempting the takeover.

police department In communities where this is the formal name, capitalize *police department* with or without the name of the community: *the Los Angeles Police Department, the Police Department.*

If a police agency has some other formal name such as *Division of Police,* use that name if it is the way the department is known to the public. If the story uses *police department* as a generic term for such an agency, put *police department* in lowercase.

If a police agency with an unusual formal name is known to the public as a *police department*, treat *police department* as the name, capitalizing it with or without the name of the community. Use the formal name only if there is a special reason in the story.

If the proper name cannot be determined for some reason, such as the need to write about a police agency from a distance, treat *police department* as the proper name, capitalizing it with or without the name of the community.

Lowercase *police department* in plural uses: *the Los Angeles and San Francisco police departments.*

Lowercase *the department* whenever it stands alone.

police titles See **military titles** and **titles**.

policymaker, policymaking

polio The preferred term for *poliomyelitis* and *infantile paralysis*.

Politburo Acceptable in all references for the *Political Bureau of the Communist Party*.

political divisions Use Arabic figures and capitalize the accompanying word when used with the figures: *1st Ward, 10th Ward, 3rd Precinct, 22nd Precinct, the ward, the precinct.* See **numerals**.

political parties and philosophies Capitalize both the name of the party and the word *party* if it is customarily used as part of the organization's proper name: *the Democratic Party, the Republican Party.*

Include the political affiliation of any elected officeholder.

Capitalize *Communist, Conservative, Democrat, Liberal, Republican, Socialist,* etc., when they refer to a specific party or its members. Lowercase these words when they refer to political philosophy (see examples below).

Lowercase the name of a philosophy in noun and adjective forms unless it is the derivative of a proper name: *communism, communist; fascism, fascist.* But: *Marxism, Marxist; Nazism, Nazi.*

EXAMPLES: *John Adams was a Federalist, but a man who subscribed to his philosophy today would be described as a federalist. The liberal Republican senator and his Conservative Party colleague said they believe that democracy and communism are incompatible. The Communist Party member said he is basically a socialist who has reservations about Marxism.*

Generally, a description of specific political views is more informative than a generic label like *liberal* or *conservative*.

See **convention** and **party affiliation**.

politicking

politics Usually it takes a plural verb: *My politics are my own business.*

As a study or science, it takes a singular verb: *Politics is a demanding profession.*

Ponzi scheme A fraudulent investing technique that promises high rates of return with little risk to investors. In the scheme, money provided by new investors is used to pay seeming high returns to early-stage investors to suggest the enterprise is prosperous. The scheme collapses when required redemptions exceed new investments.

pope Capitalize when used as a formal title before a name; lowercase in all other uses: *Pope Francis spoke to the crowd. At the close of his address, the pope gave his blessing. Pope Emeritus Benedict XVI* or *Benedict XVI, the pope emeritus. Benedict* alone on second reference.

Use *St. John Paul II* and *St. John XXIII* on first reference for the canonized popes. On second reference *John Paul* and *John*. Make clear in the body of a story they were popes.

See **Catholic, Catholicism**; **Roman Catholic Church** and **religious titles** in the **Religion** chapter.

populism Political philosophy or ideas that promote the rights and power of ordinary people as opposed to political and intellectual elites. Avoid labeling politicians or political parties as *populist*, other than in a quote or paraphrase: *He calls himself a populist.* Using the term in a general context is acceptable: *The panelists discussed the rise of populism in Europe. She appealed to populist fervor.*

pore, pour The verb *pore* means to gaze intently or steadily: *She pored over her books.*

The verb *pour* means to flow in a continuous stream: *It poured rain. He poured the coffee.*

Porteno The people and culture of the city of Buenos Aires, Argentina. The term for the province of the same name is *Bonaerense.*

port, starboard Nautical for left and right (when facing the bow, or forward). Port is left. Starboard is right. Change to *left* or *right* unless in direct quotes.

Portuguese names The family names of both the father and mother usually are considered part of a person's full name. In everyday use, customs sometimes vary with individuals and countries.

The normal sequence is given name, mother's family name, father's family name: *Maria Santos Ferreira.*

On second reference, use only the father's family name (*Ferreira*), unless the individual prefers or is widely known by a multiple last name (*Ferreira Castro*).

Some Portuguese use an *e* (for *and*) between the two names: *Joao Canto e Castro.* This would not be split on second reference, but would be *Canto e Castro.*

When a surname is preceded by *da, do, dos,* or *das,* include it in the second reference. *Jorge da Costa,* for example, would be *da Costa* on second reference.

A married woman adds her husband's surname to the end of hers. If *Maria Santos Ferreira* married *Joao Costa da Silva,* her full name would be *Maria Ferreira da Silva.*

Occasionally, a woman may choose not to take her husband's surname for personal reasons or because the mother's family has an aristocratic or famous surname. Use both surnames if the individual's choice is not known.

possessives Follow these guidelines:

PLURAL NOUNS NOT ENDING IN S: Add *'s*: *the alumni's contributions, women's rights.*

PLURAL NOUNS ENDING IN S: Add only an apostrophe: *the churches' needs, the girls' toys, the horses' food,*

p

the ships' wake, states' rights, the VIPs' entrance.

NOUNS PLURAL IN FORM, SINGULAR IN MEANING: Add only an apostrophe: *mathematics' rules, measles' effects.* (But see **INANIMATE OBJECTS** below.)

Apply the same principle when a plural word occurs in the formal name of a singular entity: *General Motors' profits, the United States' wealth.*

NOUNS THE SAME IN SINGULAR AND PLURAL: Treat them the same as plurals, even if the meaning is singular: *one corps' location, the two deer's tracks, the lone moose's antlers.*

SINGULAR NOUNS NOT ENDING IN S: Add *'s: the church's needs, the girl's toys, the horse's food, the ship's route, the VIP's seat.*

Some style guides say that singular nouns ending in *s* sounds such as *ce, x,* and *z* may take either the apostrophe alone or *'s.* See **SPECIAL EXPRESSIONS,** but otherwise, for consistency and ease in remembering a rule, always use *'s* if the word does not end in the letter *s: Butz's policies, the fox's den, the justice's verdict, Marx's theories, the prince's life, Xerox's profits.*

SINGULAR COMMON NOUNS ENDING IN S: Add *'s: the virus's reach, the virus's spread; the witness's answer, the witness's story.* (A change from previous guidance calling for just an apostrophe if the next word begins with *s.*)

SINGULAR PROPER NAMES ENDING IN S: Use only an apostrophe: *Achilles' heel, Agnes' book, Ceres' rites, Descartes' theories, Dickens' novels, Euripides' dramas, Hercules' labors, Jesus' life, Jules' seat, Kansas' schools, Moses' law, Socrates' life, Tennessee Williams' plays, Xerxes' armies.*

SPECIAL EXPRESSIONS: The following exceptions to the general

rule for words not ending in *s* apply to words that end in an *s* sound and are followed by a word that begins with *s: for appearance' sake, for conscience' sake, for goodness' sake.* Use *'s* otherwise: *the appearance's cost, my conscience's voice.*

PRONOUNS: Personal interrogative and relative pronouns have separate forms for the possessive. None involve an apostrophe: *mine, ours, your, yours, his, hers, its, theirs, whose.*

Caution: If you are using an apostrophe with a pronoun, always double-check to be sure that the meaning calls for a contraction: *you're, it's, there's, who's.*

Follow the rules listed above in forming the possessives of other pronouns: *another's idea, others' plans, someone's guess.*

COMPOUND WORDS: Applying the rules above, add an apostrophe or *'s* to the word closest to the object possessed: *the major general's decision, the major generals' decisions, the attorney general's request, the attorneys general's request.* See the **plurals** entry for guidelines on forming the plurals of these words.

Also: *anyone else's attitude, John Adams Jr.'s father, Benjamin Franklin of Pennsylvania's motion.* Whenever practical, however, recast the phrase to avoid ambiguity: *the motion by Benjamin Franklin of Pennsylvania.*

JOINT POSSESSION, INDIVIDUAL POSSESSION: Use a possessive form after only the last word if ownership is joint: *Fred and Sylvia's apartment, Fred and Sylvia's stocks.*

Use a possessive form after both words if the objects are individually owned: *Fred's and Sylvia's books.*

DESCRIPTIVE PHRASES: Do not add an apostrophe to a word ending in *s* when it is used primarily in a descriptive sense: *citizens band radio,* *a Cincinnati Reds infielder, a teachers college, a Teamsters request, a writers guide.*

Memory aid: The apostrophe usually is not used if *for* or *by* rather than *of* would be appropriate in the longer form: *a radio band for citizens, a college for teachers, a guide for writers, a request by the Teamsters.*

An *'s* is required, however, when a term involves a plural word that does not end in *s*: *a children's hospital, a people's republic, the Young Men's Christian Association.*

DESCRIPTIVE NAMES: Some governmental, corporate and institutional organizations with a descriptive word in their names use an apostrophe; some do not. Follow the user's practice: *Actors' Equity, Diners Club, Ladies' Home Journal, the National Governors Association.*

QUASI POSSESSIVES: Follow the rules above in composing the possessive form of words that occur in such phrases as *a day's pay, two weeks' vacation, three months' work, five years' probation.* The apostrophe is used with a measurement followed by a noun (a quantity of whatever the noun is). The examples could be rephrased as *a day of pay, two weeks of vacation, three months of work, five years of probation.*

No apostrophe when the quantity precedes an adjective: *six months pregnant, three weeks overdue, 11 years old.*

DOUBLE POSSESSIVE: Two conditions must apply for a double possessive — a phrase such as *a friend of John's* — to occur: 1. The word after *of* must refer to an animate object, and 2. The word before *of* must involve only a portion of the animate object's possessions.

Otherwise, do not use the possessive form of the word after *of:*

The friends of John Adams mourned his death. (All the friends were involved.) *He is a friend of the college.* (Not *college's,* because *college* is inanimate.)

Memory aid: This construction occurs most often, and quite naturally, with the possessive forms of personal pronouns: *He is a friend of mine.*

INANIMATE OBJECTS: There is no blanket rule against creating a possessive form for an inanimate object, particularly if the object is treated in a personified sense. See some of the earlier examples, and note these: *death's call, the wind's murmur.*

In general, however, avoid excessive personalization of inanimate objects, and give preference to an *of* construction when it fits the makeup of the sentence. For example, the earlier references to *mathematics' rules* and *measles' effects* would better be phrased: *the rules of mathematics, the effects of measles.*

post- Follow Webster's New World College Dictionary. Hyphenate if not listed there.

Some words without a hyphen:

postdate	*postnuptial*
postdoctoral	*postscript*
postgame	*postwar*
postgraduate	

Some words that use a hyphen:

post-bellum	*post-election*
post-convention	*post-mortem*

Post-it A trademark for small pieces of paper with an adhesive strip on the back that can be attached to documents.

post office It may be used but it is no longer capitalized because the

p

agency is now the *U.S. Postal Service.*
Use lowercase in referring to an individual office: *I went to the post office.*

postpartum depression A form of depression experienced by some women in the first weeks or months after childbirth. Describe a person as *having postpartum depression* only if relevant to the story, and if a medical diagnosis has been made or the person uses the term. If relatives or others use the term, ask how they know, then consider carefully whether to include the information. Do not use the term *baby blues.* See **disabilities; depression; mental illness**.

post-traumatic stress disorder A condition arising from shocking, dangerous or terrifying experiences including war, disasters, physical or sexual assault or abuse, fires, car crashes, etc. Symptoms may include flashbacks, nightmares and severe anxiety that last more than a few months. The shorthand *PTSD* is acceptable on first reference, but spell out on second reference. Describe a person as *having PTSD* only if relevant to the story, and if a medical diagnosis has been made or the person uses the term. If relatives or others use the term, ask how they know, then consider carefully whether to include the information. See **disabilities; mental illness**.

pound (monetary) The English pound sign is not used. Convert the figures to dollars in most cases. Use a figure and spell out *pounds* if the actual figure is relevant.

pound (weight) Equal to 16 ounces. The metric equivalent is approximately 454 grams, or 0.45 kilograms.
See **gram** and **kilogram**.

poverty level An income level judged inadequate to provide a family or individual with the essentials of life. The figure for the United States is adjusted regularly to reflect changes in the Consumer Price Index.

pre- Follow *Webster's New World College Dictionary.* Hyphenate if not listed there. A 2019 change: In recognition of common usage and dictionary preferences, do not hyphenate double-e combinations with *pre-* and *re-*. Examples: *preeclampsia, preelection, preeminent, preempt, preestablished, preexisting* and those listed in **re-**. Other rules in **prefixes** apply.
Some examples:

prearrange	*prehistoric*
precondition	*preignition*
precook	*prejudge*
predate	*premarital*
predecease	*prenatal*
predispose	*prenuptial*
preflight	*pretax*
pregame	*pretest*
preheat	*prewar*

Some hyphenated coinage, not listed in the dictionary:
pre-convention pre-noon

preferred stock An ownership in a company that has no voting rights but pays a fixed dividend and has a higher claim on the company's assets and earnings than common stock.

prefixes See separate listings for commonly used prefixes.
The Stylebook's preferences on whether to use a hyphen following a prefix are based largely on usage and *Webster's New World College*

p

Dictionary. Generally we do not hyphenate when using a prefix with a word starting with a consonant. But there are exceptions. See individual entries and the dictionary.

Three rules are constant:
— Use a hyphen if the prefix ends in a vowel and the word that follows begins with the same vowel. Exceptions: *cooperate, coordinate,* and double-e combinations such as *preestablish, preeminent, preeclampsia, preempt.*
— Use a hyphen if the word that follows is capitalized.
— Use a hyphen to join doubled prefixes: *sub-subparagraph.*

pregnant people Phrasing like *pregnant people* or *people who seek an abortion* seeks to include people who have those experiences but do not identify as women, such as some *transgender* men and some *nonbinary* people. Such phrasing should be confined to stories that specifically address the experiences of people who do not identify as women. See **gender, sex and sexual orientation.**

preheat Acceptable to refer to heating an oven to a specific temperature before cooking. (A change in 2020.)

premiere A first performance.

premier, prime minister These two titles often are used interchangeably in translating to English the title of an individual who is the first minister in a national government that has a council of ministers.

Prime minister is the correct title throughout the Commonwealth, formerly the British Commonwealth. See **Commonwealth** for a list of members.

Prime minister is the best or traditional translation from most other languages. For consistency, use it throughout the rest of the world with these exceptions:
— Use *chancellor* in Austria and Germany.
— Follow the practice of a nation if there is a specific preference that varies from this general practice. For example, use *premier* in China.

Premier is also the correct title for the individuals who lead the provincial governments in Canada and Australia.

See **titles.**

presently Use it to mean *in a little while* or *shortly,* but not to mean *now.*

presidency Always lowercase.

president Capitalize *president* only as a formal title before one or more names: *President Joe Biden, former Presidents Donald Trump and Barack Obama.*

Lowercase in all other uses: *The president said Monday he will look into the matter. He is running for president. Lincoln was president during the Civil War.*

See **titles.**

FULL NAMES: Use the first and family name on first reference to a current or former U.S. president or the president-elect: *former President Barack Obama, President Joe Biden, President-elect Joe Biden.* On subsequent references, use only the last name.

For presidents of other nations and of organizations and institutions, capitalize president as a formal title before a full name: *President Emmanuel Macron of France, President Amanda Nabih of Acme Corp.*

On second reference, use only the

last name.

presidential Lowercase unless part of a proper name.

Presidential Medal of Freedom

The United States' highest civilian honor. It is given by the president to people who have made exceptionally meritorious contributions to the security or national interests of the United States, to world peace, or to cultural or other significant public or private endeavors.

Presidents Day No apostrophe is an exception to Webster's New World College Dictionary, in keeping with the descriptive phrases guidance in possessives. The term is not adopted by the federal government as the official name of the Washington's Birthday holiday. However, some federal agencies, states and local governments use the term.

presiding officer Always lowercase.

press conference *News conference* is preferred.

pretax

pretense, pretext A *pretext* is something that is put forward to conceal a truth: *He was discharged for tardiness, but the reason given was only a pretext for general incompetence.*

A *pretense* is a false show, a more overt act intended to conceal personal feelings: *My profuse compliments were all pretense.*

preventive

price-earnings ratio The price of a share of stock divided by earnings per share for a 12-month period.

Ratios in AP stock tables reflect earnings for the most recent 12 months.

For example, a stock selling for $60 per share and earning $6 per share would be selling at a price-earnings ratio of 10-to-1. *P/E* is acceptable on second reference.

See **profit terminology**.

Pride, pride Capitalize *Pride* when referring to events or organizations honoring LGBTQ communities and on subsequent references. *Twin Cities Pride. "Are you going to Pride?" she asked. It's Pride day. Several cities are holding Pride events this weekend.* Lowercase *pride* when referring to generic events or the general concept of LGBTQ pride. *He attended a gay pride parade.*

See **gender, sex and sexual orientation**.

priest A vocational description, not a formal title. Do not capitalize.

See **Catholic, Catholicism** and the entries for **Episcopal Church**; **religious titles**; **Roman Catholic Church** in the **Religion** chapter.

primary Do not capitalize: *the New Hampshire primary, the Democratic primary, the primary.*

primary day Use lowercase for any of the days set aside for balloting in a primary.

prime rate A benchmark rate used by banks to set interest charges on a variety of corporate and consumer loans, including some adjustable home mortgages, revolving credit cards and business loans extended to their most creditworthy customers. Banks almost always raise or lower their rates by a similar amount on the same day Federal Reserve policymakers change their target for overnight loans between banks, known as the *federal funds rate*.

Primero de Mayo May Day, the labor day holiday in Latin America and Spain.

prime time (n.) **prime-time** (adj.)

Prince Edward Island One of the three Maritime Provinces of Canada. Do not abbreviate.
See **datelines**.

prince, princess Capitalize when used as a royal title before a name; lowercase when used alone: *Prince Charles, the prince.*
See **nobility**.

principal, principle *Principal* is a noun and adjective meaning someone or something first in rank, authority, importance or degree: *She is the school principal. He was the principal player in the trade. Money is the principal problem.*

Principle is a noun that means a fundamental truth, law, doctrine or motivating force: *They fought for the principle of self-determination.*

In a business context, *principal* refers to the amount of money that is borrowed in a loan, as distinct from interest that is paid.

prior to *Before* is less stilted for most uses. *Prior to* is appropriate, however, when a notion of requirement is involved: *The fee must be paid prior to the examination.*

prison, jail Do not use the two words interchangeably.
DEFINITIONS: *Prison* is a generic term that may be applied to the

maximum security institutions often known as *penitentiaries* and to the medium security facilities often called *correctional institutions* or *reformatories*. All such facilities usually confine people serving sentences for felonies.

A *jail* is normally used to confine people serving sentences for misdemeanors, people awaiting trial or sentencing on either felony or misdemeanor charges, and people confined for civil matters such as failure to pay alimony and other types of contempt of court.
See **felony, misdemeanor**.
The guidelines for capitalization:
PRISONS: Many states have given elaborate formal names to their prisons. They should be capitalized when used, but commonly accepted substitutes should also be capitalized as if they were proper names. For example, use either *Massachusetts Correctional Institution-Walpole* or *Walpole State Prison* for the maximum security institution in Massachusetts.

Do not, however, construct a substitute when the formal name is commonly accepted: It is the *Colorado State Penitentiary*, for example, not *Colorado State Prison*.

On second reference, any of the following may be used, all in lowercase: *the state prison, the prison, the state penitentiary, the penitentiary*.

Use lowercase for all plural constructions: *the Colorado and Kansas state penitentiaries*.

JAILS: Capitalize *jail* when linked with the name of the jurisdiction: *Los Angeles County Jail*. Lowercase *county jail*, *city jail* and *jail* when they stand alone.

FEDERAL INSTITUTIONS: Maximum security institutions are known as *penitentiaries: the U.S. Penitentiary at*

p

Lewisburg or *Lewisburg Penitentiary* on first reference; *the federal penitentiary* or *the penitentiary* on second reference.

Medium security institutions include the word *federal* as part of their formal names: *the Federal Correctional Institution at Danbury, Connecticut.* On second reference: *the correctional institution, the federal prison, the prison.*

Most federal facilities used to house people awaiting trial or serving sentences of a year or less have the proper name *Federal Detention Center.* The term *Metropolitan Correctional Center* is being adopted for some new installations. On second reference: *the detention center, the correctional center.*

prisoner(s) of war *POW(s)* is acceptable on second reference.

Hyphenate when used as a compound modifier: *a prisoner-of-war trial.*

privacy Special care should be taken with regard to publishing the names of juveniles involved in crimes, or of people who may have been the victims of sexual assault or other abuse.

Generally, we do not identify juveniles (under 18) who are accused of crimes or transmit images that would reveal their identity. However, regional editors or their designates may authorize exceptions to this practice.

Considerations in granting exceptions may include the severity of the alleged crime; whether police have formally released the juvenile's name; and whether the juvenile has been formally charged as an adult. Other considerations might include

public safety, such as when the youth is the subject of a manhunt; or widespread publication of the juvenile suspect's name, making the identity de facto public knowledge.

In some situations, state or national laws may determine whether the person's name can be published.

We normally do not identify, in text or through images, juveniles who are witnesses to crimes.

We also do not identify, in text or through images, persons who may have been sexually assaulted (unless they have come forward and voluntarily identified themselves). We should also use discretion in naming victims of other extremely severe abuse.

Sometimes a person may be identified by AP in an abduction or manhunt situation, and it develops later that — because of a sexual assault or other reason — the name should not be used. In such cases we have sometimes refrained from using the identification in future coverage.

privatization The process of transferring a government-owned enterprise to private ownership.

pro- Use a hyphen when coining words that denote support for something. Some examples:

pro-labor	*pro-business*
pro-peace	*pro-war*

No hyphen when *pro* is used in other senses: *produce, profile, pronoun, proactive,* etc.

producer price index An index of changes in wholesale prices, produced by the Bureau of Labor Statistics, U.S. Department of Labor, and used as a gauge of inflation. Spell the index name lowercase.

p

professor Never abbreviate. Lowercase before a name, but capitalize *Professor Emeritus* as a conferred title before a name: *Professor Emeritus Susan Johnson.* Do not continue in second reference unless part of a quotation.

See **academic titles**, **emeritus** and **titles**.

profit-sharing (n. and adj.) The hyphen for the noun is an exception to Webster's New World College Dictionary.

profit-sharing plan A plan that gives employees a share in the profits of the company. Each employee receives a percentage of those profits based on the company's earnings.

profit-taking (n. and adj.) Avoid this term. It means selling a security after a recent rapid rise in price. It is inaccurate if the seller bought the security at a higher price, watched it fall, then sold it after a recent rise but for less than he bought it. In that case, he would be cutting his losses, not taking his profit.

profit terminology Note the meanings of the following terms in reporting a company's financial status. Always be careful to specify whether the figures given apply to quarterly or annual results.

The terms, listed in the order in which they might occur in analyzing a company's financial condition:

dividend The amount paid per share per year to holders of common stock. Payments generally are made in quarterly installments.

If a company shows no profit during a given period, it may be able to use earnings retained from profitable periods to pay its dividend on schedule.

earnings per share (or **loss per share**, for companies posting a net loss) The figure obtained by dividing the number of outstanding shares of common stock into the amount left after dividends have been paid on any preferred stock.

extraordinary loss, extraordinary income An expense or source of income that does not occur on a regular basis, such as a loss due to a major fire or the revenue from the sale of a subsidiary. Extraordinary items should be identified in any report on the company's financial status to avoid creating the false impression that its overall profit trend has suddenly plunged or soared.

gross profit The difference between the sales price of an item or service and the expenses directly attributed to it, such as the cost of raw materials, labor and overhead linked to the production effort.

income before taxes Gross profits minus companywide expenses not directly attributed to specific products or services. These expenses typically include interest costs, advertising and sales costs, and general administrative overhead.

net income, profit, earnings The amount left after taxes and preferred dividends have been paid.

Some of what remains may be paid in dividends to holders of common stock. The rest may be invested to obtain interest revenue or spent to acquire new buildings or equipment to increase the company's ability to make further profits.

To avoid confusion, do not use the word *income* alone — always specify whether the figure is *income before taxes* or *net income.*

The terms *profit* and *earnings*

commonly are interpreted as meaning the amount left after taxes. The terms *net profit* and *net earnings* are acceptable synonyms.

return on investment A percentage figure obtained by dividing the company's assets into its net income.

revenue The amount of money a company took in, including interest earned and receipts from sales, services provided, rents and royalties.

The figure also may include excise taxes and sales taxes collected for the government. If it does, the fact should be noted in any report on revenue. The singular form is preferable in most uses.

sales The money a company received for the goods and services it sold.

In some cases the figure includes receipts from rents and royalties. In others, particularly when rentals and royalties make up a large portion of a company's income, figures for these activities are listed separately.

pro forma In the financial world, it describes a method of calculating a company's sales and earnings as if changes in circumstances existed throughout an entire period covered by a financial report. Pro forma figures are often given for companies that have been involved in a merger or acquisition, gone public or emerged from bankruptcy reorganization. Unlike earnings based on generally accepted accounting principles, pro forma earnings do not comply with any standardized rules or regulations.

Prohibition Capitalize when referring to the period that began when the 18th Amendment to the Constitution prohibited the manufacture, sale or transportation of alcoholic liquors.

The amendment was declared ratified Jan. 29, 1919, and took effect Jan. 16, 1920. It was repealed by the 21st Amendment, which took effect Dec. 5, 1933, the day it was declared ratified.

pronouncers When necessary to use a pronouncer, put it in parentheses immediately following the word or name. The syllable to be stressed should be in caps with an apostrophe: *acetaminophen (a-see-tuh-MIHN'-oh-fen)*.

Here are the basic sounds represented by AP phonetic symbols:

Vowels	Consonants
a — apple, bat	g — got, beg
ah — father, hot	j — gem, job
ahr — part, car	k — cap, keep
aw — law, long	ch — chair
ay — ace, fate	s — see
eh — bed	sh — shut
ehr — merry	y — yes
ee — see, tea	z — zoom
ih — pin, middle	zh — mirage
oh — go, oval	kh — guttural "k"
oo — food, two	
or — for, torn	
ow — cow	
oy — boy	
u — foot, put	
uh — puff	
ur — burden, curl	
y, eye — ice, time	

pronouns Growing numbers of people, including some transgender, nonbinary, agender or gender-fluid people, use *they/them/their* as a gender-neutral singular personal pronoun.

As much as possible, AP also uses *they/them/their* as a way of accurately describing and representing a person who uses those pronouns for themself.

Here are some guidelines and perspectives.

They as a singular pronoun may

be confusing to some readers and amount to a roadblock that stops them from reading further. At the same time, though, efforts to write without pronouns to avoid confusion may make people feel censored or invisible.

How to balance those priorities? Try to honor both your readers and your story subjects. As in all news writing, clarity is paramount.

Often a sentence can be sensitively and smoothly written with no pronoun. For example: *Hendricks said the new job is a thrill* (instead of *Hendricks said Hendricks is thrilled about the new job* or *Hendricks said they are thrilled about the new job*).

When using *they/them/their* as a singular pronoun, explain if it isn't clear in context: *Morales, who uses the pronoun they, said they will retire in June.*

Be sure that the phrasing does not imply more than one person. Rephrase if needed to avoid confusion about the antecedent.

Don't refer to *preferred* or *chosen* pronouns. Instead, *the pronouns they use, whose pronouns are, who uses the pronouns*, etc.

Don't make assumptions about a person's gender identity based on their pronouns, or vice versa. Don't assume a person's pronouns based on their first name.

In general, do not use neopronouns such as *xe* or *zim*; they are rarely used and are unrecognizable as words to general audiences.

They/them/their take plural verbs even when used as a singular pronoun, and the singular reflexive *themself* is also acceptable when referring to people who use *they/them/their*.

—

Do not presume maleness in constructing a sentence by defaulting to *he/his/him*.

When necessary, use *they* rather than *he/she* or *he or she* for an unspecified or unknown gender (*a person, the victim, the winner*) or indefinite pronoun (*anyone, everyone, someone*). But rewording to avoid a pronoun is preferable. For example: *The foundation gave grants to anyone who lost a job this year* (instead of *anyone who lost their job*).

A singular *they* may also be used when an anonymous source's gender must be shielded: *The person feared for their own safety and spoke on condition of anonymity.*

propeller

prophecy (n.) **prophesy** (v.)

proportions Always use figures: *2 parts powder to 6 parts water.*

proposition Do not abbreviate unless in quotations. Capitalize when used with a figure in describing a ballot question: *He is uncommitted on Proposition 15.*

prosecutor Capitalize before a name when it is the formal title. In most cases, however, the formal title is a term such as *attorney general, state's attorney* or *U.S. attorney*. If so, use the formal title on first reference.

Lowercase *prosecutor* if used before a name on a subsequent reference, generally to help the reader distinguish between prosecutor and defense attorney without having to look back to the start of the story.

See **titles**.

prostate gland A gland that surrounds the urethra at the base of the bladder in males. Blood tests to measure *PSA*, or *prostate specific antigen*, are sometimes used for screening but do not indicate the presence of cancer — just the possible need for more definitive tests. *PSA* can be high for reasons other than cancer. *PSA blood test* is acceptable on all references.

prostitute Avoid terms like *child*, *underage* or *teenage prostitute*, except in quotations or in referring to criminal charges that may use these terms. The phrasing can suggest that a child is voluntarily trading sex for money. Minors are not able to consent.

protective tariff A duty high enough to assure domestic producers against any effective competition from foreign producers.

protester

prove, proved, proving Use *proven* only as an adjective: *a proven remedy*.

provinces Names of provinces are set off from community names by commas, just as the names of U.S. states are set off from city names: *They went to Halifax, Nova Scotia, on their vacation.*

Do not capitalize *province*: *They visited the province of Nova Scotia. The earthquake struck Shaanxi province.* See **datelines**.

provost marshal The plural: *provost marshals.*

proxy An authorization for someone else to vote on behalf of a shareholder at a company's annual shareholder meeting. *Proxy fight* is a strategy used by an acquiring company or investor group in its attempt to gain control of a target company; the acquirer tries to convince other shareholders that the management of the target company should be replaced or a specific corporate action be taken. *Proxy statement* is a document that disclosed important information about issues to be discussed at an annual meeting. It includes the qualifications of management and board directors, serves as a ballot for elections to the board of directors and provides detailed information about executive compensation.

pseudonyms, nicknames A nickname should be used in place of a person's given name in stories only when it is the way the individual prefers to be known: *Jimmy Carter, Bill Clinton, Babe Ruth, Tiger Woods, Magic Johnson.*

When a nickname is inserted into the identification of an individual, use quotation marks: Sen. Henry M. "Scoop" Jackson, Paul "Bear" Bryant.

Capitalize without quotation marks such terms as *Sunshine State, the Old Dominion, Motown, the Magic City, Old Hickory, Old Glory, Galloping Ghost.* See **names**.

PTA Acceptable in all references for *Parent Teacher Association.*

public schools Use figures and capitalize *public school* when used with a figure: *Public School 3, Public School 10.*

If a school has a commemorative name, capitalize the name: *Benjamin Franklin School.*

Puerto Rico Do not abbreviate. See **datelines** and **U.S. territories**.

Pulitzer Prizes These yearly awards for outstanding work in journalism and the arts were endowed by the late Joseph Pulitzer, publisher of the old New York World, and first given in 1917. They are awarded by the trustees of Columbia University on recommendation of an advisory board.

Capitalize *Pulitzer Prize,* but lowercase the categories: *Pulitzer Prize for public service, Pulitzer Prize for fiction,* etc.

Also: *She is a Pulitzer Prize winner. He is a Pulitzer Prize-winning author.*

punctuation The punctuation entries in this book refer to guidelines rather than rules. Guidelines should not be treated casually, however.

See **Punctuation** chapter for separate entries under: **apostrophe**; **brackets**; **colon**; **comma**; **dash**; **ellipsis**; **exclamation point**; **hyphen**; **parentheses**; **periods**; **question mark**; **quotation marks**; **semicolon**; and **slash**.

p

q

Q&A format Use *Q&A* within the body of a story. See **question mark** in the **Punctuation** chapter.

QE2 Acceptable on second reference for the ocean liner Queen Elizabeth 2.

(But use a Roman numeral for the monarch: *Queen Elizabeth II*.)

Q-tips A trademark for a brand of cotton swabs.

quart (dry) Equal in volume to 67.2 cubic inches. The metric equivalent is approximately 1.1 liters.

See **liter**.

quart (liquid) Equal in volume to 57.75 cubic inches. Also equal to 32 fluid ounces. The approximate metric equivalents are 950 milliliters or 0.95 of a liter.

See **liter**.

quasar Acceptable in all references for a *quasi-stellar astronomical object*, often a source of radio waves.

Quebec Use *Quebec City* without the name of the province in datelines.

Do not abbreviate any reference to the province of *Quebec*, Canada's largest in area and second largest in population.

The people are *Quebecois*.

See **datelines**.

Quechua An Andean ethnic group in Peru and Bolivia. The language of these people.

queen mother A widowed queen who is mother of the reigning monarch. See **nobility**.

question mark See entry in the **Punctuation** chapter.

questionnaire

quiet period Avoid using this term. In the investing world, it is commonly thought to be the period following a company's initial public offering or just before earnings are reported in which it is subject to possible sanctions by the U.S. Securities and Exchange Commission for making public disclosures. But since SEC rules only prohibit disclosures that go beyond what the company has stated in SEC filings, the term *quiet period* is a misnomer.

quotation marks See entry in the **Punctuation** chapter.

quotations in the news Never alter quotations even to correct minor grammatical errors or word usage. Casual minor tongue slips may be removed by using ellipses but even that should be done with extreme caution.

Do not use (*sic*) to show that quoted material or person's words include a misspelling, incorrect grammar or peculiar usage. (This is a change from previous guidance.) Instead, paraphrase if possible. If the quoted material is essential, simply use it as spoken or written, in line with the guidance below.

In AP stories, use an editor's note to confirm for other editors: *Eds: The spelling "Cristina" instead of "Christina" in the ransom note is as the note reads.*

If there is a question about a quote, either don't use it or ask the speaker to clarify.

If a person is unavailable for comment, detail attempts to reach that person. (*Agarwal was out of the country on business; Park did not return phone messages left at the office.*)

Do not use substandard spellings such as *gonna* or *wanna* in attempts to convey regional dialects or informal pronunciations, except to convey an emphasis by the speaker.

When quoting spoken words, present them in the format that reflects AP style: *No. 1, St., Gov., $3.* But quotes should not be changed otherwise for reasons of style. If the speaker says *towards*, do not change it to *toward*.

When quoting written words, retain the style used by the writer; do not alter the written words even if they don't match AP style.

Use quotations only if they are the best way to tell the story or convey meaning. Often, paraphrasing is preferable.

In general, avoid using parenthetical clarifications in quoted material. If such a clarification is needed, it's almost always better to paraphrase. If the quote is essential, include the unclear word or phrase before the parenthetical clarification; deleting it creates questions in a reader's mind.

For example: *"I heard him (the second attacker) yell, 'The sky is falling! Chicken Little was right!' before he drew the knife."* Not: *"I heard (the second attacker) yell, 'The sky is falling! Chicken Little was right!' before he drew the knife."* Better: *The witness said he heard the second attacker yell: "The sky is falling! Chicken Little was right!" before drawing the knife.*

FULL VS. PARTIAL QUOTES: In general, avoid fragmentary quotes. If a speaker's words are clear and concise, favor the full quote. If cumbersome language can be paraphrased fairly, use an indirect construction, reserving quotation marks for sensitive or controversial passages that must be identified specifically as coming from the speaker.

CONTEXT: Remember that you can misquote someone by giving a startling remark without its modifying passage or qualifiers. The manner of delivery sometimes is part of the context. Reporting a smile or a deprecatory gesture may be as important as conveying the words themselves.

SOCIAL MEDIA POSTS AND TEXT MESSAGES: Social media posts and text messages often contain *emoji*, *GIFs* or other imagery that need to be conveyed to readers using words. Treat the visual material as context or gestures when important to include, describing by paraphrasing:

Chavis sparked a flurry of responses against the airline after tweeting a GIF of large crowds at the gate, with the message "#missinghoneymoon" and an emoji string of a worried smiley, a ring, an hourglass and an umbrella propped on a beach.

Be aware that some GIFs, emoji or other images may contain hidden meanings and nuances requiring consideration and more than just a simple description of the image posted.

Do not use parentheses to describe an emoji within a direct quote, to avoid confusing readers by making it seem as if the person being quoted wrote out the description in text.

Many story platforms support displaying posts as they actually appear, or hyperlinking to posts on social networks, giving journalists several options to let readers see material for themselves. For example, some production systems may allow you to directly insert emoji into the text of a story. Additionally, most social networks allow for direct embedding of such material, and screen captures may also be acceptable if images are displayed in accordance with your newsroom's visual standards.

OFFENSIVE LANGUAGE: See the **obscenities, profanities, vulgarities** entry.

PUNCTUATION: See the **quotation marks** entry in the **Punctuation** chapter.

Quran The preferred spelling for the Muslim holy book. Use the spelling *Koran* only if preferred by a specific organization or in a specific title or name.

q

R&B Acceptable in all references to the music genre *rhythm and blues*.

race-related coverage Reporting and writing about issues involving race calls for thoughtful consideration, precise language, and discussions with others of diverse backgrounds whenever possible about how to frame coverage or what language is most appropriate, accurate and fair.

Avoid broad generalizations and labels; race and ethnicity are one part of a person's identity. Identifying people by race and reporting on actions that have to do with race often go beyond simple style questions, challenging journalists to think broadly about racial issues before having to make decisions on specific situations and stories.

In all coverage — not just race-related coverage — strive to accurately represent the world, or a particular community, and its diversity through the people you quote and depict in all formats. Omissions and lack of inclusion can render people invisible.

Be aware that some words and phrases that seem innocuous to one group can carry negative connotations, even be seen as slurs, to another. As with all news coverage, be sensitive to your varied audiences and their different perceptions of language and the larger world.

For instance, many people see *thug* as code for a racial slur; *Black boy* has a loaded history and should be avoided in referring to Black males of any age; *unarmed Black man* could be seen as assuming the default is for Black men to be armed.

Do not write in a way that assumes *white* is default. Not: *The officer is accused of choking Owens, who is Black*. Instead: *The white officer is accused of choking Owens, who is Black*.

Some guidelines:

race Consider carefully when deciding whether to identify people by race. Often, it is an irrelevant factor and drawing unnecessary attention to someone's race or ethnicity can be interpreted as bigotry. There are, however, occasions when race is pertinent:

— In stories that involve significant, groundbreaking or historic events, such as being elected U.S. president, being named to the U.S. Supreme Court or other notable occurrences. *Barack Obama was the first Black U.S. president. Sonia Sotomayor is the first Hispanic justice of the U.S. Supreme Court. Jeremy Lin was the first American-born NBA player of Chinese or Taiwanese descent.*

— In cases where suspects or missing people are being sought, and the descriptions provided are detailed and not solely racial. Any racial reference should be removed when the individual is apprehended or found.

— When reporting a demonstration, disturbance or other conflict involving race (including verbal conflicts), or issues like civil rights.

In other situations when race is an issue, use news judgment. Include racial or ethnic details only when they are clearly relevant and that relevance is explicit in the story.

Do not use a derogatory term except in rare circumstances — when it is crucial to the story or the understanding of a news event. Flag the contents in an editor's note.

See the **Inclusive Storytelling chapter**; the **Religion chapter**; and **obscenities, profanities, vulgarities**.

racist, racism Racism is a set of attitudes, beliefs, and actions asserting racial differences in character, intelligence, etc., and asserting the superiority of one race over another, or racial discrimination or feelings of hatred or bigotry toward people of another race.

The terms *systemic racism*, *structural racism* and *institutional racism* refer to social, political and institutional systems and cultures that contribute to racial inequality in areas such as employment, health care, housing, the criminal justice system and education. Avoid shortening this use to simply *racism*, to avoid confusion with the other definition.

Some use the term *racist* to refer to anyone who benefits from *systemic racism* and doesn't actively work to dismantle it. Avoid this use unless essential in a direct quotation; if used, explain it.

Deciding whether a specific statement, action, policy, etc., should be termed *racist*, or characterized in a different way, often is not clear-cut. Such decisions should include discussion with colleagues and/or others from diverse backgrounds and perspectives. At the AP, that conversation should also include senior managers.

Begin by assessing the facts: Does the statement, action, policy, etc., meet the definition of *racism*? That assessment need not involve examining the motivation of the person who spoke or acted, which is a separate issue that may not be related to how the statement or action itself can be characterized.

In general, avoid using *racist* or any other label as a noun for a person; it's far harder to match the complexity of a person to a definition or label than it is a statement or action. Instead, be specific in describing the person's words or actions. Again, discuss with senior managers, colleagues and others from diverse backgrounds when the description may be appropriate for a person.

Cases in which the term *racist* might be used include identifying as racist support for avowed racist organizations, statements calling another race or ethnic group inferior, or employing negative stereotypes for different racial or ethnic groups. *The video shows the candidate wearing blackface and making racist statements including, "You're not white so you can't be right."*

If *racist* is not the appropriate term, give careful thought to how best to describe the situation. Depending on the specifics of what was said or done, alternatives may include *xenophobic, bigoted, biased, nativist, racially divisive*, or in some cases, simply *racial*.

Avoid *racially charged, racially motivated* or *racially tinged*, euphemisms which convey little meaning.

Always provide specifics to describe the words or actions in question; using a broad and descriptive term such as *racist* requires supporting details and context. In doing so, avoid repeating derogatory terms except in the rare circumstances when it is crucial to the story or the understanding of a news event.

Provide context and historical perspective when appropriate to help convey the impact or implications of the words or actions. For example, a story about a candidate wearing blackface should include context about performers in the 1800s who darkened their faces to create bigoted caricatures of Black people. A story about comments that certain members of Congress should "go back" to their "broken and crime-infested" countries should include the context that "go back to where you came from" is a racist insult aimed for decades at immigrants and African Americans in the United States.

See **racially charged, racially motivated, racially tinged**, and other entries in **race-related coverage**.

racially charged, racially motivated, racially tinged Avoid using these vague phrases to describe situations in which race is or is alleged or perceived to be a central issue, but that do not meet the definition of *racist* or *racism*. As alternatives, terms including *xenophobic, bigoted, biased, nativist* or *racially divisive* may be clearer, depending on the context. In some cases, the term *racial* is appropriate: *racial arguments, racial tensions, racial injustice*. Always give specifics about what was done, said or alleged.

Do not use euphemisms for *racist* or *racism* when the latter terms are truly applicable. *Mississippi has a history of racist lynchings*, not *a history of racially motivated lynchings*.

He is charged in the racist massacre of nine people at a Black church, not *the racially motivated massacre of nine people at a Black church*. See **racist, racism**, and other entries in **race-related coverage**.

critical race theory An academic framework dating to the 1970s that centers on the idea that racism is systemic in the nation's institutions and that those institutions maintain the dominance of white people. The theory is a way of analyzing American history through the lens of racism. It has become a catch-all political buzzword for any teaching in schools about race and American history, and a rallying cry for some conservatives who take issue with how schools have addressed diversity and inclusion. The theory itself is not a fixture of K-12 education.

Those opposed to critical race theory say it divides society by defining people as oppressors and oppressed based on their race. They call it an attempt to rewrite American history and make white people believe they are inherently racist.

Explain the term when used. Don't use *CRT* on later references.

BIPOC, BAME, POC See **people of color**.

biracial, multiracial Acceptable, when clearly relevant, to describe people with more than one racial heritage. Usually more useful when describing large, diverse groups of people than individuals. Avoid *mixed-race*, which can carry negative connotations, unless a story subject prefers the term. Be specific if possible, and then use *biracial* for people of two heritages or *multiracial* for those of two or more on subsequent references

r

if needed. Examples: *She has an African American father and a white mother* instead of *She is biracial.* But: *The study of biracial people showed a split in support along gender lines.* *Multiracial* can encompass people of any combination of races.

brown (adj.) Avoid this broad and imprecise term in racial, ethnic or cultural references unless as part of a direct quotation. Interpretations of what the term includes vary widely. Be specific.

Caucasian Avoid as a synonym for *white*, unless in a quotation.

dual heritage No hyphen for terms such as *African American, Asian American* and *Filipino American*, used when relevant to refer to an American person's heritage. The terms are less common when used to describe non-Americans, but may be used when relevant: *Turkish German* for a German of Turkish descent. For terms denoting dual citizenship, use the hyphen: *a dual U.S.-Australian citizen.*

minority, racial minority The term is acceptable as an adjective in broad references to multiple races other than white in the United States: *We will hire more members of minority groups.*

Be sure the term is accurate in each circumstance, since what constitutes a racial minority varies by location.

Be specific whenever possible by referring to, for instance, *Black Americans, Chinese Americans* or *members of the Seminole Tribe of Florida.* Examples: *The poll found that Black and Latino Americans are bearing the brunt of the pandemic's financial impact*, not *minorities are bearing the brunt of the pandemic's financial impact. Most of the magazine's readers are Black women,*

not *most of the magazine's readers are minority women.*

Do not use *minority* as a noun in the singular. Limit use of the plural *minorities* unless needed for reasons of space or sentence construction. Phrasing such as *minority students* or *minority groups* is preferable.

people of color The term is acceptable when necessary in broad references to multiple races other than white: *We will hire more people of color. Nine playwrights of color collaborated on the script.*

Be aware, however, that many people of various races object to the term for various reasons, including that it lumps together into one monolithic group anyone who isn't white.

Be specific whenever possible by referring to, for instance, *Black Americans, Chinese Americans* or *members of the Seminole Tribe of Florida.* Examples: *The poll found that Black and Latino Americans are bearing the brunt of the pandemic's financial impact*, not *people of color are bearing the brunt of the pandemic's financial impact. Most of the magazine's readers are Black women*, not *most of the magazine's readers are women of color.*

In some cases, other wording may be appropriate. Examples: *people from various racial and ethnic backgrounds; diverse groups; various heritages; different cultures.*

Do not use *person of color* for an individual.

Do not use the term *Black, Indigenous* and *people of color*, which some see as more inclusive by distinguishing the experiences of Black and Indigenous people but others see as less inclusive by diminishing the experiences of everyone else. Similarly, do not use the term *Black, Asian* and *minority ethnic*.

Do not use the shorthand *POC, BIPOC* or *BAME* unless necessary in a direct quotation; when used, explain it.

reverse discrimination A term sometimes used to describe bias or perceived bias against majority groups. Limit its use to quotes; generally just *discrimination* will suffice to describe such allegations or practices.

transracial The term should not be used to describe people who have adopted a different racial identity.

—

Aborigine An outdated term referring to Aboriginal people in Australia. It is considered offensive by some and should be avoided.

—

African American No hyphen for this and other dual-heritage terms. Acceptable for an American Black person of African descent. The terms are not necessarily interchangeable. Americans of Caribbean heritage, for example, generally refer to themselves as *Caribbean American*. Follow a person's preference.

Black (adj.) Use the capitalized term as an adjective in a racial, ethnic or cultural sense: *Black people, Black culture, Black literature, Black studies, Black colleges*.

African American is also acceptable for those in the U.S. The terms are not necessarily interchangeable. Americans of Caribbean heritage, for example, generally refer to themselves as *Caribbean American*. Follow a person's preference if known, and be specific when possible and relevant. *Minneapolis has a large Somali American population because of refugee resettlement. The author is Senegalese American.*

Use of the capitalized *Black* recognizes that language has evolved, along with the common understanding that especially in the United States, the term reflects a shared identity and culture rather than a skin color alone.

Also use *Black* in racial, ethnic and cultural differences outside the U.S. to avoid equating a person with a skin color.

Use *Negro* or *colored* only in names of organizations or in rare quotations when essential.

See **obscenities, profanities, vulgarities**.

Black(s), white(s) (n.) Do not use either term as a singular or plural noun. Instead, use phrasing such as *Black people, white people, Black teachers, white students. Black* and *white* are acceptable as adjectives when relevant.

boy, girl Generally acceptable to describe males or females younger than 18. While it is always inaccurate to call people under 18 *men* or *women* and people 18 and older *boys* or *girls*, be aware of nuances and unintentional implications. Referring to Black males of any age and in any context as *boys*, for instance, can be perceived as demeaning and call to mind historical language used by some to address Black men. Be specific about ages if possible, or refer to *Black youths, child, teen* or similar.

Black Lives Matter A global movement launched in 2013 after the acquittal in the killing of Trayvon Martin with a goal to eradicate systemic racism and white supremacy and to oppose violence committed against Black people. Either *Black Lives Matter* as a noun or *the Black Lives Matter movement*

r

is acceptable. *BLM* is acceptable on second reference. Although there are many groups that use *Black Lives Matter* or *BLM* in their names, only 16 are considered affiliates of the *Black Lives Matter Global Network*. *The Black Lives Matter Global Network Foundation*, which provides organizational infrastructure and funding to the affiliate chapters, was founded in 2014 after what is known as the Ferguson uprising over the August 2014 police shooting death of Michael Brown in Ferguson, Missouri. *The BLM network* is acceptable on second reference.

Some respond to the Black Lives Matter movement by saying "all lives matter" or "blue lives matter," the latter in reference to police officers. Neither is a formal movement, so lowercase and enclose in quotes.

slaves, enslaved people The term *slaves* denotes an inherent identity of a person or people treated as chattel or property. The term *enslaved people* underlines that the slave status has been imposed on individuals. Many prefer the term *enslaved person/people* to separate people's identity from their circumstances. Others prefer the term *slave* as a way to make a point of the circumstances. Either term is acceptable. Try to determine a person's preference.

Juneteenth June 19, the traditional commemoration date of the emancipation of enslaved people in the United States. On June 17, 2021, President Joe Biden signed legislation making it a U.S. federal holiday. The holiday also has been called *Juneteenth Independence Day* or *Freedom Day*. President Abraham Lincoln first issued the Emancipation Proclamation declaring all slaves free in Confederate territory on Sept. 22,

1862, but the news took time to travel. June 19, 1865, is the date when word of the proclamation reached African Americans in Texas.

historically Black colleges and universities U.S. colleges and universities established before 1964 with the mission of educating Black Americans. The schools were founded at a time when Black students were barred from many institutions that served white people. Before these accredited, degree-granting institutions were created, no structured higher education system for Black students existed. There are approximately 100 such schools now, and they admit students of any race.

HBCUs is acceptable on second reference and in headlines. *HBCU* is acceptable as a modifier on second reference: *HBCU students*. Refer to an individual school as *a historically Black college* or *a historically Black university*. Don't use *HBCU* for one college or university.

—

Arab American No hyphen for this and other dual-heritage terms. Acceptable for an American of Arab descent. When possible, refer to a person's country of origin or follow the person's preference. For example: *Lebanese American* or *Egyptian American*.

Although most Arabs worldwide are Muslim, many Arab Americans are not.

Don't assume that everyone from a predominantly Arab country identifies as Arab; ask them.

Arab Americans are classified as white by the U.S. government on federal forms and in the census. Many Arab Americans reject that classification, saying it does not reflect their life experiences or the way they are regarded in American society. Some argue it renders their communities invisible.

As a result, many Arab Americans simply check "other" on forms. Arab American organizations say that contributes to what they say is a chronic undercounting of their numbers in America.

—

Asian American No hyphen for this and other dual-heritage terms. Acceptable for an American of Asian descent. When possible, refer to a person's country of origin or follow the person's preference. For example: *Filipino American* or *Indian American*. Do not describe *Pacific Islanders* as *Asian Americans, Asians* or *of Asian descent*. Avoid using *Asian* as shorthand for *Asian American* when possible.

AAPI *Asian Americans and Pacific Islanders*. The acronym is widely used by people within these communities but is not as well known outside of them. Spell out the full term; use *AAPI* only in direct quotations and explain the term.

anti-Asian sentiment Avoid this euphemism, which conveys little meaning. Alternatives may include *anti-Asian bias, anti-Asian harassment, anti-Asian comments, anti-Asian racism* or *anti-Asian violence*, depending on the situation. Be specific and give details about what happened or what someone says happened.

Orient, Oriental Do not use when referring to East Asian nations and their peoples. *Asian* is the acceptable term for an inhabitant of those regions.

Pacific Islander Used to describe the Indigenous people of the Pacific Islands, including but not limited to Hawaii, Guam and Samoa. Should be used for people who are ethnically Pacific Islander, not for those who happen to live in Pacific Islands. Be specific about which communities you are referring to whenever possible. Do not use *Asian Pacific Islander* unless referring to Pacific Islanders of Asian descent. Do not describe *Pacific Islanders* as *Asian Americans, Asians* or *of Asian descent*.

Stop AAPI Hate A movement that was launched in March 2020 in response to a rise in anti-Asian bias and racism stemming from the coronavirus pandemic that originated in China. The Asian Pacific Planning and Policy Council, Chinese for Affirmative Action and the Asian American Studies Department of San Francisco State University created a reporting center under the name Stop AAPI Hate to track and respond to cases of hate, violence, harassment and discrimination against Asian Americans and Pacific Islanders in the United States.

—

Latino, Latina, Latinx *Latino* is often the preferred noun or adjective for a person from, or whose ancestors were from, a Spanish-speaking land or culture or from Latin America. *Latina* is the feminine form.

Some prefer the gender-neutral term *Latinx*, which should be confined to quotations, names of organizations or descriptions of individuals who request it and should be accompanied by a short explanation. *Hernandez prefers the gender-neutral term Latinx.* For groups of females, use the plural *Latinas*; for groups of males or of mixed gender, use the plural *Latinos*. *Hispanics* is also generally acceptable for those in the U.S. Use a more

r

specific identification when possible, such as *Cuban, Puerto Rican, Brazilian* or *Mexican American*.

Hispanic A person from — or whose ancestors were from — a Spanish-speaking land or culture. *Latino, Latina* or *Latinx* are sometimes preferred. Follow the person's preference. Use a more specific identification when possible, such as *Cuban, Puerto Rican* or *Mexican American*.

Chicano A term that Mexican Americans in the U.S. Southwest sometimes use to describe their heritage. Use only if it is a person's preference.

—

Native Americans, American Indians Both are acceptable terms in general references for those in the U.S. when referring to two or more people of different tribal affiliations. The term *Natives* is acceptable on second reference (see below).

For individuals, use the name of the tribe; if that information is not immediately available, try to obtain it. *He is a Navajo commissioner. She is a member of the Nisqually Indian Tribe. He is a citizen of the Cherokee Nation of Oklahoma.* Some tribes and tribal nations use *member*; others use *citizen.* Try to determine the correct term in each case. If that can't be determined, use *citizen.*

In Alaska, the Indigenous groups are collectively known as *Alaska Natives.*

First Nation is the preferred term for tribes in Canada.

Indian is used to describe the peoples and cultures of the South Asian nation of India. Do not use the term as a shorthand for *Native Americans* or *American Indians*, either a single person or a group. However, *Indian* is acceptable when part of a proper name, such as *Indian Country, the Gila River Indian Community in Arizona* or *the Metlakatla Indian Community in Alaska.*

Native, Natives Acceptable on second reference for *Native Americans.* Also acceptable as an adjective — *Native music, Native art* — but if the story is not generally about *Native Americans*, use *Native American music, Native American art*, etc.

tribe Refers to a sovereign political entity, communities sharing a common ancestry, culture or language, and a social group of linked families who may be part of an ethnic group. Capitalize the word *tribe* when part of a formal name of sovereign political entities, or communities sharing a common ancestry, culture or language. Identify tribes by the political identity specified by the tribe, nation or community: *the Apache Tribe of Oklahoma, the Cherokee Nation.* The term *ethnic group* is preferred when referring to ethnicity or ethnic violence.

tribal affiliation The 574 federally recognized tribes as of early 2022 determine how to count their own citizens or members. The primary means are calculating the percentage of one's ancestry related to a specific tribe, known as *blood quantum*; or tracing ancestry to a list of names kept by a tribe. Verify tribal enrollment with the source and, if needed, the tribe itself. Ensure proper context is used when writing about whether someone is enrolled.

Alaska Native corporations Created under the 1971 Alaska Native Settlement Claims Act, which transferred Native land to for-profit corporations. Alaska Natives from 229 federally recognized tribes are shareholders in the corporations that run oil, gas, mining and other enterprises, and provide services to Alaska Natives. The Metlakatla Indian Community opted out of the settlement act and has the only reservation in Alaska. The corporations are not synonymous with *tribal governments*, which continue to exist independently.

Indian Country A widely accepted reference for land within the boundaries of a reservation, including private property, land that has been placed into trust for tribes and to communities of people indigenous to the United States.

Indigenous (adj.) Capitalize this term used to refer to original inhabitants of a place. *Aboriginal leaders welcomed a new era of Indigenous relations in Australia. Bolivia's Indigenous peoples represent some 62% of the population.*

Indigenous peoples Groupings of people who are the original inhabitants of their countries. Use *peoples* when referring to multiple Indigenous groups. Use *people* when referring to multiple individuals from different Indigenous groups.

language Do not use the word *squaw* in any sense, including quotes, to refer to individual Native Americans. The word is acceptable if necessary as a first reference in referring to a place, but limit its use. Do not use terms such as *Indian summer* and *Indian giver*. Avoid words such as *warpath* and *powwow*, or phrases such as *circle the wagons* and *hold down the fort*, which can be disparaging and offensive. They are appropriate if used in the proper context and not meant casually or disparagingly.

Missing and Murdered Indigenous Women A grassroots movement to draw attention to disproportionate violence against Indigenous people, particularly women and children, and the lack of data in law enforcement agencies. The movement is symbolized by a red hand over the mouth that reflects solidarity with victims whose voices have been silenced. On second reference use *the movement*, not *MMIW*. The term *murder* is acceptable in this group's name. Otherwise, follow general Stylebook guidance: Do not say that a victim was *murdered* until someone has been convicted in court. Instead, say that a person was *killed* or *slain*.

Native American names For tribal affiliations, use the person's preference and clarify with the official name of the tribe if necessary. For example, some members of the Navajo Nation refer to themselves as *Diné*, the Navajo word for *the people*.

tipi (not teepee) A traditional dwelling among Native Americans in the northern Great Plains region.

tribal colleges and universities The roughly three dozen schools on or near Native American reservations that seek to incorporate culture and tradition into education. The schools, primarily in the Southwest and Midwest, are a mix of two-year and four-year institutions. The Navajo Nation, which extends into Arizona, New Mexico and Utah, opened the first tribal college in the United States in 1968. The schools are represented by the American Indian Higher Education Consortium.

r

racket Not *racquet*, for the light bat used in tennis and badminton.

rack, wrack The noun *rack* applies

to various types of framework; the verb *rack* means *to arrange on a rack, to torture, trouble* or *torment*: *He was placed on the rack. She racked her brain.*

The noun *wrack* means *ruin* or *destruction*, as in *wrack and ruin* and *wracked with pain.* Also *nerve-wracking.*

The verb *wrack* has substantially the same meaning as the verb *rack*, the latter being preferred.

radar A lowercase acronym for *radio detection and ranging. Radar* is acceptable in all references.

radical In general, avoid this description in favor of a more precise definition of an individual's political views.

When used, it suggests that an individual believes change must be made by tearing up the roots or foundation of the present order.

Although *radical* often is applied to individuals who hold strong socialist or communist views, it also is applied at times to individuals who believe an existing form of government must be replaced by a more authoritarian or militaristic one.

See **leftist, ultra-leftist** and **rightist, ultra-rightist**.

radio Capitalize and use before a name to indicate an official or state-funded broadcast voice: *Radio Free Europe, Radio France International.*

Lowercase and place after the name when indicating only that the information was obtained from broadcasts in a city. *Mexico City radio*, for example, is the form used in referring to reports that are broadcast on various stations in the Mexican capital.

raised, reared Only humans may be *reared.*

All living things, including humans, may be *raised.*

Ramadan The Muslim holy month, marked by daily fasting from dawn to sunset, ending with the Islamic holiday of Eid al-Fitr. Avoid using *holiday* on second reference to Ramadan.

ranges The form: *$12 million to $14 million.* Not: *$12 to $14 million.* Also: *a pay increase of 12%-15%* or *12% to 15%* or *between 12% and 15%.* For full calendar years, hyphenated *2019-20* is acceptable.

rank and file (n.) **rank-and-file** (adj.)

rarely It means *seldom. Rarely ever* is redundant, but *rarely if ever* often is the appropriate phrase.

ratings agency A company that measures the creditworthiness of companies, municipalities and countries. A ratings agency gauges an entity's ability to repay its debt and assigns a rating based on that assessment. The better the rating, the lower the cost for an entity to borrow money.

ratios Use figures and hyphens: *the ratio was 2-to-1, a ratio of 2-to-1, a 2-1 ratio, 1 in 4 voters.* As illustrated, the word *to* should be omitted when the numbers precede the word *ratio.*

Always use the word *ratio* or a phrase such as *a 2-1 majority* to avoid confusion with actual figures.

See **numerals**.

ravage, ravish *To ravage* is to wreak great destruction or devastation:

r

Union troops ravaged Atlanta.

To ravish is to abduct, rape or carry away with emotion: *Soldiers ravished the women.*

Although both words connote an element of violence, they are not interchangeable. Buildings and towns cannot be *ravished.*

re- Follow Webster's New World College Dictionary. Hyphenate if not listed there unless a hyphen would distort the sense (see the list below). A 2019 change: In recognition of common usage and dictionary preferences, do not hyphenate double-e combinations with re- and pre-. Those include *reelect, reemerge, reemphasize, reemploy, reenact, reengage, reenlist, reenter, reequip, reestablish, reexamine* and those listed in **pre-**.

Other rules in **prefixes** apply.

For some words, the sense is the governing factor: *recover (regain); re-cover (cover again); resign (quit); re-sign (sign again).*

Realtor The term *real estate agent* is preferred. Use *Realtor* only if there is a reason to indicate that the individual is a member of the National Association of Realtors.

rebut, refute *Rebut* means *to argue to the contrary: He rebutted his opponent's statement.*

Refute connotes success in argument and almost always implies an editorial judgment. Instead, use *deny, dispute, rebut* or *respond to.*

receivership A legal action in which a court appoints a *receiver* to manage a business while the court tries to resolve problems that could ruin the business, such as insolvency. *Receivership* is often used in federal bankruptcy court proceedings. But it also can be used for nonfinancial troubles such as an ownership dispute.

In bankruptcy proceedings, the court appoints a trustee called a *receiver* who attempts to settle the financial difficulties of the company while under protection from creditors.

recession A falling-off of economic activity that may be a temporary phenomenon or could continue into a depression.

recipes Always use figures. See **fractions** and **numerals**.

Do not use abbreviations. Spell out *teaspoon, tablespoon,* etc.

See the **food** entry for guidelines on when to capitalize the names of foods.

reconnaissance

Reconstruction The process of reorganizing the Southern states after the Civil War.

record Avoid the redundant *new record.*

record, recorded, recording Use *record* (or *album* or *LP*) for the vinyl discs used to play back audio. Use *recording* and *recorded* for audio also available in other formats such as *CDs* and *digital downloads.* For example: *I still have several Beatles records in the attic. Streaming services account for most of the recording industry's revenue for recorded music.*

recur, recurred, recurring Not *reoccur.*

Red Capitalize when used as a

r

political, geographic or military term: *the Red Army*.

red carpet The ceremonial gantlet where guests arriving at award shows strut their finery, greet fans and give media interviews. Red carpets may sometimes be other colors.

Reddit A social network that features message board-style posts, organized into topic-based pages called *subreddits*, where users share and converse about content. Users can vote up or down individual conversation threads and comments, determining which ones are most prominently displayed on the site. *"Ask me anything"* posts give users an opportunity to pose questions to public figures, topic experts and people who have had interesting experiences. *AMA* is acceptable on second reference.

red-haired, redhead, redheaded All are acceptable for a person with red hair.

Redhead also is used colloquially to describe a type of North American diving duck.

redneck Do not use this term, generally considered derogatory, to refer to poor, white, rural people.

referable

reference works Capitalize their proper names.

Do not use quotation marks around the names of books that are primarily catalogs of reference material. In addition to catalogs, this category includes almanacs, directories, dictionaries, encyclopedias, gazetteers, handbooks, school yearbooks and similar publications.

EXAMPLES: Congressional Directory, Webster's New World College Dictionary, the AP Stylebook. But: "The Elephants of Style" and "The Elements of Style."

See the **Bibliography** for the principal reference works used in preparing this book.

referendum, referendums

reform The word is not synonymous with *change*. It generally implies faults or shortcomings in the subject at hand. Use care in deciding whether *reform* is the appropriate word or whether a more neutral term is better. Use similar caution with words such as *improvement* or *overhaul*.

reggaeton A genre of music that originated in Puerto Rico and fuses hip-hop with Latin American and Caribbean rhythms. Its vocals include rapping and singing.

reign, rein The leather strap for controlling a horse is a *rein*, hence figuratively: *seize the reins, give free rein to*.

Reign is the period a ruler is on the throne: *The king began his reign*.

religious references See entry in the **Religion** chapter.

religious titles See entry in the **Religion** chapter.

reluctant, reticent *Reluctant* means *unwilling to act*: *He is reluctant to enter the primary*.

Reticent means *unwilling to speak*: *The candidate's husband is reticent*.

representative, Rep. See **legislative**

r

titles and **party affiliation**.

republic Capitalize *republic* when used as part of a nation's full, formal name: *the Republic of Argentina*.
See **datelines**.

Republican Governors Association
No apostrophe.

Republican National Committee
On second reference: *the national committee, the committee* and *the RNC*.
Similarly: *Republican State Committee, Republican County Committee, Republican City Committee, the state committee, the county committee, the city committee, the committee*.

Republican, Republican Party *GOP*
may be used on second reference.
See **political parties and philosophies** and **GOP**.

rescission

Reserve Capitalize when referring to U.S. armed forces, as in *Army Reserve*. Lowercase in reference to members of these backup forces: *reserves*, or *reservists*.

Reserve Officers' Training Corps
The *s'* is military practice. *ROTC* is acceptable in all references.
When the service is specified, use *Army ROTC, Navy ROTC* or *Air Force ROTC*, not *AROTC, NROTC* or *AFROTC*.

resistible

restaurateur

retail sales The sales of retail stores, including merchandise sold and receipts for repairs and similar services.
A business is considered a *retail store* if it is engaged primarily in selling merchandise for personal, household or farm consumption.

retweet The practice, on Twitter, of sharing an existing tweet with your followers. When using the retweet button, users have the option of writing a new tweet and appending the retweeted item — what's known as a *quote tweet*. Spell out *retweet* in all references, though it's commonly called an RT on Twitter.

Rev. When this description is used before an individual's name, precede it with the word *the* because, unlike the case with *Mr.* and *Mrs.*, the abbreviation *Rev.* does not stand for a noun. Always use the abbreviation, *the Rev.*, not the full word *reverend*, before a name.
If an individual also has a secular title such as *Rep.*, use whichever is appropriate to the context.
See **religious titles** in the **Religion** chapter.

revaluations Occur when a country's government pushes up the value of its currency in relation to another currency. (When market forces, not the government, push a currency up, it is known as appreciation.)
Suppose China revalues its currency, the yuan, against the U.S. dollar. To calculate the revaluation, you'd look at the value of 1 yuan to the U.S. dollar before the revaluation and the value afterward and calculate the percentage difference.
Example: On Day One, 1 yuan is worth 15.8 cents (or $0.158). The next day, the Chinese government revalues the currency and 1 yuan is equal to 16.1 cents ($0.161). That is

r

a 1.9% revaluation — the yuan has risen 1.9% against the U.S. dollar.

Currencies are often reported the other way, showing how much $1 is worth in another currency. In the example above, $1 went from being worth 6.32 yuan to being worth only 6.21 yuan. To find out what 1 yuan is worth — so you can show the yuan rising, not the dollar falling — divide 1 by 6.32 and 6.21 respectively.

reverse auction An auction where the winning bidder is the one willing to take the lowest price. In a reverse auction for subprime mortgage loans, for instance, a bank offering to sell a bundle of bad loans for 50 cents on the dollar would beat a bank offering to sell its loans for 60 cents on the dollar.

Reverse 911 Capitalized trademark for an automated phone alert system.

Use the generic form if the brand is uncertain.

revolution Capitalize when part of a name for a specific historical event: *the American Revolution, the Bolshevik Revolution, the French Revolution.*

The Revolution, capitalized, also may be used as a shorthand reference to the *American Revolution*. Also: *the Revolutionary War.*

Lowercase in other uses: *a revolution, the revolution, the American and French revolutions.*

revolutions per minute The abbreviation *rpm* is acceptable on first reference in specialized contexts such as an auto column. Otherwise do not use it until second reference.

revolving credit Describes an

account on which the payment is any amount less than the total balance, and the remaining balance carried forward is subject to finance charges.

Rh factor Also: *Rh negative, Rh positive.*

Rhodes scholar Lowercase *scholar* and *scholarship.*

Richter scale No longer widely used. See **earthquakes**.

RICO An acronym for *Racketeer Influenced and Corrupt Organizations Act.* Acceptable on second reference, but *anti-racketeering* or *anti-corruption law* is preferred.

ride-hailing, ride-sharing *Ride-hailing services* such as Uber and Lyft let people use smartphone apps to book and pay for a private car service or, in some cases, a taxi. They may also be called *ride-booking services. Ride-sharing* refers to app-based services that let people book a shared shuttle. Zipcar and similar companies are *short-term car rental services.*

rifle, riffle *To rifle* is to plunder or steal.

To riffle is to leaf rapidly through a book or pile of papers.

rightist, ultra-rightist In general, avoid these terms in favor of more precise descriptions of an individual's political philosophy.

Ultra-rightist suggests an individual who subscribes to rigid interpretations of a conservative doctrine or to forms of fascism that stress authoritarian, often militaristic, views.

See **radical** and **leftist, ultra-leftist**.

r

right of way, rights of way

"right-to-work" (adj.) A "right-to-work" law prohibits a company and a union from signing a contract that would require workers to pay dues or fees to the union that represents them. Use only in direct quotes or with quote marks for the purpose of explaining the term. Avoid using this phrase generically and without definition, since employees covered by union contracts can freely work with or without such laws.

right wing (n.) **right-winger** (n.) **right-wing** (adj.) Generally try to avoid in describing political leanings.

Rio Grande Not *Rio Grande River. Rio* means river in Spanish.

riot, unrest, protest, demonstration, uprising, revolt

Use care in deciding which term best applies:

A **riot** is a wild or violent disturbance of the peace involving a group of people. The term *riot* suggests uncontrolled chaos and pandemonium. Focusing on rioting and property destruction rather than underlying grievance has been used in the past to stigmatize broad swaths of people protesting against lynching, police brutality or for racial justice, going back to the urban uprisings of the 1960s. Inciting to riot is a longstanding criminal offense involving two or more people. In the United States, a federal criminal anti-riot act was enacted in 1968 in response to violent civil disturbances and protests of that era.

Unrest is a vaguer, milder and less emotional term for a condition of angry discontent and protest verging on revolt.

Protest and **demonstration** refer to specific actions such as marches, sit-ins, rallies or other actions meant to register dissent. They can be legal or illegal, organized or spontaneous, peaceful or violent, and involve any number of people.

Revolt and **uprising** both suggest a broader political dimension or civil upheavals, a sustained period of protests or unrest against powerful groups or governing systems.

river Capitalize as part of a proper name: *the Mississippi River.*

Lowercase in other uses: *the river, the Mississippi and Missouri rivers.*

road Do not abbreviate. See **addresses**.

robot, robotics A *robot* is a mechanical device that typically can move and perform actions on its own using motors, sensors and computing. Examples include robotic arms used in factories or autonomous wheeled vacuum cleaners. Some *robots* are mostly remote-controlled, such as those used in surgery.

A *humanoid* is a *robot* that physically resembles a person, though it's still uncommon outside science fiction and research labs. Avoid calling something a *robot* if it is more like a remote-controlled puppet.

Artificial intelligence software can be a component of a *robot*, but avoid calling something a *robot* or *robotic* if it is entirely software-based, such as automated systems used in online conversation or to help make decisions. However, the term *bot* can be used to describe such software-based systems. A *chatbot* is a *bot* that can engage in conversations with

r

people.

Robotics is the study and development of robots and similar machines such as drones and self-driving cars.

rock 'n' roll But *Rock & Roll Hall of Fame.*

Rocky Mountains Or simply: *the Rockies,* for the mountain range that extends more than 3,000 miles in the western United States and western Canada.

roll call (n.) **roll-call** (adj.)

Rollerblade A trademark for a brand of in-line skates.

roller coaster

rollover The selling of new securities to pay off old ones coming due or the refinancing of an existing loan.

Rolls-Royce Note the hyphen in this trademark for a make of automobile.

ROM Acronym for *read-only memory,* computer memory whose contents cannot be modified. *ROM* acceptable in all references.

Roman Catholic Church *Roman Catholic,* which refers to the Latin branch of Catholicism, is not the appropriate first reference when referring to the pope, the Vatican or the universal church. *Catholic Church* should be used instead, since it encompasses believers belonging to the Latin (Roman) and Eastern churches. Similarly, the U.S. Conference of Catholic Bishops includes bishops from Eastern churches as well as Roman Catholic bishops. See **Catholic, Catholicism**

and more detail in the **Religion** chapter.

Romani, Roma, Gypsy, gypsy, gypsy moth, spongy moth
Use the term *Romani* or the more informal *Roma* for the traditionally itinerant ethnic group, and *Romani* for an individual. Do not use *Gypsy,* which is considered offensive.

Use *spongy moth* for the invasive pest formerly known as *gypsy moth,* a change approved by the Entomological Society of America in 2022. *Gypsy moth* is acceptable in a first reference explaining the new name until it becomes better known: *spongy moths, formerly known as gypsy moths.*

Do not use *gyp* in any sense.

See **race-related coverage**.

Roman numerals The Roman letters (*I, X,* etc.) were used as numerals until the 10th century.

Use Roman numerals for wars and to establish personal sequence for people and animals: *World War I, Native Dancer II, King George V.* Also for certain legislative acts (*Title IX*).

Pro football Super Bowls should be identified by the year, not the Roman numerals: *1969 Super Bowl,* not *Super Bowl III.*

Use Arabic numerals in all other cases. See **Arabic numerals** and **numerals**.

In Roman numerals, the capital letter *I* equals 1, *V* equals 5, *X* equals 10, *L* equals 50, *C* equals 100, *D* equals 500 and *M* equals 1,000.

Other numbers are formed from these by adding or subtracting as follows:
— The value of a letter following another of the same or greater value is added: *III* equals 3.
— The value of a letter preceding

one of greater value is subtracted: *IV* equals 4.

room numbers Use figures and capitalize *room* when used with a figure: *Room 2, Room 211.*

rooms Capitalize the names of specially designated rooms: *Blue Room, Lincoln Room, Oval Office, Persian Room.*

Rosh Hashana The Jewish new year. Occurs in September or October.

roundtable (n. or adj.), **round table** (n.), **Round Table** (n.) The *Knights of the Round Table* will hold a *roundtable discussion* after seating themselves at a *round table.* They likely will refer to their meeting as a *roundtable.*

route numbers Do not abbreviate *route.* Use figures and capitalize route when used with a figure: *U.S. Route 70, state Route 1A.*
    See **highway designations**.

RSVP The abbreviation for the French *repondez s'il vous plait*, it means *please reply.*

rubber stamp (n.) **rubber-stamp** (v. and adj.)

rubella Also known as *German measles.*

runner-up, runners-up

running mate

Russian names When a first name in Russian has a close phonetic equivalent in English, use the equivalent in translating the name: *Alexander Solzhenitsyn* rather than *Aleksandr*, the spelling that would result from a transliteration of the Russian letter into the English alphabet.
    When a first name has no close phonetic equivalent in English, express it with an English spelling that approximates the sound in Russian: *Dmitry, Nikita, Sergei*, for example. If an individual has a preference for an English spelling that is different from the one that would result by applying these guidelines, follow the individual's preference. Example: *Foreign Minister Sergey Lavrov.*
    For last names, use the English spelling that most closely approximates the pronunciation in Russian. Exception: the *"ev"* ending of names like Gorbachev may be pronounced "yov."
    If an individual has a preference for an English spelling that is different from the one that would result by applying these guidelines, follow the individual's preference.
    Women's last names often have the feminine ending *"-a."* But use this ending only if the woman is not married or if she is known under that name (the tennis player *Anna Kournikova*). Otherwise, use the masculine form.
    Russian names never end in *off*, except for common mistransliterations such as *Rachmaninoff.* Instead, the transliterations should end in *ov*: *Romanov.* Also, Russian names end in *"sky,"* rather than *"ski"* typical of Polish surnames.

Russian Revolution Also: *the Bolshevik Revolution.*

Rust Belt Areas of the Midwest and Northeast where factories are old and closed.

S

saboteur

Saddam Use *Saddam* in second reference to Iraq's former leader Saddam Hussein.

safety belt Also: *seat belt*.

saint Abbreviate as *St.* in the names of saints, cities and other places: *St. Jude*; *St. Paul, Minnesota*; *St. John's, Newfoundland*; *St. Lawrence Seaway*.
But see the entries for **Saint John** and **Sault Ste. Marie**.

Saint John The spelling for the city in New Brunswick.
To distinguish it from *St. John's, Newfoundland*.

salable

Sallie Mae Commonly used for SLM Corp., a publicly traded financial services company specializing in student loans.

salvo, salvos

SAM, SAMs Acceptable on second reference for *surface-to-air missile(s)*.

Sanaa The capital of Yemen. The double-a reflects the Arabic pronunciation of *San'a*.

S&P 500 Use in all references for what was formerly known as the *Standard & Poor's 500 index*. It is the market indicator most professional investors use to determine how stocks are performing. It encompasses 500 top companies in leading U.S. industries. Many mutual funds use it as the benchmark they measure their own performance against.

San Marino Use alone in datelines on stories from the Republic of San Marino.

Santa Claus, Santa Nice in any reference. Naughty: Using *Claus* on second reference. *Mrs. Claus* is acceptable for Santa's wife. See **Kriss Kringle**.

Sardinia Use instead of Italy in datelines on stories from communities on this island.

Saskatchewan A province of Canada north of Montana and North Dakota. Do not abbreviate.
See **datelines**.

SAT Use only the initials in referring to the previously designated Scholastic Aptitude Test or the Scholastic Assessment Test. Example: *The students scored above average on the SAT*.

Satan But lowercase *devil* and *satanic*.

satellites See **spacecraft designations**.

Saudi Arabia Use *Saudi* as the adjective in referring to the people or culture of Saudi Arabia. It's *Saudi diplomacy*, not *Saudi Arabian diplomacy*. For the Saudi monarchy, follow the style on British and other monarchies.

Sault Ste. Marie, Michigan; Sault Ste. Marie, Ontario The abbreviation is *Ste.* instead of *St.* because the full name is *Sault Sainte Marie.*

savings and loan associations Also called *thrifts* or *savings and loans.* Differ from banks in that they are required by law to have a large proportion of their lending in mortgages and other consumer loans. They are regulated by the Federal Deposit Insurance Corp. and the Treasury Department's Office of the Comptroller of the Currency.

scene numbers Capitalize scene when used with a figure: *Scene 2; Act 2, Scene 4.*
 But: *the second scene, the third scene.* See **numerals**.

scheme Do not use as a synonym for *a plan* or *a project.*

Schengen Area A group of European countries that have agreed to abolish passport and customs controls among one another. Created by the 1985 Schengen Agreement, it has grown to encompass 26 countries: Austria, Belgium, Czech Republic, Denmark, Estonia, Finland, France, Germany, Greece, Hungary, Iceland, Italy, Latvia, Liechtenstein, Lithuania, Luxembourg, Malta, Netherlands, Norway, Poland, Portugal, Slovakia, Slovenia, Spain, Sweden and Switzerland.

school Capitalize when part of a proper name: *Public School 3, Madison Elementary School, Doherty Junior High School, Crocker High School.*

school choice An umbrella term for education strategies that give parents the option of enrolling children in schools other than the assigned district public school, often using public funding. Advocates praise it as a way to save children from those public schools that are struggling. Opponents note that it diverts money from those same schools. Avoid using the general term when possible; specifics are better: *The teachers union objects to the charter school bill; a proposed school voucher bill will be debated next week.*

 School choice options include:
 charter schools: Publicly funded, privately run, tuition-free public schools that operate independently of the local school district and with some autonomy over scheduling and curricula. Most charter schools are operated by nonprofit organizations but some states allow for-profit organizations to manage them.

 A handful of states lack charter school laws and do not allow them.

 Like traditional public schools, charter schools receive public funding based on the number of students they enroll.

 They operate under a charter or performance contract authorized, depending on state law, by local school districts, the state, a higher education institution or nonprofit organization.

 magnet schools: Public schools outside of the neighborhood public school that offer specialized curricula and to which students must apply.

 vouchers: Allocations of per-child public funding that can be used toward private-school tuition.

 Education Savings Accounts: Government-authorized accounts

S

into which public funds are deposited for families who withdraw their children from public school. They can be used for private-school tuition, online learning tutoring or approved higher education expenses.

home schooling (n.) home-schooler (n.) home-school (v.) home-schooled (adj.): An alternative to public or private school, typically conducted at home by a parent. Oversight of student evaluations, curricula and parental qualifications varies by state.

private schools: Operate independently of local, state or federal governments and without public money. Funding comes from student tuition, endowments, donations and grants from religious or other organizations.

Some schools are using alternatives to the traditional classroom model in their instruction. Among them:

distance learning: An alternative to in-person classroom education. Student and instructor are physically separated and students complete much of the coursework online. Popular in adult education and for college-level courses.

online learning: Lessons are conducted via the internet, with or without an instructor present. It can either supplement or replace in-person learning at every level of education, from prekindergarten through college. Students may complete single lessons or courses online, or in the case of online schools, an entire curriculum.

blended learning: A combination of in-person and online instruction used in K-12 and college classrooms.

scissors Takes plural verbs and pronouns: *The scissors are on the table.*

Leave them there.

Scotch tape A trademark for a brand of transparent tape.

Scotland Use *Scotland* after the names of Scottish communities in datelines. See **datelines** and **United Kingdom**.

Scot, Scots, Scottish A native of Scotland is a *Scot*. The people are the *Scots*, not the *Scotch*.

Somebody or something is *Scottish*.

scraping Copying online data or content, manually or using automated scraping tools, for use or display elsewhere. Depending on what's being scraped, this can raise intellectual property, security or privacy issues, though there are legitimate uses of the technique.

Screen Actors Guild-American Federation of Television and Radio Artists *SAG-AFTRA* is acceptable on second reference.

National offices in Los Angeles and New York.

screen saver

Scripture, Scriptures Capitalize when referring to the religious writings in the Bible. See **Bible**.

scuba Lowercased acronym for *self-contained underwater breathing apparatus*.

Scud missile

scurrilous

SEAL(s) A special operations force of the Navy. The acronym is for *sea, air,*

land.
See **special forces**.

search engine optimization Any of
a number of methods, both human-
and machine-powered, used to
improve the prominence of online
content in search engines, thus
increasing traffic to the content. *SEO*
is acceptable on second reference.

seasonal affective disorder A form
of depression that occurs during the
winter, when there is less sunlight.
Describe a person as *having seasonal
affective disorder* only if verified
and relevant. *SAD* is acceptable on
second reference. See **disabilities**;
depression; mental illness.

seasons Lowercase *spring, summer,
fall, winter* and derivatives such as
springtime unless part of a formal
name: *Dartmouth Winter Carnival,
Winter Olympics, Summer Olympics*.

seat belt Two words.

second reference When used in
this book, the term applies to
all subsequent references to an
organization or individual within a
story.
Acceptable abbreviations
and acronyms for organizations
frequently in the news are listed
under the organization's full name. A
few prominent acronyms acceptable
on first reference also are listed
alphabetically according to the
letters of the acronym.
The listing of an acceptable term
for second reference does not mean
that it always must be used after the
first reference. Often a generic word
such as *the agency, the commission* or
the company is more appropriate and
less jarring to the reader. At other

times, the full name may need to be
repeated for clarity.
For additional guidelines
that apply to organizations, see
abbreviations and acronyms and
capitalization.
For additional guidelines that
apply to individuals, see **courtesy
titles** and **titles**.

secretary Capitalize before a name
only if it is an official corporate
or organizational title. Do not
abbreviate.
See **titles**.

secretary-general With a hyphen.
Capitalize as a formal title before a
name: *Secretary-General Ban Ki-moon*.
See **titles**.

secretary of state Capitalize as a
formal title before a name.
See **titles**.

secretary-treasurer With a hyphen.
Capitalize as a formal title before a
name.
See **titles**.

Secret Service A federal agency
administered by the Department of
Homeland Security.
The *Secret Service Uniformed
Division*, which protects the
president's residence and offices
and the embassies in Washington,
formerly was known as the Executive
Protective Service.

section Capitalize when used with a
figure to identify part of a law or bill:
Section 14B of the Taft-Hartley Act.

**Securities and Exchange
Commission** *SEC* is acceptable on
second reference.
The related legislation is the

Securities Exchange Act (no *and*).

securitization Bundling together individual assets, such as mortgages, and selling stakes to investors.

Security Council (U.N.) *Security Council* may be used on first reference in stories under a United Nations dateline. Use *U.N. Security Council* in other first references.

Retain capitalization of *Security Council* in all references.

Lowercase *council* whenever it stands alone.

Seeing Eye dog See **service animal, assistance animal, guide dog**.

self- Always hyphenate:
self-assured   self-government
self-defense

selfie A self-portrait photo generally taken with a camera-equipped phone or webcam.

semi- The rules in **prefixes** apply, but in general, no hyphen.

Some examples:
semifinal   semiofficial
semi-invalid   semitropical
But semi-automatic , semi-autonomous.

semiannual Twice a year, a synonym for *biannual*.

Do not confuse it with *biennial*, which means *every two years*.

semicolon See entry in the **Punctuation** chapter.

semitrailer Or *semitractor-trailer*, but not *semi-tractor trailer*.

Senate Capitalize all specific references to governmental legislative bodies, regardless of whether the name of the state or nation is used: *the U.S. Senate, the Senate, the Virginia Senate, the state Senate, the Senate*.

Lowercase plural uses: *the Virginia and North Carolina senates*.

See **governmental bodies**.

Lowercase references to non-governmental bodies: *the student senate at Yale*.

senatorial Always lowercase.

senator, Sen. See **legislative titles** and **party affiliation**.

sentences Capitalize the first word of every sentence, including quoted statements and direct questions:
Patrick Henry said, "I know not what course others may take, but as for me, give me liberty or give me death."

Capitalize the first word of a quoted statement if it constitutes a sentence, even if it was part of a larger sentence in the original: *Patrick Henry said, "Give me liberty or give me death."*

In direct questions, even without quotation marks: *The story answers the question, Where does true happiness really lie?*

Use a single space between sentences.

See **ellipsis** in the **Punctuation** chapter and **poetry**.

Sept. 11 The term for describing the attacks in the United States on Sept. 11, 2001. Use *2001* if needed for clarity. Also acceptable is *9/11*. See **9/11**.

Sept. 11 memorial Acceptable in all references to the *National September 11 Memorial & Museum* at *ground zero*. Add location for other memorials

S

with similar names.

sergeant-at-arms

serial numbers Use figures and capital letters in solid form (no hyphens or spaces unless the source indicates they are an integral part of the code): *A1234567*.

serviceable

service animal, assistance animal, guide dog An animal, usually a dog, that aids a person with a disability. Examples include guiding a person who is blind, alerting a deaf person to the presence of another person, retrieving dropped items, pulling a wheelchair, providing help with balance. *Seeing Eye dog* is a trademark for a guide dog trained by Seeing Eye Inc. of Morristown, New Jersey. *Emotional support animals* or *therapy animals* are sometimes used to help a person with depression, anxiety or other conditions. They are not considered service animals under the Americans with Disabilities Act. See **disabilities**.

Service Employees International Union A Washington, D.C.-based labor organization that represents a wide array of service-industry workers in the United States, Puerto Rico and Canada. *SEIU* is acceptable on second reference.

sesquicentennial A 150-year period.

Seven Seas Arabian Sea, Atlantic Ocean, Bay of Bengal, Mediterranean Sea, Persian Gulf, Red Sea, South China Sea.

Seven Wonders of the World The Egyptian pyramids, the hanging gardens of Babylon, the Mausoleum at Halicarnassus, the temple of Artemis at Ephesus, the Colossus of Rhodes, the statue of Zeus by Phidias at Olympia and the Pharos or lighthouse at Alexandria.

sewage Use this term, not *sewerage*, for both the waste matter and the drainage system.

sexual abuse, sexual assault, sexual harassment, sexual misconduct Proceed with care when using these terms, along with others such as *rape, molestation, unwanted sex, sexual relationship*, etc. Authorities, people making accusations and people who stand accused use a variety of language and terminology to cover a wide spectrum of actions or behavior. Interpretations can vary widely. Do not simply repeat those terms.

Instead, pay close attention to legal definitions, which vary by jurisdiction, and the wording of criminal charges or convictions. Consider the nuance of each situation and what may be conveyed or perceived by the language used.

As with all accusations, allegations should be well documented and corroborated. Always seek comment from accused individuals or their representatives.

We generally do not identify, in text or images, those who say they have been sexually assaulted or subjected to extreme abuse. We may identify victims of sexual assault or extreme abuse when victims publicly identify themselves. Decisions on identifying people who say they have been subject to other forms of sexual misconduct should be made on a case-by-case basis, depending on the nature of the allegations.

S

Among points to consider:
— Terms such as *rape, sexual assault* and *sexual harassment* have legal definitions that vary by jurisdiction. Knowing the definitions is essential when deciding which term(s) are accurate and appropriate. Depending on state law, *rape* and *sexual assault* can include sexual contact by force, threat or coercion, or after the accuser's incapacitation due to drugs or alcohol.
— When reporting on court cases, use the language contained in the charges and/or conviction. If a defendant is charged with *sexual assault*, do not say he is charged with *rape*. If a defendant is convicted on a charge of *sexual misconduct*, do not say he was convicted of *having unwanted sex* with the victim or convicted of *rape*. If someone is charged with *sexual harassment*, do not say they are accused of *sexual assault*.
— It may be appropriate to explain why a story does or does not use certain terms: *The woman said she was raped; prosecutors charged the man with sexual assault under the definitions in state law*. Another example: *He was convicted of taking indecent liberties, which is the formal criminal charge*.
— The term *sexual relationship* implies consent. Under state laws, a minor cannot give sexual consent to an adult. Thus, do not write that an adult *had a sexual relationship with* or *had sex with* a minor or vice versa. (The age of consent varies by jurisdiction; know the law of the state or jurisdiction in question.) In other cases, consider carefully whether *relationship* is an appropriate term.
— A key issue in many cases is the element of consent, and definitions of what constitutes consent vary. Refer to the laws of the jurisdiction in question.
— The terms *sexual harassment* and *sexual misconduct* generally denote behavior that does not include *rape, sexual assault, sexual abuse* or *sexual violence. Sexual misconduct* is preferred over *sexual harassment*, as it encompasses a broader range of misbehavior and does not run the risk of diminishing an alleged act. Use *sexual harassment* when reporting on a specific legal charge or formal Equal Employment Opportunity Commission complaint.
— The term *sexual violence* may occasionally be used in broad references to *sexual assault, rape* and *sexual abuse*. Use the more specific wording for individual cases.
— After using a broad term such as *sexual misconduct* or *sexual assault*, describe generally the kinds of behavior alleged or admitted to — such as groping, unwanted kissing, disrobing, verbal abuse, digital penetration, oral sex, etc. Provide enough detail to make clear the alleged crimes, while avoiding a level of detail that could be perceived as gratuitous.
— Do not refer to a person making an accusation as a *victim* unless the accused person has been convicted. Avoid the term *alleged victim*. The term *accuser* is acceptable, especially when referring to a group of people: *Bill Cosby's accusers*. Limit its use when referring to an individual in favor of the correct pronoun. *The*

S

woman said the defendant forcibly kissed her.
RESOURCES:
https://www.eeoc.gov/harassment
https://apps.rainn.org/policy/
See **anonymous sources**; **privacy**.

sexually transmitted disease STD is acceptable on second reference. Consider using the phrase *a disease spread through sex* instead.

shah Capitalize when used as a title before a name: *Shah Mohammad Reza Pahlavi of Iran.*

The Shah of Iran commonly is known only by this title, which is, in effect, an alternate name. Capitalize *Shah of Iran* in references to the holder of the title; lowercase subsequent references as *the shah.*

The practice is based on the guidelines in the **nobility** entry.

shake-up (n. and adj.) **shake up** (v.)

shall, will Use *shall* to express determination: *We shall overcome. You and he shall stay.*

Either *shall* or *will* may be used in first-person constructions that do not emphasize determination: *We shall hold a meeting. We will hold a meeting.*

For second- and third-person constructions, use *will* unless determination is stressed: *You will like it. She will not be pleased.*

See **should, would** and **subjunctive mood**.

she Do not use this pronoun in reference to nations, ships, storms or voice assistants except in direct quotes. Use *it* instead.

Sheetrock A trademark for a brand of gypsum wallboard or plasterboard.

sheikh A title for a religious or tribal leader. Also used as a term of respect. For second references, follow local practices regarding whether *sheikh* should be repeated, and which name or names should be used after the term: *Sheikh Mohammad.*

sheriff Capitalize when used as a formal title before a name. See **titles**.

short An investment term used to describe the position held by individuals who sell stock that they do not yet own by borrowing from their broker in order to deliver to the purchaser.

A person selling short is betting that the price of the stock will fall.

short covering The purchase of a security to repay shares of a security borrowed from a broker.

shorthand descriptions Think carefully before using such descriptions, taking into consideration whether they are relevant, full and fair. For example, labels such as *socialite, playboy, grandmother* or *former football star* should not be the first or only description of a person whose life or career has included other notable endeavors. Jill Biden is a college professor with a doctorate in education, in addition to being the U.S. first lady. Doug Emhoff is a lawyer as well as the U.S. second gentleman. Amal Clooney can be described as a *lawyer, human rights activist* or *author*, not simply as *George Clooney's wife*. Bill Clinton is a *former president*, not simply *Hillary Rodham Clinton's husband.*

See **doctor**; **academic degrees**.

S

short sale In financial markets, a sale of securities that are not owned by the sellers at the time of sale but which they intend to purchase or borrow in time to make delivery. *Short selling* is a bet that a stock's price will fall. In real estate, a *short sale* is when a bank lets homeowners sell their homes for less than they owe on the mortgage.

short ton Equal to 2,000 pounds. See **ton**.

should, would Use *should* to express an obligation: *We should help the needy.*

Use *would* to express a customary action: *In the summer we would spend hours by the seashore.*

Use *would* also in constructing a conditional past tense, but be careful:

Wrong: *If Soderholm would not have had an injured foot, Thompson would not have been in the lineup.*

Right: *If Soderholm had not had an injured foot, Thompson would not have been in the lineup.*

See **subjunctive mood**.

showcase, showroom, showtime

shrapnel Small metal balls from explosive artillery shells or hurled pieces of bombs, hand grenades or similar devices. Use *fragments* to describe particles from objects other than armaments that detonate or disintegrate.

shrubs See **plants**.

shutdown (n.) **shut down** (v.)

Sicily Use instead of Italy in datelines on stories from communities on this island.

Sierra Nevada, the Not *Sierra Nevada mountains* or *Sierra Nevada mountain range*. (*Sierra* means mountain range.)

sightseeing, sightseer

Signal Secure messaging service offering *end-to-end encryption*. That improves message security, although the service requires users to sign up with their real phone numbers. See **internet security**.

Silicon Valley High-tech region encompassing the northern Santa Clara Valley and adjacent areas of Northern California.

Sinai Not *the Sinai*. But: *the Sinai Desert, the Sinai Peninsula*.

Sina Weibo Chinese social networking service focused on short messages, similar to *Twitter*.

Siri Name of Apple's *voice assistant*. Do not refer to Siri with feminine pronouns.

sit-in (n. and adj.) **sit in** (v.)

sizable

sizes Use figures: *a size 8 dress, size 40 long, 10 1/2B shoes, a 34 1/2 sleeve.* Also: *S, M, L, XL, XXL*, etc.

skillful

ski, skis, skier, skied, skiing Also: *ski jump, ski jumping*.

Skype A service, owned by Microsoft Corp., that allows users to communicate by voice, video and instant message over the internet. *Skype* is used informally as a verb for

S

Slack A workplace chat service used to exchange messages and files. Often used instead of email in some settings. Do not use as a verb unless in a direct quote, in which case it needs explanation. *"She Slacked me about the upcoming meeting," he said, referring to a message sent via the workplace chat service.*

slang In general, avoid slang, the highly informal language that is outside of conventional or standard usage.

See **colloquialisms** and **dialect**.

slowdown (n.) **slow down** (v.)

smart devices General term for a category of electronic gadgets that typically connect to the internet and offer advanced features.

In general, use two words except for *smartphone* and *smartwatch*. Many such devices are also referred to as *connected*, as in *connected cars* or *connected TVs*, though *internet-connected* is preferred.

Examples of *smart devices* include:

smartphones Mobile phones, such as an *iPhone* or *Samsung Galaxy* phone, that can be used to check email, browse the web and launch applications.

smartwatches Digital wristwatches that can act as companions for *smartphones*, displaying notifications, news and weather, tracking heart rates and fitness workouts and enabling text messaging and phone calls. Some models have cellular connections that allow users to retrieve data without having the companion phone nearby.

smart appliances Examples include thermostats that can sense when people are in a room and use that information to customize a heating or cooling schedule; refrigerators with cameras to keep track of food inside; and light bulbs that can adjust light levels and colors or turn on or off through an app. These devices can be separately referred to as *smart thermostats* and *smart refrigerators*.

smart TVs Television sets with internet connection, mostly for watching streaming video without the need for separate streaming TV device.

smart locks Locks that can control entry to the garage or front door through an app or digital code. Many also permit temporary digital keys for guests and contractors.

Smart appliances, smart locks and other *smart devices* in homes make up a *smart home*.

A *smart city* refers to a municipality that has installed internet-connected sensors in parking meters, traffic lights and other infrastructure to communicate and coordinate with each other.

While manufacturers have been promoting the conveniences of having *smart devices* such as refrigerators and door locks, such devices also carry security and privacy risks. Hackers, for instance, might be able to access mics and cameras on some devices to spy on their owners. They also might be able to unlock doors remotely, although it may also be easier for an intruder to break a window. And some companies collect data on usage that can be used to piece together when someone is home or how often the person has exercised. Such data can also be sought in police investigations and lawsuits.

Smithsonian Institution Not
Smithsonian Institute.

smoke bomb, smoke screen

smokejumper One word, lowercase,
for the firefighter who gets to fires
by aircraft and parachute.

Smokey Or *Smokey Bear*. Not *Smokey
the Bear*.
But: *A smoky room*.

SMS An abbreviation for *Short Message
Service*. *Text messaging* is preferred.

snafu Acceptable despite its vulgar
origin.

Snapchat A service that lets users
capture and share photos or video
clips, often with text, drawings or
other adornments. Popular among
younger people, it is best known
for messages that automatically
disappear a few seconds after
viewing. Use lowercase *snap* for a
Snapchat posting. The company
name is Snap Inc. Headquarters is in
Santa Monica, California.

sneaked Preferred as past tense of
sneak. Do not use the colloquial
snuck.

**snowdrift, snowfall, snowflake,
snowman, snowplow, snowshoe,
snowstorm, snowsuit**

so called (adv.) **so-called** (adj.)
Use sparingly. Do not follow with
quotation marks. Example: *He is
accused of trading so-called blood
diamonds to finance the war.*

socialist, socialism See **political
parties and philosophies**.

social media An umbrella term for
online services that people use to
share posts, photos and videos with
small or large groups of people,
privately or publicly. *Facebook* is the
largest one. Other major services
include *Twitter*, *Snapchat* and Meta's
Instagram. Newer ones include
TikTok, a popular video-sharing
service owned by a Beijing company,
ByteDance. Others, such as China's
Sina Weibo, are popular regionally.
Concerns about social media
include user privacy, as companies
collect troves of data to target
ads. Social media services often
emphasize viral but polarizing
content in order to keep users
engaged and returning. And while
social media companies have taken
steps to combat hate speech and
misinformation, many problematic
posts still slip through. The issue
came to the forefront after Russians
bankrolled thousands of fake
political ads during the 2016 U.S.
elections to sow discord among
Americans.
Messaging services such as
WhatsApp and *Signal* are often
lumped with social media but are
not technically social media services.
But the line has blurred in recent
years, as chat services such as
Apple's *iMessage*, *WeChat* from the
Chinese company Tencent and the
Japan-based *Line* take on broader
functions, such as payments and
group sharing.
While major companies report
usage numbers, be careful about
making direct comparisons because
each company uses a different
measure.
Some social services use a check
mark or a similar icon to denote
accounts that have been verified
to belong to the named celebrity,

journalist, government official or other public figure. Keep in mind that accounts without such a check mark may have been created by a third party for fraudulent, parody or other reasons. See **Social Media and Web-Based Reporting Guidelines** chapter.

Social Security Capitalize all references to the U.S. system.

The number groups are hyphenated: *123-45-6789*

Lowercase generic uses such as: *Is there a social security program in Sweden?*

Society for the Prevention of Cruelty to Animals *SPCA* is acceptable on second reference.

The *American Society for the Prevention of Cruelty to Animals* is limited to the five boroughs of New York City.

The autonomous chapters in other cities ordinarily precede the organization by the name of the city: On first reference, *the San Francisco Society for the Prevention of Cruelty to Animals*; on second, *the San Francisco SPCA* or *the SPCA* as appropriate in the context.

solvency The ability to pay expenses and debt on time and continue operating. An insolvent company typically has to seek bankruptcy protection from creditors.

Somali A person from Somalia, or an adjective for something linked to Somalia. Do not use *Somalian*.

SOS The distress signal.

S.O.S (no final period) is a trademark for a brand of soap pad.

sound barrier The speed of sound

is no longer a true barrier because aircraft have exceeded it. See **Mach number**.

soundstage

source Avoid the term if possible. Be as specific as possible about the source of information. If space is limited, use *source* as a last resort. *Official* or a similar word will often suffice, including in headlines. See **anonymous sources**.

source code The basic blueprint of a computer program.

South Use *South* to describe the 16-state region as defined by the U.S. Census Bureau that is broken into three divisions. Capitalize *Southern* as an adjective describing the region.

The four *East South Central* states are Alabama, Kentucky, Mississippi and Tennessee.

The eight *South Atlantic* states are Delaware, Florida, Georgia, Maryland, North Carolina, South Carolina, Virginia and West Virginia.

The four *West South Central* states are Arkansas, Louisiana, Oklahoma and Texas.

There is no official U.S. Census Bureau definition of *Southeast*.

For directions, *south* and *southern*. See **directions and regions**.

See **Midwest**, **Northeast** and **West** for the bureau's other regional breakdowns.

Southeast Asia The nations of the Indochina Peninsula and the islands southeast of it: Cambodia, Indonesia, Laos, Malaysia, Myanmar, Papua New Guinea, the Philippines, Singapore, Thailand and Vietnam.

S

south, southern, southeast, southwest See **directions and regions**.

Space Age It began with the launching of Sputnik 1 on Oct. 4, 1957.

spacecraft designations Use Arabic figures and capitalize the name: *Gemini 7, Apollo 11, Pioneer 10*. See **numerals**.

spacecraft, spaceship, spacesuit, spacewalk

space shuttle Lowercase *space shuttle*, but capitalize a proper name: *space shuttle Discovery*.

The space shuttle was a reusable winged spaceship capable of carrying people and cargo into Earth orbit. NASA's shuttles flew from 1981 until 2011, logging 135 missions. Two of the five shuttles were destroyed in flight, Challenger in 1986 and Columbia in 2003.

spam, Spam Use *spam* in all references to unsolicited commercial or bulk email, often advertisements. Use *Spam*, a trademark, to refer to a canned meat product.

Spanish-American War

Spanish names The family names of both the father and mother usually are considered part of a person's full name. In everyday use, customs sometimes vary with individuals and countries.

The normal sequence is given name, father's family name, mother's family name: *Gabriel Garcia Marquez*.

On second reference, use only the father's family name (*Garcia*), unless the individual prefers or is widely known by a multiple last name

(*Garcia Marquez*).

Some individuals use a *y* (for *and*) between the two surnames to ensure that both names are used together (including second references): *Gabriel Garcia y Marquez*.

A married woman sometimes uses her father's name, followed by the particle *de* (for *of*) and her husband's name. A woman named *Irma Perez* who married a man named *Anibal Gutierrez* would be known as *Irma Perez de Gutierrez*.

See **accent marks**.

speaker Capitalize as a formal title before a name. Generally, it is a formal title only for the speaker of a legislative body: *Speaker John Boehner*.

See **titles**.

special forces Do not use interchangeably with *special operations forces*. Capitalize when referring specifically to the *U.S. Army Special Forces*, also known as Green Berets. Others, such as Navy SEALs or Army Rangers, should be called *special operations forces*.

special needs, special education When possible, avoid these terms. While they remain in wide use in education and law, many view them as euphemistic and offensive. Instead, aim to be specific about the needs or services in question. See **disabilities**.

Special Olympics Organization that offers 30-plus Olympic-style individual and team sports for people with intellectual disabilities. The organization supports over 5 million athletes and more than 100,000 competitions each year in more than 170 countries, as

S

well as other activities, events and services. Athletes are called Special Olympians. See **disabilities**.

species Same in singular and plural. Use singular or plural verbs and pronouns depending on the sense: *The species has been unable to maintain itself. Both species are extinct.*
See **genus, species**.

speeches Capitalize and use quotation marks for their formal titles, as described in **composition titles**.

speechmaker, speechmaking

speed of sound See **Mach number**.

speeds Use figures. *The car slowed to 7 mph, winds of 5 to 10 mph, winds of 7 to 9 knots, 10-knot wind.*
See **numerals**.

spelling The basic rule when in doubt is to consult this book followed by, if necessary, a dictionary under conditions described in the **dictionaries** entry.
Memory aid: Noah Webster developed the following rule of thumb for the frequently vexing question of whether to double a final consonant in forming the present participle and past tense of a verb:
— If the stress in pronunciation is on the first syllable, do not double the consonant: *combat, combating, combated; cancel, canceling, canceled.*
— If the stress in pronunciation is on the second syllable, double the consonant unless confusion would result: *incur, incurred, incurring.* An exception, to avoid confusion with *buss*, is *bus, bused, busing.*
Avoid spelling simplifications

such as *lite*. Exception: *thru* allowed in some compounds: *drive-thru, writethru.*
British spellings, when they differ from American, are acceptable only in particular cases such as formal or composition titles: *Jane's Defence Weekly, Labour Party, Excel Centre, London Palladium Theatre, Wimbledon's Centre Court.*

spill, spilled, spilling Not *spilt* in the past tense.

spinoff (n.) A distribution that occurs when the company forms a separate company out of a division, a subsidiary or other holdings. The shares of the new company are distributed proportionately to the parent company holders.

sportsbook Use one word for places where sports bets are accepted either in person or online, unless part of a formal name. The shorthand *book* is acceptable on second reference: *The sportsbook opened in December; the book stopped taking bets just before kickoff.*

sports writer This is an exception to Webster's New World College Dictionary.

sport utility vehicle No plural *s* in *sport*; no hyphen.
SUV is acceptable on first reference.

spot market A market for buying or selling commodities or foreign exchange for immediate delivery and for cash payment.

spot price The price of a commodity available for immediate sale and delivery. The term is also used to refer to foreign exchange transactions.

spree This term is usually applied to shopping or revelry. Do not use in other circumstances: *killing spree*.

springtime

sputnik Usually lowercase, but capitalize when followed by a figure as part of a proper name: *Sputnik 1*. It is Russian for *satellite*.

square Do not abbreviate. Capitalize when part of a proper name: *Washington Square*.

SRO Acceptable on second reference for *standing room only*.

SST Acceptable in all references for *supersonic transport*.

stadium, stadiums Capitalize only when part of a proper name: *Dodger Stadium*.

Stalin, Josef Not *Joseph*.

stall Use care when using *stall* in this sense: when an automobile *stalls*, the engine stops. This may not be true when an airplane *stalls*; it pitches forward or sideways because of a lack of air speed.

stamp, stomp Both are acceptable, but *stamp* is preferred.

stanch, staunch Stanch is a verb: *He stanched the flow of blood.*
Staunch is an adjective: *She is a staunch supporter of equality.*

stand-alone (adj.)

standard time Capitalize *Eastern*

Standard Time, Pacific Standard Time, etc., but lowercase *standard time* when standing alone.
See **time zones**.

starboard Nautical for *right*, when facing the bow, or forward. See **port, starboard**.

"The Star-Spangled Banner" But lowercase *the national anthem*.

startup One word (n. and adj.) to describe a new business venture. An exception to Webster's New World College Dictionary preference.

"Star Wars" Enclosed in quotes in references to the movie series, entertainment spinoffs and the Strategic Defense Initiative against nuclear attack of the 1980s. Also: *"Star Wars" Day, "Star Wars" Canyon.*

state Lowercase in all *state of* constructions: *the state of Maine, the states of Maine and Vermont.*
Four states — Kentucky, Massachusetts, Pennsylvania and Virginia — are legally commonwealths rather than states. The distinction is necessary only in formal uses: *The commonwealth of Kentucky filed a suit.* For simple geographic reference: *Tobacco is grown in the state of Kentucky.*
Do not capitalize *state* when used simply as an adjective to specify a level of jurisdiction: *state Rep. William Smith, the state Transportation Department, state funds.*
Apply the same principle to phrases such as *the city of Chicago, the town of Auburn*, etc.
See also **state names**.

statehouse Capitalize all references

S

to a specific statehouse, with or without the name of the state: *The Vermont Statehouse is in Montpelier. The governor will visit the Statehouse today.*

Lowercase plural uses: *the Massachusetts and Rhode Island statehouses.*

state names Follow these guidelines:

SPELL OUT: The names of the 50 U.S. states should be spelled out when used in the body of a story, whether standing alone or in conjunction with a city, town, village or military base. No state name is necessary if it is the same as the dateline. This also applies to newspapers cited in a story. For example, a story datelined Providence, R.I., would reference the *Providence Journal*, not the *Providence (Rhode Island) Journal*. See **datelines**.

EIGHT NOT ABBREVIATED: The names of eight states are never abbreviated in datelines or text: *Alaska, Hawaii, Idaho, Iowa, Maine, Ohio, Texas* and *Utah*.

Memory aid: Spell out the names of the two states that are not part of the contiguous United States and of the continental states that are five letters or fewer.

IN THE BODY OF STORIES: Except for cities that stand alone in datelines, use the state name in textual material when the city or town is not in the same state as the dateline, or where necessary to avoid confusion: *Springfield, Massachusetts,* or *Springfield, Illinois*. Provide a state identification for the city if the story has no dateline, or if the city is not in the same state as the dateline. However, cities that stand alone in datelines may be used alone in stories that have no dateline if no confusion would result.

ABBREVIATIONS REQUIRED: Use the state abbreviations listed at the end of this section:

— In conjunction with the name of a city, town, village or military base in most datelines. See **datelines** for examples and exceptions for large cities.
— In lists, agate, tabular material, nonpublishable editor's notes and credit lines.
— In short-form listings of party affiliation: *D-Ala., R-Mont.* See **party affiliation** entry for details.

Following are the state abbreviations, which also appear in the entries for each state (postal code abbreviations in parentheses):

Ala. (AL)	Md. (MD)	N.D. (ND)
Ariz. (AZ)	Mass. (MA)	Okla. (OK)
Ark. (AR)	Mich. (MI)	Ore. (OR)
Calif. (CA)	Minn. (MN)	Pa. (PA)
Colo. (CO)	Miss. (MS)	R.I. (RI)
Conn. (CT)	Mo. (MO)	S.C. (SC)
Del. (DE)	Mont. (MT)	S.D. (SD)
Fla. (FL)	Neb. (NE)	Tenn. (TN)
Ga. (GA)	Nev. (NV)	Vt. (VT)
Ill. (IL)	N.H. (NH)	Va. (VA)
Ind. (IN)	N.J. (NJ)	Wash. (WA)
Kan. (KS)	N.M. (NM)	W.Va. (WV)
Ky. (KY)	N.Y. (NY)	Wis. (WI)
La. (LA)	N.C. (NC)	Wyo. (WY)

These are the postal code abbreviations for the eight states that are not abbreviated in datelines or text: AK (Alaska), HI (Hawaii), ID (Idaho), IA (Iowa), ME (Maine), OH (Ohio), TX (Texas), UT (Utah). Also: District of Columbia (DC).

Use the two-letter Postal Service abbreviations only with full addresses, including ZIP code.

PUNCTUATION: Place one comma between the city and the state name, and another comma after the state name, unless ending a sentence or indicating a dateline: *He was traveling from Nashville, Tennessee, to Austin, Texas, en route to his home in Albuquerque, New Mexico. She said*

S

Cook County, Illinois, was Mayor Daley's stronghold.

HEADLINES: Avoid using state abbreviations in headlines whenever possible.

MISCELLANEOUS: Use *New York state* when necessary to distinguish the state from New York City.

Use *state of Washington* or *Washington state* within a story when it's necessary to differentiate the state name from the U.S. capital, Washington. It's written Washington, D.C., with the added abbreviation only if the city might be confused with the state.

State of the Union Capitalize all references to the president's annual address.

Lowercase other uses: *"The state of the union is confused," she said.*

state police Capitalize with a state name if part of the formal description for a police agency: *the New York State Police, the Virginia State Police.*

In most cases, state police standing alone is a shorthand reference for *state police officers* rather than a reference to the agency. For consistency and to avoid hairline distinctions about whether the reference is to the agency or the officers, lowercase the words *state police* whenever they are not preceded by a state name.

states' rights

statewide

stationary, stationery To stand still is to be *stationary.*

Writing paper is *stationery.*

St. Barts, St. Martin In general,

use the English spellings for these Caribbean islands. *St. Martin* is divided by its northern French side, called *Saint-Martin* in French, and its southern Dutch side, called *Sint Maarten* in Dutch. In some uses, if referring specifically to the French half of the island it can be *Saint-Martin*, and if referring specifically to the Dutch side it can be *St. Maarten.* But explain in copy: *The island known as St. Martin in English is divided between French Saint-Martin and Dutch Sint Maarten.* For *St. Barts*, use *Saint Barthelemy* only if needed in quotes, and explain that it is the French name.

stealth When used in connection with military aircraft, ships and vehicles it means the equipment is masked from various types of electronic detection. Stealth equipment can range from radar wave absorbing paint to electronic jamming devices. Like the *cruise missile*, always lowercase, no quotation marks.

stem cell

stepbrother, stepfather Also: *stepsister, stepmother.*

STEM Acceptable on first reference for *science, technology, engineering and math*, but spell out the full phrase shortly thereafter.

St. John's The city in the Canadian province of Newfoundland and Labrador.

Not to be confused with *Saint John, New Brunswick.*

stockbroker

stock index futures Futures contracts valued on the basis of

S

indexes that track the prices of a specific group of stocks. The most widely traded is the future based on the S&P 500. Speculators also trade options on index futures.

stock prices Prices are quoted in dollars and cents. Use active verbs: *Microsoft stock fell 10 cents to $38.01 in afternoon trading.* Avoid rounding individual stock prices in stories. If individual stock prices are rounded, the story should include context. *The stock rose above $100 for the first time.* In headlines, rounding down is acceptable.

When writing about indexes, carry out decimals two places. *The Dow Jones Industrial Average rose 78.73 points, or 0.5%, to close at 16,438.91.* However, it is acceptable to round down in shorter stories. *The Dow rose to 16,438.*

stopgap

stormwater

storyline

storyteller

straight-laced, strait-laced Use *straight-laced* for someone strict or severe in behavior or moral views.

Reserve *strait-laced* for the notion of confinement, as in a corset.

strait Capitalize as part of a proper name: *Bering Strait, Strait of Gibraltar.*

But: *the Bosporus* and *the Dardanelles.* Neither is followed by *Strait.*

straitjacket

Strategic Arms Reduction Treaty

START is acceptable on first reference to the treaty as long as it is made immediately clear which is being referred to.

Use the *strategic arms treaty* or the *treaties* in some references to avoid alphabet soup.

There are three START treaties:
— START I, signed in 1991.
— START II, signed in 1992. Ratified by U.S. Senate, but never took effect because Senate did not adopt the 1997 protocol and several amendments to Anti-Ballistic Missile treaty demanded by Russian Duma. Shelved by Russia in 2002 after U.S withdrew from ABM treaty.
— New START, signed in 2010.
— Do not confuse with the *Strategic Arms Limitation Treaty* of 1979, known as *SALT.*

streaming audio The broadcasting of audio content over the internet, offering music or *podcasts* on demand to listeners through mobile apps and websites. Many of these services also offer social sharing options.

street Abbreviate only with a numbered address. See **addresses**.

strikebreaker

stutter A condition that involves significant problems with flow of speech, such as repetitions of syllables, elongations of sounds or prolonged stops. The term *stutter* is generally used rather than *stammer* in the United States. Refer to the condition only if relevant. For example: President Joe Biden has spoken frequently about how overcoming a stutter was one of the hardest things he's done in life.

S

Do not use the term *stutterer* for a person. Instead, *a person who stutters* or *she has* (or *had*) *a stutter*.

If using a direct quotation in which a person has stuttered, do not call attention to the stutter. Instead, treat it as you would any other: *"Tomorrow is a new day," he said.* Not *"T-t-tomorrow is a new day," he said.* See **disabilities**.

Styrofoam A trademark for a brand of plastic foam. Use the term *plastic foam* unless referring specifically to the trademarked product. (Note: Cups and other serving items are not made of *Styrofoam* brand plastic foam.)

sub- The rules in **prefixes** apply, but in general, no hyphen.

subcommittee Lowercase when used with the name of a legislative body's full committee: *a Ways and Means subcommittee.*

Capitalize when a subcommittee has a proper name of its own: *the Senate Permanent Subcommittee on Investigations.*

subjunctive mood Use the subjunctive mood of a verb for contrary-to-fact conditions, and expressions of doubts, wishes or regrets:

If I were a rich man, I wouldn't have to work hard.

I doubt that more money would be the answer.

I wish it were possible to take back my words.

Sentences that express a contingency or hypothesis may use either the subjunctive or the indicative mood depending on the context. In general, use the subjunctive if there is little

likelihood that a contingency might come true:

If I were to marry a millionaire, I wouldn't have to worry about money.

If the bill passes as expected, it will provide an immediate tax cut.

See **should, would**.

subpoena, subpoenaed, subpoenaing

subprime A class of borrowers characterized by tarnished credit histories. These borrowers usually entail greater risk for lenders so they are charged a higher interest rate for a loan.

successor

Sudan Use *Sudan* for the East African country whose capital is *Khartoum. South Sudan* is the country in the southern region that declared independence July 9, 2011. Its capital is *Juba.*

sue To avoid any suggestion that someone is being judged before a trial, do not use a phrase such as *sued for malfeasance.* Instead, say *the lawsuit accuses her of malfeasance* or *he was named in a lawsuit accusing him of libel.*

suffixes See separate listings for commonly used suffixes.

Follow Webster's New World College Dictionary for words not in this book.

If a word combination is not listed in Webster's New World College Dictionary, use two words for the verb form; hyphenate any noun or adjective forms.

suicide Generally, AP does not cover suicides or suicide attempts, unless

S

the person involved is a well-known figure or the circumstances are particularly unusual or publicly disruptive.

Suicide stories, when published, should not go into detail on methods used. Suicide prevention experts believe, based on experience and some studies, that the less said in the media about the methods of suicide, the less likelihood that a death will prompt at-risk people from taking their lives by that same method in the days immediately after.

If police or family members announce publicly the method of a suicide, it is acceptable to describe the method. But do not specify the method in the headline or lead, and do not go into specific details, such the type of gun used.

If the method is not initially announced but becomes public in later days, put that detail lower in the story or consider whether a story is necessary at all.

Often, it may not be necessary to say anything other than that the person died by suicide.

Avoid using the phrase *committed suicide*. Alternate phrases include *killed himself*, *took her own life* or *died by suicide*. The verb *commit* with *suicide* can imply a criminal act. Laws against suicide have been repealed in the United States and many other places.

Notes or letters are another area for caution. Generally avoid reporting the contents.

Some experts recommend including in stories the National Suicide Prevention Lifeline: 988 after July 2022, or 1-800-273-8255 before then.

Do not refer to an *unsuccessful suicide attempt*. Refer instead to an *attempted suicide*.

Medically assisted suicide is permitted in some states and countries. Advocacy groups call it *death with dignity* or *right-to-die*, but AP doesn't use those phrases on their own. When referring to legislation whose name includes *death with dignity*, *right-to-die* or similar terms, say the law or proposal allows *people who are terminally ill to end their own lives*. If the term is in the name of a bill or law, make that clear. *Euthanasia* should not be used to describe *medically assisted suicide* or *physician-assisted suicide*.

More resources: https://www.reportingonsuicide.org.

suit, suite You may have a *suit* of clothes, a *suit* of cards, or be faced with a *lawsuit*.

There are *suites* of music, rooms and furniture.

summertime

sun Lowercase. See **heavenly bodies**.

sunbathe The verb forms: *sunbathed*, *sunbathing*. Also: *sunbather*.

Sun Belt Generally those states in the South and West, ranging from Florida and Georgia through the Gulf states into California.

super- The rules in **prefixes** apply, but in general, no hyphen. Some frequently used words:

superagency   superhighway
supercarrier   superpower
supercharge   supertanker

As with all prefixes, however, use a hyphen if the word that follows is capitalized: *super-Republican*.

Super Bowl

S

superconducting super collider

superintendent Do not abbreviate. Capitalize when used as a formal title before a name.
See **titles**.

supersede

supersonic See **Mach number**.

supersonic transport *SST* is acceptable in all references.

superspreader (n., adj.) An individual who spreads a virus or disease to an unusually large number of people, or a setting or event where an infection is spread to a large number of people: *a superspreader event.*

supervised injection sites

Acceptable terminology, along with *safe injection sites, overdose prevention centers* and similar terms, for places where people are allowed to use illicit drugs while being medically monitored. Avoid abbreviations such as *SIS* and disparaging terms like *shooting gallery.*
See **addiction; drugs**.

Supreme Court of the United States

Capitalize *U.S. Supreme Court* and also *the Supreme Court* when the context makes the *U.S.* designation unnecessary.

The chief justice is properly the *chief justice of the United States*, not *of the Supreme Court*: *Chief Justice John Roberts.*

The proper title for the eight other members of the court is *associate justice*. When used as a formal title before a name, it should be shortened to justice unless there are special circumstances: *Justice Ruth Bader Ginsburg, Associate Justice Ruth Bader Ginsburg.*
See **judge**.

supreme courts of the states

Capitalize with the state name (*the New Jersey Supreme Court*) and without the state name when the context makes it unnecessary: *the state Supreme Court, the Supreme Court.*

If a court with this name is not a state's highest tribunal, the fact should be noted. In New York, for example, the Supreme Court is a trial court. Appeals are directed to the Appellate Division of the Supreme Court. The state's highest court is the Court of Appeals.

surface-to-air missile(s) *SAM(s)* may be used on second reference. Avoid the redundant *SAM missiles.*

survivor, victim Use these terms with care because they can be imprecise and politically and legally fraught.

Survivor can denote someone who has lived through an injury or disease, but also can apply to someone who endured a threat but escaped injury altogether. Example: *a mass shooting survivor.* Likewise, *victim* can create confusion because it can variously mean someone killed, injured or subjected to mistreatment such as sexual misconduct.

Be specific if there is room for confusion: *The ceremony honored people wounded in the mass shooting*, not *The ceremony honored victims* and/or *survivors of the mass shooting. The play told the story of those killed in the hurricane*, not *The play told the stories of the hurricane's victims.*

Also be alert to potential biases and assumptions inherent in the word *victim.* A phrase such as *AIDS*

S

victim, for instance, not only makes it unclear whether the subject is alive or dead, but many AIDS patients do not consider themselves victims. Instead, use neutral, precise descriptions: *He has AIDS. She has hepatitis.* In crime stories, avoid *alleged victim* if possible; it is too easily construed as skepticism. In stories in which sexual misconduct or other allegations are leveled, consider calling the person making the allegations an *accuser* instead of a *victim* if shorthand is needed, to avoid implications of guilt on the part of the accused.

Survivor is often used to describe people who have lived through physical or emotional trauma, as in *abuse* or *rape survivor*. It is best to be specific when referring to individuals, especially if the person was never in danger of death. Use of *survivor* gets more latitude when describing groups. *A group of Holocaust survivors met at the memorial.*

See **diseases**; **homicide, murder, manslaughter**; **allege**; **sexual abuse, sexual assault, sexual harassment, sexual misconduct**.

suspect The word refers to a person who police, prosecutors or other authorities believe or say committed a crime. Do not use it to mean a person of unknown identity who definitely committed a crime. In other words, don't substitute *suspect* for *robber, killer, rapist,* etc., in describing an event, even if authorities phrase it that way. Correct: *Police said the robber stole 14 diamond rings; the thief ran away.* Incorrect: *Police said the suspect stole 14 diamond rings; the suspect ran away.* Conversely, don't substitute *robber, killer, rapist,* etc., when *suspect* is

indeed the correct word. Correct: *Police arrested the suspect the next day.* Incorrect: *Police arrested the robber the next day.*

Also see separate **allege** and **accused, alleged, suspected** entries. For guidance on related terms, see **arrest** and **indict**.

swag Sometimes used to describe the free stuff at gift suites and in gift bags given to presenters and other award-show participants.

swastika

SWAT Acronym for *Special Weapons and Tactics*.

swing states States where voters have vacillated between Republican and Democratic candidates in the last three or four presidential elections.

syllabus, syllabuses

synagogue The preferred term for a Jewish house of worship. Many Reform synagogues (and some others) have the word *temple* in their names, a usage deemed archaic by some — it harks back to the early 19th century, when German Jews used it to assert that they no longer yearned to restore the ancient Temple in Jerusalem. Orthodox Jews often use the word *shul*, Yiddish for *school*. Avoid the redundant *Jewish synagogue. Congregation* can be used generically: *The congregation met every Sabbath to worship.*

sync Short for synchronization; not *synch*. Also, *syncing*.

Syria A Middle Eastern nation on the Mediterranean bordered by Iraq, Lebanon, Jordan, Turkey and

Israel. Syria is a predominantly Sunni Muslim country with minority Alawite, Christian, Shiite, Druze and other communities. Its ethnic groups include Arab, Kurdish, Armenian and Turkmen people.

The country has been ruled by the Assad family since 1971, when Hafez Assad came to power in a coup. A popular uprising against his son, President Bashar Assad, erupted in March 2011 and eventually turned into an armed insurgency and civil war following a brutal military crackdown. Hundreds of thousands have been killed and half of the country's prewar population of 23 million has been displaced by that war.

S

t

tablespoon, tablespoonfuls Equal to three teaspoons or one-half a fluid ounce.

    The metric equivalent is approximately 15 milliliters. See **liter** and **recipes**.

tabular matter Exceptions may be made to the normal rules for abbreviations as necessary to make material fit. But make any abbreviations as clear as possible.

Taiwan An island off the coast of China that is self-governed by an elected government but also claimed by the People's Republic of China, which has viewed it as sovereign territory since a 1949 split amid civil war. See **China**; **"One-China" policy**.

takeoff (n. and adj.) **take off** (v.)

takeover (n. and adj.) **take over** (v.)

Taliban Extremist Islamic movement in Afghanistan. The *Taliban* held most of the country from 1996 to 2001, when they were ousted by a U.S.-led coalition in the wake of the Sept. 11 attacks. Over the next two decades the group pressed an insurgency that culminated in 2021 with the withdrawal of foreign troops and a return to power. The name derives from the Arabic word for students. The word *Taliban* normally takes a plural verb. Historically, the *Taliban* have enforced a strict form of Islamic law that, among other things, limits the participation of women in education and other activities, and places Draconian restrictions on the arts.

Talmud The collection of writings that constitute the Jewish civil and religious law.

tanks Use Arabic figures, separated from letters by a hyphen: *M-60*. Plural: *M-60s*.

taps Lowercase (without quotation marks) the bugle call for "lights out," also sounded at military funerals.

Taser Trademark for stun gun. Use the generic form if the brand is uncertain. Don't use verbs like *tasered*. Exception: When verb forms appear in direct quotations, use lowercase.

tax-free (adj.)

teachers college No apostrophe.

team Use singular verb and pronoun "it" when referring to the team as a collective unit. However, the team name takes a plural verb: *The Orlando Magic are close to setting a franchise record.*

    See **collective nouns**.

teamster Capitalize *teamster* only if the intended meaning is that the individual is a member of the International Brotherhood of Teamsters, Chauffeurs, Warehousemen and Helpers of America.

Teamsters union Acceptable in all references to the *International Brotherhood of Teamsters*.

See the entry under that name.

tea party Movement in the United States that opposes the Washington political establishment and espouses conservative and libertarian philosophy, including reduced government spending, lower taxes and reduction of the national debt and the federal budget deficit. Adherents are *tea partyers*. Formally named groups in the movement are capitalized: *Tea Party Express*.

tear gas Two words. See also **Chemical Mace**.

teaspoon Equal to one-sixth of a fluid ounce, or one-third of a tablespoon.

The metric equivalent is approximately 5 milliliters.

See **liter**.

teaspoonful, teaspoonfuls Not *teaspoonsful*. See **recipes**.

technology Broadly speaking, *technology* encompasses all practical applications of scientific knowledge, especially in the development of tools, machinery, materials and methods of production.

These days, the term is usually shorthand for *information technology* such as computing, robotics, communications and artificial intelligence, as well as the tools and processes used to manufacture devices from computer chips to smartphones to satellites. In daily usage, *technology* is most often used to describe internet-connected smart devices, especially smartphones; the apps they run; and the services and platforms they connect to.

Technology-related terms are listed as individual entries throughout the Stylebook, reflecting the prominence of these terms in everyday life. Examples include **internet security; smart devices; app, platform, service, site**. Both technology and the language and terms associated with it are rapidly evolving; AP Stylebook Online provides the most current guidance.

Consider your audience carefully when describing technology. Younger generations have grown up with technology and require less explanation of terms and services they find familiar, while the same language may bewilder some older readers. It is safe to assume that services in widespread use — such as Facebook and Google, for instance — will be recognized by all demographics. Other terms, such as *zero-day vulnerability*, are not familiar to many and should be explained for general audiences. When in doubt, explain potentially unfamiliar terms and avoid online or technical jargon.

There are, of course, many other forms of *technology*. *Biotechnology*, for instance, is short for *biological technology*, and refers to the development of medical therapies using modern understanding of genetics, immunology and other biological processes. Explain more specific uses of the term, usually by supplying an appropriate modifier: *industrial technology, software technology, environmental technology* and so forth.

High technology is an outdated term for *information technology*. The modifier *high-tech* remains appropriate as a signifier of novel or unfamiliar technological developments: *The restaurant's robotic chefs prepare high-tech cuisine*

t

and serve it to diners with a minimum of fuss.

In common usage, the *technology industry* includes companies engaged in the development of information technologies. *Technology stocks* are the shares of publicly traded companies in the *technology industry*.

teen, teenager (n.) **teenage** (adj.)
Do not use *teen-aged*.

Teflon A trademark for a type of nonstick coating.

telephone numbers Use figures. The form: *212-621-1500*. For international numbers use *011* (from the United States), the country code, the city code and the telephone number: *011-44-20-7535-1515*. Use hyphens, not periods.

The form for toll-free numbers: *800-111-1000*.

If extension numbers are needed, use a comma to separate the main number from the extension: *212-621-1500, ext. 2*.

teleprompter A generic term for an electronic device that rolls a prepared speech or script in front of politicians, award show hosts, presenters and other speakers.

television program titles Follow the guidelines in **composition titles**.

Put quotation marks around *show* only if it is part of the formal name. The word *show* may be dropped when it would be cumbersome, such as in a set of listings.

(Italics are used here only to illustrate examples; do not use italics on the wires.)

In text or listing, treat programs named after the star in any of the following ways: *"The Mary Tyler Moore Show," "Mary Tyler Moore"* or *the Mary Tyler Moore show*. But be consistent in a story or set of listings.

Use quotation marks also for the title of an episode: *"The Clean Room Infiltration," an episode of "The Big Bang Theory."* Also: *"NBC Nightly News," the "Today" show, "The Tonight Show."*

television station The call letters alone are frequently adequate, but when this phrase is needed, use lowercase: *television station WTEV*.

temperatures Use figures for all except *zero*. Use a word, not a minus sign, to indicate temperatures below zero.

Right: *The day's low was minus 10.*
Right: *The day's low was 10 below zero.*
Wrong: *The day's low was -10.*
Right: *The temperature rose to zero by noon.*
Right: *The day's high was expected to be 9 or 10.*
Also: *5-degree temperatures, temperatures fell 5 degrees, temperatures in the 30s* (no apostrophe).

Temperatures get higher or lower, but phrasing such as *warmer temperatures* or *cold temperatures* is also acceptable.

In recipes: *450 F or 232 C.*

See **Fahrenheit**; **Celsius**; **numerals** and **weather terms**.

Temple Mount See entry in the **Religion** chapter.

tenfold

Ten Most Wanted Fugitives The FBI's official list.

Tennessee Valley Authority *TVA* is acceptable on second reference.

Headquarters is in Knoxville, Tennessee.

tera- A prefix denoting 1 trillion units of a measure.

terrace Do not abbreviate. See **addresses**.

terrorism The calculated use of violence, especially against civilians, to create terror to disrupt and demoralize societies for political ends. Because the word is often used loosely by governments and leaders to condemn any rival political group or act of resistance or protest, the word is best used with caution. Instead, describe specific actions that are being perpetrated and attribute the use of the word *terrorism* or *terrorist* to authorities or others except when talking about significant historical events widely acknowledged as terrorist actions, such as the 9/11 attacks, the London tube bombings, the Bali bombings or the Oklahoma City bombing.

text, texting, texted Acceptable in all usages as a verb for *to send a text message*.

texts, transcripts Follow normal style guidelines for capitalization, spelling and abbreviations in handling a text or transcript. Do not use a dateline.

Use quotation marks only for words or phrases that were quoted in the text or by the person who spoke.

Identify a change in speakers by starting a paragraph with the new speaker's name and a colon. Use normal second-reference forms if the speaker has been identified earlier; provide a full name and identification if the individual is being mentioned for the first time.

Use Q: for *question* and A: for *answer* at the start of paragraphs when these notations are adequate to identify a change in speakers.

See **ellipsis** in the **Punctuation** chapter for guidelines on condensing texts and transcripts.

Thai A native or the language of Thailand.

Siam and *Siamese* are historical only.

Use *siamese* for the cat.

Thanksgiving, Thanksgiving Day The fourth Thursday in November.

than, then *Than* is a conjunction used to compare things; *then* is an adverb used to place events in time or things in order. *He wrote a volume that was longer than the AP Stylebook, and then published it.*

that (conjunction) Use the conjunction *that* to introduce a dependent clause if the sentence sounds or looks awkward without it. There are no hard-and-fast rules, but in general:

— *That* usually may be omitted when a dependent clause immediately follows a form of the verb *to say*: *The president said he had signed the bill.*
— *That* should be used when a time element intervenes between the verb and the dependent clause: *The president said Monday that he had signed the bill.*
— *That* usually is necessary after some verbs. They include: *advocate, assert, contend, declare, estimate, make clear, point out, propose* and *state.*

t

— *That* is required before subordinate clauses beginning with conjunctions such as *after, although, because, before, in addition to, until* and *while*: *Haldeman said that after he learned of Nixon's intention to resign, he sought pardons for all connected with Watergate.*

When in doubt, include *that.* Omission can hurt. Inclusion never does.

that, which (pronouns) Use *that* and *which* in referring to inanimate objects and to animals without a name. Use *that* for essential clauses, important to the meaning of a sentence, and without commas: *I remember the day that we met.* Use *which* for nonessential clauses, where the clause is less necessary, and use commas: *The team, which finished last a year ago, is in first place.*

(Tip: If you can drop the clause and not lose the meaning of the sentence, use *which*; otherwise, use *that.* A *which* clause is surrounded by commas; no commas are used with *that* clauses.)

See the **essential clauses, nonessential clauses** entry for guidelines on using *that* and *which* to introduce phrases and clauses.

theater Use this spelling unless the proper name is *Theatre*: *Shubert Theatre.*

theatergoer

their, there, they're *Their* is a plural possessive pronoun that, in general, should agree in number with the antecedent. For exceptions, see **pronouns**.

There is an adverb indicating direction: *We went there for dinner.*

There also is used with the force of a pronoun for impersonal constructions in which the real subject follows the verb: *There is no food on the table.*

They're is a contraction for *they are.*

thermos Formerly a trademark, now a generic term for any vacuum bottle, although one manufacturer still uses the word as a brand name.

Lowercase *thermos* when it is used to mean any vacuum bottle; use *Thermos* when referring to the specific brand.

they, them, their See **pronouns**.

Third World Avoid use of this term. *Developing nations* is more appropriate when referring to the economically developing nations of Africa, Asia and Latin America. Do not confuse with *nonaligned*, which is a political term. See **nonaligned nations**.

3D

three R's They are: *reading, 'riting and 'rithmetic.*

Tiananmen Square Large public square in central Beijing. Site of pro-democracy demonstrations in 1989 that ended in bloodshed.

tie, tied, tying

TikTok Video service popular with teens and young adults. Many of the short videos are set to music and are distinguished by their lighthearted, goofy style. Parent company is Chinese tech giant ByteDance, which also has a version of the app for Chinese users, called *Douyin.*

t

In 2020, the Trump administration attempted to force a sale of TikTok's U.S. subsidiary to U.S. companies on national security grounds. The Biden administration revoked that effort, but then drafted rules that would expand government oversight of apps that could be exploited by foreign adversaries to steal data in the U.S.

till Or *until*. But not *'til*.

time element Use the days of the week, not *today* or *tonight*, in news stories.

Use *Monday*, *Tuesday*, etc., for days of the week within seven days before or after the current date.

Use the month and a figure where appropriate. See **months** for forms and punctuation.

Avoid such redundancies as *last Tuesday* or *next Tuesday*. The past, present or future tense used for the verb usually provides adequate indication of which Tuesday is meant: *He said he finished the job Tuesday. She will return Tuesday.*

Avoid awkward placements of the time element, particularly those that suggest the day of the week is the object of a transitive verb: *The police jailed Tuesday.* Potential remedies include the use of the word *on* (see the **on** entry), rephrasing the sentence, or placing the time element in a different sentence.

See **today, tonight** for further discussion, including usage other than in news stories.

time of day The exact time of day that an event has happened or will happen is not necessary in most stories. Follow these guidelines to determine when it should be included and in what form:

SPECIFY THE TIME:
— Whenever it gives the reader a better picture of the scene: Did the earthquake occur when people were likely to be home asleep or at work? A clock reading for the time in the datelined community is acceptable although *pre-dawn hours* or *rush hour* often is more illustrative.
— Whenever the time is critical to the story: When will the rocket be launched? When will a major political address be broadcast? What is the deadline for meeting a demand?

DECIDING ON CLOCK TIME: When giving a clock reading, use the time in the datelined community.

If the story has no dateline, use the clock time in force where the event happened or will take place.

The only exception is a nationwide story or tabular listing that involves television or radio programs. Always use Eastern time, followed by *EDT* or *EST*, and specify whether the program will be broadcast simultaneously nationwide or whether times will vary because of separate transmissions for different time zones. If practical, specify those times in a separate paragraph.

ZONE ABBREVIATIONS: Use *EST*, *CDT*, *PST*, etc., after a clock time only if:
— The story involves travel or other activities, such as the closing hour for polling places or the time of a televised speech, likely to affect people or developments in more than one time zone.
— The item involves television or radio programs. (See above.)
— The item has no dateline.
— The item is an advisory to editors.

CONVERT TO EASTERN TIME? Do not convert clock times from other time zones in the continental United States to Eastern time. If there is high interest in the precise time, add *CDT*, *PST*, etc., to the local reading to help readers determine their equivalent local time.

If the time is critical in a story from outside the continental United States, provide a conversion to Eastern time using this form: *The kidnappers set a 9 a.m. (3 a.m. EDT) deadline.*

See **time zones** for additional guidance on forms.

times Use figures except for *noon* and *midnight*. Use a colon to separate hours from minutes: *11 a.m., 1 p.m., 3:30 p.m., 9-11 a.m., 9 a.m. to 5 p.m.*

Avoid such redundancies as *10 a.m. this morning, 10 p.m. tonight* or *10 p.m. Monday night*. Use *10 a.m.* or *10 p.m. Monday*, etc., as required by the norms in time element.

The construction *4 o'clock* is acceptable, but time listings with *a.m.* or *p.m.* are preferred.

See **midnight**; **noon**; **numerals** and **time zones**.

time sequences Spell out: *50 hours, 23 minutes, 14 seconds.* When using the abbreviated form, as in sports statistics or similar agate use, or subsequent references, the form is: *2:30:21.65* (hours, minutes, seconds, tenths, hundredths).

timeshare (n.) A property with multiple owners who each has rights to use it at certain times of year; typically an apartment or condo-type unit located in a resort or vacation destination.

time zones Capitalize the full name of the time in force within a particular zone: *Eastern Standard Time, Eastern*

Daylight Time, Central Standard Time, etc.

Lowercase all but the region in short forms: *the Eastern time zone, Eastern time, Mountain time,* etc.

See **time of day** for guidelines on when to use clock time in a story.

Spell out *time zone* in references not accompanied by a clock reading: *Chicago is in the Central time zone.*

The abbreviations *EST, CDT*, etc., are acceptable on first reference for zones used within the continental United States, Canada and Mexico only if the abbreviation is linked with a clock reading: *noon EST, 9 a.m. PST.* (Do not set off the abbreviations with commas.)

Spell out all references to time zones not used within the contiguous United States: *When it is noon EDT, it is 1 p.m. Atlantic Standard Time and 8 a.m. Alaska Standard Time.*

One exception to the spelled-out form: *Greenwich Mean Time* may be abbreviated as *GMT* on second reference if used with a clock reading. See **GMT**.

tipoff (n. and adj.) **tip off** (v.)

titleholder

titles In general, confine capitalization to formal titles used directly before an individual's name.

The basic guidelines:

LOWERCASE: Lowercase and spell out titles when they are not used with an individual's name: *The president issued a statement. The pope gave his blessing.*

Lowercase and spell out titles in constructions that set them off from a name by commas: *The vice president, Kamala Harris, was elected in 2020. Pope Francis, the current pope,*

t

was born in Argentina.

FORMAL TITLES: Capitalize formal titles when they are used immediately before one or more names: *Pope Francis, President Joe Biden, Vice Presidents Yukari Nakamura and Vanessa Smith.*

A formal title generally is one that denotes a scope of authority, professional activity or academic activity: *Sen. Catherine Cortez Masto, Dr. Benjamin Spock, retired Gen. Colin Powell.*

Other titles serve primarily as occupational descriptions: *astronaut Sally Ride, poet Maya Angelou.*

A final determination on whether a title is formal or occupational depends on the practice of the governmental or private organization that confers it. If there is doubt about the status of a title and the practice of the organization cannot be determined, use a construction that sets the name or the title off with commas.

ABBREVIATED TITLES: The following formal titles are capitalized and abbreviated as shown when used before a name both inside and outside quotations: *Dr., Gov., Lt. Gov., Rep., Sen.* and certain military ranks listed in **military titles**.

All other formal titles are spelled out in all uses.

GOVERNMENT OFFICIALS: In stories with U.S. datelines, do not include *U.S.* before the titles of secretary of state or other government officials, except where necessary for clarity.

In stories with international datelines, include *U.S.* before the titles.

ROYAL TITLES: Capitalize *king, queen,* etc., when used directly before a name. See individual entries and **nobility**.

TITLES OF NOBILITY: Capitalize a full title when it serves as the alternate name for an individual. See **nobility**.

PAST AND FUTURE TITLES: A formal title that an individual formerly held, is about to hold or holds temporarily is capitalized if used before the person's name. But do not capitalize the qualifying word: *former Secretary of State Condoleezza Rice, deposed King Constantine, Attorney General-designate Griffin B. Bell, acting Mayor Peter Barry.*

LONG TITLES: Separate a long title from a name by a construction that requires a comma: *Omar Robinson, the undersecretary for economic affairs, spoke.* Or: *The undersecretary for economic affairs, Omar Robinson, spoke.*

UNIQUE TITLES: If a title applies only to one person in an organization, insert the word *the* in a construction that uses commas: *Adama Bimou, the deputy vice president, spoke.*

ADDITIONAL GUIDANCE: Many commonly used titles and occupational descriptions are listed separately in this book, together with guidelines on whether and/or when they are capitalized. In these entries, the phrases *before a name* or *immediately before a name* are used to specify that capitalization applies only when a title is not set off from a name by commas.

See **academic titles; composition titles; legislative titles; military titles; and religious titles**.

today, tonight Use the day of the week, not *today* or *tonight*, in news stories. In news stories, use *today* or *tonight* only in direct quotations, and in phrases that do not refer to a specific day: *Customs today are different from those of a century ago.*

In other types of writing, *today, this morning, this afternoon* and *tonight* are acceptable if using the day of the week would be awkward. For example, in an internal note Wednesday to company staff: *Xin Chen took over as vice president for human resources today*. In an external announcement: *Xin Chen took over as vice president for human resources Wednesday*.

See **time element**.

tomorrow Use only in direct quotations and in phrases that do not refer to a specific day: *The world of tomorrow will need additional energy resources*.

Use the day of the week in other cases.

ton There are three types:

A *short ton* is equal to 2,000 pounds.

A *long ton*, also known as a *British ton*, is equal to 2,240 pounds.

A *metric ton* is equal to 1,000 kilograms, or approximately 2,204.62 pounds.

See **metric system**.

See **kiloton** for units used to measure the power of nuclear explosions.

Tony Awards The most prestigious awards for Broadway shows of the past season, presented by The Broadway League and the American Theatre Wing, both based in New York City. Plural form: *the Tonys*.

top Capitalize the word top if it's part of the formal name of a list or a shortened version of a formal list: *The AP Top 25, Spotify's Global Top 50; the rapper has a number of Top 10 pop hits*. Lowercase in informal uses: *It's widely regarded as one of the top five restaurants in the city*.

Tory, Tories An exception to the normal practice when forming the plural of a proper name ending in *y*.

The words are acceptable on second reference to the Conservative Party in Britain and its members.

total, totaled, totaling The phrase *a total of* often is redundant.

It may be used, however, to avoid a figure at the start of a sentence: *A total of 650 people were killed in holiday traffic accidents*.

touch screen (n.) **touch-screen** (adj.)

Tourette syndrome A neurological disorder characterized by involuntary, repetitive movements and vocalizations.

toward Not *towards*.

town Apply the capitalization principles in **city**.

town council Apply the capitalization principles in **city council**.

toxic substances, toxins A *toxic substance* is one that is likely to be poisonous, depending on the amount of exposure to it. *Toxins* are poisonous substances that come from plants or animals.

trademark A trademark is a brand, symbol, word, etc., used by a manufacturer or dealer and protected by law to prevent a competitor from using it: *AstroTurf*, for a type of artificial grass, for example.

In general, use a generic equivalent unless the trademark name is essential to the story.

Many trademarks are listed

t

separately in this book, together with generic equivalents.

The International Trademark Association, located in New York, is a helpful source of information about trademarks. See **brand names**.

traffic, trafficked, trafficking

trans- The rules in **prefixes** apply, but in general, no hyphen. Some examples:

*transcontinental transsship
transmigrate trans-Siberian
transoceanic*

Also: *trans-Atlantic* and *trans-Pacific*. These are exceptions to Webster's New World College Dictionary in keeping with the general rule that a hyphen is needed when a prefix precedes a capitalized word.

transfer, transferred, transferring

transgender (adj.) See **gender, sex and sexual orientation**. Follow guidelines for **obscenities, profanities, vulgarities** as appropriate.

Transportation Communications International Union Formerly the Brotherhood of Railway, Airline and Steamship Clerks, Freight Handlers, Express and Station Employees. *TCU* is acceptable on second reference.

Headquarters is in Rockville, Maryland.

transsexual Do not use. See **gender, sex and sexual orientation**.

transvestite Use *cross-dresser* instead.

trauma Avoid the vague medical jargon *trauma* when it is possible to use more specific words like *injury*, *wound*, *bruise* or *shock*. Acceptable in medical diagnoses such as *traumatic brain injury* or *post-traumatic stress disorder*, and in references to emotional injury. See **disabilities**.

travelogue Not *travelog*.

travel, traveled, traveling, traveler

treasurer Capitalize when used as a formal title immediately before a name. See **titles**.

Caution: The secretary of the U.S. Department of the Treasury is not the same person as the U.S. treasurer.

Treasurys Securities sold by the federal government to investors to fund its operations, cover the interest on U.S. government debt and pay off maturing securities. Because they carry the full backing of the government, Treasurys are viewed as the safest investment.

trending (v. or adj.) Used to indicate that a particular topic, word, phrase or piece of content is getting a lot of attention on a social network, search engine or website. Do not use without context and explanation, including describing the location of users where the topic is trending. *The Oscars are trending worldwide on Twitter today.*

Trinidad and Tobago In datelines on stories from this nation, use a community name followed by either *Trinidad* or *Tobago* — but not both — depending on which island the community is located.

Trojan horse, Trojan War

troop, troops, troupe A *troop*, in its

singular form, is a group of people, often military, or animals. *Troops,* in the plural, means several such groups. But when the plural appears with a large number, it is understood to mean individuals: *There were an estimated 150,000 troops in Iraq.* (But not: *Three troops were injured.*)

Use *troupe* only for ensembles of actors, dancers, singers, etc.

Truman, Harry S. With a period after the initial. Truman once said there was no need for the period because the S did not stand for a name. Asked in the early 1960s about his preference, he replied, "It makes no difference to me."

AP style has called for the period since that time.

trustee A person to whom another's property or the management of another's property is entrusted.

Do not capitalize if used before a name.

trusty A prison inmate granted special privileges as a trustworthy person.

TSA PreCheck The Transportation Security Administration's expedited screening program that lets approved travelers get through airport security lines faster. *TSA* is acceptable on first reference in this usage, but spell out the agency's full name later. In other uses, *TSA* should be used only on second reference.

tsar Use *czar.*

T-shirt Acceptable to use *tee* on subsequent references.

tuberculosis *TB* is acceptable on second reference to describe this lung disease.

Turkmen, Turkmens Used to describe the people of Turkmenistan and neighboring regions. *He is Turkmen. They are Turkmens.*

turnpike Capitalize as part of a proper name: *the Pennsylvania Turnpike.* Lowercase *turnpike* when it stands alone.

See **highway designations**.

tweet (n. or v.) A short posting on Twitter.

21-gun salutes True 21-gun salutes are conducted not with rifles but with artillery batteries. In the United States, they are reserved for the arrivals and departures from military installations of the president, president-elect or former presidents, and for their funerals. Visiting foreign heads of state also receive 21-gun salutes. The firing of rifles three times at a military funeral is often incorrectly described as a 21-gun salute. Properly, it should be called a *rifle salute* or *the three volleys.*

20-something

24/7

twin towers The two tallest buildings in the World Trade Center complex destroyed in the 9/11 attack. Also lowercase *north tower* and *south tower.*

Twitter Inc. A social network on which users share text, photos, video and links with their followers, in short messages, or *tweets. Twitter* is acceptable on first reference. The verb is *to tweet, tweeted.* Twitter is based in San Francisco.

Twitter is used by many influential people, including

t

journalists, policymakers and celebrities. It is not necessarily reflective of the general population. Twitter can be a tool for gauging people's moods and interests, but it should not be a substitute for traditional interviews and reporting outside of Twitter. Also beware of judging an account's influence based solely on the number of followers. Some companies offer services to boost that number through the use of automatically generated accounts and other techniques.

two-by-four Spell out the noun, which refers to any length of untrimmed lumber approximately 2 inches thick by 4 inches wide.

typhoons Capitalize typhoon when it is part of the name that weather forecasters assign to a storm: *Typhoon Tilda.*

But use *it* and *its* — not *she, her* or *hers* — in pronoun references.

See **weather terms**.

t

u

U-boat A German submarine. Anything referring to a submarine should be *submarine* unless directly referring to a German vessel of World War I or II vintage.

UFO, UFOs Acceptable in all references for *unidentified flying object(s)*.

ultra- The rules in **prefixes** apply, but in general, no hyphen.

U.N. Use periods in *U.N.*, for consistency with U.S. within texts. In headlines, it's *UN* (no periods). See **United Nations**.

un- The rules in **prefixes** apply, but in general, no hyphen. Some examples:
un-American   unnecessary
unarmed   unshaven

under- The rules in **prefixes** apply, but in general, no hyphen. Some examples:
underdog   undersheriff
underground   undersold

undersecretary One word. See **titles**.

underwater In the housing industry, the term for homeowners who owe more on their mortgages than their homes are worth.

underway One word in all uses.

unemployment rate In the United States, this estimate of the number of unemployed residents seeking work is compiled monthly by the Bureau of Labor Statistics, an agency of the Labor Department.

Each month the bureau selects a nationwide cross section of the population and conducts interviews to determine the size of the U.S. workforce. The workforce is defined as the number of people with jobs and the number looking for jobs.

The unemployment rate is expressed as a percentage figure. The essential calculation involves dividing the total workforce into the number of people looking for jobs, followed by adjustments to reflect variable factors such as seasonal trends.

UNESCO Acceptable in all reference for the *United Nations Educational, Scientific and Cultural Organization*.

unfollow To remove an account from the list of accounts that populate one's feed on a social network.

unfriend To remove someone from a list of friends that one is connected to, usually on Facebook.

UNICEF Acceptable in all references for the *United Nations Children's Fund*. The words *International* and *Emergency*, originally part of the name, have been dropped.

unidentified flying object(s) *UFO* and *UFOs* are acceptable in all references.

Uniform Code of Military Justice The laws covering members of the

U.S. armed forces.

union Capitalize when used as a proper name of the Northern states during the Civil War: *The Union defeated the Confederacy*.

union names The formal names of unions may be condensed to conventionally accepted short forms that capitalize characteristic words from the full name followed by union in lowercase.

Follow union practice in the use of the word worker in shortened forms: United Auto Workers, United Mine Workers.

When worker is used generically, make autoworkers and steelworkers one word in keeping with widespread practice; use two words for other job descriptions: bakery workers, mine workers.

unique It means one of a kind. Do not describe something as *rather unique*, *most unique* or *very unique*.

United Arab Emirates Spell out on first reference in stories and in datelines. *UAE* (no periods) is acceptable on second reference.

United Auto Workers The shortened form of the United Automobile, Aerospace and Agricultural Implement Workers of America is acceptable in all references. Headquarters is in Detroit.

United Farm Workers Headquarters is in Keene, California.

United Kingdom It consists of *Great Britain* and *Northern Ireland*. *Great Britain* (or *Britain*) consists of *England*, *Scotland* and *Wales*. *Ireland* is independent of the *United Kingdom*.

The abbreviation *U.K.* is acceptable as a noun or adjective. Use *UK* (no periods) in headlines.
See **datelines**, **Ireland** and **England**.

United Mine Workers of America The shortened forms *United Mine Workers* and *United Mine Workers union* are acceptable in all references.

UMW and *Mine Workers* are acceptable on second reference.

Use *mine workers* or *miners*, lowercase, in generic references to workers in the industry.

Headquarters is in Washington.

United Nations Abbrev: *U.N.* (no space). Use periods in *U.N.*, for consistency with U.S. within texts. In headlines, it's *UN* (no periods).

In datelines: *UNITED NATIONS (AP)* —

Use *U.N. General Assembly*, *U.N. Secretariat* and *U.N. Security Council* in first references not under a United Nations dateline.

General Assembly, *the Secretariat* and *Security Council* are acceptable in all references under a United Nations dateline and on second reference under other datelines.

Lowercase *the assembly* and *the council* when they stand alone.
See **UNESCO** and **UNICEF**.

United Service Organizations *USO* is acceptable in all references.

United States Use periods in the abbreviation, *U.S.* within texts. In headlines, it's *US* (no periods).

United Steelworkers The shortened form of the *United Steel, Paper and Forestry, Rubber, Manufacturing, Energy, Allied Industrial and Service*

u

Workers International Union is acceptable in all references. Headquarters is in Pittsburgh.

unprecedented It means *having no precedent, unheard of.* Often misused.

-up Follow Webster's New World College Dictionary. Hyphenate if not listed there.

Some frequently used words (all are nouns, some also are used as adjectives):

breakup	*makeup*
call-up	*mix-up*
change-up	*mock-up*
checkup	*pileup*
cleanup	*pushup*
close-up	*roundup*
cover-up	*runners-up*
crackup	*setup*
follow-up	*shake-up*
frame-up	*shape-up*
grown-up	*smashup*
hang-up	*speedup*
holdup	*tie-up*
letup	*walk-up*
lineup	*windup*

Use two words when any of these occurs as a verb.

See **suffixes**.

up- The rules in **prefixes** apply, but in general, no hyphen.

uppercase One word (n., v., adj.) when referring to the use of capital letters, in keeping with printers' practice.

UPS Inc. Acceptable in all references to *United Parcel Service Inc.* Headquarters is in Atlanta.

upstage

upstate Always lowercase: *upstate New York.*

up-to-date, up to date Hyphenate as a compound modifier before a noun: *We bring you the most up-to-date news.* Otherwise, no hyphen: *Stay up to date with Stylebook Online. My calendar is up to date.*

upward Not *upwards.*

URL Acceptable in all references for *Uniform Resource Locator*, an internet address.

U.S. The abbreviation is acceptable as a noun or adjective for *United States.* In headlines, it's *US* (no periods).

USA No periods in the abbreviated form for *United States of America.*

U.S. Agency for International Development *USAID* is acceptable on second reference.

U.S. Air Force See **air force**; **military academies**; and **military titles**.

U.S. Army See **army**; **military academies**; and **military titles**.

USB Acceptable on all references for *universal serial bus*, used to designate a kind of standard interface for connecting peripherals to a computer. When the type of *USB* needs to be noted, use hyphen: *USB-C.*

U.S. Chamber of Commerce On second reference, *the Chamber* is acceptable. For a local chamber of commerce, capitalize the full name: *the Seattle Metropolitan Chamber of Commerce.* But on second reference, *the chamber* is lowercase.

U.S. Coast Guard See **coast guard**; **military academies**; and **military**

U

titles.

U.S. Conference of Mayors The members are the mayors of cities with 30,000 or more residents.

Use *the conference* or *the mayors' conference* on second reference.

There is no organization with the name *National Mayors' Conference*. See **National League of Cities**.

U.S. Court of Appeals The court is divided into 13 circuits.

REFERENCE FORMS: A phrase such as a *federal appeals court* is acceptable on first reference.

On first reference to the full name, use *U.S. Court of Appeals* or a full name: *8th U.S. Circuit Court of Appeals* or *the U.S. Court of Appeals for the 8th Circuit*.

U.S. Circuit Court of Appeals without a circuit number is a misnomer and should not be used.

In shortened and subsequent references: *the Court of Appeals, the 2nd Circuit, the appeals court, the appellate court(s), the circuit court(s), the court*.

Do not create nonexistent entities such as *the San Francisco Court of Appeals*. Make it *the U.S. Court of Appeals in San Francisco*.

JURISTS: The formal title for the jurists on the court is *judge*: *U.S. Circuit Judge Homer Thornberry* is preferred to *U.S. Appeals Judge Homer Thornberry*, but either is acceptable.

See **judge**.

U.S. Court of Appeals for the Armed Forces This court, not part of the judicial branch as such, is a civilian body established by Congress to hear appeals from actions of the Defense Department. It is based in Washington. (Formerly the U.S. Court of Military Appeals.)

U.S. Court of Appeals for the Federal Circuit Commonly known as the CAFC, it replaced U.S. Court of Claims and U.S. Court of Customs and Patent Appeals. It handles lawsuits against the federal government and appeals involving customs, patents and copyright. It is based in Washington.

U.S. Customs and Border Protection An agency of the Department of Homeland Security, it includes the Border Patrol. See **immigration, migration**.

U.S. District Courts There are 94. In shortened and subsequent references: *the District Court, the District Courts, the court*.

Judge is the formal title for District Court jurists: *U.S. District Judge Frank Johnson*. See **judge**.

user interface The features of a device, program or website that enable control by a user. *UI* is acceptable on second reference. It is a key element of *user experience*, or *UX*, which is a broader term referring to how people experience a given product or service.

U.S. Immigration and Customs Enforcement See **immigration, migration**.

U.S. Marshals Service No apostrophe.

USMCA Acceptable but not preferred on first reference for the *United States-Mexico-Canada Agreement*; provide the full name and a brief definition soon after the first reference. Until the shorthand becomes more broadly known, wording such as *the North American free trade agreement* (note lowercase) or the agreement's full name is preferred on first reference when possible. USMCA replaces the *North American Free Trade Agreement*, or *NAFTA*.

U.S. Navy See **navy**; **military academies**; and **military titles**.

U.S. Postal Service Use *U.S. Postal Service* or *the Postal Service* on first reference. Retain capitalization of *Postal Service* in subsequent references to the agency.

Lowercase *the service* when it stands alone. Lowercase *post office* in generic references to the agency and to an individual office: *I went to the post office.*

USS For *United States Ship*, *Steamer* or *Steamship*, preceding the name of a vessel: *the USS Iowa.*

In datelines:
ABOARD USS IOWA (AP) —

U.S. Tax Court This court handles appeals in tax cases.

U.S. territories Do not abbreviate the names of U.S. territories. There are 16 such territories; 11 of them are small islands, reefs or atolls in the Caribbean or the Pacific, without native populations. The others — Puerto Rico, the U.S. Virgin Islands, Guam, the Northern Mariana Islands and American Samoa — are self-governing, unincorporated territories. They send nonvoting representatives to the U.S. Congress.

Residents of Puerto Rico, the U.S. Virgin Islands, Guam and the Northern Marianas are U.S. citizens; American Samoans are considered noncitizen U.S. nationals. Residents of the territories cannot vote in presidential elections, though their delegates participate in national political conventions to choose the nominees.

For datelines, use the community followed by the unabbreviated name of the territory: *SAN JUAN, Puerto Rico.*

Uyghur A Turkic ethnic group native to China's northwest Xinjiang region. Most identify as Muslims. Use this spelling for the people and its language. The previous spelling, *Uighur*, was based on an earlier romanization of the language. Plural: *Uyghurs.*

u

V

vacation rental websites Sites such as Airbnb and Vrbo that connect people offering residences or rooms with others who want to rent them for short-term stays. Other descriptions include *short-term lodging service* or *a website that lists residences or rooms for short-term rental*. Do not call them *home-sharing sites* or *room-sharing sites*.

vaccine (n.), vaccination (n.) A *vaccine* is a product that stimulates the body's immune system to make antibodies and provide immunity against a specific virus or other germ. *Vaccination* is the act of giving a vaccine.

The terms are often interchangeable, since a person is receiving the *vaccine* while getting a *vaccination*. Use the term *vaccination* if needed to be specific about the act of giving or receiving the shot: *the city's vaccination schedule*, for example. The terms *immunization* and *vaccination* can generally be used interchangeably.

Don't refer to a *vaccine* as a *drug, medicine* or *serum*.

Coronavirus vaccines are made in a wide variety of ways. It's not necessary to include the type of vaccine, unless relevant, in most stories. Use the manufacturer's name if needed to distinguish between vaccines.

Do not say *anti-COVID-19 vaccine* or *anti-coronavirus vaccine*. Instead: *COVID-19 vaccine* (or *vaccination*) or *coronavirus vaccine* (or *vaccination*). The terms *COVID-19* and *coronavirus* are both acceptable as a modifier for the vaccine or vaccination.

Valentine's Day Feb. 14. Honors the saint martyred in third-century Rome. Sweethearts mark it by exchanging valentines.

Valium A trademark for a brand of tranquilizer and muscle relaxant. It also may be called *diazepam*.

valley Capitalize as part of a full name: *the Mississippi Valley*.

Lowercase in plural uses: *the Missouri and Mississippi valleys*.

vape, vaping Inhaling vapor from an *electronic cigarette* or other *vaping device* (not *vape device*). See **electronic cigarette**.

Vaseline A trademark for a brand of petroleum jelly.

V-E Day May 8, 1945, the day the surrender of Germany was announced, officially ending the European phase of World War II.

vegetative state A condition in which the eyes are open and can move, and the patient has periods of sleep and periods of wakefulness, but remains unconscious, unaware of self or others. The patient can't think, reason, respond, do anything on purpose, chew or swallow. Reaction to a sound or a sight is reflex. Also called *unresponsive wakefulness state*.

See **coma** and **minimally conscious state**.

V-8 The engine.

Velcro A trademark for a brand of fabric fastening products that can be pressed together or pulled apart. Use a generic term such as *fabric fastener*.

verbs The abbreviation *v.* is used in this book to identify the spelling of the verb forms of words frequently misspelled.

SPLIT FORMS: In many cases, splitting the infinitive or compound forms of a verb is necessary to convey meaning and make a sentence easy to read. Such constructions are acceptable. For example: *Those who lie are often found out. How has your health been? The budget was tentatively approved.* Let readability and comprehension be your guide. If splitting a verb results in an awkward sentence, don't do it. *She wants to write clearly*, not *She wants to clearly write.*

verses See **poetry** for guidelines on how to handle verses of poetry typographically.

versus Spell it out in ordinary speech and writing: *The proposal to revamp Medicare versus proposals to reform Medicare and Medicaid at the same time* ... In short expressions, however, the abbreviation *vs.* is permitted: *The issue of guns vs. butter has long been with us.*

For court cases, use *v.*: *Marbury v. Madison.*

Veterans Affairs Formerly Veterans Administration, it became Cabinet level in March 1989 with the full title Department of Veterans Affairs. *VA* (no periods) is still used on second reference.

Veterans Day Formerly Armistice Day, Nov. 11, the anniversary of the armistice that ended World War I in 1918.

The federal legal holiday, observed on the fourth Monday in October during the mid-1970s, reverted to Nov. 11 in 1978.

Veterans of Foreign Wars VFW is acceptable on second reference.

Headquarters is in Kansas City, Missouri.

veto, vetoes (n.) The verb forms: *vetoed, vetoing.*

vice Use two words: *vice admiral, vice chairman, vice chancellor, vice consul, vice president, vice principal, vice regent, vice secretary.*

Several are exceptions to Webster's New World College Dictionary. The two-word rule has been adopted for consistency in handling the similar terms.

vice versa

video game Two words in all uses.

video on demand Spell it out; do not use VOD.

video recording Term for digital audio and visual recording. Digital has largely replaced videotaping.

Vietnam War

vie, vied, vying

village Apply the capitalization principles in **city**.

Vimeo A video-sharing network formerly owned by the internet company IAC and now an

V

independent concern.

VIP, VIPs Acceptable in all references for *very important person(s)*.

Virgin Islands Use with a community name in datelines on stories from the U.S. Virgin Islands. Do not abbreviate.

Identify an individual island in the text if relevant.

See **datelines** and **British Virgin Islands**.

virtual private network A service that shields internet users by encrypting their data traffic, preventing others from observing their web browsing and other activities. Organizations use *VPNs* for secure communications over the public internet. Individuals can also use VPN services to mask their location in order to circumvent censorship or geography-based online viewing restrictions. *VPN* is acceptable on second reference.

virtual reality, augmented reality *Virtual reality* is a computer-generated simulation of an interactive, three-dimensional environment. *Virtual reality* experiences typically require the use of headsets, hand-held controllers and other electronic equipment that allow a person to interact with the simulation. A similar concept, *augmented reality*, involves the projection of interactive computer-generated images into a person's real-world surroundings. *VR* and *AR* are acceptable on second reference.

virus, worm A computer *virus* is any malicious, invasive program designed to infect and disrupt computers. A *worm* is a type of virus that spreads on networks such as the internet, copying itself from one computer to another without human intervention.

V-J Day Sept. 2, 1945, the day of formal surrender by Japan to Allied forces in World War II. Some commemorations recognized the date as Aug. 14, 1945, the day fighting with Japan ended and the armistice was declared, but the formal proclamation was not until Sept. 2.

Vodou, Voodoo Capitalize and use the spelling *Vodou* when referring specifically to the religion as it is practiced primarily in Haiti or among the Haitian community abroad. The spelling *Voodoo* has come to be seen as pejorative in those regions and should be avoided. However, the spelling *Voodoo* is commonly used and acceptable when referring to the religion as practiced in Louisiana. Avoid using either term as shorthand for magical or superstitious beliefs. For example, do not refer to *voodoo* (lowercase) *economics* unless essential in a direct quotation, or to *voodoo rituals* unless essential and with attribution and explanation.

voicemail

Voice of America *VOA* is acceptable on second reference.

vote-getter

vote tabulations Always use figures for the totals.

Spell out below 10 in other phrases related to voting: *by a five-vote majority, with three abstentions, four votes short of the necessary two-thirds majority*.

V

For results that involve fewer than 1,000 votes on each side, use these forms: *The House voted 230-205, a 230-205 vote.*

To make totals that involve more than 1,000 votes on a side easier to read, separate the figures with the word *to* to avoid hyphenated adjectival constructions. See **election returns** for examples.

V

W

waitlist (n.) **wait-list** (v.)

Wales Use *Wales* after the names of Welsh communities in datelines. See **datelines** and **United Kingdom**.

Wall Street When the reference is to the entire complex of financial institutions in the area rather than the actual street itself, *the Street* is an acceptable short form.

war Capitalize as part of the name of a specific conflict: *the Afghanistan War, the Iraq War, the Civil War, the Cold War, the Korean War, the Vietnam War, the War of 1812, World War I, World War II, the Gulf War.*

warden Capitalize as a formal title before a name. See **titles**.

wards Use figures. See **political divisions**.

-ward, -wards Virtually none of the words ending with this suffix end with an *s*: *backward, forward, toward, downward, upward, onward, outward, inward, southward, skyward, Earthward, heavenward, homeward.*

warhead

war horse, warhorse Two words for a horse used in battle.
One word for a veteran of many battles: *He is a political warhorse.*

warlord

wartime

Washington's Birthday Capitalize *birthday* in references to the holiday.
The date President George Washington was born is computed as Feb. 22. The federal legal holiday is the third Monday in February.
Some states and some organizations refer to it as *Presidents Day,* but the formal name has not changed.

watt A unit of power. Do not confuse with *watt-hour,* a unit of energy used to describe electricity consumed or generated over time.
A *watt* is often used to describe the peak or maximum capacity of an electric device, like a light bulb or a power generator. Think of it as a snapshot of a level of electric power at any moment. Common variants include kilowatt, (1,000 watts), megawatt (1 million watts) and gigawatt (1 billion watts). Abbreviations are *W, kW, MW, GW.*
Watt-hours are used to measure power over time. One *watt-hour* is one watt of power over one hour. Most people pay for electricity by the *kilowatt-hour.* Variants are *megawatt-hours* and *gigawatt-hours.* Abbreviations are *Wh, kWh, MWh, GWh.*
Press releases about power plants usually speak of a plant's power in megawatts. However, this is usually just a reference to the plant's peak power. Power plants, particularly those that rely on renewable resources such as sun or wind, don't generate power at peak rates consistently.

The best way to describe a plant's practical ability to generate electricity is to multiply its peak capacity in kilowatts or megawatts by the plant's capacity factor (a percentage that yields the *average* amount of power actually produced by the plant, rather than what it produces just at peak moments).

To determine how many homes can be powered by a plant, multiply the peak power by the capacity factor, then multiply by 8,760 (the number of hours in a year), then divide that by the average consumption of a home over a year in kilowatt hours. In the United States, an average home consumes about 11,000 kWh per year.

Another common unit of power is horsepower. One kilowatt equals 1.34 horsepower.

Waymo The self-driving vehicle subsidiary of Google's corporate parent, Alphabet Inc. Can be described as a Google spinoff, but it's no longer a part of Google. See **autonomous vehicles**.

weapons *Gun* is an acceptable term for any firearm. Note the following definitions and forms in dealing with weapons and ammunition:

semi-automatic rifle, assault rifle, assault weapon The preferred term for a rifle that fires each time the trigger is pulled is a *semi-automatic rifle*. The term does not convey any details about a rifle's appearance, which is not integral to its function.

Avoid *assault rifle* and *assault weapon*, which are highly politicized terms that generally refer to AR- or AK-style rifles designed for the civilian market, but convey little meaning about the actual functions of the weapon. Avoid the terms preferred by advocates and gun manufacturers, such as *military-style rifles* or *modern sporting rifles*.

When reporting on guns, do not automatically repeat terms used by authorities, witnesses or others. Witnesses will often misinterpret the sound of a rapidly fired gun or base a description on the look of the weapon. Instead, seek specific and detailed information from authorities, such as a gun's make, model, caliber and magazine capacity. For example, *Authorities said the shooter used a Smith & Wesson M&P15 rifle or Authorities said the man used an AR-style semi-automatic rifle with a 30-round magazine*. Where possible, state what the gun does: *Authorities say he used a MAC-10 machine pistol, which fires a bullet and quickly reloads every time the trigger is pulled. Use more generalized descriptions*, such as *rifle* or *handgun*, until such details become available.

Often, the most important detail about a weapon used in a crime is the size of its magazine. AR- and AK-style rifles generally have magazines that carry 10 to 30 rounds, but can be fitted with specialized magazines that hold far more.

The shorthand *AR* does not stand for "assault rifle," but for ArmaLite Rifle, a reference to the company that first designed it for military use. Some military versions of an AR-style rifle can be set to fire in an automatic mode.

An *automatic rifle* continuously fires rounds if the trigger is depressed and until its ammunition is exhausted.

Under the National Firearms Act, *automatic rifles* are restricted in the United States to the military, law enforcement and civilians who have obtained special licenses to

W

own such weapons (provided the weapons were manufactured before May 19, 1986).

anti-aircraft A cannon or other weapon designed for defense against air attack. The form: *a 105 mm anti-aircraft gun.*

artillery A carriage-mounted cannon.

automatic A firearm that reloads automatically after each shot. The term should not be used to describe the rate of fire. To avoid confusion, specify *fully automatic* or *semi-automatic* rather than simply automatic. Give the type of weapon or model for clarity.

bolt-action rifle A manually operated handle on the barrel opens and closes the breech, ejecting a spent round, loading another and cocking the weapon for triggering. Popular for hunting and target-shooting. Example: *Remington 700.* Some shotguns are bolt-action.

buckshot See **shot**.

bullet The projectile fired by a rifle, pistol or machine gun. Together with metal casing, primer and propellant, it forms a *cartridge.*

caliber A measurement of the diameter of the inside of a gun barrel except for most shotguns. Measurement is in either millimeters or decimal fractions of an inch. The word caliber is not used when giving the metric measurement. The forms: *a 9 mm pistol, a .22-caliber rifle.*

cannon A weapon, usually supported on some type of carriage, that fires explosive projectiles. The form: *a 105 mm cannon.* Plural is *cannons.*

carbine A short, lightweight rifle, usually having a barrel length of less than 20 inches. The form: *an M3 carbine.*

cartridge See **bullet**.

clip Do not use this term unless in a quote. The correct term is *magazine* to describe the device used to store multiple rounds of ammunition together as a unit, ready for insertion into a firearm. A *clip* is a device that stores rounds together that can then be used to load bullets into a *magazine.* See **magazine** for a fuller description.

Colt Named for Samuel Colt, it designates a make of weapon or ammunition developed for Colt handguns. The forms: *a Colt .45-caliber revolver, .45 Colt ammunition.*

fully automatic A firearm that fires continuously as long as the trigger is depressed. Examples include *machine guns* and *submachine guns.*

gauge The measure of the size of a shotgun. Gauge is expressed in terms of the number per pound of round lead balls with a diameter equal to the size of the barrel. The bigger the number, the smaller the shotgun.

The forms: *a 12-gauge shotgun, a .410 shotgun.* The .410 actually is a caliber, but commonly is called a gauge. The ball leaving the barrel is 0.41" in diameter.

handgun A *pistol* or a *revolver.*

howitzer A cannon shorter than a gun of the same caliber employed to fire projectiles at relatively high angles at a target, such as opposing forces behind a ridge. The form: *a 105 mm howitzer.*

lever-action rifle A handle on the stock ejects and loads cartridges and cocks the rifle for triggering. A firearm often associated with the Old West. Example: *Winchester 94.*

M1, M16 These and similar combinations of a letter and figure(s) designate rifles used by the military. The forms: *an M1 rifle, an M16 rifle.*

W

machine gun A fully automatic gun that fires as long as the trigger is depressed and bullets are chambered. Such a weapon is generally so large and heavy that it rests on the ground or a mount. A submachine gun is hand-held. The form: *a .50-caliber Browning machine gun*.

magazine The ammunition storage and feeding device within or attached to a firearm. It may be fixed to the firearm or detachable. It is not a *clip*.

Magnum A trademark for a type of high-powered cartridge with a larger case and a larger powder charge than other cartridges of approximately the same caliber. The form: *a .357 Magnum, a .44 Magnum*.

mortar Device used to launch a mortar shell; it is the shell, not the mortar, that is fired.

musket A heavy, large-caliber shoulder firearm fired by means of a matchlock, a wheel lock, a flintlock or a percussion lock. Its ammunition is a musket ball.

pistol A handgun that can be a single shot or a semi-automatic. Differs from a revolver in that the chamber and barrel are one integral part. Its size is measured in calibers. The form: *a .45-caliber pistol*.

revolver A handgun. Differs from a pistol in that cartridges are held in chambers in a cylinder that revolves through the barrel. The form: *a .45-caliber revolver*.

rifle A firearm designed or made to be fired from the shoulder and having a rifled bore. It uses bullets or cartridges for ammunition. Its size is measured in calibers. The form: *a .22-caliber rifle*.

Saturday night special A compact, relatively inexpensive handgun.

semi-automatic A firearm that fires only once for each pull of the trigger. It reloads after each shot. The form: *a semi-automatic rifle, a semi-automatic weapon, a semi-automatic pistol*. The hyphen is an exception to general guidance against hyphenating words formed with *semi-*. See **semi-automatic rifle, assault rifle, assault weapon**.

shell The word applies to military or naval ammunition and to shotgun ammunition. For small arms, bullet or round is the common term for ammunition.

shot Small lead or steel pellets fired by shotguns. A shotgun shell usually contains 1 to 2 ounces of shot. Do not use *shot* interchangeably with *buckshot*, which refers only to the largest shot sizes.

shotgun A firearm typically used to fire small spherical pellets called shot. *Shotguns* usually have a smooth bore barrel, but some contain a rifled barrel, which is used to fire a single projectile. Size is measured according to gauge, except for the .410, which is measured according to caliber, meaning the ball leaving the barrel is 0.41" in diameter. The form: *a 12-gauge shotgun, a .410 shotgun*.

silencer, suppressor A device that muffles the sound of a firearm. They are colloquially known as *silencers* but are more accurately referred to as *suppressors*.

The device reduces the sound a gun makes when it's fired but does not eliminate the sound. They generally lower the sound level by 20 to 35 decibels, making most firearms still louder than the average ambulance siren.

For clarity, describe the device as a *firearm suppressor*, and note that it is *generally known in generic terms as a silencer*.

To legally purchase the device,

W

it must be bought from a licensed dealer and the buyer must undergo an extensive background check. The background check, similar to what is required to purchase fully automatic weapons, is tightly regulated under the National Firearms Act of 1934.

Each suppressor carries a serial number that can be tracked.

Suppressors were invented in the early 1900s by MIT-educated Hiram Percy Maxim, who invented a muffler for gasoline engines. The devices were brought under National Firearms Act regulations after Depression-era game wardens were concerned hunters would use them to poach.

submachine gun A lightweight fully automatic gun firing handgun ammunition.

-wear *Activewear, daywear, eveningwear, eyewear, headwear, menswear, outerwear, sportswear, swimwear, womenswear.*

weather-beaten

weather terms The following (except for **storm names**) are based on definitions used by the National Weather Service. All temperatures are Fahrenheit. The federal weather glossary is at http://forecast.weather.gov/glossary.php

blizzard Wind speeds of 35 mph or more and considerable falling and/or blowing of snow with visibility of less than one-quarter mile for three or more hours.

coastal waters The waters within 100 miles of the coast, including bays, harbors and sounds.

cyclone A storm with strong winds rotating about a moving center of low atmospheric pressure.

The word sometimes is used in the United States to mean *tornado* and in the Indian Ocean area to mean *hurricane.*

degree-day A measure of the amount of heating or cooling needed for a building. It is based on the difference between the average daily temperature and 65 degrees. Positive values are cooling degree-days and negative values are heating degree-days.

derecho A widespread and usually fast-moving straight-line windstorm. It is usually more than hundreds of miles long and more than 100 miles across. Plural: *derechos.*

dew point The temperature to which air must be cooled for dew to form. The higher the *dew point*, the more moisture in the air.

dust devil A small, rapidly rotating wind that is made visible by the dust, dirt or debris it picks up. Also called a *whirlwind*, it develops best on clear, dry, hot afternoons.

dust storm Visibility of one-half mile or less due to dust, wind speeds of 30 mph or more.

El Nino, La Nina El Nino is a naturally occurring climate phenomenon that starts with unusually warm water in the central and eastern equatorial Pacific and then changes weather worldwide. The term refers to the interaction of that warmth with the atmosphere in the region, shifting currents in the air 5 to 10 miles above sea level. These shifts affect weather for thousands of miles, leading to storm tracks and belts of strong winds. El Nino is a cause of changes in weather, with the weather it brings best referred to as "effects of El Nino." Winter is often milder and wetter in much of the U.S., with heavier winter rains often hitting California from January through

W

March, especially during stronger El Nino periods. El Nino often, but not always, triggers droughts in places like Australia and India. Elsewhere, droughts are quenched and floods may replace them. The Pacific gets more hurricanes; the Atlantic fewer. The world warms, increasing Earth's already rising thermometer from climate change. The effects in the U.S. usually don't go that deep into spring.

The flip side of El Nino is La Nina, which is an occasional but natural cooling of the equatorial Pacific that also changes weather worldwide. There is also a neutral stage with neither unusually warm water from an El Nino nor cool water from La Nina. La Nina's effects are often opposite of El Nino, so there are more hurricanes in the Atlantic and fewer in the Pacific. Parts of Australia and Indonesia get wetter. In the U.S., drier than normal conditions occur in the central Plains in the fall and the Southeast in the winter, while the Pacific Northwest is likely to be wetter than normal.

flash flood A sudden, violent flood. It typically occurs after a heavy rain or the melting of a heavy snow.

flash flood warning Warns that flash flooding is imminent or in progress or is highly likely. Those in the affected area should take necessary precautions immediately.

flash flood watch Alerts the public that conditions are favorable for flash flooding. Those in the affected area are urged to be ready to take additional precautions if a flash flood warning is issued or if flooding is observed.

flood Stories about floods usually tell how high the water is and where it is expected to crest. Such a story should also, for comparison, list flood stage and how high the water is above, or below, flood stage.

Wrong: *The river is expected to crest at 39 feet.*

Right: *The river is expected to crest at 39 feet, 12 feet above flood stage.*

freeze Describes conditions when the temperature at or near the surface is expected to be below 32 degrees during the growing season. Adjectives such as *severe* or *hard* are used if a cold spell exceeding two days is expected. A *hard freeze* is when the temperature drops to 28 degrees in areas that don't normally freeze.

A freeze may or may not be accompanied by the formation of frost. However, use of the term *freeze* usually is restricted for occasions when wind or other conditions prevent frost.

freezing drizzle, freezing rain A drizzle or rain that falls as a liquid but freezes into glaze upon contact with the cold ground or surface structures.

frost Describes the formation of very small ice crystals, which might develop under conditions similar to dew except for the minimum temperatures involved. Phrases such as *frost in low places* or *scattered light frost* are used when appropriate.

funnel cloud A violent, rotating column of air that does not touch the ground, usually a pendant from a cumulonimbus cloud.

gale Sustained winds within the range of 39 to 54 mph (34 to 47 knots).

hail Showery precipitation in the form of irregular pellets or balls of ice more than 5 mm in diameter, falling from a cumulonimbus cloud.

heavy snow It generally means:
a. A fall accumulating to 4 inches

W

or more in depth in 12 hours, or

b. A fall accumulating to 6 inches or more in depth in 24 hours.

high wind Normally indicates that sustained winds of 40 mph or greater are expected to last one hour or longer; or winds of 58 mph regardless of how long they last.

hurricane categories Hurricanes are ranked 1 to 5 according to what is known as the Saffir-Simpson Hurricane Wind Scale.

Category 1 — Hurricane has winds of 74 to 95 mph. Some damage will occur.

Category 2 — Winds from 96 to 110 mph. Extensive damage will occur.

Category 3 — Winds from 111 to 129 mph. Devastating damage will occur.

Category 4 — Winds from 130 to 156 mph. Catastrophic damage will occur.

Category 5 — Winds of 157 mph or higher. Catastrophic damage will occur.

Only four *Category 5* storms have hit the mainland United States since record keeping began: the 1935 Labor Day hurricane that hit the Florida Keys and killed 600 people; Hurricane Camille, which devastated the Mississippi coast in 1969, killing 256 and causing $1.4 billion in damage; Hurricane Andrew, which hit South Florida in 1992, killing 43 and causing $30.5 billion in damage; and Hurricane Michael, which was classified as Category 4 when it hit Florida's Gulf Coast on Oct. 10, 2018, but was later reclassified as Category 5. Michael was directly responsible for 16 U.S. deaths and about $25 billion in damage. Hurricane Katrina in 2005 reached Category 5 in open water but hit the coast as a Category 3. Most estimates put the death toll

in Katrina at more than 1,800 people, although some estimates are lower depending what deaths are included in the total. The storm caused more than $100 billion in damage; some later estimates peg that number at over $150 billion.

Categories 3, 4 and 5 hurricanes are considered major hurricanes.

hurricane eye The relatively calm area in the center of the storm. In this area winds are light and the sky often is covered only partly by clouds.

hurricane or typhoon A warm-core tropical cyclone in which the minimum sustained surface wind is 74 mph or more.

Hurricanes are spawned east of the international date line. Typhoons develop west of the line. They are known as cyclones in the Indian Ocean and Australia.

When a hurricane or typhoon loses strength (wind speed), usually after landfall, it is reduced to *tropical storm* status.

hurricane season The portion of the year that has a relatively high incidence of hurricanes. In the Atlantic, Caribbean and Gulf of Mexico, this is from June through November. In the eastern Pacific, it is May 15 through Nov. 30. In the central Pacific, it is June 1 through Nov. 30.

hurricane warning An announcement that sustained winds of 74 mph (119 km/hr) or higher are expected somewhere within the specified area in association with a tropical, subtropical or post-tropical cyclone. The warning is issued 36 hours before tropical-storm-force winds are expected to arrive.

hurricane watch An announcement that sustained winds of 74 mph (119 km/hr) or higher

W

are possible within the specified area in association with a tropical, subtropical or post-tropical cyclone. A hurricane watch is issued 48 hours in advance of the expected onset of tropical-storm-force winds.

ice storm warning Reserved for occasions when significant, and possibly damaging, accumulations of ice are expected.

ice storm, freezing drizzle, freezing rain Describes the dangerous freezing of drizzle or rain on objects as it strikes them. *Freezing drizzle* and *freezing rain* are synonyms for *ice storm*. Significant accumulations, which can take down power lines, are usually one-quarter of an inch or greater.

microburst Occurs when a mass of cooled air rushes downward out of a thunderstorm, hits the ground and rushes outward in all directions. Peak winds last less than five minutes and are less 2.5 miles wide. A plane flying through a *microburst* at low altitude, as on final approach or takeoff, would at first experience a strong headwind and increased lift, followed by a strong tail wind and sharply decreased lift.

monsoon Usually refers to a regular season of heavy rain and wind for a particular region, such as in India or Arizona and New Mexico. It is a seasonal warm wind created by temperature difference on land and nearby ocean. It reverses directions with the seasons, so there are dry phases of monsoons, but people don't usually think of the seasonal dry period as a monsoon.

National Hurricane Center The National Weather Service's National Hurricane Center in Miami has overall responsibility for tracking and providing information about tropical depressions, tropical storms and hurricanes in the Atlantic Ocean, Gulf of Mexico, Caribbean Sea and eastern Pacific Ocean.

The service's Central Pacific Hurricane Center in Honolulu is responsible for hurricane information in the Pacific Ocean area north of the equator from 140 degrees west longitude to 180 degrees.

Online: www.nhc.noaa.gov

nearshore waters The waters extended to 5 miles from shore.

nor'easter The term used by the National Weather Service for storms that either exit or move north along the East Coast, producing winds blowing from the northeast.

offshore waters The waters extending to about 250 miles from shore.

polar vortex Usually refers to the gigantic circular upper air weather pattern in the Arctic region, enveloping the North Pole (but it can apply to the South Pole, too). It is a normal pattern that is stronger in the winter and keeps some of the coldest weather bottled up near the North Pole. The jet stream usually pens the polar vortex in and keeps it north. But at times some of the vortex can break off or move south, bringing unusually cold weather south and permitting warmer weather to creep up north.

rainstorm A storm with heavy rain. Do not call it a *rain event*.

sandstorm Visibility of one-half mile or less due to sand blown by winds of 30 mph or more.

Santa Ana wind In Southern California, a weather condition in which strong, hot, dry, dust-bearing winds descend to the Pacific Coast from inland desert regions.

severe thunderstorm Describes

W

either of the following:

a. Winds — Thunderstorm-related surface winds sustained or gusts 58 mph or greater.

b. Hail — Surface hail 1 inch in diameter or larger. The word *hail* in a watch implies hail at the surface and aloft unless qualifying phrases such as *hail aloft* are used.

sleet (one form of ice pellet) Describes generally solid grains of ice formed by the freezing of raindrops or the refreezing of largely melted snowflakes before reaching the ground. Sleet, like small hail, usually bounces when hitting a hard surface.

sleet (heavy) Heavy sleet is a fairly rare event in which the ground is covered to a depth of one-half inch or more or a depth of significance to motorists and others.

squall A sudden increase of wind speed by at least 18 mph (16 knots) and rising to 25 mph (22 knots) and lasting for at least one minute.

storm names Major storm names provided by government weather agencies, the European Union or the World Meteorological Organization

Heat index

TEMP. F	40%	45%	50%	55%	60%	65%	70%	75%	80%	85%	90%	95%	100%
110	136												
108	130	137											
106	124	130	137										
104	119	124	130	137			APPARENT TEMPERATURE						
102	114	119	124	130	137								
100	109	114	118	124	129	136							
98	105	109	113	117	123	128	134						
96	101	104	108	112	116	121	126	132					
94	97	100	102	106	110	114	119	124	129	135			
92	94	96	99	101	105	108	112	116	121	126	131		
90	91	93	95	97	100	103	106	109	113	117	122	127	132
88	88	89	91	93	95	98	100	103	106	110	113	117	121
86	85	87	88	89	91	93	95	97	100	102	105	108	112
84	83	84	85	86	88	89	90	92	94	96	98	100	103
82	81	82	83	84	84	85	86	88	89	90	91	93	95
80	80	80	81	81	82	82	83	84	84	85	86	86	87

RELATIVE HUMIDITY

Wind chill factor

AIR TEMPERATURE

WIND MPH	40	35	30	25	20	15	10	5	0	-5	-10	-15	-20	-25	-30	-35	-40	-45
5	36	31	25	19	13	7	1	-5	-11	-16	-22	-28	-34	-40	-46	-52	-57	-63
10	34	27	21	15	9	3	-4	-10	-16	-22	-28	-35	-41	-47	-53	-59	-66	-72
15	32	25	19	13	6	0	-7	-13	-19	-26	-32	-39	-45	-51	-58	-64	-71	-77
20	30	24	17	11	4	-2	-9	-15	-22	-29	-35	-42	-48	-55	-61	-68	-74	-81
25	29	23	16	9	3	-4	-11	-17	-24	-31	-37	-44	-51	-58	-64	-71	-78	-84
30	28	22	15	8	1	-5	-12	-19	-26	-33	-39	-46	-53	-60	-67	-73	-80	-87
35	28	21	14	7	0	-7	-14	-21	-27	-34	-41	-48	-55	-62	-69	-76	-82	-89
40	27	20	13	6	-1	-8	-15	-22	-29	-36	-43	-50	-57	-64	-71	-78	-84	-91
45	26	19	12	5	-2	-9	-16	-23	-30	-37	-44	-51	-58	-65	-72	-79	-86	-93
50	26	19	12	4	-3	-10	-17	-24	-31	-38	-45	-52	-60	-67	-74	-81	-88	-95
55	25	18	11	4	-3	-11	-18	-25	-32	-39	-46	-54	-61	-68	-75	-82	-89	-97
60	25	17	10	3	-4	-11	-19	-26	-33	-40	-48	-55	-62	-69	-76	-84	-91	-98

APPARENT TEMPERATURE

FROSTBITE TIME   30 MIN.   10 MIN.   5 MIN.

W

are acceptable. Do not use names created by private weather agencies or other organizations. See **fire names**.

storm surge An abnormal rise of water above the normal tide, generated by a storm.

storm tide Water level rise due to the combination of storm surge and the astronomical tide.

tidal wave Often used incorrectly as a synonym for *tsunami*. A large wave created by rising tide in a funnel-shaped inlet is called a *tidal bore*. Unusually large waves at sea are sometimes called *rogue waves*.

tornado A violent rotating column of air forming a pendant, usually from a cumulonimbus cloud, and touching the ground. It is often, but not always, visible as a funnel cloud, and usually is accompanied by a loud roaring noise. On a local scale, it is the most destructive of all atmospheric phenomena. Tornadoes can appear from any direction, but in the U.S. most move from southwest to northeast.

Tornado strength is measured by an enhanced F-scale rating from EF0 to EF5, which considers 28 different types of damage to structures and trees. It updates the original scale, which estimated wind strength. An EF2 or higher is considered a significant tornado.

Plural is *tornadoes*.

tornado warning A *tornado warning* is issued by a local National Weather Service office to warn the public of an existing tornado.

tornado watch A *tornado watch* alerts the public to the possibility of a tornado in the next several hours.

traveler's advisory Alerts the public that difficult traveling or hazardous road conditions are expected to be widespread.

tropical depression A tropical cyclone in which the maximum sustained surface wind is 38 mph (33 knots) or less.

tropical storm A warm-core tropical cyclone in which the maximum sustained surface winds range from 39 to 73 mph (34 to 63 knots) inclusive.

tsunami (s.), **tsunamis** (pl.) A great sea wave or seismic sea wave caused by an underwater disturbance such as an earthquake, landslide or volcano. It can cause massive death and destruction as was seen in the Indian Ocean *tsunami* in December 2004. It is different from a tidal wave.

typhoon See **hurricane or typhoon** in this listing.

waterspout A tornado over water.

wind chill factor No hyphen.

The *wind chill* is a calculation that describes the combined effect of the wind and cold temperatures on exposed skin. The *wind chill factor* would be minus 4, for example, if the temperature was 15 degrees and the wind was blowing at 25 mph — in other words, a temperature of 4 below zero with no wind.

The higher the wind at a given temperature, the lower the wind chill reading, although wind speeds above 40 mph have little additional cooling effect.

wind shear A sudden shift in wind direction and/or speed.

windstorm A storm with heavy wind but little or no precipitation. Do not call it a *wind event*.

winter storm warning Notifies the public that a winter storm is producing, or is forecast to produce, heavy snow or significant ice accumulations.

winter storm watch Alerts the public that there is a potential

W

for heavy snow or significant ice accumulations. The watch is usually issued at least 24 to 36 hours in advance.

web Short form of *World Wide Web*, it is a part of the internet that enables the distribution of image-rich content and information. The web is not the same as the internet, but is a subset; other applications, such as email, exist on the internet. Also, *website, webcam, webcast, webfeed, webmaster, webpage*. But *web address, web browser*. See **internet**.

web browser Software for viewing and interacting with websites on a computer or another device.

website Also, *webcam, webcast, webpage, webfeed, the web*.

Webster's New World College Dictionary See **dictionaries**.

WeChat Messaging service owned by Chinese tech giant Tencent. Popular mostly in mainland China and known as *Weixin* in Chinese. Notable for combining functions and services that are traditionally separated elsewhere. WeChat offers basic chat features such as instant messaging and calling, and hosts group chats where users can discuss topics like sports, technology, social issues, investments and celebrities. *WeChat* also lets people pay for movies, food delivery, public transit and utility bills, donate to charities, and split restaurant checks with friends.

WeChat lacks end-to-end encryption found in *Signal*, Meta's *WhatsApp* and *Messenger* and Apple's *iMessages*. Chinese dissidents and activists have long suspected that authorities are able to monitor what they have been saying on the services. The company has denied keeping a record of user chats.

weeklong, weekslong One word as an adjective.

weights Use figures: *The baby weighed 9 pounds, 7 ounces. She had a 9-pound, 7-ounce boy.*

West, Western, west, western Use *West* to describe the 13-state region as defined by the U.S. Census Bureau that is broken into two divisions. Capitalize *Western* as an adjective describing the region.

The eight *Mountain* states are Arizona, Colorado, Idaho, Montana, Nevada, New Mexico, Utah and Wyoming.

The five *Pacific* states are Alaska, California, Hawaii, Oregon and Washington.

Capitalize *Western* for the film and book genre and certain genres of music: *Western swing*. But lowercase in *country-western* to avoid mixed cases. Capitalize *Old West* when referring to the 19th-century American frontier.

Capitalize *West* and *Western* when referring to the cultural and political region constituting the Western Hemisphere and Europe.

For directions, *west* and *western*. See **directions and regions**. See **Midwest**, **Northeast** and **South** for the bureau's other regional breakdowns. See **country music**.

Western Hemisphere The continents of North and South America, and the islands near them.

It frequently is subdivided as follows:

Caribbean The islands from the tip of Florida to the continent of South America, plus French Guiana, Guyana and Suriname on the northeastern coast of South America.

Major island elements are Cuba, Hispaniola (the island shared by the Dominican Republic and Haiti), Jamaica, Puerto Rico, and the West Indies islands.

Central America The narrow strip of land between Mexico and Colombia. Located there are Belize, Costa Rica, El Salvador, Guatemala, Honduras, Nicaragua and Panama.

Latin America The area of the Americas south of the United States where Romance languages (those derived from Latin) are dominant. It applies to most of the region south of the United States except areas with a British heritage: the Bahamas, Barbados, Belize, Grenada, Guyana, Jamaica, Trinidad and Tobago, and various islands in the West Indies. Suriname, the former Dutch Guiana, is an additional exception.

North America Canada, Mexico, the United States and the Danish territory of Greenland. When the term is used in more than its continental sense, it also may include the islands of the Caribbean.

South America Argentina, Bolivia, Brazil, Chile, Colombia, Ecuador, Paraguay, Peru, Uruguay, Venezuela, and in a purely continental sense, French Guiana, Guyana and Suriname. Politically and psychologically, however, the latter three regard themselves as part of the Caribbean.

West Indies An island chain extending in an eastward arc between the southeastern United States and the northern shore of South America, separating the Caribbean Sea from the Atlantic Ocean and including the Bahamas,

the Greater Antilles, and the Lesser Antilles.

Major island elements are the nations of Barbados, Grenada, and Trinidad and Tobago, plus smaller islands dependent in various degrees on:

— Britain: British Virgin Islands, Anguilla, and the West Indies Associated States, including Antigua, Dominica, St. Lucia, St. Vincent and St. Christopher-Nevis.

— France: Guadeloupe (composed of islands known as Basse-Terre and Grande-Terre, plus five other islands) and Martinique.

— Netherlands: Netherlands Antilles, composed of Aruba, Bonaire, Curacao, Saba, St. Eustatius and the southern portion of St. Martin Island (the northern half is held by France and is part of Guadeloupe).

— United States: U.S. Virgin Islands, principally St. Croix, St. John and St. Thomas.

Western Wall See entry in the **Religion** chapter.

West Point Acceptable on second reference to the *U.S. Military Academy*.
See **military academies**.
In datelines:
WEST POINT, N.Y. (AP) —

WhatsApp Messaging service owned by Meta Platforms Inc.

wheat It is measured in bushels domestically, in metric tons for international trade.

There are 36.7 bushels of wheat in a metric ton.

wheelchair user People use

W

wheelchairs for independent mobility. Do not use *confined to a wheelchair* or *wheelchair-bound*. If a wheelchair is needed and that fact is relevant to the story, make sure the relevance is clear. See **disabilities**.

wherever

which See **essential clauses, nonessential clauses**; **that, which**; and **who, whom**.

whip Capitalize when used as a formal title before a name. See **legislative titles** and **titles**.

whistleblower

white paper Two words, lowercase, when used to refer to a special report.

WHO The World Health Organization is the specialized health agency of the United Nations and is based in Geneva. It sets internationally accepted guidelines for treating diseases and coordinates responses to disease outbreaks globally. WHO is acceptable on second reference and takes a singular verb.

wholesale price index A measurement of the changes in the average prices that businesses pay for a selected group of industrial commodities, farm products, processed foods and feed for animals.

Do not capitalize when referring to the U.S. producer price index, issued monthly by the Bureau of Labor Statistics, an agency of the Labor Department.

who's, whose *Who's* is a contraction for *who is*, not a possessive: *Who's there?*

Whose is the possessive: *I do not know whose coat it is.*

who, whom *Who* is the pronoun used for references to human beings and to animals with a name. Write *the person who is in charge*, not *the person that is in charge*.

Who is grammatically the subject (never the object) of a sentence, clause or phrase: *The woman who rented the room left the window open. Who is there?*

Whom is used when someone is the object of a verb or preposition: *The woman to whom the room was rented left the window open. Whom do you wish to see?*

See **essential clauses, nonessential clauses** for guidelines on how to punctuate clauses introduced by *who, whom, that* and *which*. Also see **that, which (pronouns)**.

-wide No hyphen.

wide- Usually hyphenated. Some examples:
wide-angle   *wide-eyed*
wide-awake   *wide-open*
wide-brimmed
Exception: *widespread*.

widget In a technology context, a small module with a specific purpose that appears on a website, desktop or other interface and allows access to content or functions.

widow, widower In obituaries: A man is *survived by his wife*. A woman is *survived by her husband*.

In same-sex marriages, a man is *survived by his husband*. A woman is *survived by her wife*.

Guard against the redundant *widow (widower) of the late*.

Wi-Fi A wireless communications technology often used to connect to home and business networks, which in turn connect to the internet. Wi-Fi has a shorter range than cellular technology but is convenient for sharing one internet connection among multiple devices. A Wi-Fi connection is sometimes called a *hot spot*.

The speed of Wi-Fi connections has improved with each generation. As of early 2022, the latest version of Wi-Fi was called Wi-Fi 6E, a consumer-friendly rebranding of older and more technical references. Earlier versions of Wi-Fi such as 802.11ax, 802.11ac and 802.11n are now known respectively as WiFi 6, Wi-Fi 5 and Wi-Fi 4.

A Wi-Fi *router* manages the connection between the internet and local devices such as phones, computers and smart speakers. An emerging technology known as a *mesh network* allows several Wi-Fi routers to work together as one, increasing the range of Wi-Fi signals as more routers are added to the network.

wiki Software that allows a group of users to add, delete, edit and share information on a website.

WikiLeaks

Wikipedia An online encyclopedia whose entries are created and edited by its users, regardless of their expertise. May contain useful links but should not be used as a primary source of information. It is operated by the nonprofit Wikimedia Foundation, based in San Francisco.

wildfires Use square miles to describe the size of fires. *The fire has burned nearly 4 1/2 square miles of hilly brush land.* Use acres only when the fire is less than a square mile. When possible, be descriptive: *The fire is the size of Denver.*

will See **shall, will** and **subjunctive mood**.

Windows Operating system made by Microsoft Corp.

wines Wine names for grape varietals, such as *chardonnay* and *shiraz*, are not capitalized. Wines named for regions, such as *Champagne* or *Chianti*, are capitalized.

wintertime

wireless A set of technologies for delivering data without wires. Common types include:

cellular Access comes through a phone company, such as Verizon or AT&T. Signals can travel far, offering broad coverage, but many phone plans offer a limited amount of data before charging extra.

Wi-Fi Access comes through a residential or business broadband provider, such as Comcast. The coverage range is shorter, but home plans typically offer unlimited data. Although Wi-Fi is a wireless technology, it typically connects to a home or business network that requires physical cables.

Bluetooth A short-range wireless technology for connecting devices directly to each other, such as a smartwatch to a phone.

NFC, or **near-field communication** A wireless technology that lets two devices nearby, such as phones or sensors, communicate with each other. Its best-known use is for *mobile payments*, in which placing

W

a phone near a payment reader at a store triggers the payment. *NFC* is acceptable in all references, but explain it.

Specify the type of wireless technology when that is pertinent to a story.

wiretap, wiretapper (n.) The verb forms: *wiretap, wiretapped, wiretapping*.

-wise No hyphen when it means *in the direction of* or *with regard to*. Some examples:

clockwise   *otherwise*
lengthwise   *slantwise*

Avoid contrived combinations such as *moneywise, religionwise*.

The word *penny-wise* is spelled with a hyphen because it is a compound adjective in which *wise* means *smart*, not an application of the suffix *-wise*. The same for *street-wise* in *the street-wise youth* (an exception to Webster's New World College Dictionary).

WMD Acceptable on second reference for *weapons of mass destruction*.

woman, women See **female, male**.

workbook, workday, workforce, workhorse, workout, workplace, worksheet, workstation, workweek

workers' compensation

working class (n.) **working-class** (adj.)

World Bank Acceptable in all references for *International Bank for Reconstruction and Development*.

World Health Organization *WHO* is

acceptable on second reference. Headquarters is in Geneva.

World Series Or *the Series* on second reference. A rare exception to the general principles under **capitalization**.

World Trade Center The complex of buildings that replaced the development of the same name destroyed on Sept. 11, 2001. The complex also includes the National September 11 Memorial & Museum and the transportation hub and shopping mall known as the Oculus. The tallest building is *One World Trade Center*. If necessary for clarity, refer to the *new World Trade Center complex*, or to the *old* or *destroyed trade center complex* or *twin towers*, or to *ground zero*. See **One World Trade Center** and **Sept. 11 memorial**.

World War I, World War II

worldwide

write-down (n. and adj.) **write down** (v.) An accounting step a company makes when an asset or class of assets it holds falls in value. The decline in value is reflected in a reduction on the asset side of a company's balance sheet.

write-in (n. and adj.) **write in** (v.)

wrongdoing

W

xyz

Xbox Video game console offered by *Microsoft Corp. Xbox* also refers to related game services such as *Xbox Live.*

Xmas Don't use this abbreviation for *Christmas.*

XML For *Extensible Markup Language*, used to sort, search and format information.

X-ray (n., v. and adj.) Use for both the photographic process and the radiation particles themselves.

Yahoo An online services provider owned by Verizon Communications Inc. Do not use the exclamation point in its formal name.

yard Equal to 3 feet. The metric equivalent is approximately 0.91 meter.
See **foot; meter;** and **distances**.

year-end (n. and adj.)

yearlong, yearslong One word as an adjective.

year-round (adj. and adv.)

years When a phrase refers to a month and day within the current year, do not include the year: *The hearing is scheduled for June 26.* If the reference is to a past or future year, include the year and set it off with commas: *Feb. 14, 2025, is the target date.* Use an s without an apostrophe to indicate spans of decades or centuries: *the 1890s, the 1800s.*
Years are an exception to the general rule in numerals that a figure is not used to start a sentence: *2013 was a very good year.*
See **A.D.; B.C.; century; historical periods and events; months** and **numerals**.

yesterday Use only in direct quotations and in phrases that do not refer to a specific day: *Yesterday we were young.*
Use the day of the week in other cases.

Yom Kippur The Jewish Day of Atonement. Occurs in September or October.

Young Men's Christian Association The term *the Y* is acceptable in all references to the main organization, which has its headquarters in Chicago. Use *YMCA* when referring to a specific location: *the YMCA of Greater Louisville.*

Young Women's Christian Association *YWCA* is acceptable in all references.
Headquarters is in New York.

youth Applicable to a boy or girl from age 13 until 18th birthday. Use *man* or *woman* for individuals 18 and older. See **boy, girl**.

YouTube Video-sharing service owned by Google, which bought it in 2006. It has helped promote videos ranging from educational to whimsical and made celebrities out of ordinary people.

The company has faced backlash over what some consider hate speech or harassment in videos. The service made several policy changes to attempt to cut down on harassment and threats, though questionable videos still slip through. Separately, Google and YouTube paid $170 million in 2019 to settle allegations in the U.S. that the video service failed to screen out children from using its service, thus violating a federal law that restricts data collection on children under 13.

Yukon A territorial section of Canada. Do not abbreviate. Use in datelines after the names of communities in the territory.

See **Canada**.

Yule, Yuletide Old English name for Christmas season. Uppercase is an exception to Webster's New World College Dictionary.

zero, zeros

zigzag

Zika A virus that can cause severe birth defects if a pregnant woman becomes infected. Most people infected with the Zika virus don't get sick, and those who do usually experience mild symptoms including fever, rash, joint pain and red eyes, and rarely, Guillain-Barre, a syndrome that causes temporary muscle weakness and sometimes paralysis. But during pregnancy, the Zika virus can cause miscarriage, stillbirth, and brain defects including microcephaly, in which babies are born with abnormally small heads because their brains didn't develop

properly.

Zika is primarily spread by a type of tropical mosquito called Aedes aegypti, which can pick up the virus from an infected person's blood. It also can be transmitted by sex. There are no treatments; testing of some experimental vaccines is underway. The virus is closely related to the dengue and yellow fever viruses. The link to birth defects didn't become apparent until a large Zika outbreak was reported in Brazil in 2015 and spread rapidly through Latin America and the Caribbean.

Usage: *the Zika virus* or just *Zika*.

ZIP code Use all-caps *ZIP* for *Zone Improvement Plan*, but always lowercase the word *code*.

Run the five digits together without a comma, and do not put a comma between the state name and the ZIP code: *New York, NY 10020*.

zip line

xyz

Punctuation

Incorrect punctuation can change the meaning of a sentence, the results of which could be far-reaching.

Even if the meaning is not changed, bad punctuation, however inconsequential, can cause the reader to lose track of what is being said and give up reading a sentence.

The basic guideline is to use common sense.

— Punctuation is to make clear the thought being expressed.

— If punctuation does not help make clear what is being said, it should not be there.

"The Elements of Style" by William Strunk Jr. and E.B. White says:

"Clarity, clarity, clarity. When you become hopelessly mired in a sentence, it is best to start fresh; do not try to fight your way through against terrible odds of syntax. Usually what is wrong is that the construction has become too involved at some point; the sentence needs to be broken apart and replaced by two or more shorter sentences."

This applies to punctuation. If a sentence becomes cluttered with commas, semicolons and dashes, start over.

These two paragraphs are full of commas and clauses; all of it equals too much for the reader to grasp:

The Commonwealth Games Federation, in an apparent effort to persuade other nations to ignore the spiraling boycott, ruled Sunday that Budd, a runner who has had a storied past on and off the track, and Cowley, a swimmer who competes for the University of Texas, were ineligible under the Commonwealth Constitution to compete for England in the 10-day event to be held in Edinburgh, Scotland, beginning July 24.

The decision on Budd, who has been the object of a number of demonstrations in the past, and Cowley followed an earlier announcement Sunday by Tanzania that it was joining Nigeria, Kenya, Ghana and Uganda in boycotting the games because of Britain's refusal to support economic sanctions against South Africa's government.

apostrophe (') Follow these guidelines:

POSSESSIVES: See the **possessives** entry in main section.

PLURAL NOUNS NOT ENDING IN S: Add 's: *the alumni's contributions, women's rights.*

PLURAL NOUNS ENDING IN S: Add only an apostrophe: *the churches' needs, the girls' toys, the horses' food, the ships' wake, states' rights, the VIPs' entrance.*

NOUNS PLURAL IN FORM, SINGULAR IN MEANING: Add only an apostrophe: *mathematics' rules, measles' effects.* (But see **INANIMATE OBJECTS** below.)

Apply the same principle when a plural word occurs in the formal name of a singular entity: *General Motors' profits, the United States' wealth.*

NOUNS THE SAME IN SINGULAR AND PLURAL: Treat them the same as plurals, even if the meaning is singular: *one corps' location, the two deer's tracks, the lone moose's antlers.*

SINGULAR NOUNS NOT ENDING IN S: Add 's: *the church's needs, the girl's toys, the horse's food, the ship's route, the VIP's seat.*

Some style guides say that singular nouns ending in s sounds such as *ce, x,* and *z* may take either the apostrophe alone or 's. See **SPECIAL EXPRESSIONS,** but otherwise, for consistency and ease in remembering a rule, always use 's if the word does not end in the letter s: *Butz's policies, the fox's den, the justice's verdict, Marx's theories, the prince's life, Xerox's profits.*

SINGULAR COMMON NOUNS ENDING IN S: Add 's: *the hostess's invitation, the hostess's seat; the witness's answer, the witness's story.* (A change from previous guidance calling for just an apostrophe if the next word begins with s.)

SINGULAR PROPER NAMES ENDING IN S: Use only an apostrophe: *Achilles' heel, Agnes' book, Ceres' rites, Descartes' theories, Dickens' novels, Euripides' dramas, Hercules' labors, Jesus' life, Jules' seat, Kansas' schools, Moses' law, Socrates' life, Tennessee Williams' plays, Xerxes' armies.* (An exception is *St. James's Palace.*)

SPECIAL EXPRESSIONS: The following exceptions to the general rule for words not ending in s apply to words that end in an s sound and are followed by a word that begins with s: *for appearance' sake, for conscience' sake, for goodness' sake.* Use 's otherwise: *the appearance's cost, my conscience's voice.*

PRONOUNS: Personal interrogative and relative pronouns have separate forms for the possessive. None involves an apostrophe: *mine, ours, your, yours, his, hers, its, theirs, whose.*

Caution: If you are using an apostrophe with a pronoun, always double-check to be sure that the meaning calls for a contraction: *you're, it's, there's, who's.*

Follow the rules listed above in forming the possessives of other pronouns: *another's idea, others' plans, someone's guess.*

COMPOUND WORDS: Applying the rules above, add an apostrophe or 's to the word closest to the object possessed: *the major general's decision, the major generals' decisions, the attorney general's request, the attorneys general's request.* See the **plurals** entry for guidelines on forming the plurals of these words.

Also: *anyone else's attitude, John Adams Jr.'s father, Benjamin Franklin of Pennsylvania's motion.* Whenever practical, however, recast the phrase to avoid ambiguity: *the motion by Benjamin Franklin of Pennsylvania.*

JOINT POSSESSION, INDIVIDUAL

POSSESSION: Use a possessive form after only the last word if ownership is joint: *Fred and Sylvia's apartment, Fred and Sylvia's stocks*.

Use a possessive form after both words if the objects are individually owned: *Fred's and Sylvia's books*.

DESCRIPTIVE PHRASES: Do not add an apostrophe to a word ending in *s* when it is used primarily in a descriptive sense: *citizens band radio, a Cincinnati Reds infielder, a teachers college, a Teamsters request, a writers guide*.

Memory aid: The apostrophe usually is not used if *for* or *by* rather than *of* would be appropriate in the longer form: *a radio band for citizens, a college for teachers, a guide for writers, a request by the Teamsters*.

An *'s* is required, however, when a term involves a plural word that does not end in *s*: *a children's hospital, a people's republic, the Young Men's Christian Association*.

DESCRIPTIVE NAMES: Some governmental, corporate and institutional organizations with a descriptive word in their names use an apostrophe; some do not. Follow the user's practice: *Actors' Equity, Diners Club, the National Governors Association*.

QUASI POSSESSIVES: Follow the rules above in composing the possessive form of words that occur in such phrases as *a day's pay, two weeks' vacation, three months' work, five years' probation*. The apostrophe is used with a measurement followed by a noun (a quantity of whatever the noun is). The examples could be rephrased as *a day of pay, two weeks of vacation, three months of work, five years of probation*.

No apostrophe when the quantity precedes an adjective: *six months pregnant, three weeks overdue, 11 years old*.

DOUBLE POSSESSIVE: Two conditions must apply for a double possessive — a phrase such as *a friend of John's* — to occur: 1. The word after *of* must refer to an animate object, and 2. The word before *of* must involve only a portion of the animate object's possessions.

Otherwise, do not use the possessive form of the word after *of*: *The friends of John Adams mourned his death*. (All the friends were involved.) *He is a friend of the college*. (Not *college's*, because *college* is inanimate).

Memory aid: This construction occurs most often, and quite naturally, with the possessive forms of personal pronouns: *He is a friend of mine*.

INANIMATE OBJECTS: There is no blanket rule against creating a possessive form for an inanimate object, particularly if the object is treated in a personified sense. See some of the earlier examples, and note these: *death's call, the wind's murmur*.

In general, however, avoid excessive personalization of inanimate objects, and give preference to an *of* construction when it fits the makeup of the sentence. For example, the earlier references to *mathematics' rules* and *measles' effects* would better be phrased: *the rules of mathematics, the effects of measles*.

OMITTED LETTERS: *I've, it's, don't, rock 'n' roll, 'tis the season to be jolly. He is a ne'er-do-well*. See **contractions** in main section.

OMITTED FIGURES: *The class of '62. The Spirit of '76. The '20s*.

PLURALS OF A SINGLE LETTER: *Mind your p's and q's. He learned the three R's and brought home a report card* with *four A's and two B's. The Oakland A's won the pennant.*

DO NOT USE: For plurals of numerals or multiple-letter combinations. See **plurals**.

brackets [ ] They cannot be transmitted over news wires. Use parentheses or recast the material. See **parentheses**.

colon (:) Capitalize the first word after a colon only if it is a proper noun or the start of a complete sentence: *He promised this: The company will make good on all the losses.* But: *There were three considerations: expense, time and feasibility.*

EMPHASIS: The colon often can be effective in giving emphasis: *He had only one hobby: eating.*

LISTS: A frequent use of a colon is at the end of a sentence or phrase to introduce lists, tabulations, texts, etc. See **lists, bulleted lists**.

LISTINGS: Use the colon in such listings as time elapsed (*1:31:07.2*), time of day (*8:31 p.m.*), biblical and legal citations (*2 Kings 2:14; Missouri Code 3:245-260*).

DIALOGUE: Use a colon for dialogue. In coverage of a trial, for example:

Bailey: What were you doing the night of the 19th?

Mason: I refuse to answer that.

Q&A: The colon is used for question-and-answer interviews:

Q: Did you strike him?

A: Indeed I did.

INTRODUCING QUOTATIONS: Use a comma to introduce a direct quotation of one sentence that remains within a paragraph. Use a colon to introduce long quotations within a paragraph and to end all paragraphs that introduce a paragraph of quoted material.

PLACEMENT WITH QUOTATION MARKS: Colons go outside quotation marks unless they are part of the quotation itself.

MISCELLANEOUS: Do not combine a dash and a colon.

comma (,) The following guidelines treat some of the most frequent questions about the use of commas. Additional guidelines on specialized uses are provided in separate entries such as **dates** and **scores**.

As with all punctuation, clarity is the biggest rule. If a comma does not help make clear what is being said, it should not be there. If omitting a comma could lead to confusion or misinterpretation, then use the comma.

For detailed guidance, consult the punctuation section in the back of Webster's New World College Dictionary.

IN A SERIES: Use commas to separate elements in a series, but do not put a comma before the conjunction in most simple series: *His grandchildren are Vera, Chuck and Dave. He would nominate Marquez, Bedi, Lyman or Wong. She goes to school, plays league soccer and takes private dance lessons.*

Include a final comma in a simple series if omitting it could make the meaning unclear. *The governor convened his most trusted advisers, economist Olivia Schneider and polling expert Carlton Torres.* (If Schneider and Torres are his most trusted advisers, don't use the final comma.) *The governor convened his most trusted advisers, economist Olivia Schneider, and polling expert Carlton Torres.* (If the governor is convening unidentified advisers plus Schneider and Torres, the final comma is needed.)

Note, though, that rephrasing often is better:

The governor convened economist Olivia Schneider and polling expert Carlton Torres, his two most trusted advisers. Or *The governor convened his most trusted advisers: economist Olivia Schneider and polling expert Carlton Torres.* (If Schneider and Torres are the governor's most trusted advisers.)

The governor convened his most trusted advisers, along with economist Olivia Schneider and polling expert Carlton Torres. (If the governor is convening unidentified advisers plus Schneider and Torres.)

Put a comma before the concluding conjunction in a series if an integral element of the series requires a conjunction: *I had orange juice, toast, and ham and eggs for breakfast.*

Use a comma also before the concluding conjunction in a complex series of phrases: *The main points to consider are whether the athletes are skillful enough to compete, whether they have the stamina to endure the training, and whether they have the proper mental attitude.*

See **dash** and **semicolon** for cases when elements of a series contain internal commas.

WITH EQUAL ADJECTIVES: Use commas to separate a series of adjectives equal in rank. If the commas could be replaced by the word *and* without changing the sense, the adjectives are equal: *a thoughtful, precise manner; a dark, dangerous street.*

Use no comma when the last adjective before a noun outranks its predecessors because it is an integral element of a noun phrase, which is the equivalent of a single noun: *a cheap fur coat* (the noun phrase is *fur coat*); *the old oaken bucket; a new, blue spring bonnet.*

WITH NONESSENTIAL CLAUSES: A nonessential clause must be set off by commas. An essential clause must not be set off from the rest of a sentence by commas.

See **essential clauses, nonessential clauses** in the main section.

WITH NONESSENTIAL PHRASES: A nonessential phrase must be set off by commas. An essential phrase must not be set off from the rest of a sentence by commas.

See **essential phrases, nonessential phrases** in the main section.

WITH INTRODUCTORY CLAUSES AND PHRASES: A comma is used to separate an introductory clause or phrase from the main clause: *When he had tired of the mad pace of New York, he moved to Dubuque.*

The comma may be omitted after short introductory phrases if no ambiguity would result: *During the night he heard many noises.*

But use the comma if its omission would slow comprehension: *On the street below, the curious gathered.*

WITH CONJUNCTIONS: When a conjunction such as *and, but* or *for* links two clauses that could stand alone as separate sentences, use a comma before the conjunction in most cases: *She was glad she had looked, for a man was approaching the house.*

As a rule of thumb, use a comma if the subject of each clause is expressly stated: *We are visiting Washington, and we also plan a side trip to Williamsburg. We visited Washington, and our senator greeted us personally.* But no comma when the subject of the two clauses is the same and is not repeated in the second: *We are visiting Washington and plan to see the White House.*

The comma may be dropped if two clauses with expressly stated subjects are short. In general, however, favor use of a comma unless a particular literary effect is desired or if it would distort the sense of a sentence.

INTRODUCING DIRECT QUOTES: Use a comma to introduce a complete one-sentence quotation within a paragraph: *Wallace said, "She spent six months in Argentina and came back speaking English with a Spanish accent."* But use a colon to introduce quotations of more than one sentence. See **colon**.

Do not use a comma at the start of an indirect or partial quotation: *He said the victory put him "firmly on the road to a first-ballot nomination."*

BEFORE ATTRIBUTION: Use a comma instead of a period at the end of a quote that is followed by attribution: *"Write clearly and concisely," she said.*

Do not use a comma, however, if the quoted statement ends with a question mark or exclamation point: *"Why should I?" he asked.*

WITH HOMETOWNS AND AGES: Use a comma to set off an individual's hometown when it is placed in apposition to a name (whether *of* is used or not): *Mary Richards, Minneapolis, and Maude Findlay, Tuckahoe, New York, were there.*

If an individual's age is used, set it off by commas: *Maude Findlay, 48, Tuckahoe, New York, was present.*

WITH PARTY AFFILIATION, ACADEMIC DEGREES, RELIGIOUS AFFILIATIONS: See separate entries under each of these terms.

NAMES OF STATES AND NATIONS USED WITH CITY NAMES: *His journey will take him from Dublin, Ireland, to Fargo, North Dakota, and back. The Selma, Alabama, group saw the governor.*

Use parentheses, however, if a state name is inserted within a proper name: *The Huntsville (Alabama) Times.*

WITH YES AND NO: *Yes, I will be there.*

IN DIRECT ADDRESS: *Mother, I will be home late. No, sir, I did not take it.*

SEPARATING SIMILAR WORDS: Use a comma to separate duplicated words that otherwise would be confusing: *What the problem is, is not clear.*

IN LARGE FIGURES: Use a comma for most figures greater than 999. The major exceptions are street addresses (*1234 Main St.*), broadcast frequencies (*1460 kilohertz*), room numbers, serial numbers, telephone numbers, and years (*1876*). See separate entries under these headings.

PLACEMENT WITH QUOTES: Commas always go inside quotation marks.

WITH FULL DATES: When a phrase refers to a month, day and year, set off the year with a comma: *Feb. 14, 2029, is the target date.*

See **semicolon**.

compound adjectives See the **hyphen** entry.

dash (—) Follow these guidelines:

ABRUPT CHANGE: Use dashes to denote an abrupt change in thought in a sentence or an emphatic pause: *Through her long reign, the queen and her family have adapted — usually skillfully — to the changing taste of the time.* But avoid overuse of dashes to set off phrases when commas would suffice.

SERIES WITHIN A PHRASE: When a phrase that otherwise would be set off by commas contains a series of words that must be separated by commas, use dashes to set off the full phrase: *He listed the qualities — intelligence, humor, conservatism, independence — that he liked in an* *executive.*

ATTRIBUTION: Use a dash before an author's or composer's name at the end of a quotation: *"Who steals my purse steals trash." — Shakespeare.*

IN DATELINES:

NEW YORK (AP) — The city is broke.

IN LISTS: See **lists, bulleted lists**.

WITH SPACES: Put a space on both sides of a dash in all uses except sports agate summaries.

See **em dash, en dash, hyphen**.

ellipsis (...) In general, treat an ellipsis as a three-letter word, constructed with three periods and two spaces, as shown here.

Use an ellipsis to indicate the deletion of one or more words in condensing quotes, texts and documents. Be especially careful to avoid deletions that would distort the meaning.

An ellipsis also may be used to indicate a thought that the speaker or writer does not complete. Substitute a dash for this purpose, however, if the context uses ellipses to indicate that words actually spoken or written have been deleted.

Brief examples of how to use ellipses are provided after guidelines are given. More extensive examples, drawn from the speech in which President Richard Nixon announced his resignation, are in the sections below marked **CONDENSATION EXAMPLE** and **QUOTATIONS**.

PUNCTUATION GUIDELINES: If the words that precede an ellipsis constitute a grammatically complete sentence, either in the original or in the condensation, place a period at the end of the last word before the ellipsis. Follow it with a regular space and an ellipsis: *I no longer have a strong enough political base. ...*

When the grammatical sense calls for a question mark, exclamation point, comma or colon, the sequence is word, punctuation mark, regular space, ellipsis: *Will you come? ...*

When material is deleted at the end of one paragraph and at the beginning of the one that follows, place an ellipsis in both locations.

CONDENSATION EXAMPLE: Here is an example of how the spacing and punctuation guidelines would be applied in condensing President Richard Nixon's resignation announcement:

Good evening. ...

In all the decisions I have made in my public life, I have always tried to do what was best for the nation. ...

... However, it has become evident to me that I no longer have a strong enough political base in ... Congress.

... As long as there was ... a base, I felt strongly that it was necessary to see the constitutional process through to its conclusion, that to do otherwise would be ... a dangerously destabilizing precedent for the future.

QUOTATIONS: In writing a story, do not use ellipses at the beginning or end of direct quotes:

"It has become evident to me that I no longer have a strong enough political base," Nixon said.

Not *"... it has become evident to me that I no longer have a strong enough political base ... ,"* Nixon said.

SPECIAL EFFECTS: Ellipses also may be used to separate individual items within a paragraph of show business gossip or similar material. Use periods after items that are complete sentences.

em dash, en dash, hyphen

References in this book to *dashes* denote what some styles call *em dashes*, *long dashes* or *thick dashes.* Because of news industry specifications for text transmission, AP has never used *en dashes,* also known as *short dashes.*

Some elaboration:

HYPHENS Use *hyphens* as joiners, such as for compound modifiers: *small-business owner.* AP also uses *hyphens* for ranges, such as *Jan. 1-4,* while some other styles use en dashes. There should be no spaces surrounding a hyphen.

EN DASHES AP does not use *en dashes.* Some other styles call for *en dashes* to indicate ranges, such as ranges of dates or times, or with some compound modifiers. An *en dash* is about half the width of an *em dash,* approximating the width of a capital letter *N.*

EM DASHES AP refers to these simply as *dashes* and covers their use in the **dash** entry. They are used to signal abrupt change; as one option to set off a series within a phrase; before attribution to an author or composer in some formats; after datelines; and to start lists. AP style calls for a space on both sides of a *dash* in all uses except the start of sports agate summaries. An *em dash* is approximately the width of a capital letter *M* in the typeface being used.

See **hyphen** and **dash.**

exclamation point (!) Follow these guidelines:

EMPHATIC EXPRESSIONS: Use the mark to express a high degree of surprise, incredulity or other strong emotion.

AVOID OVERUSE: Use a comma after mild interjections. End mildly exclamatory sentences with a period.

PLACEMENT WITH QUOTES: Place the mark inside quotation marks when it is part of the quoted material: *"How*

wonderful!" he exclaimed. "Never!" she shouted.

Place the mark outside quotation marks when it is not part of the quoted material: *I hated reading Spenser's "Faerie Queene"!*

MISCELLANEOUS: Do not use a comma or a period after the exclamation mark:

Wrong: *"Halt!", the corporal cried.*
Right: *"Halt!" the corporal cried.*

hyphen (-) Hyphens are joiners. Use them to avoid ambiguity or to form a single idea from two or more words.

Use of the hyphen is far from standardized. It can be a matter of taste, judgment and style sense. Think of hyphens as an aid to readers' comprehension. If a hyphen makes the meaning clearer, use it. If it just adds clutter and distraction to the sentence, don't use it.

If the sheer number of hyphens in a phrase, or confusion about how to use them, can daunt either the writer or the reader, try rephrasing. *It's a guide about how to use hyphens wisely,* not *it's a how-to-use-hyphens-wisely guide.*

These guidelines include changes in 2019, most notably removal of the requirement to hyphenate most compound modifiers after versions of the verb *to be.* In addition, see individual entries in this book and in Webster's New World College Dictionary.

AVOID AMBIGUITY: Use a hyphen whenever ambiguity would result if it were omitted. See COMPOUND MODIFIERS section for details. Also: *He recovered his health. He re-covered the leaky roof. The story is a re-creation. The park is for recreation.*

COMPOUND MODIFIERS: When a compound modifier — two or more words that express a single concept

— precedes a noun, you must decide: Hyphenate that modifier, or not? Often there's not one absolute answer.

Do use a hyphen if it's needed to make the meaning clear and avoid unintended meanings: *small-business owner, better-qualified candidate, little-known song, French-speaking people, free-thinking philosophy, loose-knit group, low-income workers, never-published guidance, self-driving car, bases-loaded triple, one-way street* (Think of the different possible meanings or confusion if the hyphen is removed in each of those examples.)

Other two-word terms, particularly those used as nouns, have evolved to be commonly recognized as, in effect, one word. No hyphen is needed when such terms are used as modifiers if the meaning is clear and unambiguous without the hyphen. Examples include *third grade teacher, chocolate chip cookie, special effects embellishment, climate change report, public land management, real estate transaction, emergency room visit, cat food bowl, parking lot entrance, national security briefing, computer software maker.*

Often, arguments for or against a hyphen could be made either way. Again, try to judge what is most clear and logical to the average reader. Also, consult Webster's New World College Dictionary.

Hyphenate *well-* combinations before a noun, but not after: *a well-known judge,* but *the judge is well known.*

Generally, also use a hyphen in modifiers of three or more words: *a know-it-all attitude, black-and-white photography, a sink-or-swim moment, a win-at-all-costs approach.* Consider

carefully, though, before deciding to use more than three modifiers.

No hyphen is needed to link a two-word phrase that includes the adverb *very* and all adverbs ending in *-ly*: *a very good time, an easily remembered rule.*

Many combinations that are hyphenated before a noun are not hyphenated when they occur after a noun: *She works full time. She is well aware of the consequences. The children are soft spoken. The play is second rate. The calendar is up to date.* (Guidance changed in 2019 to remove the rule that said to hyphenate following a form of the verb *to be.*)

But use a hyphen if confusion could otherwise result, especially with longer compound modifiers or those that are not as commonly used: *The steel surface should be blast-cleaned. The technology is state-of-the-art. The test was multiple choice and fill-in-the-blank. He will work arm-in-arm with the director.*

Also use hyphens to avoid nonsensical terms such as *nonlife*: Make it *non-life-threatening*, not *nonlife-threatening*. Often the better choice is to rephrase, even if it means using a few more words.

COMPOUND VERBS: Don't use a hyphen in phrasal verbs (a verb combined with an adverb, a preposition or both). It's *back up the car*, not *back-up the car*; *set out the desserts*, not *set-out the desserts*. In general, do hyphenate other compound verbs: *She speed-walked her way to victory; he spoon-fed the baby.*

COMPOUND NOUNS: Hyphenate compounds when needed to avoid confusion: *merry-go-round, sister-in-law, hand-me-downs, so-and-so.*

MODIFYING ONE-WORD COMPOUNDS: Words that are usually one-word compounds (*automaker, bookstore*) should be separated when a modifier is added: *fast-car maker*, not *fast carmaker* or *fast-carmaker*.

COMPOUND PROPER NOUNS AND ADJECTIVES: A change in 2019: Do not use a hyphen to designate dual heritage: *African American, Italian American, Mexican American.*

PREFIXES AND SUFFIXES: See **prefixes** and **suffixes**, and separate entries for the most frequently used prefixes and suffixes. Prefixes that generally require hyphens include *self-, all-, ex-, half-.* Suffixes that generally require hyphens include *-free, -based, -elect.*

AVOID DUPLICATED VOWELS, TRIPLED CONSONANTS: Examples: *anti-intellectual, shell-like.* But double-e combinations usually don't get a hyphen: *preempted, reelected.* (Exception added in 2019, reflecting common usage.)

MULTIPLE COMPOUND MODIFIERS: If the phrase is easily recognized without hyphens, use a hyphen only to link last element: *They hope to spark consumer interest in department store-based shopping. She said assistant vice president-managed courses should include real estate licensing-related materials.* (Again, rephrasing may be a better option.)

SUSPENSIVE HYPHENATION: Use these forms to shorten a compound modifier or a noun phrase that shares a common word:

When the elements are joined by *and* or *or*, expressing more than one element: *10-, 15- or 20-minute intervals; 5- and 6-year-olds.* But: *The intervals are 10, 15 or 20 minutes; the children are 5 to 6 years old.*

When the elements are joined by *to* or *by*, expressing a single element: *a 10-to-15-year prison term; an 8-by-12-inch pan.* But: *The prison term is 10*

to 15 years; the pan is 8 by 12 inches.

parentheses ( ) In general, use parentheses around logos, as shown in **datelines**, but otherwise be sparing with them.

Parentheses are jarring to the reader. Because they do not appear on some news service printers, there is also the danger that material inside them may be misinterpreted.

The temptation to use parentheses is a clue that a sentence is becoming contorted. Try to write it another way. If a sentence must contain incidental material, then commas or two dashes are frequently more effective. Use these alternatives whenever possible.

There are occasions, however, when parentheses are the only effective means of inserting necessary background or reference information. When they are necessary, follow these guidelines:

WITHIN QUOTATIONS: If parenthetical information inserted in a direct quotation is at all sensitive, place an editor's note under a dash at the bottom of a story alerting copy desks to what was inserted.

PUNCTUATION: Place a period outside a closing parenthesis if the material inside is not a sentence (*such as this fragment*).

(*An independent parenthetical sentence such as this one takes a period before the closing parenthesis.*)

When a phrase placed in parentheses (*this one is an example*) might normally qualify as a complete sentence but is dependent on the surrounding material, do not capitalize the first word or end with a period.

INSERTIONS IN A PROPER NAME: Use parentheses if a state name or similar information is inserted within a proper name: *The Huntsville (Alabama) Times*. But use commas if no proper name is involved: *The Selma, Alabama, group saw the governor.*

NEVER USED: Do not use parentheses to denote a political figure's party affiliation and jurisdiction. Instead, set them off with commas, as shown under **party affiliation**.

Do not use (*cq*) or similar notation to indicate that an unusual spelling or term is correct. Include the confirmation in an editor's note at the top of a story.

periods (.) Follow these guidelines:

END OF DECLARATIVE SENTENCE: *The stylebook is finished.*

END OF A MILDLY IMPERATIVE SENTENCE: *Shut the door.*

Use an exclamation point if greater emphasis is desired: *Be careful!*

END OF SOME RHETORICAL QUESTIONS: A period is preferable if a statement is more a suggestion than a question: *Why don't we go.*

END OF AN INDIRECT QUESTION: *He asked what the score was.*

MANY ABBREVIATIONS: For guidelines, see **abbreviations and acronyms**. For the form of frequently used abbreviations, see the entry under the full name, abbreviation, acronym or term.

INITIALS: *John F. Kennedy, T.S. Eliot* (No space between *T.* and *S.*, to prevent them from being placed on two lines in typesetting.)

Abbreviations using only the initials of a name do not take periods: *JFK, LBJ.*

ELLIPSIS: See **ellipsis**.

ENUMERATIONS: After numbers or letters in enumerating elements of a summary: *1. Wash the car. 2. Clean the*

basement. Or: A. Punctuate properly. B. Write simply.

PLACEMENT WITH QUOTATION MARKS: Periods always go inside quotation marks. See **quotation marks**.

SPACING: Use a single space after a period at the end of a sentence.

question mark (?) Follow these guidelines:

END OF A DIRECT QUESTION: *Who started the riot?*

Did he ask who started the riot? (The sentence as a whole is a direct question despite the indirect question at the end.)

You started the riot? (A question in the form of a declarative statement.)

INTERPOLATED QUESTION: *You told me — Did I hear you correctly? — that you started the riot.*

MULTIPLE QUESTIONS: Use a single question mark at the end of the full sentence:

Did you hear him say, "What right have you to ask about the riot?"

Did he plan the riot, employ assistants, and give the signal to begin?

Or, to cause full stops and throw emphasis on each element, break into separate sentences: *Did he plan the riot? Employ assistants? Give the signal to begin?*

CAUTION: Do not use question marks to indicate the end of indirect questions:

He asked who started the riot. To ask why the riot started is unnecessary. I want to know what the cause of the riot was. How foolish it is to ask what caused the riot.

QUESTION-AND-ANSWER FORMAT: Do not use quotation marks. Paragraph each speaker's words:

Q: Where did you keep it?
A: In a little tin box.

PLACEMENT WITH QUOTATION MARKS: Inside or outside, depending on the meaning:

Who wrote "Gone With the Wind"?
He asked, "How long will it take?"

MISCELLANEOUS: The question mark supersedes the comma that normally is used when supplying attribution for a quotation: *"Who is there?" she asked.*

quotation marks (" ") The basic guidelines for open-quote marks (") and close-quote marks ("):

FOR DIRECT QUOTATIONS: To surround the exact words of a speaker or writer when reported in a story:

"I have no intention of staying," he replied.

"I do not object," he said, "to the tenor of the report."

Franklin said, "A penny saved is a penny earned."

A speculator said the practice is "too conservative for inflationary times."

RUNNING QUOTATIONS: If a full paragraph of quoted material is followed by a paragraph that continues the quotation, do not put close-quote marks at the end of the first paragraph. Do, however, put open-quote marks at the start of the second paragraph. Continue in this fashion for any succeeding paragraphs, using close-quote marks only at the end of the quoted material.

If a paragraph does not start with quotation marks but ends with a quotation that is continued in the next paragraph, do not use close-quote marks at the end of the introductory paragraph if the quoted material constitutes a full sentence. Use close-quote marks, however, if the quoted material does not constitute a full sentence. For example:

He said, "I am shocked and horrified by the slaying.

"I am so horrified, in fact, that I will ask for the death penalty."

But: *He said he was "shocked and horrified by the slaying."*

"I am so horrified, in fact, that I will ask for the death penalty," he said.

DIALOGUE OR CONVERSATION: Each person's words, no matter how brief, are placed in a separate paragraph, with quotation marks at the beginning and the end of each person's speech:

"Will you go?"

"Yes."

"When?"

"Thursday."

NOT IN Q-AND-A: Quotation marks are not required in formats that identify questions and answers by Q: and A:. See **question mark** for example.

NOT IN TEXTS: Quotation marks are not required in full texts, condensed texts or textual excerpts. See **ellipsis**.

COMPOSITION TITLES: See **composition titles** for guidelines on the use of quotation marks in book titles, movie titles, etc.

NICKNAMES: See **nicknames**.

IRONY: Put quotation marks around a word or words used in an ironical sense: *The "debate" turned into a free-for-all.*

UNFAMILIAR TERMS: A word or words being introduced to readers may be placed in quotation marks on first reference:

Broadcast frequencies are measured in "kilohertz."

Do not put subsequent references to *kilohertz* in quotation marks.

See **foreign words**.

AVOID UNNECESSARY FRAGMENTS: Do not use quotation marks to report a few ordinary words that a speaker or writer has used:

Wrong: *The senator said he would

"go home to Michigan" if he lost the election.

Right: *The senator said he would go home to Michigan if he lost the election.*

PARTIAL QUOTES: When a partial quote is used, do not put quotation marks around words that the speaker could not have used.

Suppose the individual said, *"I am horrified at your slovenly manners."*

Wrong: *She said she "was horrified at their slovenly manners."*

Right: *She said she was horrified at their "slovenly manners."*

Better when practical: Use the full quote.

QUOTES WITHIN QUOTES: Alternate between double quotation marks ("or") and single marks ('or'):

She said, "I quote from his letter, 'I agree with Kipling that "the female of the species is more deadly than the male," but the phenomenon is not an unchangeable law of nature,' a remark he did not explain."

Use three marks together if two quoted elements end at the same time: *She said, "He told me, 'I love you.'"*

PLACEMENT WITH OTHER PUNCTUATION: Follow these long-established printers' rules:

— The period and the comma always go within the quotation marks.

— The dash, the semicolon, the colon, the question mark and the exclamation point go within the quotation marks when they apply to the quoted matter only. They go outside when they apply to the whole sentence.

HEADLINES: Use single quote marks in headlines.

See **comma.**

semicolon (;) In general, use the semicolon to indicate a greater separation of thought and information than a comma can convey but less than the separation that a period implies.

The basic guidelines:

TO CLARIFY A SERIES: Use semicolons to separate elements of a series when the items in the series are long or when individual segments contain material that also must be set off by commas:

He is survived by a son, John Smith, of Chicago; three daughters, Jane Smith, of Wichita, Kansas, Mary Smith, of Denver, and Susan, of Boston; and a sister, Martha, of Omaha, Nebraska.

Note that the semicolon is used before the final *and* in such a series.

Another application of this principle may be seen in the cross-references at the end of entries in this book. Because some entries themselves have a comma, a semicolon is used to separate references to multiple entries, as in: See the **felony, misdemeanor** *entry*; **pardon, parole, probation**; *and* **prison, jail**.

See **dash** for a different type of connection that uses dashes to avoid multiple commas.

TO LINK INDEPENDENT CLAUSES: Use semicolon when a coordinating conjunction such as *and, but* or *for* is not present: *The package was due last week; it arrived today.*

If a coordinating conjunction is present, use a semicolon before it only if extensive punctuation also is required in one or more of the individual clauses: *They pulled their boats from the water, sandbagged the retaining walls, and boarded up the windows; but even with these precautions, the island was hard-hit by the hurricane.*

Unless a particular literary effect is desired, however, the better approach in these circumstances is to break the independent clauses into separate sentences.

PLACEMENT WITH QUOTES: Place semicolons outside quotation marks.

slash (/) Use a slash, rather than a hyphen, for constructions such as and/or, either/or, over/under, red state/blue state, etc. No space on either side of the slash. To break up lines of a verse, use a slash with a space on each side:

Row, row, row your boat / Gently down the stream / Merrily, merrily, merrily, merrily / Life is but a dream.

Business

Our market is the individual consumer of business news. We must write in a lively, clear and accessible style that provides explanation and content for people who may not have a deep knowledge of business and finance. We must avoid insider jargon and present complex issues in an understandable, straightforward manner. No story is too small or routine to meet this standard: Each has meaning for readers and viewers. They may own a stock we are writing about, live in a community where a company is based, use a product or service or have some other connection to the news we are providing. We must keep in mind that we are writing on a global scale and make sure that our reporting reflects that and think about creative ways to tell stories.

AP business journalists must be careful with numbers; quickly grasp what those numbers mean and turn those numbers into real stories, not just about companies or profits but about people's lives.

When stories break, or when you set out to break a story yourself, you need experts or insiders who can help. And you need to know where you can find all the facts you need: in SEC filings, court documents, lists of shareholders and creditors, company histories, etc.

COVERING CORPORATE EARNINGS REPORTS

U.S. federal law requires corporations whose stock is publicly traded to report revenue and profit or losses every three months. This is what business is all about, whether a corporation made money or lost it, and why. These statements are usually released on the major public relations wire services during earnings season, a three- or four-week period that begins roughly two weeks after the end of each quarter.

Before each quarterly reporting period begins, AP business editors and reporters determine which companies will receive expanded coverage based on reader interest, corporate developments, legal or regulatory issues, and influence on financial markets and consumers. When these companies report earnings, AP typically will publish a several-hundred word report and, in some cases, additional elements such as video and graphics.

The AP automates the writing of thousands of quarterly earnings stories using software. These stories average about 200 words and provide customers with the basics: the net income and revenue that the company reported for the quarter — and year — when applicable. An algorithm that creates the stories also is designed to report if the company beat the expectations of Wall Street analysts that cover the company and to include forward-looking guidance when that information is available. The standard style for slugs is BC-US--Earns-Company Name.

While AP is automating many earnings reports, there are times when reporters can and should write original earnings stories or add to automated earnings reports. The decision to add original reporting depends on many factors including the stock activity following an earnings announcement.

Many of the following principles should be followed whether a reporter writes an earnings story from the beginning or adds to one that was automatically generated.

— We should tell the reader what the company does and give the increase or decline of net income either in percentage or absolute terms, along with the reason. Net income is synonymous with profit or earnings. The story should also include the company's revenue, which is sometimes called sales. In AP copy, however, this should always be referred to as revenue.

— Comparisons of profits or losses and revenues/sales should be made with the same period a year earlier, expressed both as a total and as earnings per share, which is simply the profit divided by the number of shares of stock outstanding. Company statements sometimes express this figure as fully diluted. Many company statements also include basic earnings per share, but AP uses fully diluted as a more meaningful figure.

— Use active verbs — *rose, fell* and the like — not passive constructions like *were up/down*. And to calculate the percentage change in profit, use the year-over-year change in net income, not the earnings-per-share numbers. The number of shares outstanding can, and often does, change year to year, which doesn't make it a clear apples-to-apples comparison.

— Include comments on the corporation's performance from the chief executive or outside analysts, and any background that puts the performance in perspective.

— Be alert to announcements of job cuts, executive resignations, acquisitions, changes in strategy, data about key products, warnings of a reduction of future earnings or upward revisions of earnings forecasts.

Why net income is important

Net income truly is the bottom line and the benchmark for companies' performance over time. It's what they are required to report to the SEC in accordance with generally accepted accounting principles, and it gives us a standard reporting format that brings a consistency to our news report.

In the rare cases where companies don't provide the net income number in their news release, we need to press their representatives for those numbers. And if they are not immediately available, we need to be as transparent as possible in explaining to readers why we are providing pro forma or some other adjusted or non-GAAP representation of the company's results instead of the net income figures, which were not disclosed.

Wall Street analysts have been much more concerned in recent years with operating earnings per share, which are calculated by excluding one-time *extraordinary* gains or charges, and revenue totals. Operating earnings may exclude the costs of a big reorganization, such as severance payments to laid-off workers or penalties for breaking leases on factories that are closed. If a company has no extraordinary events, operating earnings and net earnings can be identical.

In the days and weeks before earnings reports, analysts issue EPS predictions, and these predictions are compiled into a consensus figure by research companies such as FactSet and Zacks Investment Research.

On the day of the report, investors compare the consensus prediction for operating earnings per share with the actual number and the stock price often moves up or down based on whether the company falls short of, meets or exceeds expectations. When AP says in a story "Company X's performance beat Wall Street analysts' predictions," this is the number we're referring to. In most stories we explain how the adjusted number was calculated and immediately compare the adjusted earnings per share to the consensus, or average, analyst forecast.

It's worth noting that the analysts' forecast for earnings and revenue in a quarter often reflects the guidance provided by companies about what they expect their earnings and sales will be. That's why it's important to not only review what the analysts' consensus forecast is, but to determine whether a company has made a public forecast. When earnings or revenue disappoint, it's a much more powerful statement for us to say the company's earnings fell short of its own forecast, as well as analysts' expectations — assuming those facts are obtainable.

Operating earnings is sometimes confused with *earnings from continuing operations*. Continuing operations is a subset of operations. It refers to business units that existed in the past and will exist in the future. It excludes *discontinued operations* which represent businesses that have been sold or shut down in the past year. Companies often downplay earnings of these operations since they are no longer relevant to future profits.

Importance of the conference call

Stocks often move within seconds of an unexpected pronouncement by the CEO or CFO on the analyst conference call after the earnings are released. It could come from their response to a question about a big contract, the reason for a revised sales or earnings forecast, or any number of other reasons. That's information we obviously will want in a quick writethru of the story. But even if there are no dramatic announcements, it's important to listen to the call to gain a more complete understanding of how the company is positioning itself going forward. And it may provide a colorful key quote from a top company executive.

Make the company come to life

Earnings are the report cards for top corporate executives. The results, more often than not, are a consequence of decisions they made — acquisitions they engineered, factories they convinced their boards of directors to build or shutter, advertising campaigns they approved. Including detail about the decisions corporate executives have made helps us show that companies are made up of people who win or lose based on the decisions they make.

How to assemble a wrap story

When two or more companies in the same industry report earnings on the same day, we often want an earnings wrap story after the separate earnings stories are out and updated with details from the conference calls. These should read like a seamless narrative with one or more thematic elements holding them together. And in almost every case, a wrap should have a forward-looking element that gives readers a sense of whether the good or bad earnings are likely to get better or worse in future quarters, and why.

The basis for the thematic element may come from one or more of the conference calls that company executives hold after releasing earnings. Or there may be cases where your reporting will take you in a different direction in identifying the unifying theme. Talk to money managers who own the stock, competitors and others who you think can provide insight into what is going on. There also may be cases where the earnings are so divergent that the theme could be that the industry appears to be in disarray. But in all cases, our aim should be to convey to readers who is winning, who is losing and why. That often means that the wrap story may have a more complete explanation of how specific decisions made by executives impacted the earnings.

It also isn't necessary to repeat in the wrap version every number that is in the separate earnings stories. Instead, you should use a common sense approach that asks the question: Is this number necessary to convey the main points we are trying to make? They don't have to be lengthy expositions; if you can tell the tale in 400 or 500 words, all the better.

INTERNATIONAL BUREAUS

Currency Conversions

Currency conversions are necessary in stories that use foreign currency to make clear for readers how a number translates into dollars. But conversions should be used sparingly and preferably not in the lead unless it's a significant part of a story. A conversion is generally needed only the first time a currency is mentioned. The reader can make the necessary conversions after that.

Do not convert amounts that are not current because exchange rates change over time. If necessary for clarity in the story, specify that the conversion is at current exchange rates.

When conversions are needed, use the $ sign to report U.S. dollar amounts and write euros in the form *100 euros*. Do not use the euro symbol (€). Examples:

AMSTERDAM (AP) — Anheuser-Busch InBev, the world's largest brewer, says its third quarter profits rose as the takeover of new brands and higher selling prices offset the impact of lower sales volumes.

The company, based in Leuven, Belgium, said Thursday that net profit was up 31% to $2.37 billion (1.73 billion euros), from $1.81 billion in the same period a year earlier.

The gain largely reflects the company's $20 billion purchase in June of the 50% of Mexico's Grupo Modelo it didn't already own.

PARIS (AP) — French cosmetics giant L'Oreal says sales of its Maybelline makeup, Garnier shampoo and other beauty aids helped lift earnings to a new record in 2013.

The company behind Lancome cosmetics and the Body Shop retail chain reported net profit of 2.96 billion euros ($4 billion) last year, up 3.2% from 2.87 billion in 2012.

For all other currencies, following the amount, spell out the name of the currency followed in parentheses by the equivalent in U.S. dollars. *Japan approved a 1.8 trillion yen ($18 billion) extra budget to partially finance an economic stimulus* *package.*

When dealing with a dollar currency of a country other than the United States, use the following abbreviations before the amount on second and subsequent references:

AU$ Australian dollars
CA$ Canadian dollars
SG$ Singapore dollars
NZ$ New Zealand dollars
HK$ Hong Kong dollars
NT$ New Taiwan dollars
ZW$ Zimbabwe dollars

Treasurer Wayne Swan approved a 16 billion Australian dollar ($10.74 billion) deal. Swan said AU$8 billion would be reserved for capital expenditure.

Different Accounting Rules

In some countries, companies don't report every quarter. The reports may come out every six months or even annually. Many foreign companies don't report *net income* or *earnings per share*. Some report *earnings before taxes.* If that's all they report, call them to see if they will give you net income. If they won't, use whatever number seems closest.

For the companies that report only half-year and full-year results, add a line saying, "The company did not break out quarterly results," so it's clear why we're not using them. Similarly, when reporting sales results for French companies, note that they often report sales a week or two before profit.

Foreign companies that sell shares in the United States (called American depositary receipts) often issue a separate earnings statement using American accounting standards. Use this when you can.

BANKRUPTCY

Bankruptcy categories – personal and business

Federal courts have exclusive jurisdiction over bankruptcy cases, and each of the 94 federal judicial districts handles bankruptcy matters. The primary purposes of the federal bankruptcy laws are to give an honest debtor a "fresh start" in life by relieving the debtor of most debts, and to repay creditors in an orderly manner to the extent that the debtor has property available for payment. Bankruptcies can also be **voluntary** or **involuntary**.

Chapter 7 of the Bankruptcy Code is available to both individual and business debtors. Its purpose is to achieve a fair distribution to creditors of the debtor's available non-exempt property. It provides a fresh financial start for individuals, although not all debt is wiped away; debts for certain taxes, fraudulently incurred credit card debt, family support obligations — including child support and alimony — and most student loans must still be repaid. And the new bankruptcy law that took effect in October 2005 limits Chapter 7 as an option for many

Americans: Those deemed by a **"means test"** to have at least $100 a month left over after paying certain debts and expenses will have to file a 5-year repayment plan under the more restrictive Chapter 13 instead. **When a company files for Chapter 7, it usually leads to liquidation.** But a company in Chapter 7 proceedings can continue to operate under the direction of a court trustee until the matter is settled, and if it can settle with creditors in the interim, it may not have to be liquidated.

Chapter 11 of the Bankruptcy Code is available for both business and consumer debtors. Its purpose is to rehabilitate a business as a going concern or reorganize an individual's finances through a **court-approved reorganization plan**. When we refer to such a filing, we should say the company is **seeking Chapter 11 protection**. This action frees a company from the threat of creditors' lawsuits while it reorganizes its finances. The debtor's reorganization plan must be accepted by a majority of its creditors. Unless the court rules otherwise, the debtor remains in control of the business and its assets.

Chapter 12 of the Bankruptcy Code is designed to give special debt relief to a family farmer with regular income from farming.

Chapter 13 of the Bankruptcy Code is likely to be required for an increasing percentage of individuals seeking to wipe the slate clean. As mentioned above, those deemed by a "means test" to have at least $100 a month left over after paying certain debts and expenses will have to file a 5-year repayment plan under Chapter 13 that allows **unsecured creditors to recover part or all of what they are owed**. Supporters believe the changes will help rein in consumers who pile up credit card debt only to wipe it out with a Chapter 7 filing. Opponents say the law will hurt those who incur debt unexpectedly such as with health problems or lost jobs.

Chapter 15 of the Bankruptcy Code is a new section added in the 2005 reforms that deals with foreign bankruptcies. It is a way for companies with U.S. assets that are organized or nominally headquartered overseas to file bankruptcy in that foreign jurisdiction and in the U.S. as well, and have the U.S. court recognize the foreign bankruptcy as the primary one. The chapter is based on a model law developed by the United Nations in 1997. It has thus far been relatively uncommon, but **may be used more in the future, particularly by hedge funds that are organized overseas but operate in the U.S.**

How to prepare if a big corporate bankruptcy filing seems imminent

Burdensome debt and the refusal of lenders to extend new loans are the common denominators for most companies seeking bankruptcy court protection. Those tend not to crop up suddenly, which means you should be able to judge the likelihood that one of your companies may be filing. That's why we encourage all reporters to set up **SEC filing alerts** for key companies using their own user name and password on the Morningstar Document Research service. Bankruptcy should be one of the keywords you choose because outside auditors often force companies to tip their hands by flagging to investors the possibility of a bankruptcy filing. One expression you'll want to add to your company alert setup is **"going concern."** That's the term companies use when they note that their outside auditors are questioning their ability to remain in business.

Beyond that, you need to have a good understanding of the **balance sheet** and the **income statement** of the major companies you cover to answer these questions: How much debt do they have and how much of it must be repaid or refinanced in this quarter or the quarters to come? Have they demonstrated an inability to raise fresh cash through the sale of stock or debt financing? Has cash flow gone negative?

After a company seeks Chapter 11 protection, **holders of the company's debt** are often the best source of information about the status of bankruptcy negotiations since they often stand to gain control of the company in the reorganization process.

Few companies will be chatty about bankruptcy filings ahead of time, but it's still a good idea to plant the seed with company spokesmen that you want to be alerted as soon as a filing is made, that you want to know in which court it will come (more and more of the big ones seem to be ending up in the Southern District of New York in Manhattan), and that you would like a full set of documents if possible.

Another question to ask is: What will happen to the company's employees? When a company seeks bankruptcy protection, it often pushes for job cuts, pay cuts and reductions in benefits. If any workers are represented by unions, those unions will likely fight those cuts. A company seeking Chapter 11 protection will sometimes try to use bankruptcy court to achieve concessions if it can't reach an agreement on its own with unions. So stay in contact with union representatives to keep up with out-of-court negotiations, and check docket reports on Pacer for requests for permission to impose wage concessions, to reject union contracts or anything similar.

Also, companies seeking bankruptcy protection often turn over their pension plans to the Pension Benefit Guaranty Corporation, the federal pension insurance agency (http://www.pbgc.gov). But eliminating pension plans altogether is also common — United Airlines, US Airways, TWA and Pan Am, among others, all canceled their pension plans in bankruptcy.

And a reminder on tracking a company's stock after it files for bankruptcy: Companies are usually **delisted** by the New York Stock Exchange and the Nasdaq stock market after they seek bankruptcy court protection. That means they usually begin trading on the over-the-counter market known as the **Pink Sheets**. The **letter Q** at the end of a ticker signifies that the company is operating under bankruptcy protection and **PK** means it trades on the Pink Sheets. (Example: Delphi Corp. went from DPH on the New York Stock Exchange to DPHIQ.PK — four letters required in the ticker symbol for bankrupt companies — on the Pink Sheets.)

Is it a reorganization or a liquidation?

Knowing the answer to this question is key to how we describe the filing in our story. If it's a Chapter 11 filing and the company hopes to stay in business, don't say "Company XX filed for bankruptcy on DATE TK ..." Instead, we should say "Company XX **sought bankruptcy court protection** on DATE TK ..."

If a company closes its doors, says it's unable to raise new cash and is **going out of business** via a Chapter 7 filing, spell that out in the lead.

Secured and unsecured creditors

When you borrow money to buy a car, the lender is a **secured creditor**; they get to reclaim the car if you stop making payments. Similarly, companies usually have to pledge some kind of **collateral** when they sell bonds or otherwise borrow money. There can be several levels or rankings of security pledged for various categories of a company's debt. For our purposes, we need to know which creditor stands first, second and so on in line for repayment if a company files for bankruptcy because their claims and desires often conflict with what management wants to happen.

In a bankruptcy reorganization, secured lenders and debt holders obviously want to be repaid 100 cents on the dollar. Management often is against that idea, because they need whatever money they still have to continue operating the company. What often happens is that after extensive negotiations (and big lawyer bills) secured debt holders agree to **exchange their securities for new shares of stock** (i.e., equity) in the post-bankruptcy company, which emerges as a consequence with a much-reduced debt load.

So what happens to **existing shareholders**? In most cases, **their shares become worthless**. But every so often, secured debt holders' claims can be satisfied in a way that leaves some residual equity value in the company. But even then, existing shareholders' ownership stake in the company is often **severely diluted** by the issuance of new shares to former debt holders. That's why the stocks of companies seeking bankruptcy protection often continue to trade at a few dollars a share. It's mostly a fool's game, but something we need to be able to explain as part of our reporting and writing.

Prepackaged bankruptcies and DIP financing

Companies heading toward bankruptcy sometimes start negotiations with major secured creditors on what is known as a **prepackaged bankruptcy** filing. If a company can reach agreement on key details before the bankruptcy court supervision begins, it can speed its eventual reorganization and exit from bankruptcy. Known as an out-of-court restructuring plan, it is filed simultaneously with a Chapter 11 petition. But such plans require the approval of at least two-thirds in amount and more than one-half in the number of allowed claims held by creditors.

One study makes the case that the prepackaged bankruptcy approach is taken most often by companies that had a higher ratio of operating income to total debt in the years before financial stress set in, and when long-term debt represents a larger percentage of total debt (which makes sense because there typically would be fewer debt holders to negotiate with).

These prepackaged plans, as well as regular Chapter 11 reorganizations, often are accompanied by what is known as **debtor-in-possession financing**. This is a term for new money extended by a lender in Chapter 11 cases. Investopedia.com describes DIP financing as being unique from other financing methods in that it usually has priority over existing debt, equity and other claims.

Why should we care about DIP financing? It's a profitable line of business for banks. And companies' ability to obtain it often is a critical factor in whether they continue to operate or have to shut down.

Emerging from bankruptcy

When the reorganization is completed and a company emerges from bankruptcy, we should be able to spell out how much of the company's debt has been wiped away. If debt holders swap their holdings for shares of the reorganized company, spell that out and explain what role they will play. Also include whether the company attracted new equity holders as part of the reorganization.

MERGERS AND ACQUISITIONS

Is it a merger or a takeover?

Few business combinations are truly a merger of equals, so we need to be precise and sparing in the use of the word "merger." It is **not a synonym for an acquisition or takeover**, which should be the preferred descriptive used in most of our stories. But how do we first decide whether or not it's a merger, and if the answer is not, what are the rules that should guide us in concluding who's buying whom?

The AP M&A Checklist:

1. Is one of the companies' stock being used as the currency? If the answer is yes, that's usually a good sign that company is the acquirer and it is not a merger.

2. What is the message from the exchange ratio in stock transactions? Typically when shareholders of Company A are offered new shares in a combined company at a 1-for-1 ratio, and Company B shares are exchanged at something less or more (i.e., each Company B share will be exchanged for 0.47% of a share of the new company), it's an indication that Company A's stock is being used as the basis for the transaction. But it also could be a sign that the companies' boards have agreed to a merger that uses a formula to compensate for the differing market value (total number of shares multiplied by the closing stock price the day before the announcement) of the two companies to come up with an exchange ratio for stock in the new company.

3. What is the message from the stock movements after the announcement? Shares of companies being acquired typically rise and shares of the acquirer often fall after the announcement. Not always, of course, but that's usually the case because most bidders **pay a premium**, or an above-market price, for the shares of the company being acquired, and investors often are worried about the amount of debt the acquirer is taking on to complete the transaction.

4. Whose cash is being used to fund the cash portion of a transaction? If the announcement says Company A's cash will be used or that its existing lines of credit will be tapped to pay for Company B's shares, that's a pretty strong indication that Company A is the acquirer.

5. Which company's executives are filling most of the top management roles? The key distinction usually is who gets the CEO slot. But if one of the two CEOs is named to head the company for a limited period (say two years or less) before his fellow CEO takes over, that's a good sign of a political compromise to paper over the fact that the second CEO's company is going to be in charge long-term.

6. Which company will end up with the majority of the seats on the new board of directors? This is often a key tiebreaker. It's a good indication of which outfit is going to be in charge if one ends up with 60% of the board and the other gets 40%. Also, make sure to get not only the short-term makeup of the board of the combined company, but also whether there were any deals cut for some members to retire in short order.

7. Whose name will be on the big sign outside the headquarters? Usually an obvious tell, but not always. First Union clearly was the acquirer of Wachovia, but the board members decided for their own reasons to use the Wachovia name when the two North Carolina banks combined operations. It may have been a deal killer for some Wachovia board members if their name didn't survive, or it may have simply been a marketing decision by First Union's brass that the name Wachovia had a better chance of standing out in the crowded banking space. Wachovia, incidentally, was acquired by Wells Fargo in 2008.

8. Where will the company be headquartered? Since CEOs typically do the negotiating and they typically aren't anxious to move, this can be an informative tell.

How to value the transaction

Our basic rule is to **exclude the debt** of the acquired company when calculating the value of a takeover. If Company A has agreed to pay $50 a share in cash for all of the stock of Company B, you would multiply $50 times the fully diluted number of shares outstanding of Company B to come up with transaction's total value. Companies often include the debt in their news release, which places a higher total value on the transaction. In cases like that, if they spell out the debt total, back it out and fashion a lead something like this:

Company A, the world's largest TK, agreed Monday to pay $XX million to acquire Company B, whose product line XXX will do XXXX. The transaction, valued at $50 per share, or a X.X premium to Friday's closing price, includes the assumption of $XXX million of Company B's debt.

Unfortunately, news releases sometimes only provide the per-share number for the transaction. So in addition to calling the company to get the key numbers we need to value the transaction, we should backstop by reviewing the latest 10-Q filing of the acquired company to get the number of fully diluted shares outstanding so we can do the math ourselves. In some cases, companies only give the per-share number because they don't want to call attention to the fact that there are an enormous number of options of the acquired company that can be exercised as part of a transaction.

When stock is the currency used in the transaction, or is part of a stock and cash offer, the valuation equation changes. If Company A offers 1 share of its stock for each share of Company B, you would multiply the previous day's closing price of Company A by the number of fully diluted shares outstanding of Company B. When there is a cash component per share, or if the exchange ratio is greater or lesser than 1-for-1, the math gets a little more complicated, but it's also straightforward. First calculate the value of the stock portion (If Company A is offering 0.47 of a share of its stock that was trading at $50 yesterday, the stock portion is worth 50 x .47, or $23.50.) Then add whatever will be paid in cash per share (say $10) to give a total value of $33.50 per Company B share and multiply that times the total number of shares of Company B outstanding.

Any time stock of the acquirer is used as a currency in a takeover, the value of the transaction obviously can change throughout the day based on the stock movement of the acquirer. But for our purposes, on the day the takeover is announced, we should stay with our initial valuation (based on the closing price of the acquirer a day earlier) until the markets close.

Then we should redo the math based on that day's closing value of the acquirer's stock — and make it clear to readers why the total has changed from what they have been reading throughout the day.

What needs to be in the first version of the story

Lead with the **full name of the buyer** and include a descriptive size and scope, **explain the terms** and **value of the deal** as simply as possible (all cash? cash and stock? all stock?) while adding the name of the company to be acquired, and **provide a reason why** the deal is happening — or, if the release is mum on that point, a description of what the combined company will look like or the capabilities it will have (making it the world's biggest maker of fish tacos).

If there are **job cuts** or other major corporate developments, including a warning that future earnings will be lower because of **earnings dilution**, aim to get those in the initial story. Dilution occurs when a stock-based transaction increases the number of shares of the acquirer without a near-term corresponding increase in earnings per share.

Specify where the two companies are **headquartered**. Also include **stock price history** and **premarket trading**, if it is available, for both the acquirer and the acquiree. And if it is easily obtainable, specify what the **premium** that the acquiring company is offering and whether it is a **hostile bid**.

As the urgent series continues, include any pertinent details about potential antitrust issues, contingencies like the need for board approval, government approval, shareholder approval, court approval, break-up fees, **due diligence** (the review by the acquirer of a target company's internal books and operations), and **nondisclosure/confidentiality agreements**.

Also specify the **stage of the transaction** — letter of intent, definitive agreement, closing, etc. And if not added already, provide details about how the acquirer will finance the takeover, what the seller's plans are for the proceeds it will be receiving, the projected effect on future sales/earnings, other details on how the companies will change as a result of the deal (layoffs, management changes, etc.), and when the deal is expected to close.

Add historical perspective. A news story showed a good example: In early 2003, Overture bought Altavista from CMGI for $140 million in cash and stock. That didn't look like much of a deal until they added the needed perspective that

CMGI bought Altavista from Compaq only four years earlier for $2.3 billion.

What is the stock reaction telling us?

If Company A offers $50 in cash for Company B and the share price of Company B rises to $55 or $60, that's a pretty strong indication that some investors are betting at least one **competing bid** will emerge. Alternatively, if Company B's shares trade way below $50, we need to find out why investors are skittish about the deal closing.

It also should be standard practice to keep track of the stock prices of both the acquirer and the target in the days and weeks after the initial announcement. Depending on how they perform, you may want to write additional stories about whether investors are betting the deal is on track or in trouble. And when stock is used as part or all of the currency for a proposed takeover, it's a good idea to build the formula into a spreadsheet and track it daily to see whether the spread between the market price is narrowing or widening from the offer's valuation.

Some investors make and lose millions on these bets, so be careful when you interview them about these deals — and make sure to explain what they have at stake if we quote them either speaking in support of or objecting to the transaction.

Assessing the deal's chances for success

Besides the market implications about whether a deal will close or not, we should also from the first day be sharpening our analysis about whether the proposal makes business sense. There are several ways to approach this. Are the promised cost cuts doable, and what will they cost in human terms (jobs lost) and the effects on local economies? Will it deliver the higher profits the acquirer is promising? Will it position the acquirer's stock for future market gains? We should be asking these questions as part of our first-day coverage and come back as often as needed for deals both pending and completed.

Inclusive storytelling

Inclusive storytelling seeks to truly represent all people around the globe. It gives voice and visibility to those who have been missing or misrepresented in traditional narratives of both history and daily journalism. It helps readers and viewers both to recognize themselves in our stories, and to better understand people who differ from them in race, age, gender, class and many other ways.

It makes our work immeasurably stronger, more relevant, more compelling, more trustworthy.

It is essential to accuracy and fairness.

It is not a "topic" to be siloed or explored here and there.

Inclusive storytelling should be part of everyday conversations, decision-making and coverage. That means integrating these goals in all aspects of conversations, from the beginning of the story idea to garnering reaction (and more story ideas) after publication.

Being an inclusive storyteller calls on all of us to stretch beyond our accustomed ways of thinking, our usual sources, our regular, go-to topics or angles for coverage. It challenges us to recognize and examine our unconscious biases, and find ways to overcome them.

It aims to infuse every aspect of coverage, both in text and in visuals, with diverse voices and faces, perspectives and context. It is considerate of language, sources and diverse audiences. It often relies on teamwork and collaboration.

Among the considerations: the stories we choose to convey; the sources we talk with; the images we select; the framing, approach and specific words we use; the details we include or don't include — and the understanding that all of those various parts of a story can be seen and interpreted very differently, depending on a person's background and experiences.

A notable example: The very terms *diversity* and *inclusivity* or *inclusion* can be interpreted as implying that the norm or the standard is being white, male, straight, not disabled, not poor, etc.

That is not the intent in this chapter's use of those terms. Rather, we strive for storytelling that both represents all people and shines a brighter light on those who have been underrepresented in traditional narratives.

Those traditional narratives — in history books, daily journalism and much of popular media — are versions of the world and specific events conveyed for decades or centuries through the perspectives of what has been the dominant demographic. That means those narratives generally reflect what is traditional for dominating groups, but not for underrepresented people and groups.

In other words, not for much of the world. Not for much of our audience.

Such narratives have always fallen short. In today's world, the inaccuracies and misrepresentations grow ever greater as the diversity of our audiences increases.

As journalists, we are used to asking the questions, not answering them. It's important to shift mindsets and interrogate our own assumptions and decisions.

That means creating a culture where we can have candid conversations that will lead to richer, more meaningful and more accurate stories. And it means considering, with every story, the points raised here — plus other points for reflection and action that might arise as we expand and deepen our storytelling.

Below are additional concepts and pointers. Many separate Stylebook entries also have guidelines relevant to inclusive storytelling. They include: **disabilities**; **diseases**; **gender, sex and sexual orientation**; **gender-neutral language**; **immigration, migration**; **older adults**; **race-related coverage**; **shorthand descriptions**; the **Religion chapter**; the **Health and Science chapter**.

TWO PATHS

Inclusive reporting and storytelling includes two distinct and equally important paths.

One: Cast a wide net when looking for voices and images for any story, whether it's on education, health, politics, marathon running, architecture, or whatever your beat or your daily assignment is.

— If a story requires some kind of expert commentary, such as a political scientist or an academic focusing on a particular area, don't stick to the same people you've always spoken to. Widen your search, perhaps by going to institutions that aren't as well known instead of the big-name universities, or smaller community groups instead of the biggest nonprofits. Don't pigeonhole people by assuming, for example, that you should only talk to a Black academic for a story about race, or to a woman about parenting.

— When looking for voices from people on the street or in the general public, be conscious of who you're reaching out to. Are you talking only to men? Women? White people? Black people? Young? Old? Citizens? Voters? Only particular neighborhoods or geographic regions? Don't settle for the people who are quickest or easiest to interview. Be intentional about hearing from a range of people.

— Be equally intentional about the subjects of your photos and videos. Whose images are you showing? Do they represent the diversity of the topic or the community?

Two: Home in on individual communities or voices in stories focused on that group. A few examples of ways in which this can be done:

— Describing the unique obstacles faced by gay people who come out later in life.

— Explaining what has led women of color to become a growing force as so-called mom influencers, a multibillion-dollar world that has long been overwhelmingly white.

— Focusing on hourly workers, not just white-collar workers, in talking about economic pressures and gains.

— Writing obituaries for people who were barrier-breakers or well known for certain groups, even if they aren't known as well in the general public.

— Examining how a larger issue, like abortion, or an institution, like the military, can be experienced differently based on race, gender, class, age, etc.

TYPES OF EXPERIENCES

A person who lives an experience personally has a different perspective from someone who merely observes it or is involved at arm's length (or from a much greater distance). Some use the term *lived experiences*: a person's firsthand experiences, and how those experiences affect the person and their understanding of the world and of other people. This is distinct from general experiences, which can be secondhand or indirect.

For example, a Black woman's white friend may feel empathy and anger when a stranger shouts a racist slur. That is a different experience than the lived experience of the woman who was the target of that slur that day, and of other slurs (or worse aggressions) on many other days.

Both types of experiences are valid and worthy of exploration. But the fact that they are different needs to be understood as a part of accurate reporting and conveyed as a part of full and inclusive storytelling. A person's lived experiences can be very different from versions of life that are conveyed by other people.

NOT TOKENISM

The point is not to make a cursory effort to include a diverse voice or two in order to check a box, but to develop a fuller picture of people's varied experiences and perspectives.

By extension, no one group should be treated as a monolith. And one person does not represent an entire group: One person who uses a wheelchair or one gay person, for example, doesn't speak for all people who use wheelchairs or for all gay people.

Among Latino populations, how people of Mexican descent vote may differ from how Cuban Americans vote. Even within each of those populations, there are differences in voting behavior. Republicans vary in their backgrounds, including socioeconomic status and geography. So do Democrats.

Interviewing a broad cross-section of people within a certain population gives us a better sense of how their views may differ. For example, coverage of a lawsuit accusing Harvard University of discriminating against Asian Americans would best include voices of Asian Americans on all sides of the affirmative action issue, and capture perspectives from different Asian diasporas.

It is also important to add nuance and context around experiences that people share. For instance, a Black man who says he has never been stopped by police and doesn't believe that police brutality is a problem may be accurately describing his own experiences and beliefs. But those views may be inconsistent with data and polling. It doesn't mean he shouldn't be included in coverage; it means his perspective should be situated in the proper context.

CONTEXT AND BACKGROUND

Context and background are vital in stories to give readers a full, accurate picture of the issues. Don't assume readers already know. Include the appropriate information to establish the origins of a story, its movement through time and a look ahead. Consider historical, political, economic, social, cultural, and other context and background for stories.

For example, don't focus on the percentage of one's ancestry when writing about a Native American tribe that doesn't use so-called blood quantum for enrollment. The Cherokee Nation requires citizens to trace ancestry to a list of names kept by the tribe.

Seek to answer whether something is a first, part of a trend or an anomaly. Look at data and statistics to determine whether one group might be disproportionately affected by decisions or actions.

For example, racist attacks against Americans of Asian descent rose amid the coronavirus pandemic. Asian Americans pointed to other times in history when they were targeted, including in the Chinese Exclusion Act of 1882, when the U.S. government put a moratorium on immigration from China; the World War II incarceration of Japanese Americans; and the 1982 beating death of Vincent Chin in Detroit.

Be careful about drawing comparisons between two seemingly similar events, such as the removal of Confederate statues and the removal of statues commemorating Spanish colonizers and missionaries, without including the appropriate context. The events that gave rise to the statues occurred hundreds of years apart and in different regions of what's now the U.S.

UNCONSCIOUS/IMPLICIT BIAS

Everyone has unconscious or implicit biases; they form without our even realizing it, through repetition and reinforcement of stereotypes and assumptions over a lifetime.

They even can contradict what we understand and declare to be our beliefs.

These biases influence the way we assess a person or a situation before we have the facts. From there, they can shape which facts we gather — and which ones we don't — and how we interpret them. They can affect the words we choose, how we cast a headline, what angle we take in photographing a person or scene.

They can include implicit assumptions that we might not even realize are biases: that adults should be employed, married, parents, romantically active, sexually active, omnivores, Christian, and/or religious, for example.

Even seemingly positive assumptions grounded in stereotypes, such as of Asian Americans being smart and hardworking, are overgeneralizations that can gloss over complex realities.

While you may not always be aware of your own implicit biases, there are ways that you can check yourself:

— Understand and question your own world view and what it is based on, and its limitations in the assumptions you form, decisions you make, sources you choose and perspectives you take in your storytelling.
— Explore any preconceived notions you might have about the person and/or topic.
— Ask yourself how your own life experiences affect how you see this topic.
— Consider how all of that affects how you approach the story – how you frame it, who you talk to or photograph.
— Recognize that people of any race are capable of racist behavior and assumptions (both explicit and implicit). Women as well as men are capable of sexist behavior and assumptions. Older adults may view younger people through a lens of ageism, as well as vice versa.
— Ask yourself: What steps have you taken to overcome assumptions in your reporting and storytelling once you've identified them?

LANGUAGE

The words — even a single word — that we choose to describe a person or convey a scene shape the thoughts and perceptions of readers and listeners.

The term *immigration sweep*, for example, could sound as if something or someone dirty needs to be cleaned up. Is a person *an addict*, or *a person with a drug dependency*? Is the woman *elderly*, or *a 70-year-old marathon runner*?

Much of the guidance throughout the Stylebook is grounded on the principle of thoughtful and precise wording. What we say about language in one entry generally applies to all areas.

For example, our guidance about **disabilities** also applies broadly to other coverage areas: People's perceptions of disabilities vary widely, as do the ways in which disabled people, or people with disabilities, describe themselves. Use care and precision, considering the impact of specific words and the terms used by the people you are writing about.

Other points:

— Use precise language, not imprecise generalizations or labels. Be as specific as possible. *Japanese American women in their 20s*, for example, not *young Asian women*. *People over 80*, not *older adults*. Rather than *hero* or *traitor*, give details: *The monument depicts Gen. Robert E. Lee, a slave owner and commander of the Confederate forces after they seceded from the United States.*

— Limit use of the term *community* in reference to groups of people. While sometimes it is the best word, it also can imply homogeneity and the idea that all members of a particular "community" think and act alike. This is similar to the concept of avoiding any type of generalization or stereotype.

— Don't use dehumanizing *"the"* terms such as *the homeless, the blind, the mentally ill, the poor*, etc.

— Understand the difference between *person-first language (people with disabilities*, for example) and *identity-first language (disabled people)*. Whenever possible, determine which approach a person prefers. When preferences can't be determined, aim for a mix of *person-first* and *identity-first language*.

— Be sensitive to the various meanings and implications of words: *insane schedules, lame ideas, turning a blind eye, he must be deaf*, etc. Generally there are better, and more specific, ways of saying it. At the least, take a moment to pause and consider before using such words in unrelated situations.

VISUALS

For video, photo and graphics, approach assignments through an inclusion lens even before arriving on scene. Continue to assess throughout the shoot, while producing, and when editing:

— Think about the people who are affected. When covering a new infrastructure bill, for example, find the people of various backgrounds who have been harmed by poor infrastructure. Go beyond just politicians and policymakers.

— Seek out a diverse range of voices and faces for an assignment, particularly for stories that don't specifically have to do with a person's identity. For example, seek a Black female researcher focusing on vaccination rates among children, or a Latino teacher on strike in Chicago, or a gay couple struggling to make ends meet during the pandemic.

— Make sure the person's humanity is depicted with care and attention paid to lighting, angling of shots, etc.

— For video, let the subjects speak for themselves through soundbites that are

STORYTELLING

chosen for the final edit.

— Be mindful not to fall into stereotypical traps. For example, avoid choosing to focus on a home in disarray when telling the story of a low-income family without spending time capturing a deeper picture of the family's story.

— When dealing with a community that has suffered a loss or trauma, or historically has been marginalized and misrepresented by the media, be respectful of hesitancy to appear on camera. Work to establish trust before pointing a camera at people.

— Accurately represent a scene. For example, if a pro-gun rally includes mostly white men with guns and a few Black men, don't focus on the Black men in your shots as though they represented what the gathering looked like as a whole.

— Question who or what might be missing while on a shoot and when editing.

— In the editing phase, consider whether a diverse range of views, voices and faces are making the final cut. Remember that who and what you choose to exclude can be as important as who and what you include.

STRENGTHENING YOUR STORYTELLING

Consider and collaborate

— At every stage of storytelling — from generating story ideas to the final editing, and all steps in between — ask whose voice or perspective is missing or should be represented more robustly. Seek to include voices and experiences from a variety of lenses.

— Consider and reflect the wide range of interests, needs and voices of people reading and viewing your stories.

— Think about race, gender, socioeconomic status, age, geography, sexual orientation, gender identity, disabilities, education levels, religion and political affiliation.

— Diversify the sources and voices presented as important and credible.

— Avoid falling into stereotypes (going to Chinatown to get the "Asian" perspective) or relying on always-heard voices such as male financial analysts or female teachers.

— Collaborate from the outset with colleagues in all formats — and bring in perspectives from others not involved with the coverage. They will bring additional insights and can help identify inclusion holes. They also bring expertise in how a finished product will look. But they can do that effectively only if brought in early in the process.

— Remember that talking with people from all sorts of backgrounds not only improves a particular story, but also expands your understanding of the experiences and perspectives of people with backgrounds other than yours.

— If the editor who assigned you the story is not the one editing it, be sure to communicate your efforts to broaden your storytelling and the perspective and voices the story cannot do without.

Expand your circle

— Leave your bubble and stretch yourself. Explore places you've never been that aren't in the news. Find sources and new voices in places you don't normally

look – then make them part of your source lists for the future.
— Follow new people from a wide variety of backgrounds on social media.
— But don't rely too much on social media. Many excellent sources don't use it and have valuable and often entirely different perspectives.
— Ask people you meet for other sources, including people who might have differing opinions.
— Ask colleagues — including those from other departments — for sources, then use that as a jumping-off point to expand and cultivate your own sources.
— Take time to get to know diverse sources before you need them, particularly in areas that are traditionally dominated by a particular gender, race, etc.
— Watch, read and listen to content from a variety of political views – particularly views different from your own. Find sources of different races, ages, genders, sexual orientations and geographies.

Invest the time
— Research your subjects ahead of time. This shows that you care and will help you ask more informed questions. Consider creating a Twitter list of groups and people related to the topic to get into their worlds, find new subjects, understand the context and find more story ideas.
— Take time to get to know your sources. Don't rush through interviews. Listen carefully to what they're saying and seek to understand their perspective, especially if it doesn't conform to what you thought they would say.
— If possible, observe people in their environment. You likely will learn things you wouldn't from an interview only.
— Be someone who shows up – and not just when news is breaking or you have a specific need. You'll likely reap the benefits of a rich relationship (and story ideas and new contacts) with people who trust your motivations.
— Evaluate your work. Ask yourself: What can I do next time to be even more inclusive? Ask others for feedback on your work. What might you have missed?

ACCESSIBILITY
Make sure stories on your website and social media are as accessible as possible. Measures include:
— Alternative text on visuals: a short written description of an image for people who are blind or have low vision, and/or use screen readers.
— For video, closed or open captioning for deaf or hard-of-hearing people, as well as for people who process written information better than audio. See https://www.w3.org/WAI/media/av/captions/.
— For video, consider audio descriptions for people who are blind or have low vision. An audio description is narration added to the soundtrack to describe important visual details that cannot be understood from the main soundtrack. See https://www.w3.org/WAI/WCAG21/Understanding/audio-description-prerecorded.html.
— For podcasts and other audio, a transcript for deaf and hard-of-hearing people.
— For text-based graphics, the contrast ratio between the text and the image should be at least 4.5 to 1 as recommended by the Web Content Accessibility Guidelines. For large text, the contrast ratio should be at least 3 to 1.

STORYTELLING

— As in all news writing, use simple, plain language free of jargon, cliches and generalities. Favor smaller words over bigger words (*try*, not *attempt*; *bold*, not *audacious*; *use*, not *utilize*.) Write short, direct sentences with strong verbs. Aim for one idea per sentence. Break sentences with lots of punctuation into two sentences. Or three. Avoid strings of modifiers.

ADDITIONAL RESOURCES

As noted above, these Stylebook entries contain additional guidance: **disabilities**; **diseases**; **gender, sex and sexual orientation**; **gender-neutral language**; **immigration, migration**; **older adults**; **race-related coverage**; **shorthand descriptions**; the **Religion chapter**; the **Health and Science chapter**.

A selection of other detailed guidance, which in some cases may differ from AP's approach:

Guidelines for Inclusive Journalism, by The Seattle Times (with links to a number of other guides and resources): http://st.news/inclusivejournalism

Inclusive Language Guidelines, by the American Psychological Association: https://www.apa.org/about/apa/equity-diversity-inclusion/language-guidelines.pdf

Conscious Style Guide: https://consciousstyleguide.com/

The Diversity Style Guide, San Francisco State University: https://www.diversitystyleguide.com/

Disability Language Style Guide, by the National Center on Disability and Journalism: https://ncdj.org/style-guide/

For a partial list of additional print and online resources used by the Stylebook team, see the **Bibliography**.

Data journalism

Why this section

Data journalism has become a staple of reporting across beats and platforms. The ability to analyze quantitative information and present conclusions in an engaging and accurate way is no longer the domain of specialists alone. Government agencies, businesses and other organizations alike all communicate in the language of data and statistics. To cover them, journalists must become conversant in that language as well.

Acquiring data

Data can come from a variety of public and private sources, each presenting its own benefits and challenges. Some data sets might be downloadable from public websites, while some might depend on negotiation with government officials or other sources. Journalists should evaluate data sources as critically as they would any other source of information.

Requesting government data

SOURCES OF GOVERNMENT DATA: All government agencies collect data that can be useful to reporters. The Briefing on Media Law section includes a useful introduction to the Freedom of Information Act, which can be used to request data from agencies in the executive branch of the U.S. federal government. The National Freedom of Information Coalition maintains a list of resources about similar laws that cover state and local governments: http://www.nfoic.org/state-foi.

DATA FORMAT REQUEST: In a records request for data, be sure to ask for data in an "electronic, machine-readable" format that can be interpreted by standard spreadsheet or database software. The alternative, which is the default for many agencies, is to provide records in paper form or as scans of paper pages, which present an obstacle to analysis. Public records laws vary significantly from federal to state and local governments; some state governments do not require records to be provided in searchable form, for example. In some cases paper records may be the only option.

Whenever possible, ask to speak with technical experts who manage the data as well as "domain experts" who can provide insight about idiosyncrasies of a data set, its place within a regulatory framework, and other important background information.

Scraping data from websites

Sometimes, a data provider's website allows users to browse or search a data set but fails to provide direct download of the data. In this situation it may be possible to use software to step through the pages of the site and extract the data in a process known as web scraping.

Some website operators sanction this practice, and others oppose it. A website with policies limiting or prohibiting scraping often will include them in its terms of service or in a "robots.txt" file, and reporters should take these into account when considering whether to scrape.

Scraping a website can cause its servers to work unusually hard, and in extreme cases, scraping can cause a website to stop working altogether and treat the attempt as a hostile attack. Therefore, follow these precautions:

— Scraping should be seen as a last resort. First try to acquire the desired data by requesting it directly.
— Limit the rate at which the scraper software requests pages in order to avoid causing undue strain on the website's servers.
— Wherever feasible, identify yourself to the site's maintainers by adding your contact information to the scraper's requests via the HTTP headers.

Legal and ethical considerations of leaked or hacked data

Reporters may come into possession of data that was not intended to be released to the public. Such data may have been leaked by a person within the company or agency that collected it, or it might have been released by a third party who hacked into the company or agency.

Treat data sets obtained in this manner with skepticism and extreme caution. Leaked and hacked data sets can contain private information of people who individually might not be relevant to the story. The data files themselves may contain malicious programs that can compromise computer networks. And the authenticity and accuracy of any hacked or leaked data sets should be confirmed before their use. If the subject of a leak has refused to confirm its authenticity, provide appropriate caveats. See the Briefing on Media Law section for other relevant legal considerations, and seek legal advice before using such data or publishing findings based on it.

Evaluating data sources

Data sources, much like human sources, should be evaluated for reliability, currency, scope and bias. Before working with a data set, take time to background it:

— If the data collectors used a data entry form, ask to see a copy of the form and any directions they received about how to enter the data.
— Request a record layout (also known as a data dictionary) for any data used. This document should describe the fields, the types of data they contain and details such as the meaning of any codes in the data and how missing data is indicated.
— Determine whether the data set is up to date, how frequently it is normally updated and when it will be updated next.
— Look for any anomalies in the data that would invalidate the analysis, such as outliers, blank values, placeholder values or different types of data appearing in the same field.
— As with any other release of information, consider the source. Did the data come from a government agency or from an advocacy group? Examine the methodology used for data collection. The purpose and methods of the original data collection will determine what is included and excluded from a

data set. These decisions can affect the usefulness of the data.
— If possible, compare the data against another source of similar information. Does the data for a parallel industry, organization or region look similar? If not, what could explain the discrepancy? It might also be possible to verify the consistency of summary statistics included with the data, such as sums and percentages; consider calculating a few of them by hand to check whether they agree with the values provided.

Reproducible analysis and transparency

As a general rule, all assertions in a story based on data analysis should be reproducible. The methodology description in the story or accompanying materials should provide a road map to replicate the analysis. Such a road map provides visibility into the analysis for editors, story subjects and the public. It also allows the reporter or others to more easily update and expand upon the work in the future.

If at all possible, an editor or another reporter should attempt to reproduce the results of the analysis and confirm all findings before publication. This crucial step can help avoid significant errors and is made much easier by maintaining a log of all steps in the analysis.

At a minimum, maintain a data log including:
— Details on data source(s), such as URLs to download the data or copy of a formal records request for the data. Note: Keep original copies of all data used in analysis, and annotate/transform data only in copies of the originals.
— Copies of the data dictionary and any other documentation that accompanied the original data set.
— Description of all steps required to transform the data and perform the analysis.

Sharing data and methodology

PRE-PUBLICATION SHARING: When applicable, key results of an analysis, along with the code or a description of the methodology, should be shared with data providers or subjects of a story before publication, so they can answer questions based on the findings and offer a response. Share the results only, not the full story.

METHODOLOGY STATEMENT: If the methodology behind an analysis can be explained in one or two sentences, include the full explanation in the story. If the methodology is more complex, provide a separate text box or story that accompanies the main piece. A similar explanation should accompany any interactive graphics based on a data analysis.

Guidelines for publishing data

Where possible, provide the source data for download along with the story or visualization. When distributing data consider the following guidelines:
— The data should be distributed in a machine-readable, widely useable format, such as a spreadsheet.
— The data should be accompanied by thorough documentation that explains data provenance, transformations and alterations, any caveats with the data analysis and a data dictionary.

Reporting on data

When performing data analysis and conveying conclusions, strive for accuracy and simplicity. Do not obfuscate analysis with technical terms or overstate conclusions.

Compared with what?

A number alone does not signify much. It must be compared against something (a previous year's figure, measures from other places, a benchmark or goal, etc.). Make sure your comparison is weighing two similar types of values and that units of measurement and means of collecting the data are similar. When reporting numbers, provide the comparison for context: About 40% of male students passed the test compared with 55% of female students.

— Per capita and related calculations allow you to compare values among groups of different sizes. Per capita values are calculated by dividing the value of interest by the population of interest. For larger populations, calculating the rate per 10,000 may be more instructive.
— Rankings should include raw numbers to provide a sense of relative importance.
— When comparing dollar amounts across time, be sure to adjust for inflation or seasonal adjustment
— Data should reflect the appropriate population for the topic: For example, use voting-age population as a base for stories on demographic voting patterns.

Conveying measures of change

— Actual change: When measuring actual change over time, subtract the older number from the newer number. However, this raw measure of difference may not be the best way to convey change to the reader. For example, if a town's budget went up $200 million from one year to the next, that may not tell much.
— Percent change: Percent change describes the relative change of the new number from the old number. To calculate percent change, take the actual change, divide by the old number and multiply by 100. If that same town had a budget last year of $1.5 billion, an increase of $200 million would represent around a 13% change. This number can then be compared to other towns or other years.
— Percentage point change: Do not confuse percent change and percentage point change. A change from 10% to 13% is a rise of 3 percentage points. This is not equal to a 3% change.
— Avoid percentage and percent change comparisons from a small base. Use the raw numbers in these cases.

Understanding averages

— Measures of central tendency: Calculating an average or measure of central tendency is an attempt to represent a set of numbers using a value that best describes the group as a whole. There are three common ways to measure a typical or central value for a set of numbers. One measure may be more appropriate for a given data set:
    — Mean: The most common measure of central tendency is the mean,

commonly called the average. To calculate the mean of a group of numbers, add them together and divide the sum by the quantity of numbers in the group. The mean of 20, 6 and 4 would be (20+6+4)/3 or 10. The mean is very sensitive to outliers. If the data set contains some values that are much larger or much smaller than the bulk of the values, use the median as a representative value for the set.

— Median: The median is the middle value of a set of numbers when arranged from smallest to largest. The median of 20, 6 and 4 is 6. The median is more resistant to outlier values than the mean and so often better represents the center point of the set.

— Mode: Another common measure used to indicate a typical value is the mode, which simply means the most frequent value. In a histogram or bar chart, it is the value that is represented by the highest bar.

— When communicating average values, indicate if you are using the median or mode as opposed to the mean. For example, if you are reporting the median, use a median income of $35,000 instead of an average income of $35,000.

— Do not average averages. Be aware that taking the mean of a set of mean values is not appropriate. If the groups represented are of different sizes, adding their means and dividing by the number of groups will not provide an accurate overall mean.

Correlation and causation

When exploring the relationship between two variables in a data set, be careful to distinguish correlation from causation.

— Correlation indicates that two variables are related to each other: When one changes, the other appears to change, as well.

— Causation implies that a change in one variable caused the change in the other.

Many variables have a connection, but which variable causes a change in the other can be inconclusive or unknown. The common change in both variables may be caused by a third factor or even by random chance. When reporting on correlations, look for an explanatory basis of the causal relationship and consider lurking factors that may better explain the relationship.

Writing with numbers

— When possible, round numbers to avoid overemphasizing precision in reporting. Supplying the full number may signal to the reader that each digit is important, when that is not the case.

— Avoid overloading a sentence or paragraph with numbers. While there is no absolute maximum, a good rule of thumb is to use no more than eight or 10 digits in a single paragraph.

— Use fractions, ratios, and percentages to make numbers understandable: Reformulating numbers in these ways helps to limit the number of digits per paragraph: 75% can be written as three of four, ¾, etc. (See fractions, ratios, percent.)

— Add appropriate cautions or caveats to numbers. Providing this information can make stories more credible and reduce the need to publish updates when new data become available.

— Include measures of uncertainty. Often, calculations are based on

DATA JOURNALISM

measurements that include some level of uncertainty. Uncertainty can be communicated using confidence intervals or a margin of error. (See polls and surveys.)
— Mention sample sizes of surveys, particularly if small. (See polls and surveys.)

Data visualization

Data visualization should be both compelling and nondeceptive. Published visuals must serve a concrete narrative purpose and present data in a straightforward and clear fashion. Visuals used for analysis must be checked carefully to make sure they accurately represent the underlying data.

— A visual experience should require as little external explanation or background knowledge as possible. Avoid creating both low-information graphics and graphics that are so complex that they require detailed explanation.
— Bar charts should set the baseline of the y-axis at zero. The y-axis of a line chart should fall within the normal expectations. For example, gas prices tend to range between \$1.50 and \$4 per gallon. A line chart visualizing these prices could have a y-axis stretching from \$1 to \$4 in increments of \$1. In all cases, clearly indicate the scale of both axes.
— Remove outliers from the visualization only with extremely good justification (e.g. a known data entry error).
— Circles and other 2D shapes used in visualization should be scaled using their area, rather than the radius or side length.
— Don't involve 3D elements unnecessarily. Perspective can distort the visualization.

Clarity in design

— Use as few fonts as possible. Use either bold or italic to differentiate but not both.
— Use color to convey or highlight information, not as decoration.
— Use as few elements as possible to keep visuals clean and crisp. Complexity should be added only when it conveys additional information.

Mapping

Maps are useful visualizations for an analysis in which geography is critical. If geography is not central to the story, consider alternative ways to present the information. Beware of using maps to compare frequency by place, as such maps often reflect the population distribution rather than a meaningful rate.

Polls and surveys

Reporting on public opinion research requires rigorous inspection of a poll's methodology, provenance and results. The mere existence of a poll is not enough to make it news. Do not feel obligated to report on a poll or survey simply because it meets AP's standards.

Poll results that seek to preview the outcome of an election must never be the lead, headline or single subject of any story. Preelection horse race polling can and should inform reporting on political campaigns, but no matter how good the poll or how wide a candidate's margin, results of preelection polls always reflect voter opinion before all ballots are cast. Voter opinions can change before Election Day, and they often do.

When evaluating a poll or survey, be it an election poll or a survey on a topic unrelated to politics, the key question to answer is: Are its results likely to accurately reflect the opinion of the group being surveyed?

Generally, for the answer to be yes, a poll must:
— Disclose the questions asked, the results of the survey and the method in which it was conducted.
— Come from a source without a stake in the outcome of its results.
— Be representative of the population surveyed, usually by randomly sampling from that population and appropriately correcting for the fact that some types of people are more likely to respond to polls than others.
— Report the results in a timely manner.

Polls that pass these tests are suitable for publication.

Do not report on surveys in which the pollster or sponsor of research refuses to provide the information needed to make these assessments. In stories relying heavily on the results of a poll, always include a short description of how that poll meets the standards, allowing readers and viewers to evaluate the results for themselves: *The AP-NORC poll surveyed 1,020 adults from Dec. 7-11 using a sample drawn from NORC's probability-based AmeriSpeak Panel, which is designed to be representative of the U.S. population.*

Some other key points:
— Comparisons between polls are often newsworthy, especially those that show a change in public opinion over time. But take care when comparing results from different polling organizations, as difference in poll methods and question wording — and not a change in public opinion — may be the cause of differing results. Only infer that a difference between two polls is caused by a change in public opinion when those polls use the same survey methodology and question wording, and after taking into account the survey's margin of sampling error.
— Some organizations publish poll averages or aggregates that attempt to

combine the results of multiple polls into a single estimate in an effort to capture the overall state of public opinion about a campaign or issue. Averaging poll results does not eliminate error or preclude the need to examine the underlying polls and assess their suitability for publication. In election polling, survey averages can provide a general sense of the state of a race. However, only those polls that meet these standards should be included in averages intended for publication, and it is often preferable to include the individual results of multiple recent surveys to show where a race stands.

— Some pollsters release survey results to the first decimal place, which implies a greater degree of precision than is possible from scientific sampling. Poll results should always be rounded to whole numbers. Margins of sampling error can be reported to the first decimal place.

— Take care to use accurate language when describing poll results. For example, only groups comprising more than 50% of the population can be said to be the majority. If the largest group includes less than 50% of the surveyed population, it is a plurality. For survey estimates, the poll's margin of sampling error should be taken into account before describing a result as a majority. See **majority, plurality**.

— In most cases, *poll* and *survey* may be used interchangeably.

Polls are not perfect

When writing or producing stories that cite survey results, take care not to overstate the accuracy of the poll. Even a perfectly executed poll does not guarantee perfectly accurate results.

It is possible to calculate the potential sampling error of a poll of a random sample of a population, and that detail must be included in a story about a poll's results: *The margin of sampling error for all respondents is plus or minus 3.7 percentage points.* See **Margin of error** later in this entry.

Sampling error is not the only source of survey error, merely the only one that can be quantified using established and accepted statistical methods. Among other potential sources of error: the wording and order of questions, interviewer skill and refusal to participate by respondents selected for a sample. As a result, total error in a survey may exceed the reported margin of error more often than would be predicted based on simple statistical calculations.

Be careful when reporting on the opinions of a poll's subgroup — women under the age of 30, for example, in a poll of all adults. Find out and consider the sample size and margin of error for that subgroup; the sampling error may be so large as to render any reported difference meaningless. Results from subgroups totaling fewer than 100 people surveyed should not be reported.

Very large sample sizes do not preclude the need to rigorously assess a poll's methodology, as they may be an indicator of an unscientific and unreliable survey. Often, polls with several thousand respondents are conducted via mass text message campaigns or website widgets and are not representative of the general population.

Margin of error

A scientific survey of a random sample of a population will have a margin of sampling error. This margin is expressed in terms of *percentage points*, not *percent*.

For example, consider a poll with a margin of error of 5 percentage points. Under ideal circumstances, its results should reflect the true opinion of the population being surveyed, within plus or minus 5 percentage points, 95 of every 100 times that poll is conducted.

Sampling error is not the only source of error in a poll, but it is one that can be quantified. See the first section of this entry.

The margin of error varies inversely to the poll's sample size: The fewer people interviewed, the larger the margin of error. Surveys with 500 respondents or more are preferable.

Evaluating the margin of error is crucial when describing the results of a poll. Remember that the survey's margin of error applies to every candidate or poll response. Nominal differences between two percentages in a survey may not always be meaningful.

Use these rules to avoid exaggerating the meaning of poll results and to decide when to report that a poll finds one candidate is leading another, or that one group is larger than another.

— If the difference between two response options is more than twice the margin of error, then the poll shows one candidate is leading or one group is larger than another.
— If the difference is at least equal to the margin of error, but no more than twice the margin of error, then one candidate can be said to be *apparently leading* or *slightly ahead*, or one group can be said to be *slightly larger* than another.
— If the difference is less than the margin of error, the poll says a race *is close* or *about even*, or that two groups *are of similar size.*
— Do not use the term *statistical dead heat* or *statistical tie*, which is inaccurate if there is any difference between the candidates. If the poll finds the candidates are exactly tied, say *they are tied*. For very close races that aren't exact ties, the phrase *essentially tied* is acceptable, along with descriptions like *close* or *about even.*

There is no single established method of estimating error for surveys conducted online among people who volunteer to take part in surveys. While they may not report a margin of error, these surveys are still subject to error, uncertainty and bias.

Evaluating polls and surveys

When evaluating whether public opinion research is suitable for publication, consider the answers to the following questions.

— Has the poll sponsor fully disclosed the questions asked, the results of the survey and the method in which it was conducted?

Reputable poll sponsors and public opinion researchers will disclose the methodology used to conduct the survey, including the questions asked and the results of each, so that their survey may be subject to independent examination and analysis by others. Do not report on surveys in which the pollster or sponsor of research refuses to provide such information.

Some public opinion researchers agree to publicly disclose their methodology as part of the American Association for Public Opinion Research's transparency

POLLS AND SURVEYS

initiative. Participation does not mean polls from these researchers are automatically suitable for publication, only that they are likely to meet the test for disclosure. A list of transparency initiative members can be found on the association's website at: http://www.aapor.org/Standards-Ethics/Transparency-Initiative/Current-Members.aspx

– Does the poll come from a source without a stake in the outcome of its results?

Any poll suitable for publication must disclose who conducted and paid for the research. Find out the polling firm, media outlet or other organization that conducted the poll. Include this information in all poll stories, so readers and viewers can be aware of any potential bias.

Polls paid for by candidates or interest groups may be designed to produce results that are beneficial to that candidate or group, and they may be released selectively as a campaign tactic or publicity ploy. These polls should be carefully evaluated and usually avoided.

– How are people selected to take part in the poll? Does the poll rely on a random sample of a population, in which every member of that population has a known probability of inclusion?

These are known as *probability-based polls*, and they are the best method of ensuring the results of a survey reflect the true opinion of the group being surveyed.

Those conducted by telephone must include people interviewed on their cellphones. Those that only include landline interviews have no chance of reaching the more than half of American adults who have only a mobile phone.

Avoid polls in which computers conduct telephone interviews, sometimes referred to as IVR (for *interactive voice response*), *automated* or *robopolls*. These surveys cannot legally dial cellphones, and while they sometimes are supplemented with online interviews to reach cellphone users, such supplements are usually of dubious quality. These surveys also cannot randomly select respondents within a household, which can lead to underrepresentation of some demographic groups such as younger adults.

Polls conducted online are valid if the poll is of a panel of respondents recruited randomly from the entire population, with internet access or the option to take surveys over the phone provided to those who don't have internet access.

Many online polls are conducted using opt-in panels, which are composed of people who volunteer to take part, often in response to online advertisements. Research into such surveys has found that traditional demographic weighting is often insufficient to make such opt-in panels representative of a population as a whole. Results among demographic groups such as African Americans and Hispanics can be especially inaccurate, and biases within these groups are especially difficult to correct. These surveys lack representation of people without internet access, a population that differs in key ways from those who do have internet access.

However, opt-in surveys that use additional variables as part of their weighting schemes have shown more promising results, particularly those that use a probability-based sample that is supplemented and/or combined with other sample sources. Because of the difficulty in assessing such approaches and ongoing research into how well they work to reduce bias, the results from such polls should be published only after careful consideration of the techniques used to ensure the results are truly representative. The sample selection and weighting process must be disclosed in detail before they can be considered for publication.

Do not accept assurances from pollsters that use "proprietary" sampling and weighting methods that are not made available for review and scrutiny.

Balloting of visitors to a website, of a company's email list or polls conducted by Twitter users rely on self-selected samples that should always be avoided. They are both unrepresentative of a broader population and subject to manipulation.

For surveys conducted by mail and sent to a random selection of addresses, pay especially close attention to how long it took to field these polls, especially if they include topics in the news or pertaining to elections. Before publishing results of polls by mail, carefully consider whether the results of time-sensitive questions may be outdated. To overcome this issue, some U.S. surveys are now conducted by contacting people through the mail and allowing them to take the survey online or by phone.

Outside of the United States, many polls are conducted using in-person interviews of people at randomly selected locations. Many are of high quality. Pay close attention to how the pollsters tried to include rural and other hard-to-reach places in the survey sample.

Many political polls are based on interviews with registered voters, since registration is usually required for voting. Polls may be based on likely voters closer to an election; if so, ask the pollster how that group was identified. Polls that screen for likely voters at the sample level by only attempting to interview those who have a history of voting may include fewer nonvoters, but may also exclude some potential new voters.

— Has the poll been weighted to correct for the fact that some types of people are more likely to respond than others? What variables have been used, and where did the targets come from?

Most polls are weighted, or adjusted, to make sure that people who are less likely to respond are appropriately represented in the survey. Polls that do not weight to correct for nonresponse are likely to underrepresent key groups in the population that are harder to reach, including younger adults, members of minority groups and those without college degrees.

Find out what variables were used to weight the poll, and where the weighting targets came from. The best weighting targets usually come from high-quality government surveys such as the U.S. Census Bureau's American Community Survey or Current Population Survey. Take care with surveys that weight results among likely voters to estimates of demographics or partisan identification from a previous election. Those estimates themselves can be subject to considerable error, as turnout in one election may not reflect turnout in the next.

Polls that are not weighted on variables such as age, sex, race/ethnicity and education should be able to demonstrate how their survey samples compare with known demographics of the population being surveyed. These surveys may not be suitable for publication.

— Are the results being reported in a timely manner?

Public opinion can change quickly, especially in response to events. Make every

POLLS AND SURVEYS

effort to report results from a poll as close to the period when the survey was conducted as possible.

Be careful when considering results from polls fielded immediately after major events, such as political debates, that often sway public opinion in ways that may only be temporary. Similarly, if events directly related to a poll's questions have taken place since they were asked, the results may no longer reflect the opinion of the populations being surveyed. That does not mean they are no longer valid, but must be placed into the proper context. Often, such results are valuable in describing how public opinion has changed — or remained consistent — in the wake of such events.

In all cases, consider whether it is useful to inform readers and viewers directly when the poll was conducted: *The poll was taken three days after the president proposed new tax cuts. The poll was conducted the week before Congress passed the new health care legislation.*

The timeliness of results is especially crucial in reporting on pre-election polls.

Voter opinions often change during the course of a political campaign, and results from questions asked several weeks or in some cases days prior may no longer provide an accurate picture of the state of a race.

When describing voter opinions about candidates for political office, it's best to summarize results from several recent polls, or the trend in polls over time, rather than cite the results of a single survey in isolation.

Exit polls

Any poll seeking to project the outcome of an election on the day of the election itself — including exit polls — should be assessed both on its methodology and its historical accuracy, and consideration should be given to how much value the poll results add to the understanding of the election before any actual votes are counted.

It is important to take care with these surveys, especially when they predict a relatively narrow victory for a candidate or party. As with all surveys, exit polls and other election day surveys are subject to potential error. That potential error exists even among polls that are historically highly accurate; a poll's actual error may exceed its reported margin of sampling error.

In the United States, The Associated Press sponsors its own election survey, AP VoteCast. While this survey is used by AP to aid in declaring the winners of elections, its primary use is to explain the election. Never use AP VoteCast to say definitively who has won or lost an election. At AP, election outcomes in the U.S. should not be described as definite until AP has called a race and declared a winner.

In all cases, do not describe a candidate or party as having won or lost with certainty based only on exit poll results. Instead, consider saying that initial exit poll data shows a candidate ahead or suggests that a candidate has won.

In assessing whether an election poll such as an exit poll is suitable for publication, consider the following questions.

How was the poll conducted? Most traditional exit polls are conducted using random samples of voters exiting their polling places at a representative set of locations. Exit polls may not work well in countries where it is difficult to select a representative sample of polling places, where a significant proportion of voters

POLLS AND SURVEYS

cast their ballots by mail or in person before the day of the election, or where voters for some parties are significantly more or less likely than voters for other parties to respond to the exit poll. Other types of Election Day surveys should be carefully assessed to determine if their methodology makes them suitable for publication.

Has the poll been accurate in previous elections? If an exit poll has historically been inaccurate, it is likely better not to use the poll at all than to risk publishing incorrect projections. If results from the poll are published, extra care should be taken in describing its results and clearly explaining how the poll has failed in the past to accurately reflect the ultimate result.

Health and science

These fields offer incredibly interesting and universally appealing topics to cover, and there is never a shortage of good ideas or pitches vying for attention. But with this bonanza of opportunity comes unique responsibility. A misleading or incorrect story could lead someone to make unwise, harmful choices. It's impossible to be too careful, yet there's no need to fear these topics, either. The skills that make for good science or medical writing are the same as those for good reporting on any topic.

Chief among them is critical thinking: to question rather than accept a claim, to check what's already been written about it, to ask for evidence to evaluate the claim and to seek the help of experts to put it into context. Is it the first treatment for a disease or the fifth? The biggest rise in average temperature in a decade or the ninth? Does it change what scientists have long understood?

Anyone can write a recap of results. The journalist's job is to help readers understand what they mean.

CHOOSING STORIES

News stories are aimed at the public, not at scientists, doctors, investors or policymakers. They must be useful to general readers and written in clear language free of jargon.

In health and medicine, topics that affect a lot of people appeal to a larger audience than those that affect a few (heart disease versus a rare disease) unless there's a great human interest story or major advance that makes it newsworthy.

In science, advances that help further understanding of our world (or distant worlds) in ways that can be made relevant or interesting to general readers can be worth covering. Also worthy of coverage are stories that hold some other special appeal because of the subject or scientific approach.

News stories should have value for readers, not just give credit to a researcher, university or hospital. A good test: whether it would be talked about at the dinner table.

When initially evaluating potential stories, here are things to look for, and to look out for:

— Important science usually is made public in journals or at scientific meetings where a researcher's methods and results have been deemed acceptable by outside experts (a process called peer review). That gives their findings more credibility, though rigorous checking by reporters is still essential. Reputable scientists rarely announce their findings solely in a press release or at a press conference.

— Consider the source. Is it from an established research institution? A large, reputable journal, or one without peer review? Off-the-beaten-path places and minor journals can have good science, but reporting on it requires even more care than usual.

— Reports conducted by advocacy and industry groups, even though many employ accomplished scientists, should be treated with caution. That research is generally designed to make a point, not to look for an answer objectively.

— Beware of "breakthroughs" because few things truly are. Exaggeration makes readers and viewers distrust the media and science.

— Be skeptical of "first" and "only," and use these words only when you're sure they're true. It's often difficult or impossible to verify that something is a first. Or it may be a first for a certain research institution or hospital yet has been done elsewhere, or it's an incremental step that's technically a first but in reality is of small import.

— Be skeptical of health claims based on testimonials or anecdotes. They are not science. Many people ascribe benefits to something when it is really a placebo effect — when a person responds to a dummy treatment. Conversely, many people also ascribe their health problems to something without any way to know if that is truly the cause. Readers are not served well from one person's belief, experience or understanding of the effectiveness or safety of a treatment, a medical device, a diet or a chemical.

— Keep in mind that scientists are not infallible. They are human, with their own biases, and can make mistakes even when they're very careful.

SCIENTIFIC JOURNALS, MEETINGS AND EMBARGOES

Science and medical journals are written for scientists, researchers and doctors, offering professionals in the field findings that further research can build on.

Sometimes these findings are important or interesting enough for general readers. These are usually published in major journals and provided several days in advance under embargo to registered journalists to allow time to prepare stories and consult experts.

Understand, however, that institutions use embargoes to drum up interest. Science happens continuously, not just when journals or universities announce findings. Avoid embargoes that do not allow you to speak to sources outside of the institution that is promoting their work.

Never use information obtained under embargo for any other purpose besides journalism. Do not discuss with family, friends or others while the information is under embargo. Drug company stocks rise and fall on such news, and journalists can be liable like anyone else if insider trading happens because of improper or premature disclosure of results.

There are thousands of journals, some with more rigorous standards than others. Research that has not been peer-reviewed, including articles posted on preprint servers, should be reported with extreme care. Even studies published in respected peer-reviewed journals require journalistic vetting with experts unconnected with the research because the process of peer review is not foolproof.

Research sometimes is presented first at scientific or medical conferences and meetings. Coverage of this research requires extra care because often only partial results are released and they haven't been subjected to full peer review. If reporting findings presented at meetings, it's best to be there in person so you can consult outside experts who have seen the presentation.

TYPES OF STUDIES

How a study was done helps determine how reliable its results are. Here are things to consider about some common study designs:

EXPERIMENTS: The strongest studies are experiments in which researchers can directly test a hypothesis while considering alternative explanations. In medicine, the best ones randomly assign a group of people to get either the treatment being tested or a fake version of it or a current standard of care. Neither the participants nor their doctors know who got what until the study ends (which is why they are called "double blind"). Sometimes experiments, especially early-stage ones, lack a comparison group, and that limits what can be known from the results.

OBSERVATIONAL STUDIES: Observational studies examine a group of people or compare groups based on such factors as how much they weigh or what medicines they take. A common version is a study that looks for links between lifestyle habits or exposures to chemicals and diseases or conditions. Some things can be learned only from observational studies. For example, it would be unethical to assign one group to a medical test involving radiation every year and watch for 20 years to see how many develop cancer, and compare the results to a group that didn't get the annual test. Drawing conclusions from observational studies is hard because many other things can affect results besides the factor being examined. This is called *confounding*. It is a particular problem with food, nutrition and diet studies because it is almost impossible to account for all the other things a person does over long periods. But sometimes, especially when multiple observational studies reach the same conclusion, the evidence is strong enough to establish a cause-and-effect relationship. This is how scientists originally showed that smoking causes lung cancer. *Prospective* (forward-looking) observational studies, in which the study population is carefully tracked over time, are more reliable than retrospective studies, in which researchers must take a "best guess" approach by relying on questionnaires and looking back at records.

META-ANALYSES: Another type of study is a meta-analysis, when researchers compile results of many related studies that individually are not big or strong enough to establish a point but that might suffice collectively. Reporting on these requires great care; much depends on which studies researchers include or leave out. Big numbers give statistical power to observe an effect, but combining studies also magnifies the flaws in each one's methods.

MODELS: In a modeling study, scientists use computer simulations to play out thousands of scenarios to see what could happen when changes are made to complex systems, like ecosystems, climate or cosmic events.

The mathematics of the model should be checked with outside experts, along with the assumptions that go into the calculations. Researchers should show that they have rigorously tested the model by running it over and over — and, if possible, by applying it retroactively and seeing if the results match real-world observations from the past (such as air temperature or sea level, for climate models).

RESEARCH STAGES: Drug studies usually are conducted in three phases in humans. In phase 1, small numbers of people are given an experimental treatment to see if it's safe. In phase 2, more are treated to further test safety and determine appropriate dosages. Phase 3 studies are large tests of safety and effectiveness.

HEALTH AND SCIENCE

It's often best to wait to report until then because many things that look good early on fail at this stage. They're also what regulators usually rely on for approval decisions. Note: While it's important for the reporter to understand this, there's usually no need to bog down news stories with these terms. Instead of *phase 1*, for example, call it *early research*.

JUDGING STUDIES

Here are some things to consider when evaluating a study:

— Is it in people or animals? Results in animals frequently don't extend to humans.

— How large is it? Bigger is almost always better, but it depends on the type of study. An experiment that tests drug X in 1,000 people and includes a comparison group is much more definitive than a 5,000-person observational study that notes just who took drug X and how they fared. In rare situations, studies of these size are impossible, and small studies are just as valid statistically.

— Is there something else that might explain or influence the results, such as age, other medical conditions, genetic differences or where people live? If so, did researchers adjust results to consider these in a way outside experts think is valid?

— Is it consistent with prior studies? Studies with results that contradict earlier, well-regarded research should be treated with more skepticism. That doesn't mean you should ignore studies with outlier results, but you should vet them even more thoroughly than usual.

— Does the effect increase with the dose? In an environmental study, for instance, does the occurrence or severity of a health problem increase as the amount of toxic exposure increases? There may be a special reason if it doesn't, but it may be a red flag.

— Is there a plausible biological explanation? A study result has more credibility if researchers can point to how it occurred. For example, a study finding that left-handed people are more likely to suffer from athlete's foot should be regarded with great skepticism if researchers cannot suggest a credible explanation. On the other hand, a researcher who found that adding fluoride to a city's water supply reduced tooth decay can credibly point to experiments showing that fluoride bonds with the outer layer of tooth enamel and strengthens it.

— Does it add to knowledge, or is it a "marketing study" designed to encourage doctors to use a company's drug in the guise of a clinical trial? Similarly, be aware of awareness campaigns that may push readers to be tested for conditions they shouldn't be, to create more "worried well," and sell more drugs or boost donations to advocacy groups.

NUMBERS

Numbers can help you tell health, science and environment stories — and help you tell if there is a story to be told. First, we want to know whether the results of a study are statistically significant, which means that the risk they are just a fluke is acceptably low. Then we need to carefully show readers just how much difference in outcome the study found. Patients "did better" tells us little; "60 out of 100 patients who took the drug survived, compared with just 30 of 100 who did not" is much more informative.

Here are some statistics you will encounter in studies. You will probably never tell your audience about p-values or confidence intervals, but they help you evaluate whether a study result is worth reporting. You probably will include risks and percentages because they can give your audience important context — as long as you handle them properly.

RELATIVE RISK: Relative risk is the risk of something happening to one group compared with the risk of it happening to another. This is often expressed in a fraction or ratio in scientific studies. If there is no difference, the ratio is 1. For example, if a study finds that the relative risk of a group of smokers getting a disease is 1.5 compared with a group of nonsmokers, it means the smokers are 1.5 times as likely — or 50% more likely — to develop the disease. But it doesn't say how likely it is that either group gets the disease. For that, you need absolute risk.

ABSOLUTE RISK: Absolute risk is the risk of something happening at all. For example, the nonsmoking group in the above example may have had a 4 in 100 chance of getting the disease, while the smokers had a 6 in 100 chance of getting a disease. Another example: A drug that extends life by 50% (a relative risk) sounds impressive, but that might mean living six months on average on a treatment versus four months without. Readers deserve both views of the results.

P-VALUE: A p-value (or probability value) is a measure that scientists use to gauge whether a result reflects a real, reliable difference or is just a fluke. Generally, a p-value of less than 0.05 suggests the result is reliable. So if a study reports that a drug lowered cholesterol and the result has a p-value of 0.04, it has met the test. This number is nearly always included in medical studies and in some science studies if relevant. Keep in mind, however, that such statistics can be gamed, in what is known as "p-hacking," or cherry-picking experimental conditions until there is a statistically significant result. Ask researchers whether they tested more variables than they report.

CONFIDENCE INTERVAL: In addition to a single result (often expressed as a relative risk), many medical, environmental and science studies include a confidence interval that encompasses the range of likely results. If a confidence interval ranges from below 1 to over 1, it means the result is not statistically significant. For example, if a drug lowered the risk of a heart attack but the confidence interval was 0.85 to 1.25, it fails the test; there is a meaningful chance that the drug did not actually lower the risk of heart attack. Another warning sign is if the upper and lower bound of a confidence interval are far apart (1.2 to 15.3, for example). In this sense, you can think of confidence intervals like margins of error in an opinion poll: the tighter the range, the better.

SIGNIFICANT: *Significant* when referring to statistics means the results have passed statistical tests. But that does not mean the results are automatically noteworthy — or significant — for readers. Even though a study finds a statistically significant benefit from a treatment, that doesn't necessarily mean it makes people feel noticeably better or is worth using. Study results that are not statistically significant should be treated with great skepticism, though there may occasionally be circumstances where a result is newsworthy even if it falls short of statistical significance.

PERCENTAGES: There is a big difference between percent and percentage points, so be careful when using these terms to report results (see **percent, percentage, percentage points**). If a drug changes the number of people in a group who have high blood pressure from 80% to 40%, that's a 50% decline but a difference of 40 percentage points.

REPORTING HEALTH AND SCIENCE

Among the most critical parts of reporting a story that involves health, science or the environment is getting comments from outside experts who know the subject well. When reporting a study, you should find experts who had no role in the work.

Ideally, consult more than one about the methods, the results and the conclusions being made by the study's authors. This helps reveal whether the study is worth reporting and if so, why, even though the study has already been reviewed by peers.

To find independent experts, check a study's footnotes and references for who has previously researched the topic. PubMed and Google Scholar can also point to experts and previous studies for context. Ask them: Do you believe the conclusions? Does the evidence strongly support them? What are the problems with the study or conclusions? What other factors could be at play? Is this a big deal and why? How does this fit with what we knew before?

Don't rely solely on a press release about a study; always read the actual study. Sometimes press releases hype or exaggerate claims and conclusions beyond what a study really showed.

Other important reporting tips and considerations include:

FINANCIAL DISCLOSURES: Find out who paid for the research, and report it when it is relevant, which is almost always the case with studies of treatments. Much if not most medical research is paid for by private companies, or advocacy or special interest groups; governments increasingly fund a smaller share. This doesn't mean the work is bad or wrong, but stories need to report what role the sponsor played (supplied the drug? compiled the results?). Include what ties, if any, the researchers had to the sponsor or its competitors, and whether the researchers might profit through patents or royalties. Sometimes sponsorship is a reason not to write, such as a health claim for a food based on an industry-funded study.

CAVEATS: Science is rarely definitive. There often are other potential explanations for a phenomenon or competing interpretations of what a fossil tells us about the past. As long as those alternatives also have a sound scientific underpinning, they should be noted.

SIDE EFFECTS: There always are risks or side effects to treatments. If a news release or a meeting abstract doesn't mention that, it's a red flag — and you need to find out. Any story reporting a treatment's benefits also should include its risks and any serious side effects.

COSTS: Always try to include the cost of a treatment. If it's experimental and the cost hasn't been set, often you can discuss context, such as the cost of other similar treatments. Also try to find out if insurers are likely to cover it, or note that it is still unclear whether they will and that insurance policies and out-of-pocket costs vary. Often, that's what patients need to know.

TIME TO MARKET: Remember that it can take many years for a drug to move from testing to government approval and commercial use. Many drugs never make the transition because of concerns about profitability or effectiveness. Readers often assume that they will be able to use an experimental drug immediately after it has been tested. Avoid giving them false hope. Instead, explain the steps that lie ahead and how long they are likely to take.

PITFALLS

FALSE BALANCE: Do not give a platform to unqualified claims or sources in the guise of balancing a story by including all views. This perpetuates denialism. For example, coverage of a study describing effects of climate change should not seek "other side" comment that humans have no influence on the climate; in reporting about lung cancer deaths, do not pursue comment that smoking does not cause cancer.

On the other hand: Recognize when statements are false but also newsworthy and necessary to report. Examples include a key policymaker rejecting mainstream climate science, or parents lobbying Congress with the argument that vaccines cause autism. Such statements or actions need to be reported — but such stories must prominently include fact-checking material making clear that science shows the statements are wrong.

PATIENTS AND FAMILIES: When writing about the medical conditions of patients or public figures, it's important to verify information supplied by the patient, friends or family with medical records or their doctor. Without confirmation, attribute the information to its source. This is not to say that patients are not worth talking to; quite the opposite. Patients' experiences and their struggle to understand and navigate their condition and how it is being treated is often interesting and newsworthy. But quote patients on their lives and their feelings; quote scientists on science. Use care when featuring patients in anecdotes to make sure they are truly representative or typical of what you're writing about. Be wary of patients suggested by drug or device makers to speak with journalists because they may have been compensated or coached.

NONEXPERTS: Don't report medical advice from celebrities or sports figures. They're often paid by companies or advocacy groups to pitch products or a point of view, such as the need for certain cancer screenings or a diet or "wellness" product, and they are not scientific or medical experts.

TOXIC CHEMICALS, RADIATION, CARCINOGENS: Living down the street from a dump doesn't necessarily raise someone's risk for a disease. Working with a known cancer-causing substance for decades might. Reporting on these topics requires consulting toxicologists, public health researchers and other specialists. As with general reporting, avoid reporting claims that are based on advocacy or made by lawyers or people who claim to be affected rather than science. When news requires coverage, for example when a major lawsuit is filed, be sure to note if the claims have not yet been proven. Treat all claims made by sources — whether they are made by polluters or by those who claim to be affected — with the same level of scrutiny. Making sure to include absolute risk (discussed above) when reporting on these subjects is critical to provide readers an accurate understanding of danger.

CANCER CLUSTERS: Most suspected clusters, after investigation, turn out to be either baseless or unverifiable. That's especially true if they involve many types of cancer, which have many different causes. Other factors such as a family history of the disease, genes that predispose people to it and habits such as smoking all affect cancer risk. It requires public health expertise and training to sort out these risks, so always seek out qualified independent experts when reporting on alleged clusters.

CURES: Avoid calling a disease cured, especially cancer. An infection or temporary condition can be cured, but doctors can't be sure that a cancer won't recur, so they say "remission" for that reason.

WRITING TIPS

We are translators between people who speak the language of science and ordinary readers who don't. If you don't understand a term or know for certain that you can replace a technical term with a more reader-friendly one, ask an expert for help. You can write *high blood pressure* instead of *hypertension*, for example, but you cannot refer to a *cardiac arrest* as a *heart attack*, because they are two different things.

As in all writing, avoid jargon and cliches — even in quotes.

Some common science and medical jargon that can be said more simply include: *clinician* (use *doctor* instead), *efficacy* (just say how well it works or not), *literature* (*other studies*), *pathogen* (*germs*), *proportion* (*share*), *prevalence* (say how common something is), *trials* or *clinical trials* (*studies, research*), *underlying condition* (*other conditions, other medical conditions*).

Some common cliches in science writing include: *cutting edge, holy grail, game changing, low-hanging fruit, outside of the box, paradigm shift, perfect storm, sci-fi, sea change, silver bullet, smoking gun, tip of the iceberg, wake-up call.*

INDIVIDUAL TERMS

Specific health and science terms are in the Stylebook's alphabetical section.

HEALTH AND SCIENCE

Social media and web-based reporting guidelines

With its global and cultural reach, social media is embedded in daily life. It is often the first place people go to share photos, videos and their accounts of major events. Public conversations have migrated onto digital forums. And it's a go-to spot for news consumers. In short, journalists need to pay close attention to social media – and use it wisely.

While a vital space for reporting, online platforms can also be rife with misinformation. Journalists must separate truth from fiction. Verification can be challenging. But it is essential when reporting through online sources.

Finding people and information online requires the same critical thinking skills that reporters use in the field. Quick, smart reactions to breaking news can be key to locating witnesses, photos and videos. Often, social media is the easiest, fastest — and sometimes only — way to reach people.

Some tips and best practices:

How do we use social media in our work?
— To track down sources — in particular, people who witnessed a news event or who have a direct stake in a reporting topic.
— To gather user-generated content, like photos or videos.
— To get a sense of how people are reacting to an event.
— To look for news tips or discussion trends that might lead to or form a story.
— To diversify our sources, including seeking voices of underrepresented people, groups and communities.
— To directly report news developments to the public and to promote our work.
— To produce and distribute original content that's tailored to a given platform.

Some things to consider
— There are no one-size-fits-all answers to how we as journalists should manage our social media accounts with respect to our personal privacy. But consider various factors, including your newsroom's conduct and ethics policy, and approach social networks with clarity regarding your personal feelings and professional needs.
— Posts or messages that are intended to be personal can easily be shared, just like emails can be forwarded and conversations recorded. Never violate your organization's conduct or ethics policy under the assumption that your posts are personal, not professional. Social networks bring into clear focus that

journalists are considered journalists by the public 24/7.
— Don't reach out online to people who could be in imminent danger. You don't want to distract them from staying safe or give away their location with an alert on their phone. The safety of others is more important than a scoop.

User-generated content

User-generated content, or UGC, is photos, videos or other content with news or editorial value that has been produced by anyone who isn't working as a professional journalist. Sometimes this is also referred to as citizen journalism, when members of the public capture news events on their own devices either by chance or by pursuing a story. User-generated content may be found on social networks or pursued by a reporter on the scene of a news event.

It is essential to hold UGC to the same standards as any other information in a reporter's notebook. Journalists handling UGC face a number of challenges, including verification. Reporters should seek to tell the story of each piece of video and audio and every photo we acquire. For AP reporters, this can mean tapping into the organization's considerable knowledge base, drawing on the expertise of staff around the world.

Securing access to content can often be a challenge, especially in a breaking news situation when video or photos have been widely circulated on social networks. Always look for the original source of the media. Reposts are common. Users sometimes post content they got from family, friends or other apps. So it's important to be sure who shot the photo or video. Once that content owner has been identified, ask for permission to use the material. Also ask tough questions about when they captured material, why they were there, and anything else that can help you determine the authenticity of the content. Searching a person's social media profile can also help establish whether that person is trustworthy.

When publishing UGC, make every effort to give due credit to the person who has created that content. Use the person's name if allowed to, or a username if it is that person's preference.

How do you vet sources found through social media?

In general, apply the same principles used in vetting a source found any other way. But there are additional challenges, like private circulation of content, users concealing their identities or content being posted by accounts other than the original source.

Most importantly, avoid lifting photos or videos from social networking sites without identifying the content creator first. Most social media sites offer a way to communicate with a user. Use this to establish direct contact, so you can explain what you're working on, how you plan to use the material and get more detailed information about the source and their claims.

Some social networks use a check mark or a similar icon to denote accounts that have been verified to belong to the named celebrity, journalist, government official or other public figure. Verification is helpful in authenticating an account but should not be blindly trusted. Keep in mind that accounts without such a check mark may have been created by a third party for fraudulent, parody or other reasons.

Beware of fake accounts or ones that seem to have been created specifically for an event. If the source provides factual information that's central to a story, always pursue at least one additional source for confirmation.

Companies and other organizations regularly use social media to post announcements and press releases. One way to verify an account is to see if a website known to represent the same group links to that account. Also look for the verified check mark if that service offers it. But keep in mind that a password to an account could be compromised, and someone may have temporarily taken over a legitimate account. If there are any suspicions, verify the post directly with the individual or group, using contact information independently obtained.

If you come across photos, videos or other content that you would like to use in your news report, you'll need to verify the authenticity of the piece of content. You'll also need to determine who controls the copyright of the material and get permission from that person or organization to use it.

Verifying UGC

Reverse image search is the use of a search engine to find websites where an image appears. It is the gold standard and should be used for all UGC and third-party photos and videos. Platforms like Google Images, Yandex and TinEye offer different tools for searching the internet for past versions of images. This can help find original sources, but also flush out old visuals being recirculated in relation to recent events.

Verify the **credibility of the story** by cross-referencing UGC against your organization's own reporting, reporting from trusted media outlets or posts from other independent sources on social media.

Local knowledge can help determine whether images are from the **location** they claim. If not possible or the location is too obscure, compare it against online maps, satellite and street views. The devil lies in the details, so check flags, uniforms, road signs, license plates or shop names for leads. Listen for spoken languages, accents and any other audible details in videos. Make sure the images match the **time** of day or night the event is meant to have happened and look for clues in weather conditions, people's clothing or trees and greenery.

What information can be gleaned from looking at social media profiles?

Social media sites each format their accounts differently, but they all have a few common elements that are important to look at when trying to verify users' identities or assess their proximities to a news event:

HANDLE/USERNAME: People sometimes use their first and last names when setting up profiles. Many will use the same handle on different platforms. A simple Google search of their username can offer valuable information. Some people don't use their full names on their accounts, however, so other profile details need to be assessed in those instances.

BIO/"ABOUT" SECTION: Details shared can include but are not limited to the person's location, occupation, workplace, educational background and birthday. Each user determines how much personal information they make public.

PROFILE PICTURE: A person's profile picture or other photos of themselves posted on their account can help connect them to a photo or video from a news event. Running a reverse image search of a profile picture can also help spot fake accounts.

CONTACT INFORMATION: Profiles can include users' email addresses or phone numbers. They're also likely to include a way to message the person directly. If the user is sharing information about a breaking news event, it's best to publicly reply to their post first and follow up in direct messages as needed. Message requests don't always send notifications.

RECENT POSTS: A user's most recent activity on their account, whether text posts or photos and videos, can also help determine who they are and how relevant they are to a story. Check to see whether they've written about topics you're covering or shared visuals they took themselves from where they're located. Context clues in the photos or videos, such as street signs or landmarks, can help determine if the user is actually close to a situation you're looking into.

Searching social media

There are many platforms out there, with new ones regularly emerging. Here we examine best practices in searching for content on some of the biggest social media platforms.

To get strong results, be thoughtful about your search terms and refine them as you go. People who aren't journalists don't write like journalists, so try to think of what they might say. Speed is also key in finding content when news breaks.

Twitter

The Twitter Advanced Search is simple but powerful. Try different combinations of keywords to find what you're looking for. Search results can be sorted to show most recent tweets first or filtered to limit the tweets to photos or videos. You can use "and" and "or" in the searches and choose among several languages. The "People" search area lets you look for tweets from, or to, specific user accounts. You can also specify a date range for when the tweets were originally sent. Twitter Lists are a great way for teams to narrow down news feeds to accounts from their coverage area, while the Twitter application TweetDeck is a place for teams to collaborate on searches under one account. TweetDeck allows users to view lists of news feeds, messages, notifications and more in a digestible dashboard.

Facebook

The Facebook search field makes it easy to type in what you're looking for and then refine the search by type of result (people, photos, videos, etc.). When you find someone, message them privately or comment on the post that you're contacting them about, identify yourself and give the person a way to reach you through phone or email. Note that Facebook messages sent to strangers will generate "message requests," which recipients may or may not notice among their notifications. You can also try to find other ways to contact users — maybe they have a link to a blog or an email address, or perhaps you can find the same person on Twitter or LinkedIn. Facebook Live videos can be a great way to follow a breaking news event using the same search functions.

Instagram

Instagram allows you to search for photos and videos by hashtag, user, or geographic location. Search results on Instagram are tailored toward the searching account's trends and interests, so make sure to be specific in your search. Look through results organized by "most recent" for chronologically ordered posts. Instagram Stories, a tool that allows users to post moments of their day, can be a useful place to find breaking news, but make sure to verify any videos as original content. Beware of reposts.

Google Images

The search by image function on Google Images can be a handy tool for tracking down original content. Press the camera icon near the search bar and upload an image URL or saved file. Google will show you "visually similar images," and will list websites where the image was posted. This should help track down the original and find old postings that could debunk images.

YouTube

YouTube can be a good place to find developing news videos and background footage for general newsgathering. Conduct a search using the box and click "Filter" when the results are returned. You can then narrow the results by time frame or change how they are displayed. Consider the keywords someone uploading video may use, as well as the city and specific streets or landmarks they may refer to. To message the person who posted the video, click on their username and go to their "About" page. Some users will list contact information, others may not. Try Googling their username or reverse-image search their avatar/profile picture to try to find them on other networks.

TikTok

TikTok has become the go-to social media site for many people. It is buzzing with viral content that can regularly be found reposted on other social media sites, with the TikTok logo and username overlaid. To search TikTok, toggle to the "Discover" page to find trending videos, hashtags and specific content creators. Make sure to check the user's bio for linked social media accounts or contact information.

Referencing user-generated content

When using or referencing UGC in the AP report, we must be consistent about how we refer to the content. Here is some recommended language for use in various formats.

Video scripts and shotlists

Use what's applicable from the following caveats before each UGC shot:

++USER GENERATED CONTENT: This video has been authenticated by AP based on the following validation checks:
++Video and audio content checked by regional experts against known locations and events
++Video is consistent with independent AP reporting
++Video cleared for use by all AP clients by (content creator or third-party

SOCIAL MEDIA

granting authorization)

Restrictions should also be added if applicable. For example, ++Editorial use only, no archive, no resale – for content acquired as handout.

Photos
Stills should be marked as (Name of source via AP) and MANDATORY CREDIT is the standard.

Audio reports
Sound from validated UGC of (fill in as appropriate). COURTESY: ((mandatory on-air credit))

Aside from social media, what about the internet in general?

Anything you find in this sprawling information repository should be assessed and vetted with the same care that you use for everything else. Even what may look like an official press release issued by a company can be doctored or fabricated. Be leery of press releases posted on sites other than an organization's own known website or an established clearinghouse such as PR Newswire or Business Wire.

Be especially careful about websites and social networks that allow anyone to contribute text, photos and other information.

Some points to consider:
— Whom does a webpage belong to? Is the owner's identity verifiable, or is that person pretending to be someone else? Avoid anonymous pages just as you would avoid a source whose identity you could not verify.
— Is there contact information in case you want to follow up? One way to check who owns a domain name is through a "Whois" query at a website such as www.networksolutions.com/whois/index.jsp. Keep in mind, however, that data is self-reported and could be incorrect. In addition, many site owners now register for domain names anonymously.
— The source for the information on the page should be clearly stated. Is it a primary or secondary source? Can it be checked somewhere else?
— Does the website accept user contributions? If so, is there a vetting process? Wikipedia, for instance, allows individuals to contribute to encyclopedia entries regardless of expertise. It may provide a good starting point for research, but you should follow the footnotes for the source material and look for additional sources of information.
— Based on what you know, how accurate does the information seem? If there's something on the site that you know is incorrect, there may be other errors.
— Are there any obvious signs of bias? One possible clue: the type of sites linked to.
— Is the page current? If it hasn't been updated lately, the information may be outdated.
— Be wary of information in email because the sender's address can be easily forged. Again, it is best to verify information directly with the person you believe is the sender.

SOCIAL MEDIA

— Don't believe everything you see. Software such as Photoshop makes it easy to alter or manufacture photographs or video clips that look real to the untrained eye. Deepfake videos generated by artificial intelligence are also difficult to distinguish from the real thing.

— Use common sense. Just as you wouldn't necessarily trust an anonymous flyer you pick up on the street, be wary of websites and social accounts you stumble across. Do not assume that a site belongs to a particular company or group just because its name is in the web address.

See **domain name; misinformation, fact checks, fake news; internet security;** and the **Digital Security for Journalists** chapter.

Digital security for journalists

It's impossible to be productive as a journalist without extensive use of digital communications. That also involves securing devices, online accounts and your reporting material to protect your sources and your work.

Anyone dealing with sensitive material should follow certain basic practices. You may not be able to stop sophisticated state-backed hackers, but you can complicate their efforts — maybe enough to make them give up, and certainly enough to frustrate their less sophisticated counterparts.

Good practices can also help you avoid online harassment — malicious trolling and message-bombing — and doxxing, the malicious publication of information such as home addresses, phone numbers and email addresses. You also want to be careful what data you share with social media platforms and make it as difficult as possible for malicious hackers to hijack your accounts there.

Here are some techniques, tools and resources to help you secure your data and protect yourself online. Many may already be familiar. Most security compromises stem from lapses in digital hygiene — not high-tech hacking.

1) Use secure passwords. Strongly consider multifactor authentication

First, secure your smartphone with a strong PIN/passcode — ideally, at least eight digits. Yes, facial recognition and fingerprints are also options. But an intimidating security agent could force you to use them against your will. And there are privacy concerns.

Always use unique passwords for every online service or device. Reusing passwords means that any single hack could end up granting the bad guys access to much of your online life. If that happens, an attacker could gain control of all your accounts and change the passwords to lock you out. Good luck challenging that form of identity theft.

Passwords should also be complex. Automated password crackers can quickly defeat simple passwords based on dictionary words, even when strung together or with letters replaced by numbers ("0" for "o," "3" for "e," etc.). Many experts say the safest option is to use passwords made from random strings of letters, numbers and symbols — and a different one for every account.

Such random passwords are almost impossible to remember, so give serious consideration to an online password manager such as 1Password or Dashlane. These programs can typically generate random passwords, store them, and even fill them into website logins automatically.

You'll still need a "master password" to access the password manager. One safe option is to choose a passphrase — a short, personally memorable and hard-to-guess phrase such as "myRabb1tquincy!AteG4rbageFries." (Now that it's published here, though, definitely don't use that one.)

In the absence of a password manager, try to include at least one capital letter, one lowercase letter, one number and one symbol in every password. Exercise particular care with passwords to online email and social-network accounts, since they may grant access to sources and could let others masquerade as you.

Your email password is often your most important, especially if it also grants access to a wide array of other online tools, such as Microsoft Office or Google services. Protected social-networking passwords are also crucial, as they may offer access to sources — and could allow others to masquerade as you online.

Multifactor authentication is also highly recommended. Most people are familiar with two-factor authentication, in which you need to enter a code texted to your phone in addition to your password. But those texted codes can be intercepted. And your phone number can be hijacked. Instead, consider apps from Google or Microsoft that can generate codes directly on your phone or turn the phone itself into the authenticator.

When reporting on highly sensitive subjects, it may also be worth adding a third factor in the form of a physical electronic key. Such devices can fit on a keychain and use USB or Bluetooth technology. Google offers a free Advanced Protection Program for users at high risk, though security keys must be purchased.

To protect your privacy, you should also consider getting a virtual phone number instead of your real cellphone number when signing up for online services or making calls to shady and potentially hostile sources. Google Voice is a good option here, though it only works in the U.S. for those with a personal Google account. There is also a tradeoff, as Google collects data on and profits from your online activities. But Google also has some of the best security in the industry and is good about alerting users to suspicious activity.

2) Remember: Some computers and channels are more secure than others

Always be aware of how your phone or computer is connecting to the internet and how you're communicating with others. Seemingly minor choices can inadvertently expose your messages, browser history and more.

Different networks have different levels of security. A wired office connection is reasonably secure from eavesdropping. So is your workplace Wi-Fi — as long as you have to log into it with your employee credentials or a similar method. Open Wi-Fi networks, however — such as those at coffee shops, hotels and airports — usually aren't secure, which means that anyone in the area could be reading your communications and copying the passwords you enter into sites you visit.

If you're ever in doubt, use VPN software, which creates a "virtual private network" — an encrypted tunnel to a safe computing environment such as your organization's intranet. (In authoritarian nations, VPNs can also provide an on-ramp to the open internet.) VPNs are quite secure as long as you trust the VPN provider and the computer you are running it on. Be careful about your choice of provider. Organizations including Consumer Reports publish guides and can help you choose a reliable VPN.

Avoid doing sensitive work on machines you can't vouch for, as unfamiliar computers might have viruses, key-logging software or other malware installed. Especially try to avoid typing your passwords on a public computer or other untrusted system. If you must log in from such a machine, change any passwords you used once you're at a secure computer.

Phones are harder to intercept over the air, although mobile carriers have full access to your connections and your location, even when you're not making calls. If you're meeting with sensitive sources or otherwise looking to avoid surveillance, leave your phone behind or put it in a "Faraday pouch" that blocks both incoming and outgoing signals. (Simply powering down your phone may not protect you from tracking.)

All devices should be immediately updated as soon as software patches and updates become available. Falling behind risks being exposed to newly discovered vulnerabilities.

3) Stay anonymous online and protect communications

Journalists are right to be concerned about surveillance. So pay similar attention to your means of communication. Email, for instance, has the weakest security of any method. Unless it's encrypted en route, it's no more secure than sending a postcard.

Most email is not encrypted in transit, although software add-ons like Virtru can provide encryption using your existing email service. Email encrypted using the popular tool Pretty Good Privacy can be very secure, but PGP is difficult to set up and use correctly — and can be compromised after the fact if your private key leaks. Email services such as Protonmail, Tutanota, Startmail (Europe-based) and Riseup use encryption and are reasonably well established.

Standard text messages also travel unencrypted, though a growing number of instant-messaging apps including Apple's iMessage encrypt messages. Other good options include Signal, WhatsApp and Wickr.

Signal is the gold standard for private calls and messaging on smartphones. WhatsApp employs the same encryption technology but is owned by Meta, which can track who you contact, though not the contents of conversations or messages.

Both Signal and WhatsApp offer group text and video chats; Apple now also offers secure group video chats on FaceTime. Wickr lacks video but handles messaging and calls. For secure videoconferencing via browser, try Jitsi, which uses PGP and doesn't track participants.

The first time you connect, use the phone or some other channel simultaneously to ensure that the person on the other end is really who you think it is. Also be aware that no amount of communication security will help if someone later reads the message history stored on your phone or computer (see point 5 below).

If you visit a website directly from your personal computer or smartphone without tools that mask your browsing, your identity can easily be determined. One option for use on both phones and computers is The Onion Router, or Tor, which is designed to hide your IP address, conceal your location and erase your online footprints. It's a best used with a VPN.

And a reminder: Third-party collaboration programs including Slack and Microsoft Teams can't be trusted for secure communications such as sharing confidential sources or information. Much like unencrypted email, what's

DIGITAL SECURITY

discussed there can be obtained from the providers themselves by authorities with a subpoena.

4) Beware of phishing, still the top means of malware infection. Always read the URL

Phishing is the tactic of tricking people into divulging their passwords or allowing malicious software onto their phone or computer. A common phishing tactic is to send an email or a text message — often forged to look like a legitimate communication from someone you know or trust — containing a link. Clicking it could take you to a counterfeit website — perhaps one that resembles your bank — which can harvest your password if you try to log in. Clicking the link or opening an attachment might also surreptitiously install software that lets hackers take control of your device.

To avoid phishing, never open a link or file from an unknown or untrusted source; double-check it even if the sender seems legitimate. Read the website address in the link and don't click if it looks even remotely suspicious. Flag the message and send it to an expert if you believe it might be malicious.

In the meantime, keep your browser, computer and phone operating systems up to date; that minimizes your vulnerability to attack.

A sophisticated state-backed hacker also can break into your phone, read everything on it and eavesdrop in real time without any action by you — no need for clicked links or opened attachments. For that reason, these intrusions are known as zero-clicks. The Israeli spyware company NSO Group is the best-known seller of such software and dozens of journalists have been hacked with it.

5) Think about what data is stored and where — especially if it's in the cloud

Many communications programs make automatic copies. How many copies of sensitive chat logs, photographs and private messages are floating around on your laptop? And on your phone? Are any copies stored in the cloud? Do you back up your entire phone or computer to the cloud? You should know the answers if you need to protect sensitive material.

Your organization may already have data retention policies or guidance on best practices. If it doesn't, consult an attorney about what data to keep while reporting. You may want to avoid storing some types of data electronically in the first place, especially if you are traveling in a war zone or a country with repressive rulers where sources' lives are at risk. Some journalists have dusted off typewriters for delicate investigations.

Ask similar questions about data stored in the cloud. Is it encrypted both in transit and at rest in the cloud? If not, consider switching to a provider that will protect data this way, or use a program that encrypts files and folders before they are saved to the cloud.

Don't forget that many providers of online services, including giants like Meta and Google, will turn over cloud-stored data to authorities when served with a subpoena. This can take place without judicial oversight, and you might not be notified. Because many governments operate massive internet surveillance operations, assume that any information transmitted without encryption is in the hands of one state agency or another.

6) Consider what might happen if your equipment falls into the wrong hands

Communication security is important, but many people neglect physical security. A laptop or phone can be lost or stolen; someone might enter your office while you are at lunch or even sneak into your hotel room. Computers and other electronics are also routinely seized by authorities at international borders.

Encrypt your hard drive if you have sensitive material on your computer. Be careful to track all copies of critical files, including those on thumb drives, camera memory cards or other portable media.

Bear in mind that even if you regularly delete sensitive data from your computer, it can still be read unless it is securely wiped. Use so-called military-grade deletion software for wiping, which overwrites hard drives and solid-state storage devices. Also consider deleting your digital tracks, including your browsing history and digital "cookies" uploaded to your computer during online activity. When traveling, your phone and laptop can be your worst enemies if they are not encrypted and protected by strong passwords.

In countries with heavy surveillance regimes, consider traveling with burner phones and cheap laptops that contain no sensitive data. In public spaces such as trains and airports, use a privacy screen — a film overlay for your device display that inhibits peripheral viewing — while working on your laptop to discourage prying eyes.

7) If a security breach might cause serious harm, get expert advice

Digital security is just one part of operational security — it takes more than technology to keep secrets.

This short guide is no substitute for specialized training, technology and procedures. That includes training in how to examine potentially newsworthy content downloaded from the internet that may be boobytrapped with malicious software. When the stakes are high — or the data of dubious provenance — you need to consult an expert.

DIGITAL SECURITY

Religion

a

abaya Robe-like outer garment worn by Muslim women.

Advent Period including the four Sundays preceding Christmas.

Adventist See **Seventh-day Adventist Church**.

African Methodist Episcopal Church Historically African American Methodist denomination based in the United States.

The church grew out of the Free African Society, founded in 1787 by Black churchgoers in Philadelphia who objected to segregation policies at their Methodist church, where the congregation included white and Black members.

The denomination experienced major growth during the Civil War and Reconstruction. Today, its members are in 39 countries on five continents. The *AME* and *AME Church* are acceptable on second reference.

agnostic, atheist An *agnostic* believes it is impossible to know whether any deities exist. An *atheist* believes that no deities exist. See **"nones."**

Al-Aqsa Mosque The mosque completed in the eighth century atop the Haram al-Sharif, or *Noble Sanctuary*, in the Old City of Jerusalem; Arabs also use *Al-Aqsa* to refer to the whole area, which houses the Dome of the Rock shrine, too. To Jews the area is known as the *Temple Mount*, the site of the ancient Jewish temples.

Allah The Arabic word for *God*. The word *God* should be used, unless the Arabic name is used in a quote written or spoken in English.

Allahu akbar The Arabic phrase for *God is great*.

altar, alter An *altar* is a tablelike platform used in a religious service.

To *alter* is to change.

Amish A separatist Christian group formed in 17th century Europe in a schism with other *Anabaptists*. They began immigrating to North America in the 18th century and are no longer in Europe.

The Amish, named for early leader Jakob Ammann, mainly sought a greater degree of separation from outside society and shunning of transgressors.

Almost all are *Old Order Amish*, with shared beliefs including tight church discipline and shunning of those excommunicated; a refusal to do military service or take oaths; and a strict interpretation of the Bible.

Known as part of the *Plain People*, they are marked by plain, modest dress and grooming — including long dresses and head coverings for women and beards but no mustaches for married men. They speak Pennsylvania German or a Swiss

German dialect as a first language and are also fluent in English. They make limited use of technology, often staying off electricity grids and driving horses and buggies rather than cars.

Old Order Amish typically worship in homes rather than church buildings and affiliate with one of dozens of networks with differing rules. They attend Amish-run schoolhouses through the eighth grade. In a landmark 1972 case, Wisconsin v. Yoder, the Supreme Court ruled that the state could not require compulsory school attendance among the Amish people past the eighth grade without violating their freedom of religion.

A bishop is typically the highest authority in a congregation.

As of 2021, there were about 360,000 Amish in 31 states and Canada, with the highest concentrations in Pennsylvania, Ohio and Indiana, according to the Young Center for Anabaptist and Pietist Studies at Elizabethtown College in Pennsylvania.

See **Anabaptists**.

Anabaptists The term refers to members of a Christian tradition that emerged from the radical edge of the Protestant Reformation in Europe.

Core beliefs have included separation of church and state, adult (not infant) baptism, church discipline, separation from the corruption of the larger society, nonresistance to evil (a term many prefer to *pacifism* and including a refusal to do military service) and a strict interpretation of the Bible, particularly Jesus' Sermon on the Mount with its demanding requirements for forgiveness, simplicity and love of enemies.

Interpretations of these principles vary widely among modern-day Anabaptists in four main movements: traditionalist *Amish* and *Hutterites* and the more diverse *Brethren* and *Mennonites*, who range from traditionalist to highly assimilated. Conservative Anabaptists sometimes describe themselves as *Plain People*, marked by separatism from mainstream society and modest, plain dress that includes head coverings for women.

The term *Anabaptist* — originally pejorative but now widely accepted — means *rebaptizer* because early Anabaptist converts rejected the validity of their baptism as infants in a state church, then underwent baptism as adults when joining the new movement. Not part of the Baptist tradition, though they share some beliefs.

Anglican Communion The name for the worldwide association of national Anglican churches.

Each national church is independent. A special position of honor is accorded to the archbishop of Canterbury, as the preeminent officer in the original Anglican body, the Church of England.

The test of membership in the Anglican Communion traditionally has been whether a church has been in communion with the See of Canterbury. No legislative or juridical ties exist, however.

Anglicans have traditionally considered themselves Catholic, but not Roman Catholic, because they believe they are part of the universal church with their bishops in direct succession from the original apostles. A principal difference between Roman Catholics and

RELIGION

Anglicans is still the dispute that led to the formation of the Church of England — refusal to acknowledge that the pope, as bishop of Rome, has ruling authority over other bishops. See **Catholic, Catholicism**.

ANGLICAN CHURCHES: The term refers to churches in the tradition of the Church of England, which formed in a split with the papacy during the Protestant Reformation. Traditionally it referred to members of the Anglican Communion, in addition to the Church of England, including the Scottish Episcopal Church, the Anglican Church of Canada, the Episcopal Church in the U.S. and numerous branches in other countries. Some traditionalists left the U.S. and Canadian denominations to form the Anglican Church in North America. Although not recognized by the Anglican Communion, the denomination describes itself as Anglican and is on friendly terms with many national churches that are part of the Anglican Communion.

See **Episcopal Church**.

Antichrist, anti-Christ *Antichrist* is the proper name for the individual the Bible says will challenge Christ.

The adjective *anti-Christ* would be applied to someone or something opposed to Christ.

Antiochian Orthodox Christian Archdiocese of North America

Formed in 1975 by the merger of the Antiochian Orthodox Christian Archdiocese of New York and All North America and the Archdiocese of Toledo, Ohio, and Dependencies in North America. It is under the jurisdiction of the patriarch of Antioch, based in Damascus, Syria.

See **Eastern Orthodox churches**.

antisemitism (n.), antisemitic (adj.)
Prejudice or discrimination against Jews. A 2021 change from previous style (*anti-Semitism* and *anti-Semitic*).

The term was coined in the 19th century by the German writer Wilhelm Marr, who opposed efforts to extend the full rights of German citizenship to Jews. He asserted that Jews were Semites — descended from the Semitic peoples of the Middle East and thus racially different from (and threatening to) Germany's Aryans. This racist pseudoscience was applied only to Jews, not Arabs.

The previous style was based on common usage. In recent years, that style has come under criticism from those who say it could give credence to the idea that Jews are a separate race. In response, a growing number of Jewish organizations and others have settled on the style *antisemitism*.

Avoid using the term *antisemite* for an individual other than in a direct quotation. Instead, be specific in describing the person's words or actions.

Apostles' Creed A statement of core Christian beliefs developed a few centuries after Christ's death.

apostolic delegate, papal nuncio
An *apostolic delegate* is a Catholic diplomat chosen by the pope to be his envoy to the church in a nation that does not have formal diplomatic relations with the Vatican.

A *papal nuncio* is the pope's envoy to a nation with which the Vatican has diplomatic relations.

archbishop See **Episcopal Church**; **Catholic, Catholicism**; **Roman Catholic Church**; and **religious titles**.

archbishop of Canterbury In general, lowercase *archbishop* unless it is used before the name of the individual who holds the office.

Capitalize *Archbishop of Canterbury* standing alone only when it is used in a story that also refers to members of Britain's nobility. See **nobility** in the A-Z section for the relevant guidelines.

archdiocese Capitalize as part of a proper name: *the Archdiocese of Chicago, the Chicago Archdiocese.* Lowercase when it stands alone.

See the entry for the particular denomination in question.

Armenian Apostolic Church of America, Armenian Church of America See **Oriental Orthodox churches**.

Ashoura The Shiite Muslim commemoration marking the death of Hussein, the grandson of the Prophet Muhammad, at the Battle of Karbala in present-day Iraq in the seventh century.

Ash Wednesday The first day of Lent for many churches, 46 days before Easter.

See **Easter** and **Lent**.

Assemblies of God The world's largest Pentecostal denomination, founded in 1914 in Hot Springs, Arkansas, with 300 people at the founding convention. It now encompasses more than 12,000 churches in the U.S. and claims more than 69 million members worldwide.

b

Baha'i A monotheistic religion founded in the mid-19th century by Baha'u'llah, a Persian nobleman considered a prophet by the Baha'is. Baha'u'llah taught that all religions represent progressive stages in the revelation of God's will, leading to the unity of all people and faiths. The Baha'is have no clergy; they are governed by local, national and international elected councils. The international governing body, the Universal House of Justice, is based in Haifa, Israel. Its U.S. offices are in Evanston, Illinois.

baptism See **sacraments**.

Baptist churches There are a wide range of Baptist bodies in the U.S. with varied beliefs and practices. The largest is the Southern Baptist Convention; most of its members are in the South, although it has churches nationwide.

The largest predominantly Northern body is American Baptist Churches USA.

Three other large Baptist bodies are predominantly African American: the National Baptist Convention of America, the National Baptist Convention U.S.A. Inc., and the Progressive National Baptist Convention Inc.

Other Baptist groups include the Cooperative Baptist Fellowship, formed in the 1990s by Southern Baptists who disagreed with the denomination's conservative direction, and the Baptist World Alliance, an international voluntary association for Baptists located in the Washington, D.C., area.

It is incorrect to apply the term *church* to any Baptist unit except the local church.

CLERGY: All members of the Baptist clergy may be referred to as *ministers*. *Pastor* applies if a minister leads a congregation.

On first reference, use *the Rev.* before the name of a man or woman. On second reference, use only the last name.

See **religious titles**.

See **religious movements** for definitions of some descriptive terms that often apply to Baptists but are not limited to them.

bar mitzvah The Jewish rite of passage and family celebration that marks a boy's 13th birthday. A similar ceremony for girls is held at age 12 or 13 and called the *bat mitzvah* or *bas mitzvah*. Many, but not all, branches of Judaism hold the ceremony for girls. Judaism regards the age as a benchmark of religious maturity. Bar mitzvah translates as "one who is responsible for the Commandments."

beatification See **canonization**.

Bible Capitalize, without quotation marks, when referring to the Scriptures in the Old Testament or the New Testament. Capitalize also related terms such as the *Gospels, Gospel of St. Mark, the Scriptures, the Holy Scriptures*.

Lowercase *biblical* in all uses.

Lowercase *bible* as a nonreligious term: *My dictionary is my bible.*

Do not abbreviate individual books of the Bible. Capitalize book in such uses as *Book of Genesis*.

Old Testament is a Christian designation; Hebrew Bible or Jewish Bible is the appropriate term for stories dealing with Judaism alone.

The standard names and order of Old Testament books as they appear in Protestant Bibles are: Genesis, Exodus, Leviticus, Numbers, Deuteronomy, Joshua, Judges, Ruth, 1 Samuel, 2 Samuel, 1 Kings, 2 Kings, 1 Chronicles, 2 Chronicles, Ezra, Nehemiah, Esther, Job, Psalms, Proverbs, Ecclesiastes, Song of Solomon, Isaiah, Jeremiah, Lamentations, Ezekiel, Daniel, Hosea, Joel, Amos, Obadiah, Jonah, Micah, Nahum, Habakkuk, Zephaniah, Haggai, Zechariah, Malachi.

Jewish Bibles contain the same 39 books, in different order. Catholic Bibles follow a different order, usually use some different names and include the seven Deuterocanonical books (called the Apocrypha by Protestants): Tobit, Judith, 1 Maccabees, 2 Maccabees, Wisdom, Sirach, Baruch. Orthodox churches have a slightly different scriptural list.

The books of the New Testament, in order: Matthew, Mark, Luke, John, Acts, Romans, 1 Corinthians, 2 Corinthians, Galatians, Ephesians, Philippians, Colossians, 1 Thessalonians, 2 Thessalonians, 1 Timothy, 2 Timothy, Titus, Philemon, Hebrews, James, 1 Peter, 2 Peter, 1 John, 2 John, 3 John, Jude, Revelation.

Citations listing a chapter number and verse(s) use this form: *Matthew 3:16, Luke 21:1-13, 1 Peter 2:1.*

Bible-believing Do not use the term to distinguish one faction from another, because all Christians believe in the Bible. The differences are over interpretations.

Bible Belt Those sections of the United States, especially in the South and Midwest, where strictly conservative Christian beliefs prevail. The term was believed to be coined by H.L. Mencken as a derisive commentary on fundamentalism. The term should be used with care, because in certain contexts it can give offense.

bishop See **religious titles** and the entry for the denomination in question.

Blessed Sacrament, Blessed Virgin

B'nai B'rith See **fraternal organizations and service clubs** in the A-Z section.

Buddha, Buddhism The religion founded in India around 500 B.C. based on the teachings of Siddhartha Gautama, who was called *Buddha*, or *enlightened one*, by his followers.

Buddhism is considered the world's fourth-largest religious tradition after Christianity, Islam and Hinduism. The overwhelming majority of Buddhists live in the Asia-Pacific region. About half live in China.

Countries with Buddhist majorities include Thailand, Cambodia and Myanmar. Small communities of Buddhists can be found in North America and Europe.

Buddhists believe that right, or virtuous, thinking and behavior can liberate people from suffering. Nirvana is the state of ultimate enlightenment and peace. Until nirvana is reached, believers cannot be freed from the cycle of death and rebirth.

There are many variants of Buddhist practice and teaching, but scholars generally categorize the streams as:
— Mahayana Buddhism. Prevalent in China, Japan, South Korea and Vietnam. Stresses enlightenment is possible for all.
— Theravada Buddhism. Found in Cambodia, Laos, Thailand, Myanmar and Sri Lanka. Stresses monastic discipline and meditation.
— Vajrayana Buddhism. Concentrated in Tibet, Nepal and Mongolia. Sometimes called Tibetan Buddhism.

C

canonization The process of declaring a person a saint in the Catholic Church. It involves a church investigation of whether, after the person dies, miracles can be attributed to their intercession from heaven. When the church confirms a first miracle, the person is *beatified*, then is *canonized* after confirmation of a second miracle. The process can take years, but can be shortened by the pope.

cantor See **Jewish congregations**.

cardinal See **Catholic, Catholicism**; **Roman Catholic Church**.

Catholic, Catholicism Use *Catholic Church*, *Catholic* or *Catholicism* in the first references to those who believe that the pope, as bishop of Rome, has the ultimate authority in administering an earthly organization founded by Jesus Christ.

Given the majority of Catholics belong to the Latin (Roman) rite, it is acceptable to use *Roman Catholic Church* on first reference if the context is clearly referring to the

RELIGION

Latin rite. For example: *the Roman Catholic Archdiocese of Indianapolis.* However, when referring to the pope, the Vatican or the universal church, *Catholic Church* should be used since it encompasses believers belonging to the Latin and Eastern churches that are in communion with Rome. Similarly, the U.S. Conference of Catholic Bishops includes bishops from Eastern churches as well as Roman Catholic bishops.

Lowercase *catholic* where used in its generic sense of general or universal, meanings derived from a similar word in Greek.

See **Roman Catholic Church**.

celebrant, celebrator Reserve *celebrant* for someone who conducts a religious rite: *He was the celebrant of the Mass.*

Use *celebrator* for someone having a good time: *The celebrators kept the party going until 3 a.m.*

Central Conference of American Rabbis See **Jewish congregations**.

charismatic groups See **religious movements**.

Christian Church (Disciples of Christ) The parentheses and the words they surround are part of the formal name.

The body owes its origins to an early-19th-century frontier movement to unify Christians.

The Disciples, led by Alexander Campbell in western Pennsylvania, and the Christians, led by Barton W. Stone in Kentucky, merged in 1832.

The local church is the basic organizational unit.

National policies are developed by the General Assembly, made up of representatives chosen by local churches and regional organizations.

All members of the clergy may be referred to as *ministers. Pastor* applies if a minister leads a congregation.

On first reference, use *the Rev.* before the name of a man or woman. On second reference, use only the last name. See **religious titles**.

Christian Science Church See **Church of Christ, Scientist**.

Christmas, Christmas Day Dec. 25. The federal legal holiday is observed on Friday if Dec. 25 falls on a Saturday, on Monday if it falls on a Sunday.

Never abbreviate *Christmas* to *Xmas* or any other form.

Christmastime One word.

Christmas tree Lowercase *tree* and other seasonal terms with *Christmas*: *card, wreath, carol,* etc. Exception: *National Christmas Tree.*

church Capitalize as part of the formal name of a building, a congregation or a denomination; lowercase in other uses: *St. Mary's Church, the Roman Catholic Church, the Catholic and Episcopal churches, a Roman Catholic church, a church.*

Lowercase in phrases where the church is used in an institutional sense: *She believes in the separation of church and state. The pope says climate change is a crucial issue for the church.*

See **religious titles** and the entry for the denomination in question.

Churches of Christ Thousands of independent U.S. congregations cooperate under this name supporting ministries such as children's homes, Bible camps,

Christian universities and disaster relief organizations. Each local church is autonomous and operates under a governing board of elders. The ministers do not use clergy titles. Do not precede their names by a title.

The churches do not regard themselves as a denomination. Rather, they stress a nondenominational effort to preach what they consider basic Bible teachings and they restrict worship activities to those they've identified in the New Testament. For this reason, they generally exclude instrumental music from worship. The churches also teach that baptism by immersion is essential for salvation.

It is one of the Stone-Campbell faith traditions, which emerged from the early "Restoration" movement formed amid 19th century revivals led by Alexander Campbell and Barton W. Stone.

Within the U.S., the churches are concentrated in the South and Southwest. But many of the churches are located overseas, in countries such as India.

See **religious movements**.

churchgoer

Church of Christ, Scientist This denomination was founded in 1879 by Mary Baker Eddy. Her teachings are contained in "Science and Health with Key to the Scriptures," which, along with the Bible, she ordained as the "dual and impersonal pastor" of the church.

The Mother Church in Boston is the international headquarters. Its government provides for a board of directors, which transacts the business of the Mother Church.

A branch church, governed by its own democratically chosen board, is named First Church of Christ, Scientist, or Second Church, etc., according to the order of its establishment in a community.

The terms *Christian Science Church* or *Churches of Christ, Scientist*, are acceptable in all references to the denomination.

The word *Christian* is used because its teachings are based on the word and works of Jesus Christ. The word *Science* is used to reflect the concept that the laws of God are replicable and can be proved in healing sickness and sin. Therefore, members are taught to avoid conventional medical treatment.

The church is composed entirely of lay members and does not have clergy in the usual sense. Both men and women may serve as *readers*, *practitioners* or *lecturers*.

The terms *reverend* and *minister* are not applicable. Do not use *the Rev.* in any references.

See **religious titles**.

Church of England See Anglican Communion.

Church of Jesus Christ of Latter-day Saints, The Note the
capitalization and punctuation of *Latter-day*. The church in 2018 began moving away from the widely recognized terms *Mormon church* and *LDS church*, and now prefers that its full name be used and that members be referred to as *Latter-day Saints*.

Use the full name of the church on first references, with *the church*, *church members*, *members of the faith* preferred on second and later reference. When necessary for space or clarity or in quotations or proper names, *Mormon*, *Mormons* and *Latter-day Saints* are acceptable.

The term *Mormon* is based on the church's sacred Book of Mormon and remains in common use by members of the faith. When using the church's full name, include a short explanation such as, *the church, widely known as the Mormon church* ...

The church is based on revelations that Joseph Smith said were given to him by heavenly messengers beginning in the 1820s and codified through 1843. These constitute scripture alongside the Bible in the King James Version.

The headquarters is in Salt Lake City, but millions of its members live outside the U.S.

Church hierarchy is composed of men known as *general authorities*. Among them, the policymaking body is the First Presidency, made up of a president and two or more counselors. With the Quorum of the Twelve Apostles, it has final authority in all church matters.

CLERGY: All worthy young men over the age of 12 are members of the priesthood though they are not called priests. They can be ordained elders after age 18, usually after graduating from high school and before serving as missionaries. They may later become high priests, or bishops.

Formal titles include *president* (for members of the First Presidency), *bishop* (for members of the Presiding Bishopric and for local bishops) and *elder* (for other general authorities and church missionaries). Capitalize these formal titles before a name on first reference; use only the last name on second reference.

The terms *minister* or *the Rev.* are not used.

See **religious titles**.

RELATED GROUPS: The term *Mormon* is not properly applied to the other Latter Day Saints churches that resulted from the splits after Smith's death. This includes groups that call themselves "fundamentalist" and others that perpetuate Smith's practice of polygamy, which the church renounced in 1890.

One offshoot group is the Community of Christ, headquartered in Independence, Missouri. For many decades, it was called the Reorganized Church of Jesus Christ of Latter Day Saints (note the lack of a hyphen and the capitalized Day).

College of Cardinals See **Catholic, Catholicism**; **Roman Catholic Church**.

Communion, Holy Communion See **sacraments**.

conclave A private or secret meeting. In the Catholic Church it describes the private meeting of cardinals to elect a pope.

confirmation See **sacraments**.

Conservative Judaism See **Jewish congregations**.

Coptic Christian The Coptic Orthodox Church traces its origins to the Apostle Mark in first-century Alexandria. The word Copt is derived from the Greek word for Egypt.

The Coptic church is part of the *Oriental Orthodox* tradition, which generally shares the beliefs of Eastern Orthodox churches, but has some distinct teachings, mainly concerning Christology, or the nature of Christ. There are no definitive statistics for the Coptic Christian population, but they are considered to be the largest Christian community in the Mideast, including millions in Egypt. Significant diaspora Coptic Christian communities can be found in the United States, Canada and Australia.

cult A loaded term to be used with caution.

curate See **religious titles**.

Curia See **Catholic, Catholicism; Roman Catholic Church**.

d

dalai lama The traditional spiritual leader of Tibetan Buddhism. *Dalai lama* is a title rather than a name, but it is all that is used when referring to the man. Capitalize *Dalai Lama* in references to the holder of the title, in keeping with the principles outlined in the **nobility** entry. The title is lowercase in generic references to the religion and history.

deacon See the entry for the individual's denomination.

deity Lowercase. See **gods** and **religious references**.

denomination Use with caution; some Christian bodies object to this label.

devil But capitalize *Satan*.

devout Use sparingly if at all; better to be specific about a person's religious practice, i.e. *He attends Mass daily.*

diocese Capitalize as part of a proper name: *the Diocese of Rochester, the Rochester Diocese, the diocese.*
See **Episcopal Church; Catholic, Catholicism** and **Roman Catholic Church**.

Diwali The festival of lights, also called *Deepavali*, gets its name from the row (avali) of clay lamps (deepa) that are lit to symbolize the victory of inner light over spiritual darkness. The holiday is celebrated by Hindus, Jains, Sikhs and Buddhists.

For Hindus in southern India, Diwali is the day Lord Krishna slew the demon, Naraka. In the northern states it's observed as the day Lord Rama returned from a 14-year exile to the forest. For Jains, it marks the day Lord Mahavira (the religion's founder) attained nirvana or spiritual awakening. In Sikhism, Diwali honors the day the Guru Hargobind, the sixth of 10 Sikh gurus, was released from prison during Mughal rule. Some Buddhists celebrate Diwali as the commemoration of the day when Emperor Ashoka converted to Buddhism in third century B.C. It is observed mostly by the Vajrayana Buddhist minority among the Newar people of Nepal.

Diwali falls between October and November, but the exact date varies based on the lunar calendar. Celebrations last for several days featuring fireworks and worship of Lakshmi, the goddess of wealth.

Druze A tradition that developed from a medieval sect of Shiite Islam. The religion draws from Christian, Muslim and Jewish beliefs and was influenced by gnosticism, with believers divided into two main classes: the "initiated" who have studied the faith's sacred writings

RELIGION

and serve as authorities, and the "uninitiated" who comprise the majority of Druze.

The Druze call themselves the "People of Unity." The exact number of Druze is not known, but they are concentrated in Syria, Lebanon and Israel, with diaspora populations in Europe, North America, Australia and elsewhere.

e

Easter Christian holy day commemorating the resurrection of Jesus Christ. Christians believe Jesus was raised from the dead three days after his crucifixion.

Western Christian churches and most Orthodox Christian churches follow different calendars and often observe Easter on different dates.

Eastern Orthodox churches The term applies to a group of churches that have roots in the earliest days of Christianity. They teach that their bishops have been established as the successors of the apostles through generations of ceremonies, but unlike their Roman Catholic counterparts, they do not recognize papal authority.

Churches in this tradition were part of the undivided Christendom that existed until the Great Schism of 1054. At that time, many of the churches in the western half of the old Roman Empire accorded the bishop of Rome supremacy over other bishops. The result was a split between eastern and western churches.

The churches that constitute Eastern Orthodoxy are organized along mostly national lines. They recognize the ecumenical patriarch of Constantinople (modern-day Istanbul) as first among equals. He convenes councils but has no authority over individual churches except those under his direct authority, such as the Greek Orthodox Church.

Eastern Orthodox churches include the Russian, Greek, Romanian and Serbian Orthodox churches.

In the United States, organizational lines are rooted in the national backgrounds of various ethnic groups, such as the Greek Orthodox Archdiocese of America. But many U.S. churches now have members of varied ancestries, and cooperate through the Assembly of Canonical Orthodox Bishops.

Eastern Orthodox churches share a common faith, spelled out by seven ancient church councils, and members participate in communion together.

Fourteen Eastern Orthodox churches in Eastern Europe and the Middle East are universally recognized as *autocephalous* (entirely self-governing) under their own patriarchs. Most other Orthodox churches are under the authority of one of these patriarchs, with a small number considered *autonomous* (largely self-governing). Additional churches' claims to full self-governance are recognized by some patriarchs but disputed by others, including the Orthodox Church in America and the Orthodox Church of Ukraine.

Eastern Orthodox have their own disciplines on matters such as married clergy — a married man may be ordained, but a priest may not marry after ordination. Married men cannot become bishops.

Some of these churches call the archbishop who leads them a *metropolitan*; others use the term *patriarch*. He normally heads the principal archdiocese within a nation. Working with him are other archbishops, bishops, priests and deacons.

Archbishops and bishops frequently follow a monastic tradition in which they are known only by a first name. When no last name is used, repeat the title before the sole name in subsequent references.

Some forms: *Metropolitan Tikhon, archbishop of Washington and metropolitan of America and Canada.* On second reference: *Metropolitan Tikhon. Archbishop* may be replaced by *the Most Rev.* on first reference. *Bishop* may be replaced by *the Rt. Rev.* on first reference.

Use *the Rev.* before the name of a priest on first reference.

Another family of churches, known as *Oriental Orthodox churches*, agreed to only the first three councils, though they share many practices and cooperate at times. They include churches of Armenia, Egypt, Ethiopia and India.

See **religious titles**.

Eastern Rite churches The term applies to a group of Catholic churches that accept the authority of the pope but have considerable autonomy in ritual and questions of discipline such as married clergy — a married man may be ordained, but marriage is not permitted after ordination. They use ancient liturgies similar to those of Orthodox and other churches with heritages in Eastern Europe, Africa and Asia.

Among the Eastern Rite churches are those using the Byzantine or "Greek Catholic" rite, such as those with Melkite, Romanian, Ruthenian and Ukrainian roots, as well as Armenian, Chaldean, Coptic and Maronite churches.

ecumenical This term is not interchangeable with interfaith; it refers to collaboration among different Christian denominations.

Eid al-Adha Meaning "Feast of Sacrifice," this most important Islamic holiday marks the willingness of the Prophet Ibrahim (Abraham to Christians and Jews) to sacrifice his son. During the holiday, which in most places lasts four days, Muslims slaughter sheep or cattle, distribute part of the meat to poor people and eat the rest. The holiday begins on the 10th day of the Islamic lunar month of Dhul-Hijja, during the annual hajj pilgrimage to Mecca.

Eid al-Fitr A three-day holiday marking the end of Ramadan, Islam's holy month of fasting.

elder For its use in religious contexts, see the entry for an individual's denomination.

encyclical A high-level papal teaching document on faith and morals. Always lowercase "e" except when starting a sentence.

Episcopal Church Acceptable in all references for *the Episcopal Church*, the U.S. national church that is a member of the Anglican Communion.

Some traditionalists left the U.S. denomination to form the Anglican Church in North America.

The *Episcopal Church* is governed

nationally by two bodies — the permanent Executive Council and the General Convention, which meets every three years.

After the council, the principal organizational units are, in descending order of size: provinces, dioceses or missionary districts, local parishes and local missions.

The Executive Council is composed of bishops, priests, laypeople. One bishop is designated leader of the church and holds the formal title of presiding bishop.

The General Convention has final authority in matters of policy and doctrine. All acts must pass both of its houses — the House of Bishops and the House of Deputies. The latter is composed of an equal number of clergy and lay delegates from each diocese.

A province is composed of several dioceses. Each has a provincial synod made up of a house of bishops and a house of deputies. The synod's primary duty is to coordinate the work of the church in its area.

Within a diocese, a bishop is the principal official. The bishop is helped by the Diocesan Convention, which consists of all the clergy in the diocese and lay representatives from each parish.

The parish or local church is governed by a vestry, composed of the pastor and lay members elected by the congregation.

The clergy consists of bishops, priests and deacons. A priest who heads a parish is described as a *rector* rather than a pastor.

For first reference to bishops, use *Bishop* before the individual's name: *Bishop Rob Wright*. An acceptable alternative in referring to U.S. bishops is *the Rt. Rev.* The designation *the Most Rev.* is used before the names of the archbishops of Canterbury and York.

For first references, use *the Rev.* before the name of a priest, *Deacon* before the name of a deacon.

See **Anglican Communion** and **religious titles**.

Episcopal, Episcopalian *Episcopal* is the adjective form; use *Episcopalian* only as a noun referring to a member of the Episcopal Church: *She is an Episcopalian.* But: *She is an Episcopal priest.*

Capitalize *Episcopal* when referring to the Episcopal Church. Use lowercase when the reference is simply to a body governed by bishops.

Ethiopian Orthodox Tewahedo Church See **Oriental Orthodox churches**.

evangelical See **religious movements**.

Evangelical Friends Alliance See **Quakers**.

evangelism See **religious movements**.

evangelist Capitalize only in reference to the men credited with writing the Gospels: *The four Evangelists were Matthew, Mark, Luke and John.*

In lowercase, it means a preacher who makes a profession of seeking conversions. Often confused with the term *evangelical*. See **evangelical**.

exorcise, exorcism

f

father Use *the Rev.* in first reference

before the names of Episcopal, Orthodox and Catholic priests. Use *Father* before a name only in direct quotations. Capitalize *father* in *God the Father* and similar phrases.

See **religious titles**.

fundamentalist See **religious movements**.

g

gentile Generally, any person not Jewish; often, specifically a Christian.

gods and goddesses Capitalize *God* in references to the one unique deity of all monotheistic religions. Capitalize all noun references to the deity: *God the Father, Holy Ghost, Holy Spirit, Allah,* etc. Lowercase personal pronouns.

Lowercase *gods* and *goddesses* in references to the deities of polytheistic religions.

Lowercase *god, gods* and *goddesses* in references to false gods: *He made money his god.*

See **religious references**.

Good Friday The Friday before Easter.

Gospel(s), gospel Capitalize when referring to any or all of the first four books of the New Testament: *the Gospel of John, the Gospels.*

Lowercase in other references: *She is a famous gospel singer.*

Greek Orthodox Church See **Eastern Orthodox churches**.

gurdwara A house of worship in the Sikh religion where the faith's scriptures are stored.

h

Hades But lowercase *hell.*

Haggadah The text Jews use during Passover.

hajj The pilgrimage to Mecca required once in a lifetime of every Muslim who can afford it and is physically able to make it. Some Muslims make the journey more than once. The hajj occurs once a year during the Islamic lunar month of Dhul-Hijja, the 12th and final month of the Islamic calendar year. The person making the *hajj* is a *hajji* (male) or *hajjah* (female).

halal Arabic for *permitted* or *lawful.* The word is used to describe foods allowed under Islamic dietary laws. Always lowercase.

hallelujah Lowercase the biblical praise to God, but capitalize in composition titles: Handel's "Hallelujah" chorus.

Hanukkah The Jewish Festival of Lights, an eight-day commemoration of rededication of the Temple by the Maccabees after their victory over the Syrians.

Usually occurs in December but sometimes falls in late November.

Haram al-Sharif Arabic for *Noble Sanctuary*, the Muslim name for the walled, elevated area in Jerusalem's Old City that was the site of the ancient Jewish temples. Also known as the *Temple Mount*, the area now houses the centuries-old Dome of the Rock shrine and Al-Aqsa mosque. Muslims believe Prophet Muhammad made his night journey to heaven from the site.

RELIGION

Haredi, Haredim (plural) A Hebrew term for ultra-Orthodox Jews. The word translates literally as "trembling" in awe of God.

Hasidic A term describing a movement within ultra-Orthodox Judaism. Its origins are rooted in Jewish mysticism and spiritual revival. Often used as an umbrella term for all ultra-Orthodox. Members are collectively referred to as *Hasidim*.

heaven

hell But capitalize *Hades*.

High Holidays, High Holy Days
Both are acceptable for the period of the Jewish calendar that includes Yom Kippur and Rosh Hashana. See **Jewish congregations**.

Hindu, Hinduism The dominant religion of India and the world's third-largest religion, after Christianity and Islam.

Nearly all the world's 1.1 billion Hindus live in India, Nepal, Bangladesh, Indonesia, Malaysia and the United States. They are a majority in India, Nepal and Mauritius. The original Hindu scriptures are called the Vedas.

Hindus believe the soul never dies, but is reborn — in either human or animal form — each time the body dies. Under the Hindu rule of karma, a person's every action and thought will affect how the soul is reborn. The cycle of death and rebirth continues until a soul reaches spiritual perfection, and can then be united in total enlightenment and peace, known as nirvana, with the supreme being, ending the cycle.

Hindus believe in one supreme being who is represented in different gods and goddesses. The primary gods are Brahma, the creator; Vishnu, the preserver; and Siva, the destroyer. Vishnu has had important human incarnations such as Krishna and Rama.

The primary goddess is Devi, who has several manifestations including Durga, Kali, Sarasvati and Lakshmi. She represents in her forms either motherhood and good fortune or destruction. There are thousands of other deities and saints that also may receive prayers and offerings.

Hindus also believe that animals have souls and many are worshipped as manifestations of god.

Holy Communion, Communion See **sacraments**.

Holy Father The preferred form is to use *the pope* or *the pontiff*, or to give the individual's name.

Use *Holy Father* in direct quotations or special contexts where a particular literary effect is desired.

Holy Land Capitalize the biblical region. It does not have a formal geographic designation, but encompasses Israel, the West Bank and parts of nearby countries.

holy orders See **sacraments**.

Holy See The headquarters of the Catholic Church in Vatican City.

Holy Spirit Preferred over *Holy Ghost* in most usage.

Holy Week The week before Easter.

humanism, humanist A philosophy emphasizing the importance of human beings, without relying on belief in deities or supernatural forces.

i

iftar The breaking of the daily fast during the holy Islamic month of Ramadan.

imam Lowercase when describing the leader of a prayer in a Muslim mosque. Capitalize before a name when used as the formal title for a Muslim leader or ruler.
See **religious titles**.

Inner Light See **Quakers**.

Islam Followers are called Muslims. Their holy book is the Quran, which according to Islamic belief was revealed by God (Allah in Arabic) to the Prophet Muhammad in the seventh century in Mecca and Medina. The place of worship is a mosque, also called a masjid in Arabic. The weekly holy day is Friday. The Five Pillars are profession of faith, prayer, almsgiving, fasting and pilgrimage, known in Arabic as *hajj*.

It is the religion of more than 1.8 billion people in the world, making it the world's second-largest faith, after Christianity. Although Arabic is the language of the Quran and Muslim prayers, not all Arabs are Muslims and not all Muslims are Arabs. Most of the world's Muslims live in a wide belt that stretches halfway around the world: across West Africa and North Africa, through the Arab countries of the Middle East and on to Turkey, Iran, Afghanistan, Pakistan and other Asian countries, parts of the former Soviet Union and western China, to Indonesia and the southern Philippines.

There are two major divisions in Islam:
— *Sunni* The biggest single branch in Islam, comprising about 85% of all Muslims. Nations with Sunni majorities include Egypt, Saudi Arabia and most other Arab nations, as well as non-Arab Turkey and Afghanistan. Most Palestinian Muslims and most West African Muslims are Sunnis.
The austere form of Islam that was espoused by the Saudi kingdom for decades is often referred to as *Wahhabism* and its Sunni Muslim adherents as *Wahhabis*.
— *Shiite* The second-largest branch. Iran's population is overwhelmingly Shiite; other countries with large Shiite communities include Iraq, Lebanon and Bahrain.
The schism between Sunni and Shiite stems from the early days of Islam and arguments over Muhammad's successors as caliph, the spiritual and temporal leader of Muslims during that period. The Shiites wanted the caliphate to descend through Ali, Muhammad's son-in-law. Ali eventually became the fourth caliph, but he was murdered; Ali's son al-Hussein was massacred with his fighters at Karbala, in what is now Iraq. Shiites considered the later caliphs to be usurpers. The Sunnis no longer have a caliph.

Titles for the clergy vary from branch to branch and from country to country, but these are the most common:
Grand Mufti — The highest authority in Quranic law and interpretation, a title used mostly by Sunnis.
Sheikh — Used by most clergymen in the same manner that *the Rev.* is used as a Christian clerical title,

RELIGION

especially common among Sunnis. (Not all sheikhs are clergymen. *Sheikh* can also be a secular title of respect or nobility.)

Ayatollah — Used by Shiites, especially in Iran, to denote senior clergymen, such as *Ayatollah Ruhollah Khomeini.*

Hojatoleslam — A rank below ayatollah.

Mullah — Lower-level clergy.

Imam — Used by some branches as a title for the prayer leader at a mosque. Among the Shiites, it usually has a more exalted connotation.

The adjective is *Islamic. Islamist* is an advocate of political Islam, the philosophy that the Quran should rule all aspects of life — religious, political and personal. *Islamic fundamentalist* should not be used as a synonym for *Islamic militant* or *radical.*

Islamic holy days See **Ashoura**, **Eid al-Adha**, **Eid al-Fitr** and **Ramadan**. Because the Muslim faith operates on the lunar calendar, these commemorations fall on different days each year on the Western calendar.

Islamist An advocate or supporter of a political movement that favors reordering government and society in accordance with laws prescribed by Islam. Do not use as a synonym for *Islamic fighters, militants, extremists* or *radicals,* who may or may not be Islamists. Where possible, be specific and use the name of militant affiliations: *al-Qaida-linked, Hezbollah, Taliban,* etc. Those who view the Quran as a political model encompass a wide range of Muslims, from mainstream politicians to militants known as jihadis.

j

Jehovah's Witnesses The denomination was founded in Pittsburgh in 1872 by Charles Taze Russell, a former Congregationalist layman. On second reference, *Witnesses* is acceptable.

Witnesses do most of their work through three legal corporations: the Watch Tower Bible and Tract Society of Pennsylvania, the Watchtower Bible and Tract Society of New York Inc., and, in England, the International Bible Students Association. A governing body consisting largely of the principal officers of the corporations oversees the denomination.

Jehovah's Witnesses believe that they adhere to the oldest religion on Earth, the worship of Almighty God revealed in the Bible as Jehovah.

They regard civil authority as necessary and obey it "as long as its laws do not contradict God's law." Witnesses refuse to bear arms, salute the flag or participate in secular government.

They refuse blood transfusions as being against the Bible, citing the section of Leviticus that reads: "Whatsoever man ... eats any manner of blood, I will cut him off from among his people."

There are no formal titles, but there are three levels of ministry: *publishers* (baptized members who do evangelistic work), *regular pioneers* (who devote greater time to activities) and *special pioneers* (full-time workers).

Jesus The central figure of

Christianity, he also may be called *Jesus Christ* or *Christ*.

Personal pronouns referring to him are lowercase.

Jewish congregations A Jewish congregation is autonomous. No synods, assemblies or hierarchies control the activities of an individual synagogue.

Among the major expressions of Judaism in North America are:

1. Orthodox Judaism. The Orthodox Union is the umbrella organization for modern or centrist Orthodox congregations whose rabbis are represented by the Rabbinical Council of America. Many additional Orthodox congregations and rabbis in North America are part of strictly observant communities whose adherents are often called Haredi. They also are referred to as ultra-Orthodox , although some object to the term.

2. Reform Judaism. Congregations are represented by the Union for Reform Judaism, and clergy by the Central Conference of American Rabbis.

3. Conservative Judaism. Congregations are represented by the United Synagogue of Conservative Judaism, and clergy are represented by the Rabbinical Assembly.

Reform is the largest organized movement in Judaism in the U.S., while Orthodoxy is the fastest-growing.

The spiritual leader of a congregation is called a *rabbi*, while the individual who leads the congregation in song is called a *cantor*. Capitalize these titles before an individual's full name on first reference. On second reference, use only the last name.

See **religious titles** and **Zionism**.

Jewish holy days See separate listings for **High Holidays, High Holy Days; Hanukkah; Passover; Purim; Rosh Hashana; Shavuot; Sukkot;** and **Yom Kippur**.

The High Holy Days are Rosh Hashana and Yom Kippur. All Jewish holy days and the Jewish Sabbath start at sunset before the day marked on most calendars.

jihad Arabic noun used to refer to the Islamic concept of the struggle to do good. In particular situations, that can include holy war, the meaning extremist Muslims commonly use. Use *jihadi* and *jihadis*. Do not use *jihadist*.

k

Koran Use *Quran* in all references except when preferred by an organization or in a specific title or name. See **Quran**.

kosher Describes any food that complies with Judaism's strict set of dietary regulations.

Kwanzaa A seven-day celebration, based on African festivals, from Dec. 26 through Jan. 1.

l

Last Supper

Latin Rite See **Catholic, Catholicism; Roman Catholic Church.**

Latter Day Saints, Latter-day

RELIGION

Saints See **Church of Jesus Christ of Latter-day Saints, The**.

layperson, laypeople See **gender-neutral language**.

lecturer A formal title in the Christian Science Church. An occupational description in other uses.

Lent The period from Ash Wednesday through Holy Saturday, the day before Easter. The 40-day Lenten period for penance, suggested by Christ's 40 days in the desert, does not include the six Sundays between Ash Wednesday and Easter.

Lord's Supper See **sacraments**.

Lutheran churches The basic unit of government in Lutheran practice is the congregation. It normally is administered by a council, headed either by the senior pastor or a layperson elected from the membership of the council. The council customarily consists of a congregation's clergy and elected laypeople.

The Evangelical Lutheran Church in America is the largest Lutheran group in the U.S.

The Lutheran Church-Missouri Synod, founded in 1847, is a separate and distinct body.

Lutheran teachings go back to Martin Luther, a 16th-century Roman Catholic priest whose objections to elements of Roman Catholic practice began the movement known as the Protestant Reformation.

Members of the clergy are known as *ministers*. *Pastor* applies if a minister leads a congregation.

On first reference, use *the Rev.* before the name. On second reference, use only the last name.

See **religious titles**.

Magi Wise men who brought gifts to the infant Jesus at Epiphany, celebrated Jan. 6.

mark of the beast A phrase in the New Testament's Book of Revelation conveying an allegiance to Satan.

Mass It is *celebrated*, not *said*. Always capitalize when referring to the ceremony, but lowercase any preceding adjectives: *high Mass*, *low Mass*, *requiem Mass*.

In Eastern Orthodox churches the correct term is *Divine Liturgy*.

See **Catholic, Catholicism; Roman Catholic Church**.

matrimony See **sacraments**.

megachurch Generally used to describe a Protestant church with an average of 2,000 or more attendees at weekly worship services.

Melkite Church See **Eastern Rite churches**.

Mennonites A diverse group of *Anabaptists* who emerged soon after the start of the Protestant Reformation. Named for early leader Menno Simons.

Core beliefs have historically included separation of church and state, adult (not infant) baptism and nonresistance to evil (a term many prefer to *pacifism*).

Interpretation varies widely across dozens of Mennonite groups in North America and the world. Some, including *Old Order Mennonites*, resemble the Amish in their plain dress and use of horse-and-buggy transportation. Other traditionalists are more open to modern technology but maintain conservative theology. More assimilated groups wear modern dress, use technology and modern worship music and resemble other evangelical or liberal Protestant denominations.

The most progressive group, the Mennonite Church USA, is active in ecumenical and peacemaking efforts. The Mennonite World Conference, an umbrella group of many denominations, counted about 1.5 million people in member churches globally in 2018, about half in Africa and about 250,000 in North America.

See **Anabaptist** and **Amish**.

menorah The seven-branch candelabrum from the ancient temple in Jerusalem. Also the popular term for the nine-branch candelabrum, or hanukkiah, used on the Jewish holiday of Hanukkah.

Messiah, messiah Capitalize in religious uses, such as references to the promised deliverer of the Jews or to Jesus in Christianity. Lowercase when referring to the liberator of a people or country.

Messianic Jews Messianic Jews follow Jewish law but believe that Jesus is the Messiah. The major denominations of Judaism reject Messianic Judaism as a form of Judaism.

Methodist churches The term *Methodist* originated as a nickname applied to a group of 18th-century Oxford University students known for their methodical application to Scripture study and prayer.

The principal Methodist body in the United States is the United Methodist Church, which also has member conferences in other countries.

The General Conference, which meets every four years, has final authority in all matters.

United Methodist bishops have extensive administrative powers in their regions, including the authority to place, transfer and remove local church pastors, usually in consultation with district superintendents.

Districts in each region are responsible for promotion of mission work, support of colleges, hospitals and publications, and examination of candidates for the ministry.

Methodism in the United States also includes three major black denominations: the African Methodist Episcopal Church, the African Methodist Episcopal Zion Church and the Christian Methodist Episcopal Church.

Church officeholders include *elders*, who are ordained to ministry, and *bishops*. *Pastor* applies if a minister leads a congregation.

For first references to bishops use the word: *Bishop W. Kenneth Goodson* of Richmond, Virginia.

For first reference to ministers, use *the Rev.* before the name. On second reference, use only the last name.

See **religious titles**.

minister It is not a formal title in most religions, with exceptions such as the Nation of Islam, and is not capitalized. Where it is a formal title, it should be capitalized before the name: *Minister John Jones.*

RELIGION

See **religious titles** and the entry for an individual's denomination.

monotheism A religion espousing the belief in only one god. See **polytheism**.

monsignor See **Catholic, Catholicism**; **Roman Catholic Church**.

Mormon church See **Church of Jesus Christ of Latter-day Saints, The**.

Muhammad The chief prophet and central figure of the Islamic religion, *Prophet Muhammad*. Use other spellings only if preferred by a specific person for his own name or in a title or the name of an organization.

mullah An Islamic leader or teacher, often a general title of respect for a learned man.

Muslims The preferred term to describe adherents of Islam. The term *Black Muslim* has been used in the past to describe members of predominantly African American Islamic sects that originated in the United States. However, the term is considered derogatory.

n

National Baptist Convention of America See **Baptist churches**.

National Baptist Convention U.S.A. Inc. See **Baptist churches**.

National Council of the Churches of Christ in the U.S.A. This interdenominational, cooperative body includes most major Protestant and Eastern Orthodox denominations in the United States.

The shortened form *National Council of Churches* is acceptable in all references.

Headquarters is in Washington. See **World Council of Churches**.

Nation of Islam The nationalist religious movement traces its origins in 1930 to W.D. Fard, also known as Wali Fard, who called for racial separation. Elijah Muhammad took over the leadership in 1934, holding the post until his death in 1975. A son, Warith (Wallace) Dean Muhammad, succeeded to the leadership and pointed the movement toward integration and traditional Islam. Louis Farrakhan led a separatist movement to reconstitute the Nation of Islam in the late 1970s.

The Nation of Islam does not release membership figures.

Use the title *minister* on first reference to clergy: *Minister Louis Farrakhan*.

Nativity scene Only the first word is capitalized.

New Testament See **Bible**.

Noah's Ark

nondenominational Term used by Protestants to describe churches or ministries that are not affiliated with a specific denomination. *Independent* is also acceptable. Always lowercase.

"nones" The *"nones"* are the fastest-growing group in surveys asking Americans about their religious identity. They describe themselves as atheists, agnostics or "nothing in particular" — though the term is not interchangeable with atheist nor agnostic. Define the term when used. Use quote marks in first use and no quote marks thereafter. For example: *The poll found that 30% of the "nones" — people who describe themselves as atheists, agnostics or "nothing in particular" — meditate.* See **agnostic, atheist**.

O

Old Testament See **Bible**.

Oriental Orthodox churches The term applies to a group of churches that have roots in the earliest days of Christianity and split from other churches after the Council of Chalcedon in the year 451 due to differing interpretations of the divinity of Jesus. They are distinct from *Eastern Orthodox churches*, though they share many practices and cooperate in some areas.

Major churches in this tradition include the Ethiopian Orthodox Tewahedo Church; the Coptic Orthodox Church, based in Egypt; and the Armenian Apostolic Church. Most have parishes in the United States and other areas of the diaspora.

Orthodox, orthodox Capitalize when referring to membership in or the activities of an Eastern Orthodox church. See **Eastern Orthodox churches**.

Capitalize also in phrases such as *Orthodox Judaism* or *Orthodox Jew*. See **Jewish congregations**.

Do not describe a member of an Eastern Orthodox church as a *Protestant*. Use a phrase such as *Orthodox Christian* instead.

Lowercase *orthodox* in nonreligious uses: *an orthodox procedure.*

Orthodox Church in America See **Eastern Orthodox churches**.

P

papal nuncio Do not confuse with an *apostolic delegate*. See **apostolic delegate, papal nuncio**.

parish Capitalize as part of the formal name for a church congregation or a governmental jurisdiction: *St. John's Parish, Jefferson Parish*.

Lowercase standing alone or in plural combinations: *the parish, St. John's and St. Mary's parishes, Jefferson and Plaquemines parishes.*

parishioner Note this spelling for the member of a parish, an administrative district of various churches, particularly Catholic and Anglican. Do not use for Judaism or non-hierarchal Protestant denominations.

Passover The weeklong Jewish commemoration of the deliverance of the ancient Hebrews from slavery in Egypt. Occurs in March or April.

Capitalize *Seder* in references to the Passover feast commemorating the exodus.

pastor See **religious titles** and the entry for the individual's denomination.

patriarch Lowercase when describing someone of great age and dignity.

Capitalize as a formal title before a name in some religious uses. See

RELIGION

Eastern Orthodox churches; religious titles; Catholic, Catholicism and **Roman Catholic Church**.

Pentecost A Christian holy day occurring on the seventh Sunday after Easter, corresponding to the Jewish feast of Shavuot.

Pentecostalism See **religious movements**.

polytheism A religion espousing the belief in more than one god. See **monotheism**.

pontiff Not a formal title. Always lowercase.

pope Capitalize when used as a formal title before a name; lowercase in all other uses: *Pope Francis spoke to the crowd. At the close of his address, the pope gave his blessing. Pope Emeritus Benedict XVI* or *Benedict XVI, the pope emeritus. Benedict* alone on second reference.

Use *St. John Paul II* and *St. John XXIII* on first reference for the canonized popes. On second reference *John Paul* and *John*. Make clear in the body of a story they were popes.

See **Catholic, Catholicism; Roman Catholic Church** and **religious titles**.

practitioner See **Church of Christ, Scientist**.

preacher A job description, not a formal religious title. Do not capitalize.

See **titles** and **religious titles**.

Presbyterian churches Presbyterian churches in the U.S. have roots in Calvinism and in churches in Scotland and England, and are distinguished in part by how they govern their church. They typically have four levels of authority — individual congregations, presbyteries, synods and a general assembly.

Congregations are led by a pastor and a session composed of ruling elders who represent congregants on matters of government and discipline.

Presbyteries, composed of a district's ministers and ruling elders, form a synod, which generally meets once a year to decide matters not related to doctrine or the church constitution.

A general assembly, composed of delegations of pastors and ruling elders from each presbytery, meets every two years to decide issues of doctrine and discipline.

The northern and southern branches of Presbyterianism merged in 1983 to become the Presbyterian Church (U.S.A.).

There are also several distinctly conservative Presbyterian denominations, such as the Presbyterian Church in America. Be careful to specify the denomination being written about.

Presbyterians believe in the Trinity and the humanity and divinity of Christ. Baptism, which may be administered to children, and the Lord's Supper are the only sacraments.

All Presbyterian clergy may be described as *ministers*. Pastor applies if a minister leads a congregation.

On first reference, use *the Rev.* before the name of a man or woman. On second reference, use only the last name.

See **religious titles**.

priest A vocational description, not a

formal title. Do not capitalize.

See **religious titles** and the entries for **Catholic, Catholicism; Roman Catholic Church** and **Episcopal Church**.

prophet Capitalize when used before the name of a person considered by a religious group to be divinely inspired: *Prophet Elijah, Prophet Muhammad.*

Protestant Episcopal Church See Episcopal Church.

Protestant, Protestantism

Capitalize these words when they refer either to denominations formed as a result of the break from the Roman Catholic Church in the 16th century or to the members of these denominations.

Church groups covered by the term include Anglican, Baptist, Congregational, Methodist, Lutheran, Presbyterian and Quaker denominations. See separate entries for each.

Protestant is not applied to Christian Scientists, Jehovah's Witnesses or members of The Church of Jesus Christ of Latter-day Saints.

Do not use *Protestant* to describe a member of an Eastern Orthodox church. Use a phrase such as *Orthodox Christian* instead.

See **religious movements**.

Purim The Jewish Feast of Lots, commemorating Esther's deliverance of the Jews in Persia from a massacre plotted by Haman. Occurs in February or March.

q

Quakers This informal name may be used in all references to members of the *Religious Society of Friends,* but always include the full name in a story dealing primarily with Quaker activities.

The denomination originated with George Fox, an Englishman who objected to Anglican emphasis on ceremony. In the 1640s, he said he heard a voice that opened the way for him to develop a personal relationship with Christ, described as the Inner Light, a term based on the Gospel description of Christ as the "true light."

Brought to court for opposing the established church, Fox tangled with a judge who derided him as a "quaker" in reference to his agitation over religious matters.

The basic unit of Quaker organization is the weekly meeting, which corresponds to the congregation in other churches. Quaker practices and beliefs vary from a more Bible-centered Christianity with pastors as worship leaders to a more liberal approach with less structured worship and a wide range of teachings.

Quaker associations include the Friends United Meeting, which has a global membership focused on evangelism, communications and other projects; Evangelical Friends Church International and the more liberal Friends General Conference.

Fox taught that the Inner Light emancipates a person from adherence to any creed, ecclesiastical authority or ritual forms.

There is no recognized ranking of clergy over laypeople. However, there are meeting officers, called

RELIGION

elders or *ministers*. Quaker ministers sometimes use *the Rev.* before their names and describe themselves as *pastors*.

Capitalize *elder*, *minister* or *pastor* when used as a formal title before a name. Use *the Rev.* before a name on first reference if it is a minister's practice. On second reference, use only the last name.

See **religious titles**.

Quran The preferred spelling for the Muslim holy book. Use the spelling *Koran* only if preferred by a specific organization or in a specific title or name.

r

rabbi See **Jewish congregations**.

Rabbinical Assembly See **Jewish congregations**.

Rabbinical Council of America See **Jewish congregations**.

Ramadan The Muslim holy month, marked by daily fasting from dawn to sunset, ending with the Islamic holiday of Eid al-Fitr. Avoid using *holiday* on second reference to Ramadan.

rector See **religious titles**.

Reform Judaism See **Jewish congregations**.

religious movements The terms that follow have been grouped under a single entry because they are interrelated and frequently cross denominational lines.

evangelical Historically, *evangelical*

was used as an adjective describing Protestant dedication to conveying the message of Christ. Today it also is used as a noun, referring to a category of doctrinally conservative Protestants. They emphasize the need for a definite, adult commitment or conversion to faith in Christ and the duty of all believers to persuade others to accept Christ.

Evangelicals make up some conservative denominations and are numerous in broader denominations. Evangelicals stress both doctrinal absolutes and vigorous efforts to win others to belief.

The National Association of Evangelicals is an interdenominational, cooperative body of relatively small, conservative Protestant denominations.

evangelism The word refers to activity directed outside the church fold to influence others to commit themselves to faith in Christ, to his work of serving others and to infuse his principles into society's conduct.

Styles of evangelism vary from direct preaching appeals at large public meetings to practical deeds of carrying the name of Christ, indirectly conveying the same call to allegiance to him.

The word *evangelism* is derived from the Greek *evangelion*, which means the gospel or good news of Christ's saving action on behalf of humanity.

fundamentalist The word gained usage in an early-20th century fundamentalist-modernist controversy within Protestantism. In recent years, however, *fundamentalist* has to a large extent taken on pejorative connotations except when applied to groups that stress strict, literal interpretations of Scripture and separation from other

Christians.

In general, do not use *fundamentalist* unless a group applies the word to itself.

neo-Pentecostal, charismatic These terms apply to a movement that has developed within mainline Protestant and Catholic denominations since the mid-20th century. It is distinguished by its emotional expressiveness, spontaneity in worship, speaking or praying in "unknown tongues" and healing. Participants often characterize themselves as "spirit-filled" Christians.

Unlike the earlier Pentecostal movement, which led to separate denominations, this movement has swelled within major churches.

Pentecostalism A movement that arose in the early 20th century and separated from historic Protestant denominations. It is distinguished by the belief in tangible manifestations of the Holy Spirit, often in demonstrative, emotional ways such as speaking in "unknown tongues" and healing.

Pentecostal denominations include the Church of God in Christ, Assemblies of God, the Pentecostal Holiness Church, the United Pentecostal Church Inc. and the International Church of the Foursquare Gospel founded by Aimee Semple McPherson.

religious orders Capitalize the names and the related terms applied to members of the orders: *He is a member of the Society of Jesus. He is a Jesuit.*

religious references The basic guidelines:

DEITIES: Capitalize the proper names of monotheistic deities: *God,*

Allah, the Father, the Son, Jesus Christ, the Son of God, the Redeemer, the Holy Spirit, etc.

Lowercase pronouns referring to the deity. Avoid use of pronouns outside of direct quotes. Most monotheistic religions do not ascribe a gender to God; avoiding pronouns is accurate and respectful in all cases.

Lowercase *gods* in referring to the deities of polytheistic religions.

Capitalize the proper names of pagan and mythological gods and goddesses: *Neptune, Thor, Venus,* etc. Lowercase such words as *god-awful, godlike, godliness, godsend. God* is often capitalized in such phrases as *thank God* and *oh my God,* but lowercase *god* may be acceptable in some instances.

LIFE OF CHRIST: Capitalize the names of major events in the life of Jesus Christ in references that do not use his name: *The doctrines of the Last Supper, the Crucifixion, the Resurrection and the Ascension are central to Christian belief.*

But use lowercase when the words are used with his name: *The ascension of Jesus into heaven took place 40 days after his resurrection from the dead.*

Apply the principle also to events in the life of his mother: *He cited the doctrines of the Immaculate Conception and the Assumption.* But: *She referred to the assumption of Mary into heaven.*

RITES: Capitalize proper names for rites that commemorate the Last Supper or signify a belief in Christ's presence: *the Lord's Supper, Holy Communion, Holy Eucharist.*

Lowercase the names of other sacraments. See **sacraments**.

Capitalize *Benediction* and *Mass.* But: *a high Mass, a low Mass, a requiem Mass.*

HOLY DAYS: Capitalize the names

RELIGION

of holy days. See separate entries for major Christian, Jewish and Muslim feasts.

OTHER WORDS: Lowercase *heaven, hell, devil, angel, cherub, an apostle, a priest*, etc.

Capitalize *Hades* and *Satan*.

For additional details, see **Bible**, entries for frequently used religious terms, the entries for major denominations, **religious movements** and **religious titles**.

Religious Society of Friends See Quakers.

religious titles The first reference to member of the clergy normally should include a capitalized title before the individual's name.

In many cases, *the Rev.* is the designation that applies before a name on first reference.

On second reference, use only a last name: *the Rev. Billy Graham* on first reference, *Graham* on second. If known only by a religious name, repeat the title: *Pope John XXIII* on first reference, *John, the pope* or *the pontiff* on second; *Pope Emeritus Benedict XVI* or *Benedict XVI, the pope emeritus. Benedict* alone on second reference. *Metropolitan Herman* on first reference, *Metropolitan Herman* or *the metropolitan* on second.

Detailed guidance on specific titles and descriptive words such as *priest* and *minister* is provided in the entries for major denominations. In general, however:

CARDINALS, ARCHBISHOPS, BISHOPS: The preferred form for first reference is to use *Cardinal, Archbishop* or *Bishop* before the individual's name: *Cardinal Daniel DiNardo, archbishop of Galveston-Houston.* On second reference: *DiNardo* or *the cardinal.*

Substitute *the Most Rev.* if applicable and appropriate in the context: *He spoke to the Most Rev. Jose Gomez, archbishop of Los Angeles.* On second reference: *Gomez* or *the archbishop.*

Entries for individual denominations tell when *the Most Rev., the Very Rev.*, etc., are applicable.

MINISTERS AND PRIESTS: Use *the Rev.* before a name on first reference.

Substitute *Monsignor* before the name of a Catholic priest who has received this honor.

Do not routinely use *curate, father, pastor* and similar words before an individual's name. If they appear before a name in a quotation, capitalize them.

RABBIS: Use *Rabbi* before a name on first reference. On second reference, use only the last name.

NUNS: Always use *Sister*, or *Mother* if applicable, before a name: *Sister Agnes Rita* in all references if the nun uses only a religious name; *Sister Mary Ann Walsh* on first reference if she uses a surname. *Walsh* on subsequent references.

OFFICEHOLDERS: The preferred first-reference form for those who hold church office but are not ordained clergy in the usual sense is to use a construction that sets the title apart from the name by commas. Capitalize the formal title of an office, however, if it is used directly before an individual's name.

FORMER: Do not use *former* for job titles that are bestowed in perpetuity, such as *bishop*, unless those designations have been officially revoked. Instead use language like *retired bishop* to indicate that people are no longer actively serving.

Reorganized Church of Jesus Christ

of Latter Day Saints Now called *the Community of Christ*. Not properly described as a *Mormon church*. See the explanation under **Church of Jesus Christ of Latter-day Saints, The**.

Rev. When this description is used before an individual's name, precede it with the word *the* because, unlike the case with *Mr.* and *Mrs.*, the abbreviation *Rev.* does not stand for a noun. Always use the abbreviation, *the Rev.*, not the full word *reverend*, before a name.

If an individual also has a secular title such as *Rep.*, use whichever is appropriate to the context.

See **religious titles**.

Roman Catholic Church The church teaches that its bishops have been established as the successors of the apostles through generations of ceremonies in which authority was passed down by a laying-on of hands.

Responsibility for teaching the faithful and administering the church rests with the bishops. However, the church holds that the pope has final authority over their actions because he is the bishop of Rome, the office it teaches was held by the Apostle Peter at his death.

The Curia serves as a form of governmental cabinet. Its members, appointed by the pope, handle both administrative and judicial functions.

The pope also chooses members of the College of Cardinals, who serve as his principal counselors. When a new pope must be chosen, they meet in a conclave to select a new pope by a two-thirds majority vote. In practice, cardinals are mostly bishops, but there is no requirement that a cardinal be a bishop.

In the United States, the church's principal organizational units are archdioceses and dioceses. They are headed, respectively, by archbishops and bishops, who have final responsibility for many activities within their jurisdictions and report directly to Rome.

A caution: *Roman Catholic*, which refers to the Latin branch of Catholicism, is not the appropriate first reference when referring to the pope, the Vatican or the universal church. *Catholic Church* should be used instead, since it encompasses believers belonging to the Latin (Roman) and Eastern churches. Similarly, the U.S. Conference of Catholic Bishops includes bishops from Eastern churches as well as Roman Catholic bishops. See **Catholic, Catholicism**.

The church counts more than 1 billion members worldwide. In the United States estimates vary, but it is the largest single body of Christians in the nation.

Roman Catholics believe in the Trinity — that there is one God who exists as three divine persons — the Father, the Son and the Holy Spirit. They believe that the Son became man as Jesus Christ.

In addition to the Holy Eucharist, there are six other sacraments — baptism, confirmation, penance (often called the sacrament of reconciliation), matrimony, holy orders, and the sacrament of the sick (formerly extreme unction).

The clergy below pope are, in descending order of prominence, cardinal, archbishop, bishop, monsignor, priest and deacon. In religious orders, some men who are not priests have the title *brother*.

Capitalize *pope* when used as a title before a name: *Pope John XXIII*,

RELIGION

418

Pope Francis. Lowercase in all other uses. See **religious titles**.

The first-reference forms for other titles follow. Use only last names on second reference.

CARDINALS: *Cardinal Daniel DiNardo*. The usage *Daniel Cardinal DiNardo*, a practice traceable to the nobility's custom of identifications such as *William, Duke of Norfolk*, is still used in formal documents but otherwise is considered archaic.

ARCHBISHOPS: *Archbishop Gregory Aymond*, or *the Most Rev. Gregory Aymond, archbishop of New Orleans*.

Bishops: *Bishop Thomas Paprocki*, or *the Most Rev. Thomas Paprocki, bishop of Springfield, Illinois*.

MONSIGNORS: *Monsignor Martin Krebs*. Do not use the abbreviation *Msgr*. Do not use *the Rt. Rev.* or *the Very Rev.* — this distinction between types of monsignors no longer is made.

PRIESTS: *the Rev. James Martin*. See **religious titles**.

rosary It is *recited* or *said*, never *read*. Always lowercase.

Rosh Hashana The Jewish new year. Occurs in September or October.

Russian Orthodox Church See **Eastern Orthodox churches**.

S

Sabbath Capitalize in religious references. A day traditionally set aside for rest and worship. It is observed from sunset Friday to sunset Saturday in Judaism and on Sunday by most Christians.

sacraments Capitalize the proper names used for a sacramental rite that commemorates the life of Jesus Christ or signifies a belief in his presence: *the Lord's Supper, Holy Communion, Holy Eucharist*.

Lowercase the names of other sacraments: *baptism, confirmation, penance* (now often called the *sacrament of reconciliation*), *matrimony, holy orders*, and *the sacrament of anointing the sick* (formerly *extreme unction*).

See entries for the major religious denominations and **religious references**.

sacrilegious

Satan But lowercase *devil* and *satanic*.

savior Use this spelling for all senses, rather than the alternate form, *saviour*.

Seventh-day Adventist Church The denomination, with headquarters in Silver Spring, Maryland, has its roots in the preaching of William Miller of New Hampton, New York, a Baptist layman who said his study of the Book of Daniel indicated the end of the world would come in the mid-1840s.

When Christ did not return as predicted, the Millerites split into smaller groups. One, influenced by the visions of Ellen Harmon, later the wife of James White, is the precursor of the Seventh-day Adventist practice today.

The term *Adventist* reflects the belief that a second coming of Christ is near. *Seventh-day* reflects the church teaching that the Bible requires observing the Sabbath on the seventh day of the week.

Baptism, by immersion, is reserved for those old enough to

RELIGION

understand its meaning.

The head of the General Conference, the top church administrative authority, is the *president*. Ministers are *pastor* or *elder*. Capitalize immediately before a name on first reference. On second reference, use only the last name.

The designation *the Rev.* is not used.

See **religious titles**.

Shariah Islamic law. The phrase *Shariah law* is redundant.

Shavuot The Jewish Feast of Weeks, commemorating the receiving of the Ten Commandments. Occurs in May or June.

Shiite The spelling for this branch of Islam. Plural is *Shiites*. The alternate spelling *Shia* is acceptable in quotes. See **Islam**.

Sikhi, Sikhism A distinct, independent religion founded in the Punjab region of South Asia in the late 15th century by Guru Nanak, who promoted the idea of a singular divine (God) and a life of spiritual reflection and selfless service.

Guru Nanak propagated Sikhi through the composition of devotional hymns and by challenging conventional religious practices such as purifications, image worship, pilgrimages and religious austerities. With more than 27 million Sikhs worldwide, it is among the world's largest religions.

The most visible aspect of Sikh identity is the turban, which covers a Sikh's unshorn hair, and can be worn by men and women alike. Take care not to imply that only Sikh men wear turbans or keep their hair long. Sikh men and Sikh women are equally forbidden from cutting their hair.

The initiated Sikh identity includes five articles of faith — *kesh* (unshorn hair), *kanga* (small comb), *kara* (steel bracelet), *kirpan* (religious article resembling a knife) and *kachera* (soldier-shorts) — and distinguishes someone who has formally committed to the values of Sikhism by accepting initiation.

Sikhi was founded and established by 10 successive leaders (gurus) who lived from 1469-1708. The last of those leaders, Guru Gobind Singh, passed the authority of guruship to two entities for eternity—the Guru Granth Sahib (the scriptural canon) and the Guru Khalsa Panth (the community of initiated Sikhs).

Sikhi recognizes no clergy. Individuals have direct access to their own spiritual experience, and any Sikh can play a leadership role in the worship. A Sikh leader trained in all aspects of maintaining decorum in a *gurdwara* (Sikh house of worship), including reading from and caring for Guru Granth Sahib, is called a *granthi*.

While the vast majority of Sikhs live in Punjab, and most Sikhs living elsewhere are of Punjabi background, not all Sikhs are Punjabi, and not all Punjabis are Sikh.

Sikhi is the term Sikhs use for their faith. *Sikhism* and the *Sikh religion* are also acceptable.

sister Capitalize in all references before the names of nuns.

If no surname is given, the name is the same in all references: *Sister Agnes Rita*.

If a surname is used in first reference, drop the given name and sister on second reference: *Sister Mary Ann Walsh* on first reference,

Walsh in subsequent references.

Use *Mother* the same way when referring to a woman who heads a group of nuns.

See **religious titles**.

Society of Friends See **Quakers**.

Sukkot The Jewish Feast of Tabernacles, celebrating the fall harvest and commemorating the desert wandering of the Jews during the Exodus. Occurs in September or October.

synagogue The preferred term for a Jewish house of worship. Many Reform synagogues (and some others) have the word *temple* in their names, a usage deemed archaic by some — it harks back to the early 19th century, when German Jews used it to assert that they no longer yearned to restore the ancient Temple in Jerusalem. Orthodox Jews often use the word *shul*, Yiddish for *school*. Avoid the redundant *Jewish synagogue*. *Congregation* can be used generically: *The congregation met every Sabbath to worship*.

synod A council of churches or church officials. See the entry for the denomination in question.

t

Talmud The collection of writings that constitute the Jewish civil and religious law.

Temple Mount The walled, elevated area in Jerusalem's Old City that was the site of the ancient Jewish temples. It now houses the centuries-old Dome of the Rock shrine and Al-Aqsa Mosque and is known to Muslims as the *Haram al-Sharif*, or *Noble Sanctuary*. Muslims believe the Prophet Muhammad made his night journey to heaven from the site.

Ten Commandments Do not abbreviate or use figures. Not all faith groups organize the Ten Commandments in the same order.

Twelve Apostles The disciples of Jesus. An exception to the normal practice of using figures for 10 and above.

u

Ukrainian Catholic Church See **Eastern Rite churches**.

Unitarian Universalist Association The central organization for the Unitarian Universalist religious movement in the United States, which welcomes people with a wide range of spiritual beliefs.

United Church of Christ The Evangelical and Reformed Church merged with the Congregational Christian Churches in 1957 to form the United Church of Christ.

The word *church* is correctly applied only to an individual local church. Each such church is responsible for the doctrine, ministry and ritual of its congregation.

Jesus is regarded as man's savior, but no subscription to a set creed is required for membership.

Members of the clergy are known as *ministers*. *Pastor* applies if a minister leads a congregation.

RELIGION

On first reference, use *the Rev.* before the name. On second reference, use only the last name. See **religious titles**.

United Methodist Church See **Methodist churches**.

United States Conference of Catholic Bishops Formerly the National Conference of Catholic Bishops, it is the national organization of Catholic bishops. *U.S. Conference of Catholic Bishops* is acceptable on first reference.

United Synagogue of Conservative Judaism Not *synagogues*. See **Jewish congregations**.

V

Very Rev. See **Episcopal Church**; **religious titles**; **Catholic, Catholicism** and **Roman Catholic Church**.

Vodou, Voodoo Capitalize and use the spelling *Vodou* when referring specifically to the religion as it is practiced primarily in Haiti or among the Haitian community abroad. The spelling *Voodoo* has come to be seen as pejorative in those regions and should be avoided. However, the spelling Voodoo is commonly used and acceptable when referring to the religion as practiced in Louisiana. Avoid using either term as shorthand for magical or superstitious beliefs. For example, do not refer to *voodoo* (lowercase) *economics* unless essential in a direct quotation, or to *voodoo rituals* unless essential and with attribution and explanation.

W

Wahhabi Follower of a strict Muslim sect that adheres closely to the Quran; it's most powerful in Saudi Arabia.

Western Wall The last remaining part of the second temple complex of the biblical period and the holiest site where Jews can pray. *The Western Wall* is located in Jerusalem's Old City, on the edge of the site known as the *Temple Mount* to Jews and *Haram al-Sharif* (*the Noble Sanctuary*) to Muslims. Some non-Jews refer to the site as the *Wailing Wall*.

Wicca Religion shaped by pagan beliefs and practices. The term encompasses a wide range of traditions generally organized around seasonal festivals, and can include ritual magic, a belief in both female and male deities, and the formation of covens led by priestesses and priests. *Wiccan* is both an adjective and a noun. Uppercase in all uses.

World Council of Churches An international, interdenominational cooperative body of Anglican, Eastern Orthodox, Protestant and old or national Catholic churches.

The Catholic Church is not a member but cooperates with the council in various programs.

Headquarters is in Geneva.

worship, worshipped, worshipper

Y

Yom Kippur The Jewish Day of Atonement. Occurs in September or

RELIGION

October.

Z

Zionism The effort of Jews to regain
and retain their biblical homeland.
It is based on the promise of God
in the Book of Genesis that Israel
would forever belong to Abraham
and his descendants as a nation.

The term is named for Mount
Zion, the site of the ancient temple
in Jerusalem.

Zoroastrianism A monotheistic
religion predating Christianity and
Islam founded some 3,800 years ago
by Zoroaster. It was the dominant
religion in Persia before the Arab
conquest. It stresses good deeds, and
fire plays a central role in worship
as a symbol of truth and the spirit of
God.

Sports

SPORTS IDENTIFICATION CODES

ARC — Archery
ATH — Athletics (Track & Field)
BAD — Badminton
BBA — Baseball-American League
BBC — Baseball-College
BBM — Baseball-Minor Leagues
BBN — Baseball-National League
BBO — Baseball-Other
BBH — Baseball-High School
BBI — Baseball-International
BBW — Baseball-Women's
BBY — Baseball-Youth
BIA — Biathlon
BKC — Basketball-College
BKH — Basketball-High School
BKL — Basketball-Women's Pro
     (WNBA)
BKN — Basketball-NBA
BKO — Basketball-Other
BKW — Basketball-Women's College
BOB — Bobsled
BOX — Boxing
BVL — Beach Volleyball
CAN — Canoeing
CAR — Auto Racing
CRI — Cricket
CUR — Curling
CYC — Cycling
DIV — Diving
EQU — Equestrian
FEN — Fencing
FIG — Figure Skating
FHK — Field Hockey
FBC — (American) Football-College
FBH — (American) Football-High
     School
FBN — (American) Football-NFL
FBO — (American) Football-Other
FRE — Freestyle skiing
GLF — Golf

GYM — Gymnastics
HNB — Handball
HKC — (Ice) Hockey-College
HKN — (Ice) Hockey-NHL
HKO — (Ice) Hockey-Other
HKW — (Ice) Hockey-Women's
JUD — Judo
JUM — Ski Jumping
LAC — Lacrosse
LUG — Luge
MMA — Mixed Martial Arts
NOR — Nordic combined
PEN — Modern Pentathlon
MOT — Motorcycling
OLY — Olympics (with a specific sport
     code added where applicable)
RAC — (Horse) Racing
ROW — Rowing
RGL — Rugby League
RGU — Rugby Union
SAI — Sailing
SHO — Shooting
SKE — Skeleton
SKI — Alpine Skiing
SPD — Speedskating and Short Track
     Speedskating
SBD — Snowboarding
SOC — Soccer
SOF — Softball
SQA — Squash
SUM — Sumo Wrestling
SWM — Swimming
TAE — Taekwondo
TEN — Tennis
TRI — Triathlon
TTN — Table Tennis
VOL — Volleyball
WPO — Water Polo
WEI — Weightlifting
WRE — Wrestling
XXC — Cross-Country Skiing

a

abbreviations It is not necessary to spell out the most common abbreviations on first reference: *NFL, AFC, NFC, NBA, NHL, NCAA, PGA, LPGA, USGA, NASCAR, MLB, AL, NL, FIFA.*

Achilles tendon No apostrophe for the tendon connecting the back of the heel to the calf muscles. But it's *Achilles' heel*, with an apostrophe, for a vulnerable spot.

ACL When describing injuries, acceptable in all references to the *anterior cruciate ligament.*

-added Follow this form in sports stories: *The $500,000-added sweepstakes.*

agate See **basic summary** and **match summary**.

All-America, All-American The Associated Press recognizes only one All-America football and basketball team each year. In football, only Walter Camp's selections through 1924, and the AP selections after that, are recognized. Do not call anyone not listed on either the Camp or AP roster an *All-America* selection.

Similarly do not call anyone who was not an AP selection an *All-America basketball player*. The first All-America men's basketball team was chosen in 1948.

Use *All-American* when referring specifically to an individual: *All-American Breanna Stewart*, or *She is an All-American.*

Use *All-America* when referring to the team: *All-America team*, or *All-America selection.*

all-star, All-Star, All-Star Game Use uppercase All-Star only when referring to players who have been officially named All-Stars in a sport that refers to its best players each season as All-Stars. The term does not apply in pro football, where players selected to The Associated Press NFL All-Pro team should be referred to as *All-Pro*, while those selected to the Pro Bowl should be referred to as *Pro Bowl players* or *Pro Bowlers*. Use lowercase all-star sparingly to refer informally to performances or players in casual constructions. Use All-Star Game in references where it is the official title of the game.

Alpine skiing In Olympics, slalom, giant slalom, super-G, downhill, Alpine combined

apostrophe See the **possessives** entry in main section and the **apostrophe** entry in the **Punctuation** chapter, including its descriptive phrases section. Use only in constructions where warranted: *Patriots quarterback Tom Brady* doesn't get an apostrophe as a descriptive but *Tom Brady, the Patriots' starting quarterback*, gets an apostrophe as a possessive.

archery At the Summer Olympics, individual and team events for men and women. Use a **basic summary**.

AstroTurf A trademark for a type of artificial grass.

athlete's foot, athlete's heart

athletic club Abbreviate as *AC* with the name of a club, but only in sports summaries: *Illinois AC*. See **match**

summary for an example of such a summary.

athletic director Use the singular *athletic* unless otherwise in a formal title.

athletic teams Capitalize teams, associations and recognized nicknames: *Red Sox, the Big Ten, the A's, the Colts.*

athletic trainers Health care professionals who are licensed or otherwise regulated to work with athletes and physically active people to prevent, diagnose and treat injuries and other emergency, acute and chronic medical conditions including cardiac abnormalities and heat stroke. Specify where necessary to distinguish from personal trainers, who focus primarily on fitness.

auto racing Common terms include *victory lane, pit road.*

Follow the forms below for all major auto races:

NASCAR

LINEUP

NASCAR-Sprint Cup-Daytona 500 Lineup
By The Associated Press
After Thursday qualifying; race Sunday
At Daytona International Speedway
Daytona Beach, Fla.
Lap length: 2.5 miles
(Car number in parentheses)
1. (99) Carl Edwards, Ford, 194.738.
2. (16) Greg Biffle, Ford, 194.087.
3. (14) Tony Stewart, Chevrolet, 193.607.

RESULTS

NASCAR Sprint Cup-Daytona 500 Results
By The Associated Press
Monday
At Daytona International Speedway
Daytona Beach, Fla.
Lap length: 2.5 miles
(Start position in parentheses)

1. (4) Matt Kenseth, Ford, 202 laps, 100.9 rating, 47 points, $1,589,387.
2. (5) Dale Earnhardt Jr., Chevrolet, 202, 99.5, 42, $1,102,175.
3. (2) Greg Biffle, Ford, 202, 126.2, 42, $804,163.

For cars not finishing the race, include reason:
41. (17) Robby Gordon, Dodge, engine, 25, 30.5, 3, $268,150.
42. (8) Jimmie Johnson, Chevrolet, accident, 1, 28.3, 2, $327,149.
43. (25) David Ragan, Ford, accident, 1, 25.9, 1, $267,637.

After the final driver, add:

Race Statistics
Average Speed of Race Winner: 140.256 mph.
Time of Race: 3 hours, 36 minutes, 2 seconds.
Margin of Victory: 0.210 seconds.
Caution Flags: 10 for 42 laps.
Lead Changes: 25 among 13 drivers.
Lap Leaders: G.Biffle 1-9; R.Smith 10-11; G.Biffle 12-14; P.Menard 15-16; D.Hamlin 17-40; J.Burton 41-57; J.Gordon 58; T.Stewart 59-60; J.Burton 61-67; G.Biffle 68-76; M.Truex Jr. 77-81; G.Biffle 82; T.Labonte 83-85; G.Biffle 86-99; M.Truex Jr. 100-101; D.Hamlin 102-129; G.Biffle 130; M.Martin 131-132; G.Biffle 133-138; D.Hamlin 139-143; J.Logano 144-145; M.Kenseth 146-157; G.Biffle 158; D.Blaney 159-164; M.Kenseth 165-202.
Leaders Summary (Driver, Times Led, Laps Led): D.Hamlin, 3 times for 57 laps; M.Kenseth, 2 times for 50 laps; G.Biffle, 8 times for 44 laps; J.Burton, 2 times for 24 laps; M.Truex Jr., 2 times for 7 laps; D.Blaney, 1 time for 6 laps; T.Labonte, 1 time for 3 laps; P.Menard, 1 time for 2 laps; J.Logano, 1 time for 2 laps; M.Martin, 1 time for 2 laps; T.Stewart, 1 time for 2 laps; R.Smith, 1 time for 2 laps; J.Gordon, 1 time for 1 lap.
Top 12 in Points: 1. M.Kenseth, 47; 2. D.Earnhardt Jr., 42; 3. G.Biffle, 42; 4. D.Hamlin, 42; 5. J.Burton, 40; 6. P.Menard, 39; 7. K.Harvick, 37; 8. C.Edwards, 36; 9. J.Logano, 36; 10. M.Martin, 35; 11. C.Bowyer, 33; 12. M.Truex Jr., 33.

Formula One-Abu Dhabi Grand Prix Results

By The Associated Press
Sunday
At Yas Marina circuit
Abu Dhabi, United Arab Emirates
Lap length: 3.45 miles
1. Kimi Raikkonen, Finland, Lotus, 55 laps, 1:45:58.667, 107.421 mph.
2. Fernando Alonso, Spain, Ferrari, 55, 1:45:59.519.

Constructors Standings
1. Red Bull, 460 points.
2. Ferrari, 400.

IndyCar-MAVTV 500 Results

By The Associated Press
Saturday

SPORTS

At Auto Club Speedway
Fontana, Calif.
Lap length: 2 miles
(Starting position in parentheses)

1. (5) Ed Carpenter, Dallara-Chevrolet, 250, Running.
2. (9) Dario Franchitti, Dallara-Honda, 250, Running.
24. (13) Will Power, Dallara-Chevrolet, 66, Contact.
25. (11) E.J. Viso, Dallara-Chevrolet, 65, Mechanical.

Race Statistics
Winners average speed: 168.939.
Time of Race: 2:57:34.7433.
Margin of Victory: Under Caution.
Cautions: 7 for 43 laps.
Lead Changes: 29 among 12 drivers.
Lap Leaders: Kanaan 1, Andretti 2-4, Hildebrand 5-35, Briscoe 36-37, Sato 38-39, Newgarden 40, Hildebrand 41-65, Carpenter 66-75, Jakes 76-85, Carpenter 86-109, Dixon 110, Carpenter 111-122, Dixon 123-133, Kanaan 134-147, Castroneves 148-149, Sato 150-152, Kanaan 153-184, Dixon 185-195, Carpenter 196, Dixon 197-198, Carpenter 199-203, Tagliani 204-217, Carpenter 218, Tagliani 219-223, Franchitti 224-225, Tagliani 226-227, Sato 228, Carpenter 229-236, Franchitti 237-249, Carpenter 250.
Points: Hunter-Reay 468, Power 465, Dixon 435, Castroneves 431, Pagenaud 387, Briscoe 370, Franchitti 363, Hinchcliffe 358, Kanaan 351, Rahal 333.

NHRA Results

By The Associated Press
Sunday
At Firebird International Raceway
Chandler, Ariz.
Final Results

Top Fuel_Tony Schumacher, 4.606 seconds, 213.20 mph def. Morgan Lucas, 4.652 seconds, 258.67 mph.
Funny Car_Ron Capps, Dodge Charger, 4.064, 314.90 def. Matt Hagan, Charger, 4.158, 300.33.
Pro Stock_Erica Enders-Stevens, Chevy Cobalt, 6.538, 211.99 def. Mike Edwards, Chevy Camaro, 6.520, 213.74.

b

backboard, backcourt, backfield, backhand, backspin, backstop, backstretch, backstroke Some are exceptions to Webster's New World, made for consistency in handling sports stories.

badminton Games are won by the first player to score 21 points, unless it is necessary to continue until one player has a two-point spread. Most matches go to the first winner of two games.

Use a **match summary**.

ball carrier

ballclub, ballgame, ballpark, ballplayer

baseball The spellings for some frequently used words and phrases, some of which are exceptions to Webster's New World College Dictionary:

backstop	*pinch hit*
baseline	*pinch hitter (n.)*
bullpen	*pitchout*
center field (n., adj.)	*put out (v.) putout*
center fielder	*(n.)*
designated hitter	*RBI (s.), RBIs (pl.)*
doubleheader	*right field (n., adj.)*
double play	*rundown (n.)*
fair ball	*sacrifice*
fastball	*sacrifice fly*
first baseman	*sacrifice hit*
foul ball line	*shortstop*
foul tip	*shut out (v.)*
ground-rule double	*shutout (n., adj.)*
home plate	*slugger*
home run	*squeeze play*
left field (n., adj)	*strike*
line drive	*strike zone*
line up (v.)	*Texas leaguer*
lineup (n.)	*third base coach*
major league(s) (n.)	*triple play*
major league (adj.)	*twinight*
major leaguer (n.)	*doubleheader*
outfielder	*walk-off*
passed ball	*wild pitch*

NUMBERS: Some sample uses of numbers: *first inning, seventh inning stretch, third inning single, 10th inning, first base, second base, third base, first home run, 10th home run, first place, one RBI, 10 RBIs. The pitcher's record is now 6-5. The final score was 1-0.*

LEAGUES: Use *American League, National League, American League West, National League East,* or *AL West* and *AL East,* etc. On second reference: *the league, the pennant in the West, the league's West Division,* etc.

Note: No hyphen in *major league, minor league, big league* (n. or adj.).

PLAYOFFS: Use *American League Championship Series,* or *ALCS* on second reference; *National League Championship Series,* or *NLCS; AL Division Series,* or *ALDS;* and *NL Division Series,* or *NLDS.* In the early rounds, use *series* lowercase. Use uppercase *Series* only to refer to the World Series.

ERA Acceptable in all references for earned run average.

Green Monster Acceptable in all references to the left field wall at Fenway Park, home of the Boston Red Sox.

BOX SCORES: A sample follows.

The visiting team always is listed on the left, the home team on the right.

Only one position, the first he played in the game, is listed for any player.

BC-BBN--BOX-Atl-SD

BRAVES 8, PADRES 3

ATLANTA	ab	r	h	bi	SAN DIEGO	ab	r	h	bi
Ogllen ss	5	1	1	1	QVeras 2b	4	1	0	0
Lckhrt 2b	5	2	2	0	SFinley cf	4	0	1	0
ChJnes 3b	4	2	2	1	Gwynn rf	4	1	1	1
Glrrga 1b	2	1	1	4	Cminiti 3b	3	0	1	0
Klesko lf	4	0	1	1	Leyritz 1b	3	1	2	2
Rocker p	0	0	0	0	Joyner 1b	1	0	1	0
Perez p	0	0	0	0	CHrndz c	4	0	1	0
Seanez p	0	0	0	0	RRivra lf	3	0	1	0
Lgtnbr p	0	0	0	0	MaSwy ph	1	0	0	0
JLopez c	4	1	1	1	Gomez ss	3	0	0	0
AJones cf	4	1	2	0	Miceli p	0	0	0	0
Tucker rf	2	0	1	0	Bhrngr p	0	0	0	0
GerWm rf	2	0	1	0	Lngstn p	0	0	0	0
Neagle p	2	0	0	0	GMyrs ph	0	0	0	0
DeMrtz p	0	0	0	0	JHmtn p	2	0	0	0
Clbrnn ph	1	0	0	0	RayMys p	0	0	0	0
DBtsta lf	1	0	0	0	Sheets ss	1	0	0	0
VnWal ph	1	0	0	0					
Totals	**36**	**8**	**12**	**8**		**34**	**3**	**8**	**3**

Atlanta 000 101 600 - 8
San Diego 000 200 000 - 2

DP_Atlanta 1, San Diego 2. LOB_Atlanta 4, San Diego 7. 2B_ChJones (1), Gwynn (1), RRivera (2). 3B_Lockhart (1). HR_Galarraga (1), JLopez (1), Leyritz (1).

	IP	H	R	ER	BB	SO
Atlanta						
Neagle	5 2-3	7	3	3	1	7
DeMrtz W, 1-0	1-3	0	0	0	0	0
Rocker	1 1-3	0	0	0	0	3
Perez	0	1	0	0	1	0
Seanez	2-3	0	0	0	0	0
Ligtenberg	1	0	0	0	1	2
San Diego						
JHamilton L, 0-1	6	7	4	4	2	5
RaMyers	2-3	2	3	3	1	0
Miceli	1-3	1	1	1	0	1
Boehringer	1	2	0	0	0	0
Langston	1	0	0	0	0	0

Perez pitched to 2 batters in the 8th, JHamilton pitched to 2 batters in the 7th.

Umpires_Home, Bonin; First, Davis; Second, Rippley; Third, Tata; Left, Poncino; Right, Hallion.

T_2:58. A_65,042 (59,772).

Example of an expanded box score:

BC-BBA--EXP-BOX-Ana-Tex

Rangers 3, Angels 2

Anaheim	AB	R	H	BI	BB	SO	Avg.
Erstad cf	4	0	3	2	0	0	.750
Gil ss	3	0	0	0	0	0	.000
a-OPalmeiro ph	1	0	0	0	0	0	.000
Nieves ss	0	0	0	0	0	0	.000
Salmon rf	4	0	1	0	0	1	.250
Glaus 3b	4	0	1	0	0	1	.250
GAnderson lf	3	0	1	0	1	0	.333
GHill dh	4	0	0	0	0	1	.000
BMolina c	4	1	1	0	0	1	.250
Spiezio 1b	3	1	1	0	0	1	.333
Eckstein 2b	3	0	1	0	0	0	.333
Totals	**33**	**2**	**9**	**2**	**1**	**5**	

Texas	AB	R	H	BI	BB	SO	Avg.
Greer lf	3	0	0	1	0	1	.143
Velarde 2b	4	0	1	0	0	1	.250
ARodriguez ss	4	0	1	0	0	3	.375
RPalmeiro 1b	2	0	0	0	2	0	.167
IRodriguez c	4	1	2	0	0	0	.250
Galarraga dh	3	1	1	1	0	0	.167
Caminiti 3b	2	0	1	0	1	0	.500
Curtis cf	2	1	1	0	0	0	.500

SPORTS

| Mateo rf | 3 | 0 | 1 | 0 | 0 | 1 | .429 |

| ^Totals | 27 | 3 | 8 | 2 | 3 | 6 | |

| **Anaheim** | 001 000 010_2 9 2 | | | | | | |
| **Texas** | 020 000 10x_3 8 0 | | | | | | |

a-grounded into double play for Gil in the 8th.

LOB_Anaheim 5, Texas 5. 2B_Erstad 2 (2), Glaus (1), BMolina (1), Spiezio (1), Velarde (1), IRodriguez (1), Galarraga (1). RBIs_Erstad 2 (2), Greer (1), Galarraga (1). SB_ARodriguez (1). SF_Greer. GIDP_OPalmeiro, GHill 2, IRodriguez, Curtis, Mateo.

Runners left in scoring position_Anaheim 4 (Salmon, Glaus, BMolina 2); Texas 3 (Greer, RPalmeiro, Caminiti). RISP_L.A. Angels 2 for 12; Texas 2 for 9.

Runners moved up_Gil 2, Eckstein.

DP_Anaheim 3 (Gil, Eckstein and Spiezio), (Gil, Eckstein and Spiezio), (Eckstein, Gil and Spiezio); Texas 3 (ARodriguez, Velarde and RPalmeiro), (Velarde, ARodriguez and RPalmeiro), (Caminiti, IRodriguez and RPalmeiro).

	IP	H	R	ER	BB	SO	NP	ERA
Anaheim								
Schoeneweis L, 0-1	7	8	3	3	3	5	108	3.86
Weber	1	0	0	0	0	1	13	0.00
Texas								
Rogers W, 1-0	7 1-3	7	2	2	0	5	96	2.45
JRZimmermn H, 4	2-3	0	0	0	0	2	0.00	
Crabtree S, 1	1	2	0	0	1	0	12	0.00

Inherited runners-scored_JRZimmermn 2-0.

IBB_off Crabtree (GAnderson) 1. HBP_by Schoeneweis (Curtis).

Umpires_Home, Rippley; First, Winters; Second, Barrett, Ted; Third, Marquez.

T_2:31. A_49,512 (49,115).

LINESCORE: When a bare linescore summary is required, use this form:

Philadelphia	010 200 000 - 3 4 1
San Diego	000 200 000 - 2 9 1

K. Gross, Tekulve (8) and Virgil; Dravecky, Lefferts (3) and Kennedy. W - KGross, 4-6. L-Dravecky, 4-3. Sv - Tekulve (3). HRs - Philadelphia, Virgil 2 (8).

LEAGUE STANDINGS:
The form:

All Times EDT

NATIONAL LEAGUE

	W	L	Pct.	GB
EAST				
Pittsburgh	92	69	.571	-
Philadelphia	85	75	.531	61/2
WEST				
	W	L	Pct.	GB
Cincinnati	108	54	.667	-
Los Angeles	88	74	.543	20

Monday's Results

Chicago 7, St. Louis 5

Atlanta at New York, ppd., rain

Tuesday's Games

Cincinnati (Gullett 14-2 and Nolan 4-4) at New York (Seaver 12-3 and Matlack 6-1) 2, 6 p.m.

Wednesday's Games

Cincinnati at New York, 7:05 p.m.

Chicago at St.Louis, 8:05 p.m.

Only games scheduled.

In subheads for results and future games, spell out day of the week as: *Tuesday's Games*, instead of *Today's Games*.

BASE jumping Acceptable on first reference for the extreme sport, but explain later in the story. *BASE* is an acronym for *building*, *antenna*, *span* (such as a bridge) and *earth* (such as a cliff).

basic summary This format for summarizing sports events lists winners in the order of their finish. The figure showing the place finish is followed by an athlete's full name, his affiliation or hometown, and his time, distance, points or whatever performance factor is applicable to the sport.

If a contest involves several types of events, the paragraph begins with the name of the event.

A typical example:

60-yard dash - 1, Steve Williams, Florida TC, 6.0. 2, Hasley Crawford, Philadelphia Pioneer, 6.1. 3, Mike McFarland, Chicago TC, 6.2. 4

100 - 1, Steve Williams, Florida TC, 10.1. 2, ...

Most basic summaries are a single paragraph per event, as shown. In some competitions with large fields, however, the basic summary is supplied under a dateline with each winner listed in a single paragraph. See the **auto racing** and **bowling** entries for examples.

Other examples:

Archery
(After 3 of 4 Distances)

1. Darrell Pace, Cincinnati, 914 points.

2. Richard McKinney, Muncie, Ind. 880.

—

Bobsled, Women

1. Kaillie Humphries and Jennifer Ciochetti, Canada, 3 minutes, 48.57 seconds (57.10- 57.07-57.22-57.18).

2. Sandra Kiriasis and Petra Lammert, Germany, 3:48.90 (57.30-57.28-57.21-57.11).

3. Elana Meyers and Katie Eberling, United States, 3:49.57 (57.22-57.45-57.41-57.49).

—

Canoeing, Men

Kayak Singles, 500 meters

Heat 1 - 1, Rudiger Helm, Germany, 1:56.06. 2, Zoltan Sztanity, Hungary, 1:57.12. Also: 6, Henry Krawczyk, New York, 2 04.64. First Repechage - 1, Ladislay Soucek, Czech Republic, 1:53.20. 2, Hans Eich, Germany, 1:54.23.

—

Gymnastics:

Parallel Bars - 1, Joe Smith, Houston, 9.675 points. 2, Ed Jones, Albany, N.Y., 9.54. 3, Andy Brown, Los Angeles, 9.4.

—

ATHENS, Greece (AP) - Final results Saturday of the weightlifting event from the Summer Olympics:

Men's 85kg

1. Juan Jose Madrigal, Costa Rica, 472.5 kg.

2. Rampa Mosweu, Botswana, 470.0.

Additional examples are provided in the entries for several of the sports that are reported in this format.

For international events in which U.S. competitors are not among the leaders, add them in a separate paragraph as follows:

Also: 14, Dick Green, New York, 6.8.

In events where points, rather than time or distance, are recorded as performances, mention the word points on the first usage only:

1. Jim Benson, Springfield, N.J., 150 points. 2. Jerry Green, Canada, 149.

basketball The spellings of some frequently used words and phrases:

air ball	*half-court pass*
alley-oop	*hook shot*
backboard	*jump ball*
foul line	*jump shot*
foul shot	*layup*
free throw	*man-to-man*
free-throw line	*pivotman*
frontcourt	*tip off (v.)*
full-court press	*tipoff (n., adj.)*
goaltending	

NUMBERS: Some sample uses of numbers: *in the first quarter, a second quarter lead, nine field goals, a 3-pointer, 3-point play, 10 field goals, the 6-foot-5 forward, the 6-10 center. He is 6 feet, 10 inches tall.*

LEAGUE: *National Basketball Association* or NBA.

For subdivisions: *the Atlantic Division of the Eastern Conference, the Pacific Division of the Western Conference,* etc. On second reference: *the NBA East, the division, the conference,* etc.

PLAYOFFS: In the NBA, *Eastern Conference first round, Western Conference semifinals, Eastern Conference finals, Western Conference finals, NBA Finals.*

NCAA Tournament It is acceptable to refer to the regional semifinals as the *Sweet 16,* the regional finals as the *Elite Eight* and the national semifinals as the *Final Four.* For early-round games, use *round of 64* or *round of 32* if needed, though it is easier in many cases to say a team's first or second game if they begin in the round of 64: *California won its opening game of the NCAA Tournament. First Four* is acceptable to refer to the NCAA Tournament games played to reach the round of 64.

BOX SCORE: A sample follows. The visiting team always is listed first.

In listing the players, begin with the five starters — two forwards, center, two guards — and follow with all substitutes who played.

Figures after each player's last name denote field goals made and attempted, free throws made and attempted and total points.

EXAMPLE:

Hornets-Bulls, Box

NEW ORLEANS (95)

Ariza 7-12 0-0 16, Ayon 2-6 1-2 5, Kaman 7-18 3-4 17, Vasquez 4-10 4-4 12, Belinelli 3-7 0-0 6, Jones 4-10 2-2 10, Aminu 0-4 2-2 2, Jack 4-9 0-0 10, Henry 3-10 6-7 12, Thomas 2-3 1-1 5. Totals 36-89 19-22 95.

CHICAGO (99)

SPORTS

Deng 6-16 1-2 14, Boozer 7-14 0-0 14, Noah 7-12 1-3 15, Rose 11-24 9-11 32, Hamilton 2-5 1-1 5, Brewer 3-6 0-0 6, Gibson 2-4 1-2 5, Watson 0-2 0-0 0, Korver 2-6 0-0 5, Asik 1-1 1-1 3. Totals 41-90 14-20 99.

New Orleans 26•24•20•25_95

Chicago 30•17•29•23_99

3-Point Goals_New Orleans 4-9 (Jack 2-2, Ariza 2-2, Henry 0-1, Vasquez 0-1, Belinelli 0-3), Chicago 3-18 (Korver 1-5, Deng 1-5, Rose 1-5, Brewer 0-1, Hamilton 0-1, Watson 0-1). Fouled Out_None. Rebounds_New Orleans 55 (Kaman 11), Chicago 56 (Noah 16). Assists_New Orleans 22 (Kaman 5), Chicago 25 (Rose 9). Total Fouls_New Orleans 18, Chicago 16. Technicals_Boozer, Noah. A_21,919 (20,917).

An expanded box example:

BC-BKN--Lakers-Nuggets, Long Box

NUGGETS 119, LAKERS 108

		FG	FT	Reb			
L.A. LAKERS	**Min**	**M-A**	**M-A**	**O-T**	**A**	**PF**	**PTS**
World Peace	30:53	6-11	1-2	2-2	0	3	15
Clark	22:40	4-9	0-2	0-1	0	2	8
Howard	38:20	6-8	3-14	4-14	1	2	15
Nash	34:03	6-8	4-5	0-3	5	3	16
Bryant	38:44	12-23	5-6	0-6	9	3	29
Jamison	24:15	5-12	1-2	0-3	1	0	14
Meeks	31:34	3-5	0-0	2-5	1	3	8
Blake	19:31	1-2	0-0	0-2	4	1	3
Totals	240:00	43-78	14-31	8-36	21	17	108

Percentages: FG .551, FT .452.

3-Point Goals: 8-19, .421 (Jamison 3-4, Meeks 2-4, World Peace 2-5, Blake 1-2, Bryant 0-1, Nash 0-1, Clark 0-2).

Team Rebounds: 13. Team Turnovers: 15 (22 PTS).

Blocked Shots: 5 (Howard 4, Clark).

Turnovers: 15 (Nash 6, Bryant 4, World Peace 2, Blake, Howard, Meeks).

Steals: 6 (World Peace 3, Clark, Jamison, Meeks).

Technical Fouls: World Peace, 11:37 first; Defensive three second, 10:02 first; Bryant, 12:00 third.

		FG	FT	Reb			
DENVER	**Min**	**M-A**	**M-A**	**O-T**	**A**	**PF**	**PTS**
Chandler	25:24	10-18	0-0	2-4	1	3	23
Faried	31:48	6-10	0-0	4-10	0	5	12
Koufos	14:24	3-4	2-4	3-5	0	5	8
Lawson	40:30	8-19	5-7	0-4	8	3	22
Iguodala	36:45	6-9	2-5	0-4	12	0	14
Brewer	25:40	6-15	3-5	0-2	3	3	16
McGee	23:19	3-4	1-2	2-7	0	3	7
AMiller	27:41	3-4	3-4	0-3	5	0	9
Randolph	6:18	3-3	0-0	2-4	0	1	6
Hamilton	4:15	0-1	0-0	0-1	1	0	0
Mozgov	3:56	1-1	0-0	0-0	0	2	2
Totals	240:00	49-88	16-27	13-44	30	25	119

Percentages: FG .557, FT .593.

3-Point Goals: 5-18, .278 (Chandler 3-5, Brewer 1-5, Lawson 1-6, Iguodala 0-1, A.Miller 0-1).

Team Rebounds: 9. Team Turnovers: 10 (16 PTS).

Blocked Shots: 7 (McGee 4, Faried 2, Iguodala).

Turnovers: 9 (Lawson 4, Iguodala 2, Brewer, Faried, McGee).

Steals: 13 (Faried 3, McGee 2, A.Miller 2, Brewer, Chandler, Iguodala, Koufos, Lawson, Randolph).

Technical Fouls: Coach Karl, 7:27 first; Defensive three second, 3:56 second; Defensive three second, 4:17 third.

L.A. Lakers 29 25 29 25_108

Denver 35 32 28 24_119

A_19,155 (19,155). T_2:14.

Officials_Joe Crawford, David Guthrie, Josh Tiven.

STANDINGS: The format for professional standings:

Eastern Conference

Atlantic Division

	W	L	Pct.	GB
Boston	43	22	.662	–
Philadelphia	40	30	.571	5 1/2

In college boxes, the score by periods is omitted because the games are divided only into halves.

No. 19 CONNECTICUT 74, No. 8 SYRACUSE 66

CONNECTICUT (15-5)

Villanueva 9-13 3-7 21, Boone 2-4 3-5 7, Brown 0-2 5-6 5, Williams 3-11 1-2 9, Gay 6-13 4-4 18, Armstrong 2-2 2-2 6, Kellogg 0-0 0-0 0, Anderson 1-4 2-3 4, Nelson 1-1 2-3 4. Totals 24-50 22-32 74.

SYRACUSE (21-3)

Warrick 6-13 4-7 16, Pace 7-9 0-0 14, Forth 0-1 0-0 0, McNamara 4-18 0-0 9, McCroskey 2-5 0-0 4, Watkins 2-2 0-0 4, Edelin 3-8 1-2 7, Roberts 4-10 4-5 12. Totals 28-66 9-14 66.

Halftime_Connecticut 37-36. 3-Point Goals_Connecticut 4-14 (Gay 2-5, Williams 2-5, Brown 0-2, Anderson 0-2), Syracuse 1-9 (McNamara 1-9). Fouled Out_Roberts. Rebounds_Connecticut 36 (Villanueva 10), Syracuse 34 (Warrick 7). Assists_Connecticut 14 (Williams 6), Syracuse 17 (Edelin, McNamara 6). Total Fouls_Connecticut 15, Syracuse 24. A_27,651.

The format for college conference standings:

	Conference			All Games		
	W	L	Pct.	W	L	Pct.
Missouri	12	2	.857	24	4	.857

betting odds Use figures and a hyphen: *The odds were 5-4, he won despite 3-2 odds against him.*

The word *to* seldom is necessary, but when it appears it should be hyphenated in all constructions: *3-to-2 odds, odds of 3-to-2, the odds were 3-to-2.*

bettor A person who bets.

billiards Use a **match summary**.

bobsledding, luge Scoring is in minutes, seconds and tenths of a second. Extend to hundredths if available.

Identify events as *two-man, four-man, men's luge, women's luge*. In Olympics, *women's bob, two-man bob, four-man bob, men's luge, women's luge*.

Use a **basic summary**. Example:

Women

1. Kaillie Humphries and Jennifer Ciochetti, Canada, 3 minutes, 48.57 seconds (57.10- 57.07-57.22-57.18).

2. Sandra Kiriasis and Petra Lammert, Germany, 3:48.90 (57.30-57.28-57.21-57.11).

3. Elana Meyers and Katie Eberling, United States, 3:49.57 (57.22-57.45-57.41-57.49).

bowl games Capitalize them: *Cotton Bowl, Orange Bowl, Rose Bowl*, etc.

bowling Scoring systems use both total points and won-lost records.

Use the **basic summary** format in paragraph form. Note that a comma is used in giving pinfalls of more than 999.

EXAMPLES:

ST. LOUIS (AP) — Second-round leaders and their total pinfalls in the $100,000 Professional Bowlers Association tournament:

1. Bill Spigner, Hamden, Conn., 2,820.

2. Gary Dickinson, Fort Worth, Texas, 2,759.

ALAMEDA, Calif. (AP) — The 24 match play finalists with their won-lost records and total pinfall Thursday night after four rounds — 26 games — of the $65,000 Alameda Open bowling tournament:

1. Jay Robinson, Los Angeles, 5-3, 5,937.

2. Butch Soper, Huntington Beach, Calif., 3-5, 5,932.

boxing The four major sanctioning bodies for professional boxing are the World Boxing Association, the World Boxing Council, the World Boxing Organization and the International Boxing Federation.

Weight classes and titles by organization:

105 pounds — Mini Flyweight, WBF, IBF, WBO; Strawweight, WBC

108 pounds — Light Flyweight, WBA, WBC; Junior Flyweight, IBF, WBO

112 pounds — Flyweight, WBA, WBC, IBF, WBO

115 pounds — Super Flyweight, WBA, WBC; Junior Bantamweight, IBF, WBO

118 pounds — Bantamweight, WBA, WBC, IBF, WBO

122 pounds — Super Bantamweight, WBA, WBC; Junior Featherweight, IBF, WBO

126 pounds — Featherweight, WBA, WBC, IBF, WBO

130 pounds — Super Featherweight, WBA, WBC; Junior Lightweight, IBF, WBO

135 pounds — Lightweight, WBA, WBC, IBF, WBO

140 pounds — Super Lightweight, WBA, WBC; Junior Welterweight, IBF, WBO

147 pounds — Welterweight, WBA, WBC, WBO, IBF

154 pounds — Super Welterweight, WBA, WBC; Junior Middleweight, IBF, WBO

160 pounds — Middleweight, WBA, WBC, IBF, WBO

168 pounds — Super Middleweight, WBA, WBC, IBF, WBO

175 pounds — Light Heavyweight, WBA, WBC, IBF, WBO

190 pounds — Cruiserweight, WBA, WBC, IBF, WBO

More than 200 pounds — Heavyweight, WBA, WBC, IBF, WBO

Some other terms:

kidney punch A punch to an opponent's kidney when the puncher has only one hand free. It is illegal. If the puncher has both hands free, it is legal.

knockout (n. and adj.) **knock out** (v.) A fighter is knocked out if he takes a 10-count.

If a match ends early because one fighter is unable to continue, say that the winner stopped the loser. In most boxing jurisdictions there is no such thing as a technical knockout.

outpointed Not *outdecisioned*.

rabbit punch A punch behind an opponent's neck. It is illegal.

box office (n.) **box-office** (adj.)

bullfight, bullfighter, bullfighting

C

canoeing Scoring is in minutes, seconds and tenths of a second. Extend to hundredths if available.

In Olympics, slalom and sprint events for both men and women. See **basic summary**.

chronic traumatic encephalopathy A degenerative brain disease that researchers have linked to concussions or repeated blows to the head. It is most closely associated with football but also has been diagnosed in some athletes from other contact sports and military combat veterans. It can be identified only posthumously through an examination of the brain. *CTE* is acceptable on second reference, and in headlines if essential.

cliches A team losing a game is not a "disaster." *Home runs* are *homers*, not "dingers," "jacks" or "bombs." A player scored 10 *straight points*, not 10 "unanswered" points. If a football team scores two touchdowns and the opponent doesn't come back, say it "never trailed" rather than "never looked back." In short, avoid hackneyed words and phrases,

redundancies and exaggerations.

coach See **titles** entry in sports guidelines.

collective nouns Nouns that denote a unit take singular verbs and pronouns: *class, committee, crowd, family, group, herd, jury, orchestra, team*.

However, team names such as *the Jazz, the Magic, the Avalanche* and *the Thunder* take plural verbs.

Many singular names take singular verbs: *Boston is favored in the playoffs. Stanford is in the NCAA Tournament.*

College Football Playoff Use *the playoff* or *the national championship* as applicable on second reference. The abbreviation *CFP* is acceptable only when referring directly to rankings, whether or not the term has been spelled out earlier in a story. In game stories, reflect the committee's ranking when referring to a team's record: *Alabama (7-1, 4-1, No. 3 CFP)*. Do not use the abbreviation in other forms in stories or in headlines. The AP Top 25 ranking should be used in headlines and at the top of stories, and can be used without distinction: *No. 1 Alabama, top-ranked Alabama*. While deferring to AP ranking, stories should later make note of where a team stands in the College Football Playoff rankings because the measurement matters for playoff and bowl placement, and fans will be aware of both rankings. When writing about the committee that determines the College Football Playoff, use *the committee, the selection committee* or *playoff selection committee*.

conferences Major college basketball and football conferences are listed

Major College Basketball Conferences

AMERICA EAST CONFERENCE – Albany (N.Y.); Binghamton; Hartford; Maine; Mass.-Lowell; New Hampshire; Stony Brook; UMBC (Maryland-Baltimore County); Vermont.

AMERICAN ATHLETIC CONFERENCE – Cincinnati; ECU (East Carolina); Houston; Memphis; SMU; South Florida; Temple; Tulane; UCF (Central Florida); UConn; Tulsa.

ATLANTIC 10 CONFERENCE – Davidson; Dayton; Duquesne; George Mason; Fordham; George Washington; LaSalle; Richmond; St. Bonaventure; Saint Joseph's; Saint Louis; Rhode Island; UMass; VCU (Virginia Commonwealth).

ATLANTIC COAST CONFERENCE – Boston College; Clemson; Duke; Florida State; Georgia Tech; Louisville; Miami; North Carolina; North Carolina State; Notre Dame; Pittsburgh; Syracuse; Virginia; Virginia Tech; Wake Forest.

ATLANTIC SUN CONFERENCE – Florida Gulf Coast; Jacksonville; Kennesaw St.; Lipscomb; North Florida; Northern Kentucky; S.C. Upstate; Stetson.

BIG 12 CONFERENCE – Baylor; Iowa State; Kansas; Kansas State; Oklahoma; Oklahoma State; Texas; TCU; Texas Tech; West Virginia.

BIG EAST CONFERENCE – Butler; Creighton; DePaul; Georgetown; Marquette; Providence; St. John's; Seton Hall; Villanova; Xavier.

BIG SKY CONFERENCE – Eastern Washington; Idaho; Idaho State; Montana; Montana State; North Dakota; Northern Arizona; Northern Colorado; Portland State; Sacramento State; Southern Utah; Weber State.

BIG SOUTH CONFERENCE – North Division: Campbell; High Point; Liberty; Longwood; Radford. South Division: Charleston Southern; Coastal Carolina; Gardner-Webb; Presbyterian; UNC-Asheville; Winthrop.

BIG TEN CONFERENCE – Illinois; Indiana; Iowa; Maryland; Michigan; Michigan State; Minnesota; Nebraska; Northwestern; Ohio State; Penn State; Purdue; Rutgers; Wisconsin.

BIG WEST CONFERENCE – Cal Poly; Cal State Fullerton; CS Northridge; Hawaii; Long Beach State; UC Davis; UC Irvine; UC Riverside; UC Santa Barbara.

COLONIAL ATHLETIC ASSOCIATION – College of Charleston; Delaware; Drexel; Elon; Hofstra; James Madison; Northeastern; Towson; UNC-Wilmington; William & Mary.

CONFERENCE USA – Charlotte; East Carolina; FAU (Florida Atlantic); FIU (Florida International); Louisiana Tech; Marshall; Middle Tennessee; North Texas; Old Dominion; Rice; Southern Mississippi; Tulane; Tulsa; UAB (Alabama-Birmingham); UTEP; UTSA (Texas-San Antonio); Western Kentucky.

HORIZON LEAGUE – Cleveland State; Detroit; Green Bay; Illinois-Chicago; Milwaukee; Oakland; Valparaiso; Wright State; Youngstown State.

IVY LEAGUE – Brown; Columbia; Cornell; Dartmouth; Harvard; Pennsylvania; Princeton; Yale.

METRO ATLANTIC ATHLETIC CONFERENCE – Canisius; Fairfield; Iona; Manhattan; Marist; Monmouth (N.J.); Niagara; Quinnipiac; Rider; St. Peter's; Siena.

MID-AMERICAN CONFERENCE – East Division: Akron; Bowling Green; Buffalo; Kent State; Miami (Ohio); Ohio. West Division: Ball State; Central Michigan; Eastern Michigan; Northern Illinois; Toledo; Western Michigan.

MID-EASTERN ATHLETIC CONFERENCE – Bethune-Cookman; Coppin State; Delaware State; Florida A&M; Hampton; Howard; Maryland-Eastern Shore; Morgan State; Norfolk State; N.C. A&T; N.C. Central; Savannah State; S.C. State.

MISSOURI VALLEY CONFERENCE – Bradley; Drake; Evansville; Illinois State; Indiana State; Loyola of Chicago; Missouri State; Northern Iowa; Southern Illinois; Wichita State.

MOUNTAIN WEST CONFERENCE – Air Force; Boise State; Colorado State; Fresno State; Nevada; New Mexico; San Diego State; San Jose State; UNLV; Utah State; Wyoming.

NORTHEAST CONFERENCE – Bryant; CCSU (Central Connecticut State); Fairleigh Dickinson; LIU Brooklyn; Mount St. Mary's (Md.); Robert Morris; Sacred Heart; St. Francis (NY); St. Francis (Pa.); Wagner.

OHIO VALLEY CONFERENCE – East Division: Belmont; Eastern Kentucky; Jacksonville State; Morehead State; Tennessee State; Tennessee Tech. West Divsion: Austin Peay; Eastern Illinois; Murray State; SIU-Edwardsville; Southeast Missouri State; UT-Martin.

PACIFIC-12 CONFERENCE – Arizona; Arizona State; California; Colorado; Oregon; Oregon State; Southern California; Stanford; UCLA; Utah; Washington; Washington State.

PATRIOT LEAGUE – American U.; Army; Boston U.; Bucknell; Colgate; Holy Cross; Lafayette; Lehigh; Loyola (Md.); Navy.

SOUTHEASTERN CONFERENCE – Alabama; Arkansas; Auburn; Florida; Georgia; Kentucky; LSU; Mississippi; Mississippi State; Missouri; South Carolina; Tennessee; Texas A&M; Vanderbilt.

SOUTHERN CONFERENCE – Chattanooga; ETSU (Eastern Tennessee State); Furman; Mercer; Samford; UNC Greensboro; Western Carolina; The Citadel; VMI; Wofford.

SOUTHLAND CONFERENCE – Abilene Christian; Central Arkansas; Houston Baptist; Incarnate Word; Lamar; McNeese State; New Orleans; Nicholls State; Northwestern State; Oral Roberts; Sam Houston State; Southeastern Louisiana; Stephen F. Austin; Texas A&M-Corpus Christi.

SOUTHWESTERN ATHLETIC CONFERENCE – Alabama A&M; Alabama State; Alcorn State; Arkansas-Pine Bluff; Grambling State; Jackson State; MVSU (Mississippi Valley State); Prairie View; Southern U.; Texas Southern.

SUMMIT LEAGUE – Denver; IPFW (Indiana-Purdue-Fort Wayne); IUPUI (Indiana-Purdue-Indianapolis); Nebraska-Omaha; North Dakota State; Oral Roberts; South Dakota; South Dakota State; Western Illinois.

SPORTS

SUN BELT CONFERENCE – Appalachian State; Arkansas State; Georgia State; Georgia Southern; Louisiana-Lafayette; Louisiana-Monroe; South Alabama; Texas-Arlington; Texas State; Troy; UALR (Arkansas-Little Rock).

WEST COAST CONFERENCE – BYU; Gonzaga; Loyola Marymount; Pacific; Pepperdine; Portland; Saint Mary's (Calif.); San Diego; San Francisco; Santa Clara.

WESTERN ATHLETIC CONFERENCE – CS Bakersfield; Chicago State; Grand Canyon; New Mexico State; Seattle; Texas-Pan American; UMKC (Missouri-Kansas City); Utah Valley.

INDEPENDENTS – NJIT.

Major College Football Conferences

FOOTBALL BOWL SUBDIVISION

AMERICAN ATHLETIC CONFERENCE – Cincinnati; East Carolina; Houston; Memphis; Navy; South Florida; SMU; Temple; Tulane; Tulsa; UCF (Central Florida).

ATLANTIC COAST CONFERENCE – Atlantic Division: Boston College; Clemson; Florida State; Louisville; N.C. State; Syracuse; Wake Forest. Coastal Division: Duke; Georgia Tech; Miami; North Carolina; Pittsburgh; Virginia; Virginia Tech.

BIG 12 CONFERENCE – Baylor; Iowa State; Kansas; Kansas State; Oklahoma; Oklahoma State; Texas; TCU; Texas Tech; West Virginia.

BIG TEN CONFERENCE – East Division: Indiana; Maryland; Michigan; Michigan State; Ohio State; Penn State; Rutgers. West Division: Illinois; Iowa; Minnesota; Nebraska; Northwestern; Purdue; Wisconsin.

CONFERENCE USA – East Division: Charlotte; Florida Atlantic; Florida International; Marshall; Middle Tennessee; Old Dominion; Western Kentucky. West Division: Louisiana Tech; North Texas; Rice; Southern Mississippi; UAB; UTEP; UTSA.

MID-AMERICAN CONFERENCE – East Division: Akron; Bowling Green; Buffalo; Kent State; Miami (Ohio); Ohio. West Division: Ball State; Central Michigan; Eastern Michigan; Northern Illinois; Toledo; Western Michigan.

MOUNTAIN WEST CONFERENCE – Mountain Division: Air Force; Boise State; Colorado State; New Mexico; Utah State; Wyoming. West Division: Fresno State; Hawaii; Nevada; San Diego State; San Jose State; UNLV.

PACIFIC-12 CONFERENCE – North Division: California; Oregon; Oregon State; Stanford; Washington; Washington State. South Division: Arizona; Arizona State; Colorado; Southern California; UCLA; Utah.

SOUTHEASTERN CONFERENCE – East Division: Florida; Georgia; Kentucky; Missouri; South Carolina; Tennessee; Vanderbilt. West Division: Alabama; Arkansas; Auburn; LSU; Mississippi; Mississippi State; Texas A&M.

SUN BELT CONFERENCE – East Division: Appalachian State; Coastal Carolina; Georgia Southern; Georgia State; Troy. West Division: Arkansas State, Louisiana-Lafayette; Louisiana-Monroe; South Alabama; Texas State.

INDEPENDENTS – Army; BYU; Liberty; UMass; New Mexico State, Notre Dame, UConn.

on the previous pages.

cover A team that *covers the spread* beats the expectation of oddsmakers for that game, regardless of an actual win or loss. *The Warriors beat the Kings but failed to cover the 12-point spread. The Kings lost but covered.*

cross-country Note hyphen, which is an exception to the practices of U.S. and international governing bodies for the sport.

Scoring for this track event is in minutes, seconds and tenths of a second. Extended to hundredths if available.

National AAU Championship

Cross-Country

Frank Shorter, Miami, 5:25.67; 2. Tom Coster, Los Angeles, 5:30.72

Adapt the **basic summary** to paragraph form under a dateline for a field of more than 10 competitors.

See **auto racing** and **bowling** for examples.

cross-country skiing Events include freestyle sprint, classical-style event; 10-kilometer race, also abbreviated 10km or 10K.

cycling Use the **basic summary** format.

d

day to day Hyphenate only as a compound modifier preceding a noun: *Aaron Rodgers will be evaluated on a day-to-day basis.* Otherwise, no hyphen: *Candace Parker was day to day with an injured right ankle.*

decathlon Summaries include time or distance performance, points earned in that event and the cumulative total of points earned in previous events.

Contestants are listed in the order of their overall point totals. First name and hometown (or nation) are included only on the first and last events on the first day of competition; on the last day, first names are included only in the first event and in the summary denoting final placings.

Use the **basic summary** format. Include all entrants in summaries of each of the 10 events.

An example for individual events:

Decathlon

(Group A)

100 – 1, Fred Dixon, Los Angeles, 10.8 seconds, 854 points. 2, Bruce Jenner, San Jose State, 11.09, 783.

Long jump – 1, Dixon 14-7 (7.34m), 889, 1,743. 2, Jenner, 23-6 (7.17m), 855, 1,638.

Decathlon final – Bruce Jenner, San Jose State, 8,524 points. 2, Fred Dixon, Los Angeles, 8,277.

discus The disc thrown in track and field events.

diving Use a **basic summary**.

e

esports Acceptable in all references to competitive multiplayer video gaming. Use alternate forms like *eSports* or *e-sports* only if part of a formal name, like an organization or arena. Capitalize at the start of sentences. Like other collective nouns that are plural in form, *esports* takes singular form when the group or quantity is regarded as a unit. *Some gamers are finding esports is a viable profession; nine esports were added to the competition.* It is also acceptable to refer to individual esports events as *games* or *events*.

event names See **sports sponsorship**.

f

fast break

favorite, underdog, upset The
terms *favorite, underdog, upset* and
variations should be used only
based on actual odds offered by a
sportsbook. For individual games in
team sports and head-to-head events
like boxing or tennis, the *favorite*
is the team or player oddsmakers
say is most likely to win, while the
underdog is most likely to lose.
An *upset* happens only when an
underdog beats a clear favorite. *UFC
fighter Holly Holm was a more than 8-1
underdog when she knocked out Ronda
Rousey to give the superstar her first
loss.*

A team should not be called
an underdog unless its opponent
is favored by oddsmakers, even
if rankings, location or other
factors seem to give the team a
disadvantage. For example, teams
in the NCAA Tournament are
seeded numerically 1-16, but lower
seeds are sometimes favored over
teams seeded higher. When No. 9
seed Florida State beat No. 8 seed
Missouri in 2018, it was not an upset
because Florida State was a slight
favorite.

In events with large fields like
tennis tournaments or auto races,
as well as future-looking bets like
NFL or MLB championships or MVP
races, it sometimes makes sense to
refer to teams and players as *among
the favorites* if they are one of several
top contenders but not necessarily
the top favorite: *The Kansas City
Chiefs and Los Angeles Rams were
among the favorites to win the Super
Bowl as the playoffs began, though
behind the New Orleans Saints, an 11-4
overall favorite.* In horse races, golf
tournaments and similar events, a
top contender winning shouldn't be
termed an upset even if the very top
favorite loses.

FBS Abbreviation for *Football Bowl
Subdivision*. The higher level of
NCAA Division I football. Formerly
known as the I-A Division. *FBS* is
used on second reference.

FBS (Football Bowl Subdivision)
conferences: Atlantic Coast, Big 12,
Big East, Big Ten, Conference USA,
Mid-American, Mountain West,
Pacific-12, Southeastern, Sun Belt,
Western Athletic, Independents
(Army, Navy, Notre Dame)

FCS Abbreviation for *Football
Championship Subdivision*. The
lower level of NCAA Division I
football. Formerly known as the
I-AA Division. *FCS* is used on second
reference.

FCS (Football Championship
Subdivision) conferences: Big
Sky, Big South, Colonial Athletic
Association, Great West, Ivy League,
Mid-Eastern Athletic, Missouri
Valley, Northeast, Ohio Valley,
Patriot League, Pioneer League,
Southern, Southland, Southwestern
Athletic, Independents (North
Carolina Central, Old Dominion,
Savannah St.)

field goal

fencing Identify epee, foil and saber
classes as: *men's individual foil,
women's team foil*, etc.

Use **match summary** for early
rounds of major events, for lesser
dual meets and for tournaments.

Use **basic summary** for final
results of major championships.

For major events, where
competitors meet in a round-robin

SPORTS

and are divided into pools, use this form:

Epee, first round (four qualify for semi-finals) Pool 1 – Joe Smith, Springfield, Mass., 4-1. Enrique Lopez, Chile, 3-2.

figure skating All jumps, spins and other moves are lowercase even if named after someone: *double axel, triple flip-triple toe loop, triple lutz, triple salchow, sit spin, camel spin, death spiral*. Use a **basic summary**.

first quarter, first-quarter *He scored in the first quarter. The team took the lead on his first-quarter goal.*

football The spellings of some frequently used words and phrases:

blitz (n., v.)   *out-of-bounds (adj.)*
cornerback   *pick six (n.) pick-six*
end line   *(adj)*
end zone   *pitchout (n.)*
fair catch   *place kick*
fourth-and-1 (adj.)   *place-kicker*
fullback   *play off (v.)*
goal line   *playoff (n., adj.)*
goal-line stand   *quarterback*
halfback   *runback (n.)*
handoff   *running back*
kick off (v.)   *split end*
kickoff (n., adj.)   *tailback*
left guard   *tight end*
linebacker   *touchback*
lineman   *touchdown*
line of scrimmage   *wideout*
nickel back   *wide receiver*
onside kick   *X's and O's*
out of bounds (adv.)

NUMBERS: Use figures for yardage: *The 5-yard line, the 10-yard line, a 5-yard pass play, he plunged in from the 2, he ran 6 yards, a 7-yard gain; a fourth-and-2 play.*

Some other uses of numbers: *The final score was 21-14. The team won its fourth game in 10 starts. The team record is 4-5-1.*

PLAYOFFS: *wild-card round,* *wild card, divisional round, NFC championship game, AFC championship game.*

SUPER BOWL: Refer to the Super Bowl by the year of the game, not by Roman numeral. If a counter is needed, use cardinal numbers: *2017 Super Bowl* preferred over *Super Bowl 51*; do not use *Super Bowl LI*.

LEAGUE: *National Football League,* or *NFL.*

TD Acceptable in all references to touchdown.

O-line, D-line Acceptable abbreviations for offensive line, defensive line.

STATISTICS: All football games, whether using the one- or two-point conversion, use the same summary style.

The visiting team always is listed first.

Field goals are measured from the point where the ball was kicked — not the line of scrimmage. The goal posts are 10 yards behind the goal lines. Include that distance.

Abbreviate team names to four letters or fewer on the scoring and statistical lines as illustrated.

The passing line shows, in order: completions-attempts-interceptions.

A sample agate package:

Jets-Giants Stats

N.Y. Jets	7	10	7	0_24
N.Y. Giants	0	7	14	14_35

First Quarter
NYJ_Rhodes 11 fumble return (Nugent kick), 8:36.
Second Quarter
NYG_Ward 8 run (Tynes kick), 10:54.
NYJ_B.Smith 16 pass from Pennington (Nugent kick), :33.
NYJ_FG Nugent 47, :00.
Third Quarter
NYG_Jacobs 19 run (Tynes kick), 11:17.
NYJ_L.Washington 98 kickoff return (Nugent kick), 11:03.
NYG_Shockey 13 pass from Manning (Tynes kick), :33.
Fourth Quarter
NYG_Burress 53 pass from Manning (Tynes kick), 7:52.
NYG_Ross 43 interception return (Tynes kick), 3:15.
A_78,809

SPORTS

	NYJ	NYG
First downs	16	21
Total Net Yards	277	374
Rushes-yards	22-55	39-188
Passing	222	186
Punt Returns	2-20	2-16
Kickoff Returns	5-200	3-62
Interceptions Ret.	1-1	3-68
Comp-Att-Int	21-36-3	13-25-1
Sacked-Yards Lost	1-7	0-0
Punts	4-45.3	5-46.8
Fumbles-Lost	0-0	1-1
Penalties-Yards	6-40	3-37
Time of Possession	26:15	33:45

INDIVIDUAL STATISTICS

RUSHING_N.Y. Jets, T.Jones 13-36, L.Washington 9-13, Pennington 2-6, B.Smith 1-0. N.Y. Giants, Jacobs 20-100, Ward 13-56, Manning 4-17, Droughns 2-15.

PASSING_N.Y. Jets, Pennington 21-36-3-229. N.Y. Giants, Manning 13-25-1-186.

RECEIVING_N.Y. Jets, Coles 8-89, Cotchery 4-31, Baker 3-52, B.Smith 3-44, T.Jones 2-14, L.Washington 1-(minus 1). N.Y. Giants, Burress 5-124, Ward 3-8, Shockey 2-33, Moss 1-10, Matthews 1-6, Hedgecock 1-5.

MISSED FIELD GOAL_N.Y. Jets, Nugent 42 (WL).

The rushing and receiving paragraph for individual leaders shows attempts and yardage gained. The passing paragraph shows completions, attempts, interceptions and total yards gained.

STANDINGS: The form for **professional standings**:

American Conference
East

	W	L	T	Pct.	PF	PA
y-New England	12	3	0	.800	464	321
N.Y. Jets	8	7	0	.533	360	344
Buffalo	6	9	0	.400	351	385

y-clinched division

The form for college **conference standings**:

Atlantic Coast Conference
Atlantic Division

	Conference				All games			
	W	L	PF	PA	W	L	PF	PA
Wake Forest	6	2	175	145	11	2	289	191
Boston College	5	3	189	133	9	3	313	180

In college conference standings, limit team names to nine letters or fewer. Abbreviate as necessary.

fractions In general, follow **fractions** entry in the Stylebook's main section, writing fractions with two numerals separated by a forward slash: 1/2, 2/3 or 3/4. Do not use single fractional characters, which do not appear properly for some computer systems. For mixed numbers, separate the whole integer from the fraction with a space: *J.J. Watt had 2 1/2 sacks, Matt Cain pitched 7 2/3 innings.* In baseball, avoid using fractions to describe outings of less than an inning. Simply write: *Craig Kimbrel got the last two outs for the save.*

free agent, free agent signing

freestyle skiing Events are *halfpipe, moguls, aerials.*

g

game day Two words rather than one. *The commissioner said he expects a strong game day atmosphere in Mexico City.* Use one word only if part of a formal title or other name.

game plan

golf Some frequently used terms and some definitions:

birdie, birdies, birdied One stroke under par.

bogey, bogeys One stroke over par. The past tense is *bogeyed.*

caddie

eagle, eagled Two strokes under par.

fairway

green fee A fee paid to play on a golf course. Not *greens fee. Green* refers to all parts of a golf course, not just the putting green.

SPORTS

hole-in-one

Masters, Masters Tournament
No possessive. Use *the Masters* on second reference.

tee, tee off

NUMBERS: Some sample uses of numbers:

Use figures for handicaps: *He has a 3 handicap; a 3-handicap golfer, a handicap of 3 strokes; a 3-stroke handicap.*

Use figures for par listings: *He had a par 5 to finish 2-up for the round, a par-4 hole; a 7-under-par 64, the par-3 seventh hole.*

Use figures for club ratings: *a 5-iron, a 7-iron shot, a 4-wood, 3-hybrid.*

Miscellaneous: *the first hole, a nine-hole course, the 10th hole, the back nine, the final 18, the third round. He won 3 and 2.*

ASSOCIATIONS: *Professional Golfers' Association of America* (note the apostrophe) or *PGA*. Headquarters is in Palm Beach Gardens, Florida. Members teach golf at golf shops and teaching facilities across the country.

The *PGA Tour* is a separate organization made up of competing professional golfers. Use *tour* (lowercase) on second reference.

The PGA conducts the PGA Championship, the Senior PGA Championship, and the Ryder Cup as well as other golf championships not associated with the PGA Tour.

The *United States Golf Association* or *USGA* is headquartered in Far Hills, New Jersey. It conducts the United States' national championships. These include the U.S. Open, the U.S. Women's Open, the U.S. Senior Open, 10 national amateur championships and the State Team Championships.

SUMMARIES — Stroke (Medal) Play: List scores in ascending order. Ties are listed in the order in which they were played. Use a dash before the final figure, hyphens between others.

On the first day, use the player's score for the first nine holes, a hyphen, the player's score for the second nine holes, a dash and the player's total for the day:

First round:

Lorena Ochoa	35-34 – 69	
Se Ri Pak	36-33 – 69	

On subsequent days, give the player's scores for each day, then the total for all rounds completed:

Second round:

Rory McIlroy	66-69 – 135	
Tiger Woods	65-71 – 136	

Final round, professional tournaments, including prize money:

Final Round:

(FedExCup points in parentheses)

J.B. Holmes (4,500), $1,080,000 68-65-66-70 – 269

Phil Mickelson (2,700), $648,000 68-68-67-67 – 270

Use hometowns only on national championship amateur tournaments. For tournaments including both amateurs and professionals, indicate amateurs with an "a-" before the name:

a-Stacey Lewis, The Woodlands, Texas 70-69 – 139

The form for cards:

Par out	444 343 544-35
Watson out	454 333 435-34
Nicklaus out	434 243 544-33
Par in	434 443 454-35 – 70
Watson in	434 342 443-31 – 65
Nicklaus in	433 443 453-33 – 66

SUMMARIES — Match Play: In the first example that follows, "and 2" means that the 17th and 18th hole were skipped because Rose had a three-hole lead with two to play. In the second, the match went 18 holes. In the third, a 19th and 20th hole were played because the golfers were tied after 18.

Justin Rose def. Charles Howell III, 3 and 2.

Paul Casey def. Shaun Micheel, 2 up.
Nick O'Hern def. Tiger Woods, 20 holes.

Grey Cup The Canadian Football League's championship game.

Group of Five Spell out the number when referring to the group of NCAA conferences that are not among the Power Five but play at the highest level of college football. The group includes the American Athletic Conference, Conference USA, the Mid-American Conference, the Mountain West and the Sun Belt Conference.

Gulfstream Park The racetrack.

gymnastics Scoring is by points. Identify events by name: Men: *floor exercise, vault, pommel horse, still rings, horizontal bar* (or *high bar*), *parallel bars.* Women: *floor exercise, vault, balance beam, uneven bars.*
Use a **basic summary**. Example:
Parallel Bars — 1, Joe Smith, Houston, 9.675 points. 2, Ed Jones, Albany, N.Y., 9.54. 3, Andy Brown, Los Angeles, 9.4.

h

halftime

handball Use a **match summary**.

heatstroke

hit-and-run (n. and adj.) **hit and run** (v.) *The coach told him to hit and run. He scored on a hit-and-run.*

hockey The spellings of some frequently used words:

blue line	penalty box
crease	power play
face off (v.)	power-play goal
faceoff (n., adj.)	red line
goalie	short-handed
goal line	slap shot
goal post	two-on-one break

hat trick Three goals in one game. *Natural hat trick* means three goals scored consecutively by one player in a game or period. *Gordie Howe hat trick* refers to a goal, an assist and a fight by one player. Use sparingly and with explanation.

Stanley Cup The trophy awarded to the NHL champion, the Cup on second reference. It is a traveling trophy awarded to the league champion for one year and then passed to the next winner. Accordingly, it should never be plural: *Mark Messier won six Stanley Cup titles.*

LEAGUE: *National Hockey League* or *NHL.*
For NHL subdivisions: *the Central Division of the Western Conference, the division, the conference,* etc.

SCORING: A player's points total is equal to the sum of his goals and assists. The format G-A--P may be used on second reference and in notes. *Anze Kopitar led the Kings in scoring (29-41--70) en route to the team's 2014 Stanley Cup championship.*

RECORDS: In the NHL, a team's record is expressed in the Win-Loss-Overtime Loss format in which a win is worth 2 points, an overtime loss is worth 1 point and a loss is zero. In college and international play, records are written in the Win-Loss-Tie format. Unless there is a likelihood of confusion, no further explanation is necessary. *The Bruins went 54-19-9 last season to finish with 117 points, the most in the league. Rick DiPietro had an 18-5-5 record in college*

SPORTS

before going 130-138-28 with eight ties in his NHL career.

PLAYOFFS: *Stanley Cup* or *NHL playoffs* until the final round, then *Stanley Cup Final*. Note singular *Final*. But *final* or *finals*, lowercase, when used alone.

SUMMARIES: The visiting team always is listed first in the score by periods.

Note that each goal is numbered according to its sequence in the game.

The figure after the name of a scoring player shows his total goals for the season.

Names in parentheses are players credited with an assist on a goal.

The final figure in the listing of each goal is the number of minutes elapsed in the period when the goal was scored.

Senators-Flyers, Sums

Ottawa	1 1 1_3
Philadelphia	3 1 1_5

First Period_1, Ottawa, Neil 8 (Simpson, Havlat), 4:07. 2, Philadelphia, Lapointe 4 (Somik, Slaney), 10:41. 3, Philadelphia, Recchi 25 (LeClair, Handzus), 11:11. 4, Philadelphia, Markov 6 (Handzus, LeClair), 16:10. Penalty_Amonte, Phi (ob.-holding), 5:17.

Second Period_5, Philadelphia, Johnsson 9 (Zhamnov, Slaney), 5:22 (pp). 6, Ottawa, Chara 15 (Spezza, Schaefer), 14:32 (pp). Penalties_Fisher, Ott (tripping), 3:57; Simpson, Ott (holding), 6:06; Somik, Phi (slashing), 13:08; Fisher, Ott (high-sticking), 17:07.

Third Period_7, Philadelphia, Zhamnov 10 (Gagne, Amonte), 6:54. 8, Ottawa, Bondra 23 (Alfredsson, Schaefer), 19:47 (pp). Penalties_Alfredsson, Ott (rough) 9:03; Zhamnov, Phi (roughing), 9:03; Smolinski, Ott (roughing), 12:18; Sharp, Phi (roughing), 12:18; Simpson, Ott (slashing), 14:21; Philadelphia bench, served by Sharp (too many men), 15:57; Van Allen, Ott, major-double game misconduct (fighting), 18:15; Ray, Ott, major (fighting), 18:15; Lalime, Ott, minor-major-game misconduct (leaving the crease, fighting), 18:15; Simpson, Ott, major-game misconduct (fighting), 18:15 Brashear, Phi, double minor-double major-misconduct-game misconduct; (instigator, roughing, fighting), 18:15; Radivojevic, Phi, major-double game misconduct (fighting), 18:15; Esche, Phi, minor-major-double game misconduct (leaving the crease, fighting), 18:15; Markov, Phi, major-game misconduct (fighting), 18:15; Chara, Ott, minor-major-misconduct-game misconduct (instigator, fighting), 18:18; Neil, Ott, major (fighting), 18:18; Somik, Phi, major (fighting) 18:18; Timander, Phi, major (fighting), 18:18.

Shots on goal_Ottawa 7-9-10_26. Philadelphia 13-11-6_30.

Power-play Opportunities_Ottawa 2 of 6; Philadelphia 1 of 4.

Goalies_Ottawa, Lalime 22-19-7 (30 shots-25 saves), Prusek (18:15 third, 0-0). Philadelphia, Esche 18-7-5 (22-20), Burke (18:15 third, 4-3).

A_19,539 (19,519). T_2:39.

Referees_Marc Joannette, Dan Marouelli. Linesmen_Jonny Murray, Tim Nowak.

STANDINGS: The form:

Eastern Conference
Atlantic Division

	GP	W	L	OT	Pts.	GF	GA
Philadelphia	71	47	10	14	108	314	184
NY Islanders	71	45	17	9	99	310	192

home field (n.) home-field (adj.)

horse races Capitalize their formal names: *Kentucky Derby, Preakness, Belmont Stakes*, etc.

horse racing Some frequently used terms and their definitions:

across the board A bet on a horse to win, place and show. If the horse wins, the player collects three ways; if second, two ways; if third, one way.

also-ran Fails to finish in the money: first, second or third.

backstretch Straight portion of the far side of the racing surface between the turns.

Belmont Stakes First run in 1867, the Belmont is three weeks after the Preakness at Belmont Park on Long Island. The distance is 1 1/2 miles on a dirt track.

broodmare A female horse used for breeding.

bug boy An apprentice jockey, so-called because of the asterisk beside the individual's name in a program. It means that the jockey's mount gets a weight allowance.

colt A male thoroughbred horse 4 years old and under, or a standardbred 3 years of age.

daily double Wager calling for the selection of winners of two

SPORTS

consecutive races, usually the first and second.

entry Two or more horses owned by same owner running as a single betting interest. In some states two or more horses trained by same person but having different owners also are coupled in betting.

exacta Wager in which the first two finishers in a race, in exact order of finish, must be picked.

filly A female horse under the age of 5.

furlong One-eighth of a mile. Race distances are given in furlongs up through seven furlongs (spell out the number), after that in miles, as in *one-mile, 1/1-16 miles*.

gelding A castrated male horse.

graded stakes A thoroughbred race that derives its name from the stake, or entry fee, that owners must pay. There are three levels, assigned by the American Graded Stakes Committee. *Grade 1* is the highest level, the most prestigious, based partly on purse but also on such considerations as previous winners and race history. The other levels are *Grade 2* and *Grade 3*. Do not use Roman numerals. *Grade 2*, not *Grade II*.

half-mile pole The pole on a racetrack that marks one-half mile from the finish. All distances are measured from the finish line, meaning that when a horse reaches the quarter pole, he is one-quarter mile from the finish.

horse A male horse over 4 years old.

Kentucky Derby Dating from 1875, the "Run for the Roses" is held on the first Saturday in May at Churchill Downs. The race distance is 1 1/4 miles on a dirt track.

length A measurement approximating the length of a horse,

used to denote distance between horses in a race.

maiden A horse that has not won a race.

mare A female horse 5 years and older.

margin of victory Expressed in lengths of a horse, or other part of the horse's anatomy at the finish line: by a nose, by a neck, or in a photo finish: *Seattle Slew won by three lengths*.

mutuel field Not *mutual field*. Two or more horses, long shots, that have different owners and trainers. They are coupled as a single betting interest to give the field not more than 12 wagering interests. There cannot be more than 12 betting interests in a race. The bettor wins if either horse finishes in the money.

Preakness Stakes First run in 1873, the Preakness is two weeks after the Derby at Pimlico Race Course in Maryland. The distance is 1 3/16 miles on a dirt track.

race distances Under a mile expressed in furlongs: six furlongs (3/4ths of a mile); more than a mile in figures: 1 1/4 miles, 1 3/16 miles.

stallion A male horse used for breeding.

trifecta A wager picking the first three finishers in exact order.

Triple Crown Annual series of races for 3-year-old horses: the Kentucky Derby, the Preakness Stakes and Belmont Stakes.

winning times Expressed In minutes, seconds and hundredths of a second: *I'll Have Another's winning time in the Derby was 2:01.83*.

wire-to-wire A horse leading a race from start to finish.

i

IC4A Abbreviation for *Intercollegiate Association of Amateur Athletes of America*. In general, spell out on first reference. A phrase such as *IC4A tournament* may be used on first reference, however, to avoid a cumbersome lead. If this is done, provide the full name later in the story.

indoor (adj.) **indoors** (adv.) *He plays indoor tennis. He went indoors.*

injuries Be precise in describing injuries. Instead of knee injury describe how a player hurt his or her left knee, right knee or both knees. Avoid medical jargon as much as possible and try to define injuries as simply as information allows without just parroting team or league language if vague.

"integrity fee" In sports betting stories, the term *"integrity fee"* should be used in quotation marks on first reference and only with explanation. Generally, this refers to a proposed cut paid directly to leagues like the NBA and MLB on wagers or proceeds from bets in each sport. Some leagues argue that their products provide the backbone for sports betting and that they should be compensated to make sure players, referees and other team and league officials do not cheat.

j

judo Use the **basic summary** format by weight divisions for major tournaments; use the **match summary** for dual and lesser meets.

k

Kentucky Derby *The Derby* on second reference. An exception to normal second-reference practice. Plural is *Derbys* — an exception to Webster's New World College Dictionary.
See **capitalization** in main section.

knuckleball One word is an exception to Webster's New World College Dictionary.

l

lacrosse Scoring in goals, worth one point each.
The playing field is 110 yards long. The goals are 80 yards apart, with 15 yards of playing area behind each goal.
A match consists of four 15-minute periods. Overtimes of varying lengths may be played to break a tie.
Adapt the summary format in **hockey**.

Ladies Professional Golf Association No apostrophe after *Ladies*. Use *LPGA Tour* in all references.

left hand (n.) **left-handed** (adj.) **left-hander** (n.)

long shot Use two words for this term describing a big underdog.

m

marathon Use the formats illustrated in the **cross-country** and **track and field** entries.

SPORTS

match summary This format for summarizing sports events applies to individual contests such as tennis, match play golf, etc.

Give a competitor's name, followed either by a hometown or by a college or club affiliation. For competitors from outside the United States, a country name alone is sufficient in summaries sent for U.S. domestic use.

Rafael Nadal, Spain, def. Jarkko Nieminen, Finland, 7-5, 6-3, 6-1.

Serena Williams, United States, def. Nicole Vaidisova, Czech Republic, 6-3, 6-4.

Some other examples:

Billiards

Minnesota Fats, St. Paul, Minn., def. Pool Hall Duke, 150-141.

Handball

Bob Richards, Yale, def. Paul Johnson, Dartmouth, 21-18, 21-19.

Tom Brenna, Massachusetts, def. Bill Stevens, Michigan, 21-19, 17-21, 21-20.

MCL When describing injuries, acceptable in all references to the *medial cruciate ligament.*

midcourt, midfield

minicamp

mixed martial arts *MMA* acceptable in all references.

motor sports Two words unless different in the official name of an event.

motorboat racing Scoring may be posted in miles per hour, points or laps, depending on the competition.

In general, use the **basic summary** format. For some major events, adapt the basic summary to paragraph form under a dateline. See **auto racing** for an example.

motorcycle racing Follow the formats shown under **auto racing**.

MVP Acceptable in all references for most valuable player.

n

NASCAR Acceptable in all references for *National Association for Stock Car Auto Racing.*

NCAA Acceptable in all references for *National Collegiate Athletic Association.*

New Year's Six Spell out the number when referring to the group of college football bowl games that rotate the College Football Playoff semifinal games. The games include the Orange Bowl, the Fiesta Bowl, the Peach Bowl, the Cotton Bowl, the Rose Bowl and the Sugar Bowl and are typically played on or around New Year's Eve or New Year's Day.

nonconference No hyphen.

numerals In general, follow numerals entry in main section, spelling out one through nine in most uses and using figures for 10 or above. Use figures whenever preceding a unit of measure or points, as well as for team records or game numbers. Some sample uses of numbers: *first place; second quarter; 10th inning; a 3-pointer with 0.2 seconds left; 3-of-8 shooting; he made 3 of 4; the 6-foot-5 player; the 6-5 tight end; the 5-yard line; Game 6; The final score was 21-14. The team won its fourth game in 10 days. The team's record is 4-5-1. Johnson had seven catches for 188 yards. Stafford was 8 for 18 for 200 yards and two touchdowns.* See entries for individual sports for specialized uses, as well as entries for **fractions** and **time**.

o

odds-on For a strong favorite to win, odds of less than even money: *The horse was sent off as a 4-5 favorite.* An odds-on favorite means casinos believe the event is more likely to happen than not.

offseason No hyphen.

overtime, double overtime, triple overtime

over/under, total Use a slash, not a hyphen, for the gambling phrase that describes wagers on a total set by oddsmakers, such as combined total points in a game or total wins for a team in a season. *Total* is also acceptable. *Bettors drove the over/under down to 58 points for the Alabama-Clemson national title game after Nevada casinos initially set the total higher. The total for the Eagles-Bears playoff game opened at 41 1/2 points.*

p

pari-mutuel

performance-enhancing drugs Avoid using abbreviations *PEDs*, *PED* in stories and headlines unless in direct quotes. Whenever possible, be more specific in describing drugs considered performance-enhancing, including anabolic steroids, stimulants and human growth hormone.

play Use names for set plays or packages but do not automatically capitalize. Instead use standard AP style for the descriptive word: *wildcat package, West Coast offense, triangle offense.*

playoff (n.) play off (v.)

possessives See **apostrophes** in Punctuation Guide.

postgame, pregame

postseason, preseason No hyphen.

Power Five Spell out the number when referring to the group of conferences that generate the most athletic revenue in the NCAA and have some autonomy to create rules. The group includes the Big Ten, Big 12, Atlantic Coast Conference, Southeastern Conference and Pac-12.

r

racket Not *racquet*, for the light bat used in tennis and badminton.

racquetball Amateur games are played to 15 points in a best-of-three match. Professional matches are played to 11 points, unless it is necessary to continue until one player has a 2-point spread. Most matches go to the winner of three of five games.
Use a **match summary**.

record Avoid the redundant *new record*.

right hand (n.) **right-hander** (n.) **right-handed** (adj.)

rodeo Use the **basic summary** format by classes, listing points.

rowing Scoring is in minutes, seconds

and tenths of a second. Extend to hundredths if available.

Use a **basic summary**. An example, for a major event where qualifying heats are required:

Single Sculls Heats (first two in each heat qualify for Monday's quarterfinals, losers go to repechage Friday): Heat 1 — 1, Peter Smith, Australia, 4:24.7. 2. Etc. Heat 2 — 1, John Jones, Canada, 4:26.3. 72

runner-up, runners-up

S

school names A list of university names as used for sports is under **Major College Basketball Conferences, Major College Football Conferences and Football Championship Subdivision**. Use abbreviations on first reference only for well-known schools with unique acronyms that can easily stand alone without being mistaken for other universities. Abbreviations for other schools on second reference are permissible when the shorthand is commonly used and clear.

scores Use figures exclusively, placing a hyphen between the totals of the winning and losing teams: *The Reds defeated the Red Sox 4-3, the Giants scored a 12-6 football victory over the Cardinals, the golfer had a 5 on the first hole but finished with a 2-under-par score.*

Use a comma in this format: *Boston 6, Baltimore 5.*

See individual listings for each sport for further details.

series Best-of-seven series, best of seven. Hyphenate when used as a modifier with the number spelled out: *best-of-seven matchup*. On its own, no hyphens in the term: *The*

Red Sox and Phillies meet in a best of seven.

shoestring catch

short-course swimming Use *short-course* on second reference.

short-handed

skiing Identify events as: *men's downhill, women's slalom*, cross-country (note hyphen), etc. In ski jumping, note style where two jumps and points are posted.

Use a **basic summary**. Example:

90-meter special jumping — 1, Karl Schnabel, Austria, 320 and 318 feet, 234.8 points. 2, Toni Innauer, Austria, 377-299, 232.9. 3, Etc. Also; 27, Bob Smith, Hanover, N.H., 312-280, 201. 29

ski, skis, skier, skied, skiing Also: *ski jump, ski jumping*.

soccer Soccer is the preferred term in the United States, but around the world the sport is referred to as football.

The spellings of some frequently used words and phrases:

AFC Asian Football Confederation.

backpass A pass that a player makes back toward his own goal, to the goalkeeper on his team. The goalkeeper is unable to pick up the ball if the pass comes from the player's foot.

Bundesliga German League first division.

CAF Confederation Africaine de Football. Refer to it as the governing body of African soccer rather than spelling out French acronym.

Champions League

coach Also known as *manager* on British teams and *technical director* on some Latin American teams.

CONCACAF The Confederation of North, Central American and

Caribbean Association Football.

Conference National Fifth-highest division of English soccer.

Conference North, Conference South Sixth-highest division of English soccer.

CONMEBOL Confederacion Sudamerica de Futbol. Refer to it as South America's governing body rather than spelling out Spanish acronym.

Copa America South American national team championship. Use the Spanish name, not *America Cup*.

Copa Libertadores South American club championship. Use the Spanish name, not *Liberators Cup*.

corner A kick taken from the corner of the field by an attacking player. Awarded when the ball has passed over the goal line after last touching a defensive player. The shot is taken from the corner nearest to where the ball went out.

defender Do not use *defenseman*.

Eredivisie Netherlands first division.

FA Cup Acceptable on first reference for The Football Association Cup.

false nine A forward player who appears to be playing as a team's main attacker but who drops back, closer to the midfield. It leaves the defense of the opposing team with no one to mark.

FIFA Federation Internationale de Football Association. *FIFA* acceptable on first reference. Refer to it as the international soccer governing body rather than spelling out French acronym.

forward or **striker**

4-2-3-1 formation The typical lineup of a modern-day soccer team, with four defenders, two deep midfielders, three attacking midfielders and a lone forward.

free kick A kick awarded to a team if its player is fouled by an opponent anywhere on the field except for the two penalty areas near the goals. The kick can either be direct (able to shoot straight into the net) or indirect (cannot shoot into the net).

friendly An exhibition game.

goalkeeper *Goalie* is acceptable. Do not use *goaltender*.

hand ball A foul awarded when a player deliberately touches the ball with his hand or any part of his arm.

La Liga Spanish first division.

League Championship Second-highest division of English soccer.

League Cup The No. 2 cup competition in England. Do not refer to as *Carling Cup*.

League One Third-highest division of English soccer.

League Two Fourth-highest division of English soccer.

Ligue 1 French first division.

midfielder

MLS Major League Soccer. *MLS* acceptable on first reference.

OFC Oceania Football Confederation.

offside Offside occurs when a player is nearer to his opponent's goal line than the second-to-last opponent when a ball is passed to him by a teammate. It does not apply if the player is in his half of the field. A free kick is awarded to the opposing team at the place where the offside happened.

one-two When a player passes the ball to a teammate, who then returns it to the same player with his first touch. A move usually done on the run, making it hard to defend against.

parking the bus A phrase used to describe how a team packs its defense to protect a lead or a draw.

penalty A refereeing decision

SPORTS

awarded if a player from the defensive team fouls a player from the attacking team inside the penalty area. The attacking team chooses a player to have a free shot at goal from the penalty spot, 12 yards from the goal line.

penalty area Sometimes referred to as *penalty box*. Do not refer to solely as *box* on U.S. wires.

Premier League Top league in England. Also the name of the top league in Scotland. Note that England, Scotland, Wales and Northern Ireland have separate national teams. Do not refer to *Premiership* or *Barclay's Premier League*.

red card Issued to a player who commits a serious foul or who has been issued with two yellow cards in the same game. The player must leave the field and cannot be replaced.

Serie A Italian League first division.

sideline *Touchline* for international wires.

throw-in When a player restarts play by throwing the ball back onto the pitch from its perimeter. The player must keep both feet on the ground and have both hands behind his head as he throws the ball.

"tiki-taka" A system of intricate, one-touch and rapid passing artistry developed by Spanish club Barcelona and eventually adopted by Spain's national soccer team.

total football The label given to a tactical theory, pioneered in international soccer by the Netherlands in the 1974 World Cup, in which any outfield player can take over the role of any of his teammates.

UEFA Union of European Football Associations.

wall A line of defensive players that protects the team's goalkeeper at a free kick.

World Cup Not *World Cup Finals*.

zonal marking A system of defending at corners where players from the defensive team mark areas rather than opposition players. An alternative to man-to-man marking.

In summaries and key lines for international wires, the home team is listed first; on U.S. wires, the visiting team is listed first.

SUMMARY:

At Saint-Denis, France

Italy 0 2 – 2

France 2 0 – 2

(France won 4-3 on penalty kicks)

First half – 1, France, Zidane 4 (Djorkaeff), 12th minute. 2, France, Deschamps (penalty kick), 45th minute.

Second half – 3, Italy, own goal, 88th minute. 4, Italy, R. Baggio 6 (D. Baggio), 90th minute.

First overtime – None.

Second overtime – None.

Penalty kicks – France 4 (Zidane G, Lizarazu NG, Trezeguet G, Henry G, Blanc G); Italy 3 (Baggio G, Albertini NG, Costacurta G, Vieri G, Di Biagio NG).

Yellow Cards – Italy, Del Piero, 26th minute; Bergomi, 28th; Rostacurta, 113th. France, Guivarc'h, 53rd minute; Deschamps, 63rd.

Referee – Dallas (Scotland). Linesmen – Grigorescu (Romania),

Warren (England).

A –77,000

Lineups

Italy – Gianluca Pagliuca; Giuseppe Bergomi, Fabio Cannavaro, Alessandro Costacurta, Paolo Maldini; Francesco Moriero, Dino Baggio (Demetrio Albertini, 52nd), Luigi Di Biagio, Gianluca Pessotto (Angelo Di Livio, 90th); Christian Vieri, Alessandro Del Piero (Roberto Baggio, 67th).

France – Fabien Barthez; Lilian Thuram, Laurent Blanc, Marcel Desailly, Bixente Lizarazu; Didier Deschamps, Emmanuel Petit, Zinedine Zidane, Christian Karembeu (Thierry Henry, 65th); Stephane Guivarc'h (David Trezeguet, 65th), Youri Djorkaeff.

Lineup order is goalkeepers, defenders, midfielders, forwards.

Separate the different positions with semicolons and the players within a position with commas.

STANDINGS:
Scores and standings move in separate files.

Schedule on world wires has times GMT instead of EST or EDT.

Schedule lists home teams first.

Sunday, Jan. 31
Bari vs. Lazio of Rome, 0130
Cagliari vs. Juventus of Turin, 0130
Fiorentina vs. Vicenza, 0130

Standings for international leagues have a different style: *GP* (games played), *W* (wins), *D* (draws), *L* (losses), *GF* (goals for), *GA* (goals against) and *Pts* (points). Standings for Major League Soccer follow the same style as National Football League: *W* (wins), *L* (losses), *T* (ties), *Pts* (points), *GF* (goals for) and *GA* (goals against).

Spanish Soccer At A Glance

By The Associated Press
La Liga

Team	GP	W	D	L	GF	GA	Pts
Real Madrid	25	8	2	5	54	21	56
Barcelona	25	16	6	3	49	17	54
Villarreal	25	14	4	7	43	35	46

Major League Soccer

By The Associated Press
EASTERN CONFERENCE

	W	L	T	Pts	GF	GA
D.C. United	16	7	7	55	56	34
New England	14	8	8	50	51	43
New York	12	11	7	43	47	45

Special Olympics Organization that offers 30-plus Olympic-style individual and team sports for people with intellectual disabilities. The organization supports over 5 million athletes and more than 100,000 competitions each year in more than 170 countries, as well as other activities, events and services. Athletes are called Special Olympians. See **disabilities**.

speedskating Scoring is in minutes, seconds and tenths of a second.

Extend to hundredths if available. Use a **basic summary**.

sportsbook Use one word for places where sports bets are accepted either in person or online, unless part of a formal name. The shorthand *book* is acceptable on second reference: *The sportsbook opened in December; the book stopped taking bets just before kickoff.*

sports editor Capitalize as a formal title before a name. See **titles** in main section.

sports sponsorship If the sponsor's name is part of the event name, such as Buick Open, use the name in the title. If there is a previously established name commonly accepted for the event — *Orange Bowl, Sugar Bowl* — use that name even if there currently is a corporate sponsor. *Orange Bowl*, not *Discover Orange Bowl*. However, mention the sponsor somewhere in the story or in a self-contained paragraph after a 3-em dash at the bottom of the story.

sports writer Two words. An exception to Webster's New World College Dictionary.

spread, line It's often not necessary to use the word *spread* itself; simply say whether a team is favored or not: *The Lakers were favored by 8 1/2 at home against the Knicks.* When necessary, numbers for spreads, totals and other wagers should generally be expressed as mixed numbers rather than decimals. The term *line* is also acceptable: *The Patriots opened as a heavy favorite, but the line tightened to 1 after coaches said star quarterback Tom Brady was injured and would not play.*

SPORTS

stadium, stadiums Capitalize only when part of a proper name: *Yankee Stadium.*

swimming Scoring is in minutes, if appropriate, seconds and tenths of a second. Extend to hundredths if available.

Most events are measured in metric units.

Identify events as *men's 4x100 relay, women's 100 backstroke*, etc.

See **track and field** for the style on relay teams and events where a record is broken

Use a **basic summary**. Examples, where qualifying heats are required:

100 Butterfly
Final
1, Michael Phelps, United States, 50.77. 2, Ian Crocker, United States, 50.82. 3, Albert Subirats, Venezuela, 51.82.

t

table tennis Do not use the synonym *pingpong* to refer to the sport. The trademark name is *Ping-Pong.*

tennis Some commonly used terms: *double-fault, double-faulted. Love, 15, 30, 40, deuce, advantage, tiebreaker.* Report set scores thusly: *Serena Williams defeated Madison Keys 7-6 (5), 6-2.* Indicate tiebreakers in parentheses after the set score, using only the loser's total points in the tiebreaker.

time Follow advice in **time sequences** and **times** entries in Stylebook's main section. Use common descriptions for time frames in sports events unless the exact time is truly relevant: *Midway through the second quarter rather than 6:28 into the second quarter.* Precise times down to the second are usually

reserved for the final minute or two minutes of each period, depending on the sport.

titles Capitalize or use lowercase according to guidelines in **titles** in Stylebook's main section. Job descriptions, field positions and informal titles are lowercase: *coach John Calipari; forward Alex Morgan; general manager John Elway.* Some other informal titles commonly used in sports include *general manager, trainer, team doctor, manager, captain.*

Tommy John surgery Acceptable when referring to *ulnar collateral ligament reconstruction surgery* in the elbow, more commonly referred to as *surgery to repair a torn ligament in the elbow.*

track and field Scoring is in distance, time or height, depending on the event.

For time events, spell out *minutes* and *seconds* on first reference, as in *3 minutes, 26.1 seconds.* Subsequent times in stories and all times in agate require a colon and decimal point: *3:26.1.* For a marathon, it would be *2 hours, 11 minutes, 5.01 seconds* on first reference then the form *2:11:5.01* for later listings.

In running events, the first event should be spelled out, as in *men's 100-meter.* Later references can be condensed to phrases such as *the 200, the 400*, etc.

For hurdle and relay events, the progression can be: *100-meter hurdles, 400 hurdles*, etc.

For field events — those that do not involve running — use these forms: *26 1/2* for *26 feet, one-half inch; 25-10 1/2* for *25 feet, 10 1/2 inches*, etc.

In general, use a **basic summary**. For the style when a record is broken, note the mile event in the example below. For the style in listing relay teams, note 4x400 meter relay.

60-yard dash – 1, Steve Williams, Florida TC, 6.0. 2, Hasley Crawford, Philadelphia Pioneer, 6.2. 3, Mike McFarland, Chicago TC, 6.23.

100 – 1, Steve Williams, Florida TC, 10.1. 2.

Mile – 1, Filbert Bayi, Tanzania, 3:55.1, meet record, old record 3:59, Jim Beatty, Los Angeles TC, Feb. 27, 1963. 2, Paul Cummings, Beverly Hills TC, 3:56.1.

Women's 880 – 1, Johanna Forman, Falmouth TC, 2:07.9.

4x400 relay – 1, St. John's (John Kennedy, Doug Johnson, Gary Gordon, Ordner Emanuel), 3:21.9. 2, Brown, 3:23.5. 3, Fordham, 3:24.1.

Team scoring – Chicago TC 32, Philadelphia Pioneer 29.

Where qualifying heats are required:

Men's 100-meter heats (first two in each heat qualify for Friday's semifinals): Heat 1 – 1, Steve Williams, Florida TC, 10.1.

U

Ultimate Fighting Championship

UFC is acceptable in all references to the company that promotes mixed martial arts fights. Do not use *UFC* to refer to MMA fights held by other promoters. See **mixed martial arts**.

untracked Do not use this term for an athlete or team now performing well after a slow period. Use clearer expressions such as *back on track*.

up-tempo

USGA Acceptable in all references for the *United States Golf Association*.

V

versus Follow guidance under **versus** in the main section, spelling out the word in ordinary speech and writing, as well as in quotes: *Belichick's unconventional passing game versus Seattle's secondary*. It is permissible to abbreviate as *vs.* in short expressions: *Clippers vs. Warriors*.

volleyball In all indoor international, U.S. college and USA Volleyball games, each of the first four sets is won by the first team to score 25 points. If the match is tied in sets after the first four sets, a deciding fifth set will be played to 15 points. In all five sets, teams must win by 2 points without a cap on points.

Use a **match summary**. Example:

U.S.-Women def. Korea 21-25, 25-16, 29-27, 16-25, 15-12.

volley, volleys

W

warmup (n.) warm up (v.)

water polo Scoring is by goals. List team scores. Example:

World Water Polo Championship
First Round

United States 7, Canada 1

Britain 5, France 3

water skiing Scoring is in points. Use a **basic summary**. Example:

World Water Skiing Championships
Men

Overall – 1, George Jones, Canada, 1,987 points. 2, Phil Brown, Britain, 1,756.

Slalom – 1, George Jones, Canada, 73 buoys (two rounds).

water sports

weight In agate listings, use abbreviations for some sports, such as *lbs.* for pounds and *kg.* for kilograms.

weightlifting Use a **basic summary**. Example:

ATHENS, Greece (AP) – Final results Saturday of the weightlifting event from the Summer Olympics:

Men's 85kg

SPORTS

1. Juan Jose Madrigal, Costa Rica, 472.5 kg.
2. Rampa Mosweu, Botswana, 470.0.

wild card (n.) **wild-card** (adj.)

World Athletics The international governing body for track. The organization had been the International Association of Athletics Federations, or IAAF, until October 2019.

World Series Or *the Series* on second reference. A rare exception to the general principles under **capitalization**.

wrestling Identify events by weight division.

y

yachting Use a **basic summary**, identifying events by classes.

yard Equal to 3 feet.
　　The metric equivalent is approximately 0.91 meter.
　　To convert to meters, multiply by 0.91 (5 yards x 0.91 = 4.55 meters).
　　See **foot**; **meter**; and **distances**.

yard lines Use figures to indicate the dividing lines on a football field and distance traveled: *40-yard line, he plunged in from the 2, he ran 6 yards, a 7-yard gain.*

yearling An animal 1 year old or in its second year. The birthdays of all horses arbitrarily are set at Jan. 1. On that date, any foal born in the preceding year is considered 1 year old.

Z

zone, zone defense

Briefing on media law

INTRODUCTION

The courts significantly changed the legal standards governing the work of reporters and editors during the era of the civil rights movement and the Vietnam War, applying the First Amendment's protection of speech and press with new force and meaning.

In *New York Times v. Sullivan* (1964), the Supreme Court held for the first time that the First Amendment limits the ability of states to impose damages for the publication of a statement even when it is false, in some circumstances. Sixteen years later, in *Richmond Newspapers v. Virginia* (1980), the court reached the equally unprecedented conclusion that the First Amendment establishes an affirmative right of the press and public to compel access to certain information concerning the exercise of government power. The fallout from these two watershed cases has reshaped a great deal of the law that governs the publication of the news and the way it is gathered.

This chapter addresses some of the key legal issues facing journalists. With respect to newsgathering *activity*, it explores three topics of direct significance:

Access to government information, including the rules governing reporter access to the courts and to government information generally;

Confidential sources, including the law relating to promises of confidentiality and the reporter's privilege; and

Newsgathering conduct, including common law and statutory rules that may create liability for actions taken while a reporter is seeking out the news.

With respect to news *content*, this chapter addresses the legal principles in three branches of the law that govern liability for the publication of information:

Defamation, including the elements of a claim arising from the publication of a *false* statement, and the common law and constitutional defenses to liability;

Privacy, including claims for the disclosure of private facts, misappropriation and "false light," which can arise when the facts reported are *true*; and

Copyright infringement, including the elements of a copyright claim and the "fair use" defense.

While the law can vary in significant ways from one state to another, particularly in its details, the broad principles affecting newsgathering and reporting in the United States are largely consistent, due in part to the federal constitutional principles protecting speech and the press that overlay state law. Reporters and editors naturally will become familiar over time with the particulars of media law in the places where they work, and this chapter is intended only as a general primer on some basic principles that are likely to apply across a range of situations. It should not be construed as legal advice and should not substitute for obtaining legal guidance when you are in doubt.

LEGAL PRINCIPLES OF NEWSGATHERING

Several legal rules have special importance to the way the news is gathered. This chapter takes up three of them: the affirmative rights that can be invoked to compel access to government *proceedings* and the release of government documents; the legal protections that often allow reporters to obtain information through a promise of confidentiality; and the "laws of general applicability," such as intrusion, trespass, and misrepresentation, that reporters must usually follow, even when they inhibit the ability to seek out the news.

Access to government information

Public access to information about the actions of government is essential in a democracy. James Madison made just this point in 1832:

"A Popular Government, without popular information, or the means of acquiring it, is but a Prologue to a Farce or a Tragedy; or perhaps both. Knowledge will forever govern ignorance: And a people who mean to be their own Governors, must arm themselves with the power which knowledge gives."

The press and public have affirmative rights, both constitutional and statutory, to compel access to the type of government information that is essential to the functioning of our democracy. A right of access extends to official *proceedings*, including court trials, hearings, and the meetings of some legislative bodies and administrative agencies. Access rights also extend to the inspection of *documents* held by the government, with only specific exceptions. Given the independence of the three branches of government, the scope of access to judicial proceedings and court records is largely governed by constitutional and common law principles articulated by judges, while access to information in the executive and legislative branches is largely governed by statutes and administrative regulations.

These access rights are not absolute; they can be abridged in a number of situations. Nonetheless, clear legal standards define the scope of these rights and the procedures available to reporters to enforce them.

— Recognition of a First Amendment right of access

The articulation by the Supreme Court in 1980 of a constitutional *right* to certain information about the exercise of government power, and the delineation of the proper scope and application of that right over the ensuing years, would provide a fascinating case study of the meaning of a "living constitution." In *Richmond Newspapers v. Virginia*, the Supreme Court ruled for the first time that the First Amendment encompasses an affirmative, enforceable right of public access to criminal trials. As the court later explained the rationale for this new constitutional right, "a major purpose" of the First Amendment's protection of free speech, a free press and the right to petition the government is the public's need to know what the government is up to, if democracy is to function. Just as other provisions of the Bill of Rights have been read to imply the right to travel, a right to privacy, and the right to be presumed innocent, the court concluded that the First Amendment implies a right of the public to certain information concerning the direct exercise of government power.

In a series of rulings following *Richmond Newspapers*, the Supreme Court reaffirmed the existence of this constitutional right of access and defined its scope. In *Globe Newspaper Co. v. Superior Court* (1982), the court said that the right to attend a criminal trial applies even during the testimony of a minor victim of a sex crime. The court in that case struck down as unconstitutional a Massachusetts statute mandating closed proceedings during all such testimony, saying that the First Amendment right of access requires a judge to determine on a case-by-case basis whether the privacy concerns of a particular victim outweigh the public's right to attend and observe the proceedings. In 1984, the Supreme Court held that the right of public access extends to the proceedings to select a jury in a criminal case, *Press-Enterprise Co. v. Superior Ct. I*, and two years later said the right extends to preliminary hearings in a criminal prosecution. *Press-Enterprise Co. v Superior Ct. II*. The First Amendment protects the public's right to attend such judicial proceedings unless specific findings are made, on the record, demonstrating that a closed proceeding is essential in order to "preserve higher values," and any limitation imposed on public access must be narrowly tailored to serve that interest. In 2010, in *Presley v. Georgia*, the court held a trial judge must ensure that these standards are satisfied before a courtroom is closed to the public, even if no one objects to the closure.

While the Supreme Court has not substantively revisited the right of access in detail since 1986, lower federal and state courts have considered and applied the right to a wide variety of judicial and administrative proceedings over the intervening years. Courts have recognized a constitutional right to attend a given type of proceeding if public access will generally play a positive role in the performance of the proceeding (encouraging diligent attention by officials, ensuring that proper procedures are followed, preventing perjury or other misconduct, facilitating public understanding of decisions made), and if it is the type of proceeding that historically has been open to the public. This right has been held also to apply to administrative proceedings conducted like trials, such as deportation hearings and agency adjudications.

The constitutional right is generally recognized to apply to all aspects of a criminal prosecution, except to matters involving a grand jury. Grand jury investigations historically have been completely secret, and this secrecy itself advances the important public policy of protecting innocent people in those cases where an investigation does not result in any criminal charge being filed. The right of access has been held to extend to civil trials and proceedings, although in some states there are important exceptions. Family Court proceedings, for example, raise significant privacy concerns, as do juvenile delinquency matters, and these are often closed to the public.

— Limits on constitutional access

As noted, the constitutional right to attend government proceedings is not absolute. That a First Amendment right protects public access to a type of proceeding does not mean that such a proceeding can never be closed to the press and public. The Supreme Court has identified four factors that must each be satisfied before the right of access may be restricted:

1. Those who want to close a proceeding must prove that holding a public proceeding would directly threaten some compelling interest, such as a defendant's right to a fair trial or the right of privacy, that outweighs the public interest in openness.

2. There must be no alternative short of closing the proceeding that could protect the threatened interest.

3. Any limitation on access must be as narrow as possible.

4. The limitation imposed must be effective in protecting the threatened interest or else closure may not be ordered.

Applying these factors, courts have required journalists and the public to be excluded from proceedings in a number of situations, such as during the testimony of a sexual assault victim whose identity has not previously been disclosed to the public, or during testimony by an undercover police officer whose effectiveness or safety would be jeopardized by public identification.

Sidebar conferences between the attorneys and the judge generally involve discussions intended to be kept confidential from the jury, but these discussions should usually be available to the press. A transcript is generally kept of such sidebar discussions and should be available for inspection as part of the record of the proceeding. To withhold the transcript of such a sidebar conference held during an open proceeding, the same four-part test would need to be met.

One recurring but unsettled issue concerns reporters' access to information identifying jurors, and their right to speak to jurors after a verdict. The Supreme Court has said specifically that the First Amendment right of access extends to jury selection proceedings, where names and other identifying information are normally disclosed. Some lower courts have concluded that this principle also requires disclosures of written juror questionnaires when they are used. Nonetheless, in some high profile cases such as the prosecutions of Martha Stewart, Michael Jackson, Illinois Gov. Rod Blagojevich, and baseball slugger Barry Bonds, courts have sought to keep the identities of jurors private during the trial or to minimize press contact with jurors following a verdict. Sometimes a judge will conduct jury selection by reference only to juror numbers, to prevent public disclosure of juror names or addresses before a trial is over. The U.S. Court of Appeals in Philadelphia concluded in *United States v. Wecht* (2008) that the public access right requires juror names to be disclosed before the start of a trial, but this position is not universally embraced. In other cases, courts have barred reporters from speaking with jurors long after a verdict is returned. Limitations on disclosure of juror identities before a verdict is returned are sometimes permitted, but restrictions after a verdict is returned can rarely be squared with the First Amendment right of access.

Reporters confronted with such court orders should seek legal advice on the validity of the restriction imposed.

— What to say if a hearing is about to be closed without prior notice

Because a constitutional right is at stake, the press has a right to be heard before a proceeding is closed to the public. The following statement should be read in court when confronted with an attempt to close a hearing without advance notice. It allows a reporter, when permitted to address the court, to state the basic concerns and to seek time for counsel to appear to make the legal argument. Any parts of the statement that are not applicable to a specific case can be changed or omitted:

May it please the Court, I am (name) of The Associated Press (or other news organization). I respectfully request the opportunity to register on the record an objection to closing this proceeding to the public. The Associated Press (or other organization) requests a hearing at which its counsel may present to the Court legal authority and arguments showing why any closure in this proceeding would be improper.

The press and the public have a constitutional right to attend judicial proceedings, and may not be excluded unless the Court makes findings, on the record, that: (1) closure is required to preserve a compelling constitutional interest, (2) no adequate alternatives to closure exist, and (3) the closure ordered is narrowly tailored to protect the threatened interest effectively.

The Associated Press (or other news organization) submits that these findings cannot be made here, especially given the public interest in this proceeding. The public has a right to be informed of what transpires in this case, the positions being argued by the parties, and the factual basis for rulings made by the Court. The Court should avoid any impression that justice is being carried on in secret. The Associated Press (or other news organization) objects to any closure order and respectfully requests a hearing at which it can present full legal arguments and authority in support of this position. Thank you.

If the court will not allow a reporter to be heard, a brief written statement — handwritten is fine — should be delivered to the courtroom clerk, making these same points.

— A word about gag orders

The tension between the right of a free press and the right of a fair trial is nothing new. Finding an impartial jury for the treason trial of Aaron Burr in 1807 was difficult, the Supreme Court has noted, because few people in Virginia "had not formed some opinions concerning Mr. Burr or his case, from newspaper accounts." Nonetheless, an apparently increasing number of cases involving celebrity defendants or notorious crimes generating intense publicity have led to an increased number of orders preventing lawyers, parties to a case, and sometimes even witnesses, from discussing the case outside of the courtroom.

The Supreme Court has said that speech by attorneys, as officers of the court, may be regulated to protect the integrity of the judicial system. Orders more broadly barring the speech of other trial participants, including the parties and witnesses, are permitted only when absolutely necessary to ensure an accused's right to a fair trial. Such orders have been entered in cases involving extraordinary press coverage that threatens the ability to select an impartial jury, when other measures are not likely to mitigate the effects of unrestrained pretrial publicity.

A typical gag order does not prevent a reporter from asking questions, but it does bar trial participants and court officers from answering them. Because a gag order restricts access to news, most courts acknowledge that a reporter has legal standing to challenge an order, and may be successful if a gag order was entered without adequate factual findings to justify the need for the specific restraint on speech imposed by the court, or if the order is overbroad in the categories of individuals restrained or the range of topics they are prohibited from discussing.

— Media protocols in high-profile cases

Over the years "decorum orders" have been entered by some courts to regulate the conduct of reporters covering high profile trials. Sometimes requested by the parties and sometimes imposed unilaterally by the court, these orders may restrict the use of cameras and recording devices at specific locations in and around the courthouse, direct that witnesses or jurors not be photographed as they come and go from court, restrict the use of cellphones, or impose other restrictions to protect the decorum of a trial and operations at the courthouse. In the aborted Kobe Bryant prosecution, for example, a Colorado state judge imposed a decorum order specifying such details as where cameras could be positioned outside the courthouse, limiting the times when reporters could enter or leave the courtroom, and specifying where reporters could sit, where they could park their cars and how they could enter the courthouse.

Restrictions on the actions of journalists that directly affect their ability to gather news must be narrowly tailored to protect a compelling governmental interest. Decorum orders that become necessary in high-profile cases to ensure safety, protect physical access to the courts by the public, or prevent interference with the integrity of the proceedings in the courtroom, are likely to be allowed as long as their terms are reasonable, content-neutral and limited to clearly defined restrictions on conduct within the courthouse and its immediate environs. A decorum order likely goes too far, however, if it also controls the content of a news report rather than just the conduct of a reporter. For example, for privacy reasons a court might restrict the taking of photographs of jurors as they enter or leave the courthouse, but could not properly bar the press from ever publishing the image of a juror, even if it were obtained through other sources. One restriction is limited to conduct at the courthouse; the other is aimed at the content of a news report.

— The right to attend other types of proceedings

In some instances, the constitutional right of access has been held to extend to proceedings beyond court hearings. For example, the U.S. Court of Appeals in Cincinnati has held that the public had a constitutional right to attend deportation proceedings conducted by the Immigration and Naturalization Service. (*Detroit Free Press v. Ashcroft*, 2002.) The U.S. Court of Appeals in New York has held that the right of access applies in transit agency tribunals to assess fines. (*New York Civ. Lib. Union v. N.Y.C. Transit Authority*, (2011)). The First Amendment right of access similarly has been found to extend to military courts-martial, proceedings of judicial review boards and hearings of the Federal Mine Safety and Health Administration.

Most states and the federal government also have statutes known as "open meetings laws" or "government in the sunshine" acts that protect the right of the public and the press to attend meetings of public authorities. These laws essentially provide that every meeting where a public board or public authority convenes to conduct business must be open to the public, with only limited exception. The federal law, for example, allows a meeting to be closed only if one of 10 identified categories of information is to be discussed, such as personnel and salary decisions. Even when a portion of a meeting is closed, a transcript or minutes must be prepared, and must be disclosed to the extent that disclosure would not reveal the exempt information.

These access laws typically apply to executive agencies, but not to the legislative bodies, in most cases. Most state constitutions separately require open legislative sessions, although each house is usually free to make its own rules about access to committee meetings.

— The right of access applies to court records

The right of access generally includes the right to inspect transcripts of open proceedings, evidence introduced at a trial and most motion papers, orders and other records of open court proceedings. Some courts have concluded that this right to inspect judicial records is implicit in the First Amendment right of access, holding that the right covers any documents relating to a proceeding that is itself subject to the First Amendment right of access.

Other courts analyze the right of access to documents filed with the court as a common law right that may be more easily restricted, sometimes with unfortunate results. For example, in the famous case of *McConnell v. Federal Election Commission* (2003), a challenge to the constitutionality of the McCain-Feingold campaign finance reform act was decided by the courts entirely on the basis of written submissions, without any public evidentiary hearing. A massive record of some 100,000 pages was presented to the court, apparently detailing the types of campaign abuses that Congress found to justify restrictions on election speech. Despite the public interest in knowing the factual basis for the competing arguments being made, the District of Columbia court concluded that the public had only a common law right to inspect the documents presented to the court, and that this right extended only to information "relied upon" by the court in reaching its decision. The court therefore rejected an application by several news organizations to inspect the evidence filed with the court, saying the public was only entitled to inspect specific pages of the record actually cited in the court's opinions. Other courts have rejected this limitation and have found a constitutional right of access to records submitted to courts in support of requests for judicial action, regardless of whether the court ultimately relies on the record, an approach embraced by the U.S. Court of Appeals in New York (*Lugosh v. Pyramid Corp.*).

Whether the right to inspect court records is a constitutional right or a common law right is not fully settled in some areas of the country. Whatever the scope of the right to inspect court records, however, it does not generally extend to pretrial discovery documents and other litigation records that are not filed with the courts. While compelled public access to discovery has been afforded on rare occasions, involving highly newsworthy disputes, reporters generally have no right to require parties to a lawsuit to allow inspection of litigation material that is never filed with the court.

— Access to other government records

The federal Freedom of Information Act (FOIA), originally passed by Congress in 1966, creates a presumptive right of access to all documents held in the executive branch, other than documents in the possession of the president and his immediate staff. It does not cover Congress or the courts. All Cabinet agencies, independent agencies, regulatory commissions and government-owned corporations are covered.

Records made available for inspection under the act include virtually anything recorded in a physical medium that can be reproduced. This includes all documents, papers, reports, and letters in the government's possession, as well as films, photographs, sound recordings, databases, computer disks and tapes. A 1996 law expanded FOIA to require federal agencies, whenever possible, to share data in a specific format, such as on computer diskette or CD-ROM. The 1996 amendments also broadened citizen access to government by placing more information directly online.

The act contains nine exemptions that permit — but do not require — agencies to withhold information. Those exemptions are: (1) national security; (2) internal agency personnel rules; (3) information specifically exempt from disclosure by another law; (4) trade secrets; (5) internal agency memorandums and policy deliberations; (6) personal privacy; (7); law enforcement investigations; (8) federally regulated bank information; and (9) oil and gas well data.

Different agencies apply these exemptions in different ways even when issues ostensibly have already been settled in court. If you want something, ask for it. Let the government decide whether it has any grounds or willingness to deny your request. The statutory exemptions allow information to be withheld, but do not require it. Even an exempt document can be released at the government's discretion.

Because of the various exemptions, documents are often produced with large sections blacked out as "exempt." And, because of a lack of manpower assigned to implement the act, there are often long delays in getting documents at all. Under the law, information is supposed to be produced within 20 days, but there is no effective enforcement mechanism when an agency misses this deadline, short of going to court.

— Making a request under FOIA

There is no set format for making a FOIA request for documents. Although most agencies have adopted regulations describing specific steps to follow, any reasonably precise identification of the information sought, submitted to the proper person, will trigger an obligation for an agency to respond. Here are a few elementary steps to consider in making a FOIA request that may help avoid problems:

— Call the public information office of the agency you believe has the records before filing your request, to make sure you have the right agency and the right address for filing it. Ask if the information you are seeking could be released without a written FOIA request.

— Be as specific as possible about what you want. Give dates, titles, and authors for documents if you know them. In your letter, provide your telephone number, email address, and offer to supply any other information that might help narrow the search.

— Even if you are using the letterhead stationery of a news organization, state specifically that you are a reporter for that organization and plan to use the material in news stories. The act does not require you to state your purpose, but disclosures in the public interest are eligible for fee waivers, exemption waivers and in some cases expedited handling.

— Request a waiver of search and copying fees. To avoid delays if the waiver is denied, also state a limit you are prepared to pay, such as $100, without the agency's need to obtain your prior, specific consent.
— If you want field office files checked as well as those at headquarters, be sure to request that specifically. Some agencies, such as the FBI, will not check beyond the office where the request is submitted, unless asked. It is good practice to send a separate request directly to the FOI officer at the field office of an agency in any event, if you think relevant documents exist there.
— Ask the agency to cite specific exemptions for each item it withholds in the event that any part of the request is denied.
— Request that redacted copies of documents be provided if only a specific portion of a document is subject to an exemption.
— If your initial request is denied, file an administrative appeal. Some agencies take a very different view on appeal. The denial letter will specify to whom the appeal must be sent and the deadline for making an appeal. If you do not first pursue an administrative appeal, you cannot go to court to compel release of the information.
— An appeal can be made through a simple letter that explains why the public will benefit from disclosure and asks for a review of the grounds on which the request was denied. Several exemptions require a balancing of private and public interests, and reviewers on an administrative appeal may be more likely to exercise their right to waive an exemption if a good case for disclosure is made.

You may want to consult FOIA experts or manuals before proceeding with a request. A FOI Service Center is maintained by the Reporters Committee for Freedom of the Press. The committee publishes a pamphlet with sample FOIA letters and appeal forms as well as analyses of the act. (Available on the web at: http://www.rcfp.org/foiact/index.html.) The committee maintains a toll-free hot line (800-336-4243), 24 hours a day, seven days a week, with attorneys available to provide FOIA advice to journalists.

On the web, the U.S. Department of Justice publishes a "Guide to the Freedom of Information Act," which gives the current government understanding of what is covered and not covered by each exemption, http://www.justice.gov/oip/foia-guide.html. Also on the web, the U.S. Department of Justice publishes a collection of "FOIA Resources," which includes up-to-date copies of relevant statutes and recent court decisions, http://www.justice.gov/oip/foia-resources.

It is advisable to check on specific state freedom of information laws. Each individual state has its own freedom of information laws that apply to state and local government agencies.

Issues concerning sources

For better or worse, some sources who possess important information of great public significance will speak to a journalist only if they are promised confidentiality. This has been true from the earliest history of an independent press in America. John Peter Zenger, whose New York trial in 1735 is best remembered for establishing the principle that truth is a defense to a claim for libel, was also the first American newspaperman to establish the tradition that journalists will protect their sources to the point of imprisonment. Zenger refused to divulge to British authorities the identities of those who made the statements that authorities considered libelous.

The use of confidential sources remains an important means for reporters to uncover the news. Such sources make available to the public more than the sanitized "spin" of government and corporate press releases. Yale professor Alexander Bickel noted:

"Indispensable information comes in confidence from officeholders fearful of superiors, from businessmen fearful of competitors, from informers operating at the edge of the law who are in danger of reprisal from criminal associates, from people afraid of the law and government — sometimes rightly afraid, but as often from an excess of caution — and from men in all fields anxious not to incur censure for unorthodox or unpopular views." ("The Morality of Consent," 1975.)

In one study of some 10,000 news reports conducted in 2005, 13% of the front-page newspaper articles reviewed were based, at least in part, on anonymous sources.

Promising confidentiality to a source always raises a number of issues, legal and journalistic. If a reporter refuses to identify a source, there is always the potential that a publisher may be hauled into court or a reporter thrown into jail. If a publisher is sued for libel, having a story based on sources that were promised confidentiality creates an entirely separate set of concerns: it is hard to prove the "truth" of a statement if the source of the information cannot be revealed. In one case, a Massachusetts court entered a default judgment against the Boston Globe for refusing to reveal its confidential source for a story that became the subject of a libel claim. A jury subsequently awarded the plaintiff $2.1 million — a hefty price to pay to uphold a promise to a source.

— A promise to a source creates an enforceable agreement

A reporter who reveals the name or identity of someone who was promised confidentiality can be held liable for breach of the agreement.

The Supreme Court decided just this issue in *Cohen v. Cowles* (1991), a case involving "dirt" on one political candidate that was provided to a newspaper reporter on the eve of the election by a political consultant for the candidate's opponent. The reporter promised the consultant confidentiality. His editors, however, considered the identification of the source necessary for the public to weigh the significance of the new disclosures, and overruled the reporter. As a result, the no-longer confidential source lost his job, and sued. A jury verdict of $200,000 in favor of the spurned source was upheld by the Supreme Court, which found the First Amendment no defense to a claim for the damages caused by breaking a promise freely made.

The same result was reached by a New York court in a case involving a promise to mask someone's identity in a photograph. A journalist promised a man receiving treatment in an AIDS clinic that he would not be "identifiable" if he allowed his photograph to be taken. The journalist used a rear-angle setup and retouching techniques to obscure his identity, but the man's friends still recognized him when the photograph was published. The New York court held that the burden of carrying out the promise to disguise rested with the journalist who made the promise, and upheld the jury's award of damages to the patient.

Reporters can unwittingly create problems for themselves in making agreements with sources to protect confidentiality, or in failing to clarify with the source the meaning of an agreement. A few common-sense steps can minimize the risk that problems with sources will develop:

— Before making any promise, consider whether it is worth doing: How important is the information that the source is going to provide? Can the information be obtained or confirmed from any "on-the-record" source?

— If a promise of some protection is to be made, express it in terms of the steps that will be taken to protect the source rather than the result to be achieved. For example, promise a source to not use the name, or agree on how the source will be identified in the story (a "high-ranking military officer," or a "knowledgeable Defense Department official"), rather than promising "no one will know you gave me this information." If a photograph or videotape is involved, the key is still to promise a specific action ("I will photograph you only from behind") rather than promising a result ("no one will recognize you").

— Make sure the source has the same understanding of the scope of the promise made as you do. Avoid using ambiguous terms as a shorthand for an agreement, such as "this will be off the record," or this is "confidential." Instead, be specific about the terms of the agreement and how far the promise extends. Must confidentiality be maintained if litigation results? If a court order requires disclosure? Or, will the source allow disclosure in certain situations?

— Follow through with any agreement, making sure to inform editors and others who need to know to carry out the promise. The broader the promise, the more the effort needed to make sure that it is upheld.

The bottom line is this: promises of confidentiality or anonymity should be made cautiously, and only after a determination that the risk of such promises is outweighed by the need for the information. When a promise is made, make sure it is as precise as possible, and then make sure it is carried out.

— Reporter's privilege

Given the importance of confidential sources, reporters have long asserted a right to protect the identity of those to whom confidentiality was promised. All states except Wyoming have provided some level of protection for reporters who are called to testify about their sources. Thirty-nine states and the District of Columbia have enacted "shield laws" that provide legal protection against the disclosure of sources; Hawaii's statute expired under a sunset provision and it has not as of this writing been re-enacted; nine additional states have recognized some form of a "reporter's privilege" through judicial decisions. About half of the state shield laws provide reporters with an absolute privilege not to disclose confidential sources, while the remainder establish a high standard that must be met before a reporter's promise of confidentiality can be pierced.

The existence and scope of the reporter's privilege is more confused in federal courts. Although significant efforts have been made in recent years, there is no federal shield law, and the Supreme Court has addressed the "reporter's privilege" only once — in a ruling that is far from clear.

In *Branzburg v. Hayes* (1972), the Supreme Court considered claims of privilege asserted by three journalists who had been subpoenaed to reveal confidential information and sources before grand juries investigating possible criminal activity. The reporters had written stories describing the synthesizing of hashish, conversations with admitted drug users, and eyewitness accounts of events at Black Panther headquarters at a time of civil unrest in the surrounding neighborhood. In each instance, the journalist claimed a privilege under the First Amendment not to answer questions concerning confidential information and sources.

A closely divided Supreme Court held in a 5-4 ruling that it did not violate the First Amendment to require these journalists to testify in the grand jury investigations, conducted in good faith, concerning the identities of persons allegedly engaged in criminal conduct. The court, however, did not reject altogether the notion of a First Amendment privilege. To the contrary, the majority opinion expressed the view that its narrow focus should not apply to "the vast bulk of confidential relationships between reporters and their sources," and emphasized that even grand juries "must operate within the limits of the First Amendment as well as the Fifth."

Justice Lewis Powell cast the decisive fifth vote and wrote separately to underscore further the "limited nature" of the court's holding. He explained that reporters would still have access to the courts, and could move to quash a subpoena if confidential source information were being sought "without a legitimate need of law enforcement."

Court decisions over the ensuing decades have embraced a qualified reporter's privilege that accommodates the interests of the press and those who seek to obtain information through judicial process. The United States Courts of Appeals in 10 of the 12 federal circuits have specifically applied the First Amendment reporter's privilege in civil lawsuits.

Courts, however, have read *Branzburg* more restrictively in the criminal context, sometimes declining to recognize a privilege at all, or allowing only a very limited balancing of interests. Three different federal appellate courts affirmed contempt citations requiring reporters to be jailed for refusing to reveal confidential sources sought in criminal investigations. In 2001, freelance writer Vanessa Leggett served nearly six months in a Texas prison for declining to reveal sources of information related to a notorious murder, almost four times longer than any prison term previously imposed on any reporter by any federal court. In 2004, James Taricani, a reporter for WJAR-TV in Rhode Island, completed a four-month sentence of home confinement for declining to reveal who leaked a videotape capturing alleged corruption by public officials in Providence. And, in 2005 The New York Times reporter Judith Miller was jailed in Virginia for several months for refusing to disclose her confidential source for a story she never wrote about CIA operative Valerie Plame.

Most recently, the U.S. Court of Appeals for the Fourth Circuit rejected any First Amendment-based or common law reporter's privilege in a criminal proceeding in which the subpoenaed journalist, James Risen, was an "eyewitness" to a crime. In this case, a confidential source allegedly leaked classified information to Risen and Risen was then subpoenaed to testify whether the criminal defendant was, in fact, his source. (*U.S. v. Sterling*). The U.S. Court of Appeals in Richmond held that Risen had no privilege whatsoever to refuse to testify in this context, and the Supreme Court refused to review the holding. When the case against the source went to trial, however, Attorney General Eric Holder decided that Risen's testimony was not needed, and Risen was not forced to testify. The CIA officer accused of being the source was convicted without compelling the reporter to testify or go to jail.

The aggressive court actions in criminal investigations have encouraged private litigants and federal courts adjudicating their civil cases also to demand confidential information from reporters. In one civil suit, five reporters (including two Pulitzer Prize winners) were held in contempt and subjected to fines of $500 per day each for declining to reveal their confidential sources of information about Dr. Wen Ho Lee, who claimed information about him was provided to reporters by government agents in violation of the Privacy Act.

Because the scope of a reporter's privilege in the federal courts is unsettled, reporters have been aided in federal investigations by Department of Justice guidelines that severely limit the circumstances under which U.S. attorneys may attempt to subpoena or search members of the news media. These guidelines were first enacted in 1970, but were most recently revised in 2014 and 2015 after public uproar over revelations that the department had secretly subpoenaed the telephone records of the AP in connection with a national security leak investigation and had obtained a search warrant for the email of a Fox News reporter in another leak investigation.

The guidelines currently in effect apply to subpoenas and similar compulsory process, court orders issued pursuant to 18 U.S.C. § 2703(d) or 18 U.S.C. § 3123, and warrants intended either "to obtain information from members of the news media" or to procure "communications records" or "business records" of members of the news media that are held by third parties. A notable limitation is that the guidelines protect only information related to "newsgathering activity," a term which is left undefined.

Where the guidelines apply, they generally require that all members of the department obtain the approval of the attorney general or relevant assistant attorney general before issuing a subpoena or requesting a court order seeking documents or information covered by the guidelines. They make clear that steps to seek information from a member of the news media are considered "extraordinary measures, not standard investigatory practices."

In deciding whether to authorize such a subpoena or seek a court order, the attorney general considers (a) in criminal matters, whether there are reasonable grounds to believe that a crime has occurred, and whether the information sought is essential to a successful investigation or prosecution; (b) in civil matters, whether there are reasonable grounds to believe that the information is essential to the successful completion of the investigation or litigation in a case of substantial importance; and (c) in all matters, whether the government has made all reasonable attempts to obtain the information from alternative, non-media sources. The government is also generally required to give reasonable notice to the journalists implicated before seeking a subpoena or court order, and to negotiate with them. The attorney general will generally limit any authorization to seeking evidence needed to verify the accuracy of published information and the circumstances surrounding such information, and requires all requests for information from the news media to be "narrowly drawn" to avoid imposing an undue burden.

These regulations provide the same types of protection contained in some state shield laws, and the Department of Justice has demonstrated a serious desire to enforce these regulations strictly. Any time a subpoena is received by a reporter from a U.S. attorney, the first question to ask the attorney is: Did you comply with the media guidelines at 28 C.F.R. 50.10 before issuing this subpoena? Not infrequently, just asking the question results in the subpoena being withdrawn.

— Liability for newsgathering conduct

A reporter for Mother Jones won a national award in 1984 for posing as a job applicant at a chemical factory and covertly taking photographs documenting illegal pesticides being manufactured for the export market. That conduct today would more likely win a lawsuit.

In holding that a reporter's promise of confidentiality is legally binding, the Supreme Court in *Cohen v. Cowles* (1991) announced that "generally applicable" laws having only "incidental effects" on the ability of the press to gather the news do not offend the First Amendment. Ever since, a flow of lawsuits have been filed against reporters asserting claims for such "generally applicable" torts as intrusion, trespass, and fraud, and more recently, asserting claims for accessing password-protected computers or voicemail. From the muzzling effect of the tobacco industry's threat of "tortious interference" liability against CBS for an expose based on a confidential source who was party to a standard confidentiality agreement as an employee of a tobacco company, through *Food Lion's* claim of trespass, fraud and breach of duty leveled against ABC and a spate of other hidden camera lawsuits, reporters since *Cohen v. Cowles* have faced an increased number of claims alleging misconduct in the gathering of the news.

This section highlights briefly some of the legal theories that can create problems for the unwary reporter.

— Intrusion upon seclusion

A claim for intrusion exists in most states if someone intentionally commits a "highly offensive" intrusion upon another's solitude or seclusion, invading either a physical space or the private affairs of the plaintiff, such as reviewing private financial statements or personal email without permission. Intrusion claims against the press most commonly arise in three contexts: (1) surreptitious surveillance; (2) trespass of private property, and (3) instances where consent to enter a private setting for one purpose has been exceeded (as where a reporter gains access to information under false pretenses).

Intrusion is a branch of the law of privacy. Where the potentially offending conduct occurs is therefore important. For example, in the United States a person generally has no legitimate basis to complain if a picture is taken in a public place, but if the picture is taken in or around the person's home, a claim for intrusion may exist if the person had a "reasonable expectation" of privacy where the photograph was taken.

In one noted lawsuit a few years back, the family of an officer of a large health care corporation successfully obtained an injunction against the elaborate efforts of a news organization that was seeking information about the family. The organization's camera crew followed the children to school, and sat in a boat outside the family's Florida home with a camera equipped with a high-powered telescopic lens. In issuing an injunction, the court concluded that "a persistent course of hounding, harassment and unreasonable surveillance, even if conducted in a public or semi-public place," could support a claim for intrusion upon seclusion.

A claim for intrusion generally requires (1) an intentional intrusion, (2) that impinges upon the solitude or seclusion of another, or his private affairs, and (3) that would be highly offensive to a reasonable person. The term "highly offensive" is ill-defined, but can include harassing behavior, surreptitious surveillance, or the use of high-power lenses and listening devices to invade typically private places.

The tort of intrusion is based on wrongful conduct rather than on the publication of any information, so a claim may exist even when the news story being pursued is never published. For this reason, in many states it is no defense to an intrusion claim to assert the newsworthiness of the information that was being sought. The issue is whether a reasonable person would view the conduct as highly offensive under all the circumstances.

Some examples where courts have upheld claims for intrusion illustrate the nature of the tort:

—Two journalists in California, without discussing who they were, gained access to the home of a disabled veteran who purported to provide healing aids in the form of clay, minerals and herbs. While there, they surreptitiously photographed and tape-recorded the veteran, for use in a magazine report. The court allowed a claim for intrusion even though the reporters were invited into the home by the veteran. While a person takes the risk that someone allowed into their home is not what he seems, and even though a visitor is free to repeat anything he sees or hears, the court held that the homeowner's risk does not extend to the risk that secret photographs and recordings will be transmitted to the world at large.

—The unauthorized recording of an unplanned interview conducted when the plaintiff answered his own front door has similarly been held to constitute an actionable "intrusion," while secretly recording an interview of a person who stepped from their home onto a public sidewalk was held not to be an intrusion.

—Televising an image of a person's home is not an intrusion if the broadcast shows no more than what can be seen from the street, and secretly recording a conversation in a place of business was held not to be an intrusion if the reporter was invited into the office and the state wiretap law permitted the secret recording.

— Trespass

A person commits a trespass by entering property that is in the possession of another, without authorization or consent. To avoid a claim, permission must be obtained by an owner, a tenant or someone acting on their behalf. Like intrusion, a trespass claim arises from conduct in gathering news, not from the content of any report that may subsequently be published.

Permission to be on private property can be implied by custom or by the nature of the premises. For example, someone has implied permission to enter a store or restaurant during business hours, even though it may be located on private property. There is similarly an implied right to approach someone's house on a driveway or sidewalk to see if they are home. Permission, whether express or implied, can also be revoked. If a posted sign says "Do Not Enter," or if the owner came to the door and said to leave, remaining on the property likely would be a trespass.

Trespass is also a strict liability tort. Entering on someone's property without permission, even by accident or mistake, will constitute a trespass. On the other hand, trespass protects only against a physical invasion of property; it does not limit the collection or use of information gathered while on the property. The law of trespass does not restrict a reporter on a public sidewalk from using what can be seen or heard on the adjacent private property.

The impact of trespass on newsgathering is also tempered by the nature of the damages that may be recovered through a claim for trespass. The trespass tort is intended to protect property, not privacy or reputation. A trespasser therefore can be held responsible only for physical harm done while on the land and other injury that is a "natural consequence" of the trespass. Courts generally will not recognize injury to reputation or emotional distress caused by the later publication of a photograph obtained during a trespass to be a "natural consequence" of the trespass itself.

A vivid example of a trespass claim involved a television camera crew that was preparing a report on credit card fraud. The United States Secret Service obtained a warrant to search an apartment for evidence of credit card fraud, and a news magazine camera crew followed the Secret Service into the apartment. Part of the search was taped, including a sequence of a mother and child cowering on the couch asking not be photographed. In refusing to dismiss a lawsuit asserting claims for trespass and a constitutional tort (for improperly accompanying federal agents in executing a search warrant), an outraged court said the reporters "had no greater right than that of a common thief to be in the apartment." Like intrusion, the trespass was complete once the invasion of private property occurred. The trespass claim could be asserted even though the news report being pursued was never broadcast.

In situations rife with the potential for trespass, common sense can once again minimize the risk of litigation:

— Whenever possible, ask the property owner or those who appear to be in charge for permission to enter, or seek their approval to remain. In situations where police or fire officials have taken control of a crime or disaster scene, they may stand in for the owner and grant or deny access. Their presence does not defeat the owner's rights, however, and the owner can still require a reporter to leave private property.

— Always identify yourself — verbally, by displaying a press credential, and through insignias on clothing and cameras — so that those present know you are a reporter and will not assume you are part of any police or emergency response team. If not asked to leave, the fact that your status as a reporter was disclosed may be sufficient to establish an implied consent to remain.

— If asked to leave, retire to the sidewalk, street, or other position on public property.

— Consent obtained through fraud or misrepresentation will not be considered

valid consent and will not defeat a claim for trespass.
— Consent obtained from minors or others who are not legally capable of giving consent (mentally incapacitated people, for example) will not defeat a claim for trespass.

— Electronic eavesdropping

Both state and federal law regulate the electronic recording of conversations, including telephone conversations.

Under the federal law, a conversation may not be recorded without the consent of at least one of the participants. That means reporters are not prohibited by federal law from recording any conversation in which they participate, whether or not they disclose that the conversation is being recorded. But, leaving a hidden tape recorder in a room to record a conversation between others, secretly listening in on an extension phone and recording the conversation, or recording a telephone call picked up on a scanner or listening device, is a violation of federal law if done without permission of one of the parties.

The law in most states is similar to the federal law, allowing a conversation to be recorded so long as one party to the conversation consents. The laws in a minority of states are more strict, and prohibit recording any conversation unless permission is given by all the parties to the conversation. This requirement of consent extends only to conversations where there is some expectation of privacy, and does not prohibit tape-recording at speeches, press conferences and similar public events.

— Misrepresentation and similar forms of wrongdoing

Laws of general applicability govern the actions of reporters, yet conduct that might sometimes be deemed "deceit," "misrepresentation" or "fraud" can be useful in ferreting out the news. Reporters are often less than candid in dealing with those from whom they want information. Recognizing this reality, some courts have held that claims such as fraud and misrepresentation cannot be pursued against journalists unless the wrong is "particularly egregious," or part of a broader pattern of wrongdoing. For example, courts have rejected claims for fraud based on a false message left on a telephone answering machine to induce the disclosure of information, and for falsely promising that no "ambush" techniques would be used if an interview were granted.

Other courts have been less willing to weigh the public interest in a news report against the allegedly wrongful conduct. In one instance, a judge allowed claims for fraud and breach of contract to proceed against Business Week after a reporter gained access to records of a credit reporting agency by misrepresenting that a subscription to the credit service was being sought in order to conduct background checks on potential Business Week employees. In reality, information was sought for an exposé on the credit-reporting industry, and the reporter promptly obtained the credit history of then-Vice President Dan Quayle without his consent. The court held that such "wanton misconduct" can result in liability, and allowed a recovery of the costs incurred by the credit agency as a result of the misrepresentation.

Remember, the basic rule is that reporters must obey rules and regulations when they are gathering the news. While there are some exceptions, the First

Amendment will not generally provide a defense to a reporter who violates the law while gathering the news.

— Special Considerations When Dealing with National Security Issues

The Espionage Act (of 1917) makes it a federal crime to publish classified information that either (a) reveals the communications intelligence activities of the United States or any foreign country, or (b) discloses classified information obtained from a foreign government or military force through the "processes of communications intelligence." The Espionage Act also broadly makes it a crime for any unauthorized person either to communicate to another, or to retain possession of "information relating to national defense" if there is "reason to believe" the information could harm the U.S. or help a foreign nation or military force.

In the decades since the statute was enacted, there has never been a prosecution of a news organization for violating the Espionage Act, but there has been saber-rattling from time to time. In December 2010, for example, Sen. Joseph Lieberman publicly called upon the Justice Department to investigate whether The New York Times had violated the Espionage Act by publishing confidential U.S. diplomatic cables it had obtained from WikiLeaks. And, in June 2013, Rep. Peter King, chairman of the House Subcommittee on Counterterrorism, repeatedly called for the prosecution of journalists who "severely compromise national security," singling out Glenn Greenwald, then a journalist for The Guardian, for publishing news reports based on the documents leaked by Edward Snowden. The application of the Espionage Act to a news organization would raise significant First Amendment issues and might well run afoul of the doctrine barring application of criminal sanctions against the press for publishing truthful information on matters of public concern. It would also raise a number of significant issues, including the propriety of the classification of the information at issue; the vagueness and breadth of the statute when applied to the press; and the lack of the meaning of "harm" to our national security and the burden of proving it.

Given the continuing uncertainty surrounding the Espionage Act, special care should be taken before accepting or communicating information known to be classified, and legal guidance sought where appropriate. Because the act is not literally limited to "classified" information, special care should be taken with any nonpublic information concerning official intelligence activities or communications with foreign governments.

In order to avoid exposure for possible conspiracy and "aiding and abetting" liability or both, it is also important to maintain a traditional source-news organization relationship with those individuals who may provide you with national security information, although this is no guarantee of immunity from prosecution.

In 2011, as part of a national security leak investigation, the Justice Department obtained a search warrant for the email of a Fox News reporter who allegedly obtained classified information from a State Department source. In applying for the warrant, the department told the court that the reporter had asked the source to disclose newsworthy information he knew to be classified, and asserted that in doing so the reporter was aiding and abetting a violation of the Espionage Act.

When the search warrant application was made public months later, a firestorm erupted over the assertion that a reporter had committed a crime simply by asking for information. Attorney General Holder subsequently acknowledged that the department had never intended to prosecute the reporter and had over-stepped its bounds in making the allegation of criminality. Holder vowed that no reporter would go to jail for "engaging in journalism" so long as he was attorney general. Holder then revised the departmental guidelines to prevent a search warrant from being sought for a reporter's records unless the reporter is indeed the target of an active criminal investigation. Holder's successor, Loretta Lynch, indicated that she would stand by his policy of not jailing journalists for doing their jobs. The Trump administration's position in this regard is uncertain, though Attorney General Jeff Sessions has declined to "make a blanket commitment" endorsing the prior approach.

LEGAL PRINCIPLES OF PUBLICATION

When a news report is published, the nature of its content poses three principal legal risks to a journalist: that the report contains incorrect information that harms someone's reputation, contains correct information that invades someone's privacy, or contains material that is subject to someone else's copyright. This section provides an overview of the law of defamation, privacy and copyright infringement, by examining what a plaintiff is required to prove against news organizations to succeed on such claims and the defenses that are available.

Defamation

In 1967, shortly after *New York Times v. Sullivan* was handed down, Associate Justice John Harlan remarked that "the law of libel has changed substantially since the early days of the Republic." Unfortunately, the news stories that still generate the most claims of injury to reputation — the basis of libel — are still the run-of-the-mill.

Perhaps 95 of 100 libel suits result from the routine publication of charges of crime, immorality, incompetence or inefficiency. A Harvard Nieman report makes the point: "The gee-whiz, slam-bang stories usually aren't the ones that generate libel, but the innocent-appearing, potentially treacherous minor yarns from police courts and traffic cases, from routine meetings and from business reports."

Most lawsuits based on relatively minor stories result from factual error or inexact language — for example, getting the plea wrong or inaccurately making it appear that all defendants in a case face identical charges. Libel even lurks in such innocent-appearing stories as birth notices and wedding announcements. Turner Catledge, former managing editor of The New York Times, noted in his autobiography, "My Life and the Times," that people sometimes would "call in the engagement of two people who hate each other, as a practical joke." The fact that some New York newspapers have had to defend suits for such announcements illustrates the care and concern required in every editorial department.

In publishing, no matter what level of constitutional protection, there is just no substitute for accuracy.

— What is libel?

Libel is one side of the coin called "defamation," slander being the flip side. At its most basic, defamation means injury to reputation. Libel is generally distinguished from slander, in that a libel is written, or otherwise printed, whereas a slander is spoken. While defamation published in a newspaper universally is regarded as libel, it is perhaps not so self-evident that, in many states, defamation broadcast by television or radio also is considered libel, rather than slander: Because broadcast defamation is often recorded on tape and carried to a wide audience, it is viewed as more dangerous to reputation than a fleeting, unrecorded conversation, and so is classed with printed defamation. In any case, the term defamation generally includes both libel and slander. Words, pictures, cartoons, photo captions and headlines can all give rise to a claim for defamation.

The various states define libel somewhat differently, but largely to the same effect. In Illinois, for example, libel is defined by the courts as "the publication of anything injurious to the good name or reputation of another, or which tends to bring him into disrepute." In New York, a libelous statement is one that tends to expose a person to hatred, contempt or aversion or to induce an evil or unsavory opinion of the person in the minds of a substantial number of people in the community.

In Texas, libel is defined by statute as anything that "tends to injure a living person's reputation and thereby expose the person to public hatred, contempt or ridicule, or financial injury or to impeach any person's honesty, integrity, virtue, or reputation or to publish the natural defects of anyone and thereby expose the person to public hatred, ridicule, or financial injury."

— Liability for republication: the 'conduit' fallacy

A common misconception is that one who directly quotes a statement containing libelous allegations is immune from suit so long as the quoted statement was actually made, accurately transcribed and clearly attributed to the original speaker. This is not so. In fact, the common law principle is just the opposite — a republisher of a libel is generally considered just as responsible for the libel as the original speaker. That you were simply an accurate conduit for the statement of another is no defense to a libel claim.

In many circumstances, therefore, a newspaper can be called to task for republishing a libelous statement made by someone quoted in a story. This rule can lead to harsh results and therefore exceptions exist. For example, reporting the fact that a plaintiff has filed a libel suit against a defendant could, in certain circumstances, lead to a claim against a newspaper for repeating the libel alleged in the complaint. In most states, a "fair report privilege" shields the publisher of an accurate and impartial report of the contents of legal papers filed in court to avoid this result.

Many states also recognize that newspapers under the pressure of daily deadlines often rely on the research of other reputable news organizations in republishing news items originally appearing elsewhere. In such cases, reliance on a reputable newspaper or news agency often is recognized as a defense to a libel claim. Of course, this so-called "wire service defense" may not be available if the republisher had or should have had substantial reason to question the accuracy or good faith of the original story.

The fair report privilege and the wire service defense are exceptions to the basic rule. When the press reports that X has leveled accusations against Y, the press may be held to account not only for the truth of the fact that the accusations were made, but also for the steps taken to verify the truth of the accusations. Therefore, when accusations are made against a person, it generally is prudent to investigate their truth as well as to obtain balancing comment with some relation to the original charges. Irrelevant countercharges can lead to problems with the person who made the first accusation.

In short, always bear in mind that a newspaper can be held responsible in defamation for republishing the libelous statement made by another, even when the quote is correct.

— The five things a successful libel plaintiff must prove

Although the terminology may differ from state to state, a libel plaintiff suing a reporter or a news organization will have to prove five things in order to prevail on a claim for defamation:

1. A defamatory statement was made.
2. The defamatory statement is a matter of fact, not opinion.
3. The defamatory statement is false.
4. The defamatory statement is about ("of and concerning") the plaintiff.
5. The defamatory statement was published with the requisite degree of "fault."

By developing an understanding of the legal elements of a claim for libel, reporters and editors can fashion guideposts that will assist them in practicing their craft in a way that avoids wrongfully injuring the reputation of the subjects of their stories — and thereby reducing the legal risk to the publications for which they write.

1. A defamatory statement was made

It may seem self-evident that a libel claim cannot exist unless a defamatory statement was made, but subjects of news stories (and their lawyers) often bring claims for libel without being able to demonstrate that what was written about them is capable of conveying a defamatory meaning. Put differently, not every negative news report is defamatory.

Generally, statements accusing someone of being a criminal, an adulterer, insane or infected with a loathsome disease are considered automatically "capable of defamatory meaning," as are statements that injure someone's professional reputation (such as that they are corrupt or incompetent). However, to determine whether any particular statement is susceptible of defamatory meaning, reference must be made, first, to the definition of libel adopted in the relevant state, and second, to the full context in which the challenged statement appeared when it was published.

For example, a New York court found that a statement identifying an attorney as a "flashy entertainment lawyer" was not, without more, defamatory, although a statement that a lawyer was an "ambulance chaser" with an interest only in "slam dunk" cases would be. The reasoning is that the first statement would not necessarily damage a lawyer's reputation, while the latter would. Likewise, in New York, allegations of drunkenness, use of "political clout" to gain governmental benefit, membership in the "Mafia," communist affiliation or that someone has cancer may or may not be defamatory, depending on the circumstances of the case.

In Illinois, courts make determinations about defamatory meaning on a case-by-case basis, though in Illinois, most statements will not be considered defamatory unless they charge a person with commission of a crime, adultery/fornication, or incompetence or lack of integrity in their business or profession. Under this approach, the statement that plaintiff left his children home at night and lost his job because of drinking was held to be defamatory as an accusation of child neglect and inability to discharge the duties of his job due to alcoholism. Similarly, reporting that an alderman had disclosed confidential information was held to be defamatory as indicating that the official lacked the integrity to properly discharge the duties of his office.

In Texas, a statement may be false, abusive and unpleasant without being defamatory. For example, a Texas court held that describing someone as resembling a "hard boiled egg," referring to baldness and pudginess, was not defamatory. Likewise, describing a political candidate as a "radical," "backed and financed by big-shot labor bosses" was not considered defamatory in Texas. On the other hand, an insinuation that a person is connected with gambling and prostitution was found to be defamatory. The assertion that a person who had made an allegation against another of child molestation had fabricated and since recanted the allegation was defamatory when no recantation had, in fact, been made.

While each potentially defamatory statement must be assessed in its own context, particular caution is in order where the statement involves allegations of crime or similar wrongdoing, incompetence or unprofessionalism, or infidelity.

2. The defamatory statement is a matter of fact, not opinion

To be actionable as libel, a defamatory statement must be provably false (or carry a provably false implication). Stated differently, only factual statements that are capable of being proven true or false can form the basis of a libel claim. "Opinions" that do not include or imply provably false facts cannot be the basis of a libel claim. Similarly, epithets, satire, parody and hyperbole that are incapable of being proven true or false are protected forms of expression.

The Supreme Court, in *Gertz v. Robert Welch Inc.* (1974), recognized a constitutional dimension to the prohibition of libel claims based on opinion, stating that "there is no such thing as a false idea." In a later case, *Milkovich v. Lorain Journal Co.* (1990), the Supreme Court denied that there is a distinct constitutional "opinion privilege," but held that any claim for libel must be based on a statement of fact that is provably false, thus shielding purely subjective opinions from liability. Under this approach, a statement is not protected "opinion" merely because it contains qualifying language such as "I think" or "I believe," if what follows contains an assertion of fact that can be proven true or false (e.g., "I believe he murdered his wife.").

Some examples of actual cases can provide a better sense of the distinction between an actionable false fact and a protected opinion:

In Virginia, "pure expressions of opinion" cannot be the basis of a claim for defamation. Under this standard, the statement "I wouldn't trust him as far as I could throw him" and the caption "Director of Butt-Licking" were held to be nonactionable opinion. The Virginia Supreme Court has found words charging that an architect lacked experience and charged excessive fees, or accusing a charitable foundation with failing to spend a "reasonable portion" of its income on program services, also to be protected opinions rather than to be verifiable facts.

In New York, the test for distinguishing a fact from an opinion asks whether: (1) the statement has a precise core of meaning on which a consensus of understanding exists; (2) the statement is verifiable; (3) the textual context of the statement would cause an average reader to infer a factual meaning; and (4) the broader social context signals usage as either fact or opinion. The first two factors focus on the meaning of the words used, the latter two factors consider whether the content, tone and apparent purpose of the statement should signal to the reader that the statement reflects the author's opinion.

Under these principles, calling a doctor a "rotten apple," for example, is incapable of being proved true or false and is therefore protected as an expression of opinion. Similarly, a statement that someone lacked "talent, ambition, initiative" is a nonactionable expression of opinion, since there is no provable, common understanding of what quantum of talent or ambition constitutes a "lack." In one New York case, a letter to the editor published in a scientific journal submitted by the International Primate Protection League and which warned that a multinational corporation's plans for establishing facilities to conduct hepatitis research using chimpanzees could spread hepatitis to the rest of the chimpanzee population was, given its overall context, protected as opinion.

Even when a fact is implicit in an opinion, the common law often protects the statement from liability. In many states, a statement of opinion based on true facts that are themselves accurately set forth is not actionable. Where the facts underlying the opinion are reported inaccurately, however, and would adversely affect the conclusion drawn by the average reader concerning the opinion expressed, the publication may give rise to a claim for libel. For example, the statement, "I believe he murdered his wife because he was found with a bottle of the same kind of poison that killed her," likely would not be actionable even if the plaintiff could prove he did not murder his wife *if* it is true that he was found with a bottle of the same kind of poison that killed her. The true facts on which the (erroneous) opinion was based were disclosed to the readers. If there was no bottle of poison, however, the suggestion that he was a murderer would certainly be actionable. If an opinion suggests or appears to rely on an undisclosed fact, however, a libel claim may still be brought upon the unstated, implied facts if they are both false and defamatory.

The statement that a sports commentator was a "liar" without reference to specific facts, under this approach, was considered to be protected opinion. Taken in the total context of an article, the statement that the plaintiff was a "neo-Nazi" was protected as opinion. Likewise, a statement calling a plaintiff a "commie," suggesting that he does not understand the subject he teaches and that he is "not traveling with a full set of luggage," was also protected as opinion. Statements accusing doctors of being "cancer con-artists," of practicing "medical quackery," and of promoting "snake oil remedies," were also protected. A newspaper column and editorial characterizing a nudist pageant as "pornography" and as "immoral" were also protected.

One federal appeals court has held that three questions should be considered to distinguish opinion from fact: (1) does the statement use figurative or hyperbolic language that would negate the impression that the statement is serious? (2) does the general tenor of the statement negate the impression that the statement is serious? (3) can the statement be proved true or false?

Under this test, a commentator's statement that a product "didn't work" was not an opinion because, despite the humorous tenor of the comment, it did not use figurative or hyperbolic language, it could reasonably be understood as asserting an objective fact and the fact could be proven true or false. Likewise, a statement made in a newspaper interview that plaintiff was an "extortionist" was not protected as opinion.

The common thread to these variations is that opinions offered in a context presenting the facts on which they are based will generally not be actionable. On the other hand, opinions that imply the existence of undisclosed, defamatory facts (i.e., if you knew what I know) are more likely to be actionable. In addition, a statement that is capable of being proven true or false, regardless of whether it is expressed as an opinion, an exaggeration or hyperbole, may be actionable.

3. The defamatory statement is false

In almost all libel cases involving news organizations, the plaintiff has the burden of proving that the defamatory statement is false. (The states are divided on whether a purely private individual has to prove falsity when the defamatory statement does not involve a matter of public concern.) Nonetheless, as a practical matter, a libel defendant's best defense is often to prove that the statement is true. While this may sound like six-of-one-half-dozen-of-the-other, there is considerable significance to placing on the plaintiff the legal burden of proving falsity: Where a jury feels it cannot decide whether a statement is true or false because the evidence is mixed, it is required to rule against the plaintiff — ties go to the defendant.

In almost all states, the question is not whether the challenged statement is literally and absolutely true, in every jot and tittle, but whether the statement as published is "substantially true." That is, a court will consider whether the gist or sting of the defamatory statement is accurate, or whether the published statement would produce a different effect in the mind of a reader than would the absolutely true version.

For example, most courts will dismiss a libel claim brought by a person charged with second degree burglary, if a newspaper mistakenly reported that he had been charged with first-degree burglary: The gist of the story (that the man is an accused burglar) is true, and most readers would not form a better opinion of the man had they been correctly informed that it was only second degree burglary with which he had been charged. But, where a newspaper mistakenly reports that the accused burglar has been charged with murder (or that a person thus far only accused of murder has been convicted of it), a court might well conclude that the "sting" of the statement is not substantially accurate, and that readers would think less of the person based on the false statement than they would have had the published report been accurate.

4. The defamatory statement is about the plaintiff

Since the law of libel protects the reputation of an individual or a business entity, only the individual or entity whose reputation has been injured is entitled to complain. Thus, a libel plaintiff must prove that the defamatory statement was "of and concerning" the plaintiff. It often is obvious whether a statement is about a particular person (for example, because it gives his or her full name, place of residence and age). But even where no name is used, a libel claim may be brought if some readers would reasonably understand the statement to be about the plaintiff. For example, the statement referring to "the woman who cooks lunch at the diner," when there is only one woman who cooks at that diner, will be considered "of and concerning" the female cook.

In a recent Illinois case, a news report on the commencement of a murder trial referred to the defendant as "suburban car dealer John Doe." While "John Doe" was indeed on trial for murder, he was not a suburban car dealer. His brother, "Joe Doe," was a suburban car dealer, but was not on trial for murder. The court concluded that reasonable readers could have understood the report to be about Joe (despite the fact that Joe's name was never mentioned, while John's was correctly used), and that Joe therefore would have the opportunity to show the statement was understood to be "of and concerning" him.

A few words about "group libel." Where a statement impugns a group of persons, but no individual is specifically identified, no member of the group may sue for libel if the group is large. For example, the statement, in a large city, that "all cab drivers cheat their customers out of money," does not allow any cab driver to sue for libel as a result, no matter how many fares the plaintiff cab driver may have lost because of the published statement. But, beware of publishing the same statement in a newspaper in a town with only a handful of cab drivers, where a court might well conclude the readers would reasonably think the statement was specifically referring to each of the town's four cab drivers, despite the absence of their names in the statement. Some courts have questioned whether the First Amendment permits claims for group libel under any circumstances, because the Supreme Court has said that the requirement that the statement be "of and concerning" the plaintiff is constitutionally required.

In this regard, it is worth noting, most courts have held that a statement about a company is not, without more, "of and concerning" its officers, directors or employees (provided it is not a sole proprietorship). By the same token, a statement about a CEO or other corporate official is not, without more, "of and concerning" the company itself.

Finally, a word about the dead: It is mostly correct that you cannot defame the dead. Again, because libel protects personal reputation, and one has no practical need for a good personal reputation in this world after one has departed it, most states do not permit a person's survivors to bring a claim for statements made after the person's death.

5. The defamatory statement was published with the requisite degree of fault

For almost 200 years, libel in this country was a tort of strict liability. It did not matter whether the defendant was at fault or had acted in some improper way. The mere fact that a libel was printed was sufficient to establish liability

New York Times v. Sullivan changed everything. In that case the Supreme Court first recognized the constitutional requirement that a public official must demonstrate not only that an error was made, but also a high degree of fault by the publisher in order to prevail on a libel claim. Somewhat confusingly referred to as "actual malice," what such a plaintiff is required to prove is that the defendant published a "calculated falsehood" — that is, that the defendant knew the statement was false when published, or published the statement despite having a high degree of awareness that it probably was false (the latter is sometimes called "reckless disregard" for the truth). This additional burden was required under the First Amendment, the court said, in order to provide the "breathing room" for the exercise of free speech that is essential to public discussion by citizens on matters concerning their self-government.

The court considered the *Sullivan* case "against the background of a profound national commitment to the principle that debate on public issues should be uninhibited, robust and wide-open, and that it may well include vehement, caustic and sometimes unpleasantly sharp attacks on government and public officials."

The ruling in *Sullivan* with respect to libel claims by public officials was extended three years later to libel claims by public figures, in *The Associated Press v. Walker*. The court reversed a $500,000 libel judgment won by former Maj. Gen. Edwin A. Walker in a Texas state court against the AP, after it had reported that Walker "assumed command" of rioters at the University of Mississippi and "led a charge of students against federal marshals" when James H. Meredith was admitted to the university in September 1962. Walker alleged those statements to be false.

In ruling for the AP, the Supreme Court found: "Under any reasoning, Gen. Walker was a public man in whose public conduct society and the press had a legitimate and substantial interest." It therefore held that Walker, too, was required to prove higher fault by the publisher even though he was not a public official.

The rulings in the *Sullivan* and *Walker* cases were landmark decisions for freedom of the press and speech. They established safeguards not previously defined, but they did not provide news organizations with absolute immunity against libel suits by officials who are criticized. Rather, they stand for the principle that, to encourage public debate on matters of public concern, when a newspaper publishes information about a public official or public figure and publishes it without "actual malice," it should be spared a damage suit even if some of the information turns out to be wrong.

The *Walker* decision made an additional important distinction concerning the context in which an article is prepared. In a companion case consolidated before the Supreme Court, Wallace Butts, former athletic director of the University of Georgia, had obtained a libel verdict against Curtis Publishing Co. His suit was based on an article in the Saturday Evening Post accusing Butts of giving his football team's strategy secrets to an opposing coach prior to a game between the two schools.

The Supreme Court found that Butts was a public figure, but said there was a substantial difference between the two cases. Unlike the AP report on the actions of Walker, "the Butts story was in no sense 'hot news' and the editors of the magazine recognized the need for a thorough investigation of the serious charges. Elementary precautions were, nevertheless, ignored."

Chief Justice Earl Warren, in a concurring opinion, referred to "slipshod and sketchy investigatory techniques employed to check the veracity of the source" in the Butts case. He said the evidence disclosed "reckless disregard for the truth."

The differing outcomes against The Associated Press and the Saturday Evening Post should be noted carefully. Although both involved public figures who were required to establish "actual malice," the evidence sufficient to make this showing differed in the context of a "hot news" report from investigative reporting.

By 1974, in *Gertz v. Robert Welch, Inc.*, the Supreme Court had extended the requirement that a libel plaintiff show some fault on the part of the defendant to include all defamation claims against news organizations, although not all types of plaintiffs must show the highest degree of fault. The level of "fault" that a plaintiff must prove will vary depending on who the plaintiff is.

— Fault required for public officials and public figures

If the plaintiff is a public official or public figure, the plaintiff must establish by clear and convincing evidence that the publication was made with "actual malice," which, as noted, is an unfortunate choice of phrase by the Supreme Court for a concept that might better have been called "constitutional fault," since the standard has little to do with whether a reporter harbored spite or ill will against the plaintiff.

The first type of actual malice, "knowing falsity," is easy to understand. "Reckless disregard" has required further elaboration by the courts, the best description of which perhaps is publication of a statement "with a high degree of awareness of its probable falsity." Put differently, a reporter may act with reckless disregard for truth if he or she publishes despite holding serious doubts about the truth of the published statement.

The test for actual malice thus looks to the subjective state of mind of the reporter/publisher at the time of publication. It inquires into whether the reporter or publisher believed the statement was false or whether he/she proceeded to publish despite recognizing that there was a good chance that the statement was false. Because most reporters and publishers are not in the business of publishing news reports unless they have good grounds to believe them to be true, generally speaking, it is difficult for a plaintiff to show that a newspaper published a story with actual malice.

As one Illinois court phrased it, actual malice is shown only when a reporter's investigation "has revealed either insufficient information to support the allegations in good faith or information which creates substantial doubt as to the truth of published allegations."

Thus, as interpreted by most states, "actual malice" cannot be proven simply by showing that a reporter made mistakes (either by getting facts wrong or by failing to talk to one or more key sources), or that the reporter disliked the plaintiff, or that the newspaper frequently published items critical of the plaintiff. Rather, the test focuses on whether the reporter in fact disbelieved, or strongly doubted the truth of, the published statement. In some cases, plaintiffs may establish actual malice if they can show that a reporter willfully turned a blind eye to the truth and, if acting in good faith, would have known that the statement was false.

— Fault required for private individuals

Under the First Amendment, even private individuals must show some degree of fault before they can recover for a libel by a news organization in a report on a matter of public concern. States are free to set the standard of care that must be met in reporting on private individuals, so long as they require at least a showing of negligence.

A number of states have decided to adopt the minimum standard and require a private libel plaintiff to show only that a reporter was negligent. That means the plaintiff must show that the reporter's conduct was less careful than one would expect of a reasonable journalist in similar circumstances. In Texas and California, for example, the question in a private figure libel case is whether the defendant should have known, through the exercise of reasonable care, that a statement was false.

The courts have looked at a number of factors to evaluate whether "negligence" exists. The considerations include:

— Did the reporter follow the standards of investigation and reporting ordinarily adhered to by responsible publishers? In many libel cases plaintiffs will use "expert" witnesses to testify about what are the "acceptable journalistic practices."

— Did the reporter follow his or her own normal procedures? Any time that you do something differently from what you usually do in reporting a story — particularly if the change involves exercising less care, rather than more care — you had better have a good explanation for why that was done.

— Did the reporter have any reason to doubt the accuracy of a source, or any advance warning that the story might not be right? Was it possible to find out the truth? This — like many of the factors the courts consider — is a matter of common sense. If you have received information that just does not ring true to you, and it is something that is easily checked, check it out before you run with the story!

— How *much* did the reporter do to check out the facts? Did the reporter take steps to confirm the information received, or simply run with the story without verifying the facts?

— Who are your sources of information? Are they reliable, and objective — or known "flakes" or people with a clear ax to grind? Are they anonymous sources? How many independent sources do you have (and how do they know the information they are giving you)?

Some courts set different fault levels for private figures depending on whether the publication at issue involved a matter of "public concern" or of "private concern." New York, for example, has held that if the plaintiff is a private individual involved in a matter of legitimate public concern, the plaintiff must establish by a preponderance of the evidence that the publication was made in a "grossly irresponsible" manner without due regard for the standards of information gathering and dissemination ordinarily followed by responsible parties involving similar matters. In cases involving matters of private concern,

New York, too, applies a negligence standard, although New York courts typically defer to the press in determining what constitutes a matter of "public concern" (and thus the vast majority of New York private figure cases apply the "gross irresponsibility" standard).

— Who is who?

Needless to say, being able to determine whether the subject of a news story is a public official or figure or a private figure bears directly on the amount of legal risk posed by the story.

While it is clear that not every government employee will be considered a public official for purposes of what they must prove in a libel case, the Supreme Court has yet to lay down definitive standards. Thus, the definition varies somewhat from state to state.

In New York, public officials are those who are elected or appointed to office and who appear to have substantial responsibility for control over public and governmental affairs. Judges, police officers, state troopers and corrections officers have all been held to be public officials under this standard. Similarly, a public official is defined in California to be someone who has, or appears to the public to have, substantial responsibility for or control over the conduct of governmental affairs. In California, people found to be public officials have included a police officer, an assistant public defender and an assistant district attorney.

Texas, in contrast, looks to the following criteria as relevant to determine whether a libel plaintiff is a public official: (1) the public interest in the public position held by the plaintiff; (2) the authority possessed by the plaintiff to act on behalf of a government entity; (3) the amount of governmental funds controlled by the plaintiff; (4) the number of employees the official supervises; (5) the amount of contact between the plaintiff and the public, and (6) the extent to which the plaintiff acts in a representative capacity for the governmental entity or has any direct dealings with the government.

Under this standard, (1) a county sheriff; (2) a Child Protective Services specialist with authority to investigate charges of child abuse, remove children from their homes and place them in foster care; (3) an undercover narcotics agent employed by the state's law enforcement agency; (4) a ranking officer in charge of a narcotics squad of four men; (5) an individual who was a high school athletic director, head football coach and teacher; (6) an assistant regional administrator of a branch office of the Securities and Exchange Commission, and (7) a part-time city attorney have all been found to be public officials.

But under the same Texas test, the following people were found not to be public officials: (1) a high school teacher; (2) a prominent member of two private organizations affiliated with a state university; (3) a former special counsel for a court of inquiry into county fund management; (4) a court reporter, and (5) an appointed justice of the peace (where the article appeared in a city where plaintiff was not justice of the peace and did not refer to plaintiff's official capacity).

While, at least at higher ranks, it is relatively easy to identify public officials, both reporters and the courts have confronted substantial difficulty in the area of public figures, particularly in separating those who are merely socially or professionally prominent from those who, because of their influence over public matters, are properly considered public figures for libel purposes.

For example, the 1976 case of *Time v. Firestone* stemmed from Time magazine's account of the divorce of Russell and Mary Alice Firestone. The magazine said she had been divorced on grounds of "extreme cruelty and adultery." The court made no finding of adultery. She sued. The former Mrs. Firestone was a prominent social figure in Palm Beach, Florida, and held press conferences in the course of the divorce proceedings. Yet, the Supreme Court said she was not a public figure because "she did not assume any role of special prominence in the affairs of society, other than perhaps Palm Beach society, and she did not thrust herself to the forefront of any particular public controversy in order to influence resolution of the issues involved in it."

Similarly, Sen. William Proxmire of Wisconsin was sued for $8 million by Ronald Hutchinson, a research scientist who had received several public grants, including one for $50,000. Proxmire gave Hutchinson a "Golden Fleece" award, saying Hutchinson "has made a fortune from his monkeys and in the process made a monkey of the American taxpayer." The Supreme Court held in 1979 that, despite the receipt of substantial public funds, Hutchinson was not a public figure because he held no particular sway over the resolution of matters of public concern.

Note also the case of Ilya Wolston, who pleaded guilty in 1957 to criminal contempt for failing to appear before a grand jury investigating espionage. A book published in 1974 referred to these events. Wolston alleged that he had been libeled. In ruling on *Wolston v. Reader's Digest*, the Supreme Court said that he was not a public figure. The court said people convicted of crimes do not automatically become public figures. Wolston, the court said, was thrust into the public spotlight unwillingly, long after the events of public concern had ended.

At bottom, although the Supreme Court has yet to definitively resolve the issue, the point appears to be that public figures are those who seek the limelight, who inject themselves into public debate, and who seek to influence public opinion. A person who has widespread influence over public opinion on many matters may be deemed a "general purpose public figure" and required to prove actual malice no matter the subject of a particular allegedly defamatory statement. Oprah Winfrey is an example of someone who likely would be deemed a general purpose public figure.

A person who seeks to influence public opinion in only one area (such as, for example, by leading a campaign to enact animal rights legislation), however, may be deemed a "limited purpose public figure" and required to prove actual malice only with respect to allegedly defamatory statements about his or her animal rights activities. Limited purpose public figures have included: a prominent attorney; religious groups; a belly dancer; and a "stripper for God," among others.

Texas courts generally ask three questions in order to determine whether someone is a limited purpose public figure: (1) is the controversy truly a public controversy? (i.e., (a) are people talking about the controversy and (b) are people other than those immediately involved in the controversy likely to feel the impact of its resolution?); (2) does the plaintiff have more than a trivial or tangential role in the controversy?; (3) is the alleged defamation relevant to the plaintiff's participation in the controversy? Under this standard, an abortion protester on a public street in the vicinity of an abortion clinic was considered a limited purpose public figure, as was a zoologist who appeared on television shows and gave interviews on his controversial work.

On the other hand, a public school teacher whose participation in public controversy did not exceed that which she was required to do by school district regulations (except that she responded to media inquiries), was not a public figure in California. Similarly, a corporation which conducted a closeout sale for a landmark department store was not a public figure simply because it was doing business with a party to a controversy.

A note on corporations: In many states, the same standards that determine whether an individual is a public figure apply to corporations. Some states, however, conclude that corporations are always public figures, while others apply a narrower standard. For example, a British corporation that did not deal in consumer goods and had not received significant past publicity was a private figure for the purposes of a Texas libel claim.

In addition, a few lower courts have embraced the concept of an "involuntary public figure," in which an otherwise private person becomes a public figure by virtue of his or her having become drawn into a significant public controversy.

While this area of the law is freighted with subtleties to which lawyers and judges devote considerable energy, the practical bottom line is that, while public officials and public figures always bear a high burden of proof in making out a libel claim, where a news story concerns a private individual, whether involved in a matter of public concern or not, his or her burden is likely to be lower, perhaps much lower, if the story is wrong. Accordingly, there are more legal risks to publishing reports about private individuals (especially where the matter is not of legitimate public concern).

— Defenses commonly available to news organizations

Where a news story is written in such a way that a plaintiff might be able to prove all five of the elements of a libel, the law nevertheless affords defenses to news organizations in certain circumstances. Among the most prominent are the "fair comment privilege," the "fair and accurate report privilege," and the "neutral report privilege." They are referred to as privileges because, where properly invoked, a news organization is "privileged" to print what otherwise would be an actionable libel.

1. Fair comment

The fair comment (sometimes, "fair criticism") privilege long predates the opinion doctrine and continues, in most states, to exist as an independent matter of state law. The right of fair comment has been summarized as follows: "Everyone has a right to comment on matters of public interest and concern, provided they do so fairly and with an honest purpose. Such comments or criticism are not libelous, however severe in their terms, unless they are written maliciously. Thus it has been held that books, prints, pictures and statuary publicly exhibited, and the architecture of public buildings, and actors and exhibitors are all the legitimate subjects of newspapers' criticism, and such criticism fairly and honestly made is not libelous, however strong the terms of censure may be." (*Hoeppner v. Dunkirk Pr. Co.*, 1930.)

Some states, such as Texas, have recognized the fair comment privilege as a matter of statutory law. The Texas statute protects reasonable and fair comment or criticism of the official acts of public officials and of other matters of public concern when published for general information.

Not all states recognize this privilege, and the specifics of its application vary among the states that do recognize it. But where an otherwise potentially libelous story is important to the public interest, careful consideration of whether this privilege might protect publication of the report may be appropriate.

2. Fair and accurate report

Under this privilege, a fair and accurate report of a public proceeding (such as a city council hearing) or document (such as a pleading filed in court) generally cannot be the basis of a libel suit.

Pursuant to the Texas fair report statute, for example, the privilege applies to "a fair, true and impartial account" of: (a) judicial proceedings; (b) an official proceeding to administer the law; (c) all executive and legislative proceedings; and (d) the proceedings of public meetings dealing with public purposes. New York and several other states likewise have created the privilege by statute along similar lines; in some states, the privilege is a product of judge-made law.

In order to qualify for the privilege in the states that recognize it, the account must be both substantially accurate and fair. This does not mean the newspaper is required to publish a verbatim account of an official proceeding or the full text of a government document, but any abridgement or synopsis must be substantially accurate and fairly portrayed. Where it applies, the privilege relieves a news organization of responsibility for determining the underlying truth of the statements made by the participants in these contexts, precisely because the very fact that the comments were made in an official proceeding is newsworthy regardless of whether the statements are actually true.

Some jurisdictions require that, to be privileged, the report expressly identify the official proceeding or document being reported upon.

It bears emphasis that the privilege is limited to statements made in the contexts defined under state law, and it behooves reporters to learn the particulars of the privilege in the states in which they practice journalism.

Statements made by government officials outside of official proceedings (e.g., statements by police or a prosecutor or an attorney on the courthouse steps), or in documents that have not been officially made part of the government record (e.g., a draft pleading provided by a lawyer that has not yet been filed with the court) may or may not qualify as privileged, depending on what state you are in and on the circumstances in which the statements are made. Some states only extend the privilege to such out of court statements if made by specified top officials. At least one New York trial court, however, has applied this fair report privilege to a news report based on information provided "off the record" by police sources.

In New York and some other states, court rules provide that the papers filed in matrimonial actions are sealed and thus not open to inspection by the general public. It is not clear whether the fair report privilege will attach to publication of the contents of such papers, which by court rule, or order of the judge, are to be kept confidential.

In one case where this very situation arose, the vice president of a company filed a libel suit in New York alleging that he was fired because a newspaper published his wife's charges of infidelity set forth in divorce proceedings. The newspaper responded that its report was a true and fair account of court proceedings. The New York Court of Appeals rejected that argument on grounds that the law makes details of marital cases secret because spatting spouses frequently make unfounded charges.

The lesson of this case is that information gleaned from "confidential" court documents might not be covered under the fair report privilege. In such a case, the paper will be put to the test of proving that it made a reasonable effort to determine the truth of the allegations before publishing them.

Similarly, not all U.S. states recognize a privilege for reporting the contents of foreign government proceedings or documents, at least in part because, according to some courts, it is not clear that the records of foreign governmental entities are as reliable as the records of American governmental units.

There are other "traps" to be aware of when relying on this privilege. For example, statements made on the floor of convention sessions or from speakers' platforms organized by private organizations may not be privileged under the fair report privilege. Strictly speaking, conventions of private organizations are not "public and official proceedings" even though they may be forums for discussions of public questions.

Similarly, while statements made by a governor in the course of executive proceedings have absolute privilege for the speaker (even if false or defamatory), the press' privilege to report all such statements is not always absolute. For example, after a civil rights march, George Wallace, then governor of Alabama, appeared on a television show and said some of the marchers were members of communist and communist-front organizations. He gave some names, which newspapers carried. Some libel suits resulted.

3. Neutral reportage

Once viewed as a promising development in the law likely to spread across most states, the advancement of the neutral report privilege has not proceeded as once anticipated. Many states have declined to consider whether the privilege should exist, while others have rejected it outright (including in Pennsylvania in 2004). Where recognized, the neutral report privilege protects a fair, true and impartial account of newsworthy statements, regardless of whether the reporter knows or believes those statements to be true, if the statements have been made by prominent and typically responsible persons or organizations. The rationale is that some statements are newsworthy, and should receive public attention just because of who has made them.

Thus, for example, a news report concerning a statement by Michael Jordan concerning corruption in basketball, or by the NAACP regarding discrimination committed by a business, likely would be privileged as a neutral report, even if it should later turn out that Jordan or the NAACP were mistaken, since the mere leveling of charges by such prominent sources typically is of public concern.

Significantly, the privilege, where it exists, does not apply when the author of an article goes beyond reporting the fact the statements were made and espouses or adopts the charges as the author's own.

California is one of the few states to recognize the neutral report privilege.

There, the privilege is available when the plaintiff is a public figure, the defamatory statement is made by one who is a party to a public controversy and the publication is accurate and neutral. One California court applying the privilege found that a newspaper's account of an accusation that a police officer had improperly obtained a false confession to a crime from a person later released as innocent was not actionable where the newspaper also printed the officer's denial of the charge.

In some states, courts appear to have applied the principle without naming the privilege as such. In one 1997 case in Texas, for example, the court held that a story that accurately reported that parents of school children had accused a school teacher of physically threatening and verbally abusing their children was substantially true regardless of whether the parents' allegations themselves were accurate. More recently, in 2013, the Texas Supreme Court initially cast doubt on this line of cases, but then later clarified that it was not completely "foreclosing" the possibility that a news report, the sole purpose of which was to report allegations, could be tested for truth by examining whether it had accurately conveyed the allegations. Similarly, in Illinois, a federal appeals court in 2004 held that several stories that accurately reported that a charitable organization was the target of a federal investigation into terrorism funding were not actionable because the fact that the organization was under investigation was true, regardless of whether it was actually guilty of funding terrorism.

New York state courts do not recognize a privilege for neutral reportage, though a federal court in New York has actually found a neutral reportage privilege grounded in the U.S. Constitution. As the federal court described the neutral report privilege in that case, "when a responsible, prominent organization ... makes serious charges against a public figure, the First Amendment protects the accurate and disinterested reporting of those charges, regardless of the reporter's private views regarding their validity." (*Edwards v. National Audubon Society*, 1977.)

— *Summary of practical points*

Although every AP story is expected to be accurate and fair, stories that involve negative reports about individuals or companies warrant particular attention. When evaluating such a story, it usually is prudent to ask these questions:

1. Are any statements in the story capable of defamatory meaning? In this regard pay close attention to the use of certain "red flag" words that may sound more negative (and thereby more defamatory) than if a different, but similar, word had been chosen. Words such as "fraud," "crony," "linked," "suspicious" and "contaminated" may suggest or imply bad conduct or have criminal connotations (like: "connected" to the Mafia or organized crime). Careful editing can ensure that the facts get reported without the use of "buzz words" that may trigger a libel claim.

— Remember that the fact that police are questioning someone about a crime does not necessarily justify the label suspect. Witnesses are obviously also questioned about a crime.

2. Are those statements ones of fact (capable of being proven true or false), or protected as opinion, or simply rhetorical hyperbole that no reasonable reader would understand as a statement of fact?

3. Could someone reading the report reasonably understand it to be about a specific person, whether or not the person is actually named? Could readers understand it to be about more than one person – the person we intend, but also someone else?

— Remember to be careful of descriptive phrases that may give rise to cases of mistaken identity. A report that "an elderly janitor for a local school" was arrested could lead to suits from every elderly janitor in the school district.

4. Could you prove that the statements in question are true (and do so without violating promises to any confidential sources)?

5. If it turns out that you have the facts wrong, would a jury think you failed to do something that any reasonable journalist would have done to get it right?

6. Assuming there is some possibility that the first five questions could be answered in the plaintiff's favor, is there a privilege that nevertheless justifies proceeding to publish? For example, is the report a fair and accurate report of an official government proceeding or document?

— If a privilege applies, remember that the privilege does not remove the need for careful reporting and the use of editorial judgment. In many cases, courts have held that it is up to the jury to decide whether a particular publication was a fair and accurate report or whether there was "actual malice."

Headlines, photos and captions must be as accurate and objective as news stories. Remember that each of these elements of a story can also give rise to claims of libel.

— Document preservation and discovery

A 1979 Supreme Court ruling, *Herbert v. Lando*, has had a significant impact on what materials a libel plaintiff can compel a news organization to disclose. The case ruled that retired Army Lt. Col. Anthony Herbert, a Vietnam veteran, had the right to inquire into the editing process of a CBS "60 Minutes" segment, produced by Barry Lando, which provoked his suit. Herbert had claimed the right to do this so that he could establish actual malice.

The decision formalized and called attention to something that was at least implicit in *New York Times v. Sullivan*: that a plaintiff had the right to try to prove the press was reckless or even knew that what it was printing was a lie. How else could this be done except through inquiry about a reporter's or editor's state of mind?

Despite an admonition in *Herbert v. Lando* that lower courts should carefully monitor (and, if necessary, rein in) discovery in libel cases, reporters and publications involved in libel suits are often forced to expend significant time and resources on discovery concerning their newsgathering, writing and editing activities.

Different reporters follow different practices about retaining their notes. There are potential litigation advantages and disadvantages from following a policy of either keeping notes for a number of years or disposing of notes as soon as they are no longer needed for reporting. The best practice is the one that best advances a reporter's journalistic goals. Whatever practice you follow, however, should be followed uniformly. A difficult issue is presented in litigation if a reporter generally keeps notes, but just doesn't happen to have the notes for a disputed story. Similarly, a reporter who never keeps notes, but happens to save them for a story that ends in litigation, can send a message that the story posed some unique concerns. Adopt a policy and follow it consistently.

Of course, once a lawsuit arrives, no documents (including electronic files, notes, email messages and the like) should be destroyed or deleted, regardless of your usual practice. At that point any notes and drafts are potential evidence and their destruction, with knowledge of the lawsuit, may be illegal.

— Motions practice

If litigation arises, lawyers for a reporter will often seek to dispose of the claims without the necessity of a trial. A number of issues, such as whether a story is "of and concerning" the plaintiff or conveys the defamatory meaning alleged, can often be decided by a judge as a matter of law before any litigation discovery begins.

Courts also can impose "summary judgment" dismissing a case at any point when the evidence developed by the parties demonstrates that the plaintiff's claims are legally defective. A judge may not enter summary judgment if it rests on any facts in dispute. Only the jury may decide disputed issues of fact.

In a 1986 decision, *Anderson v. Liberty Lobby*, the Supreme Court held that summary judgment should be granted in libel actions against public officials and public figures unless the plaintiff can prove actual malice with "convincing clarity" or by "clear and convincing evidence." This rule further facilitates the dismissal of unmeritorious claims without the expense and burden of proceeding to trial.

Over the past twenty years, some states have gone one step further, enacting so-called anti-SLAPP statutes to bring to an end more expeditiously libel lawsuits involving issues of public concern that lack significant merit. The concept initially was to prevent baseless claims asserted by plaintiffs who did not hope to win the lawsuit, but who used litigation to intimidate and censor others. Prime examples were unscrupulous real estate developers seeking to silence opponents of a zoning variance, and others engaged in "strategic litigation against public participation." Anti-SLAPP statutes typically require a defamation plaintiff at the outset of a case to convince the court that reasonable grounds exist to believe a valid defamation claim exists, and they provide for an award of attorneys' fees to the defendant if the claim is found to be meritless. California has one of the broadest statutes, which applies its rules and procedures to any lawsuit challenging defendants for exercising their right of free speech "in connection with a public issue." The California law can be invoked in certain situations to strike lawsuits challenging news reports on public issues, and in recent years some other jurisdictions have adopted similar broad press protections.

— Trials and damages

The huge jury verdicts that sometimes occur in libel cases have caused much concern among legal commentators and the press. A number of remedies have been proposed, including statutory caps on both compensatory and punitive damages. A 1996 non-press Supreme Court case, holding that some excessive damage verdicts might violate the Constitution, holds out some possible promise of relief.

The Supreme Court addressed libel damages in *Gertz v. Robert Welch, Inc.*

(1974), and held that in private figure cases, where "actual malice" has not been proven, any award of damages must be supported by competent evidence, represent compensation only for actual damages, must not be "presumed," and must not be punitive. "Actual damages," however, may include compensation for injury to reputation and standing in the community, personal humiliation, and mental anguish and suffering — all items to which a jury assigns a dollar value. In cases where a plaintiff has proved "actual malice," he or she may also recover "presumed" and "punitive" damages.

While the First Amendment imposes severe restrictions on libel claims, and court rules encourage the dismissal of meritless cases at the earliest point, litigation can be a long, expensive, and disruptive process. The key to avoiding the distraction of litigation is always to remember AP's credo: Get it fast, but get it right.

— Invasion of privacy

The roots of the right of privacy are often traced to an article titled "The Right to Privacy" that appeared in the Harvard Law Review in 1890, and was co-authored by Louis D. Brandeis, who later became a Supreme Court justice. The article asserted that the press of the day was "overstepping in every direction the obvious bounds of propriety and decency," and urged courts to recognize a distinct cause of action that would protect the individual's "right of privacy." As a Supreme Court justice, Brandeis later wrote:

"The makers of our Constitution recognized the significance of man's spiritual nature, of his feelings and of his intellect. They knew that only a part of the pain, pleasure and satisfactions of life are to be found in material things. They sought to protect Americans in their beliefs, their thoughts, their emotions and their sensations. They conferred, as against the government, the right to be let alone — the most comprehensive of rights and the right most valued by civilized men." (*Olmstead v. United States*, Brandeis, J. dissenting.)

Over the following decades, legal commentators have vigorously debated the scope and nature of a cause of action for privacy, and identified four distinct forms of the "right of privacy:" (1) misappropriation of someone's name or likeness for a commercial purpose; (2) public disclosure of private facts; (3) unreasonable intrusion upon seclusion, and (4) false light in the public eye. In recent times, these causes of action have taken on significance to the press as plaintiffs have attempted to avoid the heavy burdens of proof placed on the libel plaintiff by alleging an invasion of a form of the right of privacy, instead.

The four distinct "branches" of the privacy tort each seek to protect a different aspect of an individual's privacy. The "intrusion" tort, which is discussed in more detail above, primarily seeks to protect against physical intrusions into a person's solitude or private affairs. The tort does not require publication of information for recovery, and it therefore is referred to as a "newsgathering tort." The other three branches of privacy all require publication of some information in order for the plaintiff to have a claim.

States vary widely both in terms of their acceptance of any of these right to privacy claims and in terms of the rules governing any such claims. Of the four forms of the "privacy" cause of action, New York only recognizes the claim for misappropriation of name or likeness for commercial purposes. Texas recognizes claims for intrusion upon seclusion, public disclosure of private facts and misappropriation of name or likeness for commercial purposes. The California state constitution expressly incorporates a right of privacy and California courts recognize all four forms of the right of privacy cause of action. Illinois courts also recognize all four privacy torts.

The right of privacy creates liability for the publication of facts that are true, and thus raises particular concerns under the First Amendment. In a number of contexts the Supreme Court has struck down rulings imposing liability for reporting information that was both true and newsworthy, but it has consistently declined to hold that the First Amendment always bars such liability altogether.

It can generally be said that when people become involved in a news event, voluntarily or involuntarily, they forfeit aspects of the right to privacy. A person somehow involved in a matter of legitimate public interest, even if not a bona fide spot news event, normally can be written about with safety. However, the same cannot be said about a story or picture that dredges up the sordid details of a person's past and has no current newsworthiness.

Paul P. Ashley, then president of the Washington State Bar Association, summarized the privacy concern for reporters at a meeting of the Associated Press Managing Editors association:

"The essence of the wrong will be found in crudity, in ruthless exploitation of the woes or other personal affairs of private individuals who have done nothing noteworthy and have not by design or misadventure been involved in an event which tosses them into an arena subject to public gaze."

— Publication of private facts

When most people speak of an "invasion of privacy," they have in mind the public disclosure of highly embarrassing private facts. In those states where such a claim is recognized, the elements of a cause of action generally include: (1) "publicity" given to private information, (2) that a reasonable person would find highly offensive, and (3) which is not of any legitimate public interest.

In some states the lack of "legitimate public interest" or lack of "newsworthiness" is an element of the tort, meaning it is a plaintiff's burden to prove. In others, this element is an affirmative defense and the defendant must show how the information was indeed a matter of legitimate public concern. In all cases, newsworthiness is a complete defense to the tort. The First Amendment bars a claim for the true and accurate disclosure of a private fact so long as the information is newsworthy.

The first element of the tort requires "publicity" given to private information. This requires some element of widespread disclosure to the general public, not simply a communication to a single person or small group of people. Conversely, facts that are already known to the general public cannot be the basis of a public disclosure claim, while facts known only to a small group can be.

For example, a California court allowed a privacy claim to be based upon the publication of a photograph of a Little League team in a national magazine to illustrate a story about the team's coach who had sexually abused some of the athletes. Although the photograph had been given to all the members of the team, the identities of the minors shown in the photograph were not known to a broader national audience. The court said their identities could therefore be considered "private" in the context of the story about sex abuse. Some courts have similarly ruled that a person who is recognizable in a picture of a crowd in a public place is not entitled to the right of privacy, but if the camera singled him out for no news-connected reason, then his privacy might be invaded.

The second element of the tort requires that the disclosure be "highly offensive" to a reasonable person. This factor goes to the embarrassing nature of the information itself. Reporting someone's age, for example, would not be highly offensive to a reasonable person, even if that information were not widely known. Reporting, over their objection, that someone was a victim of sexual abuse or suffered from an incurable disease might be.

Finally, no claim will lie if the information is newsworthy, or of legitimate public concern. Courts generally will defer to reporters and editors to determine what is "newsworthy," but the line is not always clear. Even in the context of a report on a plainly newsworthy topic, the disclosure of a highly embarrassing private fact may give rise to a claim for invasion of privacy if the facts are not logically related to the matter of public concern. For example, disclosure of the intimate sexual practices of a celebrity might support a claim for invasion of privacy if it were unrelated to any newsworthy report and amounted to prying into someone's life for its own sake.

Some examples can help to demonstrate the nature of this branch of the privacy tort:

— In a case against a Chicago newspaper, an Illinois trial court held that a mother had stated a cause of action for invasion of privacy when she alleged that she told the newspaper reporter that she did not want to make any public statement about her son's death and where the reporter nevertheless remained in the private hospital room with the mother, recorded her grief-stricken last words to her son and subsequently published a picture of the son's dead body and the mother's "last words" to her son.

— The unsavory incidents of the past of a former prostitute, who had been tried for murder, acquitted, married and lived a respectable life, were featured in a motion picture. She sued for invasion of privacy by public disclosure of private facts. The court ruled that the use of her name in the picture and the statement in advertisements that the story was taken from true incidents in her life violated her right to pursue and obtain happiness.

— Another example of spot news interest: A child was injured in an auto accident in Alabama. A newspaper took a picture of the scene before the child was removed and ran it. That was spot news. Twenty months later a magazine used the picture to illustrate an article. The magazine was sued for public disclosure of private facts and lost the case, the court ruling that 20 months after the accident the child was no longer "in the news."

— In another case, a newspaper photographer in search of a picture to illustrate a hot weather story took a picture of a woman sitting on her front porch. She wore a house dress, her hair in curlers, her feet in thong sandals. The picture was taken from a car parked across the street from the woman's home. She sued, charging invasion of privacy by intrusion upon seclusion and public disclosure of private facts. A court, denying the newspaper's motion for dismissal of the suit, said the scene photographed "was not a particularly newsworthy incident," and the limits of decency were exceeded by "surreptitious" taking and publishing of pictures "in an embarrassing pose."

— False light invasion of privacy

A claim for false light basically complains about publicity that places the plaintiff in a false light in the public eye. In those states that recognize this tort, the publicity must be of a kind that would be highly offensive to a reasonable person, and the defendant generally must have acted with the same level of fault that would be required if the plaintiff had filed a libel claim.

One form in which a claim for false light occasionally arises occurs when an opinion or utterance is falsely attributed to the plaintiff. In another version of the claim, the plaintiff's picture is used to illustrate an article to which he has no reasonable connection, as where the picture of an honest taxi driver is used to illustrate an article about the cheating propensities of cab drivers.

The Supreme Court of the United States ruled in 1967 that the constitutional guarantees of freedom of the press are applicable to claims for invasion-of-privacy by false light involving reports of newsworthy matters. *Time Inc. v. Hill* (1967). The ruling arose out of a reversal by the Supreme Court of a decision of a New York court that an article with photos in Life magazine reviewing a play, "The Desperate Hours," violated the privacy of a couple who had been held hostage in a real-life incident. In illustrating the article, Life posed the actors in the house where the real family had been held captive.

The family alleged violation of privacy by false light in the public eye, saying the article gave readers the false impression that the play was a true account of their experiences. Life said the article was "basically truthful."

The court said:

"We create grave risk of serious impairment of the indispensable service of a free press in a free society if we saddle the press with the impossible burden of verifying to a certainty the facts associated in a news article with a person's name, picture or portrait, particularly as related to non-defamatory matter."

The court added, however, that these constitutional guarantees do not extend to "knowing or reckless falsehood." A newspaper still may be liable for invasion of privacy if the facts of a story are changed deliberately or recklessly, or "fictionalized." As with The New York Times and The Associated Press decisions in the field of libel, "The Desperate Hours" case does not confer a license for defamatory statements or for reckless disregard of the truth.

An Illinois court allowed a "false light" claim to proceed where a news report allegedly broadcast the plaintiff's comments (which were covertly recorded) out of context. In a more famous case, a federal appeals court concluded that Gennifer Flowers could maintain a false light claim against James Carville for publishing facts suggesting she had lied about the nature of her relationship with President Bill Clinton. The court said the false light claim could compensate for emotional injury that would not be covered by a claim for defamation.

— Misappropriation

The final of the three "publication"-related forms of invasion of privacy recognized by the courts is misappropriation of the name or likeness of a living person for purposes of trade or advertising without that person's consent. In recent years, some states have included voice as well as name or likeness. This tort is intended to allow people to control the commercial use and exploitation of their own identities. The First Amendment provides for at least some exceptions to such a right — as where a candidate for public office includes his opponent's name and likeness in campaign advertisements.

The misappropriation tort is not generally a concern to reporters because it applies to the *commercial* exploitation of a person's name and likeness. It does not bar editorial uses and provides no remedy when a person's name or image (questions of copyright aside) is used in a news report. This branch of privacy is of little concern outside of the advertising department of a news organization.

— *Publishing on the internet and social media*

Content published on the internet in blogs, chat rooms, discussion groups, social media sites and the like is generally subject to the same rules and standards for libel, privacy and other legal actions as any print publication.

AP has adopted Social Media Guidelines that are intended to be followed by its employees. Those Guidelines require, among other things, that AP employees always "identify themselves as being from the AP if they are using [social networking site] accounts for work in any way." And, "if you or your department covers a subject . . . you have a special obligation to be even-handed in your tweets." The Guidelines also restrict AP employees from "declaring their views on contentious public issues in any public forum and must not take part in organized action in support of causes or movements."

The Guidelines say that it is acceptable to extend and accept Facebook friend requests from sources, politicians and newsmakers if necessary for reporting purposes, and to follow them on Twitter. "However, friending and 'liking' political candidates or causes may create a perception among people unfamiliar with the protocol of social networks that AP staffers are advocates. Therefore, staffers should try to make this kind of contact with figures on both sides of controversial issues. We should avoid interacting with newsmakers on their public pages — for instance, commenting on their posts."

AP employees are also cautioned to avoid retweeting in a way that makes it look like they are expressing a personal opinion on the issues of the day. "A retweet with no comment of your own can easily be seen as sign of approval of what you're relaying."

Because of the difficulty in verifying the authenticity of material posted on social media sites, it is important not simply to lift quotes, photos or video from social networking sites and attribute them to the domain or feed where the information was found. Before photos, videos or other online content is used, it is important to both verify its authenticity and ensure that any necessary rights for the reuse are obtained. (See discussion of Copyright, below).

Copyright infringement

Copyright is the right of an author to control the reproduction and use of any creative expression that has been fixed in tangible form, such as on paper or computer disk. The right of Congress to pass laws protecting copyright is itself protected in the Constitution, and the First Amendment is generally not a defense to a valid claim for copyright infringement under the Copyright Act.

The types of creative expression eligible for copyright protection include literary, graphic, photographic, audiovisual, electronic and musical works. In this context, "tangible forms" range from film to videotape to material posted on the internet. Personal letters or diaries may be protected by copyright even though they may not have been published and may not contain a copyright notice. Probably of greatest concern to reporters and editors are the copyrights in photographs and videos used to illustrate a news report.

A copyright comes into existence the moment an original work of expression is captured in a tangible form. No government approval or filing is required for a work to be protected by copyright. Upon creation of the work, ownership of the copyright in that work is vested in the "author" of a work — the person to whom the work owes its origin.

The owner will generally be the author of the work, or the photographer in the case of an image. Under certain circumstances, however, someone other than the person who actually created the work may be deemed to be the work's "author" and thereby own the copyright. Under the work made for hire doctrine, copyright ownership of a particular work vests with the employer of the author when the work is created by an employee who is acting within the scope of his or her employment.

The owner of a copyright is given the exclusive right to reproduce, distribute, display and prepare "derivative works" of the copyright material. These rights exist for the life of the author plus 70 years. In the case of a "work for hire" owned by a corporation, the right exists for 95 years from the first publication or 120 years from creation, whichever is shorter.

— Limitations on copyright

Not all uses of copyright material constitute infringement. The most important limitation on the reach of copyright law for journalists is that ideas and facts are never protected by a copyright. What is protected by the copyright law is the manner of expression. The copyright pertains only to the literary, musical, graphic or artistic form in which an author expresses intellectual concepts.

For example, an author's analysis or interpretation of events, the way the material is structured and the specific facts marshaled, the choice of particular words and the emphasis given to specific developments, may all be protected by copyright. The essence of a claim for copyright infringement lies not in taking a general theme or in covering specific events, but in appropriating particular expression through similarities of treatment, details, scenes, events and characterizations.

This printed page illustrates the distinction between protected expression and nonprotected ideas and facts. Despite the copyright protecting this page, a subsequent author is free to report any of the facts it contains. The subsequent author may not, however, employ the same or essentially the same combination of words, structure, and tone, which constitute the expression of those facts.

A second limitation on the reach of copyright is the doctrine of "fair use." This doctrine permits, in certain circumstances, the use of copyright material without its author's permission. Courts will invoke "fair use" when a rigid application of the copyright law would stifle the very creativity the law is designed to foster.

To determine whether a particular use is "fair" and hence permitted, courts are required to evaluate and balance such factors as: (1) the purpose of the use; (2) the nature of the copyrighted work that is being used; (3) the amount and substantiality of the portion used in relation to the copyrighted work as a whole; and (4) the effect of the use upon the potential value of the copyrighted work. Courts generally consider how "transformative" the use is. Uses that can be said to have transformed portions of the original work into something entirely new by "altering the first [work] with new expression, meaning or message" would factor in to a fair use finding. (See *Campbell v. Acuff-Rose Music Inc.*) Uses that merely supplant the work by presenting it essentially as it was in the original version tend not to be fair.

News reporting, criticism and comment are favored purposes under the fair-use doctrine, but "scooping" a copyright holder's first use of previously unpublished material is not. Note, though, that "purpose" is only one of the fair-use factors. Thus, a use for a proper purpose may nevertheless constitute an infringement if other factors weigh against that use being fair.

Here are some general guidelines to keep in mind when dealing with material written by others:
— Content created by the federal government is not protected by copyright, but content created by state and local governments may be. Works created for any level of government by a private contractor may be protected by copyright.
— The greater the amount of the copyrighted work used, the less likely that a court will characterize the use as fair. The amount of use alone, however, is not necessarily decisive; courts have found uses not to be fair when the portion used was small but so important that it went to the heart of the copyrighted work.
— Uses that decrease any potential market for the copyrighted work weigh against a finding of fairness. For instance, if a literary critic reproduces all five lines of a five-line poem, the potential market for the poem will be diminished because any reader of the critic's piece can also obtain a copy of the poem for free.

Reporters and editors having questions about whether their use in a news story or column of copyrighted material is a fair use should review these factors. No mathematical formula can yield the answer. Where there is a question as to whether a particular use is fair, consideration may be given to seeking permission (or a license) from the copyright owner.

If a use is not "fair" within the meaning of copyright law, it will be no defense to claim the use of the copyrighted material was newsworthy and therefore protected by the First Amendment. Moreover, proper attribution alone cannot transform an infringing use into a fair one.

In using copyrighted material in a news story or column, writers should make sure that no more of a copyrighted work than is necessary for a proper purpose is used, and that the work is not used in a way that impairs its value.

In this regard, many people who post material to the internet (photographs, descriptions of events they have witnessed, or other creative works) intend for people to copy and pass them along. It is important to remember, however, that, absent express permission, copying or distributing those works will constitute infringement of copyright unless the fair use doctrine applies. (It also may constitute breach of contract, since the terms of use of many social media sites contain restrictions on use that may be made of material posted there.) And it is often particularly difficult to determine who is the actual owner of the copyright in material posted on the internet, precisely because it is so often reproduced (or re-posted) by others. For these reasons, special care is required when considering the use of material posted by others to the web or on social media platforms.

The Associated Press statement of news values and principles

For more than 170 years, the people of The Associated Press have had the privilege of bringing news and information to the world. We have gone to great lengths, overcome great obstacles — and, too often, made great sacrifices — to ensure that the news was reported quickly, accurately and honestly, in a balanced and impartial way. Our efforts have been rewarded with trust: More than half the world's population sees AP news content on any given day.

In the 21st century, that news is transmitted in more ways than ever before — online and mobile, in print and on the air, in words, video, photographs, interactives, graphics, data and audio. No matter the platform, we insist on the highest standards of integrity and ethical behavior as we gather and deliver the news.

We abhor inaccuracies, carelessness, bias or distortions. We will not knowingly introduce rumor or false information into material intended for publication or broadcast; nor will we distort visual content. Quotations must be accurate and precise. We preserve the appropriate professional distance from those we cover.

We always strive to identify all the sources of our information. We shield them with anonymity only when they insist upon it for a valid reason and when they provide vital information — not opinion or speculation; when there is no other way to obtain that information; and when we are confident the source is reliable and in a position to know. We don't plagiarize, and we respect copyright.

We avoid behavior or activities that could be perceived as a conflict of interest, that compromise our ability to report the news fairly and accurately, uninfluenced by any person or action.

We clearly identify advertising on our platforms, and keep AP commercial activities separate from our newsroom.

We don't misidentify or misrepresent ourselves to get a story. When we seek an interview, we identify ourselves as AP journalists. We balance the newsworthiness of a story with respect for privacy and safety interests when pursuing images.

We don't pay newsmakers for interviews, to take their photographs or to film or record them. We do not provide full lists of questions in advance or allow interview subjects to approve our text or images before publication.

We must be fair. Whenever we portray someone in a negative light, we must make a real effort to obtain a response from that person.

When mistakes are made, they must be corrected — fully, quickly, transparently and ungrudgingly.

Automatically produced content must be thoroughly checked and transparent, and the sources of data clearly identified.

It is the responsibility of every one of us to ensure that these standards are upheld. Any time a question is raised about any aspect of our work, it should be taken seriously.

* * *

The policies set forth in these pages are central to the AP's mission. Any failure to abide by them could result in disciplinary action, up to and including dismissal, depending on the gravity of the infraction.

ANONYMOUS SOURCES

Transparency is critical to our credibility with the public and our subscribers. Whenever possible, we pursue information on the record. When a newsmaker insists on background or off-the-record ground rules, we must adhere to a strict set of guidelines, enforced by AP news managers.

Under AP's rules, material from anonymous sources may be used only if:

1. The material is information and not opinion or speculation, and is vital to the report.

2. The information is not available except under the conditions of anonymity imposed by the source.

3. The source is reliable, and in a position to have direct knowledge of the information.

Reporters who intend to use material from anonymous sources must get approval from their news manager before sending the story to the desk. The manager is responsible for vetting the material and making sure it meets AP guidelines. The manager must know the identity of the source, and is obligated, like the reporter, to keep the source's identity confidential. Only after they are assured that the source material has been vetted by a manager should editors and producers allow it to be used.

Reporters should proceed with interviews on the assumption they are on the record. If the source wants to set conditions, these should be negotiated at the start of the interview. At the end of the interview, the reporter should try once again to move onto the record some or all of the information that was given on a background basis.

The AP routinely seeks and requires more than one source when sourcing is anonymous. Stories should be held while attempts are made to reach additional sources for confirmation or elaboration. In rare cases, one source will be sufficient — when material comes from an authoritative figure who provides information so detailed that there is no question of its accuracy.

We must explain in the story why the source requested anonymity. And, when it's relevant, we must describe the source's motive for disclosing the information. If the story hinges on documents, as opposed to interviews, the reporter must describe how the documents were obtained, at least to the extent possible.

The story also must provide attribution that establishes the source's credibility; simply quoting "a source" is not allowed. We should be as descriptive as possible: "according to top White House aides" or "a senior official in the British Foreign Office." The description of a source must never be altered without consulting the reporter.

We must not say that a person declined comment when that person is already quoted anonymously. And we should not attribute information to anonymous sources when it is obvious or well known. We should just state the information as fact.

Stories that use anonymous sources must carry a reporter's byline. If a reporter other than the bylined staffer contributes anonymous material to a story, that reporter should be given credit as a contributor to the story.

All complaints and questions about the authenticity or veracity of anonymous material — from inside or outside the AP — must be promptly brought to the news manager's attention.

Not everyone understands "off the record" or "on background" to mean the same things. Before any interview in which any degree of anonymity is expected, there should be a discussion in which the ground rules are set explicitly. These are the AP's definitions:

On the record. The information can be used with no caveats, quoting the source by name.

Off the record. The information cannot be used for publication.

Background. The information can be published but only under conditions negotiated with the source. Generally, the sources do not want their names published but will agree to a description of their position. AP reporters should object vigorously when a source wants to brief a group of reporters on background and try to persuade the source to put the briefing on the record.

Deep background. The information can be used but without attribution. The source does not want to be identified in any way, even on condition of anonymity.

In general, information obtained under any of these circumstances can be pursued with other sources to be placed on the record.

ANONYMOUS SOURCES IN MATERIAL FROM OTHER NEWS SOURCES

Reports from other news organizations based on anonymous sources require the most careful scrutiny when we consider them for our report.

AP's basic rules for anonymous source material apply to material from other news outlets just as they do in our own reporting: The material must be factual and obtainable no other way. The story must be truly significant and newsworthy. Use of anonymous material must be authorized by a manager. The story we produce must be balanced, and comment must be sought.

Further, before picking up such a story we must make a bona fide effort to get it on the record, or, at a minimum, confirm it through our own reporting. We shouldn't hesitate to hold the story if we have any doubts. If another outlet's anonymous material is ultimately used, it must be attributed to the originating news organization and note its description of the source.

ATTRIBUTION

Anything in the AP news report that could reasonably be disputed should be attributed. We should give the full name of a source and as much information as needed to identify the source and explain why the person is credible. Where appropriate, include a source's age; title; name of company, organization or government department; and hometown.

If we quote someone from a written document — a report, email or news release — we should say so. Information taken from the internet must be vetted according to our standards of accuracy and attributed to the original source. File, library or archive photos, audio or videos must be identified as such.

For lengthy stories, attribution can be contained in an extended editor's note detailing interviews, research and methodology.

AUDIO

AP's audio content always must be accurate. We do not alter or manipulate newsmaker actuality in any way, except as provided below:

With the permission of a manager, overly long pauses by news subjects may be shortened.

To make sound clearer, the AP does permit the use of subtle, standard audio processing methods: normalization of levels, general volume adjustments, equalization and reduction of extraneous sounds such as telephone line noise. AP permits fading in and out of the start and end of sound bites. However, the use of these methods must not conceal, obscure, remove or otherwise alter the content of the audio.

Bleeping is allowed, with a manager's permission, to cover obscenities when there is no option but to use a piece of audio containing an obscenity. An employee with questions about the use of such methods or the AP's requirements and limitations on audio editing should contact the desk supervisor prior to the transmission of any audio.

We don't use sound effects or substitute video or audio from one event to another. We do not "cheat" sound by adding audio to embellish or fabricate an event. A senior editor must be consulted prior to the introduction of any neutral sound (ambient sound that does not affect the editorial meaning but corrects a technical fault).

Voice reports by AP correspondents may be edited to remove pauses or stumbles.

BYLINES AND DATELINES

A dateline tells the reader where we obtained the basic information for a story. A byline tells the reader who wrote the story.

On short, unbylined stories (routine speeches, game stories, announcements, etc.), the dateline generally should reflect where the story took place. However, when a story is longer, contains multiple elements, has analytical material or occurs at a place that is difficult for reporters to access, the dateline should be where the staffer covering the story is located.

When a datelined story contains supplementary information obtained in another location — say, when an official in Washington comments on a disaster elsewhere — we should note it in the story. The dateline for video, photos or audio must be the location where the events depicted actually occurred. For voice work, the dateline must be the location from which the reporter is speaking; if that is not possible, the reporter should not use a dateline. If a reporter covers a story in one location but does a live report from another location, the dateline is the filing point.

For text stories with datelines, bylines may be used only if the journalist was in the datelined location. If a reporter in the field works with another staffer and both deserve bylines, the name of the staffer in the field normally goes first and a tag line gives each staffer's location. We give bylines in text stories to photographers, broadcast reporters and video journalists who provide information without which there would be no story.

For stories without datelines, the byline goes to the writer, with credit in a tag line to the reporters who contributed substantial information.

For staffers who do voice or on-camera work, we do not use pseudonyms or "air names." Any exceptions — for instance, if a staffer has been known professionally by an air name for some time — must be approved by a manager.

CONFLICTS OF INTEREST

The AP respects and encourages the rights of its employees to participate actively in civic, charitable, religious, public, social or neighborhood organizations.

However, AP employees must avoid behavior or activities that could create a conflict of interest or compromise our ability to report the news fairly and accurately, uninfluenced by any person or action.

Nothing in this policy is intended to abridge any rights provided by the National Labor Relations Act.

Here is a sampler of AP practices on questions involving possible conflict of interest. It is not all-inclusive; if you are unsure whether an activity may constitute a conflict or the appearance of a conflict, consult your manager at the onset.

Expressions of opinion

Those who work for the AP must be mindful that opinions they express may damage the AP's reputation as an unbiased source of news. They must refrain from declaring their views on contentious public issues in any public forum, whether through blogs, social networks, comments pages, petitions, bumper stickers or lapel buttons. They must not take part in demonstrations in support of causes or movements- or contribute to them in any way.

Favors

Employees must not ask news sources or others they meet in a professional capacity to extend jobs or other benefits to anyone. They also must not offer jobs, internships or any benefits of being an AP employee to news sources.

Financial interests

To avoid any conflict of interest or the appearance of any such conflict, AP employees must abide by the following rules and guidelines when making personal investment and financial decisions.

Inside information

All employees may not act upon, or inform any other person of, information gained in the course of AP employment, unless and until that information becomes known to the general public. Employees must comply with federal and local laws concerning securities and financial transactions, including those prohibiting actions based upon inside information.

Family investments

Employees are expected to make every effort to ensure that no spouse or other member of their household has investment or business interests that could pose a conflict of interest. Such a conflict may make it inappropriate for the employee to accept certain assignments. Employees must consult with their managers before accepting any such assignment.

Divestiture

Employees might be asked to divest or to suspend any activity involving their holdings. They will have one year from the date of request to do so.

For business reporters and editors

Employees who regularly write or edit business news must not own stock or have any personal financial investment or involvement with any company, enterprise or industry that they regularly cover for the AP. A technology writer, for example, must not own any technology equities.

New business staff members should immediately disclose such holdings to their manager or to HR. Staff members who are temporarily assigned to such coverage must immediately notify a manager of possible conflicts to determine whether the assignment is appropriate.

Writers and editors who cover the stock markets may not own stock in any individual company. They may invest in publicly available diversified mutual funds.

Business news employees must avoid speculative, short-term investment activities such as day-trading individual stocks or commodities.

Freelance work:

Individuals who seek to engage in non-AP work are subject to the following restrictions:
— Freelance work must not represent a conflict of interest for either the employee or the AP.
— Such activities may not interfere with the employees' job responsibilities, including availability for newsgathering.
— Such activities may not exploit the name of The Associated Press or the employee's position with the AP without permission of the AP.
— Employees who wish to use material they accumulated in their AP work - notes, stories (either written or broadcast), images, videotape, graphics - for other-than-AP uses must seek written AP approval, copyright clearance and a license to syndicate. This approval must be received prior to submission to any outside publisher, purchaser, organization or broadcaster, or to posting on websites or social networks.

Under no circumstances should the AP incur expenses for research material that is not used for AP purposes.

Free tickets

We do not accept free tickets to sports, entertainment or other events for anything other than coverage purposes. If we obtain tickets for a member or subscriber as a courtesy, they must be paid for, and the member or subscriber should reimburse the AP.

Gifts

Associated Press offices and staffers often are sent or offered gifts by sources, public relations agencies, corporations and others. Sometimes these are designed to encourage or influence AP news coverage or business; sometimes they are gift bags handed out routinely to journalists covering a particular event.

Whatever the intent, we cannot accept such items; an exception is made for trinkets like caps or mugs that have nominal value, approximately $25 or less. Otherwise, gifts should be politely refused and returned, or if that is impracticable, they should be given to charity.

Books, DVDs and other items received for review may be kept for a staff member's professional reference or donated to charities, but may not be sold or raffled off for personal gain. In cases where restrictions forbid transfer to third parties, these items should be discarded. Items of more than nominal value that are provided for testing, such as electronics, must be returned.

AP staff should pay their expenses at meals with news sources. When several journalists are invited to an event with news value, such as a dinner with a senior official, staff may accept so long as an effort is made to reciprocate with the official or a staff member.

AP and its employees may accept discounts from companies only if those discounts are standard and offered to other customers.

We do not accept unsolicited contest awards from non-journalistic organizations or any organization that has a policy or financial interest in our coverage; nor do we enter such contests.

The aim in all matters involving contests should be to underscore the AP's reputation for objectivity.

Official scorers

Employees may not serve as official scorers at sports events.

Outside appearances

Employees frequently appear on radio and TV news programs as panelists asking questions of newsmakers; such appearances are encouraged.

However, there is potential for conflict if staffers are asked to give their opinions on issues or personalities of the day. Advance discussion and clearance from a staffer's supervisor are required.

Employees may speak or teach at the invitation of news industry groups and educational institutions. The AP accepts reimbursement of expenses for such appearances if the event is one that AP would not routinely participate in. AP staffers may accept honoraria, with a supervisor's approval, for appearances and teaching that require substantial preparation. We do not normally accept honoraria for routine speeches and panel discussions. We avoid addressing, or accepting fees or expenses from governmental bodies; trade, lobbying or special interest groups; businesses, or labor groups; or any group that would pose a conflict of interest.

Political activities

Editorial employees are expected to be scrupulous in avoiding any political activity, whether they cover politics regularly or not. They may not run for political office or accept political appointment; nor may they perform public relations work for politicians or their groups. Under no circumstances should they donate money to political organizations or political campaigns. They should use great discretion in joining or making contributions to other organizations that may take political stands.

Non-editorial employees must refrain from political activity and contributions unless they obtain approval from a manager.

A supervisor must be informed when a spouse or other members of an employee's household have any ongoing involvement in political causes, either professionally or personally.

Trips

If a reporting trip is organized, and we think the trip is newsworthy, we go and pay our way. If we have a chance to interview a newsmaker on a charter or private jet, we reimburse the news source for the reasonable rate of the costs incurred — for example, standard airfare. There may be exceptional circumstances, such as a military trip, where it is difficult to make other travel arrangements or calculate the costs. Consult a manager for exceptions.

CORRECTIONS

Staffers must notify supervisory editors as soon as possible of serious errors or potential errors, whether in their work or that of a colleague. Every effort should be made to contact the staffer and supervisor before a correction is sent.

When we're wrong, we must say so as soon as possible. When we make a correction, we point it out both to subscriber editors (e.g. in Editor's notes, metadata, advisories to TV newsrooms) and in ways that news consumers can see it (bottom-of-story corrections, correction notes on graphics, photo captions, etc.)

A correction must always be labeled a correction. We do not use euphemisms such as "recasts," "fixes," "clarifies," "minor edits" or "changes" when correcting a factual error.

When we correct an error from a previous day, we ask subscribers that used the erroneous information to carry the correction as well.

For live broadcasts, we correct errors in the same newscast if at all possible. If not, we make a correction in the next appropriate live segment. Audio correspondent reports that contain factual errors are eliminated and, when possible, replaced with corrected reports.

DATA

Data for stories and visual presentations must be vetted for integrity and validity. Data should be assessed in terms of the methodology behind it, sample sizes, when it was collected and the availability of other data to confirm or challenge it.

Combining more than one dataset into a presentation should be done carefully and transparently. Avoid percentage and percent change comparisons from a small base, including raw numbers when appropriate for perspective.

We must distinguish carefully between correlations and causal relationships.

FABRICATIONS

Nothing in our news report — words, photos, graphics, sound or video — may be fabricated. We don't use pseudonyms (except for established literary names or noms de guerre, which should be identified as such), composite characters or fictional names, ages, places or dates.

We don't stage or re-enact events for the camera or microphone.

Virtual reality presentations must consist of real, unmanipulated imagery and sound.

GRAPHICS AND INTERACTIVES

We use only authoritative sources. We do not project, surmise or estimate in a graphic. We create work only from what we know. Except as authorized by a manager, we do not use graphics provided by others for which we lack the underlying data.

We create charts at visually proper perspectives to give an accurate representation of data. The information must be clear and concise. We do not skew or alter data to fit a visual need.

We credit our sources on every interactive and graphic, including graphics for which AP journalists have created the database.

IMAGES

AP images must always be accurate. We do not alter or digitally manipulate the content of a photo or video except as stated below.

We avoid the use of generic photos or video that could be mistaken for imagery photographed for the specific story at hand, or that could unfairly link people in the images to illicit activity.

Photos

No element should be digitally altered except as described below.

Minor adjustments to photos are acceptable. These include cropping, dodging and burning, conversion into grayscale, elimination of dust on camera sensors and scratches on scanned negatives or scanned prints and normal toning and color adjustments. These should be limited to those minimally necessary for clear and accurate reproduction and that restore the authentic nature of the photograph. Changes in density, contrast, color and saturation levels that substantially alter the original scene are not acceptable. Backgrounds should not be digitally blurred or eliminated by burning down or by aggressive toning. The removal of "red eye" from photographs is not permissible.

Employees with questions about the use of such methods or the AP's requirements and limitations on photo editing should contact a senior photo editor prior to the transmission of any image.

Photo-based graphics, including those for television, often involve combining various photographic elements, which may mean altering portions of each photograph. The background of a photograph, for example, may be removed to leave the headshot of the newsmaker. This may then be combined with a logo representing the person's company or industry, and the two elements may be layered over a neutral background.

Such compositions must not misrepresent the facts and must not result in an image that looks like a photograph — it must clearly be a graphic. Similarly, when we alter photos to use as graphics online, we retain the integrity of the image, limiting the changes to cropping, masking and adding elements like logos.

It is permissible to display photos online using techniques such as 360-degree panoramas or dissolves as long as they do not alter the original images.

Video

For video, the AP permits the use of subtle, standard methods of improving technical quality, such as adjusting video and audio levels, color correcting due to white balance, eliminating buzzing, hums, clicks, pops, or overly long pauses or other technical faults, and equalization of audio to make the sound clearer _ provided the use of these methods does not conceal, obscure, remove or otherwise alter the content of the image.

Video can produced with titles and logos, the images toned and the audio quality improved.

When editing audio within a video, generally the specific audio associated with each video shot must be used without alteration. However in cases where music is the principal ambient sound — e.g. when the video portrays a marching band or an orchestra playing - audio may be laid unbroken and video images edited over the top, provided the video was shot contemporaneously and the meaning of the scene is not altered.

Obscuring identities

We should not use mosaics or blurring to grant anonymity in any AP-created images. Instead we should shoot the subject in silhouette or use other photo or video techniques — such as using the person's shadow naturally cast on a wall or ground — to achieve the goal of anonymity. Exceptions may be granted rarely, when other anonymity techniques have failed, with permission of a senior manager. Images may be treated so that end-users of our content cannot readjust the levels to bring a shadowed face into view. In cases in which anonymity is deemed essential for the safety of the interviewee, the voices of silhouetted persons being interviewed may be digitally distorted with a manager's permission strictly for purposes of hiding identity. However any such alteration will be noted and disclosed in the accompanying script or shot-list.

When approved by a manager, the AP allows the use of material from third parties, such as government authorities, where faces are digitally obscured. In such cases, it must be stated in the shot-list, or caption and special instructions, who is responsible for the obscuring of a face. Similarly, the caption or shot-list must clearly disclose any other manipulation of imagery by a source that otherwise would not be allowed under AP guidelines.

Posing and reenactments

We do not stage, pose or reenact events except in the circumstances described here. When we shoot B-roll "walking shot" video, "environmental" portraits of subjects at work, home, etc., or photograph subjects in a studio, care should be taken to avoid misleading viewers to believe that the moment was spontaneously captured in the course of gathering the news. The precise circumstances of such portraiture must be revealed in the shot-list or caption and special instructions box so it can't be mistaken as an attempt to deceive.

User-generated and internet content

When obtaining imagery from the internet or any other source, we must be certain it is accurate, un-manipulated, shows what it is said to show and that we have the right to use it. When acquiring user-generated content, we must give priority to the safety of providers and caution them against taking risks. We should credit them appropriately.

Offensive and gory content

AP does not seek to sanitize news events; sometimes a gory or disturbing image is essential to cover a story. However, such imagery must be appropriate and newsworthy, not gratuitous. Care must be taken with images that could be offensive toward religions, nationalities or ethnic groups. In some cases, we may decide not to send such material to consumer-facing platforms, but to distribute it to subscribers — with appropriate warnings — for them to decide on its usage.

Special warnings to consumers about disturbing content may be needed for online and virtual reality content. In the rare case that an obscene image is necessary to tell the story, we may blur the portion of the image considered offensive. This must be approved by a manager.

MUSIC

Music added to AP productions must not have an editorial effect, such as evoking sympathy, suspicion or ridicule. We must have rights to use the material.

OBSCENITIES, PROFANITIES, VULGARITIES, HATE AND PROPAGANDA

AP resists being used as a conduit for speech or images that espouse hate or spread propaganda. When hate speech or images are the basis of a news story, it is often sufficient to briefly refer to the speech or images in a text story rather than carry the speech or propaganda at length or redistribute the images. A senior manager must vet any material showing hostages or conveying kidnappers' statements or demands. Quoting from such materials should be kept to the minimum necessary to convey the story and must note that the hostage is speaking under duress.

We do not use obscenities, racial epithets or other offensive slurs in stories unless they are part of direct quotations and there is a compelling reason for them. We do not run imagery of such slurs; a manager must be consulted regarding any exceptions.

If a story cannot be told without reference to slurs, we must first try to find a way to give the reader a sense of what was said without using the specific word or phrase. If a profanity, obscenity or vulgarity is used, the content must be flagged at the top, advising editors of what the offensive material is.

Recognizing that standards differ around the world and from platform to platform, we tailor our advisories and selection of video and audio according to customer needs.

We do not refer readers to websites that are obscene, racist or otherwise offensive, and we must not directly link from stories to such sites.

We link our text content to the least offensive image necessary to tell the story. For photo galleries and interactive presentations we alert readers to the nature of the material in the link and on the opening page of the gallery or interactive.

PRIVACY OF VICTIMS

We generally do not identify, in text or images, those who say they have been sexually assaulted or subjected to extreme abuse. We may identify victims of sexual assault or extreme abuse when victims publicly identify themselves.

We generally do not identify minors who are accused of crimes or who are witnesses to them. Identification of such minors must be approved by a manager; it may depend on the severity of the alleged crime; whether police have formally released the juvenile's name; and whether the juvenile has been formally charged as an adult. Other considerations might include public safety, such as when the youth is the subject of a manhunt; or widespread publication of the juvenile suspect's name, making the identity de facto public knowledge.

QUOTATIONS

Quotes must not be taken out of context. We do not alter quotations, even to correct grammatical errors or word usage. If a quotation is flawed because of grammar or lack of clarity, it may be paraphrased in a way that is completely true to the original quote. If a quote's meaning is too murky to be paraphrased accurately, it should not be used. Ellipses should be used rarely and must not alter the speaker's meaning.

When relevant, stories should provide information about the setting in which a quotation was obtained — for example, a press conference, phone interview or hallway conversation with the reporter. The source's affect and body language — perhaps a smile or deprecatory gesture — is sometimes as important as the quotation itself.

Use of regional dialects with nonstandard spellings should generally be limited to a writer's effort to convey a special tone or sense of place. In this case, as in interviews with a people not speaking their native language, it is especially important that their ideas be accurately conveyed. Always, we must be careful not to mock the people we quote.

Quotes from one language to another must be translated faithfully. If appropriate, we should note the language spoken.

Internal editing of audio soundbites of newsmakers is not permitted. Shortened soundbites by cutaway or other video transition are permitted as long as the speaker's meaning is not altered or misconstrued.

RESPONSES

We must make significant efforts to reach anyone who may be portrayed in a negative way in our content, and we must give them a reasonable amount of time to get back to us before we send our reports. What is "reasonable" may depend on the urgency and competitiveness of the story. If we don't reach the parties involved, we must explain in the story what efforts were made to do so.

NEWS VALUES

SOCIAL NETWORKS

The use of social media by AP's journalists is held to the same high standards as reporting, communication and distribution over any other medium. Those standards include, but are not limited to:

— Avoiding expressions of opinion on contentious issues, even in supposedly password-protected conversations.
— When publishing to AP's branded accounts, staffers should get explicit permission from a senior manager before distributing third-party copyrighted material.
— Not disseminating rumors and unconfirmed reports, and attributing information.
— Carefully verifying information and content before it is distributed.
— Transparently correcting errors on all platforms on which the erroneous material was distributed.

AP journalists are encouraged to maintain accounts on social networks, and must identify themselves in their profiles as being with AP if they use the accounts for work in any way. We must not share AP proprietary or confidential information or include political affiliations or preferences. If we retweet or otherwise share opinionated material by others, we should add language that makes it clear that we're simply reporting someone else's opinions.

In social posts related to sports and entertainment, we must steer clear of both trash-talking and over-the-top, fawning praise directed at teams, athletes and celebrities.

Staffers are encouraged to share AP content in all formats to social platforms. We should do so by using the "share" buttons on apps, browsers and sites that cause an item to be posted, or by posting a link to the content. We should not manually upload or copy and paste published photos, videos or the full text of published stories into social accounts. Staffers should not upload directly to social networks images they captured that closely resemble those the AP is publishing.

Staffers may share content from other news organizations, but we should be mindful of potential competitive issues and refrain from sharing unconfirmed material. We should also keep in mind that denouncing fellow users, newsmakers or anyone else can reflect badly on AP and may one day harm a colleague's ability to get important information from a source.

AP journalists who have confirmed urgent breaking news should not share that information over social accounts until they have provided it to the appropriate AP desk and done any immediate reporting work that is asked of them. Exclusive material and important tips should not be shared online before the related story has been published.

We may follow or friend sources or newsmakers, but when doing so with politicians or political causes, we should try to connect with accounts on both sides of a given issue or campaign. AP managers should not issue friend requests to subordinates; otherwise, friend requests among AP employees are fine.

Employees must not post any information that might endanger a colleague, and shouldn't post about a missing or detained AP staffer without clearance from senior AP managers.

Posts and tweets aimed at gathering opinions for a story must make clear that we are looking for voices on all sides of an issue.

If an AP tweet or social media posting contains an error of fact, emphasis or tone, the tweet or posting promptly should be removed from the platform where it occurred, followed by a note acknowledging the deletion and a substitute corrected tweet or posting issued where appropriate.

USE OF OTHERS' MATERIAL

An AP staffer who reports and writes a story must use original content, language and phrasing. We do not plagiarize, meaning that we do not take the work of others and pass it off as our own. When we match a report that a news outlet was first with due to significant reporting effort, we should mention that the other outlet first reported it.

At the same time, it is common for AP staffers to include in their work passages from previous AP stories by other writers — generally background, or boilerplate. This is acceptable if the passages are short. Regardless, the reporter writing the story is responsible for the factual and contextual accuracy of the material.

Also, the AP often has the right to use material from its members and subscribers; as with material from other news media, we credit it.

Unless we are clearly retransmitting in full a story by a member outlet, we do not transmit stories in their original form; we rewrite them, so that the approach, content, structure and length meet our requirements and reflect the broader audience we serve.

Under no circumstances can news releases be published in their original form; we can use information, quotes and properly cleared images from releases, but we must judge the material's credibility, augment it with information from other sources, and then prepare our own stories, with the release material duly credited.

For video, if another broadcaster's material is required and distributed, we advise the name of that broadcaster on the accompanying shot list.

Pickups of audio and of television graphics are credited in billboards/captions when the source requests it.

Editing marks

HONG KONG (AP) — The organization   indent for paragraph

said Thursday. It was the first and last   paragraph

attempts.   no paragraph

With this the president tried

the Jones Smith company is not   transpose

over a period of sixty or more years   use figures

there were 5 in the group.   spell it out

former Governor Rothwell attended   abbreviate

The Ga. man was the guest of   don't abbreviate

prince edward said it was his   uppercase

as a result This will be   lowercase

the ac cuser pointed to them   remove space

In these times it is necessary   insert space

The order for the later devices   retain

The ruling a fine example   insert word

according to the this source   delete

By DONALD AMES   boldface, center

J.P. Slavens   flush right

J.P. Slavens   flush left

insert comma

insert apostrophe

insert quotation marks

insert period

hyphen

dash

Bibliography

A partial list of sources and resources used in preparation of the AP Stylebook:

Disabilities:
Disability Language Style Guide, National Center on Disability and Journalism:
https://ncdj.org/style-guide/
Disability Writing & Journalism Guidelines, Center for Disability Rights:
https://cdrnys.org/disability-writing-journalism-guidelines/
American Council of the Blind: https://www.acb.org/
American Foundation for the Blind: https://www.afb.org/
Autism Self Advocacy Network: https://autisticadvocacy.org/
National Federation of the Blind: https://nfb.org/
National Association of the Deaf: https://www.nad.org/
World Federation of the Deaf: https://wfdeaf.org/

General guidance and inclusive storytelling:
Conscious Style Guide: https://consciousstyleguide.com/
The Diversity Style Guide: https://www.diversitystyleguide.com/
Guidelines for Inclusive Journalism, The Seattle Times: http://st.news/
inclusivejournalism
Publication Manual of the American Psychological Association:
https://apastyle.apa.org/
https://apastyle.apa.org/style-grammar-guidelines/bias-free-language
https://www.apa.org/about/apa/equity-diversity-inclusion/language-guidelines.
pdf

Drugs; addictions:
Media Guide, National Institute on Drug Abuse:
https://nida.nih.gov/sites/default/files/mediaguide_web_3_0.pdf
Office of National Drug Control Policy: https://bit.ly/2X8Yz5d
International Society of Addiction Journal Editors: http://www.parint.org/
isajewebsite/terminology.htm
AMA Task Force to Reduce Opioid Abuse: https://tinyurl.com/yc8z65r6
National Institute on Drug Abuse: https://nida.nih.gov/

LGBTQ:
Stylebook, Association of LGBTQ Journalists: https:/nlgja.org/stylebook/
Style Guide, Trans Journalists Association: https://transjournalists.org/style-
guide/
GLAAD Media Reference Guide: https://www.glaad.org/reference

Medical:
AMA Manual of Style, American Medical Association: https://www. amamanualofstyle.com/
Diagnostic and Statistical Manual of Mental Disorders, American Psychiatric Association
Centers for Disease Control and Prevention: https://www.cdc.gov/
Journalism Resource Guide on Behavioral Health, the Carter Center: https://www.cartercenter.org/resources/pdfs/health/mental_health/2015-journalism-resource-guide-on-behavioral-health.pdf
National Institute of Mental Health: https://www.nimh.nih.gov
National Alliance on Mental Illness: https://nami.org/Home
The Merck Manuals Online Medical Library: https://www.merckmanuals.com/professional
U.S. National Library of Medicine and the National Institutes of Health, MedlinePlus: https://medlineplus.gov/

Race-related coverage:
Asian American Journalists Association guidance: https://www.aaja.org/news-and-resources/guidances/
Subject matter experts from AAJA: https://www.aajastudio.org/
Cultural Compliance Handbook, National Association of Hispanic Journalists: https://nahj.org/wp-content/uploads/2021/03/NAHJ-Cultural-Compliance-Handbook-Revised-12-20-2.pdf
Cultural competence guides, Michigan State University: https://news.jrn.msu.edu/culturalcompetence/
Style Guide, National Association of Black Journalists: https://www.nabj.org/page/styleguide
Tribal Nations Media Guide, Native Americans Journalists Association: https://najanewsroom.com/wp-content/uploads/2020/10/2020-NAJA-Tribal-Nations-Media-Guide-1.pdf

Religion:
Handbook of Denominations in the United States, Abingdon Press: https://www.abingdonpress.com/product/9781501822513/
Religion Stylebook, Religion Newswriters Association: http://religionstylebook.com/
World Christian Encyclopedia, Oxford University Press: https://www.worldchristiandatabase.org/
Yearbook of American and Canadian Churches, National Council of Churches of Christ in the U.S.A.: http://yearbookofchurches.org/
Sikhism: A Reporter's Guide, Sikh Coalition: https://www.sikhcoalition.org/wp-content/uploads/2018/01/Sikhism-Reporters-Guide-Electronic.pdf

Suicide:
American Foundation for Suicide Prevention: https://afsp.org/reporting-on-suicide-prevention
Reporting on suicide guidelines: https://reportingonsuicide.org/

First reference for spelling, style, usage and foreign geographic names:
Webster's New World College Dictionary, HarperCollins.

Other references for spelling, style, usage and foreign geographic names:
The American Heritage Dictionary of the English Language, HarperCollins: https://www.ahdictionary.com/
Merriam-Webster: https://www.merriam-webster.com/
Concise Oxford English Dictionary, Oxford University Press: https://www.oed.com/
National Geographic Atlas of the World, National Geographic Society: https://www.nationalgeographic.com/maps/

For federal government questions:
Congressional Directory; U.S. Government Publishing Office.
This link allows searching of the directories for the 104th Congress (1995–1996) and later: https://www.govinfo.gov/app/collection/CDIR/
For the current Congress: https://www.congress.gov

For non-U.S. government questions:
Political Handbook of the World, CQ Press, an imprint of SAGE Publications.
CIA World Factbook online: https://www.cia.gov/library/publications/the-world-factbook/

For a company's formal name:
Consult the national stock exchanges: the New York Stock Exchange, https://www.nyse.com/index, or Nasdaq, https://www.nasdaq.com/. Also consult Stylebook Online entries for individual company names, and the entry "company names," as AP usage may differ.

Other references and writing guides:
The Word, by Rene J. Cappon. The Associated Press.
Fowler's Dictionary of Modern English Usage, edited by Jeremy Butterfield. Oxford University Press.
Garner's Modern English Usage, by Bryan A. Garner. Oxford University Press.
The Chicago Manual of Style, University of Chicago Press.
The Elements of Style, by Strunk & White. The Macmillan Co.

About the AP

Since 1846, The Associated Press has been on the scene wherever news is breaking. AP is a not-for-profit newsgathering cooperative whose content — across subjects, formats and continents — is seen by half of the world's population every day. Our unmatched expertise in global newsgathering, distribution and service makes AP the most trusted, definitive source for news.

The AP's mission is to get it first but first get it right, and to be the first choice for news, by providing the fastest, most accurate reporting from every corner of the globe across all media types and platforms.

Headquartered in New York, AP delivers coverage of news, sports, business, weather, entertainment, politics, lifestyles and technology in text, audio, video, graphics, photos and interactives. AP is also a leader in developing and marketing innovative newsroom technology and newsgathering services.

AP does what it takes to get the story, even in the world's most dangerous and challenging places. Our global network of journalists work in 254 locations in 100 countries worldwide. Journalists staff every statehouse in the United States, providing unrivaled access to more sources of information and newsmakers.

The extensive network that is the AP grew from a single notion more than a century and a half ago: Cooperation can help authoritative news reach readers faster.

In late 1846, hostilities began in what would become the Mexican War. American newspapers, most based in the Northeast at the time, faced huge obstacles in reporting the conflict.

War reports for the New York Sun were sent from Mexico to Mobile, Alabama, by boat, rushed by special pony express to Montgomery and then 700 miles by U.S. Mail stagecoach to the southern terminus of the newly invented telegraph near Richmond, Virginia. That express gave the Sun an edge of 24 hours or more on papers using regular mail.

But Moses Yale Beach, the Sun's publisher, relinquished that advantage by inviting other New York publishers to join a cooperative venture that would avoid duplication of effort by sending one so-called agent, or newsgatherer, to act for the many. Five newspapers signed on: the Sun, the Journal of Commerce, the Courier and Enquirer, the Herald and the Express. It was the beginning of the AP.

AP assumed its modern legal form in 1900 when it incorporated as a not-for-profit cooperative under the Membership Corporation Law of New York state. Today, the AP membership elects the board of directors, the cooperative's governing body.

AP staffers are governed by a comprehensive ethics statement, available for viewing at https://www.ap.org/about/our-story/news-values

More than 170 years since its inception, AP remains the undisputed source for news, delivering fast, unbiased news globally to all media platforms and formats.

Index

Index entries with figures and symbols are alphabetized as if spelled out.

Entries with no page numbers refer to terms that are provided for spelling purposes only; no additional information is given in the text.

Cross-references (*See* and *See also*) generally follow the usage in the A–Z sections of the *Stylebook* and refer to entries in the index itself. For convenience, cross-references to a single entry also include the page number for that entry.

Cross-references in most indexes lead from general terms (e.g., "states") to narrower terms (e.g., "Alabama"). However, in this index, such references often lead to an entry that contains general information about treatment of the particular kind of word or phrase, e.g., "colonel. *See* military titles."

Some complex entries in the text contain indented subheadings. References to these individual sections are indicated by the form "*see* [or *see* "x"] *in y*." For example "*see* overseas territories *in* datelines" refers to the section titled "overseas territories" within the main entry "datelines."

Some terms or phrases are designated as "derogatory." They represent insulting or offensive usage and should not be used except in extremely rare circumstances.

A page number after a heading that also includes subheadings refers to the specific entry for the heading term itself.

Most terms in italics are also included in the index, except for long lists of examples given with prefixes and suffixes. The following chapters have been indexed at the section level only: Briefing on media law, Business guidelines, Inclusive storytelling, Polls and surveys. All others have been indexed in detail.

able-bodied, 2. *See also* disabilities, 84–86

ableism, 2. *See also* disabilities, 84–86

ABM, ABMs (anti-ballistic missile(s)), 2

abnormality (nonpreferred). *See* disabilities, 84–86

Aborigine (nonpreferred), 249

abortion, 2–3

abortionist (derogatory), 2–3

abou. *See* Arabic names, 21

abrupt change (in thought). *See* dash, 328

ABS (nonpreferred). *See* asset-backed security, 23

absent without leave. *See* AWOL, 26

absolute risk, in health, science and environment reporting, 374

abu. *See* Arabic names, 21

Abu Sayyaf, 3

abuser (nonpreferred). *See* addiction, 5–6

AC. *See* athletic club, 424–425

ACA. *See* Affordable Care Act, 7

academic course numbers, 208

academic degrees, 3
   abbreviation of, 1
   See also doctor; Master of Arts, Master of Science, Master of Business Administration

academic departments, 3

academic titles, 3. *See also* doctor; titles

academy. *See* military academies, 190

Academy Awards (Oscars), 3

accent marks, 3

accept, except, 3

accessibility of stories, for inclusivity, 355–356

accident, crash, 3

accommodate

accounting rules, international, 341

accounts payable, 3–4

accounts receivable, 4

accuracy (of polls and surveys), 364

accused, alleged, suspected, 4. *See also* allege; arrest; indict; suspect

Ace, 4

Achilles tendon, 4, 424

acid (lysergic acid diethylamide). *See* LSD, 91

acknowledgment

ACL (anterior cruciate ligament), 424

ACLU (American Civil Liberties Union), 14

acquired immune deficiency syndrome. *See* AIDS, 8–9

acquiring data, 357–358

acquisitions. *See* mergers and acquisitions, 345–348

acquitted. *See* innocent, not guilty, 155

acre, 4. *See also* hectare; wildfires

acronyms
   discussion of (*See* abbreviations and acronyms, 1)
   for organizations and institutions, 217
   periods in (*See* abbreviations and acronyms, 2)
   for U.S. Cabinet departments (*See* department, 78–79)

acrophobia. *See* phobia, 224

across the board (horse racing), 441

ACT (American College Testing), 4

act, amendment, bill, law, measure, ordinance, resolution, rule, statute, 4–5

acting, 5. *See also* titles, 291–292

activewear

act numbers, 5. *See also* sequential designations *in* numerals, 209

actor, 124

actress. *See* actor, 124

actual change, of data, 360

A.D., 5. *See also* B.C., 30

ADD (nonpreferred). *See* attention-deficit/hyperactivity disorder, 24

-added (suffix), 424

addict (nonpreferred). *See* addiction, 5–6

addiction, 5–6. *See also* alcoholic; diseases; drugs; health and science reporting; mental illness; naloxone; opiate, opioid; supervised injection sites

airfare

air force, 9–10. *See also* military academies; military titles

air force base. *See* air base, 9

Air Force One, 10

airline, airlines, 10

airman. *See* military titles, 191–193

Air National Guard

airport, 10

airsoft gun, 10

airstrike

air traffic controller, 10

airways. *See also* airline, airlines, 10

aka, 10

Al (in Arabic names), 21

al- (article). *See* Arabic names, 20

Al-Aqsa Mosque, 390. *See also* Haram al-Sharif; Temple Mount

alarms, 10

Alaska Native corporations, 252–253

Alaska Natives. *See* Native Americans, American Indians, 252

Alaska Standard Time, 10–11. *See also* time zones, 291

Alberta, 11. *See also* Canadian datelines, 73

albinism, albino, 11. *See also* disabilities, 84–86

albinos (nonpreferred). *See* albinism, albino, 11

album. *See* record, recorded, recording, 255

album titles. *See* composition titles, 56–57

alcoholic (nonpreferred), 11. *See also* addiction, 5–6

Alcoholics Anonymous (AA), 11

alert. *See* weather terms, 310–316

Alexa, 11. *See also* digital assistant, virtual assistant, voice assistant, 82–83

al-Fatah (improper). *See* Fatah, 107

alien (nonpreferred). *See* illegal immigration, 146–147

A-list

all- (prefix), 11. *See also* all right; all time, all-time

Allah, 11, 390

Allahu akbar, 11, 390

All-America, All-American, 424

allege, 11–12. *See also* accused, alleged, suspected; arrest; indict

Allegheny Mountains, 12

alley, 12. *See also* addresses, 6

allies, allied, 12

all right, 12

all-star, All-Star, All-Star Game, 424

all-terrain vehicle (ATV), 12

all time, all-time, 12

allude, refer, 12

allusion, illusion, 12

ally. *See* LGBTQ

Alpine skiing, 424

al-Qaida, 12

Al-Quds (the holy, Jerusalem), 12

alright (incorrect). *See* all right, 12

ALS (amyotrophic lateral sclerosis). *See* Lou Gehrig's disease, 178

al-Shabab, 12

also known as. *See* aka, 10

also-ran (horse racing), 441

altar, alter, 12, 390

alternative lifestyle (nonpreferred). *See* LGBTQ; sexual orientation

"alt-left," 13

"alt-right," 12–13. *See also* race-related coverage, 245–253

alumnus, alumni, alumna, alumnae. *See* gender-neutral language, 124–125

alumnus, alumni, alumna, alumnae, alum, 124–125

Alzheimer's disease, 13. *See also* dementia; disabilities

AMA. *See* American Medical Association, 14

AMA (ask me anything posts, Reddit). *See* Reddit, 256

Amazon.com Inc. *See* Alexa; Fire; Kindle

ambassador, 13–14

    ambassador-at-large (*See* at large, 24)

    See also titles, 291–292

Amber Alert, 14

Asperger's syndrome (nonpreferred). *See* autism spectrum disorder, autism, 24–25

assassin, killer, murderer, 22. *See also* execute, execution; homicide, murder, manslaughter

assassination, 22

assassination, date of, 22

assault, battery, 22

assault rifle, assault weapon (nonpreferred), 307–308

Assemblies of God. *See also* Pentecostalism, 415

assembly, 22–23. *See also* legislature, 173

asset-backed security, 23

asset, fixed, 23

assets, 23. *See also* goodwill, 128

assistance animal. *See* service animal, assistance animal, guide dog, 267

assistant, 23. *See also* titles, 291–292

associate, 23. *See also* assistant, 23

associate degree. *See* academic degrees, 3

Associated Press, The, 23
history of, 514
statement of news values and principles, 497–510
See also AP, 19

associate justice. *See* Supreme Court of the United States, 282

associate's degree (incorrect). *See* academic degrees, 3

Association, 23

associations, in golf, 439

assure, ensure, insure, 23

asterisk, 23

AstroTurf, 424

asylum-seekers, 147. *See also* immigration, migration, 145–153

asymptomatic (nonpreferred), 23

ATF. *See* Bureau of Alcohol, Tobacco, Firearms and Explosives, 36

atheist. *See* agnostic, atheist, 8, 390

athlete's foot

athlete's heart

athletic club (AC), 424–425. *See also* match summary, 444

athletic director, 425

athletic teams, 425

athletic trainers, 425

Atlantic Ocean

Atlantic Standard Time, Atlantic Daylight Time, 23. *See also* time zones, 291

at large, 23–24

ATM (automated teller machine), 24

ATM machine (improper). *See* ATM, 24

Atomic Age. *See* historical periods and events, 139

attache, 24

attempted suicide. *See* suicide, 281

attention-deficit disorder (nonpreferred). *See* attention-deficit/hyperactivity disorder, 24

attention-deficit/hyperactivity disorder, 24. *See also* disabilities; neurodiversity, neurodivergent, neurodiverse, neurotypical

attorney at law. *See* attorney, lawyer; lawyer

attorney general, attorneys general, 24. *See also* titles, 291–292

attorney in fact. *See* attorney, lawyer, 24

attorney, lawyer, 24. *See also* lawyer, 171–172

attribution, 24
commas before, 328
dashes with, 329
in headlines, 135
standards and practices on, 499–500

ATV. *See* all-terrain vehicle, 12

audio, standards and practices on, 500

audio reports, referencing user-generated, 383

augmented reality. *See* virtual reality, augmented reality, 304

"Auld Lang Syne," 24

Australia. *See* Down Under, 90

author, 25

autism spectrum disorder, autism, 24–25. *See also* disabilities; high functioning, low functioning; neurodiversity, neurodivergent, neurodiverse, neurotypical

automated teller machine. *See* ATM, 24

automatic (weapon), 308

automatic rifle. *See* assault rifle, assault weapon, 307–308

autonomous vehicles, 25

autopilot. *See* autonomous vehicles, 25

auto racing, 425–426

Auto Train, 25

autoworker, autoworkers, 25

autumn. *See* seasons, 265

avatar, 25

avenue, 25–26. *See also* addresses, 6

average, mean, median, norm, 26

average of, 26

averages, in data, 360–361

averse. *See* adverse, averse, 7

avian influenza (nonpreferred). *See* bird flu, 31

awards and decorations, 26. *See also* Nobel Prize, Nobel Prizes; Pulitzer Prizes

awhile, a while, 26

awkward constructions, with abbreviations or acronyms, 2

AWOL (absent without leave), 26

ax, 26

Axis, 26

Ayatollah. *See* Islam, 405–406

Aymara (people/language), 26

Azerbaijan. *See* Commonwealth of Independent States, 53

b

baby boom, baby boomer. *See* generations, 126

baby bump (nonpreferred), 27

babysit, babysitting, babysat, babysitter

baccalaureate

Bachelor of Arts, Bachelor of Science, 27. *See also* academic degrees, 3

bachelor's, bachelor's degree. *See* academic degrees; Bachelor of Arts, Bachelor of Science

backboard

backcourt

backfield

backfire (in wildfire management), 27

background (news writing), 499

backhand

backpass, 446

backspin

backstage, 27

backstop

backstretch, 441

backstroke

backward, 27

bacon, lettuce and tomato sandwich. *See* BLT, 32

bad, badly, 27. *See also* good, well, 128

Badlands (South Dakota). *See* capitalization, 41

badminton, 426. *See also* match summary, 444

Baha'i, 393

Bahamas, 27

Baha'u'llah. *See* Baha'i, 393

bail, 27

baker's dozen, 27

balance of payments, balance of trade, 28

balance sheet, 28

Balkans, in datelines, 73

ball carrier

ballclub

ballerina. *See* dancer, ballet dancer, 125

ballet dancer. *See* dancer, ballet dancer, 125

ballgame

balloon mortgage, 28

ballpark

ballplayer

ballroom

baloney, 28

BAME. *See* people of color, 248–249

Band-Aid, 28

B&B. *See* bed-and-breakfast, 30

Bank of Sweden Prize in Economic Sciences in Memory of Alfred Nobel. *See* Nobel Prize, Nobel Prizes, 204

bankruptcy, 28–29

    guidelines on covering, 341–345

bankruptcy judges. *See* judicial branch, 165

baptism. *See* sacraments, 418

Baptist churches, 393–394. *See also* religious movements; religious titles

Baptist World Alliance. *See* Baptist churches, 393–394

barbiturate

bar mitzvah, 394

baron, baroness. *See* nobility, 204–205

baronet, knight. *See* nobility, 205

barrel, 29

barrel, barreled, barreling

barrister. *See* lawyer, 171–172

baseball, 426–428

BASE jumping, 29, 428

basic summary (sports), 428–429. *See also* auto racing; bowling

basis point, 29

basketball, 429–430

   Major College Basketball
         Conferences, 433–434

bas mitzvah. *See* bar mitzvah, 394

bath salts (drugs), 90

bat mitzvah. *See* bar mitzvah, 394

battalion, 29

battery. *See* assault, battery, 22

battery-electric vehicles. *See* electric, hybrid, plug-in hybrid vehicles, 97

battlefield, 29

battlefront

battleground

battleground states, 29–30

battleship

battle station

Bauhaus. *See* artworks, 22

bay, 30

Bay Area. *See* bay, 30

bazaar. *See* bizarre, 32

BBC. *See* British Broadcasting Corp., 36

B.C., 30. *See also* A.D., 5

bearer bond, 30

bearer stock, 30

bear market, 30

beatification. *See* canonization, 395

because, since, 30

bed-and-breakfast (B&B), 30

before. *See* prior to, 235

before Christ. *See* B.C., 30

beggar (nonpreferred). *See* homeless, homelessness, 140

Belarus. *See* Commonwealth of Independent States, 53

bellwether

Belmont Stakes, 441

benefit, benefited, benefiting

Ben-Gurion International Airport, 30. *See also* airport, 10

Berlin Wall

beside, besides, 30

bestseller, bestselling, 30

betting. *See* gambling, 118

betting odds, 30, 430. *See also* odds, proportions and ratios *in* numerals, 209

bettor, 30, 430

between. *See* among, between, 15

bi- (prefix), 30

biannual, biennial, 30

bias, unconscious/implicit, 352

Bible, 394

Bible-believing (nonpreferred), 394

Bible Belt, 394–395

biblical. *See* Bible, 394

biblical citations. *See* listings *in* colon, 326

bibliography, 512–513

biennial. *See* biannual, biennial; semiannual

big brother, Big Brother, 30

Big Brothers Big Sisters of America Inc. *See* big brother, 30

Big Dipper. *See* heavenly bodies, 136

Big Tech, 31

bill. *See* act, amendment, bill, law, measure, ordinance, resolution, rule, statute, 4

billiards, 430. *See also* match summary, 444

billion, 31. *See also* millions, billions, trillions, 193

Bill of Rights, 31. *See also* Constitution, 58–59

bimonthly, 31

bin (in Arabic names). *See* Arabic names, 20–21

binary digit (bit). *See* bit, 32

bin Laden, Osama, 31. *See also* al-Qaida, 12

biological, 121

biological parents. *See* adoption, 7

biotechnology. *See* technology, 286

bioterrorism

biphobia. *See* homophobia, homophobic, 123, 141

BIPOC. *See* people of color, 248–249

bipolar disorder, 31. *See also* depression; disabilities; mental illness

biracial, multiracial, 247–248

bird flu (avian influenza), 31

birdie, birdies, birdied. *See* golf, 438

birth control pill. *See* pill, 225

birthday, 31

birth defect, 31–32. *See also* disabilities, 84–86

birthright citizenship, 148

"birth tourism," 148

bisexual, 123. *See also* sexual orientation, 122

bishops. *See* religious titles; *specific denominations*

bit (binary digit), 32

bitcoin, 67–68. *See also* cryptocurrency, 66–67

biweekly, 32

Bixby. *See* digital assistant, virtual assistant, voice assistant, 82–83

bizarre, 32

Black, 249. *See also* obscenities, profanities, vulgarities, 212

Black Lives Matter (BLM), 249–250

Black Muslim (derogatory). *See* Muslims, 410

blackout, brownout, 32

Black(s), white(s), 249

bleed. *See* hemorrhage, 137

blended learning, 264

Blessed Sacrament, Blessed Virgin

blind, limited vision, low vision/ partially sighted. *See also* deaf, Deaf, hard of hearing

blizzard, 310

BLM. *See* Black Lives Matter, 249–250

bloc, block, 32

blockchain, 68. *See also* cryptocurrency; NFT; Web3

blond, 125

blood alcohol content, 32

bloodbath, 32

BLT, 32

blue chip stock, 32

Bluetooth, 32–33, 319

Blu-ray Disc, 33

BMI. *See* body mass index, 33

B'nai B'rith. *See also* fraternal organizations and service clubs, 116

board, 33. *See also* capitalization, 40–41

board of aldermen. *See* city council, 48

board of directors, board of trustees, 33. *See also* organizations and institutions, 216–217

board of supervisors. *See* city council, 48

boards (pinboards). *See* Pinterest, 225

boats, ships, 33

USS with, 301

See also numerals, 208

bobsledding, luge, 431. *See also* basic summary, 428–429

body camera (bodycam), 33

body mass index (BMI), 33

bogey, bogeys, bogeyed. *See* golf, 438

Boko Haram, 33

bologna. *See* baloney, 28

Bolshevik Revolution. *See* Russian Revolution, 261

bolt-action rifle, 308

Bombay. *See* Mumbai, 197

Bonaerense. *See* Porteno, 229

bond, 176

bearer bond, 30

bond ratings, 33–34

book. *See* sportsbook, 275, 449

book titles. *See* composition titles, 56–57

book value, 34

Border Patrol, 152

Bosnia-Herzegovina, 34

Bosniak, Bosniaks, 34

Bosnian Croats. *See* Bosniak, Bosniaks, 34

C

534

e

g

h

INDEX

Judicial Conference of the United
States, 165
judo, 443. *See also* basic summary;
match summary
July Fourth. *See* Fourth of July, July
Fourth; Independence Day
jumbo jet, 165
jump ball
jump shot
Juneteenth, 250
Junior Chamber of Commerce, 165. *See
also* Jaycees, 162
junior, senior, 165. *See also* names, 199
junk bonds, 165. *See also* bond ratings,
33
junkie (derogatory). *See* addiction, 5
junta. *See* government, junta, regime,
administration, 129–130
Jupiter. *See* planets, 225
jury, 165. *See also* grand jury, 130
jury-rig, 165–166. *See also* jerry-built,
163–164
justice, 166. *See also* judge; Supreme
Court of the United States;
titles
justice of the peace, 166. *See also* titles,
291–292
justify, 166
juvenile delinquent, 166. *See also*
privacy, 236
juvenile diabetes (Type 1 diabetes). *See*
diabetes, 81
juveniles. *See* names; privacy

k

K (kilo-, thousand), 167
K–12. *See* kindergarten, kindergartners,
168
kaffiyeh, 167
karat. *See* carat, caret, karat, 41
Kathmandu, 167
Kazakhstan. *See* Commonwealth of
Independent States, 53
KB (kilobyte). *See* byte, 37
Kelvin scale, 167. *See also* Celsius;
Fahrenheit

Kennedy Space Center. *See* John F.
Kennedy Space Center, 164
Kentucky Derby, 442, 443. *See also*
capitalization, 41
keynote address (keynote speech), 167
keywords, 167
kg (kilogram). *See also* metric system,
189
KGB, 167
Khalsa Panth, Guru. *See* Sikhi, Sikhism,
419
Khorasan group. *See* al-Qaida, 12
kHz. *See* kilohertz, 167
kibbutz, 167
kidnap, kidnapped, kidnapping,
kidnapper
kidney punch, 431
Kiev. *See* Kyiv, 169
killer. *See* assassin, killer, murderer, 22
kilo- (prefix), 167. *See also* metric
system, 188
kilobyte (KB). *See* byte, 37
kilogram, 167. *See also* gram; metric
system; pound
kilohertz (kHz), 167
kilometer, 167. *See also* meter; metric
system; miles
kilometers per hour (kph), 167
kiloton, kilotonnage, 167
kilowatt-hour, 167–168. *See also* watt,
306
kindergarten, kindergartners, 168
Kindle, 168
Kindle Fire. *See* Fire, 110
king, queen, 168. *See also* Arabic names;
nobility; titles
Kitty Litter, 168
KKK. *See* Ku Klux Klan, 169
klan. *See* Ku Klux Klan, 169
Kleenex, 168
km (kilometer). *See* kilometer; metric
system
Knesset, 168
knight. *See* nobility, 205
K-9
knockout, knock out, 431
knots. *See* nautical miles, knots, 201
knuckleball, 443

LPGA Tour. *See* Ladies Professional
Golf Association, 443
LSD (lysergic acid diethylamide), 91
LTE. *See* 4G, 5G, LTE, 115
Lt. Gov. *See* lieutenant governor, 174
Lucite, 178
luge. *See* bobsledding, luge, 431
lunar. *See* heavenly bodies; planets
Lunar New Year, 178–179
Luther, Martin. *See* Lutheran churches,
408
Lutheran churches, 408. *See also*
religious titles, 416
Lutheran Church-Missouri Synod. *See*
Lutheran churches, 408
-ly (suffix), 179. *See also* compound
modifiers *in* hyphen, 330–331
Lycra, 179
Lyft. *See* ride-hailing, ride-sharing, 258
Lyme disease, 179
Lyndon B. Johnson Space Center, 179.
See also John F. Kennedy Space
Center, 164
lysergic acid diethylamide. *See* LSD, 91

m

m (meter). *See* metric system, 189
M.A. (Master of Arts). *See* Master of
Arts, Master of Science, Master
of Business Administration, 184
Macao, 180
Mace, 180. *See also* Chemical Mace, 44
Macedonia. *See* North Macedonia, 206
machine gun, 309
machine gun, machine-gun, machine-
gunner, machine-gun fire, 180.
See also weapons
machine learning, 180. *See also* artificial
intelligence; autonomous
vehicles; face recognition
Mach number, 180
mad cow disease, 180. *See also*
Creutzfeldt-Jakob disease, 66
Mafia, 180
magazine (for ammunition), 309
magazine names, 180

Magi, 180, 408
magistrate, 180. *See also* titles, 291–292
magnetic resonance imaging. *See* MRI,
197
magnet schools, 263
magnitudes (of earthquakes), 94–95
Magnum (weapons cartridge), 309
Mahayana Buddhism. *See* Buddha,
Buddhism, 395
maiden (horse racing), 442
mail carrier, letter carrier, 125
mailman (nonpreferred). *See* mail
carrier, letter carrier, 125
mainland China. *See* China, 45
Main Line (Philadelphia suburbs). *See*
capitalization, 40
maintenance hole, 125
major. *See* military titles, 191–193
Major College Basketball Conferences,
433–434
Major College Football Conferences,
434
major depressive disorder. *See*
depression, 79–80
majority leader, 180. *See also* legislative
titles; titles
majority, plurality, 181
Major League Soccer. *See* MLS, 447
-maker (suffix), 181
makeup, make up, 181
Maldives, 181
male. *See* boy, girl; female, male; gender,
sex and sexual orientation;
gender-neutral language
male impersonator. *See* drag performer,
drag queen, drag king, 121
Mallorca, 181
malware, 158
man. *See* boy, girl; courtesy titles;
divorce; female, male; gender-
neutral language; gentleman;
humanity, humankind,
humans, human beings, people;
husband, wife
manageable
manager, 181. *See also* titles, 291–292
manager (soccer). *See* coach, 446

nondisabled. *See* able-bodied;
    disabilities
none, 206
"nones," 410–411. *See also* agnostic,
    atheist, 8, 390
nonessential clauses, commas with,
    327. *See also* essential clauses,
    nonessential clauses, 101
nonessential phrases, commas with,
    327. *See also* essential phrases,
    nonessential phrases, 101–102
nonexperts, as pitfalls in health,
    science and environment
    reporting, 376
non-fungible token. *See* NFT, 68–69
nongovernmental organization. *See*
    NGO, 203
non-Hodgkin lymphoma. *See* Hodgkin
    lymphoma, 139
nonprofit
nonrestrictive clauses. *See* essential
    clauses, nonessential clauses,
    101
non-U.S. governmental bodies. *See*
    governmental bodies, 129
noon, 206. *See also* midnight; times
nor'easter, 313
norm. *See* average, mean, median,
    norm, 26
normal (nonpreferred). *See* disabilities,
    86
North America, 317
North Atlantic Treaty Organization,
    206
North Central region. *See* Midwest, 190
Northeast, 206. *See also* directions and
    regions; Midwest; South; West
Northern Ireland, 206. *See also*
    datelines; Ireland; United
    Kingdom
North Korea (Democratic People's
    Republic of Korea). *See* Korea,
    168
North Korean names. *See* Korean
    names, 168–169
North Macedonia, 206
north, northern, northeast, northwest.
    See directions and regions, 84

North Slope, 207
north tower. *See* twin towers, 295
Northwest Territories, 207. *See also*
    Canada, 39
note (financial), 177
notes to the editor. *See* editor's notes
not guilty. *See* innocent, not guilty, 155
notorious, notoriety, 207
nouns
    collective nouns, 51
    hyphens with compound, 331, 332
    possessives for, 229–230, 324
Nova Scotia, 207. *See also* Canadian
    datelines, 73
Novocain, 207
NOW. *See* National Organization for
    Women, 200
NRA. *See* National Rifle Association,
    200
NRC. *See* Nuclear Regulatory
    Commission, 207
NSA. *See* National Security Agency,
    200–201
Nuclear Non-Proliferation Treaty, 207
Nuclear Regulatory Commission
    (NRC), 207
nuclear terminology, 207–208
number. *See* amount, number; No.
numbers
    in baseball, 426
    in basketball, 429
    in data journalism, 261–262
    in football, 437
    in golf, 439
    in health, science and environment
        reporting, 373–374
    numbered addresses, abbreviations
        in, 2
    numbered streets, capitalization of
        (*See* addresses, 6)
    in vote tabulations, 304–305
    See also Arabic numerals; figure(s)
        (number(s)); majority,
        plurality; ranges; Roman
        numerals
numerals, 208–211
    abbreviations with, 1–2
    for aircraft name sequences, 9

p

INDEX

r

R- (Republican). *See* party affiliation, 221

R (restricted). *See* movie ratings, 197

Rabbinical Assembly. *See* Jewish congregations, 407

Rabbinical Council of America. *See* Jewish congregations, 407

rabbis. *See* Jewish congregations; religious titles

rabbit punch, 432

race, 245–246. *See also* inclusive storytelling; obscenities, profanities, vulgarities; religion

race distances (horse racing), 442

race-related coverage, 245–253

racially charged, racially motivated, racially tinged, 247. *See also* racist, racism, 246–247

racial minority. *See* minority, racial minority, 248

racism, 13

racist. *See* "alt-right," 13

racist, racism, 246–247. *See also* racially charged, racially motivated, racially tinged, 247

racket (sports), 253, 445

Racketeer Influenced and Corrupt Organizations Act. *See* RICO, 258

rack, wrack, 253–254

racquet (nonpreferred). *See* racket, 253, 445

racquetball, 445. *See also* match summary, 444

rad (nuclear measurement). *See* gray, 207

radar (radio detection and ranging), 254

radiation, 207

radical (nonpreferred), 254. *See also* leftist, ultra-leftist; rightist, ultra-rightist

radio, 254

program titles (*See* composition titles, 56–57)

radio detection and ranging. *See* radar, 254

raid. *See* immigration raid, 149

rainstorm, 313

raised, reared, 254

RAM (random access memory). *See* device memory, device storage, 81

Ramadan, 254, 414

R&B, 245

random access memory (RAM). *See* device memory, device storage, 81

ranges (for numbers), 254

rank and file, rank-and-file, 254

ranks (military), 191–193

figures in (*See* military ranks, used as titles... *in* numerals, 209)

ransomware, 158. *See* cryptocurrency, 67

rape. *See* privacy; sexual abuse, sexual assault, sexual harassment, sexual misconduct

rarely, 254

ratings agency, 254

ratios, 254. *See also* numerals, 209

ravage, ravish, 254–255

re- (prefix), 255. *See also* pre-, 232

read-only memory. *See* ROM, 260

real estate agent. *See* Realtor, 255

real-time bidding. *See* digital advertising, internet advertising, online advertising, 82

Realtor, 255

reared. *See* raised, reared, 254

rebut, refute, 255

receiver (business manager). *See* receivership, 255

receivership, 255

recession, 255

recipes, 255

figures in (*See* numerals, 209)

See also food; fractions

reconnaissance

Reconstruction, 255

record (achievement), 255, 445

in hockey, 440–441

record, recorded, recording, 255

recorded music. *See* indie, 154

S

INDEX

INDEX